The Autobiography of Noël Coward

Noël Coward was born in Teddington, Middlesex on 16 December 1899. His professional acting career began in 1911 and in 1918 he wrote the first of his plays which was subsequently to be staged. He created a sensation as playwright and actor with *The Vortex* in 1924 and followed through with *Hay Fever* and *Easy Virtue* in 1925 and the operette *Bitter-Sweet* in 1929, for which he wrote book, music and lyrics as well as directing. His *Private Lives* in 1930 launched the stage partnership with Gertrude Lawrence which was renewed later in the thirties with *Tonight at 8.30*. *Cavalcade*, *Design for Living* and an autobiography, *Present Indicative*, were the other high-points of this decade. In the early forties *Blithe Spirit* was produced in London and Coward himself toured playing the lead in this and in *Present Laughter* and *This Happy Breed* for six months in 1942/43. He also wrote, acted in, produced and co-directed the film *In Which We Serve*. The forties also saw the films *Blithe Spirit* and *Brief Encounter*. In the fifties Coward began a new career as a cabaret entertainer as well as writing *Relative Values*, *Quadrille* and *Nude With Violin* and publishing *Future Indefinite*, a second volume of autobiography. He left England and moved first to Bermuda and then to Switzerland. In the sixties he turned novelist with *Pomp and Circumstance* and published his *Collected Short Stories* and a book of verse, *Not Yet the Dodo*. His play *Waiting in the Wings* was produced together with the musicals *Sail Away* and *The Girl Who Came to Supper*. He acted his last stage role in his *Suite in Three Keys* in 1966. He was knighted in 1970 and died in Jamaica on 26 March 1973.

BOOKS BY NOËL COWARD

NOËL COWARD

Autobiography

consisting of
PRESENT INDICATIVE,
FUTURE INDEFINITE
and the uncompleted
PAST CONDITIONAL

With an Introduction by
SHERIDAN MORLEY

A METHUEN PAPERBACK

A METHUEN PAPERBACK

First published in Great Britain 1986
This paperback edition first published 1987
by Methuen London Ltd, 11 New Fetter Lane, London EC4P 4EE

Reprinted 1991

Present Indicative first published by Heinemann in 1937
Future Indefinite first published by Heinemann in 1954
Past Conditional first published in this volume.
Copyright © 1986 by the Estate of the late Noël Coward

This collection copyright © 1986 by the Estate of the late Noël Coward
Introduction copyright © 1986 by Sheridan Morley
Chronology copyright © 1986 by Martin Tickner

Printed in Finland by Werner Söderström Osakeyhtiö

British Library Cataloguing in Publication Data

Coward, Nõel
  Noël Coward: autobiography.
  1. Dramatists, English——20th century——
  Biography   2. Entertainers——Great Britain
  ——Biography
  I. Title   II. Coward, Noël. Past conditional
  III. Coward, Noël. Present indicative
  IV. Coward, Noël. Future indefiinite
  792´.092´4   PR6005.085Z/

ISBN 0-413-15830-6

Contents

PRESENT INDICATIVE

1. Aged about five years
2. Cornwall, 1907
3. As Slightly in *Peter Pan*, Duke of York's Theatre, 1913
4. As Ralph in *The Knight of the Burning Pestle*, Kingsway Theatre, 1920
5. With Lilian Braithwaite in *The Vortex*, Everyman Theatre, 1924
6. With Edna Best in *The Constant Nymph*, New Theatre, 1926
7. With Gertrude Lawrence in *Private Lives*, Phoenix Theatre, 1930
8. With Getrude Lawrence, Adrianne Allen and Laurence Olivier in *Private Lives*, Phoenix Theatre, 1930

FUTURE INDEFINITE

9. As Captain (D) in *In Which We Serve*
10. With Judy Campbell in *Blithe Spirit* (Photo: Cecil Beaton)
11. With Judy Campbell in *Present Laughter* (Photo: Cecil Beaton)
12. As Frank Gibbons in *This Happy Breed* (Photo: Cecil Beaton)
13. With the RAF, Middle East, 1943
14. Irak, 1943
15. Alderley Street, Cape Town
16. With American troops, Assam

Introduction

Gathered here together for the first time are all the autobiographies Noël Coward ever wrote. *Present Indicative*, first published in 1937, deals with Noël's childhood and his early working life up to the immense success of the anglophile chronicle that was *Cavalcade* in 1931; *Future Indefinite*, first published in 1954, deals exclusively with the war years of 1939–45 that were the years of *Blithe Spirit* and *Present Laughter* and *In Which We Serve*. But we also now have here the hitherto unpublished opening to what was going to be his third volume of memoirs, *Past Conditional*, written in the mid-1960s and dealing with the 'missing' 1930s that lay between *Present Indicative* and *Future Indefinite*.

Though only the first hundred or so typescript pages of *Past Conditional* were completed by Noël, they seem to me to contain examples of all that was best in his own autobiographical writing: a travelogue of South America, hilarious Hollywood encounters with moguls and stars of a California world Noël had always managed to avoid, Broadway success in *Design for Living* with his beloved Lunts, diversionary notes on the piano-playing techniques of Jerome Kern and Irving Berlin, and a hauntingly sad passage on the death of a brother most people never knew he had, not to mention the final recollection of a short vicar from Noël's South London childhood whose brains were, in his father's view, far too close to his bottom.

To understand Noël as an autobiographer, you have first to understand the difference between these three books and *The Noël Coward Diaries* that Graham Payn and I edited for publication in 1982 and which are now perhaps more widely known. Where they were written on a daily or weekly or monthly basis over the last thirty years of Noël's life, these autobiographies of his first forty years were far more refined and reworked typescripts written within relatively short periods from the specific viewpoint of the late 30s, the early 50s and the middle 1960s. Chronologically it has made sense to arrange them here in the correct sequence of the years they deal with: but the reader of this volume is therefore meeting Noël first in 1937, then in 1965, and only last around 1950, and must be prepared for certain alterations in character and temperament as well as one or two cast and and status changes in the immediate circle of his friends and enemies.

Present Indicative stands, in my admittedly unimpartial view, alongside Moss Hart's *Act One* and Emlyn Williams' *George* as one of the greatest autobiographies ever written about a life dedicated from an early age to the theatre. What all three books have in common, of course, is that they are largely pre-success stories: almost half of *Present Indicative* is over before we get to *The Vortex* in 1924, but it is in that half that Coward lays out the pattern of his life and explains the rules by which it was to be lived. The Teddington boyhood of genteel poverty, the failed father, the ambitious mother taking in lodgers to keep the family afloat, the child-actor meeting with Gertrude Lawrence, the desperate determination to succeed so that success could be a passport out of a suburban world he did not care for, the survival of failure and loneliness, the early passion for travel preferably by sea, the belief in work as a kind of religious discipline, the delighted discovery of New York's urgent pace and intensity, and then at 24 the success that was to change the face of London for him.

Though he was, as ever, totally discreet in print about his own sexuality, it is not hard to read, between the lines about early friendships and later bleak breakdowns, the truth about a private life that was often considerably less blithe than his own public facade would suggest. Noël himself was later to write one of the most perceptive of all the *Present Indicative* reviews: 'I read it through the other day and was pleased to find it was better written than I expected it to be. The style is sometimes convulsive, there are too many qualifying adjectives, it is technically insecure and there are several repetitive passages which slow up the narrative, but on the whole there is little in it that I regret having said: from it there emerges enough of my true character to make it valid within the limits of its intention, which was to record the factual truth about myself in relation to the world I lived in, the people I met and the rewards I worked for and often won'.

He also was in no doubt that this first autobiography had struck a chord in its readers, albeit probably the wrong one: 'For as long as it is in print or obtainable from secondhand bookshops there will be people, possibly in diminishing numbers, who will be fascinated or repelled, charmed or unimpressed by the story of an alert little boy who was talented and determined and grew up to attain many of his heart's desires and who, throughout his childhood, youth, adolescence and ten of his adult years, remained consistently fond of his mother. This fact inspired many hundred of people to write to me in glowing terms. It apparently proved to doubting minds that in spite of success and adulation, and beneath a glittering veneer of wit and vintage playboyishness, I had managed, with extraordinary strength of character, to retain a few normal human instincts. I must admit that I resent the basic assumption that the first gesture of any young man who makes good is to kick his mother in the teeth, but alas it is one of the most annoying disenchantments of success to be praised for the wrong things'.

Present Indicative ends on a similarly rueful note about the general misunderstanding of *Cavalcade* as no more than a theatrical 'Land of Hope and Glory', and in the six years that separated the end of the book from its first publication Noël went on (as will be seen from *Past Conditional*) to *Design for Living* and *Conversation Piece*, before making the film of *The Scoundrel* and writing for himself and

Gertrude Lawrence the series of one-act plays and musicals that made up *To-night at 8.30*. So by the time his first autobiography reached the bookshops he was still two years away from his fortieth birthday, but already had behind him such theatrical hits as *The Vortex*, *Hay Fever*, *Fallen Angels*, *Private Lives* and *Bitter-Sweet*. 'This' wrote St John Ervine in an *Observer* review, 'is the book of a man who according to his capacity has taken the measure of life and does not shrink from coping with it'.

Other original reviews were similarly enthusiastic about Coward as a man and an autobiographer, with only one notable exception – a notice in the *New Statesman* from Cyril Connolly which is worth quoting here if only to establish that as early in 1937 the case against Coward was already being made more eloquently, if in my view mistakenly, than in any of the subsequent 1950s rows about the angry young men of the Royal Court and Noël's temporary loss of theatrical favour.

After dismissing *Present Indicative* as 'almost always shallow and often dull', Connolly went on to wonder: 'What are we left with? The picture, carefully incomplete, of a success; probably of one of the most talented and prodigiously successful people the world has ever known – a person of infinite charm and adaptability whose very adaptability however makes him inferior to a more compact and worldly competitor in his own sphere, like Cole Porter; and an essentially unhappy man, a man who gives one the impression of having seldom really thought or really lived and who is intelligent enough to know it. But what can he do about it? He is not religious, politics bore him, art means facility or else brickbats, love wild excitement and the nervous breakdown. There is only success, more and more of it, till from his pinnacle he can look down to where Ivor Novello and Beverley Nichols gather samphire on a ledge and to where, a pinpoint on the sands below, Mr Godfrey Winn is counting pebbles. But success is all there is, and that even is temporary. For one can't read any of Noël Coward's plays now . . . they are written in the most topical and perishable way imaginable, the cream in them turns sour overnight – they are even dead before they are turned into talkies, however engaging they may seem at the time. This book reveals a terrible predicament, that of a young man with a Midas touch, with a gift that does not creep and branch and flower, but which turns everything it touches into immediate gold. And the gold melts, too'.

Thirty years after that review and *Present Indicative* were published, when in the late 1960s I was starting to write the first Coward biography, there were still a surprising number of critics around prepared to follow the Connolly line and assert that Coward was doomed to follow Lonsdale and Maugham into a theatrical mausoleum, rather than Wilde and Shaw into the ranks of the ever-revivable. Twenty years later still, at the time of this writing, it does not need a Coward apologist to point out to the unquiet grave of Mr Connolly that so far from being unreadable and unplayable, the comedies of Coward are revived more often around the country and the world than those of any other dramatist of his era.

Like Wodehouse, Coward survived to have the last laugh at his own critics; but occasional asides in *Past Conditional* indicate that their hostility especially in the mid-1950s caused him considerable unhappiness, and certainly *Future Indefinite* was originally received with a lot less critical and public enthusiasm than *Present Indicative*. There were I think several reasons for this, and the first was its timing. Rather than continue with volume two of his memoirs from where *Present Indicative* left off in 1931, which would have been logical enough, Noël had come to believe that his war experiences in Paris and then on various troop and concert tours merited a book to themselves, despite the fact that he had already published in 1944 a *Middle East Diary* which was (as he explains in *Future Indefinite*) to get him into a great deal of American trouble.

But by the time *Future Indefinite* finally appeared in 1954, readers had already had almost a decade of war memoirs and were eager to get on to something new: moreover (as his Diaries now reveal) this was a highly edited and somewhat cautious account of his war, and one inevitably lacking in any of the showbiz glamour with which his public rightly or wrongly now associated the boy wonder of *Present Indicative*. Noël's own feelings about the war and his part in it were often deeply confused, and the result, as the *Economist* reviewer noted, was that 'Coward is here painfully expatriated ... success faithfully attends him, the eminent appreciate him, Royalty thanks him, audiences applaud him; but he remains somehow not "in", not orientated, uncertain of his proper role; a figure at once more complex and more sympathetic than one would conjecture him to realize'.

If *Present Indicative* is the story of a stagestruck boy becoming a star, then *Future Indefinite* is the story of a middle-aged man trying to come to terms with a world in total disarray. In there somewhere is, I believe, a lot of the truth about the way that the war changed Coward as it did so many men and women of his generation; but his audiences in the 1950s had already proved spectacularly fickle, and they certainly did not either want or expect from him a book that was as serious a documentary as *Future Indefinite*. The diary that he began keeping in 1941 (and that forms the basis for this second complete autobiography) indicates that he started thinking seriously about it in the September of 1947: 'I found myself talking about England so very proudly, though I was talking about England in the war years when her gallantry and common sense were marred by emergency. It is all very confusing. I think I had better get after *Future Indefinite* and get some of my confusion down on paper'.

That process was to take him the next five years, with pauses along the way for such various and different projects as the musical *Ace of Clubs*, the film of *The Astonished Heart* and two rather more successful stage comedies, *Quadrille* and *Relative Values*. But he kept returning to the typescript of *Future Indefinite* as if convinced that in there somewhere, in those logs of tours and troop concerts and the filming of *In Which We Serve* and the writing of *Blithe Spirit*, lay a kind of key to the way that he and his beloved England had been changed by the Second World War. That key proved elusive: by 1952 he was noting, very unusually, the need for some major rewrites ('last part too scurried and not objective enough') and it is clear that he found it a great deal easier to write *Present Indicative* purely from childhood memory than *Future Indefinite* with the help of all his contemporary notes.

Yet what finally emerged in 1954, not to hostility, exactly, but to a politely stifled critical yawn, is important for the altogether different light it throws on Coward as a man. Here we seldom find him backstage, or concerned except tangentially with the problems of his career: instead he is out on the road, doing war work that he sometimes finds either incomprehensible or pointless, but brought up time and again against the question of who he really thinks he is and what he is supposed to be doing with his life at a time when just hanging on to that life was often a full-time occupation.

Through *Future Indefinite* there is no doubt we get to meet an older, wearier, sometimes more confused and cynical man than the youthful achiever of *Present Indicative*: but what seems to me intriguing and important about both these fully-fledged autobiographies is that they are far from the typical or predictable greasepainted cuttings jobs one might have expected. Coward was an avid reader of autobiographies, and he knew a lot about what made the best of them work: he knew that lists of names or places or plays were disastrous, and that in the end the readers wanted to know who he was and where he came from as well as what he had achieved. He constructed these books as carefully as he constructed the best of his plays, and if they are not perhaps as consistently witty or upbeat as those plays then that is simply because he was Noël Coward, not one of his own creations like Elyot Chase or Garry Essendine.

It is of course unfortunate that he never completed *Past Conditional*, because on the evidence here I think that it might have been the most intriguing of all the autobiographies. He was writing it at just the moment when he was about to come back into critical favour after a long geographic and theatrical exile, and freed from the constraints of the war diaries and his own childhood memories I believe he was beginning to write about himself in his thirties with a clarity and perception that is not always evident in the earlier volumes. But, in the words of one of his own earliest and worst songs, 'ordinary man invariably sighs for the peach out of reach', and what we have here now can be taken, along with the Diaries that cover the remaining years of his life, to represent the most complete picture of Noël that we have ever been given from his own typewriter.

Sheridan Morley

Present Indicative

PRESENT INDICATIVE: 1899-1931

WRITTEN: 1932-36
FIRST PUBLISHED: 1937

PART ONE

I was photographed naked on a cushion very early in life, an insane, toothless smile slitting my face and pleats of fat overlapping me like an ill-fitting overcoat. Later, at the age of two, I was photographed again. This time in a lace dress, leaning against a garden roller and laughing hysterically. If these photographs can be found they will adorn this book.

In due course I was baptized into the Church of England and, I believe, behaved admirably at the font. No undignified gurglings and screamings. I was carried to the church, damped, and carried back home, preserving throughout an attitude of serene resignation.

Two years later, laced and beribboned, I was conveyed to church again, and was unimpressed by everything except the music to which I danced immediately in the aisle before anyone could stop me, and upon being hoisted back into the pew, fell into such an ungovernable rage that I had to be taken home.

There are many other small incidents of my infancy, some based on hearsay, and some that I actually recall, but I will try to employ a selective economy in setting them down, for it is a tricky business tracing the development of a character along the avenues of reminiscence. Too much detailed accuracy makes dull reading. I don't believe that my own childhood, until I went on the stage at the age of ten, was very different from that of any other little boy of the middle classes, except perhaps that certain embryonic talents may have made me more precocious than the average, and more difficult to manage. Several characteristics which have been commented upon in later years evinced themselves early. I was self-assured from the first, and intolerant of undue piety. I was also uncompromising in my attitude towards people I disliked, attempting to strike them in the face, or failing this, going off into screaming fits which frequently lasted long enough for the doctor to be sent for, but invariably gave place to chubby cluckings and smiles by the time he arrived.

I cherished a woolly monkey called 'Doris' for many years. She shared my bed until I was five, despite the fact that time and friction had denuded her of her fur, her tail, and one eye. I was also excessively fond of fish.

My mother came from what is known as 'Good Family,' which means that she had been brought up in the tradition of being a gentlewoman, a difficult tradition to uphold with very little money in a small suburb, and liable to degenerate into refined gentility unless carefully watched.

The family name was 'Veitch,' and there is a genealogical tree and a crest and engravings of the house in Scotland which my mother and her sisters never saw, as it passed into alien hands before they were born. My grandfather was a captain in the Navy, and the photographs we have of him show a handsome head with curly hair, wide eyes, and side-whiskers. He was, I believe, rather short, which doesn't show in the photographs, as in all of them he is sitting down. He painted a lot in his spare time, mostly water colours, some of them very large indeed. He was good at mountains and clouds and ships, and reflections in the sea, but consciously bad at figures, so he frequently cut these out from coloured prints, and stuck them, singly and in groups, on to his blue mountains, to give the landscapes 'life.'

He died in Madeira, comparatively young, and his wife and children came home to England, where my mother was born soon afterwards. There were, in addition to Mother, three girls and two boys, and an extra relation called Barbara, or 'Borby,' who had fallen out of a port-hole on her head at the age of two, and was consequently a little peculiar. In course of time both the brothers died, and two of the sisters married, one well, the other not so well, and in the year 1883 my grandmother, Aunt Borby, Aunt Vida and my mother, came to Teddington, still quite a small village on the banks of the Thames, where they lived gently and I think a trifle sadly, making over last year's dresses and keeping up appearances.

The social activities of Teddington swirled around St Alban's Church. It was an imposing building rearing high from the ground, secure in the possession of a copper roof which had turned bright green, and a militant vicar, the Reverend Mr Boyd, who was given to furious outbursts from the pulpit, in course of which his eyes flashed fire and his fingers pointed accusingly at old ladies in the congregation. He calmed down in after-years and became Vicar of St Paul's, Knightsbridge. Apart from him and the copper roof, the church's greatest asset was the Coward family, which was enormous, active, and fiercely musical. My Uncle Jim played the organ, while my father, together with my Uncles Randolph, Walter, Percy, and Gordon, and my Aunts Hilda, Myrrha, Ida, and Nellie, graced the choir. Aunt Hilda, indeed, achieved such distinction as a 'coloratura' that she ultimately became known as 'The Twickenham Nightingale.'

It was during choir practice that my mother (also musical) met my father. He courted her for a long time through many services. I like to think of him peeping through his fingers at her during the Litany, and winking fearfully at her under cover of Mr Boyd's vitriolic sermons. They appeared together also in various discreet theatricals, notably a performance of *The Gondoliers* at the Town Hall, in which all the Cowards played principal parts, and Mother demurely tra-la-la'd in the chorus.

When they were married they continued to live at Teddington. Father was very spruce. He always wore a blue cornflower in his buttonhole, and was justly proud of having a cold bath every morning, winter and summer. He went every day to London, where he worked for Metzler's, the music publishers. A boy was born and christened 'Russell,' but he died of meningitis at the age of six, a year and a half before I appeared on the morning of December 16th, 1899.

Teddington grew steadily. A new lock was built. There was a swifter train service to London, and electric trams began to screech along the High Street. There were lots more houses everywhere, with lots more people in them, and with this onset of urban progress the Coward glory began to fade. Nearly all the sisters married and dispersed, the brothers also; Uncle Percy, indeed, actually dispersed all the way to Toronto, where he married a professional pianist, and has never been heard of since, with the exception of a few vague rumours from Australia.

In 1905 we moved to a small villa in Sutton, Surrey. It had bow windows in the front, and a slim straight garden at the back. It also had coloured glass let into the front door. Father had left Metzler's and joined a piano firm which was just beginning. His position in the firm was at first not clearly defined, but on closer analysis proved to be that of a traveller. This necessitated his being away from home a good deal. Once he even went as far afield as Naples. I remember this distinctly, because post-cards of Vesuvius fluttered daily through the letter-box.

A little while after we arrived in Sutton, my brother Eric was born. Emma, our beloved 'general' who had been with us since before my birth, took me round to have tea with some friends, and when I got back I was led upstairs by Auntie Vida to see my 'new little brother.' He seemed to me to be bright red and singularly unattractive, but everybody else was delighted with him. Various things of minor importance happened to me in Sutton. I was run over by a bicycle and had concussion. The calf of my leg was practically torn off by a bull-terrier, and I was brave when it was cauterised.

When I was six I was sent to a day school which was kept by a Miss Willington, who wore blouses with puffed sleeves, plaid skirts and her hair done over a pad. I didn't care for her. On one occasion when she had been irritating me over some little question of English grammar I bit her arm right through to the bone, an action which I have never for an instant regretted.

I made my first public appearance at a prize-giving concert at the end of the term. I was dressed in a white sailor suit and sang 'Coo' from *The Country Girl*, followed by a piping little song about the spring for which I accompanied myself on the piano. This feat brought down the house, and I had to repeat it. I remember leaning over to Mother and Father in the front row and hissing exultantly: 'I've got to sing again.' The evening ended in tears, however, because I was not given a prize. Mother tried vainly to explain to me that the prizes were for hard work during the term and not for vocal prowess, but I refused to be comforted, and was led away weeping.

Mother had an old school friend who came to stay with us sometimes. Her name was Gwen Kelly, and she was a darling. She had large mournful Irish eyes, and a white tailor-made coat and skirt, and she sang and played exquisitely. Her voice was a husky contralto with a brogue in it, and it is to her that I owe the first real enthusiasm I ever had for music. She is dead now, after devoting her life to genteel poverty and an invalid mother, but she was the first artist I knew and I shall never forget her.

We went to the seaside every summer for a fortnight. Broadstairs or Brighton or Bognor. It was at Bognor that I met Uncle George's Concert Party. I shall always remember Uncle George and his 'Merrie Men' with tenderness. They held for me a romantic attraction in their straw hats, coloured blazers, and grubby white flannel trousers. They had a small wooden stage on the sands on which they performed every afternoon and evening. Uncle George himself was the comedian and Uncle Bob, I think, was the serious vocalist. I forget the names of the others excepting Uncle Jack, who was very jaunty and sang, 'Put a little bit away for a rainy day,' swaggering up and down the stage and jingling coins in his trouser pocket.

Uncle George gave a song-and-dance competition every week for the 'Kiddies,' for which I entered my name. I don't think Mother was keen on the idea, but she gave in when she saw how eager I was. On the evening of the competition I put on my sailor suit and waited in a sort of pen with several other aspirants, noting with satisfaction that those who appeared before me were inept and clumsy. When my turn came I sang, 'Come along with me to the Zoo, dear,' and 'Liza Ann' from *The Orchid*. I also danced violently. The applause was highly gratifying, and even Mother forgot her distaste of Uncle George's vulgarity somewhat and permitted herself to bridle. At the end of the performance Uncle George made a speech and presented me with the first prize, a large box of chocolates, which, when opened in our lodgings, proved to be three parts shavings.

From the age of five onwards Mother always took me to a theatre on my birthday. We went up to London in the morning and waited in the pit queue. I saw *The Dairymaids* and *The Blue Moon*, and a Spectacle at the London Hippodrome with a dam bursting and tons of water pouring into the arena. We also went to the pantomime at Croydon which I enjoyed ecstatically from the first moment when the orchestra tuned up and the advertisement-covered safety-curtain rose, disclosing the faded old red tabs lit with an orange glow from the footlights, to the very end of the Harlequinade, when crackers were thrown by the clown and pantaloon to those fortunate enough to be in the expensive seats.

One Christmas I was given a toy theatre complete with two sets of scenery. One scene was a thick wood with a cottage in the distance, and the other was the interior of the cottage with a lot of painted beams. I used to augment this meagre *décor* with penny pantomime sheets which in those days were obtainable at any newspaper shop. There was *Cinderella*, *The Forty Thieves*, and a lurid melodrama called *Black-eyed Susan*, and many others as well. There were generally three scenes to each sheet, with all the characters brilliantly coloured and marked for each act. These had to be cut out with scissors and mounted on cardboard. I remember 'Fatima, Act III,' of the *Bluebird* sheet was one of my favourites. She was a bulbous girl with a turban. I was also very partial to 'Dandini, Act I,' in the

Cinderella set. Later on I had a bigger theatre, and Father painted me some excellent scenery, and I used dolls on wires instead of the pasteboard figures, but in my heart I liked the pantomime sheets best.

When I was seven I spent the summer with my Aunt Laura in Cornwall. She was kind, pretty, and vain, and I was very fond of her. Her garden was lovely, and there was a large lake, very deep, with an island in the middle and jungle all round with small hidden waterfalls and secret paths. There was a swing, too, and a small blue punt which sank immediately if touched.

In 1908 we moved to Number 70, Prince of Wales Mansions, Battersea Park. It was a top flat with a little balcony looking out over the park to where the iron framework of Albert Bridge and Chelsea Bridge rose in the distance above the trees. I made a few friends in the adjacent flats and together we harassed the park-keepers, rang bells and ran away, and roller-skated up and down the pavements. Sometimes in the summer we skated all the way to St George's Baths in Buckingham Palace Road and back again, with our wet bathing dresses flapping round our necks.

At this period money worries were oppressing my parents considerably. Father's income from Payne's pianos was small, and Eric and I were both growing fast and had to be clothed and fed. Mother, realising that something had to be done in order to pay off the swiftly mounting debts, decided to take in paying guests. And so a Mr Baker and a Mr Denston came to live with us, and everybody dressed for dinner for the first time for years. This was really quite a jolly period. Emma was still with us and she was a good cook. Gwen Kelly often came to dinner and played the piano afterwards. Father was gay and sang all his old songs with Mother playing his accompaniments. She would take off her rings and place them on the side of the piano and then embark with a flourish upon the introductory chords of 'Mary Adeane,' or 'She and I Together,' while I sat in an Eton collar on the sofa watching for her little grimace when she struck a wrong note, and listening to Mr Baker whispering flirtatiously to Gwen Kelly in the corner.

Father had a light tenor voice of great sweetness, and he frequently shut his eyes tightly for the top notes, reliving, I am sure in those moments, not only the past glories of Teddington drawing-rooms, but the more austere occasions when he, together with Uncle Percy, Uncle Randolph, and Uncle Walter, had awakened the sophisticated echoes of the Caxton Hall, Westminster:

> 'So dainty fair, so gentle wise,
> Young love peeped forth from heaven-blue eyes,
> The lark poured rapture from the skies
> As we went through the heather.'

2

A short while after we had settled in Battersea Park a great agitation was started as to whether or not I was to join the Chapel Royal choir. Uncle Walter, then an eminent member of it, was approached, also Dr Alcock, the organist. It was agreed that I should go to the Chapel Royal school to begin with until I was old enough to have my voice tried for the choir itself. The school was in Clapham, and was run by a Mr Claude Selfe. It was small, consisting only of the twelve Chapel Royal boys, and seven or eight outside pupils of whom I was one. Mr Selfe was kind, sometimes jocular, and nearly always noisy. He had a slight paunch and the most tremendous calves which looked as though they were about to burst exuberantly through his trousers. Manliness was his strong suit, and he did everything in his power to foster this admirable quality in us. Boyishness was all right up to a certain age, but after that manliness was the thing. He wore a black gown and a mortar-board, and when he became in the least enthusiastic or excited over anything, bubbles of foam sprang from his lips like ping-pong balls.

I travelled to school daily by tram, or rather, two trams, as I had to change half-way. The second one landed me at the 'Plough,' Clapham, and from there I walked, in anguish in the mornings, and on wings of song in the afternoon when I was on my way home, loitering on autumn days to collect 'conkers,' and occasionally ringing a few bells just to celebrate the joyful hours of freedom separating me from the next morning. There was a second-hand book-shop on the way where I could buy 'back numbers' of the *Strand Magazine* for a penny each, and I hoarded my pocket money until I could buy a whole year's worth in order to read the E. Nesbit story right through without having to wait for the next instalment. I read 'The Phoenix and the Carpet,' and 'Five Children and It,' also 'The Magic City,' but there were a few numbers missing from that year, so I stole a coral necklace from a visiting friend of Mother's, pawned it for five shillings, and bought the complete book at the Army and Navy Stores. It cost four-and-six, so that including the fare (penny half-return, Battersea Park to Victoria) I was fivepence to the good. In later years I told E. Nesbit of this little incident and I regret to say that she was delighted.

Three days a week at the Chapel Royal school the choir-boys were absent, either in the mornings or afternoons, for choir practice. These days were blissfully quiet, the class-room seemed a pleasant place relaxed in a peaceful emptiness. When I arrived in the morning and saw that those horrible little mortar-boards were not on the pegs in the lobby I knew at once that lessons would be easier, that Mr Selfe would be in an amiable mood, and that the quarter of an hour interval in the middle of the morning would be an interlude of rest rather than a strained evasion of games I didn't want to play.

On the days when the choir-boys were all present the entire atmosphere seemed charged with gloom and foreboding. They were nasty little brutes as far as I can remember, and used to bully me mildly, putting ink pellets down my collar and forcing my head down the w.c. pan. Once during one of these boyish pranks I pretended to faint, having kicked one of them in the fork, an unmanly performance which frightened everyone very much indeed.

Eventually the day came when my voice was to be tried, a lot of assiduous practice having taken place beforehand with Mother at the piano and me hooting the praises of the Lord at her side.

I was dressed in my Eton suit with a slightly larger collar than usual in case of unforeseen throat expansion, and with my hair suitably plastered, I set off clutching a roll of music and Mother's hand.

Dr Alcock was distant and extremely superior. Perhaps his position as Chapel Royal organist, which automatically brought him into contact with the Royal Family as well as the Almighty, faintly upset his balance as a human being. However, undaunted by his forbidding expression, I sang Gounod's 'There is a Green Hill Far Away' at him from beginning to end. My voice was very good and I sang it well, although perhaps a shade too dramatically. I remember giving way to a certain abandon on the line 'There was no other goo-oo-oo-ood enough to pay the price of sin,' and later, lashing myself into a frenzy over the far too often repeated – 'Arnd terust in His redeeming blood.' I think, perhaps, it was this that settled my hash with Dr Alcock, for we were ushered out rapidly with the parting words that not only was I far too young, but that there was no vacancy anyhow. Mother was bitterly disappointed, and I felt miserable at having failed, also offended that my assured talent should not have been immediately recognised, but deep down inside me I was conscious of a secret relief, a certain lifting of the heart when I reflected that my near future was not after all to be spent singing sacred music in company with those unpleasant choir-boys. Mother simmered with rage against Dr Alcock and the whole Chapel Royal for weeks, ultimately arriving at the more comforting viewpoint that my not being accepted was a great stroke of good fortune, as Dr Alcock was silly and obviously didn't know a good voice when he heard one, and that the whole choir looked extremely common, including Uncle Walter.

3

Shortly after my failure for the Chapel Royal, our paying guests departed, and Mother made another of her sudden decisions. This time it was to let the flat for six months and take a small cottage in the country. I think that during all those years in London and the suburbs she had been secretly yearning for some quieter place in which to be poor. Small poverty is a greater strain in a town than in a village, and Mother was country-bred, and weary of whining cockney tradesmen and crowded buses and genteel makeshifts. She often talked wistfully of Chobham where she had lived as a girl; where there had been a garden to the house, a real garden, not a ruled-off passage sown with a few nasturtiums. An advertisement was put in the paper and we waited anxiously for results. Fate was kindly prompt, and in a very few days a Mrs Davis arrived without warning while we were having tea. She was gay and erratic and untidy, with a large green hat and a feather boa. She immediately joined us at tea, and intercepted Mother who was trying to nip into the kitchen in order to change the jam-jar for a more impressive dish.

After tea we went into the drawing-room which smelt rather frowsy as it hadn't been used for a long time, and Mrs Davis sang 'Mifanwy,' and 'My Dear Soul' in a piercing soprano, and then, encouraged, I think, by our obvious musical appreciation, said that she would like to take the flat on the dot providing that she could move in within three days. Mother assumed a dubious expression which wouldn't have deceived a kitten, and shook her head thoughtfully, trying hard to conceal the glint of excitement in her eyes and endeavouring not to appear too eager. I personally thought that she had gone raving mad. However, it was all fixed up satisfactorily, and we spent the next three days in a state of rapture, spring-cleaning, and having our meals off one end of the kitchen table.

We went first to stay with Grandmother, Auntie Borby, and Auntie Vida in rooms at Southsea, and Eric and I were left there while Mother and Father scoured Hampshire for a cottage. There were many enchanting things to do in Southsea. Trips backwards and forwards across Portsmouth Harbour in ferry-boats, sometimes expeditions as far as Ryde in bigger steamers, concerts on the Clarence Pier, and occasionally an actual play on the South Parade Pier. It was early April, and windy, and I frequently sat for hours watching the waves sliding up the slanting stone breakwaters just below the castle. I can remember, too, trudging home at dusk across the common after a long walk, with a flick of rain in the wind, and all the lights coming up along the parade. There is for me a certain romantic desolation about Southsea and I shall always be attached to it. Whenever I revisit it now it feels familiar and friendly. The South Parade Pier and the Clarence Pier may have shrunk a trifle, the Isle of Wight may seem a little less magical and not so far away, but the forts are still there patterned like chess-boards in the sea, and the castle, and Handleys, and the Cosham trams creaking round the corners; and there are still grey warships lying out at Spithead.

About this time I took a fancy for the most tremendously hearty schoolboy literature. I read avidly week by week *Chums*, *The Boy's Own Paper*, *The Magnet*, and *The Gem*, and loved particularly these last two. *The Gem* appeared on Thursday or Friday, and was devoted to the light-hearted adventures of Tom Merry and Co. *The Magnet* came out on Tuesdays, and dealt with the very similar adventures of Harry Wharton and Co. As far as I can remember the dialogue of the two papers was almost identical, consisting largely of the words 'Jape' and 'Wheeze,' and in moments of hilarity and pain respectively: 'Ha Ha Ha!' and 'Yow Yow Yow!' There was a fat boy in each. In *The Magnet* it was Billy Bunter, who in addition to being very greedy and providing great opportunities for jam-tart fun ('Ha Ha Ha! – He He He! – Yow Yow Yow!'), was a ventriloquist of extraordinary ability, and could make sausages cry out when stabbed with a fork. They were awfully manly decent fellows, Harry Wharton and Co., and no suggestion of sex, even in its lighter forms, ever sullied their conversation. Considering their ages, their healthy-mindedness was almost frightening. I was delighted to find in a newspaper shop the other day that *The Magnet* was unchanged, excepting its cover, which used to be bright orange and is now white. I read a little of it with tender emotion. There they all were, Harry Wharton, Frank Nugent, and Billy Bunter, still 'Ha Ha Ha-ing' and 'He He He-ing' and still, after twenty-four years, hovering merrily on the verge of puberty.

Mother and Father finally discovered a minute cottage at a place called Meon in Hampshire, not far from the village of Tichfield. It had a thatch, and a lavatory at the end of the garden, the door of which always had to be kept shut because the goat liked to use it as well as the family. We lived there for six months completely happily. There was very little money, and at times I believe there wasn't enough food, but we were in the country, and so it didn't matter so much.

The sea, or rather the Solent, was only a mile away, and during Cowes Regatta Week we could see all the excitements going on just across the water. It was the year the German Emperor came and our Fleet saluted his yacht. For several nights all the warships were illuminated, and we had a moonlight picnic on the edge of the low sandy cliff, and let off some fireworks of our own that Father had bought in Fareham.

I learned a lot about the country during those six months. We went nutting and blackberrying and haymaking, and Mother and I were nearly caught stealing our landlord's plums after dark, and had to lie giggling in a ditch for half an hour.

Some little girls lived nearby, and I forced them to act a tragedy that I had written, but they were very silly and during the performance forgot their lines and sniggered, so I hit the eldest one on the head with a wooden spade, the whole affair thus ending in tears and a furious quarrel between the mothers involved.

Mrs Davis wished to keep our flat on in London for longer than she had originally intended, and at the end of our lease of the cottage we went back to Southsea for six weeks. A little while after Christmas Mother and Father became suddenly conscience-stricken over my lack of education, and so it was arranged for me to return to London a week before them in order to be in time for the first moment of the term. I was to stay with my Uncle Ran and Aunt Amy in St George's Square, and I travelled up to Victoria bleak in spirit at the prospect, not only of staying in a strange house, but of getting up early in the morning and going back to school. Mr Selfe loomed in my imagination like a black bat, the voluminous wings of his gown waiting to envelop me in the manly discipline from which I had been free for so long, and the day that I was to rejoin Mother in the flat seemed too far away in the future to be the least comfort.

That week more than came up to expectations; it was miserable beyond belief, although on looking back I am unable to discover exactly why I should have been so wretched. My aunt and uncle were kind, if somewhat remote in their attitude; perhaps if they had fussed over me a little at first and been less distantly correct in their manner towards me, or perhaps if I had not been so spoiled at home, I might have been happier there. As it was, I was conscious for the first time of being a very small boy indeed, forlorn, and badly mother-sick. There was a thick yellow fog throughout the whole week and school work was done with the gas on. The shadows of my snuffling classmates flickered over the walls, and the general smell of feet and linoleum smothered me. Mr Selfe was irascible and more frothy than ever, and one day caned me lightly on the hand which shocked and frightened me immeasurably. I remember crying all the way home in the tram to Victoria, and groping my way through the fog to St George's Square, where I managed to get to my bedroom at the top of the house without being seen by anyone but the housemaid who let me in. Once there I gave way to screaming hysterics. I was obsessed with the idea that Mother was going to have some sort of accident and die without my ever seeing her again. The dramatic scenes I visualised were terrifying: first the fatal telegram arriving at the house, and my aunt and uncle calling me into the drawing-room on the first floor to break the news, then a tear-sodden journey in the train and Auntie Vida meeting me at Fratton Junction, very small and morose, in black. Then, as a fitting climax I imagined the front bedroom enshrouded in funereal twilight with the blinds down and Mother lying still and dead under a sheet like a waxwork. 'My Aunt Amy appeared presently and admonished me kindly, she must have been startled, poor woman, at the sight of such abandoned despair. However, there was in her manner a certain dry efficiency that eventually suffocated my tears and reduced me to stillness, and a little later I dined downstairs in a state of splendid calm, and talked tremulously to the various nurses from the Westminster Hospital, several of whom were always present at meal-times. My aunt was then, and is still, a brisk dealer in nurses who, not being spoiled hysterical little boys, derive much comfort and warmth from that high clean house.

During the year 1909 my singing voice developed strongly. It was really a good voice, more full-blooded than the usual boyish treble. I occasionally sang anthems in churches but I hated doing this because the lack of applause depressed me. It irritated me when I had soared magnificently through 'God is a Spirit,' or 'Oh for the Wings of a Dove' to see the entire congregation scuffle on to their knees murmuring gloomy 'Amens' instead of clapping loudly and shouting 'Bravo.' Concerts were much more satisfactory, and I particularly enjoyed the annual church garden party at Teddington. It was a sort of fête and jumble sale, and there were stalls and amusements and a band. It was generally opened by someone suitably aristocratic, and my Aunt Myrrha ran the concerts, of which there were usually three or four in course of the afternoon. This was when I shone. I always sang a serious ballad to begin with, my principal successes being 'Through the Forest,' and 'Cherry Blossom Time.' The latter invariably was a great favourite, possibly owing to the redundance of its 'Hey Nonnys' and 'Ho Nonnys' and its winsomely pastoral sentiments. After this, I returned, smiling to the applause, and rendered a light musical comedy number with dance. It must have been surprising and, I should have thought, nauseating, to see a little boy of nine in a white sailor suit flitting about a small wooden stage, employing, with instinctive accuracy, the gestures and tricks of a professional soubrette, but they seemed to love it and encored me vociferously. Perhaps my lack of self-consciousness and my youth mitigated a little the horror of the situation, but I am certain that could my adult self have been present in that stuffy tent, he would have crept out, at the first coy gurgle, and been mercifully sick outside. I do not mean that I wasn't good. I was certainly good, far and away too good. My assurance was nothing short of petrifying, and although I look back upon myself in that saucy sailor suit with a shudder of embarrassment, there is envy in my heart as well.

The reader will probably gather from the above description that I was a brazen, odious little prodigy, over-pleased with myself and precocious to a degree; perhaps I was, but I was learning a lot, even from those kindly old ladies in their garden party finery; after all, I act to them still at matinées and I have a sad suspicion that I don't give them half as much pleasure now as I did then.

I was taken to *The King of Cadonia* on my ninth birthday, and fell in love with Gracie Leigh, and Mother bought me the *Play Pictorial*, and I cut out all the photographs and stuck them on my bedroom wall, where they remained until they turned yellow and curly at the edges and were replaced by new ones.

A little while after this, Mother, who was pleased but not surprised by my success in public, decided that my natural gift for dancing could be improved by a few lessons. So far I had tripped and flitted with much grace but little technique, often, owing to an inadequate knowledge of balance, losing control in my turns, and on one unfortunate occasion, actually finishing with my back to the audience on the final chord. The question of my going on the stage had been discussed several times. My talents and ambitions seemed obviously to lead towards it, but we were ignorant of the initial steps to take. Also I was only nine years old, and excepting a casual acquaintance with 'Mensa: A Table' in the first declension only, and a vivid mental picture of Flamborough Head, I was absolutely uneducated. The idea was therefore temporarily dismissed and lay fermenting in our minds waiting to jump out again the first moment a suitable opportunity offered itself. Meanwhile, the dancing lessons were a move in the right direction. It was no use concentrating on my voice, for that, alas, owing to certain processes in adolescence, would inevitably degenerate into humiliating croakings, and there was no physiological guarantee that when the raucous period passed, a silvery tenor would emerge in compensation for the lost soprano.

We interviewed a Miss Janet Thomas who ran a Dancing Academy in Hanover Square. Her manner was professionally brusque but sympathetic, and she seemed to take a fancy to me and agreed to give me a course of twelve lessons at a minimum fee. So, for the next six weeks I dispensed with school on Tuesday and Friday afternoons, and journeyed, first in the train from Battersea Park to Victoria, and then in a bus to the corner of Conduit Street.

It says a lot for Mother's self-control that she could sit at home, tortured by visions of street accidents, and allow me to gallivant about the town by myself at such a tender age; but she had fostered in me a spirit of independence, realising with remarkable foresight, considering how much she loved me, the valuable experience I should gain from learning to grapple early and alone with small adventures. This was brave wisdom and I profited by it. Long before I was twelve years old I was capable of buying tickets and counting change, ordering buns and glasses of milk in tea-shops, and battling in and out of trams and buses and trains. I could have found my way anywhere about London with ease, and above all, I acquired the inestimable habit of being completely happy alone. I also found that conversation with casual strangers was stimulating to the imagination. I shocked many kindly interfering old ladies with picturesque descriptions of my appalling life at home, making them cluck and shudder with horror at the drunken brutality of my father, and the squalid misery of our tenement room filled with ill-nourished brothers and sisters, many of them suffering from lingering diseases. One old body, I believe, actually went to the police about me. At any rate she said she was going, but as I had given her a false name and address, nothing ever came of it. It was also a pleasant game to be discovered sobbing wretchedly in the corners of railway carriages or buses in the hope that someone would take pity on me and perhaps give me tea at Fuller's. This was only rarely successful, the only two responses I can recall both being clergymen. One talked to me for a long time and told me to trust in God and everything would come right, and the other pinched my knee and gave me sixpence. Of the two, I preferred the latter.

I loved my dancing lessons with Miss Thomas. She started me off herself and then passed me on to her assistant, Miss Alice Hall, who put me through the whole routine of ballet dancing, including even point work for which I wore block-toed shoes. The room was long and large and smelt dimly of Ronuk. There were enormous mirrors all along one wall, and I had a fascinating view of my own front and Miss Hall's behind, which, while she was showing me the fleeter steps, jumped up and down merrily inside her black satin bloomers. There was another assistant, took named Enid, who had slightly projecting teeth and was a dear. When Miss Thomas wasn't there Miss Hall and Enid used to ask me to stay to tea which was brewed on a spirit lamp in a little curtained-off recess in the corner of the studio. This treat was only possible when I was the last pupil, and I was often bitterly disappointed when, just towards the end of my time, some gangling débutante would appear for her deportment lesson.

Frequently on my homeward journey I walked all the way from Hanover Square to Victoria, through Green Park, thereby saving a penny to buy fudge at a little shop in the Buckingham Palace Road. It was a stern principle with me never to buy the fudge at any other shop before I reached Victoria, in case I broke my leg and hadn't the penny for the bus fare.

4

One day, just before I had come to the end of my dancing course, a little advertisement appeared in the *Daily Mirror*. Mother read it aloud to me while I was having breakfast. It stated that a talented boy of attractive appearance was required by a Miss Lila Field to appear in her production of an all-children fairy play: *The Goldfish*. This seemed to dispose of all argument. I was a talented boy, God knows, and when washed and smarmed down a bit, passably attractive. There appeared to be no earthly reason why Miss Lila Field shouldn't jump at me, and we both believed that she would be a fool indeed to miss such a magnificent opportunity.

I departed for school that morning late, leaving Mother to compose a not too effusive answer to the advertisement. In due course a letter arrived from Lila Field making an appointment for us to go and see her.

On the day specified we left the house in a flurry of grandeur, Mother very impressive in grey satin with a feather boa, and me burning bright in a new Norfolk suit with an Eton collar. Miss Field received us in a small bare room in George Street, Baker Street. She was smart and attractive with a charming voice, and her large brown eyes smiled kindly at us over highly-rouged cheeks and a beauty spot. My heart sank when I noticed that there was no piano, but after a little polite conversation we surmounted that difficulty and I sang 'Liza Ann' unaccompanied, and mother la-la'd for the dance. Miss Field was delighted and said that she would engage me for the part of 'Prince Mussel' and that the fee would be a guinea and a half a week, upon which Mother became sadly red and said that she was afraid we couldn't afford to pay that. Miss Field laughed and said that the guinea and a half a week was what I would receive, and that she'd let us know soon when rehearsals started. Mother and I floated down the narrow staircase and out into the street. The moment was supreme, and we could scarcely breathe for excitement. We went straight to Selfridge's and celebrated our triumph with ice-cream sodas over which we calculated how much a year I should be earning at a guinea and a half a week. Father was impressed with our news when we reached home and we sat up very late inaccurately visualising my future. A letter was sent to Mr Selfe announcing that my school attendance would be even more convulsive than it had been hitherto, as I was now a professional actor.

The rehearsals for *The Goldfish* took place about twice a week for many months; there seemed to be a hitch over the actual production and many mothers became impatient and snatched their children away, which naturally made holes in the cast and necessitated further rehearsals of the newcomers.

Ultimately a definite production date was announced and rehearsals became less spasmodic, the 'all children' cast sang and danced, and tried on elaborate costumes at Debenham and Freebody's in a state of wild excitement. Even the most hardened and cynical of the mothers were moved to enthusiasm.

The Goldfish was a fairy play in three acts, written by Miss Field herself. I believe it had originally been produced the previous year at The Playhouse for special matinées, but the production in which I appeared was entirely reorganised.

I can only vaguely remember the plot. The first act was a children's party with a spirited opening chorus 'School, School, Good-bye to School,' which I led in company with a pretty fair girl 'Little June Tripp' (later 'June' and later still, June Inverclyde). After this came some gay provocative dialogue, only one line of which I can recall: 'Crumbs! How exciting!'

In the second act for some reason or other all the children from the first act had turned into fish. June was 'Princess Sole,' Burford Hampden 'King Starfish,' and Alfred Willmore 'King Goldfish.' I, as 'Prince Mussel,' did not appear until the third act. There were many other fish characters, and a large girl with big knees and a rich contralto voice who played 'The Spirit of the Shells.' She sang a song at the beginning of the second act which always convulsed me, there was something about her strangely adult figure swathed in green tulle weaving up and down the stage, and that strong resonant voice bursting out of her, that was ridiculously at variance with the piping refinement of the rest of the cast. She also mouthed her words in a most peculiar manner.

> 'A so-unbeam fel-ler intew the sea
> Arnd waandered far and waide
> Oonteel eet found ar leetle shell
> Whoere eet coould safely haide.'

As 'Prince Mussel,' King Starfish's court jester, I had a good song in the last act. It was sure-fire sentiment as I was supposed to be torn between my duties as a jester and my unrequited love for the queen. I sang it with tremendous passion, and at the end tore off a top B flat with a Pagliacci sob in it. I was invariably encored, sometimes twice.

The play, having opened at the Little Theatre, ran a week of matinées, and during the following six months was revived twice, first at the Crystal Palace for two performances, and later at the Court Theatre for a week, matinées and evenings, when it was condensed into two acts and was part of a triple bill, the other two items of which were performed by adults.

During the over-long intervals between my public appearances I still attended school, but with even less enthusiasm than before. I developed the adventurous habit of playing truant which was made especially easy for me by frequently genuine excuse of rehearsals. I used to leave the flat in the morning with a thrilling sensation of wickedness, and take quite a different tram and spend the whole day in Waterloo Station or Clapham Junction watching the trains. Once I bought a pennyworth of crêpe hair at a chemist's and walked up and down the embankment with a red beard.

5

After the Court Theatre engagement *The Goldfish* finally petered out, and as I had only received one week's salary I believe some acrimonious letters passed between Mother and Miss Field. My next appearance was in a less important role in a more professional atmosphere. I was sent for by Bellew and Stock, Theatrical Agents, and they (Mr Bellew) led me to E. M. Tarver, Charles Hawtrey's stage-manager at the Prince of Wales Theatre, who engaged me at two pounds a week (ten per cent commission to Bellew and Stock), to play a page-boy in the last act of a comedy called *The Great Name*. It was only three days before production, so my first rehearsal was a dress rehearsal, which should by rights have frightened me considerably although I only had one line, but I was buoyed up by some painstaking rehearsals at home with Mother. My line was to be addressed to Charles Hawtrey himself, playing the piano in the artists' room at Queen's Hall. I had to enter boldly in my buttoned suit and say: 'Stop that noise at once, please. In there they're playing *The Meistersingers*. Making such a horrible noise. We're used to good music here.' Mother and I did that scene over and over again in the dining-room of the flat with the table pushed against the wall, Mother, running the whole gamut of emotions, instructing me. 'STOP that noise at once, please,' was to be said with tremendous force, then with a barely perceptible note of awe creeping into the voice, 'in there [big gesture to the left] they're playing *The Meistersingers*' (pause for effect). Then (with biting contempt), 'Making such a horrible noise,' then (swelling with pride), 'we're used to good music here!' (rising inflection on the word 'good'). Having finally mastered this vocally to Mother's satisfaction we achieved an entrance and exit that would have been a lesson in deportment to a Ziegfeld show girl, and thus primed I bounced on to my first meeting with Charles Hawtrey. I have seldom seen a human being so astounded. He swung round on the piano stool with a glaze of horror in his eyes, while the members of the company seated in the stalls roared with laughter. After I had made my dramatic exit there was a slight pause, and I heard Mr Hawtrey say to the stage-manager in a weary voice: 'Tarver, never let me see that boy again.'

He relented later, and I was re-hearsed by Mr Tarver, and ultimately gabbled the line hurriedly in Cockney, employing the minimum of gesture.

Charles Hawtrey smelt strongly of eau-de-Cologne, was infinitely kind to me, and I worshipped him. On the strength of my association with him I bought an autograph book with glacé sweetpeas on the cover which he signed continually. I followed him about like a sheep, seizing every opportunity that offered for polite conversation. Whenever there was a vacant chair near him at the side of the stage I grabbed it and chattered at him shrilly. Once I distracted him so that he missed an entrance in the first act, after which I was not allowed on the stage at all until there was a legitimate excuse for me to be there. If I shut my eyes now his image is clear to me. I can smell the eau-de-Cologne, see the twinkle in his eye and the stripes on his Paris shirt, and hear his quiet voice edged with exasperation saying: 'Go away, boy, for God's sake leave me alone.'

The bugbear of the child actor is the business of being licensed. The law insists that no child under fourteen may appear on the professional stage without the sanction of a Bow Street magistrate; consequently, before each production, a miserable morning is spent by the business manager, the Mother, and the child, standing about tortured with anxiety in draughty passages, oppressed by an atmosphere of criminality and surrounded by policemen. The magistrates vary. Some are easy-going and give the licence without any fuss, others are obtuse and disapproving, seemingly obsessed with the idea that the child is being forced against its will to act in order to support idle and dissolute parents.

We nearly failed to get a licence for me to appear in *The Great Name* because the magistrate, who had several feet in the grave and looked like a macaw, could not be persuaded that the whole thing was not a case of sweated child labour of the worst variety. After considerable pleading on the part of Mr Fitzgerald (Hawtrey's business manager), he squawked a refusal, whereupon I burst into loud sobs, and Mother, outraged beyond endurance, sprang to her feet and delivered a vehement protest to the effect that if the licence were not granted I should be so heart-broken that I should probably go into a decline and have to be sent to a sanatorium, and that far from using my meagre two pounds a week to support the home, she would willingly pay double that amount to ensure my happiness and peace of mind. After this she sat down, very red in the face and with her hat slightly on one side. The whole Court waited expectantly in dead silence for her to be led to prison; but the old magistrate seemed crushed and, without further argument, granted the licence and we left the court tearful with relief, after a dignified bow to everybody present.

The Great Name was not a success, and ran only two months, but before it finished I was already rehearsing for Hawtrey's production of *Where the Rainbow Ends* at the Savoy. Again I was playing a page-boy, but this time a much more important part, although only in the first act.

The whole company assembled on the stage for the reading of the play.

Parts were dealt out to everybody, and we sat following them while Mr Hawtrey read. He read beautifully and it was an afternoon of enchantment, only slightly clouded for me by the fact that I wasn't playing 'Crispian,' the leading part. For this, however, Master Philip Tonge had been engaged. I scrutinised him enviously along the front row of chairs (where I had placed myself with the principals). He was the great boy actor of London. His only serious rival was Master Bobbie Andrews, who had appeared with considerable success the year previously in

Where Children Rule at the Garrick. Philip Tonge had a fresh red face; a large woolly overcoat, a 'Burglar Bill' cap with ear-flaps tied up on the top, and a formidable mother who regarded the other young juvenile males of the cast balefully, as though she expected them to rise up and fell Philip to the ground in a fury of jealousy. She proved on closer acquaintance to be kind, although domineering, and once during the run she had to be requested by the management not to monopolise our dressing-room basin for washing out her gloves, a proceeding which had become so tedious to the rest of us that we had complained.

Where the Rainbow Ends that first year was a glamorous entertainment. The leading lady was Miss Esmé Wynne, a podgy, brown-haired little girl with a bleating voice. Also in the cast was a strange fragile little thing named Mavis Yorke. She played Will-o'-the-Wisp and was exquisite; she flitted through the woods and glades of the production to Roger Quilter's gentle music, and there was in her a quality of magic. She was in no way a winsome prodigy, and utterly unlike all the other little actress children with their pert voices and black satin coats and ringlets. I often wonder what became of her, whether that tiny supple body ever became set in maturity, or whether she just snuffed out, to be remembered only as a Will-o'-the-Wisp in a children's play.

During that run several large parties were given for us, which generally took place at the Savoy. There were enormous silver trays with rows and rows of little chocolate éclairs, and crackers and paper caps and games, and our evening performances were frequently the worse for them.

The ballet mistress was Miss Italia Conti. She supplied then, as she does still, all sorts of children for all sorts of productions. They used to come shuffling into rehearsals in a great troupe, all those fairies and elves and frogs and caterpillars, gauntly escorted either by Miss Conti herself or her sister, Mrs Murray, a dragon in Astrakhan. It was a matter of constant amazement to me that she could so surely remember all their names, but she undoubtedly could and did. Mr Hawtrey winced many a time when suddenly in the middle of the ballet Miss Conti's commanding voice came shrilly out of the gloom of the dress-circle: 'Dorothy, do your coupé again,' or 'Grace, how many times have I told you never to push against Phyllis in your pirouette?'

Miss Conti insidiously suggested to me one day at the beginning of rehearsals that as my part was over after the first act, I might like to appear as a hyena and a frog in the later scenes as well. I was delighted with the idea, and rehearsed three times in a dingy basement room under the Bay Malton Hotel in Great Portland Street. Mother, having been dubious over the plan from the first, came with me to the third rehearsal and I never went any more. I was disappointed, but Mother soon convinced me that it was better to be content with my small part which was at least among the principals, than to lower my prestige by crawling about on all fours in a hot hyena skin.

6

After *Where the Rainbow Ends* finished I was out of work for a while, and I spent a good deal of time, now being an established actor, in writing in to the various theatres for free seats. I had had some professional cards printed with 'Master Noel Coward' in the middle, and 'Mr Charles Hawtrey's company, *Where the Rainbow Ends*, Savoy Theatre,' in the left-hand corner. These were sent to different managements with a stamped addressed envelope inside and a pompous little note in the third person, usually beginning, 'Master Noel Coward would be so very much obliged,' etc.

Usually, they were returned with callous regrets, but every now and then, as though to keep up my spirits, two pink dress-circle tickets would arrive with 'Complimentary' stamped across them. These were gala days. Mother used to frizz her hair and put on her evening dress. I put on my black suit and Eton collar, and off we'd go in the train and bus, always arriving far too early, long before the safety curtain had risen, but content with a box of chocolates and a programme. We used to have supper when we got home and discuss the play over it. Our greatest favourite of all was Gertie Millar. We had naturally never been able to get free seats for anything in which she was appearing, but we went in the gallery. My bedroom was plastered with photographs of her, for ever since the first time I had seen her in *The Quaker Girl*, I had adored her; and in my memory she is clearly the most graceful and charming artiste I have ever seen. Now that I know her well I can never look at her gay unchanged face without a little stab of the heart, to think that never again will she float down the stage, chuckling lightly and expressing with her hands a joy of living which was her own special charm. I often waited outside the Adelphi stage-door for hours to see her come out. She always smiled at me and said good night. Once she gave me a flower from a bouquet she was carrying which I pressed carefully in a bound volume of *Chums*.

A little while ago a party was given by Gladys and Leslie Henson – a good higgledy-piggledy theatrical party with a magnificent star cast of yesterday and to-day. Lily Elsie was there and Maurice Chevalier and Violet Loraine, and everybody balanced vol-au-vents on their knees and drank whatever they wanted, and gossiped and sang songs. Gertie Millar (the Countess of Dudley) sat on the stairs in chinchilla while I was at the piano strumming a few excerpts from bygone musical comedies in which everybody joined. Suddenly as I played 'Tony from America' the other sounds fell away, and from the semi-gloom of the stairs came 'He guessed I was all alone, so that's why he came along and found me,' in that funny, un-vocal little voice, bridging the years and for a strange instant filling our hearts with a pleasurable melancholy. Many of us cried because it was a most touching moment, and theatrical people are notoriously facile of emotion, and frequently victimised by their own foolish sentimentality.

7

During the spring of 1912 I spent a lot of time going the round of the agencies, a proceeding with which every struggling actor is bitterly well acquainted. Blackmore's, Denton's, Bellew and Stock's, crowded waiting-rooms, with spangled principal boys on the walls, triumphant in their stardom, leering down at their seedy brothers and sisters in the profession; character actors, old lady parts, straight juveniles, singing soubrettes, standing about or sitting on the few shiny chairs, talking softly to each other in corners, not so much to impress as to bolster up their tremulous faith in themselves. Every now and then a man comes in and calls a name. There is a flutter of excitement and some wizened over-made-up little woman rises to her feet, gives a defiant tug to the frayed tulle round her neck and minces into the inner office in tight glacé shoes smelling of petrol. When she comes out again she nods brightly and goes down the stairs; if her nod is too bright everybody knows that she hasn't got the job, and hope flutters anew in those that are left.

I passed hours in those horrid waiting-rooms. Twice a week I devoted a whole day to doing the rounds. I had sixpence to spend on lunch which I took, not in an ordinary Lyons', but in the Corner House. Macaroni and tomato sauce fourpence, a roll a penny, and a penny for the waitress. Sometimes I was fortunate enough to find fourpence under the plate when I arrived at the table. This meant a chocolate éclair extra and twopence for the waitress.

One day I was actually sent for by Blackmore's Agency and engaged at two pounds ten a week to play in the Prologue of a big dramatic spectacle called *War in the Air* which was to be produced at the Palladium.

The writer and producer of the show was a little grey man, I think American. He was verbose and enthusiastic and seemed convinced that the production was going to revolutionise practically everything. I played the infant Aviator in the prologue and flew a small model aeroplane, which I was supposed to have made with my own chubby hands, backwards and forwards across the stage. Unfortunately it nearly always rushed into the stalls and had to be retrieved from under old ladies' seats while I waited politely for it to be returned to me by the musical director.

The end of my scene was deeply moving. I undressed and said a prayer at my mother's knee in a white spotlight. 'Please God, bless Mummy and Daddy and Violet [my slightly Cockney playmate] and make me a great big aviator one day,' whereupon the lights faded and all hell broke loose back-stage. I was whisked violently backwards into the property room, bed and all, and my gentle grey-haired mother skipped about like a two-year-old in order to avoid being knocked down by moving scenery. The rest of the entertainment was devoted to my adventures as a 'Great big Aviator' culminating in a tremendous aerial battle in which I (grown up) and Violet (also grown up and even more Cockney) swung out into the auditorium in an aeroplane amid a lot of banging and red fire. This hair-raising effect was spoiled at the third performance by the aeroplane becoming hitched on to the front of the upper-circle, where it remained for three hours. It was finally dislodged and slid back on to the stage, after the audience had gone home. Violet, I believe, disembarked in a fainting condition. After this the effect was resolutely cut by the management.

I always got to the theatre and made up before the performance started so that I could watch from the side the variety artistes who occupied the first part of the programme. Nellie Wallace was on the bill and Phil Ray, and Maidie Scott whom I loved; she always gave me tea and cake in her dressing-room at matinées.

8

It was some time during this year, 1912, that I was engaged by Miss Ruby Ginner for some special performances of a ballet she was producing at the Savoy Theatre. It was an artistic little morsel arranged to a selection of Chopin melodies and entitled *An Autumn Idyll*, and was planned as a curtain-raiser to precede a two-act Operetta, *The Cicada*. Ruby Ginner herself was the Première Danseuse, and the *motif* of the ballet as far as I can remember was a day in the life of an Autumn Leaf (Miss Ginner) in conflict with the winter mists (members of Miss Ginner's Dancing School). As a mushroom I provided a few of the more light-hearted moments together with a little girl called Joan Carrol as a toadstool. I wore grey silk skin tights, a large grey silk hat like a gargantuan muffin, and a diaphanous frill round my middle to conceal any unaesthetic protuberances. My entrance consisted of a series of abandoned high kicks, slightly higher with the right leg than with the left, typifying the carefree *joie de vivre* of the average mushroom, until upon observing the toadstool (Joan Carrol in pink) my mood changed from gaiety to tenderness, and there ensued a refined *pas de deux* and exit to tepid applause. The really big moment of the ballet was undoubtedly Miss Ginner's valiant fight with the mists and ultimate death as the lights faded, although the effect of this was marred for me by the fact that she seemed so much larger and better developed than the mists that vanquished her.

My next engagement was with Charles Hawtrey again in a sketch *A Little Fowl Play* at the Coliseum. The magistrate refused to license me for the evening performances as the sketch didn't come on until just before eleven o'clock. I was heartbroken, and used to stand nightly in the prompt corner and listen to the assistant stage-manager playing my part (one line with a slight stutter to give character: 'I've brought the ch-ch-ch-chicken, sir'). It was typical of Hawtrey that he paid me my full salary for the whole four weeks' run when he could perfectly easily have dispensed with me altogether. I saw and learned a lot during that engagement. The entire bill was changed every Monday. The stage-manager, Mr Crocker, was kind, and allowed me to stand at the side except on Monday afternoons, when he was too harassed to bear me bobbing about under his feet. I had a close-up view of George Robey, Beattie and Babs, Madame Alicia Adelaide Needham and her choir, The Grotesques, and a Wild West show with property grass matting and cowboys and horses. During the last week Pauline Chase was on the bill with Holman Clarke in Barrie's *Pantaloon*. In this also was a small girl called Moya Nugent who played the little clown. She was by then an experienced Barrie actress as she had played Liza in *Peter Pan*, I think for two consecutive seasons. We became great friends and have remained so ever since.

In between the matinée and evening performances the Coliseum stage had an even greater allure for me; with only a few working lights left on here and there, it appeared vaster and more mysterious, like an empty echoing cathedral smelling faintly of dust. Sometimes the safety curtain was not lowered, and I used to stand down on the edge of the footlights singing shrilly into the shadowy auditorium. I also danced in the silence. Occasionally a cleaner appeared with a broom and pail, or a stage hand walked across the stage, but they never paid any attention to me. An empty theatre is romantic, every actor knows the feeling of it: complete silence emphasised rather than broken by the dim traffic noises outside, apparently hundreds of miles away; the muffled sound of a motor-horn and the thin reedy wail of a penny whistle being played to the gallery queue. As a rule there are a few exit lights left burning, casting blue shadows across the rows of empty seats. It seems incredible that within an hour or two this stillness will awake to garish red-and-gilt splendour, and be shattered by the sibilance of hundreds of voices, and the exciting discords and trills of the orchestra tuning up.

9

After *A Little Fowl Play* I was re-engaged for my original part in *Where the Rainbow Ends*. This time it was produced at the Garrick, with more or less the same cast. The run was uneventful. There were the same parties given at the Savoy, and the same kindly clergyman eager to take the younger members of the cast to tea at Lyons' Corner House. As a step in my own development this engagement was negligible except for one all-important evening when I walked with Philip Tonge all the way to his home in Baker Street, and he told me the facts of life. I was tremendously excited, not only by the facts themselves, which were confined principally to the procreation of species, but also because it was a unique experience to be able to talk to Philip alone, without the didactic presence of his mother. I can't think what she could have been doing that night, but there we were on our own, trudging up Regent Street, along Oxford Street and down Orchard Street, Philip in his Sherlock Holmes' cap and overcoat, and me in a mackintosh, gloriously immersed in a sea of pornographic mis-information. We parted opposite the Baker Street tube station, and I climbed on to the top of the last bus to Victoria in an exalted frame of mind. Presently this heady intoxication of newly acquired knowledge began to wear off and give place to a fearful remorse. I felt smirched and unclean; I felt that God was angry with me and would probably visit me with some sharp punishment in the near future. By the time I arrived home I was in a state of hysteria. Mother was in bed, slightly anxious because I was so late, but reading a book in a sensible effort to calm her fears; her relief was obvious when I charged into her room, but her expression changed to alarm when she saw my face, as with perfect sense of the theatre I gripped the bedrail and cried in a tragic voice: 'Mother, I have lost my innocence!' She hoisted herself up on the pillows and after scrutinising me carefully for a moment did the very last thing in the world that I expected: she burst out laughing. Upon looking back I consider that gesture was a brilliant stroke of psychological intuition. Her laugh pricked my swollen hysterical ego like a pin, and I am certain that it cost her a good deal to do it. I dissolved into healthy tears, and the story of my fall from spiritual grace was gradually coaxed out of me. She was wise and gentle and said that there was nothing at all for me to be upset about, and that I was bound to find out all those things sooner or later, and that the fact that it happened to be sooner was really just as well, as in order to become a good actor it was necessary to know about life as early and as thoroughly as possible. I retired to bed serene and happy after a hot cup of cocoa made on her spirit lamp.

10

In the spring of 1913 Italia Conti wrote to Mother and offered me a three weeks' engagement in Liverpool and Manchester with the Liverpool Repertory Company. Several other children were to be in it and we were all to travel together and live together under Miss Conti's personal vigilance. I was very keen to go although Mother was not enthusiastic, never having quite forgiven Miss Conti for trying to transform me into a hyena in the *Rainbow*. However, we went to interview a young man with a rasping voice and dark glasses, Basil Dean, who was to produce the play (*Hannele*, by Hauptmann), and I was engaged at a salary of two pounds a week. In due course I was seen off by Mother at Euston, and in company of about ten other children and Miss Conti, travelled to Liverpool. It was a pleasant journey. We ate sandwiches and chocolate and played card games on a travelling rug stretched across our knees. Some of the children I already knew. Gracie Seppings and two sisters, Ivy and Dorothy Moody, had been in the *Rainbow* with me, and a very perky little boy in a yachting cap called Roy Royston I had met at one or two parties. The others were strangers, and still are, with the exception of Harold French and a vivacious child with ringlets to whom I took an instant fancy. She wore a black satin coat and a black velvet military hat with a peak, her face was far from pretty, but tremendously alive. She was very *mondaine*, carried a handbag with a powder-puff and frequently dabbed her generously turned-up nose. She confided to me that her name was Gertrude Lawrence, but that I was to call her Gert because everybody did, that she was fourteen, just over licensing age, that she had been in *The Miracle* at Olympia and *Fifinella* at the Gaiety, Manchester. She then gave me an orange and told me a few mildly dirty stories, and I loved her from then onwards.

We all lived in the same digs at Liverpool, and I was violently, wretchedly homesick. Miss Conti dosed me with Epsom Salts, doubtless in the belief that the root of all woe lay in the bowels. This failed to cheer me at all and merely succeeded in making rehearsals extremely convulsive, to the great irritation of Basil Dean who was none too sweet-tempered at the best of times.

Roy Royston, Harold French and I were angels in the dream part of the play, then we did a quick change and became schoolchildren in blue smocks and hard black hats, and then back again to angels for the end of the play. The whole production was definitely advanced, in the best and worst traditions of the repertory movement. There were steps leading from the stage to the stalls, odd and not always successful lighting effects, and a lot of curtains. Gracie Seppings played Hannele, and Baliol Holloway, Gottwald, the schoolmaster.

Roy and Harold and I had a little scene of our own in the early part of the play. We appeared through the inevitable curtains at the back and read verses from scrolls. We wore short tunics with green and red hieroglyphics stencilled on them, small and uncomfortable gold fillets on our heads and bare feet, which were usually pretty dirty because we nearly always forgot the slippers which we were supposed to wear down from the dressing-room.

My homesickness got a little better after the first few days, although it never entirely left me. When once the play had opened distractions were provided for us in the shape of trips to New Brighton on the Mersey steamers, personally conducted tours around the docks, and games of rounders in the park; in course of one of these, Gertie distinguished herself by striking Miss Conti's sister, Bianca Murray, a sharp blow on the head with a wooden bat, presumably by accident.

When we had played a week in Liverpool we went to Manchester. We arrived in the afternoon and settled into rooms in Ackers Street, and after a substantial high tea went off to the theatre in the tram for an evening rehearsal. That was my first view of the little Gaiety Theatre, and whenever I face it nowadays and see the garish movie posters outside, I shudder in my heart to think that it should have fallen so sadly from the grace and quality of its early years.

On Monday morning, those of us who were under fourteen were led to the police court, where a singularly disagreeable magistrate refused to grant us a licence unless we attended school every day during the week we were in Manchester. Then ensued a flustered consultation between Mrs Murray and the manager of the theatre, and we left the court dismal and anxious. In the course of the day a school was discovered which agreed to take us in. Saturday of course was a whole holiday and Monday had gone already, so it was only for four days that we were to be incarcerated. What high cultural grace the magistrate imagined we could acquire in that time I fail to see. Anyhow, the next morning we were taken to a large red board school in the Oxford Road. Harold and Roy and I were put in a class-room and questioned by a little master with pince-nez, and when it came to my turn to answer whatever it was he asked me I stood up and announced, quivering with rage, that I had not the faintest intention of answering that question or indeed any questions, and that I was not going to learn a lesson of any sort during the four days I was forced to come to the school, and that if I was caned or punished in any way I should go straight home to London. This tirade oddly enough was effective, and for the rest of the day I sat at the back of the class-room doing nothing at all but stare with distaste at the rest of my class-mates. The next day, in spite of Mrs Murray's remonstrances (Miss Conti was in London), I took a book with me, nobody spoke to me in the school and I was allowed to keep it. Roy and Harold, more democratic-spirited, entered into everything with admirable zest and in the ten minutes' morning interval rushed out in the playground and fought and played football with the others. I think they were a trifle ashamed of me and felt self-consciously that perhaps a whole-hearted participation in everything absolved them somehow from the stigma of association with me. On the Saturday night I went to bed deliriously happy. It was all over and I was going home. The journey the next day seemed interminable, but at last, as the train slid into St Pancras Station, I saw Mother standing on the platform and knew that the purgatory of those three weeks was ended.

II

While I had been away a long-discussed move had taken place, and the flat at Battersea Park had been left in favour of an upper maisonette on the south side of Clapham Common. It was a very tall house called 'Ben Lomond,' and was owned by a Mrs White and Miss Pitney, her sister, who inhabited the ground floor and basement while we had the rest of the house. The rooms were much bigger than those we had had in the flat, and looked straight out across the common in the front, and on to a large private garden at the back. I had a tiny bedroom at the very top, situated next door to the kitchen in which we usually had our meals, because we couldn't afford a servant. Mother, I think, was unhappy but she didn't show it, and for my benefit treated the cooking and washing and floor-scrubbing as a lark. Eric, my brother, then aged eight, and I, helped with the washing up, and enjoyed it, anyhow for the first few days.

Clapham Common was a nice place to live. There was a pond opposite the house on which Father used to indulge his passion for sailing a model yacht in the intervals of travelling for Payne's pianos. He never succeeded in infecting me with enough enthusiasm to last out longer than a quarter of an hour. Eric, however, was more docile, and used to squat on the opposite side of the pond from Father and turn the boat round with a walking-stick every time it crossed successfully. We used to take our tea out under the trees during the summer and play bat-and-ball afterwards.

There were pleasant walks in Clapham along tree-shaded roads, neatly spaced with refined suburban houses, secure in small prosperity with their conservatories and stained-glass windows and croquet lawns. From the 'Plough' onwards down the Clapham Road the atmosphere became palpably commoner, but it was very lively on Saturday nights, particularly at Christmas-time when the shop windows were gay with tinsel and crackers and paper-chains, and the poulterers' and butchers' and greengrocers' were glaring yellow caves of light, with the slow-moving crowds on the shining pavements silhouetted against them.

In order to get from Clapham Common to the West End you travelled either in a Number 88 bus, which took a long time, or in the City and South London Tube, changing at the Elephant and Castle into the Bakerloo, which was quicker.

The City and South London has now been transformed into a spacious network of efficiency, but then it was unique in uncomfortable charm. The trains were smaller than any of the other tubes and rattled alarmingly, and over it all there brooded a peculiar pungent stink which will live somewhere in the back of my nostrils for ever. I am dwelling upon this particularly because for several years it was an integral part of my life. I went through every sort of emotion in the City and South London Railway. Exaltation, having been sent for by some agent. Utter despair, returning home in the evening having failed to get the job. Or else hysterical delight with a typewritten part clutched in my hand and 'Rehearsal Monday morning at 11 o'clock' flashing before my eyes like an electric light-sign along the walls of the tunnel. I also managed to get through a lot of reading during those journeys back and forth from Trafalgar Square to the 'Plough': French Revolution stories whenever possible, and a welter of Guy Boothby, Phillips Oppenheim, William Le Queux, Stanley Weyman and the early novels of Edgar Wallace.

I can close my eyes and ears now and conjure up completely the picture of Mother and myself late at night on our way home from some theatre, Mother in a dust-coloured cloak over her evening dress, with a small diamanté butterfly in her hair, and me in a scrupulously pressed dinner-jacket suit (Lockwood and Bradley in the Clapham Road), rushing from the Bakerloo side at Elephant and Castle, down tiled passages with hot draughts flying up our legs until the well-known fœtid City and South London smell met our noses and a distant screeching and rumbling soothed us with the knowledge that we had not, after all, missed the last train.

12

In the summer of 1913 Auntie Vida and Auntie Borby took a small house at Lee-on-the-Solent, and we all went down to spend a month with them. It was lovely to be able to look across at the Isle of Wight again and watch the warships and liners steaming up and down the Solent. There was nothing to do at Lee but bathe and go for bicycle rides. My favourite occupation was to spend hours on the railway embankment waiting for the rare appearance of the fussy little train which connected Lee with Fort Brockhurst and put halfpennies on the line for it to flatten into pennies, after which I tried to coax them into the slot machine on the pier, with only occasional success.

A concert party called 'The Poppy Pierrots' played twice daily on the end of the pier. The stage was under cover, but the audience sat sparsely beneath the sky and scurried to the shelters at the side whenever it rained. Miss Maud Watson ran the company. She was dark-skinned and slightly *passée* and sang a number in the second part of the programme called "Hush-a-bye, My Little Papoose," during which she perpetually rocked an imaginary child in her arms until the dance, when she callously discarded it. There were two comedians, Teddy Baird and Fred Benton, and a soprano with the fanciful name of Betley Delacoste. I forget the names of the others, but I swiftly made friends with them all and was allowed to appear with them on benefit nights and sing a couple of songs.

One day in August a post-card arrived asking me to go and see Charles Hawtrey at his office at eleven-thirty. We looked at the postmark and discovered that Mrs White must have been negligent in forwarding it, because it was four days late. Nevertheless, Mother and I went pelting up to London in an excursion train and found that Hawtrey, having tried vainly to locate me, had engaged another boy for a good part in his new comedy, *Never Say Die*, which was already in rehearsal. He was sympathetic and charming as always, and when he saw my face fall told me that he would engage me as understudy. This was definitely better than nothing, because anyhow it meant that I should be in the theatre, and be earning two pounds ten a week; so we accepted gladly, and I started attending rehearsals right away. My natural hatred of Reggie Sheffield, the boy whom I was understudying, evaporated quite soon and we became great friends, although I never ceased to pray in my heart that he would be run over by a bus. Unfortunately he was a remarkably healthy little boy and remained uninjured, and in the pink of condition throughout the entire run. Doris Lytton was in the play and Winifred Emery, and there was a good dinner scene in the second act during which real asparagus was devoured nightly. Hawtrey always loved eating on the stage and I must say the food in his productions was invariably excellent. In *Never Say Die* I used to share the remains with Nelly Ayr, the wardrobe mistress.

13

In November I satisfied a long-cherished desire to be in *Peter Pan*, which was the Mecca of all child actors. I was engaged by Dion Boucicault at four pounds a week to play 'Slightly.' It was Mother who beat him up to such a high figure; flushed with nervousness and horribly conscious of my agonised expression, she argued and insisted and finally won, and we sailed out into St Martin's Lane dizzy with triumph. Playing in *Peter Pan* was all that I hoped it would be, and more, and after the London run the entire company went on tour.

Mother's travelling expenses were paid on condition that she undertook to look after a little boy called Donald Buckley, who played 'Michael,' and allow him to share digs with me. He was nice, really, but I was highly delighted when it was discovered that he had caught lice in his head at Newcastle. He had to be tooth-combed and disinfected while I remained aloof, clean and maddeningly superior.

We played at Glasgow, Edinburgh, Newcastle and Birmingham and all the suburban dates such as Wimbledon and Hammersmith and Kennington. When we were at Kennington Mother invited a lot of the company to tea between a matinée and evening performance and we were very excited when Pauline Chase consented to come. It's only a little way from Kennington Theatre to Clapham Common, most of us went by tram, but Pauline Chase and her friend Miss Berri (who played the mermaid) drove to our house in a shining and smart yellow two-seater which threw Miss Pitney, who was peering through the ground-floor lace curtains, into transports of excitement. The tea was elaborate, the white Worcester cups (wedding present) were brought out and Mother insisted proudly that I should sing, which I did, to my own and everybody else's acute embarrassment.

The tea-party, however, on the whole was considered a great success and the remains of the home-made coffee sponge with walnuts and the Fuller's almond cake brightened our lives for the rest of the week.

14

After the run of *Peter Pan* I was out of an engagement for a long while. These periods in my memory are difficult to recapture. They seem oddly jumbled and nebulous without the chain of the theatre to hold them together. I couldn't have been very happy really, because I was never completely happy when I wasn't working.

I met an artist named Philip Streatfeild who had a studio in Glebe Place, Chelsea. He was painting a picture of Phyllis Monkman and I used to go to tea and watch it being finished. I don't really believe it could have been a very good picture, but I was most impressed by it. She was wearing the pink velvet dress in which she appeared in the 'Pom Pom' dance in the Alhambra revue; also, I think, a white feather head-dress. I met her once leaving the studio wrapped in fox fur and debated anxiously in my mind whether or not to ask her for her autograph, but by the time I had decided that I would she had hopped into a taxi and driven away. Philip also painted a model called Doris something-or-other, a pretty girl who posed casually in the nude and made tea afterwards. I soon became accustomed to the whole affair and spoke of it at home in a worldly manner.

It was about this time that an important friendship began, a friendship which for several years influenced me profoundly and is still clear to-day in spite of the fact that our two paths have diverged so definitely in opposite directions. Esmé Wynne was the little girl with the faintly bleating voice who had played the leading part in *Where the Rainbow Ends*. During the first two seasons of *The Rainbow*, I had no idea that she could ever mean anything to me in the future; in fact, I always found her pompous, podgy, and slightly superior, and although she sometimes betrayed a latent sense of humour by a misplaced giggle or so at rehearsals, these occasions were rare and her majestic deportment at parties filled me with awe and a certain indefinite dislike. In the spring of 1914 she suddenly appeared at 50, South Side, Clapham Common, wearing a white knitted jumper and skirt and hat and wheeling a brand-new bicycle of which she seemed extremely proud. She confessed that she didn't ride it very well and was terrified out of her life on any but the quietest thoroughfares. After tea I cycled back with her to Stansfield Road, Stockwell, where she lived with her family. It was a smug little road and the houses squatted back from contamination with the pavements, from which they were protected by grey strips of garden, barely enlivened here and there by dusty shrubs. The family consisted of Mother, Father, and Auntie Mona. Auntie Mona was seldom present as she was generally away on tour. But although corporeally absent, her successful aura pervaded every corner of the home and she was discussed with pride over the supper table. Esmé's mother herself was a handsome woman, who at one time had been in the original troupe of 'The Palace Girls.' I was certainly englamoured by the thought of this, but could never completely visualise her darting on and off the stage in line and waving her matronly legs with meticulous clockwork abandon, but of course my first view of her was when she was approaching fifty, and middle age had coaxed her figure into heavier shapes. I rode home that evening through the dim suburban roads, ecstatic in the thrill of new friendship, planning adventures for the future: bicycle excursions into the country, matinées at the Coliseum (early doors ninepence, with tea in the interval threepence extra). Long amicable evenings playing word games and listening to the gramophone (I had a new one that played flat disc records instead of the old-fashioned cylinders), and joyful shopping expeditions to the Woolworth's Threepenny and Sixpenny Bazaar in the Brixton Road, finishing up with the weekly melodrama at the Brixton Theatre. These romantic visions were realised quickly. Esmé and I became inseparable. Almost at the outset we gave each other nicknames, embarrassing now with the weight of years upon them, but at the time highly enjoyable. I was Poj and she was Stoj. We alternated between childishness and strange maturity. The theatre had led us far in precocity and we discussed life and death and sex and religion with sublime sophistication. We also dressed in each other's clothes and paraded the West End, rode for miles on the London and Brighton and South Coast Railway without tickets, evading station-masters, ticket-collectors and frequently even policemen. We stole chocolates from sweet-shops and cakes of soap from chemists; once Stoj got a large bottle of 'Phul-Nana' scent. We extracted, with the aid of bent hair-pins and latchkeys, packets of 'Snake Charmer' cigarettes from slot-machines and smoked them publicly with outward flamboyance and inward nausea. We explored the West End, the East End, the suburbs, and the near country with minute thoroughness. We even had baths together for the simple reason that we didn't wish to waste a moment's companionship and because it seemed affected to stop short in the middle of some vital discussion for such a paltry reason as conventional modesty. We quarrelled bitterly, usually over religion, Stoj at that time being given to spiritual ecstasies which fortunately seldom lasted long, but were remarkable alike for their violence and variety. Finally after many intensive arguments we evolved a list of rules for our 'Palship' which certainly saved us many unhappinesses and misunderstandings and was strictly adhered to for many years.

One of the most important aspects of this relationship was the fact that Stoj was determined to be a writer, an ambition that filled me with competitive fervour. She wrote poems. Reams and reams of them, love songs, sonnets, and villanelles: alive with elves, mermaids, leafy glades, and Pan (a good deal of Pan). Not to be outdone in artistic endeavour, I set many of the poems to music, sometimes, owing to the exigencies of my inspiration, changing her original scansion with disastrous results. One instance of this ruthlessness concerned a poem of which she was particularly proud, and an ugly battle ensued. The first lines were:

> "Our little Love is dying,
> On his head are lately crimson petals
> Faded quite,
> The breath of Passion withered them last night . . ."

I set these words to a merry lilt beginning: "Our little Love is dying, on his head . . ."

Very soon I began to write short stories, beastly little whimsies, also about Pan, and Fauns and Cloven Hooves. We read a lot of Oscar Wilde and Omar Khayyám and Laurence Hope. Stoj even went so far as to sing 'The Indian Love Lyrics' for a short period until I put a stop to it, not so much from aesthetic principle, but because I knew with every instinct in me that her voice was quite horrid. Apart from these small skirmishings our mutual admiration was sincere and touching. Our Egos were battling for recognition and encouragement and we supplied one another generously with praise and mild, very mild criticism.

15

In the early part of May, Philip Streatfield, who had been discussing for a long time the possibility of taking a cottage somewhere suitably picturesque where he could paint landscapes, decided to make a motor tour through the west country and to my intense excitement invited me to go too. The car belonged to a friend of Philip's, Sidney Lomer, who was kind enough not to resent my inclusion in the party, and so, in due course, on a misty drizzling afternoon we set forth, slipping out of London over glassy roads, myself bouncing blissfully about at the back among the bags. The whole two weeks' trip was enchanting, doubly so for me as I had never been in a fast car in my life. We stopped in farms and inns along the coasts of Devon and Cornwall and lingered in small fishing villages while Philip made water-colour sketches, surrounded by admiring natives.

After a fortnight of the road I was dropped off at my aunt's house in Charlestown. Philip and Sidney Lomer stayed to lunch and I suffered tortures of apprehension in case my aunt should embarrass me with over-solicitude, but she behaved beautifully and was charming and social and, I hoped, impressive. When lunch was over I waved them away in the car and spent the rest of the day exploring the lake and the garden. Everything seemed to look smaller than when I was there as a little boy, but the spell of its beauty was as strong as ever and I was very happy. There was the old blue punt, still water-logged, the deep wide lake, coffee-coloured on account of the clay soil, and the mysterious damp-smelling jungle surrounding it. I walked down every path, crossed and recrossed all the little bridges, rowed myself out to the island in the dinghy, swung myself sick in the swing, and made up little verses, gay, winsome fragments redolent of Stoj's woodland influence and rife with whimsical pixie allusion. I fancied myself for a little as a half-wild creature and darted about among the trees, occasionally crouching in the bracken in faun-like attitudes. This peculiar behaviour was of course 'play-acting', although at the time I failed to recognise it. Intermixed with this self-conscious enjoyment of myself was a completely unself-conscious enjoyment of the country and, above all, of the sea. Perhaps a few drops of quarter-deck blood had seeped into my veins from my naval ancestors; at any rate I remember feeling a deep indefinable satisfaction, even when I was quite small, whenever I was taken on to a beach and could watch the waves sliding in over the shingle. The Cornish seas were much more exciting than the refined Sunny South Coast variety. Here were no neat breakwaters and trim stone esplanades, no rompered children patting at sand castles, while fat mothers lolled near-by in deck-chairs reading novels and knitting; there was no discreet band music here to interfere with the sound of the waves. The waves had it all their own way in

Cornwall; grey and formidable, they hurled themselves endlessly against the rocks and swirled into the little sandy coves, leaving yellow suds of foam high up on the beach among the crushed shells and thick ridges of brown seaweed. There were sea-birds, too: cormorants and gulls in hundreds, wheeling and squawking round their nests on the cliffs, and diving for fish far out beyond where the waves curled and broke.

I was happy by myself in those days, a habit which I mislaid in later years, but have fortunately regained since. I spent many hours wandering along the cliffs, frequently returning drenched to the skin to eat large teas in my aunt's kitchen. Dripping-toast and splits and saffron cake, this last bright yellow and delicious.

On certain days I plastered my hair down, put on my best suit and went driving with my aunt in the dog-cart to pay calls. I was proud of her extreme prettiness and delighted that my extra years had made me more companionable to her. My uncle was seldom visible, as he was a determined invalid and preferred to stay in his room most of the time.

Later on in the same year I went again to Cornwall, this time to stay with Philip at Polperro, where he had found a pleasant little house perched up on the cliff overlooking the harbour. It was a lovely summer, hot and placid. There was nothing to do but bathe and lie on the rocks, or wander about the narrow streets of the village and talk to the fishermen. On the fourth of August we read in the paper that war had been declared, and later on in the day we saw three warships steaming slowly by, quite close in to the shore. They looked proud and invulnerable and almost smug as though they were secretly pleased.

The peace of the holiday broke at once, and I was sent back to London immediately where I was to spend one night at an hotel and then join the family and Auntie Vida at Lee-on-the-Solent. Philip saw me off at Looe and put me in the charge of Hugh Walpole, who treated me to lunch on the train and tipped me half a crown at parting.

16

The rest of that year, so eventful for the world, was quite uneventful for me. We stayed at Lee for a few weeks and I bicycled about the country and read books and went off by myself for whole day excursions into Portsmouth and Southsea. Presently we went back to Clapham and I set about looking for a Christmas engagement, a disheartening business because I was just reaching the awkward age midway between boy parts and young juveniles'. I was tall for my years and my voice was breaking, which made me croak unexpectedly in the middle of conversations, to my own mortification and Stoj's great amusement.

I was dreadfully disappointed when I heard that A. W. Baskcomb was going to play 'Slightly' in *Peter Pan* (his original part). This was my last hope gone and so I resigned myself miserably to the first Christmas I had spent without work for a long while. Mother did her best to cheer me up as much as possible and we went to one or two pantomimes, but I was really wretched until a sudden telegram arrived from Boucicault saying that Baskcomb was ill and that I could take his place immediately. It was heaven to be back in the theatre again, and I squeezed myself into my last year's furs (Act II, *Never Never Land*) and pink and black striped boots, and sniffed the grease-paint and the 'size' and that particular burnt-paper smell which always permeates every production of *Peter Pan* and is caused by the fire that the Indians make in the second act. I was immensely elated at the thought of actually appearing on the same stage with Madge Titheradge who was playing Peter; I had seen her in *Tiger Cub* at the Garrick and was deeply in love with her husky voice and swift, alert charm. That first matinée when I rejoined the company, I was going down the stairs on to the stage for the underground scene when I met her face to face; she shook hands warmly with me and said: 'My name's Madge, what's yours?' A never-to-be-forgotten, most characteristic gesture.

17

For the whole of the following year I did not work, as I developed a strange cough, which upon examination proved to be caused by a tubercular gland in my chest. Mother was very frightened, but Dr Etlinger, an old friend of the family's, assured her that it would be easily cured by a few months in the country away from theatres and smoky atmospheres. I spent a little time at the Pinewood Sanatorium at Wokingham. I was not an actual inmate of the sanatorium but stayed in Dr Etlinger's private house in the grounds. He was extremely kind to me and allowed me to accompany him on his rounds in the morning, play croquet with the patients and help him with small errands. He was a short weather-beaten man with twinkling blue eyes and a passion for Russian tea, which we used to brew at all hours of the day and night and drink out of long glasses. I learned a good deal about T.B. and its various symptoms and stages and became deeply interested. Most of the patients were officers and they were all extraordinarily cheerful, particularly the more hopeless ones. They played tennis and bowls and croquet on the lawn, dressed only in bathing trunks whenever the sun came out and in light sweaters when it didn't. It was strange to listen to these dying men talking so gaily of the future. They nearly all looked sunburned and well, and there was no trace of illness about them until they began to cough, and then in a moment their colour and vitality faded, and they seemed to shrink piteously. I remember sitting for hours in the doctor's library after dinner discussing their possible chances of recovery, and new cures and treatments and lung deflations, and the experiments of Professor Spahlinger. Then I would retire to bed rather bleakly comforting myself with the reflection that if I ever contracted T.B. seriously, I should at least know enough about it not to be fooled by false illusion when the time came for me to face the truth of dying.

My cough rapidly disappeared, and by the summer I was stronger and healthier than I had ever been in my life. The time passed slowly for me, but not really unhappily. Of course I had moments of irritable yearning for the theatre, but the sight of so much disease at close quarters had scared a lot of common sense into me, and I would have stayed away willingly for years rather than risk my cough recurring.

In June, entirely to please Mother, I consented to be confirmed and was duly prepared for this rite by Mr Tower, our Clapham vicar. I went to tea with him two or three times a week in his study and he was very affectionate and biblical.

Soon after my confirmation I received a letter written in a slanting illegible hand from Mrs Astley-Cooper, a friend of Philip Streatfield's. He had joined up and was training with the Sherwood Foresters in Essex and he had asked her to have me down to stay in the country. He seemed to think that she would like me and that I would not only derive much material benefit from her country air and excellent living, but also profit by the astringent wisdom of her friendship. He died the following year without ever realising to the full the great kindness he had done me.

I accepted her invitation to stay, and Mother came to see me off at St Pancras and left her bag in the tube, with all the money she had scraped together for my return ticket. It was a dreadful moment. Mother, however, rose above it as usual and depositing me in the waiting-room with my rather cheap suitcase, darted out of the station and asked a policeman the way to the nearest pawnshop. There happened to be one practically opposite and within five minnutes she was back, without her only remaining diamond ring but with enough money for the ticket. She stood on the platform waving as the train slid away, triumphantly pink in the face but with the suspicion of tears in her eyes. The whole thing ended up well, because she regained her bag miraculously within two days and so the ring was with her for a little while longer.

Mrs Cooper lived at Hambleton in Rutland, about three miles from Oakham in the middle of the Cottesmore country. The village stands on a hill rising abruptly out of chequered fields, polite and green and neatly hedged. The whole county of Rutland is compact and tidy. In summer it sleeps gently and a little stuffily, but in winter it wakes for hunting.

Mrs Cooper was gay company. Her principal pleasure was to lie flat on her back upon a mattress in front of the fire and shoot off witticisms in a sort of petulant wail. She draped scarves over all mirrors because she said she could find no charm in her own appearance whatever. The principal characters in the house were Uncle Clem (Captain Astley-Cooper) and Fred. Uncle Clem was handsome, charming and vague. An aura of military distinction still clung to him as he passed to and fro through the village and read the lessons in church on Sunday mornings. The status of Fred when I first saw him was difficult to define. He was too young and unimposing to be a butler, but he undoubtedly ran the house thoroughly and efficiently, Mrs Cooper with it.

It was a pleasant experience staying in a well-run country house. The trappings of life there were new to me: a fire in my bedroom every night, dinner clothes laid out neatly on the bed, brass cans of hot water, and deep baths encased in shiny brown wood. People came over and lunched or dined occasionally. A flurry of wheels in the drive announced them and the murmur of different voices echoed up from the hall as I grandly descended the polished oak staircase, very careful not to slip in my new patent-leather shoes.

During my winter visits I used to go to meets in the dog-cart, driving myself and following the hunt for as long as the pony consented to gallop. It was never amenable for more than an hour or so and had a disconcerting habit of standing stock-still for no reason at all, completely obstructing the road, and quite impervious to my shoutings and belabourings. Later on in the war Mrs Cooper and Fred ran Hambleton as a convalescent hospital and I used to go down whenever I could, sometimes only for Sunday night when I was acting, and sing and play to the soldiers.

18

Just before Christmas 1915 *Where the Rainbow Ends* was produced again at the Garrick, its fourth consecutive season. Most of the original cast were re-engaged: Esmé Wynne (Stoj), Philip Tonge, Sidney Sherwood, Mavis Yorke, and myself. This time I had grown too big for the Page-boy and was still apparently unacceptable for either 'Crispian' or 'Jim Blunders,' so I played a character part, 'The Slacker,' who was a cross between a man and a dragon. I wore a greeny-beige costume with a tail, and put on an elaborate make-up, masses of number five (yellow), cheeks carefully emaciated with blue pencil and glittering green sequins on my eyelids. The part was short but showy, and I gave a macabre performance, leading up to one of those hysterically laughing exits which never fail to get a round of applause.

After this Stoj and I were engaged to play Amy and Charlie in the spring tour of *Charley's Aunt* at salaries of two pounds and two pounds ten a week respectively. The men of the company were required to provide their own clothes, which from the point of view of elegance was an unwise decision of the management's. My undergraduate flannels in Act Two, which were remarkable both in cut and texture, shrank degradingly in the first week's wash and by the end of the tour were practically cycling knickers. The company was then, is now, and always will be run by Mr Cecil Barth, a kind man with an unbridled passion for respectability. He told us at the outset that Stoj and I were not to share rooms together because it would give the company a bad name, so I was paired off reluctantly with the leading juvenile, Arnold Raynor, who never cared for me much, while Stoj lived with a fair girl with long hair and a round face, called Norah Howard. In this Stoj was lucky, because Norah was the only other un-morose member of that exceedingly morose troupe. Kathleen Barbor (now Mrs Ernie Lotinga) was the Walking Understudy and was a little less under the pall of self-satisfied gloom that enveloped the rest, but it got her down eventually and she was only seen to smile about once a fortnight. Many of the cast of course had played the play month in, month out for years and years and years, notably James Page (Mr Spettigue), Sidney Compton (Brasset) and J. R. Crawford (Colonel whatever it was). Mr Crawford also directed rehearsals with all the airy deftness of a rheumatic deacon producing *Macbeth* for a church social. Sidney Compton had a deep rasping voice and unfolded his mouth like an Inverness cape. James Page was the gayest of these three veterans, a gossipy, slightly bibulous old thing.

In my opinion, of all the parts in that least funny of all plays 'Charley' is the worst. 'Jack' and 'Lord Fancourt Babberley' are the ones who get all the laughs and the wretched 'Charley' supplies the cues. I tried desperately at first to invest this high-spirited congenital idiot with some reality, but after a while I gave up the struggle and just bounded on to the stage nightly and said the lines with as much conviction as possible. We seemed to me to play interminably everywhere, frequently split weeks in smaller towns such as Rugby and Peterborough. These split weeks were very expensive owing to changing rooms so rapidly. Often I had only enough money for one meal a day and was forced to make do with buns and glasses of milk until after the show at night when I stuffed myself with fish and chips. The whole tour was alive with incident. In Peterborough we played during a blizzard to exactly six people. In Chester Stoj and Norah and I went rowing up the river for a picnic completely forgetting that there was a matinée. In Manchester I had a row with Arnold Raynor about the bath water and decided to share with Stoj and Norah henceforward and risk Mr Barth's disapproval.

The three of us started our alliance the following week in Hanley. The town was filthy, the rooms were filthy, and the other inmates of the house were four acrobats who used the bathroom at the same time for economy's sake and invariably left a rim of grey horror round the inside of the bath which we tried to rub off with wads of toilet paper.

Altogether that week was far from successful. No night passed without one or other of us retiring to bed in tears. I drove Stoj mad by strumming the piano and she lacerated my nerves by strumming the typewriter. I forget what poor Norah did to irritate us, but I expect she whistled, or didn't quite understand our jokes. At any rate we all quarrelled furiously to such an extent that Stoj and I (temporarily on the same side against Norah) defiantly determined to live alone together the next week and to give in our notices if there were any managerial objections.

We arrived in Chester late on Sunday afternoon in a downpour of rain. Norah, wearing a faintly superior smile, got herself and her luggage into a taxi and drove off to her combined room which she had had the forethought to reserve in advance. We left our bags at the station and set out in the rain. We trudged for miles, soaked to the skin. There was apparently only one street where theatrical rooms were available, and every room in every house seemed to be taken. We walked endlessly up and down it, averting our eyes as we passed Norah's window which was on the ground floor front. She had thoughtfully left the blind up so that we shouldn't miss the sight of her sitting by a crackling fire, cramming down hot cocoa and steak-and-kidney pudding and self-consciously reading a book propped up against the cruet. Finally we gave up the theatrical street entirely and found at the end of a lane a nice-looking house with an 'Apartments' board in the window. A flashily-dressed woman opened the door and greeted us with surprising enthusiasm. She showed us two well-furnished bedrooms and said that we could use her dining-room and that dinner was just ready. Absolutely delighted, we rushed back to the station, retrieved our luggage and within half an hour were cosily installed in pyjamas and dressing-gowns eating roast mutton and red currant jelly. It was not until three different men had walked into Stoj's room in the middle of the night that we realised that we were in a brothel. Even then we were quite eager to stay because, as I truly remarked, Stoj's appearance at night with her hair scragged back in Hinde's curlers and layers of Icilma cream plastered all over her face was so repellent that she could pass unscathed through fifty brothels. Mr Barth, however, inevitably found out and back we went to Norah, Stoj sharing her 'combined,' and I sharing meals and inhabiting a lonely single attic down the road.

The tour pursued its dreary way through February, March, April and May. In Bristol I had a religious mania lasting exactly one day and based upon an inexplicable fear of death which descended upon me abruptly in the middle of a matinée. Homesickness started it, I think, a black nostalgia for Mother and the dear familiarity of my bedroom at Clapham Common. I felt definitely that I should never see my home again. I had been away too many weeks in frowsy lodging-houses and my nerves were raw with sudden loneliness. There was thunder in the air as well, and during that night a terrific storm broke convincing me that this was my destined finish. I wept thoroughly at the vivid picture of Mother's face when she heard how the sharp lightning had struck her darling through the window of the second floor back. I murmured incoherent prayers, vowed many vows and promised many promises, if only I might live a little longer. These were apparently granted, for I woke up the next morning as bright as a button and rapidly forgot the entire episode, promises and all.

In Torquay we had charming rooms. It was May and the weather and sea were warm enough for bathing, so Stoj and I reverted to the 'Woodland' again and went for long picnics on non-matinée days. We frolicked in secluded coves and danced naked in little woods fringing the shore, shutting our aesthetic eyes to the fact that Stoj's hair always went straight as string when even slightly damped, and that owing to recent indulgences in sweets, my back was generously pimpled.

In Wolverhampton, Arnold Raynor finally lost his temper with me and knocked me down just before my entrance in the last act. I had no time to retaliate even if I had wished to, and I tottered on to the stage with my collar torn and my white tie under my left ear.

In the dressing-room afterwards he said in sinister tones: 'Now we'll have this out,' and hit me again, upon which I lost all control and threw my tin make-up box at him. He was shorter than I and much stronger. He then hit me again and I fell down and banged my head against the wall. As I did so I had the presence of mind to yell with what I hoped was enough volume and tone to indicate anger rather than stark terror; anyhow it was effective enough to bring Stoj flying into the room dressed in a brief camisole and a pair of knickers and waving a hair-brush with which she struck my aggressor so hard on the back of the head that he fell down too, whereupon everyone cried and apologised and we all went out affectionately to supper.

19

The tour came to an end in June and we said good-bye to the company with unqualified delight and rejoined our various families. The autumn tour started early in August gratefully shorn of our presence. Meanwhile I was busily preparing a single turn for the halls consisting of imitations of famous stars. This never amounted to anything as it was quite impossible for the acutest perception to distinguish one imitation from the other. I appeared at several auditions in evening clothes accompanied on the piano by Auntie Kitty (deserted in Toronto by Uncle Percy) in a black lace dress and a diamond slide in her hair. All we were ever offered was a trial week somewhere at our own expense, which I sadly and expediently refused.

A year or two before this I had met, I forget exactly where, a boy named John Ekins. He was a year older than I and had been at school at Walthamstow where I remember visiting him with Stoj and taking him a box of chocolates. We had procured this by the simple means of buying an empty box for threepence and going from sweet-shop to sweet-shop in the Clapham Road and stealing the chocolates off the counters while one of us distracted the shopkeeper's attention by asking for sweets which we knew he didn't stock. The chocolates suffered rather from joggling about in our pockets, so when we got home we rubbed them with margarine to restore their vanished shine. Anyhow, they looked alluring enough when arranged neatly with paper shavings, and John was becomingly enthusiastic about them and ate the lot. He was the son of the Rector of Rame in Cornwall and was more thoroughly stage-struck than I. He knew what every actor and actress had played in for the last thirty years, also what they had worn and whom they had married. We used to sit in the garden of the rectory overlooking the summer sea with our noses buried in back numbers of *The Play Pictorial*, staring avidly at Lily Elsie wearing a hat like a tea-cosy in *The Count of*

Luxembourg, putting her hand through a screen and being married to Bertram Wallis in a velvet coat. Kate Cutler in *Bellamy the Magnificent*, clutching her neck with both hands and looking extremely agitated; Charles Wyndham and Miss Compton in *Eccentric Lord Comberdene*, very uneasy in yachting caps, and best of all our beloved Gertie Millar in *Our Miss Gibbs*, wearing a beehive and talking to Robert Nainby as a Duke. On Wednesdays or Saturdays we used to go into Plymouth to see the matinée at the Theatre Royal. This meant walking a mile or so into Cawsand Village and catching the morning bus, which sometimes missed the ferry, forcing us to wait on the wrong side of the harbour in a fever of impatience for fear we should miss the beginning of the first act. After the matinée we always had tea in the Palm Court of the Royal, very casual and grand in our carefully pressed navy blue suits and coloured silk socks. Coming home to Rame in the late evening was lovely except for the last drag up the hill which covered our shoes with dust and generally made us slightly irritable. The scenery all the way was beautiful, particularly in the dusk with the different coloured lights springing up behind us in the harbour, and, through the giant trees of Mount Edgecombe Park, the regular flash of the Eddystone fifteen miles out to sea.

The rectory itself was cosy and lamp-lit and rather faded; all the rooms felt lived-in except the drawing-room, which retained an aloof atmosphere and smelt of moth-balls. Mr Ekins, Mrs Ekins, Christine, Audrey and John comprised the family, and it was one of the nicest households I have ever known. Audrey was consumptive and we used to have tea parties in her room to cheer her up, although she seemed to me to be happier than most people in the best of health. John finally prevailed upon his parents to allow him to live with his uncle in Lewisham and try for a stage engagement, which he succeeded in getting remarkably quickly. He appeared with Hawtrey in *Anthony in Wonderland*, played my longed-for 'Crispian' in *Where the Rainbow Ends*, and was in a melodrama at Drury Lane called *The Best of Luck*, in which Madge Titheradge was the leading lady. I often used to walk on in the crowd scenes just to give myself the feeling of being in a job. We were inseparable friends until one morning in 1917 when a letter arrived from him from Farnborough where he was training as an Air Force cadet, explaining that he had a day's leave and asking me to go to a matinée with him. By the same post there was also a letter from his mother telling me that he had died suddenly of spinal meningitis. The violence of the shock robbed the day and myself of all reality, and I went to the matinée alone, remotely cheerful and feeling myself brave. It wasn't until the second entr'acte that I began to cry foolishly and had to go home. Memory is viciously insistent on such occasions. The City and South London Tube plunged through its tunnels interminably, while I bicycled down from Rame to Cawsand with John, picnicked with him below the fort on the rocks, slid wildly up and down the frozen pond on Clapham Common and made tea late at night in his uncle's kitchen at Lewisham. The finality of death is bewildering on first acquaintance and the words 'never again' too sad to believe entirely. It took a long while for my unhappiness to disperse and even now I feel a shadow of it when I think of him.

Tragedy certainly descended swiftly on that gentle, harmless rectory. Within a year or so Christine, the healthy elder daughter, had married and died in childbirth, and there was only Audrey left to linger on for a few months. Mr and Mrs Ekins live there still and Christine's daughter is with them, but even so the house must feel empty.

20

In the summer of 1916 Robert Courtneidge engaged me to play a small part in a new musical comedy, *The Light Blues*, which was to be tried out for three weeks in Cardiff, Newcastle and Glasgow, before coming to the Shaftesbury Theatre. The play was very clean-limbed and jaunty and good-fellowish and dealt with the excruciating adventures of a jolly actress called Topsy Devigne, who dressed up as an undergraduate at Cambridge during May week and got herself into a series of roguish scrapes. Cicely Debenham played 'Topsy' and Albert Chevalier was somebody's father, and Cicely Courtneidge and Jack Hulbert supplied a second-string love interest with a couple of dance duets. I can still recall fragments of the lyrics, as for example the finale of the first act when Topsy, having successfully squeezed herself into a navy blue suit, sang:

> 'I'm Cuthbert the Coconut,
> The smartest on the tree,
> Any girl who isn't shy
> Can try a shy at me – ' etc.

And later on, Cynthia (Cicely Courtneidge), in a pink silk dress with panniers and a Dolly Varden hat, flitting backwards and forwards across the stage and singing with incredible archness:

> 'Don't you go a-counting of your chickens,
> Wait 'til they're all hatched out,
> For you never, never know
> What's going to happen next,
> And you may be vexed,
> And a little bit perplexed – ' etc.

There was also a sentimental number sung by Albert Chevalier assisted by *bouche-ferme* refrains from the whole company during which he paraded up and down in an angry white wig and sang with intense feeling:

'I see Life through rose-coloured glashes,
I see Lovers in ro-o-shy light
Billing and coo-ooing,
Tenderly woo-ooing,
Oh, if you only would tesht your shight.'

This song was extremely long, and there was ample time for Chevalier himself and the company and the whole of Cambridge to change from amber to deep pink and back again to amber before the end of it.

I played what is technically described as a 'dude' part. Morning clothes, silk hat and false moustache (insecure). I was on for about five minutes in the first act and four in the second, and I was offended at not being included in any of the musical numbers, but I was given the understudy of Jack Hulbert and learnt all his dances quickly in the forlorn hope that he would be seized with some disease on the opening night, giving me the chance to rush on and become a star immediately.

I enjoyed the three weeks' tour and shared rooms with Stephanie Stephens and her mother, who were old friends of mine. I didn't have much opportunity to enjoy the London run, as it only lasted a little while, but on the whole I learned a good deal. Mr Courtneidge was violent at rehearsals and lost his temper gloriously. On one occasion when he was reviling me for being unable to peel a banana correctly, he actually flung his hat on the stage and jumped on it, which sent me into a flurry of nervous laughter. With all his rages he was really kind and just to everybody, but he happened to belong to that school of production which considers no later rehearsal complete without tears from someone.

In Glasgow I had a painful but salutary experience. There was a full rehearsal called and I went down to the theatre with Stephanie sublimely unaware of the trouble in store for me. I have never been able to look at the bare stage of the King's Theatre since without a shudder of remembrance. On that particular morning it seemed normal enough at first with pieces of scenery littered about and the company waiting expectantly for the arrival of Mr Courtneidge. I remember being gay and jocular myself and doing a saucy imitation of somebody or other to amuse some of the minor members of the cast. Presently the 'Guv'nor' arrived and the atmosphere changed somewhat, laughter dwindled into polite smiles and there was the usual silence while he stood by the prompt table talking to the stage-manager. I must explain here that during the course of the second act I played a little scene with Shaun Glenville, who used to gag a good deal and say anything that came into his head. I was never particularly amused by these 'impromptus' but I frequently allowed myself to be convulsed with ill-repressed laughter, because I felt that it was quite a good plan to be suitably responsive to the leading comedian. Before that miserable rehearsal started Mr Courtneidge called me out before the entire company and mortified me to the dust. He informed me that I was not only a very young actor but a very bad actor, and that in addition to this I was practically a criminal for accepting a salary of four pounds a week (I had told Stephanie I was getting five) when all I did to earn it was to fool about and giggle on the stage, and that if it wasn't for the fact that we were opening in London the following week he would sack me on the spot. He said a lot more which I forget now, but it was all in the same vein, and I slunk away more utterly humiliated than I had ever been in my life. Cicely Debenham, however, lent me her handkerchief, and Cicely Courtneidge patted me on the back and said: 'You mustn't mind Father.'

The play opened in London with the mark of death emblazoned upon it, and although there were calls for author and several people made speeches, it actually ran only two weeks.

Just after this I became, briefly, a professional dancer. Not in the true 'gigolo' sense, for alas, my adolescence was too apparent, my figure too gangling and coltish to promote evil desire in even the most debauched night-club habitués. I partnered a girl named Eileen Dennis, and we were engaged by the Elysée Restaurant (now the Café de Paris) to appear during dinner and supper. A slow waltz, a tango, and a rather untidy one-step made up our programme. Later, owing to popular demand (from Eileen Dennis's mother), we introduced a pierrot fantasia for which we changed into cherry-coloured sateen and tulle ruffs. No South African millionaires threw diamond sunbursts at Eileen's feet. We were neither of us ever invited to appear naked out of pies at private supper parties, in fact the whole engagement from the point of view of worldly experience was decidedly disappointing.

Another brief engagement somewhere in those years was as a 'super' in a D. W. Griffith's film. I was paid, I think, a pound a day, for which I wheeled a wheelbarrow up and down a village street in Worcestershire with Lilian Gish. The name of the film was *Hearts of the World*, and it left little mark on me beyond a most unpleasant memory of getting up at five every morning and making my face bright yellow, and a most pleasant memory of Lilian, Dorothy and Mrs Gish who were remarkably friendly and kind to me.

21

In December 1916 I was engaged for a Christmas play by Cecil Aldin, *The Happy Family*, in which I played a Sandhurst cadet in a red-and-white-striped blazer and a pill-box hat. In the second act everybody turned into animals except Mimi Crawford and me, and I rendered a dashing military number: "Sentry Go," with a full chorus of ducks and pigs, which I drilled resonantly in the third refrain. In this play I was allowed to dance and sing for the first time since *The Goldfish*, so I was very happy. The steps I had learned from understudying Jack Hulbert came in useful, and a critic in one of the more obscure weeklies wrote that I combined the grace and movement of a Russian dancer with the looks and manner of an

English schoolboy. This thrilled me, although I couldn't help regretting that *The Times* or the *Daily Mail* hadn't displayed the same acute perception.

The first act of *The Happy Family* was remarkable for a hilarious concerted number in which every member of the company took part and sang with enthusiasm:

> 'Isn't it awfully jolly
> Doing a little revue?
> Never could be a more happy idea,
> It's nobby and nutty and new.
> Laughter and frolic and folly
> Won't we be going ahead?
> None of us stopping
> Until we are dropping
> And then we'll have breakfast in bed.'

Ten years later I quoted this to C. B. Cochran after a twenty-seven-hour dress rehearsal of *On With the Dance* in Manchester and he smiled dimly.

The following summer I went to the Gaiety, Manchester, to play in *Wild Heather*, a play by Dorothy Brandon. I lived alone in a bed-sitting-room in Lloyd Street, and was mothered by Mrs Wood, my landlady. She waited up every night for me and brought me my supper on a tray. It was usually Heinz baked beans, or welsh rarebit or something equally delicious, and she used to sit on the edge of a large feather bed and gossip with me while I ate it. It was a bright room with a permanently crooked Venetian blind veiled demurely by white lace curtains. There was an incandescent gas bracket with the mantle broken at the end, which shed an acid yellow glare over everything and almost succeeded in taking the colour out of the eiderdown. There was a 'fire-screen ornament' in the grate made of crinkled paper, and on the mantelpiece several photographs of Mrs Wood's sister as Sinbad the Sailor in tights leaning against a log of wood. The bathroom was down one flight of stairs and contained a fierce geyser which blew up occasionally, and once completely destroyed the 'fringe' of a well-known character actress.

Edyth Goodall was the leading lady in *Wild Heather*, and Helen Haye and Lyn Harding were also in it. It was a strong social drama in which everyone seemed miscast. I played Helen Haye's son, and drifted in and out until the end of the second act, when I drifted out for good, which left me free to go and watch the variety bills at the Palace and Hippodrome. During the second week of the run I went to the Palace every night to see Clara Evelyn and Ivy St Helier playing and singing at two grand pianos placed back to back. I tackled them both one day in the Midland Hotel, and was invited to tea in their sitting-room where I immediately played them some songs I had written. Miss St Helier gave me a wise little lecture on the value of 'authority' in a piano entertainer; she also showed me some good striking chords to play as introduction to almost any song. I profited a lot from that afternoon.

During the last of our three weeks' run two important events occurred. The first was the appearance at the stage door one evening of a dark enthusiastic American who said his name was Gilbert Miller, and that he had come especially from London to see my performance, as Charles Hawtrey had suggested me for a part in the new Haddon Chambers comedy *The Saving Grace*, which they were producing jointly at the Garrick. He asked me to supper at the Midland, and I was flattered and amazed that anyone so important should be so human and unmanagerial. He told me that he had feared that I should look too young for the part, and that as there was only a cast of seven including Hawtrey himself, it was necessary for everyone to be absolutely first-rate, if not actually a star. I aged visibly in manner and deportment and became almost off-hand in my efforts not to appear too youthful, but he assured me that he thought me good and that I would certainly be engaged, whereupon I was too dazed to be more than mildly astonished when he suddenly asked me quite seriously whether I would care for Marie Lohr to play opposite me. By that time I should only have given a languid nod if he had told me that Ellen Terry was going to play my baby sister.

We chatted on, and he told me several plots of plays that his father, Henry Miller, had produced in New York. He told them in detail and with tremendous vivacity, occasionally rearranging the knives and forks and plates to illustrate the more dramatic passages; at one moment he actually sprang up from his chair and shouted: 'Never, never, never!' loudly, much to the dismay of the head waiter. Finally he left me in order to catch the midnight train back to London and as I was far too inflated to contemplate the squalor of the last tram, I grandly renounced it and took a taxi all the way to Lloyd Street.

The second important event of that week was the beginning of a friendship which has lasted hilariously until now, and shows every indication of enduring through any worlds which may lie beyond us, always providing that those worlds be as redundant of theatrical jokes and humours as this one is. I stepped off a tram outside the Midland Hotel on my way to play a matinée and met Bobbie Andrews and Ivor Novello. I had not seen Bobbie since we were boy actors in the dear old romantic days of Savoy parties and teas in Lyons' Corner House. He was now definitely grown-up, as well he might be, having advanced reluctantly into his early twenties, although I must admit that his years sat but lightly upon him. He introduced me to Ivor, and we stood there chatting while I tried to adjust my mind to the shock. My illusion of this romantic handsome youth who had composed "Keep the Home Fires Burning" drooped and died and lay in the gutter between the tram-lines and the kerb. The reason for this was that I had caught him in a completely 'off' moment. He was not sitting at a grand piano. He was not in naval uniform. The eager Galahad expression which distinguished every photograph of him was lacking. His face was yellow, and he had omitted to shave owing to a morning rehearsal. He was wearing an odd overcoat with an

Astrakhan collar and a degraded brown hat, and if he had suddenly produced a violin from somewhere and played the 'Barcarole' from *The Tales of Hoffmann*, I should have given him threepence from sheer pity.

They walked along to the stage door of the Gaiety with me, and Ivor asked me to come over to the Prince's Theatre when I had finished my performance to see the last act of his musical comedy *Arlette*, which was playing there before opening in London. I remember very little about *Arlette* except the score, which was charming. Winifred Barnes was in it and Joseph Coyne and the plot was Ruritanian.

Afterwards we had tea in Ivor's rooms at the Midland, and he shaved and changed into a dinner-jacket for a company supper party. I envied thoroughly everything about him. His looks, his personality, his assured position, his dinner clothes, his bedroom and bath, and above all, the supper party. I pictured him sipping champagne and laughing gaily, warm in the conviction that he was adored by everybody at the table. I envied the easy intimacy with which he referred to Winifred Barnes as 'Betty' and Joseph Coyne (my hero of *The Quaker Girl*) as 'Joe.' I don't think honestly that there was any meanness in my envy. I didn't begrudge him his glamorous life, nobody who knew Ivor for five minutes could ever begrudge him anything. I just felt suddenly conscious of the long way I had to go before I could break into the magic atmosphere in which he moved and breathed with such nonchalance. In bed that night in my combined room I devoured minced haddock on toast with a certain distaste. A sense of frustration oppressed me. Here was I, seventeen years old, bursting with remarkable talent, a witty and delightful companion, with an interesting if not actually good-looking face and an excellent figure, just wasting time, treading water, not getting anywhere. My forthcoming engagement in *The Saving Grace* was of course comforting, but an unknown young actor in an all-star cast would not stand much chance of sending the critics into hyperboles of praise. I admit that for a little while I did toy with the vision of an unforeseen ovation on the first night at the Garrick with Hawtrey and Marie Lohr and Ellis Jeffries pushing me in front of them and imploring me to make a speech, but common sense robbed this dream of any conviction, and I looked at the photograph Ivor had given me, propped up against Sinbad on the mantelpiece, with a lowering admiration not far removed from hatred.

To know theatrical stars by their Christian names seemed to me then to be the apex of achievement. So far I had very few to my credit. Madge (Titheradge), Debbi (Cicely Debenham), Cicely and Jack (Courtneidge and Hulbert), Peggy (Edyth Goodall), and Mary (Mary Glynne). With Pauline Chase I had never got further than Miss Chase, let alone 'Polly.' This appeared to be rather a meagre list, and I resolved to embellish it as soon as possible. I dropped off to sleep in the midst of an ecstatic dream-supper-party in which Gladys (Cooper), Elsie (Janis) and Irene (Vanbrugh) were all saying: 'We must get Noel to sing us something.'

22

The Saving Grace was a gentle, witty and delightful comedy, and it is a source of great pride to me that I had the good fortune to play in it. The cast were: Charles Hawtrey, Ellis Jeffries, Emily Brooke (not Marie Lohr), May Blayney, A. E. George, Mary Jerrold and myself. We opened at the Gaiety, Manchester, which I had left only a fortnight before, and on the opening night Hawtrey made a speech mentioning each member of the company and finishing up with a brief biographical sketch of me. He told how I had played for him on and off since I was a little boy of eleven, and that the public had better watch me carefully in the future as I was undoubtedly going to be a good actor. The audience applauded and he led me forward and shook hands with me, and I fear that I cried a little, but imperceptibly.

My part was reasonably large, and I was really quite good in it, owing to the kindness and care of Hawtrey's direction. He took endless trouble with me. I was nervous and scared at rehearsals and painfully aware that I was actually too young for the part. All this I endeavoured to conceal under a manner of uppish assurance which couldn't have deceived him because he was never impatient, and taught me during those two short weeks many technical points of comedy-acting which I use to this day. The play opened at the Garrick after Manchester and was an immediate success, despite the fact that the times were unhappy, and all optimism appeared to be fading into a dreary suspicion that the war was permanent and eternal. For several weeks we had a series of air-raids. Hawtrey used to stop the first act by advancing to the footlights to tell the audience that the warning had been given, and that if those present who wished to take shelter would kindly leave as quietly as possible, the play would proceed. Whereupon, a few usually shuffled out and we continued, with forced brightness, to prove that even actors could be brave in the face of danger. The full fury of the raids invariably occurred during my love scene with Emily Brooke; this irritated us considerably. The banging of the anti-aircraft guns and the reverberations from bombs falling, not only robbed us of the attention of the audience, but destroyed any subtle *nuances* we might attempt in the scene, for in order that any of the words might be heard at all we had to bellow like bulls. On several occasions small pieces of shrapnel fell through the roof over the stage and tinkled on the thin canvas ceiling immediately above our heads.

Meanwhile, drastic changes had taken place in my family life. Mother, growing weary of the purposeless, poverty-stricken gentility of existence in a maisonette at Clapham Common, suddenly revolted and determined to do something about it. She had a series of consultations with my Aunt Ida who had been successfully running a lodging-house in Ebury Street for several years, and decided that she would do the same thing. The tenants of 111, Ebury Street, which was almost opposite to my aunt's house, wished to sell the remainder of their lease with all the furniture and what was ironically termed 'the goodwill of the business' thrown in. After a lot of discussion about inventories and instalments, and a series of scenes were enacted in the home in alternate moods of gloomy foreboding and the rosiest enthusiasm, Mother finally took the plunge, signed several incomprehensible legal documents, and we moved in *en bloc*, Auntie Vida included. There was quite a lot of additional argument over this as Auntie Vida had been nourishing a secret desire to live by herself in some sad building for deceased naval officers' daughters in Wimbledon. Poor old Auntie Borby had died the previous year, the house at Lee-on-the-Solent had long been given up and she was completely alone except for us. We jumped on the Wimbledon idea firmly, suspecting misplaced martyrdom, so she came with us and was allotted a minute bedroom under the roof next to mine.

Number 111 was a tall house with an austere personality and passably good furniture. There was a wooden room built out at the back known as 'The Bungalow' which we inhabited together with our dining-room table and chairs, the walnut davenport, the Organo piano (which imitated an organ when anyone pressed its extra pedal), an old and much beloved sofa with its intestines coming out, and a lot of family photographs; also many of Grandfather's pictures, and his sword and dirk hung horizontally on the wall with a faded photograph of Uncle Ran, as a boy, on one side of them, and me as a mushroom on the other.

We had two servants to begin with, and nearly our full complement of lodgers, most of whom had stayed on after the house had changed hands. Mother worked like a slave, cooking meals, rushing up and down the high steep stairs, organising, dealing with tradesmen, income-tax collectors, rate collectors, and in later years occasionally brokers' men. Payne's Pianos had evaporated into an inconclusive mist of failure and Father had no work to do, so he contented himself with making model yachts for his own amusement. They were beautiful yachts and, I believe, structurally accurate in every detail, and he sailed them backwards and forwards across the Clapham Common pond, and the Battersea Park pond, and the Round pond and the Serpentine, while Mother discharged servants, engaged window-cleaners, found out how to make aspic jelly from *Mrs Beeton* and anxiously added up Eric's Manor House school expenses.

We soon discovered that two servants were too expensive and so we had to make do with one, which meant a lot of housework for Mother in addition to the cooking. The lodgers were amiable and frequently serenely inconsiderate. They left every once in a while, and grave apprehension reigned in the bungalow, until the empty rooms were occupied again. Mother became more or less inured to the drudgery, but her spirit drooped a little and she looked unbearably tired.

The Saving Grace ran for several months, and I began to be recognised a little bit for the first time in my life. Occasionally I noticed people nudging one another when I passed in the street, and once a strange woman spoke to me in a bus and said that she thought I gave ever such a good performance. In addition to being in a distinguished success with a distinguished cast, I had a dressing-room to myself for the first time, which, I think, pleased me more than anything.

I had a dresser called Terry, whom I shared with A. E. George, and I gave tea-parties on matinée days. Stoj generally came and Aishie Pharall, a big girl with a fox-terrier, who had been on tour with her. After we had been running a little while Mr Camplin Smith, the stage manager, took it upon himself to use my precious dressing-room in which to interview stray applicants for small parts and understudies. He did this while I was on the stage without saying anything about it to me. One day I came up after the second act and discovered Stoj and Aishie waiting on the stairs, having been refused admittance, whereupon, swollen with the importance of my position, I lost my temper and behaved very badly. I went straight to Mr Hawtrey's room and refused to go on in the last act. Hawtrey listened patiently to my incoherent tirade, sent for Camplin Smith, and told him he was never to use my room again without my permission, and then told me gently and firmly that if I gave myself airs and talked such nonsense I should not be given the chance of going on in the last act, nor indeed in any act, as I should be immediately sacked and never be allowed to appear in a company of his again. After that he hit me quite hard on the behind and sent me up to my tea-party.

I suppose if I had been with any other management, this appalling impertinence would have done for me completely, but Hawtrey knew a whole lot of things that other managers never even suspected. He knew how to bring out young talent without storming and bullying. He knew how to conduct the most irritating rehearsals without sacrificing one atom of his dignity or authority. He also knew that very youthful actors were frequently victimised by their own frustrated conceits, and that to deal harshly with them might crush down their small confidence and suffocate any genuine talent they might have. He had humour and kindliness, and a sure expert knowledge of the theatre, and he managed, without apparent effort, to be much beloved. It is one of my lasting regrets that he died before I had time to justify a little his faith in me.

PART TWO

My career in the British Army was brief and inglorious. In 1914 and 1915, when the first patriotic call to arms had sounded, I had been too young even to wish to respond. I was too concentrated on my own struggles and ambitions to be able to view the war as anything but an inevitable background. Air raids, darkened streets, familiar names in the casualty lists, concerts for the wounded, food rations, coupons, and the universal smear of khaki over everything were so much part of everyday life that any other conditions seemed impossible to visualise.

In January, 1918, I was examined by a medical board and informed that my slight T.B. tendency of three years ago would prevent me from being passed fit for active service and would also debar me from entering any of the Officers' Training Corps, but that I would be called up for some kind of service in due course, and was to hold myself in readiness. This was almost as great a relief to me as it was to Mother. The spirit of sacrifice, the conviction of speedy victory, and even the sense of national pride had faded in the minds of most people into a cheerless resignation. Four futile years had robbed even bravery of its glamour, and the far greater gallantry of courage in the face of anti-climax was too remote for dejected civilians to grasp. It was certainly too abstract an ideal to inspire a self-centred young actor. I remained in a state of relief tinged with uneasiness until the end of the run of *The Saving Grace*, and was rehearsing a meaty dramatic part in a play by Miss Hazel May, when a horrible little grey card fluttered through the letter-box of 111, Ebury Street, summoning me immediately to a medical board at the Camberwell Swimming Baths. I sent a telegram to Mr Ayliff who was producing the play, and set off in the tram for Camberwell. At the end of several hours of beastliness during which I stood about naked on cold floors and was pinched and prodded by brusque doctors, I was told to dress myself, given an identification card, and ordered to line up with a group of about fifty men in various stages of physical and mental decay. Presently a sergeant took charge of us and marched us untidily to Whitehall, where we were shut up in a stuffy hut overlooking the Park for about two hours while lots of papers were signed. This over, the sergeant again took us in charge and we marched up Whitehall, along the Strand and over Waterloo Bridge to Waterloo Station. I kept my head averted in case any of my friends should see me on their way out from their matinées at the Adelphi and the Vaudeville. We entrained at Waterloo and finally arrived at Hounslow where we marched to the barracks and were put into one hut, all fifty of us, and dealt out slices of bread and margarine, cups of greasy cocoa, and three blankets each for the night. There was a slight scene while we were undressing because the man next to me was found to be covered with sores. After a good deal of argument he was led away protesting, and I was generously offered one of his blankets extra, which, although shivering with cold, I thought it wiser to refuse.

The next morning we were given uniforms and boots and porridge and paraded in front of an irritable officer with a wart over one eye. We were also made to swill our mouths out with some bright pink disinfectant and wash our teeth over a long trough. By this time my despair had given place to a still, determined rage. I contemplated, alternatively, fainting suddenly in the middle of the barrack square, or making a wild dash for the gates, but my common sense told me that neither of these dramatic gestures would do me any good at all, and that the only thing was to keep my head and think out some more subtle means of escape. I had made up my mind definitely that in no circumstances whatever would I spend another night in that hut. At eleven o'clock, after we had done some perfunctory drill and been shown how to put on our puttees properly, we were given half an hour's rest. I waited until all the others were sitting around in the hut and smoking and cursing, and then I went boldly up to the sergeant and asked if I could speak to him privately for a moment. He led me outside, whereupon I pressed a ten-shilling note into his hand and asked him to lead me to the commanding officer. He told me to wait for ten minutes and disappeared. Presently he came back and took me across the square and passed me on to another sergeant, who in turn took me into an office where two clerks were sitting at typewriters. Here I waited until the commanding officer arrived. He looked me up and down searchingly and asked me what was the matter. I told him that I had been called up the day before without any preliminary warning, and without any time to settle up my private affairs, and that it was essential for me to have a day's leave in order to straighten things out. Finally, after a certain amount of questioning, he said I could have the rest of the day off providing I reported back at nine o'clock p.m. A railway pass was made out for me and within an hour I was sitting in the train wearing a uniform that was far too small, and a hat that was far too big.

I went straight home, and after an hysterical reunion with Mother, who greeted me with as much fervour as if I had spent four years in the front line, I changed into my own clothes and set off in a taxi. I had a hastily composed list in my pocket of everyone I knew who might conceivably be influential enough to help me. The list numbered two generals, two colonels, and a captain; with grim persistence I saw them all, and not one of them could offer me the faintest hope. If I had come to them before, they said, it would have been quite easy, but as things were, it was too late and the only thing for me to do was to resign myself to the inevitable. The last on my list was a captain in the Air Force whom I had met casually at one or two parties. He was as affable and kindly as the others and equally hopeless, except that he gave me a note to a friend of his, Lieut. Boughey at the War Office. I arrived at the War Office just as everybody was leaving. Someone told me that Lieut Boughey had gone five minutes before, then a small corporal interfered and said that he had not gone and was still in his office. I was led into his room, and I must have looked pretty exhausted for he offered me a drink at once and told me to sit down and take it easy. I explained my troubles to him as briefly and calmly as I could, and within ten minutes he had telephoned the commanding officer at Hounslow and informed him in a sharp official voice that there had been a disgraceful muddle over N. Coward, who was perfectly fit and had no earthly right to be in a Labour corps, and that his civilian clothes were to be sent home immediately, together with any papers there were concerning him. After this we had another drink and discussed Lord Kitchener, the war, the theatre, and my immediate future in the army. Lieut Boughey said that he could get me into the Artists' Rifles O.T.C., and that he would arrange for me to have a couple of weeks' leave before joining up. I thanked him as coherently as I could and went home, marvelling that a busy man at the end of a long day's work should take such trouble to help an insignificant stranger. I never saw him again, and a few months later I heard a rumour that he had been killed.

2

In due course my papers arrived from the Artists' Rifles, and I was sent down with a batch of about twenty recruits to the training camp at Gidea Park in Essex. It was only a little way from London, and we were allowed leave every other week-end. A sergeant-major lectured us all briskly at the outset and explained that as we were now soldiers of the King, our only thoughts henceforward must be of our country and our regiment. He commanded us to turn our minds from all trivial sentimentalities such as homes and sweethearts, and wives and brothers, and concentrate upon becoming fearless, hard-bitten fighters. This little homily depressed me, and I noted with a certain wan satisfaction that it also appeared to sadden my companions. When it was over, a group of us walked dismally into the town of Romford, our duties being finished for the day. We all tried hard to march along in an upright soldiery manner but the military spirit was as yet young in us. My puttees kept on coming undone, and I dropped my cane seventeen times.

The other men in my company (Company C) were pleasant. The food wasn't good, but on the other hand it wasn't bad. The routine was hard but not callous, and those weeks should by rights have done me a lot of good. Unfortunately, however, I couldn't adapt myself to these new circumstances. It wasn't that I didn't try. I did. I made tremendous efforts, but it was no use. My stage life had ill-prepared me for any discipline other than that of the theatre, and that discipline is peculiar to itself. In almost any branch of the theatre it is individuality that counts. In the army it is exactly the opposite. You are drilled and trained and lectured as a unit, one of thousands. I did my best and learnt a lot of things. I learnt how to fold blankets into a sort of bag and how to sleep inside it. I learnt how to polish buttons, how to roll and unroll puttees, how to carry a short cane, how to salute, and also how to stab sacks of straw accurately with a bayonet under the sharp eye of a bloodthirsty corporal with a highly developed sense of drama, who lashed our imaginations to the requisite pitch of fury by shouting: 'They're bellies, they're bellies, they're all German bellies!' The one thing I never learnt was to accept it all tranquilly. The sergeant-major's words had not sunk deep enough. I couldn't wipe my mind clean of Mother and home. I twisted about miserably inside my blankets at night wondering whether Miss Daubeney was inhabiting the third floor, and whether the drawing-room suite was still vacant, and how Mother was managing to pay Eric's school expenses without the help of my weekly salary. I was tortured with the thought that I was wasting time. The needs of my King and Country seemed unimportant compared with the vital necessity of forging ahead with my own career. It was a matter of pressing urgency to me that I should become rich and successful as soon as possible – soon enough, in fact, to be able to get Mother out of that damned kitchen for ever. All this, I fully realise, was reprehensible. There were millions of young men with far graver responsibilities than mine who were sacrificing their lives daily, and there were millions of mothers in far more tragic circumstances; but these reflections were powerless to jerk my spirit free of myself and my own personal problems, and as it is my object in this book to be as truthful as I can, I must confess that I was resentful and rebellious and profoundly wretched. Oddly enough, the thought of going to the front didn't worry me particularly. To begin with, the prospect was far away in the future, after months of training as a cadet and as an officer. In addition to this, the fact that I had been graded B 2 instead of A 1 by the various medical boards, made the chance of any actual fighting even more remote. My unhappiness was concerned with the immediate present and cowardice had honestly no part in it. Soon the unfamiliarly hard routine coupled with my inward miseries began to affect me physically. I developed cracking headaches and was unable to sleep. I bought a bottle of aspirin in Romford, but it was only effective for a little while. It was ridiculous to hope for quiet in a hut with thirty men in it, and the noise every night before 'lights out' seemed to cut through my head like a saw. I used to twist string round my finger until it cut me, to prevent myself from giving way to nerves and yelling the place down.

One morning, a few weeks after I had been in the camp, we were all doubling back from musketry drill along the ribbed wooden paths that ran between the different huts. I caught my foot in one of the slats and fell heavily, striking my head against one of the stakes by the side of the path. I gather that I had concussion, because my memory of the next three days is almost completely blank, although I dimly remember Ivor's *Arlette* score running incessantly through my mind. This was accounted for a long while afterwards when someone told me that while I was lying on the corporal's bed in Hut 10 waiting for the arrival of the doctor, the regimental band was practising next door. I can only fix accurately upon two moments of consciousness. One, in the camp hospital, when I woke to the surprising vision of the company commander sitting on my bed, with his face, which was long and amiable with a moustache on it, seeming to weave up and down close to mine. I believe he asked me a lot of questions, but I forget what they were or whether or not I answered any of them satisfactorily. The only other clear moment in those strange hours was the sudden realisation that I was being conveyed rapidly backwards in bed, and that there was an orderly in khaki reading a book against a background of swiftly moving hedges. I awoke finally in the emergency ward of the First London General Hospital, with Mother bending over me and explaining tearfully that I had been unconscious for three days and nights.

3

I remained in the First London General Hospital for six weeks, in a large ward with about twenty other inmates, most of whom were shell-shock cases. I was examined by several different doctors, thoroughly, casually, suspiciously, and kindly. None of them seemed to know what was the matter with me. Some of them fired searching questions at me; abrupt and irrelevant questions obviously calculated to catch me out in the event of the whole thing being a hoax. Their suspicions were pretty adequately disproved by my temperature chart which resembled an outline of the Rocky Mountains drawn by a drunken child. They traced back my medical history and cross-examined Mother, who finally gratified them by remembering that I had been knocked down by a bicycle at the age of five. This apparently accounted for everything, and we all settled ourselves to wait until the brain tumour showed further signs of life. It didn't, and I convalesced gradually. My headaches became less frequent and less violent. My temperature returned to normal, and after a couple of weeks I was able to sleep at night without the aid of either aspirin or bromide. Mother visited me every day and brought me books and fruit, although where she found the money to pay for them I shall never know. I conceived a passion for the works of two authors, Sheila Kaye-Smith and G. B. Stern, and I wrote them both long letters of admiration to which they replied promptly. A considerable correspondence ensued, and when we ultimately met we discovered that we were already old friends.

During my really convalescent, out-of-bed period, when I wore hospital blue and helped to carry meals to the bedridden and sweep out the ward, I met in the Y.M.C.A. hut which was attached to the hospital, a young New Zealander named Geoffrey Holdsworth. He endeared himself to me by sitting wide-eyed by the rickety upright piano and imploring me to play him the "Lilac Domino" waltz. This paved the way to mutual confidences, and he took me down to the kitchens to introduce me to a friend of his who was one of the cooks; thereafter, by means of various sly devices, Geoffrey and I were always given the slightly better quality food reserved for the officers. He also showed me a broken place in the wall at the end of the grounds by which it was possible to escape after the morning duties were finished, which was generally about eleven, and not return until roll-call at six. This was a dangerous proceeding but exciting. We were only actually allowed out for one afternoon a week from two until five, but with the aid of a broken wall and a convenient tree we enjoyed many hours of extra freedom. The initial steps were the most perilous – a casual walk along the path, then a swift glance all round, and a sudden dart into the shrubbery. Once over the wall there was only the brief agony of a nonchalant stroll to the tram stop, which was the worst of all really, because the desire to run whenever a sergeant or an officer appeared had to be sternly crushed down. There was always the dread of being accosted and asked to show a 'Pass.' However, I weathered all the dangers and was never caught.

Upon arrival at Ebury Street I bathed and changed, and set out for the West End, an actor once more, wearing coloured shirts and ties and silk socks, with shoes that felt strangely light after the heavy army boots, and a heart that felt lighter still. I saw a lot of Ivor and Bobbie and Gladys Gunn (now Gladys Henson), and one day Ivor gave me a dress-circle seat for the opening matinée of his new revue at the Vaudeville, in which Beatrice Lillie was the leading lady, and Gertrude Lawrence was understudying her. In his flat there was a delicious atmosphere of slight quarrels and gossiping. Everyone drank a lot of tea and discussed what Charlot had said and what Fay (Compton) had said and how Eddie (Marsh) thought it was marvellous anyway. This would have to be changed and that would certainly have to be changed. The whole conversation swirled around all the topics I loved best, occasionally enhanced, but never interrupted by peculiar noises from the next room in which Madame Novello Davies gave interminable singing lessons to small Welsh women in grey clothes.

4

I repaid Geoffrey Holdsworth's good offices by changing the course of his life. I lent him G. B. Stern's books and also showed him some of her letters, whereupon he immediately wrote to her himself and a few months later married her. As they are now divorced, I will deny myself the pleasure of romantic digression and dissociate myself firmly from the whole affair.

On my discharge from the hospital I was given a week's leave before returning to camp. This I spent in Devonshire with Stoj and her fiancé, Lyndon Tyson. He was tall and docile, and much in love with her; otherwise I am sure he would have objected to my presence during what was undoubtedly a sort of pre-nuptial honeymoon. It was a peaceful and pleasant week enlivened by only one serious row; caused by Lyndon meeting Stoj and me face to face on the hotel landing as we issued forth blandly from the bathroom together. It took several hours of threefold hysteria and many tears and recriminations to erase the unworthy suspicions from his mind, but by tea-time everything was rosy again, and we all sat on the bench and talked about life intellectually and without resentment.

When I arrived back at the camp I was put on 'Light Duties,' which consisted of polishing practically everything, and helping to clean out the latrines. This was far from enjoyable; but I had more leisure than before, and spent most of it sitting in the canteen drinking cups of tea and eating odd messes of bright pink jelly with whipped cream on top, which the local lady workers behind the bar arranged daintily in glass dishes.

I persevered wearily with my 'Light Duties' and tried, without much success, to keep my mind from dwelling too much upon the utter futility of the situation. I felt physically well enough for about three-quarters of every day, and then suddenly, unreasonably, and without warning, a cloud of black melancholia would envelop me, draining all colour and vitality from everything and changing the friendly noises of the canteen into a nerve-racking din from which I fled to the Church hut. This, although gloomy, was at least empty and still. I lashed myself with accusations of hysteria and self-pity, aware that I was a poor weakling, a spineless creature of no integrity, unable to cope with anything more formidable than a row of footlights and a Saturday-night audience. These emotional orgies usually passed after an hour or so and I crept back, ashamed, to Hut 10, and scuffled into my blankets as unobtrusively as possible, in the hope that no one would comment upon my red-rimmed eyes.

After a few weeks my headaches began to recur, but not very badly; at least not badly enough to prevent me from applying for an afternoon's leave to attend the Theatrical Garden Party. Up to now I had helped Vane Featherstone every year with her 'Jarley's Wax-works,' and it had always been a day of ecstasy for me, hobnobbing with the stars on the more or less equal terms dictated by Charity. The company commander, with a slightly ironical smile, granted my request and I endured the next few days in a fever of anxiety in case anything should occur to prevent me from going. My anxiety was well-founded. The morning before the day of the garden party I woke with such a violent headache that I was incapable of standing up. The doctor came into the hut to examine me and I was carted off to the camp hospital. Later on in the day I was examined by two other doctors, and the next morning at eleven o'clock I was put in an ambulance and driven to the General Military Hospital at Colchester. It was a beautiful sunny day, fashioned by God for morning suits and silk hats and white gloves and flowered chiffons. I pictured the gay crowds at the Botanical Gardens, old ladies from the suburbs in black taffeta, character actresses of small standing in large feather boas, eminent male stars with button-hole cravats, and Gladys Cooper smiling immaculately, wearing shell pink and wheeling a barrow. I smelt the little 'Jarley's Wax-works' tent, hot canvas and trampled grass and tea, and knew wretchedly that I should never see any of it again, that the doctors at the first London General Hospital had been right about there being a tumour on my brain, and that I was lost for ever in frustration, misery and pain.

5

My first night in the Colchester Hospital was spent in a general ward. My head was bad and I couldn't sleep. The night nurse refused to give me aspirin because she said that I had not yet been diagnosed, so I twisted and turned and stared at the shadows the night lamp made upon the ceiling, wondering whether they would operate on my brain in the morning, and if so, whether they would use a hammer and a chisel as I heard they did in mastoid operations. I also wondered whether there would be time for Mother to get to Colchester for my death and whether I should be conscious or unconscious when she arrived.

They didn't operate on me in the morning. They thought of something far better, which was to move me straightway into an epileptic ward in the annexe. They also omitted to tell me that it was an epileptic ward, probably not wishing to deprive me of the full flavour of surprise, when the patient opposite to me proceeded to have several fits one after another before I had been in the place half an hour.

An epileptic fit is not a pleasant sight at the best of times, and as there were twelve epileptics in the ward and the moment one started they all started, my condition of acute neurasthenia showed no noticeable signs of improvement for the first week or so. As I remained there for two months I naturally became inured, and later on, even managed to be quite helpful to the nurses. I acquired the technique of squeezing the patients' tongues back into place by a deft pressure on the throat. I learnt how to hold their arms in a certain position to prevent their springing off the bed and out of the window, and I also learnt not to mind being flecked with their foam and saliva. I had a few bad moments at first, when I realised that not a single one of them suspected that he was epileptic. The minute anyone finished having a fit he generally went to sleep and woke up with no memory of it whatever. Most of them seemed rather bewildered at being there at all. The thought that I might be having fits myself all the time without knowing it was horrible, and when I questioned the nurses I wasn't quite able to believe their kindly denials, so I kept myself wide awake for twenty-four hours and checked off every ten minutes in an exercise book. I did this twice a week for the first three weeks. The strain of keeping awake all night long was awful, but the relief of finding every ten minutes safely marked was well worth it.

The rounds were made every morning by a lady doctor of bird-like appearance. She was brusque, efficient and quite idiotic. Once a week she was accompanied by the medical officer in charge of the whole annexe, and on these occasions her brusquerie became almost frantic. She yapped and poked and prodded and flounced from bed to bed, giving shrill orders to the nurses and snapping her teeth together like castanets.

Nobody seemed to consider it worth while to attempt to diagnose my case with any degree of thoroughness, and so there I remained through July and August, passing the time in bed by writing a bad novel, and reading a little and walking a little on the common whenever I could get a 'pass' for the afternoon. Sidney Lomer had a house in Colchester and I used to have tea with him sometimes. One day General (Splash) Ashmore, whom I had known when I was in *The Saving Grace*, made an official visit to the hospital. We all stood to attention when he clanked into the ward with some doctors and A.D.C.s in attendance, and he sent my stock up considerably by chatting to me for about ten minutes. Fortunately the dignity of the occasion was unimpaired by anybody having a fit, although a short while after he had left, a boy called Barnet, in the next bed to mine, had seven straight off, doubtless from sheer excitement.

Eventually the head medical officer called me into his office and told me that I was to go before the next medical board which occurred in a week's time, and that he had recommended me for complete discharge from the army. He said, reasonably, that my value as a soldier of the King amounted to a total loss, and that the sooner I got out of it the better for all concerned. I was stupefied with surprise and relief, but I retained enough sense not to give way to it too much. I believe I even managed to look a little wistful, which either deceived or amused him, for he patted me on the back and dismissed me amiably.

I went before the medical board after six days of feverish anticipation of freedom, during which I had written hysterical letters home and received correspondingly ecstatic ones back. My own medical officer was not present at the board and the doctors who were, after a cursory glance at me and my papers, marked me back for full duty with the Artists' Rifles and dismissed me curtly without argument.

I went back to the ward slowly, quite stunned, and trying to adjust my mind to the full bitterness of disappointment. To have been so near release, to have known so definitely that the futile wasteful months were at last over, and now, by the order of a few strange doctors who had glanced casually through my papers and knew nothing of my circumstances, to be sent back to the beginning again seemed too crushing a blow to realise.

I sat on my bed and opened a book, trying, while I was staring at the pages, to phrase in my mind a telegram to Mother, a telegram that would explain the truth adequately without upsetting her too much. While I was occupied with this, the head sister came in and, noting from my expression that something was wrong, called me outside and asked me what had happened. Under her sympathetic eye I managed to explain my doom more or less coherently. She thought for a moment or two and then, with surprising professional brusqueness, told me that I looked seedy and that I was to go to bed immediately for a week until the head doctor came back from his holiday; she also added stonily that it might be necessary to put me on a diet. With this she left me and I went to bed and wrote out a telegram to Mother saying that there had been a slight delay, but that she wasn't to worry as everything would be all right.

The head doctor returned from his holiday a day earlier than he was expected, and was astonished and angry to find me still littering up the ward. He interviewed me briefly in his office, and said that the medical board had behaved like bloody fools, and that not only would I be discharged within a week, but that he would see to it that I got a year's pension. Three days after this I was passed rapidly through another medical board and was signed finally out of the British Army. I still had to wait for a few days while the papers went through, but this I didn't mind in the least, as I was nominally free and could wander about the town and go to the pictures, providing I was back every night by nine o'clock.

The day before my actual discharge I was escorted up to London by a sergeant, who took me to the Pensions Office where I submitted to a good deal of questioning and was finally conceded a pension of seven shillings and sixpence a week for a term of six months. When all this was over we had a couple of hours to spare before catching the train back to Colchester, so I took the sergeant to Ebury Street and we had tea in the bungalow. Mother sent Auntie Vida round the corner to get a coffee cake at Barret and Pomeroy's and the whole occasion passed off delightfully. The sergeant, under Father's tutelage, experimented with the Organo piano and expressed great enthusiasm for Grandfather's pictures. Mother suggested that he might like a peep at my press-cutting book but I squashed this hurriedly, fearing that the early photographs of me in tights as 'Prince Mussel' might sully a hitherto successful afternoon.

The next morning, wearing a navy blue suit and carrying a kit-bag, I said good-bye to the epileptics and the nurses and my beloved head sister, and settled myself in a third-class carriage of the London train in a state of indescribable happiness. The fact that the train passed through Gidea Park and Romford gave an extra fillip to my joy. Somewhere between these two grim stations I observed a long line of Artists' Rifles tramping along the dusty road, but the train was travelling too quickly for me to be able to distinguish any familiar faces. At Liverpool Street I took a taxi and drove through the City streets. It was twelve noon, in the full tide of traffic and the hot August sun beat down upon taxis and trucks and drays and red friendly buses. It also beat down with kindly inpartiality upon the Gaiety, the Vaudeville, the Savoy, and the Adelphi theatres and I pictured as I passed them the cool pre-matinée gloom of their interiors: cleaners swishing dust-sheets from the boxes and dress circles, under-studies meandering about their stages under a working light, clutching scripts and mumbling inaudibly with an occasional sharp interruption from the stage manager at the prompt table, a genial hum of vacuum-cleaners from the front of the house, and strong shafts of alien sunlight striking down from open doors, and from the flies on to forlorn detached pieces of scenery; backings and flats against white-washed walls, unfinished staircases and shorn fragments of balustrade waiting about untidily to be set in Act One symmetry by the staff at two o'clock.

I almost wept with sentimental love for it all; it seemed that æons had passed since I had been part of it. I reflected then, without a shadow of embarrassment, upon my unworthy performance as a soldier. There was no room in my heart for anything but thankfulness that I was free again to shape my life as I wanted.

PART THREE

My first step after my discharge from the army was to look for an engagement. I sauntered into all the agents' offices and announced that I was free. I informed every management, verbally and by letter, that I was theirs for the asking, and discovered that although I had played a leading part in *The Saving Grace*, not one of them seemed to care. I appeared at crowded auditions wearing an immaculate suit and an air of amused condescension which deceived nobody and merely succeeded in irritating the other aspirants. I had written a number of light songs during the past years, and I sang them repeatedly, accompanying myself on the piano. There was a sentimental ballad: "Tamarisk Town," and a bright 'Point' number: "Forbidden Fruit," which I think is worthy of record as it was the first complete lyric I ever wrote. The perceptive reader will, I am sure, detect, even in this very youthful effort, that unfortunate taint of worldly cynicism which I am so frequently told, degrades much of my later work.

> "Every Peach, out of reach, is attractive
> 'Cos it's just a little bit too high,
> And you'll find that every man
> Will try to pluck it if he can
> As he passes by.
>
> "For the brute loves the fruit that's forbidden
> And I'll bet you half a crown
> He'll appreciate the flavour of it much, much more
> If he has to climb a bit to shake it down."

I can only suppose that this cold-blooded realism was too much for the managers, because they neither made any offers for me nor for the song. I remember on one occasion Beatrice Lillie incurred the grave displeasure of André Charlot by bringing me in to sing for him before an afternoon rehearsal. He informed her afterwards that he would not have his valuable time wasted by trivial young composers who played the piano badly and sang worse, and that never, in any circumstances, was she to do such a thing again.

In all theatrical experience I know of nothing more dispiriting than an average audition: a bleak denuded stage only illuminated by one or two glaring working lights; a weary accompanist at a rickety upright piano; in the second or third row of the stalls, with the dim auditorium stretching behind them, sit a small group of people upon whom your livelihood depends, who mutter constantly to each other and whose faces, on the rare occasions that they are turned towards the stage, register such forbidding boredom that gay words stick in the gullet, and voice-tones, so resonant and musical in the bathroom, issue forth in strangulated squeaks. An additional horror is the awareness that the sides of the stage are packed with implacable ambition. Every watching eye is steely with determination, marking with satisfaction each nervous shudder and each false note. The inexperienced of course suffer the most. They usually embark upon some lengthy song or aria and are stricken into bewildered silence half-way through by a sharp 'Thank you' from the stalls, and an abrupt cessation of all sound from the piano, after which, tremblingly, they give their names and addresses to the stage manager and go away, tortured by the knowledge that their top B flat, for which they had been conserving all their vocal energy, has not been heard at all. The wise ones sing only one refrain, sometimes only the last part of it if it happens to be over-long. Dancers have a very bad time as a rule, unless they bring their own accompanists, for in the hands of the lady provided by the management their carefully rehearsed tempos change inexorably from fast to slow and from slow to fast, heedless of their scurryings and gaspings and muttered supplications.

For most auditions ordinary day clothes are worn, embellished usually with borrowed finery. I believe that a white fox fur belonging to Beryl Norman was actually identified in the course of one month on nineteen different people. There are always a few, however, who put on fancy costumes and make up elaborately. Panniers, crinolines, insecure home-made bustles, and the inevitable pierrot suits with depressed tulle ruffles. Dancing girls used to wear imaginative 'practice dress,' but this in later years has gradually discarded its bows and frills and shrunk to nothing more or less than a plain one-piece swimming suit.

My own audition apparel was usually a navy blue suit with a coloured shirt, tie, socks, and handkerchief to match. I had not learned then that an exact duplication of colours ill becomes the well-dressed man. My bearing was a blend of assurance and professional vivacity; the fact that my bowels were as water I hope was not apparent to anybody. I used to walk on to the stage, bow politely in the direction of the stalls and say 'good morning,' sometimes, owing to nerves, a trifle more loudly than I had intended. Then, having banished the accompanist with a lordly gesture, I sat down at the piano on a stool that was invariably either too low or too high, and rattled off a few authoritative introductory chords, inwardly appalled by the tone and quality of the piano, but preserving an air of insouciance. I then swivelled round sharply, announced my song and started it before anyone had time to stop me. My voice was small but my diction clear, assisted by a violent interplay of facial expressions. My rendition of a song in those days was a model of exhaustive technique. Sustained pauses, gay laughs, knowing looks. All the paraphernalia of Harry Fragson and Margaret Cooper and Tom Clare. Fre-quently, if the dreaded 'Thank you' came in the middle of a verse, I pretended not to hear it and continued with only a faint quickening of tempo until either a second and louder 'Thank you' stopped me, or I was allowed to finish.

One day Grossmith and Laurillard held a big audition at the Shaftesbury Theatre. They were planning the production of an American musical comedy called *Oh, Boy*, with music by Jerome Kern. I received one of the usual audition cards, and arrived at the theatre in good time to force my way in front of those who had got there before me. When I had finally achieved the stage and the piano, and was half-way through my song, I noticed that Grossmith and Laurillard and all their myrmidons in the stalls were so immersed in conversation that not one of them was looking at me. I stopped dead and waited until their voices had died into silence. Then, with what I hoped was icy dignity, I said that I saw no point in wasting my time singing to them if they continued to waste their time not listening to me. There was a horrified gasp from those waiting at the side of the stage, and the stage manager nervously rustled a lot of papers. Then, George Grossmith, whose manners have always been a long way above reproach, walked down to the orchestra rail and invited me gently to start my song again from the beginning. When I had finished, they asked me to come down into the stalls, where, after a few preliminary courtesies had been exchanged, I was engaged at a salary of twelve pounds a week. The actual part I was to play would be decided upon later, but in the meantime I could rest assured that my remarkable talents should have full scope.

2

Rehearsals for *Oh, Boy*, were not scheduled to begin for a few weeks, so I wrote to G. B. Stern, who was staying at St Merryn, in Cornwall, with the Dawson-Scott family, and suggested that now was the moment for our long-deferred meeting. She replied immediately that Mrs Dawson-Scott would be delighted to lodge me for a fortnight, which, I discovered later, was a slight over-statement, and that it would be a friendly gesture on my part to offer two pounds a week for my bed and board. This seemed a perfectly satisfactory arrangement and so I set forth for Cornwall, having sent a telegram on my way to the station, a blithe, cheerful and apparently quite fatal telegram: 'Arriving Padstow five-thirty. Tall and divinely handsome in grey.' I was met at Padstow by a strange man with a cart, and as we drove along the sandy roads, I listened to the surf thundering on the beach a mile or so away, and noted, with familiar pleasure, the Cornish shapes and sounds and smells. It was a glorious summer evening, and I was extremely happy. My future was assured. A good twelve-pound-a-week job in a musical comedy, which would certainly run a year. A chance to captivate London audiences for all time with my irresistible singing and dancing. Two weeks of sunshine and bathing and picnics and brilliant literary conversation. G. B. Stern and the kindly devil-may-care Dawson-Scotts entranced with my company and responding joyously to my witty sallies. All the gods were smiling at me without a trace of irony, and there seemed to be nothing to cloud my contentment.

These anticipations were, as usual, too good to be true. That holiday, although far from dull, was an established failure from the outset. G. B. Stern herself justified and surpassed my mental picture of her, and we were friends immediately, but the Dawson-Scotts, the kindly devil-may-care Dawson-Scotts, were a bad let-down, for not only did they dislike me on sight, but they had worked up a definite distaste for me long before I arrived. I was theatrical to begin with, and it was inevitable that I would be luxury-loving, unable to swim or climb rocks, unappreciative of the country, and very affected in my speech. On to this elaborate pyramid of prejudice my telegram fluttered, my odious, conceited telegram: 'Arriving Padstow five-thirty. Tall and divinely handsome in grey.'

Mrs Dawson-Scott, a writer of 'strong' books which reeked of earth, and sea-wrack, and primitive childbirth, and hot, sweet breasts, had had, I suspected, little time to cultivate social grace. She wore a red tea-gown and no shoes or stockings, and, as far as I was concerned, a remarkably forbidding expression. Her family dutifully followed her example and my first evening with them was far from cosy. I remember, during supper, when I suggested that they should call me 'Noel,' being painfully rebuffed by the reply, 'I think, Mr Coward, we would rather wait a little.'

Marjorie, the daughter, softened a little towards me later on in the week and we had an abortive heart-to-heart talk during a 'spratting' expedition in the moonlight. This melting might be explained by the fact that I was quite adept at plunging the curved knife into the wet sand as the waves receded and, in spite of my theatrical decadence, managed to catch more sprats than any of them. She informed me with compelling frankness, as we walked along the shore, that the whole family hated me, to which I replied, with equal candour, that the hatred was entirely mutual, and that I wouldn't have stayed a day with them had it not been for Peter (G. B. Stern), and that I had paid my two pounds a week in advance.

The elder son, Christopher, was less actively unpleasant to me, his only efforts to discomfit me consisting of sharp cries of 'Bet you can't do this,' followed by a flying leap on to a slippery rock, or something equally valorous. These manly exhibitions ceased when, in addition to cutting his knee quite badly, he discovered that I was unimpressed.

The younger son, Toby, was the nicest of the lot, and actually showed traces of a sense of humour.

Peter and I managed to get away by ourselves as much as possible, and these hours were peaceful and happy. We discussed plots for plays and novels. We dwelt untiringly upon the peculiarities of the Dawson-Scotts. We watched German submarines torpedoing cargo boats far out to sea, and wandered along the beach looking for pieces of wreckage, and wondering, fearfully, whether or not we should find any dead bodies.

Peter listened and nodded, and giggled appropriately, as we sat on the beach with our backs against a rock, and I enlarged, at great length, upon my ambitions as a playwright, composer, lyric writer, and novelist. Never once did she suggest that I seemed to be taking rather too much upon myself. Never once did she trot out the 'Jack-of-all-trades-master-of-none' bugbear, from which, even at that age, I had suffered a good deal. She recognised easily in me the familiar creative urge, and permitted my Ego to strut bravely before her.

My actual achievements up to date amounted to very little. I had written quite a lot, in spare moments, during the last few years: plays, singly, and in collaboration with Stoj; short stories, verses, and one meretricious full-length novel. I had also composed a good many songs, and written lyrics for some tunes of Max Darewski's and Doris Joel's.

I stayed for my full fortnight at St Merryn, having no intention of denying myself Peter's company just because that imperceptive family failed to respond to my charms. As a matter of fact, after the first few days they became much more agreeable and even, on one or two occasions, seemed disposed to be amused at my conversation, but these moments were too rare and ephemeral to form the basis of a lasting friendship. We met a few times during the following years, generally at the 'To-morrow' Club. I also dined with them once in Hampstead.

The introduction of celebrated names into autobiographies is a rule that I am too timorous to ignore, therefore I will put on record that, between the years 1917 and 1919, I knew G. B. Stern, Sheila Kaye-Smith, Charles Scott-Moncrieff, Fay Compton, Charles Hawtrey, Ivor Novello, Gertrude Lawrence and Beatrice Lillie. I was on pleasant, but not intimate terms with Rebecca West, Hugh Walpole, W. Somerset Maugham, Yvonne Arnaud, H. G. Wells, Rose Macaulay, Olive Wadsley, Billie Carleton, Viola Tree, Ronald Colman, Madge Titheradge, Lady Carisbrooke, Lady Londesborough and Nellie Wallace. I could also nod and be nodded to by Compton Mackenzie, Irene Vanbrugh, Violet Vanbrugh, Gladys Cooper, John Galsworthy, Gerald du Maurier, Nigel Playfair, E. F. Benson, John Lane, Elsie Janis, Maurice Chevalier and Lynn Fontanne. This last name was insignificant then and belonged to a scraggy, friendly girl with intelligent brown eyes and a raucous laugh. The above list must make it obvious to the meanest intelligence that I was progressing like wild-fire. The plans nurtured in my bed-sitting-room in Manchester were blooming and I could now use a considerable number of effective Christian names without fear of swift and crushing humiliation.

3

The day before the first rehearsal of *Oh, Joy* (it had been renamed, doubtless because the arrogant Americanism of *Oh, Boy*, might stir the English public's stomach to revolt), I was stricken with a bad attack of influenza. This was a bitter blow to me, and for several days I lay feverishly visualising the thrills and excitements taking place without me. At last, very weak, but determined, I was allowed to get up and take a taxi to the theatre. My head felt light and my legs wobbly, but I walked on to the stage as firmly as possible. The morning rehearsal was just about to begin and the play was being directed by an American producer named Austin Hurgon, who, when I approached him, regarded me from a tremendously high altitude. I asked him if he had received my telegram explaining why I had not been able to attend before, and he said: 'What telegram?' I then told him my name and he said: 'Noel what?' Discouraged but persevering, I went on to explain that I had been engaged by Mr Grossmith and Mr Laurillard to play one of the principal parts. He said, with sarcasm, that he was very sorry to contradict me, but that the principal as well as the small parts had been filled ages ago, in addition to which he was regrettably forced to admit that he had never heard of me in his life. All this took place before the amused gaze of the entire company. I replied, with as much dignity as I could muster, that there was obviously some mistake, and that if he would kindly telephone the office, the muddle would be rectified. He retorted that he had no time to waste telephoning while he was rehearsing, and that I had probably been engaged for the chorus, which was rehearsing elsewhere. Trying hard to keep emotion out of my voice, I said that I had certainly not been engaged for the chorus. Whereupon he snatched up the chorus list from the prompt table, glanced through it, and triumphantly read out my name. This called forth a titter from the company, and I walked off the stage and out into the street without another word. I went into a public-house in Shaftesbury Avenue, had a glass of neat brandy to pull me together, and took a taxi to the Grossmith and Laurillard offices in Golden Square, where I demanded to see Mr Laurillard. After about twenty minutes, I was ushered into his room where my pent-up emotions broke into a full-blooded fury. I think I must have roared very loudly indeed, for he looked startled, and kept on waving his hand in the air, apparently in an effort to dam the spate of words pouring on to his head. After a while I calmed down, and he expressed great sympathy and regret, admitting that there had indeed been a mistake, as there was no part suitable for me in *Oh, Joy!* I opened my mouth to launch a fresh tirade, but he silenced me with more soothing words, explaining that my performance in *The Saving Grace* had convinced him that I was far too good a straight actor to waste my time in anything so trivial as musical comedy, and that there was a good part for me in *Scandal*, the new Cosmo Hamilton play, which was to be produced at the Strand Theatre in December with a superb cast headed by Arthur Bourchier and Kyrle Bellew. This, although better than nothing, was still not enough to compensate me for the miseries of that morning, and I went unhappily home to bed, not particularly cheered by the reflection that I had ample time to recover from my influenza, as the rehearsals for *Scandal* were not due to begin for two months.

I occupied myself during those two months by starting another novel. It was a lush work called *Cherry Pan*, dealing in a whimsical vein with the adventures of a daughter of Pan, who, born into a modern world, contrived to be arch, and elfin, and altogether nauseating, for nearly thirty thousand words. She finally petered out, owing to lack of enthusiasm on my part, and lack of stamina on hers.

4

The house in Ebury Street was, at this time, running comparatively smoothly. Our faithful standby, Miss Daubeney, was still with us on the third floor. She was a niece of Lord Brassey, and had been known to sail on his yacht, a photograph of which adorned the mantelpiece in a silver frame. She was friendly and kind, and one of our temporary housemaids, in a transport of Irish enthusiasm, described her as being 'downright aristocratic.' On the ground-floor 'dining-room suite' we had a Mr and Mrs Farina, the most charming of all our lodgers. I dined with them frequently, repressing a sense of guilt in eating the excellently cooked food that I knew Mother had been labouring over in the kitchen. Mrs Farina evinced a kindly passion for being read to, and consequently had to listen, poor woman, to everything I had ever written. She was appreciative and only occasionally critical, and did me a power of good.

I managed to sell a few magazine stories here and there, and was once led by Stoj into the presence of a Miss Ethel Mannin, who was the editor or sub-editor of the *Blue Magazine*. I met her again many years afterwards at a literary dinner party given by Mr George Doran, and was flattered to discover, upon reading her book, *Confessions and Impressions*, recently, that these two brief encounters had obviously constituted, in her mind, a delightful intimacy.

Through the influence of Max Darewski, I signed a three years' contract with his brother Herman, who at that time was the head of a music publishing firm in Charing Cross Road. The contract was for lyrics only, and I was to be paid fifty pounds the first year, seventy-five pounds the second year, and one hundred pounds the third year. I appeared dutifully every week or so, for the first few months, armed with verses, and ideas for songs. I waited many hours in the outer office, and sometimes even penetrated into the next-to-the-outer office, but seldom, if ever, clapped eyes on Herman Darewski, and nobody seemed at all interested in my lyrics. At the end of the first year I began to get a little anxious about the second instalment of seventy-five pounds. But I needn't have worried because it was paid to me without rancour, on the day specified. During the third year of my contract I was too busy with other affairs to go near the office until the last day, when I called to receive my cheque for a hundred pounds. Herman Darewski's third or fourth secretary handed it to me with a charming smile, and, after a brief exchange of social amenities, I had a cup of tea in the outer office and went home. Some while after this, the Herman Darewski publishing firm went bust, a fact that has never altogether astonished me.

On Armistice Day I wandered about the streets during the morning and afternoon, and in the evening dined with Tony and Juanita Ganderillas, whom I had met originally at one of General Ashmore's musical parties. They were Chileans, wealthy, gay and kind. After dinner we drove in a dark red Rolls-Royce through the Park and into Trafalgar Square, where we stuck, while hordes of screaming people climbed on to the roof of the car, the footboards and the radiator. We screamed with them, and shook hands with as many as we could, and I felt ignobly delighted, in this moment of national rejoicing, to be in a tail coat, a Rolls-Royce, and obviously aristocratic company. After a couple of hours in Trafalgar Square, we managed to get to the Savoy, where everybody wore paper caps, and threw streamers, and drank champagne, and Delysia, in a glittering pink dress, stood on a table and sang the "Marseillaise" over and over again to wild applause. It was a thrilling night, and I regret to say that the tragic significance of it was almost entirely lost upon me. I had not consciously suffered much from the war, apart from those unhappy months in training camps and hospitals. I had been a small boy of fourteen when it started, too young to realise what it was all about, and now that it was over, I could only perceive that life would probably be a good deal more enjoyable without it. I have noticed, just lately, a certain tendency among contemporary journalistic writers to class me with the generation that was 'ineradicably scarred by the war.' They have found, upon analysing my plays, a sense of profound disillusionment, a dreadful nerve-racked cynicism, obviously the heritage of those four black years, and I have searched myself carefully to discover any grounds for believing this dramatic implication to be true. I have found none. I was not in the least scarred by the war. It was little more to me at the time than a dully oppressive background, and although I certainly acquired a few nasty scratches from the years immediately following it, the reasons for my warped disenchantment with life must be sought elsewhere.

5

My part in *Scandal* was small, and as a character, nebulous. I made a brief appearance at the beginning of Act Two in a grey suit, and a still briefer appearance at the beginning of Act Three, dressed, I forget why, as Sir Walter Raleigh. The play was what's known as 'strong.' The 'big scene' took place in a bedroom, after all the smaller parts had gone home. Beatrice Hinchliffe (Kyrle Bellew), having tricked the strong and silent family friend (Arthur Bourchier) into a *mariage blanc*, suddenly discovered, on the wedding night, that she was deeply in love with him. This had the unfortunate effect of sending her into transports of coquetry. She bounced about on the nuptial bed, employing archness, defiance, tenderness, temper and tears, until Arthur Bourchier, goaded to a frenzy of suppressed passion, lashed her, cringing, on to her silken pillows, with a virile and dramatic speech concluding with the terrifying words: 'If you and I were alone on a desert island I wouldn't – ' etc., etc., with which he turned definitely on his heel and left her as the curtain fell. In the last act, which took place on a yacht, after a comic seasick cameo contributed by Gladys Ffolliot, everything was smoothed out satisfactorily, and everybody forgave everybody else. I never considered it a good play, but perhaps I was prejudiced by the fact that my part in it was so unimportant.

Arthur Bourchier and Kyrle Bellew were charming to me, and arranged for me to have a little dressing-room to myself. Nora Swinburne was sweet and friendly, and I loved Mary Robson dearly, from the first rehearsal onwards. Apart from these pleasant contacts, my stock was low in the company. I behaved badly, and was accused, justifiably, by Millie Hylton of making hen noises whenever she came on to the stage. I was also heartily detested by Gladys Ffolliot, who had overheard me say to someone that her dog Daphne smelt like a drain. The truth of this statement in no way mitigated her rage, and she complained about me to the management whenever possible. Clare Greet lodged a few complaints too, from time to time, but I think this was only out of loyalty to the others. The theatre was frequently divided into camps, for and against me. Mary Robson's dressing-room was my refuge, where the various skirmishes were discussed with considerable hilarity. Our laughter was sometimes over-loud, and went echoing down the passage to torment the ears of my enemies. Arthur Bourchier and Kyrle occasionally admonished me with some attempt at severity, but they were seldom able to keep going for long without a twinkle appearing in their eyes, and when their door had closed upon my unconvincingly downcast figure, I used to hear them snorting with laughter. Finally Arthur Bourchier called me very seriously into his room, and informed me that the management were going to give me my notice at the end of the week. He suggested, kindly, that it would be a good idea for me to anticipate this, by writing them a letter of resignation, thereby saving myself the humiliation of being actually sacked. He said that he, personally, would be very sorry to lose me, as he considered me an excellent actor, but that in the future, I must behave much better, and be particularly careful never to offend women in the theatre, especially the slightly older ones, as their dislike, once incurred, was implacable and very, very dangerous.

When I got home that night I spent a happy hour composing a letter to Grossmith and Laurillard. I explained with dignity that owing to the peculiar behaviour of the old ladies in the cast, I felt myself compelled to tender my resignation, and that I should be exceedingly obliged if they could see their way to accepting my fortnight's notice. I remained, theirs very sincerely. They saw their way to accepting my fortnight's notice with unflattering clearness, and when I arrived at the theatre the next night, an envelope containing the salary due to me was handed to me by the stage-door-keeper, and I was allowed only half an hour to collect my things from my dressing-room. This was a shock, but not a bad one. I was already steeled to losing my job, and two weeks one way or another didn't make much difference. I detected in this waspish gesture from the powers, a certain lack of dignity, and although I should, by rights, have left the Strand Theatre for ever, burning with shame, and with my tail between my legs, my exit was actually a jaunty affair, untinged with sadness. I packed my things, said my good-byes to the Bourchiers and Mary and Nora, rattled blithely on all the old ladies' doors, and drove off in a taxi, feeling pleasantly free and in the best of spirits.

During that engagement I formed a fixed resolution to go to America. Mary, who had played in New York several times, thrilled me by her descriptions of it. We had dinner in the grill room of the Waldorf on matinée days, and she enumerated, at great length, the delights of American theatre life. The theatres themselves were the acme of luxury. The acting was far and away superior to anything that would be seen in London. There were apparently two very attractive brothers called Shubert, who produced masses of plays every season with a lavish disregard for expense, and welcomed any English actor, however small, with enthusiasm. There was also a kindly old body named Al Woods, who produced the best melodramas in the world, outside of David Belasco, who was of course a species of divinity. In addition to these brilliant philanthropists, there was the Flat Iron Building, the Woolworth Building, which I visualised as a pyramid of scarlet and gold, rising to the clouds in tier upon tier of ten-cent magnificence, the Pennsylvania Station, Times Square, Central Park (on a grander scale than Hyde Park), the Hippodrome stage, which could support and display at least fifty elephants abreast, the Metropolitan Opera House, glittering with Astors and Belmonts and Vanderbilts, Wall Street, the Bronx Zoo, Coney Island, and, most exciting of all, Broadway by night. Broadway by night seemed to be my cup of tea entirely. Its splendours and its noise and its crowds haunted my imagination. Its gigantic sky-signs dazzled my dreams, flashing in a myriad lights, with unfailing regularity, the two words 'Noel Coward.'

Apart from the great American idea, I conceived a passably good plot for a play, and as, in those days, conception was only removed from achievement by the actual time required for putting the words on paper, it was completed inside a week. It was entitled *The Last Trick* and was a melodrama in four acts. The first and second acts were quite amusing, the third act good, and the last act weak and amateurish. The plot hinged on the 'revenge' motif and wasn't particularly original, but the dialogue was effective, and showed a marked improvement on my other work. I took the play to Gilbert Miller, and he seemed to be impressed with it. He said that he was leaving for New York in a few weeks' time and would like to take it with him, and that he might possibly be able to arrange for it to be produced. I lunched with him a few days later, and he told me the plots of several plays that he had seen in Vienna, Berlin, Paris and Budapest. He also gave me some useful pieces of advice on the art of play-writing. He said, among other things, that although my dialogue was nearly always good, my construction was 'lousy.' He said that someone had told his father, who in turn had told him, that the construction of a play was as important as the foundations of a house, whereas dialogue, however good, could only, at best, be considered as interior decoration. This I recognised immediately as being authentic wisdom. He said, on parting, that he was quite convinced that before long I would write a first-rate play, and that when I did, he would be only too delighted to produce it. He detained me for a few moments at the door by giving me an example of a really well-constructed scene. It was from the third act of a thrilling play he had recently attended in Stockholm.

Buoyed up by Gilbert Miller's encouragement, I wrote two bad plays and one better one. The first two are not worthy of discussion, but the third, *The Rat Trap*, was my first really serious attempt at psychological conflict. Even in the light of later experience, I can still see in it two well-written scenes. As a whole, of course, it was immature, but it was much steadier than anything I had done hitherto. The last act, as usual, went to pieces, but when I had finished it, I felt, for the first time with genuine conviction, that I could really write plays.

6

In the early spring of 1919, I went again to stay with Mrs Cooper at Hambleton. I drove a car for the first time. I rode a horse for the first time, with no fear but with little grace. I sang at village concerts, sometimes alone, sometimes with Mrs Cooper's daughter, Phyllis. With her soprano I harmonised breathily, making up for my lack of volume with the maximum of expression. We sang "Trot here, trot there" from *Véronique*, also "The Swing Song" from the same score. The villagers applauded us lustily, their hands and hearts warmed by the knowledge that, although my voice might seem to be a trifle reedy, I was actually, in manner and fact, a *bona fide* professional, accustomed to charming vaster multitudes from the vaster stages of the best London theatres.

Small memories are the most insistent, and I like to catch again, for a moment, the feel of the sharp spring air as we drove home at night after a concert, the smell of the wood fire in the library where we discussed, over hot soup and sandwiches, the triumphs of the evening. All the warm, comfortable ingredients of country-house life were there, the very unfamiliarity of the atmosphere enhancing its charm for me, and I felt happily aloof from the squabblings of angry old character actresses. This, I reflected, quite wrongly, was my rightful sphere, and I would go upstairs to bed, undress, and brush my teeth, still, until sleep closed down upon me, accurate in my performance of a country gentleman.

It must not be imagined that Mrs Cooper was my only contact with the shires. She was the first, but by no means the last. She, it is true, St Peter'd me into that bleak, horse-infested paradise, but once inside, I fended for myself. Other country houses opened welcoming doors to me. Some were larger and grander than Hambleton. Some were smaller and more exclusively concerned with the chase. None, however, was so individually agreeable, and I returned to the mattresses in front of the fire, the faded peach-coloured brocade curtains, and the brass hot-water-cans, with a sense of relief, a familiar home-sweet-home contentment.

Witham-on-the-Hill was one of my pleasanter excursions. It was a lovely old house, richly ordered, and belonging to the Keld Fenwicks. I was invited there, oddly enough, for a 'shoot,' I forget now what exactly was being shot, but it was probably duck. At least twenty people were staying in the house and some of them wore velvet smoking jackets in the evening, and there were two very large greyhounds, which fortunately took a fancy to me. The food was delicious, and I found several volumes of Marie Antoinette's secret memoirs in the library, which I read luxuriously during the day, while the 'shoot' was at its height. The evenings might have been a trifle dull for me if I had not been so enchanted with the authenticity of the atmosphere. The setting and the dialogue were perfect, the character performances superb, and there seemed to be, only every now and then, a suspicion of over-acting among the smaller parts.

The London managers during that year continued to disregard me, and I continued to write plays and magazine stories, occasionally selling some of the latter, and making enough money here and there to keep myself in clothes and help out with the house.

Now that I considered myself definitely 'set' as a writer, the horror of being out of an engagement was less dreadful. I could be my own master, and work alone, beholden to nobody. My plays were steadily achieving more 'body' and consistence. I flung aside all bastard whimsies and concentrated on realism. No pert elf or faun dared even to peep round a tree at me in 1919. Pan and pierrot retired, disgruntled, into oblivion as far as I was concerned and, I am glad to say, have remained there until this day. My mind, not unnaturally, jumped over-far in the opposite direction. I dealt, almost exclusively, with the most lurid types; tarts, pimps, sinister courtesans, and cynical adulterers whirled across my pages in great profusion. This phase finally passed owing to a withering lack of response from magazine editors, but it was all useful and I don't regret any of it.

Some new friends appeared. One of these was Betty Chester. Her real name was Grundtvig, and she lived with her mother and father in Chester Square.

Lorn Macnaughtan was a constant visitor at their house. She was tall and fair, with good hands and a nice speaking voice. She had been to school with Betty, and accepted a certain amount of Grundtvig patronage with slyly humorous grace. As she has been my personal secretary and close friend for nearly fifteen years, I find it difficult to describe her as I saw her then, for the first time. She seemed unremarkable in manner and personality, but there was authority in her quietness which was probably the heritage of many ancient, kilted Macnaughtans, who, in the long past, had stumped dourly over their Scottish estates. It was puzzling to try to reconcile her obvious distinction with the fact that she was, at the moment, in the chorus at the Empire, as she appeared to have no attributes whatever for that particular sphere. Her feet were large and her figure unvoluptuous; she could neither dance nor sing, and her movements were never especially graceful. She was slightly self-conscious, and her pale, clear complexion seldom conceded to wantonness more than an occasional dab of powder. When I knew her better, I discovered that her stage career was as surprising to herself as to everybody else. She had managed to get chorus and understudy jobs, sometimes through influence, sometimes through grim determination, because the Macnaughtan splendour having faded into a small house in Wellington Square, it was essential for her to make enough money to live on.

All this accounted for the strange flashes of chorus-girl jargon which sprang from Lorn's lips bawdily, at the most unexpected moments, and frequently shattered the small, tightly encased propriety of Mr Grundtvig.

By this time I had moved down from my tiny top attic in 111, Ebury Street to a more nobly proportioned room on the floor next to the top. In this, I was able to give occasional tea parties, with the social elements tastefully mixed. Gertie Lawrence used to come, bringing with her various haughty young Guards officers who sat about, puzzled by the theatrical conversation, but securely wrapped in regimental poise. Mrs Cooper came too and wailed agreeably at Stoj and Lyndon, and Peter and Sheila and Betty and Lorn. Every now and then I thoughtlessly chose the day of our housemaid's afternoon out, and was embarrassed to see Father waltzing into the room with the tea-tray. Everyone immediately rose to say 'How do you do?' and shake hands, to which he couldn't possibly respond until somebody relieved him of the tea-things. I glossed over those slight contretemps with, what I hoped, was easy Bohemian geniality, and tried not to intercept the ironic glances that any strangers present exchanged with each other.

One day a young man called Stewart Forster appeared. He was a lieutenant in the Coldstream Guards, with a deceptively guileless personality, and a timid, butter-coloured moustache, which, with the passing of time, I regret to say, has become large and quite red. Then, however, it was innocuous and faintly apologetic, as though it knew perfectly well that it had no right to be there at all, and wouldn't be, but for the exigencies of military etiquette.

Stewart asked me, on leaving, if I would care to dine with him on guard at St James's Palace the following week. I accepted with alacrity and regretted that I had no decorations other than my army discharge medal with which to adorn the occasion. I hadn't even a tail coat. I didn't mention this, but hired one from Moss Bros the day before I was due to appear at the Palace.

I arrived on the stroke of eight o'clock, and was conducted to the mess by an austere corporal. The traditional pomp of the atmosphere felt chilly at first, but there was an underlying glamour in it which thawed me presently, and, with the aid of a glass of extremely dry sherry, I expanded sufficiently to make a joke about my tail coat, which no eye, however well schooled in good manners, could possibly regard in anything but a comic light. Moss Bros had certainly let me down badly. The sleeves had a Pagliacci fullness, and the tails rebounded from my claves as I walked.

At about eleven o'clock, Stewart imposed upon himself a gigantic bearskin, which looked as though it might slip down and extinguish him entirely at the slightest sharp movement. He also buckled on his sword, and clanked out into the courtyard, where I heard his voice barking shrilly to the accompaniment of shuffling feet. When he came back I had one more glass of port, said my good-byes, and left, no longer oppressed by military tradition, but quite definitely part of it.

I walked home, down the Mall and past Buckingham Palace, much elated by my evening, and reflecting that uniform was undoubtedly very becoming to Englishmen, and that white-gloved orderlies, tawny port, a polished, shiny table decorated with silver regimental trophies, warm red-shaded lights, and large oil paintings of Their Majesties, all combined to impart to the most ordinary conversation an indescribable and imperishable charm.

7

In August 1919 I played 'Ralph' in *The Knight of the Burning Pestle* at the Birmingham Repertory Theatre.

For me, there was a quality of fantasy about the whole engagement. Nigel Playfair directed the production with a touching fidelity to Elizabethan atmosphere. No curtain. No footlights. A circular stage, fringed with uneasy gallants, who sat on stools, and smoked clay pipes. There was a musician's gallery high up on a rostrum at the back, containing a few local fiddlers, their upper parts correctly be-ruffed and be-wigged, and their lower parts more comfortably encased in their ordinary Birmingham trousers. Sometimes they forgot to leave off their pince-nez, and were flurried into doing so by urgent hisses from the conscientious gallants. I was not very good as 'Ralph,' owing to a total lack of understanding of the play. It was my first and only experience of Elizabethan comedy and, being unable to detect any great humour on it, I played that poor apprentice with a subborn Mayfair distinction which threw the whole thing out of key. This was largely Nigel Playfair's fault. He directed with more elfishness than authority, and cheered the rehearsals with many little jokes, which, although vastly appreciated by Betty Chester and me, were not actually helpful to our performances. Betty played 'The Citizen's Wife' with youth, charm and great vivacity, which, considering that she was supposed to be a bawdy matron of about forty-five, was hardly appropriate.

The Knight of the Burning Pestle could not be considered a really progressive step in my career as an actor. I had mouthed and postured my way through it with little conviction and no sense of period. I was unaware of this, however, and, even if I had realised it, I doubt whether I should have cared very much, because, in course of those three short weeks, Fortune favoured me with such a violent and unexpected slap on the back, that not only Birmingham, but the whole world, seemed to be transformed. The people in the streets, hitherto rather dingy-looking, with grim, manufacturing faces, suddenly changed into happy smiling creatures, stepping lightly over pavements, no longer grey, and wearing gay colours. Not so much as one drop of rain fell for at least three days. And even my landlady, Mrs Hunter, a woman of sad regrets if ever there was one, seemed to forget for a spell her Bright's disease, and melt into cheerfulness. All this on account of one brief cablegram from Gilbert Miller in New York informing me, in lilting, business-like terms, that Al Woods wished to pay five hundred dollars for a year's option on my play *The Last Trick*.

Five hundred dollars, after calculations in Betty's dressing-room, resolved itself into the still fantastic but more understandable sum of one hundred pounds.

I remember rushing to the Queen's Hotel in full make-up, between the first and second acts of the matinée, sending an enthusiastic reply from the hall porter's desk, and, on my way back to the theatre, buying a very large bottle of toilet water at Boots Cash Chemists.

When I returned to London, the five hundred dollars was duly paid me, in pounds, by Gilbert Miller's secretary, and within a few days another cable arrived, this time saying that Al Woods would like to buy the play outright for a further fifteen hundred dollars, as it was necessary for it to be rewritten by a more technically expert playwright than myself.

Never having received more than a few guineas for anything I had ever written, this windfall was a shock which even my self-confidence was unable to meet calmly. I couldn't believe that there wasn't some mistake, some sinister catch in it, until Mother and I had been to a bank in the City and actually watched, with glistening eyes, the money sliding over the counter to us. Even the fact that at the moment I happened to be suffering from a degrading boil on the end of my nose, failed to depress the occasion.

I burst forth rapidly into several new suits, paid a large part of our overdue quarterly instalment on the Ebury Street house and bought a second-hand grand piano at Harrods, which contributed richness and joy to my room, and considerable pain to the lodgers immediately above and below it.

I glanced back happily upon recent penury, over which the haze of distance already seemed to be shimmering (a fancy which later proved to be distinctly premature), and walked on winged feet along Bedford Street, St Martin's Lane, Garrick Street, Charing Cross Road, Wardour Street, Green Street, Coventry Street, and Shaftesbury Avenue, crossing myself devoutly outside theatrical agents' offices, and finishing up daily with an expensive lunch at the 'Ivy.'

The 'Ivy' had been a generous friend to me in the past, allowing me many meals, when it knew perfectly well that the chances of their being paid for were slender. And so now, sheathed in sudden prosperity, it seemed only fitting that I should eat there until I burst.

I went to many parties in my new tail suit, savouring to the full the sensation of being well-dressed for the first time. The days of twirling anxiously before Moss Bros' looking-glasses were over. No more hitching of the arm-pits to prevent sleeves from enveloping the hands altogether. No more bracing of out-grown trousers to their lowest, with the consciousness that the slightest movement of the arms would display a mortifying expanse of shirt between waistcoat and flies. All that belonged to the past. Now I could dance and dine securely, feeling smart and *soigné*, and very, very smooth.

When relying upon my own funds, I chose a suitably understanding partner such as Gertie Lawrence, or Meggie Albanesi, and we would dine frugally, and go to Murray's, or Rector's, or the Savoy, where it was possible to slip in by the Embankment entrance without a ticket.

When invited, I patronised the Grafton Galleries, the Ritz, Ciro's, and, on one occasion, even Claridge's.

Michael Arlen was also just beginning to blossom about this time. We used to wave languidly to each other across dance floors, shedding our worldliness later, in obscure corners. He was very dapper, and his Hawes and Curtis backless waistcoats aroused envy in me, which I soon placated, by ordering some for myself, but his exquisite pearl and platinum watch-chain was beyond competition, and all I could do was to admire it bravely, and hope, in my heart, that perhaps it was just a little bit ostentatious.

8

When Gilbert Miller returned to London, he asked me to go to see him in his office, where he continued his lecture on play construction where he had left off several months before.

He described to me the plots of *La Tosca, Fedora, The Easiest Way,* and *Within the Law,* which, incidentally, I had seen three times. He then went on to say that he himself had a good idea for a light comedy, but that he would like me to write it, preferably with Charles Hawtrey in mind, and that if I did it well enough, he would produce it in London during the following spring.

I was then, as I am now, extremely chary of the thought of writing anything based upon somebody else's idea, but I persevered, and within the next few weeks manufactured an amiable little play entitled (by Gilbert Miller) *I'll Leave It to You.*

The dialogue, on the whole, was amusing, and unpretentious, and the construction was not bad, but it was too mild and unassuming to be able to awake any really resounding echoes in the hearts of the great public, and although I was naturally entranced with it, Gilbert was not quite as enthusiastic as I had hoped he would be.

He suggested several alterations, some of which I agreed to, and all of which I made, and after a series of discussions, he departed for America again, having promised me that on his return he would arrange for a try-out production at the Gaiety Theatre, Manchester, in April. I had to content myself with this, and the reflection, that although six months was a long time to wait, I had at least had the sense to write a part in the play for myself, in which I should undoubtedly, when the moment came, score an overwhelming personal triumph.

9

In January, I went to Paris with Stewart Forster, according to a plan formulated during the summer at Rumwood, Stewart's home in Kent. We stayed at the Ritz for the first night, and at a small hotel in the Rue Caumartin for the rest of the week.

As it was the first time that we had, either of us, been out of England, our behaviour was entirely true to form.

We sipped *apértifs* outside the Café de la Paix, visited the Louvre, Napoleon's Tomb, Notre-Dame, Versailles, the Moulin Rouge, and the Folies-Bergère.

We dined at Prunier's, and the Café de Paris, and danced endlessly round the cabarets of Montmartre with metallic tarts, who persisted in mistaking us for Americans.

We even quarrelled mildly over a young lady from Cincinnati, who drove us about in her car, accepted floral offerings, and flirted with us magnificently, never for one instant deviating from that fine line of conduct which separates racy conversation from staunch moral integrity. This we recognised as a racial peculiarity, and were duly impressed by it, if a trifle irritated.

We met a Russian Prince, *soi-disant*, who owned a racing car which looked like a red pepper, and a French mistress who looked like all the pictures of flaming adventuresses in the world rolled into one, but who, on closer acquaintance, turned out to be dull and deeply sentimental.

It was an enjoyable week, and we absorbed the sights and sounds and smells of Paris thoroughly and satisfactorily, and when we left, sadly, to return to England, we possessed a certain 'manner' which had not been apparent before. Our vocabularies also were the richer by several French phrases, and three complete sentences, two of which were unrepeatable.

In February, Mrs Cooper invited me to go to Alassio with her for a fortnight, and so for the first time I slept in a *wagon-lit*, experienced the thrilling, damp coldness of a frontier station at two o'clock in the morning, and whirled through Switzerland and down on to the Lombardy plains with my nose buttoned against the railway carriage window. In Alassio we stayed at the Grand Hotel, and breakfasted daily on a balcony overlooking dusty palm trees and glittering blue sea. Behind the hotel there were plaster houses in pale colours, olive groves, cypresses, lush curtains of wistaria and bougainvillaea, and serried ranks of snow-capped mountains.

I have returned there since, more experienced in travel, having seen higher mountains, richer foliage, and bluer seas, and realised that Alassio is really nothing out of the ordinary, that there are hundreds of other little towns nestling in the shadow of the Alpes Maritimes, with just the same coloured houses and twisted streets, and just the same palm trees, and fishing boats, and pungent smells. But that was the first time, the first thrill of discovery, the first proof I had ever had, that hot sunshine was anywhere possible in February.

Upon arriving back in London, I discovered that Gilbert Miller was not returning after all, and had put the producing of *I'll Leave It to You* in the hands of Robert Oswald, the general manager of the Gaiety, Manchester. Stanley Bell was to direct the play, and the cast chosen included Kate Cutler, Farren Soutar, Muriel Pope, Stella Jesse, Douglas Jeffries, Lois Stuart, Moya Nugent, Esmé Wynne (Stoj) and myself.

The first night in Manchester was tremendously exciting. The play went well all through and, at the end, the audience cheered, and Kate pushed me forward to make a speech. I was feeling far too emotional to be able to relinquish her hand, and so I stood there, clutching it, and experiencing the curious sensation of success. There was I, and there was an audience applauding and cheering, and as I advanced a step, the applause and the cheers swelled louder and then died away into complete silence. I made quite a nice little speech. It was boyish and modest, and had been carefully rehearsed alone in my digs beforehand. I had seen too many authors hauled on to the stage on first nights, trembling and confused, with goggling eyes, to make the mistake of being caught unprepared.

When it was all over and I went out of the stage door, there was a large crowd of gallery girls waiting on the pavement, and I signed their autograph books with a flourish and enjoyed myself deeply.

Towards the end of our first week in Manchester, Mrs Charles Hawtrey and Mrs Gilbert Miller came down from London to see the play. I was very nervous, and Kate and Stanley and I prayed ardently that there would be a good audience, and no hitches in the performance. Contrary to what generally happens on those occasions, there was a good audience, and the performance was smoother and better than it had ever been, and when, at the end, I had to make my speech in response to the cheers, I was visualising clearly an immediate production at the St James's Theatre, with Hawtrey playing Uncle Daniel. The faces of Mrs Hawtrey and Mrs Miller when Stanley Bell ushered them into my dressing-room afterwards were sadly disillusioning. They both stood there, shaking their heads slowly and tenderly, like china mandarins. They were both filled and brimming over with sympathy, as though they had just been present at the greatest theatrical catastrophe of modern times. They both kissed me, said that they would have to cable to Gilbert immediately to say what they honestly and truly thought. Upon this, I lost my temper inwardly, but fortunately not outwardly, and said that I was sorry that they were so disappointed in the play, but that luckily the audiences we had played to didn't seem to be quite so hard to please. I then added with firmness and a touch of hysterical bravado, that whether Gilbert Miller and Charles Hawtrey were interested, or whether they weren't, the play would definitely be produced in London within the next few months! Upon which, they both wobbled their heads again, and went out.

When they had gone Stanley took me to supper at the Midland and did his best to cheer me up, but without much success. With both Hawtrey and Gilbert Miller ruled out, our chances of London production were small. However, I drove back to Lloyd Street, grimly determined that *I'll Leave It to You* was not going to peter out of existence with only three weeks in Manchester to its credit.

10

I'll Leave It to You opened in London at the New Theatre on July 21st, 1920, two and a half months after its try-out in Manchester. It was presented by Mary Moore (Lady Wyndham) with the same cast, excepting Farren Soutar, who had been replaced by Holman Clarke. The first night was a roaring success, and I made another boyish speech. Lots of my friends were there, including Bobbie and Ivor, neither of whom came round to see me afterwards, which hurt me bitterly. When I eventually tackled them about this, Ivor replied that the play, in the intervals of irritating him excessively, had bored him stiff. So that was that.

The critics were mostly very enthusiastic, and said a lot about it having been a great night, and that a new playwright had been discovered, etc., but unfortunately their praise was not potent enough to lure audiences to the New Theatre for more than five weeks, so the run ended rather miserably, the last week being rendered still gloomier by Lady Wyndham, who, with adamant economy, insisted that our lighting should be cut down to half.

However, I sold the amateur rights to Samuel French for a comfortable sum, and feeling much the better for my brief encouragement, both financially and spiritually, set to work with renewed vigour on a play called *Barriers Down*, which was awful.

In November, Nigel Playfair decided to produce *The Knight of the Burning Pestle* at the Kingsway Theatre, so we rehearsed it all over again, and finally opened, to tepid enthusiasm.

Mrs Patrick Campbell came one night in a box, and great excitement reigned behind the scenes. This excitement waned towards the end of the play, when it was discovered that she had been sound asleep since the beginning of the first act. I sent her an outraged message through a mutual friend, and the next night there she was again, in the same box, but far from sleepy. She wore long white gloves, and applauded wildly every time I stepped on to the stage. Elsie Janis and Mrs Janis brought a party to a matinée one day, prompted by sheer courtesy and kindness to me, and they sat, from the beginning to the end, bored and bewildered beyond relief, but infinitely polite. Many years later Elsie told me what they had really thought of the show, all of which goes to prove that Americans have very beautiful manners.

Just before Christmas, I developed suddenly a temperature of a hundred and two. The doctor forbade me to play, but, imbued with that misguided 'old trouper' bravery, I insisted, with the result that I gave sixteen members of the company 'mumps.' Nigel himself played my part for a little, but even his fine performance couldn't contend against the bad business and the 'mumps,' so the play closed, and I signed a contract to appear in Gilbert Miller's production of an American comedy, *Polly with a Past*, at the St James's Theatre. Rehearsals were not to start until February, so I had a few weeks free for a holiday.

I bought myself a second-class ticket to Rapallo, and stayed there for two days at the Casino Hotel. Then, as I knew no one at all, and couldn't speak a word of Italian, my independent spirit wilted a trifle, and I beat a hasty retreat to Alassio, where I knew Mrs Cooper was staying. She was delighted to see me, and once more I settled myself into the Grand Hotel.

After I had been there a few days, I was asked to sing at a concert at the English Club. The concert was bad, and the piano dreadful, but I sang several songs with lofty professional arrogance, only slightly deflated by a smartly dressed young woman in the front row, who appeared to be fighting an attack of convulsive giggles with singular lack of success. I remember frowning at her coldly several times, but this only seemed to send her into fresh paroxysms. When I met her afterwards with Mrs Cooper, she had regained control and was very poised indeed. Her name was Gladys Calthrop. I asked her what there was about my singing that had made her laugh so much, and, after a few evasions, she explained that it wasn't my singing exactly, but that I had looked funny.

It is strange how many really important moments in life slip by in the procession, unnoted, and devoid of prescience. No guardian angel whacks a sharp triangle in the brain, and the heavens remain commonplace. It is not my intention in this book to delve deeply into personal relationships, but as Gladys Calthrop has been so intimately concerned with all my best work, and so intrinsically part of my failures and successes, I feel that a small, retrospective fanfare is not entirely out of place. In appearance she was less atractive then than she is now. Her eyes and figure were good. Her brain was alert, and her sense of humour keen, though somewhat impaired by a slight bias towards highbrow Bohemianism.

The remaining few days of my stay in Alassio we passed almost entirely together. We went for walks. We went for drives. We sat on the beach, in olive groves, and on terraces overhanging the sea. We discussed vehemently Life, Love, Art, Marriage, Suicide and Religion. We went to a *festa* at the Combattente Club, and left politely with the English contingent, returning later when foreign constraint had fled, to enjoy ourselves. It was this *festa* that supplied the basis for my ill-fated play *Sirocco*. There was much tawdry glamour to it, contributed by sweet champagne, an electric piano, paper streamers, and the usual paraphernalia of Latin carnival.

II

Polly with a Past opened at the St James's Theatre on March 2nd. It was an American farce which had had a big success in New York, where the name part had been created by Ina Claire. In London, Polly was played by Edna Best, who was good, but appeared too adolescent in the latter part of the play when she was supposed to be a dashing French adventuress. Donald Calthrop was the leading man, and the rest of the cast consisted of Aubrey Smith, Helen Haye, Alice Moffat, Claude Rains, Arthur Hatherton, Edith Evans, Henry Kendall, and me. Donald Calthrop and Harry Kendall had the two best men parts, and, as in *Charley's Aunt*, I was the 'feed.' By the end of the run, however, I was embroidering and overacting to such an extent that they had to fight like steers to get their lines over at all.

During this run another lifelong friend made his appearance: Jeffery Amherst, or rather Jeffery Holmesdale as he was then. His father was the Earl Amherst, and he, Jeffery, held the rank of captain in the Coldstream Guards. He was small, and fair, and his gallant military record seemed slightly incongruous, until you had known him a little. He was gay and a trifle strained, and there was a certain quality of secrecy in him, entirely unfurtive, but stronger than mere reserve. It was as though he knew many things too closely, and was consequently over-wary. I dined with him several times, 'on guard' and at home with his family. I watched him twinkling and giggling through several noisy theatrical parties, but it took a long while for even me to begin to know him.

Polly with a Past bored me early in its run, but I was working hard outside the theatre. Songs, sketches, and plays were bursting out of me far too quickly, but without nearly enough critical discrimination. My best effort during that period was a comedy in three acts, *The Young Idea*, which was primarily inspired by Shaw's *You Never Can Tell*. Dolly and Phillip being my original prototypes for Sholto and Gerda, I felt rather guilty of plagiarism, however inept, and when the play was finished, J. E. Vedrenne kindly sent it to Shaw, to find out whether or not he had any objections. A short while afterwards, I received my script back from Shaw, scribbled all over with alterations and suggestions, and accompanied by a long letter, which, to my lasting regret, I was idiotic enough to lose. However, the gist of it was that I showed every indication of becoming a good playwright, providing that I never again in my life read another word that he, Shaw, had ever written. It was, as might be expected, a brilliant letter, and I took its advice only half-heartedly. But there was more than brilliance in the trouble that that great man had taken in going minutely over the work of a comparatively unknown young writer.

12

The rebirth of my determination to go to America occurred at one of Ivor's supper parties, and was caused, I think, by the presence of Jeanne Eagels, who had just made a big success in New York, in a play called *Daddies*. She talked vividly of the American theatre and I felt instinctively that she was a fine actress, and was thrilled to think that there were many others like her just on the other side of the ocean. In this I was wrong. Of all the actresses I have ever seen, there has never been one quite like Jeanne Eagels.

Ivor's parties, in those days, were great fun. In later years they seem to have become a trifle staid and less spontaneous, but perhaps the fault lies with me, perhaps I have grown blasé, and the thrill of star-gazing has turned sour and curdled. At any rate, at that time a party at 'The Flat' was a signal for general rejoicing. 'The Flat' sat, and still sits, on the very top of the Strand Theatre, and in order to reach it, a perilous ascent was made in a small, self-worked lift. Ivor's guests crushed themselves timorously together in this frightening little box, someone pulled a rope, there was a sharp grinding noise, a scream from some less hardy member of the party; then, swaying and rattling, the box ascended. Upon reaching the top, it would hit the roof with a crash and, more often than not, creak all the way down again.

Many people preferred to toil up seven long flights of stairs rather than face the lift, but I was one of the braver spirits, on one occasion actually making six complete journeys before I could induce it to stop.

The big room of the flat had a raised dais running across one end. Upon this, there were sometimes two, at other times no grand pianos, sometimes a gramophone, and nearly always Viola Tree. The high spots of the parties were reached in this room. Charades were performed, people did stunts. Olga Lynn sang, and Fay Compton immediately did an imitation of Olga Lynn singing. Visiting musicians were subtly lured to the piano. Native musicians rushed to it. Rival leading ladies had verbal scuffles. Divorced couples hobnobbed with each other, and with each other's co-respondents. Bitter enemies met face to face, and either swept majestically from the room or stayed to ruffle Ivor's hair.

Jeffery Holmesdale added an extra fillip to my American dream by telling me that he was sailing for New York at the end of May, to represent his father at some sort of centenary festival at Amherst College in Massachusetts. It seemed improbable at the moment that there could be the least chance of my going with him. *Polly with a Past* was still playing to good business, I had a run-of-the-play contract, and in addition there was the ever-present money difficulty. True, things were going better in Ebury Street, I had been earning a good salary for quite a long while, and had a certain amount in the bank, but not nearly enough to pay my return fare to America. I could, I suppose, have taken a passage on some little freight boat, but I was determined to make my first arrival as stylish as possible. I had heard a good deal about the American reverence for success, and on the strength of having had one play produced in London and having played several important parts, I felt that it would be bad policy to creep in, unannounced, by the tradesmen's entrance.

I brooded over all this for several weeks, and finally, by borrowing here and there and selling two songs to Ned Lathom, who didn't want them in the least and only bought them out of charity, I scraped together a hundred pounds, which was enough for my fare one way, on the *Aquitania*, with a little over for expenses.

The next step was to obtain permission from Gilbert Miller to leave the cast of *Polly*, which I did, a few weeks before it closed, and at the end of May, 1921, Jeffery and I set sail on the first of our many journeys together.

PART FOUR

I

To have embarked for America with a bundle of manuscripts, a one-way ticket, and only seventeen pounds to spare, was, I suppose, rather foolhardy, and when the *Aquitania* had left Cherbourg a few miles astern, fears twittered in my stomach like birds in a paper bag, and I reflected that from almost every point of view I was a fool. Admittedly, my faith in my own talents remained unwavering, but it did seem unduly optimistic to suppose that the Americans would be perceptive enough to see me immediately in the same light in which I saw myself. In this, I was perfectly right. They didn't.

However, the weather was warm, the sea calm, and I should have Jeffery to lean on for three weeks at least, so I snapped out of my despondency and sent a cheerful radio to Mother.

I appeared at the ship's concert, supporting the chief steward who sang "Mandalay," a wizened 'buck-and-wing' dancer from the second class, and a big woman in black satin, who played the fiddle, the piano, the xylophone, and, for an encore, the cornet.

New York rose out of the sea to greet us. It was a breathless June morning, and wads of cotton-wool smoke lay motionless among the high towers. The Statue of Liberty seemed insignificant but the harbour was glorious. There will always be a stinging enchantment for me in this arrival. Even now, when I know it so well in every aspect, my heart jumps a little. Then it was entirely new to me. We slid gently past Battery Park, still green with early summer, the skyscrapers moved gracefully aside to show still further vistas, and, a long way below us, platoons of straw hats passed by on ferry-boats. As we drew near the dock, several fussy little tugs came out to meet us and finally, after tremendous efforts, succeeded in coaxing and nuzzling us alongside.

We were met by Naps Alington, Gabrielle Enthoven, Cecile Sartoris and Teddie Gerrard. I knew Teddie and Naps, but had never met the other two, and was naturally unaware at the moment that I was destined to live with them for several months. Jeffery and I went, first of all, to the Algonquin, which I had heard was a comfortable, theatrical, and reasonable hotel. It was all that and more, and in later years I have grown to love it dearly. But then, in a violent heat-wave, it seemed airless and stuffy, and so, after the first night there, we moved: Jeffery to share Naps' flat in Eighth Street, and I to the Brevoort, at the lower end of Fifth Avenue.

That first evening in New York is clear in my memory. I refused to dine with

Teddie and Naps and Jeffery, because I wanted to go to a theatre. And so I promised to rejoin them all afterwards, and went off by myself. I sauntered down Broadway alone, gazing up at the sky-signs, being bumped into, pushed, and shoved by the endless, slow-moving crowds on the sidewalks. The sky was not yet quite dark and the million lights flamed against it, changing it from rich blue to deep purple. It was grander than Mary Robson had described, and more sharply beautiful than I could ever have imagined – a slightly tawdry beauty, detached, impersonal, and a little scarifying.

I walked up and down several side streets, looking at the pictures outside the theatres, and finally deciding upon one, went into the Klaw Theatre. The play was *Nice People* by Rachel Crothers, starring Francine Larrimore, and including among the smaller parts Tallulah Bankhead and Katherine Cornell. I thought the production and acting good, and the play poor, but what interested me most was the *tempo*. Bred in the tradition of gentle English comedy with its inevitable maids, butlers, flower vases, and tea-tables, it took me a good ten minutes of the first act to understand what anyone was saying. They all seemed to be talking at once. Presently I began to disentangle the threads, and learnt my first lesson in American acting, which was the technique of realising, first, which lines in the script are superfluous, and second, knowing when, and how, to throw them away.

After the play, I took a taxi down to Teddie's house in Washington Square, where I found the party in exceedingly full swing. From out of the haze of chatter, piano-playing, and cigarette smoke, I managed to extricate a dark, attractive woman, whose eyes slanted upwards at the corners, and who seemed unable to carry on a connected conversation in one language for more than three minutes. This was Poldowski, or to give her her non-professional name, Lady Dean-Paul. She had left her husband and children in England, and had come to America for much the same reason that I had: an urgent determination to make money.

Apart from her, the party bewildered me, and after a little while I crept away from it, and went back to the Algonquin, overtired and deflated after all the excitements of the day.

The first week in New York was great fun until the novelty had evaporated slightly and my spare cash had evaporated entirely. We did everything we should have done. We went up the Woolworth Building. We gaped appropriately at the majesty of the Pennsylvania and Grand Central stations. We battled our way along Wall Street during the rush hour. We went to Coney Island on a Sunday night, and were jolted and rattled and bumped at a terrific speed through pitch-black tunnels, over canvas mountains, disembarking, green in the face, to consume 'hot dogs' and non-alcoholic beer. We learnt to distinguish between 'expresses' and 'locals' in the Subway. We went to Harlem, and drifted from cabaret to cabaret, jigging to the alien rhythms, and listening to strange wailings and screechings, until our feet ached, our ears buzzed, and our eyes blinked, in the cool dawn.

We went to the New Amsterdam Theatre to see Marilyn Miller in *Sally*, and came away cheerfully enchanted. We went to the Globe Theatre to see the Ziegfeld Follies, and watched the famous, much-advertised beauties languidly boring themselves and the audience with their too perfect figures, their total lack of expression. In the same show there was, fortunately, Fanny Brice, to revive our interest in the theatre. She sang "Second-hand Rose" with that particular brand of sentimentality sacred to Jewish-American comediennes. We even went, as the guests of Averill Harriman, to watch the scions of the rich play polo.

Apart from these excursions, I delivered the three letters of introduction that I had secured before leaving England. They were addressed to Al Woods, David Belasco and Charles Dillingham respectively. Al Woods was friendly, and told me that *The Last Trick* had been rewritten several times, by several different people, but that he feared nothing could ever be done with it. He also said he was going to Europe in a month or so, and that when he returned he would be delighted to read anything that I had to show him.

Charles Dillingham was away (I think in Colorado), but his manager, Fred Latham, was very amiable and let me go and talk to him in his office on many different occasions. He gave me a lot of kind advice about writing plays, and said that he was going away for a month or so, as he badly needed a holiday.

David Belasco was impressive, and wore a purple silk dressing-gown. He also told me a great deal about play-writing, emphasising his words with striking gestures and seeming, every now and then, to digress a little from the subject in hand. I tentatively suggested that he might be interested in reading one of my scripts, and he agreed that nothing would delight him more except for the unfortunate fact that, owing to doctor's orders, he was compelled to go away for a month or so.

These three stimulating contacts emboldened me to move from the small room that I was occupying at the Brevoort, to a much smaller one, practically in the eaves.

2

A little while before leaving England I had written, in collaboration with Lorn Macnaughtan, a short book of burlesque historical memoirs entitled *A Withered Nosegay*. Lorn did the illustrations and the book was published by Christophers. Some of it was funny, and the basic idea was good, but it was written with too much zest and personal enjoyment, and, consequently, fell a long way short of success. Burlesque at any time is dangerous ground and for young and inexperienced writers usually disastrous. In this particular book there was a lot that was crude and careless, and I have often regretted that the idea didn't come to me a little later, when I should have been more aware of its pitfalls and better equipped to grapple with it.

However, I took it with me to America and sold several of the separate parts of it to *Vanity Fair*. This happened only a few weeks after my arrival, and although the payment was small, it was encouraging.

After Jeffery had gone back to England, Gabrielle Enthoven and Cecile Sartoris offered me a room in their studio in Washington Square. They said that when I sold a play, or made some money somehow, I could pay rent, but until then I was to be their guest. They were neither of them in the least well-off and this was a blessed gesture of sheer charity. I accepted and moved in immediately, grateful not only for their kindness but for their company.

The studio was small, with white-washed walls and dark, polished furniture. Occasionally, in the evenings, we went out to the pictures, but usually we stayed at home and dined quietly in pyjamas. Candles flickered in sconces on the walls whenever there was enough breeze, and we drank red wine from the little Italian grocer's round the corner.

Irene Dean-Paul and Cecile sometimes made a little money by giving 'Verlaine' recitals in the homes of the wealthy. Irene had set, exquisitely, many of the poems to music, and sang them in her husky, attractive 'musician's voice.'

Cecile recited in a rhythmic monotone, her mouth twisted a little at one corner, and her eyes, apparently far away, gazing on enchanted woods and white moons.

There were frequently quarrels, smoothed over ultimately by Gabrielle's tact. Irene flew into rages easily, and delivered vitriolic tirades against American houses, American culture, and American hostesses in particular. On one occasion, after she and Cecile had trailed all the way to Boston to give a recital, she took exception to something that had been said about *l'heure exquise*, and tearing the hard-earned cheque into little pieces, flung them dramatically in the hostess's face. Repercussions of this scene occurred at intervals for many weeks afterwards.

Irene lived in a flat in West 70th Street. It was several flights up, and panelled in sickly pitch-pine. She had a grim but tender-hearted maid, from whom she was perpetually borrowing and who lived, silently, in the back somewhere and never seemed to go out farther than the delicatessen at the corner of the street.

Sometimes, when things looked especially black, we dolled ourselves up to the nines, she in an elaborate evening dress and I in a dinner-jacket, and went to the Ritz roof or Delmonico's to dine and dance. The dining, according to a prearranged plan, consisted of my ordering some light dish, and Irene feeling suddenly ill and being unable to eat a morsel. Later, when the waiter had left us, she would plunge a fork on to my plate, and we would eat hungrily to the last scrap. Occasionally, if we were in luck, some more or less rich acquaintance appeared and took us on to a night-club. When this occurred we at once demanded vast ham sandwiches, and considered the evening definitely a success.

One day when, as usual, we were at low ebb, Irene received an invitation to go and stay the week-end with a Mrs Magee in Mount Kisco, and asked me to go with her. It was a beautiful house and a nice house-party, and we refused to allow the fact that we hadn't enough money to tip the servants to detract one whit from our enjoyment, which was wise of us because, as it turned out, I happened to play 'rummy' on the Sunday night, and made six dollars fifty.

We returned, smoothed out by luxury, and feeling much better.

With all her lightness, humour and infectious high spirits, Irene was a tragic figure. Her integrity as an artiste was fine and uncompromising, too uncompromising to be satisfied with small success, and somehow not quite steel enough, not sufficiently swaddled in egotism to shield her from the irritation of failure. Not that her work was ever a failure, far from it. Her music has a strength and sincerity beyond the reach, I think, of contemporary criticism. Her failure lay within herself, in her abrupt pride, and sudden sharp intolerance, and her inability, when in certain moods, to accept the small change of friendship, even from those whom she knew loved her deeply. All this, I believe, she realised clearly at times, but she happened to be a genuine victim of that much overworked phrase 'artistic temperament,' and suffered accordingly. Her friends also suffered accordingly, but, in my opinion, were well repaid by the privilege of knowing her.

3

At the beginning of August Cecile and Gabrielle both went away, leaving me in charge of the studio and in command of a strange negress called Gertrude, who appeared for an hour or so every morning and ambled lethargically about with a broom. Her clothes were garish, oddly shaped, and a detached stay-busk reared itself up from the small of her back like a cane.

This, actually was a bad period for me. I was penniless and very lonely. The few people that I knew in New York were away, it being midsummer. Even Irene forsook me for a while. I saw Teddie Gerrard occasionally, and Naps, but they were both, although friendly, occupied with their own affairs.

Every theatrical manager in America seemed to have vanished completely, nearly all the theatres were closed, and several of the manuscripts I had brought with me had been consigned to some secret vault by the Theatre Guild, from which it was impossible to extricate them, or even hear news of how they were faring.

I acquired many of the stock habits of the forlorn and poverty-stricken, such as tramping the streets, contemplating daring robberies, and sitting on park benches. Unfortunately, owing to my carefully conserved wardrobe, I was invariably asked for money by my brother paupers, and was once addressed as 'sir' by an obviously prosperous Chinaman. Battery Park was really the nicest place in which to sit, but it was a long walk from Washington Square. Here, however, I found the company more varied and picturesque than in Central Park, also there was the sea to look at, and it was cooler. Sentimentally, of course, it had its drawbacks, because there were nearly always ships sailing away to England, and I had to avert my eyes and do a little honest, manly fist-clenching and shoulder-squaring.

I used to get packets of bacon, on credit, from the Italian grocer just near the studio, and cook it sparingly in the kitchenette. Luckily the weather was far too hot for me to want to eat very much. The kitchenette became suffocating quickly, and so I found it more comfortable, when actually frying, to be stark naked. This aroused the moral indignation of a 'cop,' who had been observing me from the other side of the street, and he came and banged loudly on the door. I put on a dressing-gown, and ran downstairs with the bacon fork still in my hand and upon opening the door received the full force of his rage, which evaporated quickly when I asked him if he would care for a little red wine. He came up into the studio and polished off three glasses. I offered him some bacon, which he refused, but at parting he kindly lent me his revolver because, he said, it was a dangerous neighbourhood, and living there as I was, completely alone, *anything* might happen. When he had gone, I lay awake for most of the night restraining the impulse to shoot at every shadow cast by the street lamp on to the white studio wall.

Later on in the month things began to look up a bit. I sold *A Withered Nosegay* to Boni and Liveright, and got a small advance for it. I made some new friends: Horace Liveright himself, Beatrice and George Kaufman, Blythe Daly, and Tallulah Bankhead. I also spent a pleasant evening in a cafeteria with an old friend, Ronald Colman, who had just opened in a play that was a flop, and was discouraged and unhappy. We cheered each other by formulating brave ambitions. He was determined to get to the coast to try his luck in pictures, and I was equally determined not to leave America until I had had a play accepted.

On the strength of this mutual stimulus, I started immediately to write *Sirocco* with Eva Le Gallienne and Joseph Schildkraut in mind for the leading parts. They were at that moment playing in Molnar's *Liliom*. I finished it quickly, and had no particular cause to regret it until several years later.

Florence Magee invited me to Mount Kisco a number of times, and I went, gratefully, whenever I had enough for the fare. Laurette Taylor and Hartley Manners returned to town from the country with Dwight and Marguerite, Laurette's children by her first marriage, and settled themselves into an odd demi-Gothic edifice on Riverside Drive. This house possessed one enormous room below-stairs, with an open fireplace, much tortured woodwork, and stained-glass windows, and, upstairs, many small rooms on different levels, varying in décor from Laurette's gilt and belaced bedroom and a formal mahoganied dining-room, to the correct and rather heavy-handed virility of Hartley's study, with its sports trophies, pipe-racks, and sturdy writing-table.

Hartley was a charming man, but his spirit seemed to be shut up permanently inside a sort of 'iron virgin' of moral principles. This, as far as I was concerned, made any lengthy conversations difficult. I had to tread lightly, and in the few literary discussions that we had, I soon learned not to allow enthusiasm to carry me too far, and to hop aside, nimbly, from any anti-social, anti-religious, or remotely sexual allusion. Laurette, on the other hand, was frequently blunt to the point of embarrassment. She was naïve, intolerant, lovable and entirely devoid of tact. Her humour was quick as lightning, and she could pounce from a great height with all the swift accuracy of a pelican diving into the sea, seldom failing to spear some poor, wriggling fish, and disquieting considerably the other fish present. Her taste in dress was poor, and her loveliness triumphed over many inopportune bows and ostrich feathers, but her taste as an actress was unassailable.

On Sunday evenings up on Riverside Drive we had cold supper and played games, often rather acrimonious games, owing to Laurette's abrupt disapproval of any guest (whether invited by Hartley, Marguerite, Dwight or herself) who turned out to be self-conscious, nervous, or unable to act an adverb or an historical personage with proper abandon. There were also, very often, shrill arguments concerning rules. These were waged entirely among the family, and frequently ended in all four of them leaving the room and retiring upstairs, where, later on, they might be discovered by any guest bold enough to go in search of them, amicably drinking tea in the kitchen.

It was inevitable that someone should eventually utilise portions of this eccentricity in a play, and I am only grateful to Fate that no guest of the Hartley Manners thought of writing *Hay Fever* before I did.

Lynn Fontanne returned from Chicago, where she had been playing a trial run of *Dulcy*, her first star part, written especially for her by George Kaufman and Marc Connelly. Her career in America had hitherto been devoted almost entirely to supporting Laurette in various plays of Hartley's. On the strength of her comedy performance in one of these, *Dulcy* was created, and proved to be a decisive triumph for her. As yet, however, there were still two months to endure before New York production, and she was a prey to the usual nervous forebodings, her moods alternating between hysterical gaiety and the most intense melancholy.

She and Alfred Lunt were, to put it mildly, 'courting' at the moment, and lived in a theatrical lodging-house somewhere in the West Seventies, known as 'Doctor Rounds'.' Any actor, however vagrant, was welcome at Doctor Rounds'. The food was good, and the house comfortably untidy and Doctor Rounds herself quite remarkable. She had greyish hair and shrewd, wary eyes, which sized you up accurately on sight, and she would occasionally relate gruesomely medical stories from out of the mysterious limbo of her early years. There was also in the house, in addition to Barry Baxter and the other lodgers, a maid-of-all-work, *café au lait* in colour and correctly true to type in action, who crooned incessantly in and out of all the rooms, and bashed dust-pans and tin pails joyously against the banisters.

From these shabby, congenial rooms, we projected ourselves into future eminence. We discussed, the three of us, over delicatessen potato salad and dill pickles, our most secret dreams of success. Lynn and Alfred were to be married. That was the first plan. Then they were to become definitely idols of the public.

That was the second plan. Then, all this being successfully accomplished, they were to act exclusively together. This was the third plan. It remained for me to supply the fourth, which was that when all three of us had become stars of sufficient magnitude to be able to count upon an individual following of each other, then, poised serenely upon that enviable plane of achievement, we would meet and act triumphantly together.

After these prophetic orgies, we often found it necessary to bring ourselves down to earth by taking brisk walks to the corner of the street and back, or going to the pictures. Once Lynn and I even sank so low as to make a charabanc trip to Chinatown.

In the meanwhile, we all had a long way to go and there was the immediate terror of the first night of *Dulcy* looming nearer and nearer. When the actual moment arrived, Alfred and I left Lynn in her dressing-room (to employ the hour and a half before the curtain rose by making-up, and dressing, and being methodically sick), and paced miserably up and down the street. We drifted in and out of soda-fountains, consuming endless Coca-Colas and frosted chocolates, and behaving generally like anxious fathers expecting twins. Presently we watched, in panic, cars and taxis beginning to arrive at the theatre, and so we went in, and clamping ourselves to our seats in the back row of the stalls, steeled ourselves to talk casually and wave and nod to acquaintances.

From the moment that Lynn flounced on in the first act, wearing a smart black velvet gown and appearing to be completely in command of herself and the play, we knew that everything was going to be all right, as indeed it was, and by the time the applause had died away after the second act we discovered that not only were we no longer pinching each other black and blue, but that we were quite relaxed and actually enjoying ourselves.

Soon after this I struck a bad patch again and, when I could really bear it no longer, I summoned up courage to go and borrow twenty dollars from Lynn. This courage was entirely my own concern and nothing whatever to do with Lynn. I knew that she would willingly give me anything that I asked for. But of all the many borrowings I have had to do in my time, I think I loathed that one the most. It wasn't humiliated pride that oppressed me, nor yet any false shame of my bad circumstances – all these things were too clearly understood among us – but somehow, in spite of my grey suit, blue shirt and tie and brightly shined shoes, I felt vaguely bedraggled, as though my spirit hadn't been pressed properly and was shabby and creased.

I arrived at the theatre too soon, a long while before the end of the matinée, and walked up and down the alley until I could tell, by the sound of applause, that the curtain had fallen. Of course, a troop of people came round to see Lynn, and I had to wait for several more years until they left. I finally had to interrupt Lynn in the middle of a detailed description of a new bit of business she had inserted in the second act, and pop the question, almost crossly, at her. She said: 'Darling, of course, don't be so silly,' delved in her bag, and handed me the money without deviating at all from what she was saying. The next morning I received a letter from Jim Whigham, the editor of the *Metropolitan Magazine*, asking me to lunch with him at the Brook Club. He had been staying at Mount Kisco with the Magees, and had read while there a copy of *I'll Leave It to You*, which I had sent to Florence, as a sort of bread-and-butter gesture, after my first visit. He said, in course of lunch, that if I would consider turning it into a short story he would pay me five hundred dollars for it. I nearly choked, but managed to say, casually enough, that I would try, and the rest of the meal passed in a sort of haze, which was rather a pity really, as I had not had the chance of eating such good food for a long time.

I reflected gleefully, on the way home, that for five hundred dollars I would gladly consider turning *War and Peace* into a music-hall sketch.

The result of all this was that, within three days, Lynn was paid back, swooning with surprise. The Italian grocer was paid back for two months of long-since consumed eggs and bacon. Gertrude received, with her usual lethargy, six weeks' arrears of wages. And I was able to send forty pounds home to Mother, to compensate for the loss of Mrs Herriot, who had inconsiderately abandoned our drawing-room suite early in June in favour of the grave.

4

With the beginning of the autumn season New York became cooler in temperature and much hotter in theatrical activity. Broadway awoke from its summer sleep, and the first batch of 'Fall productions' opened and closed in all directions. Homburgs took the place of straw hats, and coinciding with the return of all the managers to town, came the return of all my manuscripts. I was delighted to see them again, and read them through with keen pleasure, particularly *The Young Idea*, which, like *I'll Leave It to You*, I turned into a short story and sold to the *Metropolitan* for a further five hundred dollars.

I felt now much more secure financially, which was just as well, as I had a letter from Cecile in Bar Harbour saying that she and Gabrielle were not coming back to the studio at all and were, in fact, going to give it up for good. Upon receipt of this I moved out immediately, and went back to the Brevoort.

I was rather glad to be in an hotel again, especially as I had the satisfaction of knowing that I should be able to pay my bill quite regularly every week for some time to come. The studio had, of course, been a godsend to me, but I had passed too many miserable days in it, and been too lonely there, to feel any deep regret at leaving it. Also, during the last few weeks, several unfortunate things had occurred. To begin with, my laundryman, a fat, jolly little Chinaman, had been murdered in a street fight on the next block, which depressed me, as his Monday morning vists were benign and friendly. Then, I arrived home late one night to discover that the downstairs passage window and the Yale lock on the door had both been broken, and although nothing inside had been touched, I felt, even with my carefully unloaded revolver, a little insecure. Finally, and worst of all, I had a plague of bed bugs. Having played in the pottery towns, these were not entirely strangers to me, but as, in America, the orange, apples, bananas and buildings are far bigger than anywhere else in the world, so it is with their bed bugs. I awoke one night to find the walls, the bed and myself covered with flat, slow-moving trouser buttons, which bit savagely, and, when squashed, smelt overpoweringly of almonds. I spent the hours until dawn shuddering in the kitchen, with all the lights on.

The next day, apart from a few corpses, there wasn't a sign of them, and the fumigators, when they arrived, expressed rather scornful scepticism, saying that I must have exaggerated, as the walls and ceiling and the floor showed no indications, and that there wasn't anywhere else they could possibly have come from. Nevertheless, upon my insisting, they fumigated the whole place and, in course of their labours, discovered several hundred hale and hearty bugs living cosily inside a tapestry picture of the Virgin Mary.

The various managers, although unenthusiastic about my plays, were most hospitable, asking me to lunch at the Astor, urging me to adapt sure-fire successes from the Hungarian, and sending me tickets for first nights. Even the remote Mr Belasco crashed through with a balcony seat for his revival of *The Easiest Way* with Francis Starr. This was interesting, as she gave a fine performance, and even though the play did appear to be a trifle dated, it was first-rate melodrama beautifully lit and directed. In the interval between the second and third acts, I contrived, by a casual word, to creep into the heart of Alexander Woollcott. The word was 'vexing.' I said, without any particularly witty intent, that I had found the performance of one of the actors in the play very vexing, whereupon the warm September night was instantly shattered by strange cluckings and gurglings and sharp, shrill wails of pleasure. I was unused to abandoned displays from eminent critics; as a matter of fact I was unused to eminent critics, and I regarded this capering figure on the sidewalk with astonishment. Later on I became accustomed to such outbursts, finding, to my occasional dismay, that they worked both ways. Alexander Woollcott, in a rage, has all the tenderness and restraint of a newly caged cobra, and, when striking, much the same admirable precision. He has written, during the last ten years, a good deal about me in various newspapers and magazines. He has, in criticism, brought me to the dust and raised me on to high pedestals, usually giving a sly, rococo twist to the pedestals. He has, in biographical sketches, sacrificed, without pang of conscience, many of my nobler characteristics to pertinent witticisms. He has coaxed, relentlessly, many hundreds of dollars out of me at backgammon and Russian banker, and been loudly and urgently clamorous for payment.

In 1928, when I was playing with Beatrice Lillie in *This Year of Grace*, he objected bitterly to my performance of a song, "A Room with a View." And as a final inducement to me to relinquish it to my understudy, he appeared one night in a stage box with a party, each member of which buried his and her face in a newspaper the moment I began to sing. All these gestures and many others of a like devilishness have, oddly enough, merely served to cement even more strongly my fondness for him, and there he sits, and will probably continue to sit for ever, firmly ensconced in my affections, wearing a dreadful old green dressing-gown, playing to me all the Gilbert and Sullivan records that he knows I hate, and ordering me shrilly from the house whenever I win one point from him at any game of chance.

For the moment, however, we must leave him in September 1921, whooping outside the Lyceum Theatre, and turn to more austere encounters – such, for instance, as my meeting with another critic at another first night, Mr George Jean Nathan. Him I found deeply impressive, if somewhat studied in manner, and even if I had known then how much time and ink he was going to waste in the future in roasting the pants off me, I should still have been unable to help liking the little man.

A little later on came the first really important opening of the season. This was an allstar production of *The Circle* by Somerset Maugham. Estelle Winwood, John Drew, and Mrs Leslie Carter played the parts originally created in London by Fay Compton, Allan Aynesworth and Lottie Venne. The night was particluarly englamoured by the fact that it was the return of Mrs Carter to the stage after many years' absence.

I realised, after she had been on the stage for a little while, how superb she must have been in her flamboyant 'Zazas' and 'Dubarrys' of earlier years. I could visualise her clearly, through the brilliant web of Maugham's dialogue, posturing dramatically through bravura scenes, with scarlet hair piled high and her voluptuous figure dripping with Belasco jewels, but here, with sharp modern wit to express, she seemed strained and ill at ease. The most tawny lionesses wilt in captivity, and I couldn't help feeling that Mrs Carter was wilting considerably behind the polite bars of social comedy.

Lester Donahue appeared suddenly out of the gloom at the back of the stalls and reminded me that we had met in London, and that he had given me seats of his piano recital at the Æolian Hall. I remembered it with enthusiasm, not only because he had played beautifully that afternoon, but because I was delighted to see his pink, cherubic little face again.

A few days later he moved over from wherever he was and came to the Brevoort. This was nice for me because he had a piano in his room which I used frequently.

We went to a lot of parties together, at one of which we found a childhood friend of his, Peggy Wood. Unfortunately she was not playing in anything at the moment, and so I was unable to judge for myself whether or not Lester's ecstatic descriptions of her work were justified until nearly ten years later, when she walked with such exquisite distinction through the shiny double doors in the first act of *Bitter Sweet*.

With Lester also I saw Fred and Adele Astaire for the first time, in a musical comedy called *The Love Letter*. I hadn't realised before then that such rhythm and taste in dancing were possible.

Every Thursday and Saturday there were midnight performances of *Shuffle Along*, which was playing somewhere up in the West Sixties. This was, I believe, one of the first entirely coloured revues.

Throughout the whole jumble of songs and sketches and dances there darted the swift, vivid genius of Florence Mills, at one moment moving like a streak of quicksilver, the next still against some gaudily painted back-drop, nothing animated about her at all, except her wide smile and the little pulse in her throat, throbbing like a bird while she sang:

> 'Love will find a way
> Tho' skies now are grey,
> Love like ours can never be ruled,
> Cupid's not fooled that way – '

When she died a few years ago, many thousands of people followed her to the cemetery. Most of Broadway, and all of Harlem. And when the service was over and the hymns had been sung, there was no music until, just as the small coffin was being lowered into the grave, a sudden burst of singing rose to the skies, saluting her passing with the song that she had made so famous: "Bye-bye, Blackbird."

5

On the last day of October I sailed for home on the S.S. *Cedric*, one of the smaller White Star ships.

I stood on deck until the skyline had disappeared into the rain, and retired to my cabin in which I remained, prostrate with sea-sickness, for three days. When I ultimately emerged, still faintly green, the sea was calmer and the sun was shining, and I was able to sit wanly in a deck-chair nibbling, every now and then, a little cold beef and baked potato and allowing the events of the past five months to pass in stately review before my mind's eye, over the more unpleasant of which glamour was already beginning to settle.

I relived, with slight dramatic overtones, many hours of despair. I saw a brave, tragic youth trudging through the hot streets to his accustomed bench in Battery Park, friendless and alone, gazing out over the sea to where Green England lay, and sharing, perhaps, a crust with some kindly negro.

I saw the same gallant figure attired in deep evening dress attending the smartest first nights, with not even a nickel in his trouser pocket to pay his subway fare home. I also saw him, cowering naked in the kitchen, beset on all sides by voracious bed bugs.

I sorted my new friends with genuine pleasure. Lynn and Alfred, Alec Woollcott, Lester, Cecile and Gabrielle, Florence Magee, Irene, Laurette, Beatrice and George Kaufman, the Astaires, the countless others, all of whom had been charming to me, and all of whom I knew I should be enchanted to see again at any time, anywhere.

In addition to these there were some, who for some reason or other, possibly from sheer modesty, failed to appear in my memory while I was writing the preceding pages. Perhaps they felt that by shuffling late into their places they might interfere with the flow of my narrative. However, two at least were important to me, and if the others persist in lurking in the shadows that's their look-out. The two to be specified are Hoytie Wiborg and Gladys Barbour.

I stayed with Hoytie at Easthampton, where we ate good food, played bad tennis, argued on intellectual subjects, rode the surf on a large rubber mattress, and, on one occasion, nearly drowned.

Hoytie dabbled passionately in the Arts. She talked of Picasso, Van Gogh, Scriabin and Stravinsky. She lectured me austerely upon my own talents, intimating with great firmness that if I continued along my present lines, writing lyrics, sketches, plays and music, etc., that no good could ever possibly result from it. Facile versatility, she prophesied, would lead me surely to a dilettante's grave, and that if I must go on writing so much, and so quickly, at least I must give up imagining for one moment that I had the least talent for music. This, she said, she really knew about, and that as I could neither read it nor write it, and as my execution on the piano was only erratic in the right hand and non-existent in the left, the sooner I eliminated the whole idea from my bag of tricks the better.

Years later, on the first night of *Bitter Sweet*, remembering this conversation, I smiled at her from my box with a slight gleam of triumph in my eye, but she only shook her head gloomily, as though her worst forebodings had been incontrovertibly proven.

Gladys Barbour was chalk to Hoytie's cheese. She was small and fair, whereas Hoytie was tall and dark. She preferred dancing to Picasso, and Gershwin to Stravinsky. She shared in common with Hoytie a generous heart and an infinite capacity for taking trouble to help people she liked and, incidentally, was responsible, through the kind offices of her husband, for the comfortable free cabin on the *Cedric* which I was now occupying. One night in New York, during a party at some night club, she suddenly presented me with a mascot which was nothing more or less than a twenty-dollar gold piece. I am certain to this day that she gave it to me entirely because she knew I was broke, but sentimental to the last, I refrained for two whole weeks from changing it, and when finally I could resist the temptation no longer, I found that it had been stolen by one of the bell-boys at the Brevoort. Altogether, I looked back tenderly across the sea to Gladys Barbour.

The S.S. *Cedric* was a small boat, compared with its enormous sisters, the *Majestic* and the *Olympic*, but it was comfortable enough. It was also old, and slow, and wallowed through the sea like a fat swimmer, past her prime, doing a perpetual breast stroke.

There were not many people on board. But among the few was one of definite interest, Doctor Marie Stopes. She had, appropriately, the eyes of a fanatic, but the rest of her was dim, excepting her conversation. This was surprisingly vivid, and almost exclusively concerned with the theatre. Naturally this was a comfort to me, and we discussed plays for hours in a small rustic tea-room aft of the promenade deck.

We docked at Liverpool in snow and sleet, and I went ashore hugging to myself the excitement of a surprise arrival. I couldn't resist sending Mother a telegram from Lime Street Station, and I spent the interminable five-hour journey in the train, imagining her face when she opened it and noted where it had been handed in.

The home-coming was entirely successful, and unspoiled by anti-climax. The bungalow was *en fête*. There were one or two new lodgers peering out of the windows, and a new and very young housemaid, who stood first on one leg and then on the other, and giggled loudly throughout the first flurry of reunion. Mother was flushed and hilarious, but I noticed a certain strain under her joy, and my heart sank a little, but rebounded again almost immediately with the realisation that whatever might be happening behind the scenes in that beastly house, we were at least all together again.

In so far as the complete success of my New York adventure was concerned, I felt a trifle dubious. Financially speaking, it had obviously been a failure, as I had returned with only seven pounds more than when I had landed five months before. However I had seen a lot, experienced a lot, and learned a lot. I knew New York thoroughly, better actually than I have ever known it since. The subway, the elevated, cheap cafeterias, park benches and loneliness have been no part of my later visits. But I felt, even then, certain small regrets.

To be poor in your own country is bad enough, but to be poor among strangers should, by rights, be very much worse. But, somewhat to my surprise, I realised that in my case it had not been worse at all. I remembered the Chinese laundryman, Gertrude, the Italian grocer and the Irish 'cop.' I remembered conversations in buses, and cinemas, and soda-fountains. I remembered the beauty of New York at night, viewed, not from a smart penthouse on Park Avenue, but from a crowded seat in Washington Square. And it seemed, in spite of its hardness and irritating, noisy efficiency, a great and exciting place.

PART FIVE

In reviewing the past, it is difficult to check off accurately, which, among the millions of small incidents, adventures, pleasures and pains, have been essential to the development of character, or at any rate interesting enough in themselves to be worth describing.

When this book is finished, corrected, revised and lying snugly bound in the publisher's office, I feel sure that many unrecorded events will arise to mock and torment me. Many people also. Already, I find that there are several that I have left out. Among these, oddly enough, some of considerable importance. Grace Forster, for instance, Stewart's mother. She should have made her entrance a long way back, swishing across shady lawns and night clubs, wrapped in gallant vanity, and smelling slyly of amber.

Farther back still, a hunt ball at Oakham seems to have been mislaid somehow. To this I was taken by Lady Londesborough, and was deeply, although not too rapturously impressed by it. I remember a lot of pink coats, and much deafening gaiety. I also remember a bad band and a worse floor and, more pleasantly, Burghersh, now Lord Westmorland, whose face, doubtless out of deference to the Cottesmore, seemed pinker than the pinkest coat present, and whose charm, even through the loudest din, remained inviolate.

Among other unrelated things floating in my memory, I can see clearly a man being run over by a bus just opposite the National Gallery. A Mercédès car, belonging to a gentleman called Harry Hart, which seldom got farther than Maidenhead, and a home-made turban of Joyce Barbour's fashioned saucily in 1916 from a bandana handkerchief.

The year of 1922 began for me in a welter of financial embarrassment. The hows, whys, and wherefores would make dull reading; enough that there were borrowings, mortgages on my beloved piano, pawnshops, black moments of distress, brokers' men, and worst of all, days when even Mother's invincible spirit came near to being broken.

Nobody seemed to be interested in my plays. Nobody seemed anxious to offer me parts at even reasonable salaries. Every now and then I managed to sell a short story or a song, and once I got a hundred pounds for grinding out an adaptation of a French play for Denis Eadie. Altogether it was a gloomy and depressing period.

In former days, of course, I could probably have gone out on tour or procured a small job in London, but now, having played two or three leading parts, and actually appeared in my own play in the West End, I was in the awkward situation of being too well known to be able to accept little jobs, and not well known enough to be able to command big ones.

Every morning Mother used to come and sit on my bed while I had my breakfast. This was the one hour in the day that she allowed herself to relax, and I could always tell by her face, the moment it appeared round the door, if anything awful had happened. There was a certain artificial chirpiness about her on bad days, manufactured out of a determination not to let me see that she was worried, which generally broke down before I had finished my first cup of coffee.

We were getting more and more deeply into debt, and even with the house full, which it wasn't, the income from it was not sufficient to meet the quarterly instalments, the rent, the taxes, the electric light bills, and the living expenses of Father, Mother, Auntie Vida, Eric, and me.

What worried me most was the dread that Mother would suddenly break completely and become seriously ill. Her heart was not strong, and the strain of the last few years had been appalling. This I was determined to avert at all costs, even if the brokers took possession of the house and we were all flung into the street.

I went to see Ned Lathom, knowing how kind and generous he was, and also knowing how many hundreds of people had already sponged upon him, and asked him flatly, without preliminaries, to lend me two hundred pounds. He refused almost sharply, and he added that he would willingly give me two hundred pounds, but that never, in any circumstances, would he lend money to anybody ever again, it was too dangerous a commodity, he said, to pass between friends.

I have a lot of gratitude in my heart, towards many people, but it is too special and private an emotion to spill into print. There are hundreds of ways of describing unkindness and meanness and little cruelties. A sly dig at the right moment can work wonders. But just try to write of generosity. Try to frame in words an unrelated, motiveless gesture of sheer kindness and you are lost. The warmth behind the phrases dissipates before they reach the paper, and there they lie, under your hand, sneering up at you, coldly effusive and dead as mutton.

At any rate, with Ned's cheque in my pocket, the sun shone, temporarily, with all its might. About a hundred and fifty of the two hundred went immediately to various creditors. The remaining fifty I held on to, because I had a plan in mind which, after a discussion with Gladys Calthrop, I sprang on Mother, suddenly, and clinched before she had time to argue.

The plan was that Father was to take charge of the house, and that I was to find a little cottage in the country somewhere, where she could rest completely, for several months, and where I could come for week-ends, and write. She at once made a pyramid of small difficulties which I swept grandly away. There wasn't much conviction behind them anyhow, and a few days later Gladys and I went to Dymchurch, where Athene Seyler had lent me her cottage for a fortnight, and from this we set forth daily in search of a small, inexpensive house for Mother.

Dymchurch in March was bleak, windy, cold and full of charm.

We bicycled and walked for days over the marshes, with Fred, Gladys's brown spaniel, padding along behind us, and plunging in and out of the dykes. We zigzagged backwards and forwards between Ham Street and Ivychurch, Appledore and New Romney. We climbed up on to Aldington Knoll and looked at the cliffs of France glinting in the sun across the steely grey channel. We found some early primroses and a lame sea-gull, which bit us fiercely, and messed, with the utmost abandon, all over the cottage. We went systematically through every available habitation within a radius of twenty-five miles, and finally found a small and tender one, nestling up against a public-house in the village of St Mary in the Marsh. It had four rooms, outside sanitation, a rental of ten shillings a week, and a superb view from the upper windows of unlimited sheep.

Mother seemed to be quite pleased with it, and so we moved in, and very soon the sea and the sky and the marshes began to work a little homely Kentish magic. There was nothing to do but read and write, and make expeditions into Dymchurch or New Romney to get provisions, and a lot of the tiredness was smoothed away from Mother's face within the first few weeks.

I bought a black mongrel at the Battersea Dogs' Home, and conveyed him, radiant in a new collar, to New Romney Station, where Mother met us and fell in love with him at once. He was very young and spindly in the legs, and he promptly had a violent attack of distemper, which kept him hovering between life and death for seven weeks. However, nursing him provided an occupation for Mother during the days I had to spend in London.

There were a few neighbours for her to talk to: Mrs Hinds, the owner of the inn next door, Mr and Mrs Cook, the Vicar and his wife, Miss Hammond, the local school teacher. There were also the Bodys, who owned much of the property round about, and, not very far off, at Jesson, none other than E. Nesbit, who lived with her husband, and a gentle friend, in a series of spacious huts.

I called on her very soon, and found her as firm, as nice, and as humorous as her books had led me to expect. The skipper, her husband, was a grand old man, who loved her and guarded her devotedly through her last, rather sad years.

The friend, Miss Hill, was a wispy creature, with an air of vague detachment, which inspired Athene Seyler to christen her irreverently, "The Green Hill Far Away."

During that spring I spent most of my time at St Mary's. The churchyard just across the road was a peaceful place in which to work, and it was there, propped up against a family tombstone, that I wrote *The Queen was in the Parlour*. Nothing could be further removed from that play than the surroundings in which I wrote it. Its passionate love-scenes and Ruritanian splendours emerged from my mind to the gentle cawing of rooks and the bleating of new-born lambs. When I raised my eyes from a Palace courtyard, lit by the flare of torches and brimming with revolutionaries, I saw the marshes stretching to the dark line of the sea wall, broken every now and then by dumpy little Martello towers, and slightly inland on the right, a cluster of trees and houses and a square church tower – the village of New Romney.

On long summer evenings, Mother and I used to ride up to Aldington Knoll on our bicycles, and wait there in the growing dusk until the thin line of sea, four miles away, faded and disappeared in the white mist rising from the dykes, and then looking down over the darkening country spreading all the way from Folkestone to Hastings, we would see lamps twinkling in cottage windows, bats swooping down from the high trees, and the lighthouses flashing all along the coast.

It would have been cheering had we known, then, that the land just below us would belong to us one day. That the farm-house, the five poplars, the thick woods and lush fields stretching down to the Military Canal, would all be ours to do with as we liked. But even as it was, without clairvoyance and future certainties, those evenings were lovely enough, and we pedalled home happily through the dark, our bicycle lamps making wobbling shadows across the roads, feeling that, after all, money troubles, rate collectors, and brokers' men didn't matter so very much as long as we had a water-tight ten-shilling-a-week roof over our heads.

2

In June, Robert Courtneidge took up an option on *The Young Idea*, to produce it in the early autumn for a six weeks' trial run in the provinces. This was an obvious change of fortune, and we set about casting it right away. I firmly, and very much against Courtneidge's will, insisted upon playing 'Sholto' myself. I explained patiently, and at length, that as I had taken the trouble to write the part specially for myself, it would be both illogical and foolish to allow anyone else to get so much as a smell of it. Courtneidge's argument was that I was too old for it, that my personality was too sophisticated, and that in his opinion it would be much more effective played by someone with a more cherubic cast of countenance and a more naïve charm. What he really meant, of course, was that I was not a good enough actor for it. However, he finally gave in with as good grace as possible, and we went to work on the other parts.

I had written 'Gerda' for Edna Best, but owing to some other contract she was unobtainable, and so Ann Trevor was engaged. Kate Cutler, of course, was to be Jennifer. This also had been especially written for her, and of my other old *I'll Leave it to You* friends, Muriel Pope was cast for Cicely. The rest were Herbert Marshall, Clive Currie, Naomi Jacob, Phyllis Black, Molly Maitland (then Mrs Herbert Marshall), Ambrose Manning, and Martin Lewis, who was later replaced by Leslie Banks.

Rehearsals were to begin in August, and so I had nearly two months in which to enjoy myself, relieved, for the first time for a long while, of the horrible foreboding that I was never, never going to get work again as long as I lived.

Father, much to his own and everyone else's surprise, was not only running the house successfully, but deriving, on the whole, a great deal of personal gratification from it. Always naturally gregarious, he had a grand time talking to the lodgers and hopping in and out of their rooms with breakfast trays. Apparently, he was more sociable than Mother, and not only achieved extreme popularity inside the house, but outside as well. All the tradesmen in the vicinity welcomed his morning appearance with the dog (an obsequious Pomeranian), and even the window-cleaner was accorded fortnightly a brief but intimate chat. May Weaver, the now not so new housemaid who had been present on my return from the States, relaxed into delirious gaiety with Mother's restraining influence removed. She scampered madly up and down stairs singing shrilly, and never, except very, very late in the afternoon, dreamt of wearing a cap, a small gesture to refinement upon which Mother had obdurately insisted.

3

A short while after the contract for *The Young Idea* had been signed, I was invited by Lady Colefax to Oxford, where she had taken a house for a week, to entertain a party of young people for the Bullingdon dance. I knew her then only slightly, but we have been friends ever since.

Those few days were smooth and affable, and bathed in a gentle summer peace alien to me, and yet somehow vaguely familiar, which puzzled me at first, until I realised that my sense of having seen it all before was entirely due to the books I had read.

It was all there. All the paraphernalia of the eager young novelists, and touchingly accurate in detail.

There were the shady cloisters with the sun tracing Gothic patterns across the worn paving-stones. There were the rooks cawing in the high elms, the rich, over-laden rose gardens, the green velvet lawns, and the whacks and thuds of cricket bats and tennis rackets sounding gently from the other side of yew hedges.

There, beneath aged sycamores, were spread tea-tables, cushions, wicker chairs, 'Curate's Comforts,' and large bowls of strawberries and cream, the latter to be devoured by the returning game-players who were so much, much more suitably attired for the country than I. Their shirts and flannels were yellow and well used, against which mine seemed too newly white, too immaculately moulded from musical comedy. Their socks, thick and carelessly wrinkled round their ankles, so unlike mine of too thin silk, caught up by intricate suspenders.

Their conversation, too, struck a traditional note in my ears. I seemed to know what they were going to say long before they said it. I sensed in their fledgeling jokes and light unsubtle badinage a certain quality of youthfulness that I had never known. And although I was the same age, if not younger than many of them, I felt suddenly old, over-experienced and quite definitely out of the picture.

This was not exactly an unhappy sensation. I had then, as always, no wish to change places with anyone in the world. But I felt a slight strain, as though I were playing in a scene for which I had not been sufficiently rehearsed. This evaporated soon after the first day and after I had grown to know them all a little, but I noted carefully many points, without envy or disdain or wistfulness, but merely with a keen eye on future performances.

On the night of the Bullingdon dance itself, the whole atmosphere suddenly shivered and jangled into awareness of a very unfamiliar personality indeed. The elms shuddered a little when a large car drew up at the door and disgorged, amid raucous laughter, the bouncing, Michelin figure of Elsa Maxwell. She was accompanied, sedately, by Mrs Toulmin, fair and brittle and impressively *mondaine*, with her Chanel clothes and sleek contented dressing-case. Elsa beside her looked as incongruous as a large brindle bull-dog out walking with a white Russian cat. She at once proceeded to whistle through that house like a cyclone, strumming the piano, laughing, talking and striking the rose-white youth present into a coma of dumb bewilderment.

I loved her at once. I loved her round friendly face, with its little shrewd eyes darting about like animated currants in a Bath bun. I loved her high spirits and her loud infectious laugh. It was before the days when she became the Queen of Paris, and curdled her own personality with too much *crème de la crème*. In 1922 she was still a roystering buccaneer, and with all her boastfulness and noise and shrill assertiveness, intelligent and immensely lovable.

Why she suddenly appeared at Oxford that evening I shall never know. If I felt a little out of it in so fresh and young an atmosphere, Elsa must have felt like a visitor from another planet.

To write the true story of Elsa's life would be worth doing, but unfortunately quite impossible, for the simple reason that the details of it, the real mysteries and struggles and adventures are untraceable. The only authority for data would be Elsa herself, but to appeal to her would be worse than useless. Not that she wouldn't be willing and happy to supply information, not that she wouldn't be perfectly delighted to pour treasure-troves of anecdotes and incidents and startling experiences, glittering jingling heaps of them, into a lap of anyone sympathetically disposed to listen. She is nothing if not generous in everything, a magnificent egotist into the bargain, and loves few things better than talking about herself.

But unhappily for the author engaged in these tantalising researches, one of the principal gifts that the wise Californian fairies brought to Elsa's christening was an untrammelled and peculiarly vivid imagination. This provides a complete world for her, colouring to excess, not only the things she has done, and does, but creating for her with equal reality the things she never has done and never will do.

At the height of her Paris fame, Cole Porter inscribed the following little song for her, which she pounded joyously out of most of the pianos on the Continent:

> "I met a friend of mine a week or two ago
> And he was all togged out.
> I said, 'Excuse me, but I'd really like to know
> What this is all about.
> You're over-dressed, you're absurd!'
> He answered, 'Haven't you heard?
>
> 'I'm dining with Elsa, with Elsa, supreme.
> I'm going to meet Princesses
> Wearing "Coco Chanel" dresses,
> Going wild over strawberries and cream,
> I've got Bromo Seltzer
> To take when dinner ends,
> For I'm dining with Elsa
> And her ninety-nine most intimate friends!'"

After the Bullingdon dance she departed for London, but not before she had invited me to a party the following Tuesday.

The Oxford house-party seemed a trifle flattened after she had left, a hazy indecisiveness hung about it, as though it were just coming to after an anaesthetic. But by the next day it had regained its normal composure, and proceeded pleasantly, with various diversions, to the end of the week.

4

Elsa's party was great fun, with social and Bohemian graces tactfully mixed.

Dorothy Fellows-Gordon – 'Dickie,' a lifelong friend of Elsa's – was there, tall, nice-looking, with jet-black hair and a lovely singing voice. Later on in the evening, when I was sitting talking to her in a corner, Elsa came over and joined us, and after they had both exchanged significant raised-eyebrow looks, Elsa said that they had a little proposition to make to me and that on no account was I to be offended. I couldn't imagine what on earth she was driving at, and so I laughed nervously and said that I was never offended at anything. Then she explained that she and Dickie were going for two weeks to Venice, and wanted me to go with them as their guest. She added, as a palliative to my wounded honour, that they would feel far more comfortable with a man to look after them and that I would really be doing them a great favour if I would consent.

I saw through this in a minute. I knew perfectly well that they didn't in the least need anyone to look after them, but were only trying to gloss over for me the unmentionable horror of having my expenses paid by two defenceless women. But it was sweet and sympathetic of them, and they did it beautifully. Obviously I accepted with enthusiasm and a few days later travelled over to Paris to join them.

None of us had ever been to Venice before, and the first sight of it as we walked down the station steps into a gondola, sent us all off into a clamour of excitement. Elsa led, of course. Propped up against a cushion in the back seat, she let forth a stream of enthusiasm into the gathering dusk. Superlatives flew through the air, ricochetting off mouldering Palazzos and plopping into the water, as we swept under dark little bridges, swirled round sharp corners, and finally debouched on to the Grand Canal.

We were lucky that first evening. The air was clear and pure. A 'Serenata' passed close by us on its way to the lagoon, already lit with coloured lanterns and crammed to the gunwales with stout little tenors wearing white shirts and coloured sashes. One of them was tuning a guitar, another strummed absently on a small portable piano. Our gondoliers gave sharp atmospheric cries, and the sun set considerably as we arrived at the hotel, plunging the whole scene into a misty Turneresque beauty that robbed even Elsa of further adjectives.

That was certainly a glamorous fortnight. The loveliness of Venice alone would have been enough. The strange decayed magic of old palaces rising out of green canals, the dim archways, the remote misty lagoons stretching away behind the town towards Mestre. The brilliance and warm colour of the piazza in the evenings, a military band playing chirrupy selections from Verdi, gay crowds of people passing endlessly up and down through the arcades.

All this would have enraptured a far less impressionable mind than mine, and I could have returned home happily with such memories. More happily, perhaps, without the very different memories of the Lido and the myriads of feuds and scandals and small social rumpuses which took place there daily.

I found a few new friends – Muriel Draper, with plastered straw-coloured hair and full scarlet lips; Blanche Barrymore, with farouche Byronic locks flowing in the breeze and long billowing cloaks; and Mrs Spears, a small attractive woman with deep sleepy eyes and a rather nervous smile, who said that she had completed a novel which was to be published soon, and was to be called *Jane – Our Stranger*. She omitted to tell me that her pen name was Mary Borden and so I visualised a light, slightly 'jejune' little book written to pass the time, and dealing, probably amateurishly, with the adventures of some winsome housemaid.

When I finally left Venice in order to get back to London for rehearsals of *The Young Idea*, Dickie and Elsa stayed behind for an extra week. They insisted, however, upon giving me my ticket and seeing me off at the station. I hung out of the window for a long while watching Elsa's little bobbing figure growing smaller and smaller until it seemed to dissolve into the grey platform, and reflecting that the life of a gigolo, unimpaired by amatory obligations, could undoubtedly be very delightful indeed.

5

We rehearsed *The Young Idea* in hot, smelly rehearsal rooms, and later in cool empty theatres. I felt as nervous at first as if I had never acted before. Robert Courtneidge, although milder than in the old days, could still be scarifying, and I had the uncomfortable conviction all the time that he still disapproved of my playing the part. It was typical of his generosity, however, to take me aside a few days before we opened and tell me that he had been entirely wrong and that I was giving an excellent performance. Actually I believe that his kindness overstepped the truth. Perhaps I may have been better than he thought I was going to be, but I was a long way from giving a really good performance.

There was certainly an improvement in my acting since *I'll Leave it to You*, but I was still forcing points too much and giving knowing grimaces when delivering comedy lines. I had not learned then not to superimpose upon witty dialogue the top-heavy burden of personal mannerisms. In this instance, of course, I was both author and actor, and the former suffered considerably from the antics and over-emphasis of the latter.

The play opened at Bristol. The notices and business were both good, and we settled down complacently for a pleasant little tour.

On returning to London I had a long talk with Courtneidge, who said that although there was no immediate chance of getting a theatre, it might be possible to find a suitable one after Christmas when the pantomime and fairy-play rush was over. And so, faced with November fogs and at least two months of idleness, I decided on another little excursion to foreign parts.

Ned Lathom, I knew, was in Davos recovering from his first bout of T.B. I also knew that he had only his sister Barbara with him, and that they both would be probably pleased to see me, so I sent him a telegram and waited hopefully for the reply. It was comfortingly enthusiastic, so after buying a few sweaters, thick socks and breeches, off I went; second-class on the trains, but first-class on the boat, arriving the next day, my eyes dazzled by leagues of white snow in strong sunlight and my ears pleasantly humming in the high altitude to the jingling of sleigh bells.

Ned looked better, but he still had coughing-fits from time to time. He managed, as usual, to be amazingly luxurious and had surrounded himself with books, cushions and large rich sweets which, I am sure, were bad for him.

I stayed there for three weeks with Barbara and him alone before anyone else arrived. The Christmas season had not yet begun, and the only other occupants of the hotel were T.B. patients, all in various stages of the disease. It was a strange life, gay in the evenings, when everyone made an effort to dress, dine in the restaurant and dance afterwards in the bar. During the days, of course, everybody had cures and treatments to undergo, and the whole hotel seemed dead and empty. At night, however, it regularly awoke. The gambling machine in the bar tinkled merrily, the band played, and there was the sound of corks popping and noisy conversation in many languages. Only very occasionally would someone slip away from the fun to flit upstairs, coughing, almost furtively, into a stained handkerchief.

Those evenings, with their noise and music and gaiety, were slightly macabre, but somehow not depressing. It was as though they were unrelated to ordinary existence – a few detached hours of pleasure, floating between life and death, untouchable by the sadness of either. The knowledge that practically everybody present, themselves included, would probably be dead within a year or so was, I suppose, tucked away behind the laughter of most of the people there, but it was in no way apparent. There seemed to be no strain in the air, no eager snatching at flying moments. Perhaps the disease itself carried with it a compensating illusion that ultimate cure was certain, that all the slow tedious intricate process of dying was nothing more than an interlude of small discomfort.

Ned, who had always been badly stage-struck, had financed Charlot's last revue *A to Z*, and still appeared to be avid for punishment. He made me play to him all the songs I had written, and when he realised that there were enough comparatively good ones to make up a score, he wired to Charlot commanding him to come out immediately. I was thrilled at the thought of doing a whole revue, but scared that Charlot, when he arrived, might not be quite as eager and appreciative as Ned. However, when he did arrive in due course he was expansive and benign, and a series of cigar-laden conferences ensued, during which *London Calling* was born.

I worked on sketches in the mornings, waking early when the clouds were still veiling the mountains, submitted them to Ned and Charlot in the afternoons, and within the space of a few days the whole plan of the show was roughly laid out. It was to be produced the following autumn, with Gertrude Lawrence, Maisie Gay, a comedienne as yet undecided, and myself.

Charlot took me aside and told me that he would be unable to pay me more than fifteen pounds a week, as I was inexperienced in revue work, but that as I was bound to make a great deal of money out of royalties I was not to worry about it. I didn't worry about it at the time as I was too occupied with the show as a whole, but later I gave it a certain amount of thought. Charlot went back to England, seemingly pleased with everything, and left Ned and Barbara and me in a ferment of excitement.

Christmas pounced on Davos and everything lit up. Trainloads of strange people arrived daily. A whole extra wing of the hotel was thrown open. The Kurhaus, down in the village, surprisingly produced a highly decorated bar and a jazz band. The whole place became, with abrupt thoroughness, a resort. Ned's Christmas guests, it is unnecessary to remark, were far and away the star turn of the hotel.

In order of appearance, rather than precedence, they consisted of: Clifton

Webb, Mrs Fred (Teddie) Thompson, Gladys Cooper, Dick Wyndham, Edward Molyneux, Bobbie Howard, Dickie Gordon, Elsa Maxwell and Maxine Elliott. From their advent onwards life was less peaceful but certainly more stimulating. We went on tailing parties, stringing out in a long line of sleds behind a large sleigh in which Elsa sat screaming like a banshee. We went on skating parties, Swedish Punch parties and lugeing parties. In course of one of these, quite unintentionally, I got caught up in a time test race, and to my amazement on reaching the bottom was presented with a small silver cup. Apparently I came down the two and a quarter miles in just under four minutes, not, let it be understood, because I had the least desire to do so, but because, owing to the whole run having been rebanked and iced since Barbara and I had been on it, I was completely unable to stop myself.

Gladys Cooper took a marked dislike to me, and we had several acrid tussles, notably at a lunch party at the Kurhaus, where she remarked in a tone of maddening superiority that it was ridiculous of me to go on writing plays that were never produced, and that why on earth I didn't collaborate with someone who really knew the job, she couldn't understand.

I replied that as Shaw, Barrie and Maugham didn't collaborate I saw no reason why I should. Whereupon she laughed, not without reason, and said that she had never heard of such conceit in her life and that she might just as well compare herself to Duse or Bernhardt. I jumped in here quickly on cue and retorted that the difference was not quite as fantastic as that. After which the lunch continued amid slightly nervous hilarity.

Oddly enough, after this preliminary blood-letting, Gladys and I parted glowing with mutual affection, and the glow has strengthened through the years, with never so much as a breath of disharmony.

6

The Young Idea opened at the Savoy Theatre in February to even more enthusiasm than had greeted *I'll Leave it to You*.

The play proceeded smoothly and at the end I made my usual self-deprecatory speech with a modesty which was rapidly becoming metallic, but which had the desired effect of lashing the audience to further ecstasies, and when the curtain had fallen we all rejoiced appropriately, although my personal satisfaction was edged wtih wariness. I remembered the effusions of the first night of *I'll Leave it to You* – the kindly intentioned but over-optimistic voices which had dinned into my ears that it was 'marvellous' and 'divine' and would undoubtedly 'run a year,' and decided, before giving way completely to triumph, to bide my time until I saw the returns on Saturday night. In this I turned out to be wise, for in spite of excellent press notices and a deluge of superlatives from my acquaintances, the play folded up at the end of eight weeks.

But although brief, where the company was concerned it was a happy run. There were, of course, a number of the usual rumours that business was steadily going up or that we were to be transferred to a smaller and more intimate theatre, or that a friend of Muriel Pope's had heard from a friend of hers in Keith Prowse that the libraries were about to take up a big deal stretching right into May. But being on a royalty basis, I saw the returns every night and was able to watch without illusion, the sinister little figures growing weekly smaller and smaller until ultimately, after a sad but sympathetic conversation with Courtneidge, the fatal fortnight's notice was pinned up on the board.

Nevertheless, *The Young Idea* was one more step achieved and several perquisites accrued from it, among them the sale of the publication and amateur rights to Samuel French, and a letter of the most generous praise from Mr Charles Blake Cochran.

A few days later I lunched with him at the Berkeley, flushed with perfectly chosen wine and still more perfectly chosen words of encouragement. I don't remember any premonition sitting behind my chair and nudging me into realisation that this was the first of an endless procession of similar lunches that dotted through future years, that hundreds of restaurant tables, bottles of hock and *entrecôtes minutes* were waiting for us. It only seemed an extremely pleasant hour, significant because I hoped that he might be persuaded to produce a play of mine one day.

Meanwhile things were not going so badly. Mother had returned to Ebury Street from St Mary's, happier and in better health than she had been for a long time. She occasionally snatched the reins of management from Father and after a salutary crack or two with the whip, handed them back again so that the house jogged along amicably enough, like a dreary old family coach with Auntie Vida as a diminutive postilion hopping down every now and then to open the door for the lodgers.

When *The Young Idea* closed I went off to join Gladys Calthrop and Mrs Cooper at Cap Ferrat, where the latter had rented a villa. It was a nice villa and the view from it was charming, but its peace and plenty were somewhat soured for Gladys and me by the presence of a Dominican Prior to whom Mrs Cooper was devoted, but who took a bleak dislike to us on sight. We bore his disapproval for as long as we could, and then, realising that our being there was not only making things uncomfortable for Mrs Cooper and for him but for ourselves as well, we departed in a deluge of Riviera rain for Italy.

We had very little money but it was a gay excursion and in due course we returned to Mrs Cooper and found to our horror that the Prior was still there. But this time we outstayed him and the rest of the holiday was peaceful and without incident.

7

In May a one-act comedy that I had written a year before was produced by the London Grand Guignol at the Little Theatre. It was called *The Better Half*, and was wittily played by Auriol Lee. In spite of this it was received with apathy; I think, possibly, because it was a satire and too flippant in atmosphere after the full-blooded horrors that had gone before it. Nevertheless it was quite well written and served the purpose, if only for a little, of keeping my name before the public. Meanwhile Ned was back from Davos, much improved in health and already beginning to dissipate the effects of his cure by giving the rich lunches, dinners and supper parties that he loved so much. With his return the preparations for the revue were resumed. The date was set, the title *London Calling* was set, and the cast was set, that is, with the notable exception of the leading juvenile. This state of affairs was brought about by my stubborn and unaccountable refusal to play it. At any rate it seemed unaccountable to those who had not been present during my brief fifteen-pound-a-week discussion with Charlot at Davos.

It had been arranged at the conference that I was to share the writing of the book with Ronald Jeans and the composing of the music with Philip Braham. This, although disappointing to me at first, I finally accepted as being a wise decision, as to do a whole show might have proved too heavy a burden on my inexperience. Also, during the conferences I had been unable to avoid noticing the fat and satisfying salaries that were to be received by Gertie Lawrence, Tubby Edlin and Maisie Gay, and the vision of myself, as the fourth of the quartette, earning five pounds a week less than I had received in both *I'll Leave it to You* and *The Young Idea* seemed unattractive. In consequence I announced (for which may God forgive me) that to appear in a musical show would injure irreparably my prestige as a straight actor.

After little argument my decision was accepted, but having in my contract as author a clause to the effect that I was to be consulted as to cast, I was able to raise the adequate objections to the name of every juvenile suggested, until ultimately, after many weeks' wear and tear, I allowed myself to be persuaded to change my mind.

This time my business conversation with Charlot was even briefer, but much more to the point, resulting in a salary of forty pounds a week and an additional clause permitting me to leave the cast at the end of six months if I wished.

Now I had ample time for misgivings. My dancing was rusty, but of course that could be remedied by hard practice. (My singing was rustier, and I feared could not be remedied by all the practice in the world.) However, I persuaded Fred Astaire, who was playing in *Stop Flirting*, to coach me privately, which he did with unending patience and not too frightful results.

Amid the hurly-burly of countless Charlot productions there had lived and breathed and strummed, for many years, a small sharp-eyed woman named Elsie April, whose mastery of musical technique was miraculous. She could transfer melody and harmony on to paper with the swiftness of an expert shorthand stenographer. Her physical endurance, too, was staggering. She could sit at the piano through the longest rehearsals, the most tedious auditions, seldom, if ever, playing a wrong note and only demanding for sustenance an occasional cup of tea.

When I had been working with her for some time I asked her why it was that she continued to lavish her musical talent and experience on the work of others and never composed anything herself. Her reply was evasive, 'Well, dear, I never seem to have any time.'

London Calling for me was certainly a gold mine of future alliances, for in addition to Elsie there was Dan O'Neil, the assistant stage manager. Early on in rehearsals we all found ourselves relying upon him for everything. If any props were missing, it was Danny who restored them. If there was an untraceable draught, it was Danny who discovered a window open high up in the flies and closed it. If there was a noise at the side during a quiet scene, it was Danny who silenced it. And, above all, when we were tired after rehearsing all day and most of the night, feeling discouraged and certain to the depths of our souls that the whole thing was going to be a failure, it was Danny who invariably cheered us.

The dress rehearsals of *London Calling* were hectic, and the general frenzy was in no way mitigated by the frequent appearances of Ned in the stalls, accompanied by a few gay but critical friends. True he thoughtfully brought champagne and chocolates as a rule, but our insides were too twisted with nerves to be able to respond suitably to luxuries.

Gertie and I clutched each other in corners and listened morosely to 'Pa' Braham shouting staccato instructions to the orchestra, to Carrie Graham, the ballet mistress, haranguing the chorus girls, to Maisie Gay moaning that her material was the least funny that she had yet encountered in a long and varied career, to Edward Molyneux's quiet but deadly disapproval of the way the show girls were wearing his dresses, and to the show girls' equally deadly but less quiet disapproval of the dresses themselves. The only person who seemed to be completely peaceful and at ease was Charlot, who sat with Ned and his friends in the stalls and seldom raised his voice.

At last, however, we actually opened, oddly enough, with a matinée, according to an eccentric whim of Charlot's which, nevertheless, had a certain amount of common sense to it. He figured that as we were all tired, a matinée, which didn't matter very much, would tire us just so much more and ensure us playing the first night entirely on our nerves. In this he was perfectly right. We did. We flagellated ourselves into giving a remarkably slick and good performance.

The hits of the show were primarily Maisie's singing of "What Love Means to Girls Like Me," and her performance of Hernia Whittlebot, my little burlesque on the Sitwells. Next in order of applause came Gertie singing "Carrie," and the duet, "You Were Meant for Me," which she and I did together, with a dance arranged by Fred Astaire.

Gertie sang "Parisian Pierrot" exquisitely, and Edward had made it one of the loveliest stage pictures I have ever seen. Then there was Maisie as a tired soubrette singing "Life in the Old Girl Yet."

The only complete and glorious failure of the whole show was my performance of a single number, "Sentiment," which had gone so well at the dress-rehearsal and been so enthusiastically applauded by the friendly company in the stalls, that I bounded on at the opening performance fully confident that I was going to bring the house down. It certainly wasn't from want of trying that I didn't. I was immaculately dressed in tails, with a silk hat and a cane. I sang every witty couplet with perfect diction and a wealth of implication which sent them winging out into the dark auditorium, where they fell wetly, like pennies into mud. After this, discouraged but not quite despairing, I executed an intricate dance, painstakingly sweated over by Fred Astaire, tapping, after-beating, whacking my cane on the stage, and finally exiting to a spatter of applause led, I suspected, by Mother and Gladys.

Unfortunately the number could not be taken out, owing to the running order of the revue, and so nightly the audience and I were forced to endure it.

The revue was a tremendous success, and the Press notices, although a bit pernickety and fault-finding, were excellent from the point of view of box office. They were almost unanimous over one thing, however, and that was that I should never have been allowed to appear in it.

During the first two weeks of the run, I received, to my intense surprise, a cross letter from Osbert Sitwell; in fact, so angry was it, that I first of all imagined it to be a joke. However, it was far from being a joke, and shortly afterwards another letter arrived, even crosser than the first. To this day I am still a little puzzled as to why that light-hearted burlesque should have aroused him, his brother and his sister to such paroxysms of fury. But the fact remains that it did, and I believe still does.

Soon after *London Calling* was launched, Charlot became immersed in preparations for a revue which was to be produced in partnership with Archie Selwyn in New York. This was to be a conglomeration of all the best numbers and sketches from the Charlot shows of the last few years, and in it were to be starred Beatrice Lillie, Jack Buchanan and, much to my horror, Gertrude Lawrence. This obviously meant that she would be only able to stay in *London Calling* for, at most, three months, as the new company was to sail almost immediately after Christmas.

In addition to this serious loss, we soon learned that we were also to be deprived of Danny, Carrie Graham, and several of our best chorus and small-part girls. I could only hope that it was a comfort to Ned and the other wretched backers to feel that they still had Maisie Gay, Tubby Edlin, me and the scenery.

On account of this strange managerial juggling with success, the show began to deteriorate after the first three months, and although it ran for almost a year, it continued to deteriorate by leaps and bounds under the burden of successive new editions.

When Gertie left, Joyce Barbour took her place, and Charlot sailed away to America with his troupe, leaving us completely to our own devices. We continued, however, playing to more or less adequate business until his return in February, when he decided to plan still another new edition.

This time the revue was almost entirely reconstructed. Tubby Edlin left, and A. W. Baskcomb was engaged. Teddie Gerrard came in with a vague manner, and several diamond bracelets. I decided to leave the cast too. My six months were up, in fact I had played almost seven, and I had a longing to go to America again.

It was considered by some people to be very foolish of me to chuck up a forty-pound-a-week job, merely to satisfy my mania for travel and change, but to me it wasn't foolish at all. It was the result of careful thought.

To remain hopping about in a revue for which all my spontaneous enthusiasm had died ages ago, only for the sake of the salary, seemed to be a static, over-cautious policy. I felt, sincerely enough, that my creative impulse was suffering from the monotony of eight performances a week, and although during the run I had managed to write two full-length plays, *Fallen Angels* and *The Vortex*, I was far from satisfied.

I was convinced that new experiences and inspirations and ideas were waiting for me, far away from the Duke of York's Theatre, Ebury Street, and the Ivy, and I felt that there was no time to waste, as the future was drawing near and I was already twenty-four.

8

I sailed for New York on the *Olympic* in Februray, enjoying to the full the contrast in circumstances between this and my first voyage on the *Aquitania* three years before. I had a comfortable cabin; took my meals in the Ritz restaurant; accepted small extra attentions from the ship's personnel as tributes to my fame which, although far from assured, had at least been enough to procure me a dignified pose for the White Star Line photographer at Waterloo, and an enquiry as to my American plans by the Press reporter at Southampton.

I had no premonition of what the year would bring. No seer had whispered that by the end of it I would be catapulted into real notoriety. I was pleased with the way things were going, and I had two hundred and fifty pounds to spend. Mother was well and happy; before leaving I had rented for her a cottage at Dockenfield, near Farnham in Surrey. True, we had taken it rather impulsively in a thick January fog which, when the lease was signed, lifted to disclose several villas in the too immediate vicinity. But still, it was country and cost only forty pounds a year.

I could look back cheerfully on the last six months and reflect with a certain irony how odd it was that my first two plays *I'll Leave it to You* and *The Young Idea*, having been praised almost unanimously by the critics, had failed, whereas *London Calling*, which had received only scant appreciation from them, had been a big success. The houses had been packed at every performance for the first three months. Society, with jewels and sables and white shirt-fronts, had come and come again, occasionally overflowing in driblets through the Pass door and trickling in and out of the dressing-rooms. I had observed the curious attitude of the *soi-distant* smart set towards a successful musical show, an attitude which is special and apart, and has nothing in common with that of ordinary straight play-goers. It is patronising, of course, to a certain degree, but not consciously nor disagreeably so; unaware of anything but the gay aspects of the performance and anxious to participate a little, at any rate to the extent of using Christian names and referring to 'Numbers' rather than 'Songs.' They have, these back-stage explorers, naturally no suspicion that it is a privilege for them to be there at all. They have paid for their seats, and, like children at a circus, they find it enjoyable to feed the animals afterwards. As a new animal I received many surprising visitors in my cage and learned quickly to do the little tricks that were expected of me.

London Calling had done a lot for me. For the first time I had experienced the thrill of hearing my own music played in restaurants. Also for the first time I had had the pleasure of seeing my name in electric lights outside a theatre. True, Maisie's and Gertie's names were on the best side of the sign facing down St Martin's Lane towards Trafalgar Square, while Tubby Edlin's and mine were visible only to pedestrians approaching from the direction of Seven Dials, but still there it was, 'Noel Coward' in gleaming pink bulbs, and never failed to please me every time I looked up at it, which was often.

Nineteen-twenty-four appears so far away now, much farther than earlier years. My vision of myself at eight and twelve and sixteen is clear, but at twenty-four I seem shadowy. I know how I looked, of course. The stage photographs show me in neat over-waisted suits, in pyjamas and dressing-gowns, and one in fanciful Russian dress with boots and a fur hat. My face was plumper and less lined than it is now, and my figure was good but a little weedy. Of what was going on inside me, however, there was no indication. There seems an emptiness somewhere, a blandness of expression in the eyes. There is little aggressiveness in the arranged smiles and no impatience apparent at all, and in this the cameras must have lied, for I have always been impatient. Nowadays there is more truth in my photographs. I hope there is more truth in me, too.

9

New York was still decorated with the remains of a blizzard as the *Olympic* steamed up the river. Everything was black and dirty grey; the New Jersey cliffs looked sinister, and white smoke from the ships lay heavily like clouds over the harbour. Nobody met me, which didn't matter, as I had had a wire from Jeffery at quarantine saying that he was busy on a job (*New York World*), had seats for *Rain* and would call for me at the Ritz. There was no disappointment anywhere that evening. Jeffery arrived, we dined and went to *Rain*. Jeanne Eagels had got us the management's seats in the second row. From the moment that she made her first entrance in those bedraggled trashy clothes and spoke her first lines, I knew from the timbre of her tough voice and the sullen slouch of her body that we were going to see great acting, and I was right. After we had been back-stage to see Jeanne we went to the Algonquin, for old time's sake, and had supper. Jeffery was now a full-fledged reporter on the *World* and had 'covered' a great deal of Life and Death in the raw. After his first spate was exhausted I managed tactfully to erase some of the bloodstains from his conversation and supper became more appetising.

I went home to the Ritz pleasantly tired and accepted the soft pink carpets, gold elevator doors and the general sense of rich comfort, almost as though it were all my usual background. Almost, but not quite. My small two-dollar-fifty room at the Brevoort was only two years away, still in sight and mind. I planned to revisit it soon, probably the next day. I meant to go to Washington Square, too, and sit on my old bench, jumping back for a little into loneliness and poverty, but this time with no sting of reality in it. The well-sprung mattress received me graciously, and I remember thinking just before I dropped off to sleep how sad it would be to have had Ritzes always and been denied the keen pleasure of earning them.

When I saw the bill at the end of the first week, however, I discovered that my grandeur had been both incautious and premature, and I moved hastily into Lester Donahue's flat in East 32nd Street and slept on a couch in the sitting-room. We had great fun in that little flat and gave several select cocktail parties, but I kept the Ritz as my address, feeling that as the gesture had been made it would be foolish to allow it to appear too short-lived.

The month passed swiftly with no miseries and anxieties to keep me awake at nights. It was a real holiday. I went to plays in the best seats. I experienced the mixed pain and pleasure of seeing Jack Buchanan bring the house down in the Charlot revue singing "Sentiment," watching to see why he should succeed so triumphantly where I had failed, and finding at first no adequate reason, except perhaps that it was because he apparently made no effort at all. It wasn't until later that I acknowledged to myself in secret that the truth of the matter was that his whole technique was superior to mine.

It was thrilling to see the three of them, Gertie Lawrence, Beatrice Lillie and Jack Buchanan hailed as great stars by the whole of New York. It invested them, for me, with a new glamour, as though I were discovering them too, and had never seen them before in my life. The appreciation of American audiences certainly gave an extra fillip to their performances. There was a shine on all of them, a happy gratification bursting through. I could swear that they had none of them ever been so good before.

I spent a lot of time with Lynn and Alfred, who were now married and living in a comfortable greenish apartment on Lexington Avenue. Lynn was just finishing a successful run of a comedy called *In Love with Love*. She was gay and attractive in it, utterly different from 'Dulcy' which had been a bleating, essentially comic characterisation. In *In Love with Love* she also began to be beautiful. There was a new fullness in her figure and her movements were smoother. She wore a pale pink dress in one scene which gave a warm glow to her skin, and when I noticed how she used her eyes and hands I suspected Alfred of rehearsing her in sex appeal. I think happiness and security had a lot to do with it, too. I have never known two people so happy together as the Lunts. If their whole-hearted engrossment in each other occasionally makes them a trifle remote from other people, so much the better. They could never be remote from real friendship.

Alfred was playing in *Outward Bound*. It was the first time I had ever seen him on the stage, and when I visited him in his dressing-room afterwards he went through all his hoops. I know those hoops so well now, that I can hear the paper crackling in anticipation before he dives through the first one; but then it was a surprise to me, rather a painful surprise. I had been deeply moved by his performance and was still feeling wrought up. I explained this to him from my heart, but no gleam of pleasure came into his rolling tragic eyes. He mowed down my praise with bitter self-recrimination. I had, he said, been privileged to see him give far and away the worst performance of his career. He had over-played, over-emotionalised, and used every ham trick that had ever been invented. Nothing I said could convince him to the contrary. At supper afterwards I observed that Lynn was unmoved by his despair. She said: 'Never mind, darling, you gave a lovely performance last Thursday matinée,' and went on with her scrambled eggs.

It must not be imagined that Alfred's dressing-room miseries are unreal or affected. His wretchedness, for the moment, is completely genuine, a nervous reaction from having tried too hard for perfection: an actor's disease from which we all suffer from time to time, although few can plumb the depths so wholeheartedly as he does.

In *Design for Living* we all three gave the worst performances of our careers every night together for months, and managed to be very good indeed.

I found the personality of New York completely changed by winter. The sun, although brilliant enough, was detached and without warmth. Freezing winds whipped round the corners, and the buildings took on a knife-edged sharpness, casting shadows that looked as though they had been cut out of black paper. Park Avenue and Fifth Avenue were of course immaculate, but in many of the streets snow was still piled up in dirty mounds on the sidewalks. The hotels, the houses, the theatres and even the taxis were over-heated. The sensation of undressing in luxurious warmth, opening the window the last second before getting into bed, and feeling the icy fresh air swirling into the room was delicious. I could recall without regret the airless nights in Washington Square, and the dead oppressive days when the whole city shimmered in heat haze, and the sun drained all colour from everything, softening the asphalt pavements into squelching rubber sponges, and cooking up the well-known champagne air until it felt like hot soup in the lungs.

I found several new friends, and together with them and some of my older ones I whirled through parties and trips to Harlem, and week-ends in the country. There were the Janis's, Eva Le Gallienne, Ethel Barrymore, the Kaufmans, Woollcott and many others. Among the new ones was Neysa McMein; beautiful, untidy, casual, and too difficult to know in a short month. I had actually met her during my first visit, and I think I found her rather tiresome. I was even more hasty in my judgments in those days than I am now, and as frequently inaccurate. I remembered having been taken to her studio a couple of times, where I had met a miscellaneous selection of models, journalists, actors and Vanderbilts, swimming round and in and out like rather puzzled fish in a dusty aquarium. Neysa paid little or no attention to anyone except when they arrived or left, when, with a sudden spurt of social conscience, she would ram a paint-brush into her mouth and shake hands with a kind of dishevelled politeness.

I was too inexperienced and edgy then to appreciate properly her unique talent for living, but I can salute it now.

It was at the Hartley Manners' house that I met Douglas Fairbanks and Mary Pickford. This was a big thrill, particularly as they were both charming to me. I discovered that we were sailing together on the *Olympic*, and my mind busied itself with secret plans to get to know them well. I was at that period a bad celebrity snob. Whether it was sheer undiluted snobbishness, or just part of my devouring ambition to become a celebrity myself I don't know, at any rate it was a strong passion and at least the memory of it has induced in me a quite admirable tolerance in my own dealings with lion-hunters. There is, I think, a real pleasure in reflected glory. I enjoyed it then tremendously and I enjoy it still. There is a technique to it, too. My method was always a careless indifference, so studied and practised that it could leave no doubt whatever in anybody's mind as to my easy intimacy with the object of the crowd's admiration. Other methods also can be equally successful, such as boorish irritation which I have seen used by stronger types with excellent effect – a let's-get-away-from-these-damn-fools-as-quickly-as-possible expression, apparent only when the chances of getting away are slight. With Douglas and Mary in 1924 any acquaintance of theirs could be surfeited with reflected mass-worship very swiftly. They were unable to go in or out of restaurants or theatres or hotels without dense hordes of people clamouring round them. Indeed, on the day that the *Olympic* was due to sail, the White Star Line had the forethought to send special warnings to all the passengers advising them to be on board at least two hours early. We sailed at midnight and I remember standing on deck (with Mary and Douglas, of course) as the ship moved slowly out into the river, and watching that vast sea of faces staring up from the lighted dock; hundreds of rows of pallid discs with black smudges on them where mouths were hanging open. It was an exhilarating sight, and I felt myself proudly to be the focusing point of a myriad sharp envies.

Much the same sort of thing occurred when we arrived at Southampton. The dock was black with people; so was the customs house and the station platform. Some hardy spirits actually sprinted along by the side of the train when it left, until at last the quickening pace caused them to fall back breathless, but still waving their arms like clockwork puppets that are beginning to run down a little.

Richard and Jean Norton had also been on the ship, and had planned a party for the Fairbanks to meet the Prince of Wales a few nights after their arrival in London. When they invited me too, my acceptance was so exquisitely casual that I am quite sure that it betrayed to them my obvious delight. However, I went and enjoyed it, although I must admit I suffered a little from strain afterwards. I remember that Douglas did a lot of conjuring tricks, a habit to which he was then, and still is, a keen addict, and that the Prince of Wales threw me into a frenzy by asking me to play a tune that I couldn't remember. Apart from these minor disadvantages the evening went with a swing.

10

London seemed dim to me on my return. I had not been away long enough to have missed it. Apart from seeing the family, Gladys and a few others, there was no thrill in my arrival. The weather was damp and the whole town looked sullen, as though it were cross about something. New York was hard and clear in my mind like a diamond, unsmudged as a memory by any sentimental glamour, but sharp with efficiency, strenuous ambition and achievement, in fact all the qualities that I felt were necessary to me at that time. I felt I knew London too well and had toiled in it too long, with no prospect of unexpected adventures or sudden surprises lurking round its gentle corners. It gave me a sense of frustration and a bad cold. I went to a few theatres and was irritated by both the actors and the audiences, the former lackadaisical and the latter apathetic. *London Calling* was still running, and there was an even worse air of dreariness over that. The company ambled through the show, the fade-outs and black-outs were untidy, and the smart Molyneux dresses looked as though they had been used to wrap up hot-water-bottles. I talked to Charlot about pepping it up a bit, but he wasn't interested, his mind being obviously occupied with more important plans, and so I went down to our cottage in Dockenfield and gave myself up to my cold. When this passed, my depression passed with it, and I wrote *Hay Fever*. The idea came to me suddenly in the garden, and I finished it in about three days, a fact which later on, when I had become news value, seemed to excite gossip-writers inordinately, although why the public should care whether a play takes three days or three years to write I shall never understand. Perhaps they don't. However, when I had finished it and had it neatly typed and bound up, I read it through and was rather unimpressed with it. This was an odd sensation for me, as in those days I was almost always enchanted with everything I wrote. I knew certain scenes were good, especially the breakfast scene in the last act, and the dialogue between the giggling flapper and the diplomat in the first act, but apart from these it seemed to me a little tedious. I think that the reason for this was that I was passing through a transition stage as a writer; my dialogue was becoming more natural and less elaborate, and I was beginning to concentrate more on the comedy values of situation rather than the comedy values of actual lines. I expect that when I read through *Hay Fever* that first time, I was subconsciously bemoaning its lack of snappy epigrams. At any rate I thought well enough of it to consider it a good vehicle for Marie Tempest, and so I took it up to London to read it to her. Both she and Willie Graham-Browne were kind and courteous as usual, and listened with careful attention, but when I had finished they both agreed with me that it was too light and plotless and generally lacking in action, and so back I went to the country again and wrote *Easy Virtue*. On this I worked hard and thought it excellent. I fully realised its similarity of theme to *The Second Mrs Tanqueray*, but the construction and characterisation on the whole seemed to me to be more mature and balanced than anything I had written up to date. The critics, later on, didn't agree with me, but by the time it came to their attention I was in too good a position to care. Meanwhile *The Vortex* and *Fallen Angels* were voyaging disconsolately in and out of most of the London managers' offices. H. M. Harwood at least displayed enough interest to say that he might consider producing *The Vortex* at the Ambassador's, providing that I did not play the part of 'Nicky' myself, but as one of my principal objects in writing the play had been to give myself a first-rate opportunity for dramatic acting, I refused his offer.

I had a much more hopeful nibble from Gladys Cooper, who wanted to play *Fallen Angels* with Madge Titheradge. They were both enthusiastic, and I, of course, was delighted. However, it all fell through during the next few months, more or less painlessly. Gladys had contracts to fulfil, so had Madge. When Gladys was going to be free, Madge was tied up, and vice versa, until everybody's interest and excitement died wearily, and *Fallen Angels* joined *Hay Fever* in oblivion.

Life in the Dockenfield cottage was pleasant but cramped. There was Mother and Auntie Vida, occasionally Father or Eric, and Gladys and me. I forget now where we all slept, but I do remember that no nocturnal cough nor sneeze nor digestive rumble went up unnoticed by any of us. We had a gentle wistful girl to help with the housework. Her name was Iris, and she meandered through the days in a sort of anaemic dream, from which she occasionally awoke to catch the afternoon bus for Farnham. Gladys and I drove about the countryside in a fast red tin bath which I had bought at the motor show. We visited, every now and then, acquaintances in the neighbourhood, among them one rather pompous family. Their name escapes me at the moment, but they were over-grand, and their house was large and ugly. It was filled with silver teapots, family paintings, tennis racquets, young people in flannels, sporting and hunting prints, mackintoshes, golf clubs, tweed coats, pipe-racks, and huge truculent cakes. I still retain a certain bitterness towards them, knowing that they were of the type that would fawn upon me now, and remembering how distantly, insufferably polite they were to me then. Mrs Whatever-her-name-was was quite palpably convinced to the depths of her Christian soul that Gladys and I were conducting a furtive, illicit honeymoon just a few miles away across the fields. No amount of references to Mother or Auntie Vida could budge her suspicions; I saw them in her eyes, eager and lascivious as they flickered at us over the tea-table. We left, thankfully, as soon as we could, feeling thoroughly uncomfortable and almost expecting Mother to greet us blind drunk in a dirty kimono.

11

In July I had a letter from Ruby Melville inviting me to stay with her in Deauville. Money was getting low again, but as I had enough to pay my fare, with a little over for expenses, I decided to go. So many of my earlier days seem to have been spent in a state of extreme penury among the very rich; Deauville couldn't have been smarter or wealthier or more fashionable than it was that year, at the height of its damp summer season. Nor could I have chosen a more thoroughly unsuitable place for a holiday, considering that I had about thirty pounds in the bank and no definite contracts to look forward to. However, I enjoyed myself watching people lose thousands at baccarat, and inventing thrilling dreams in which I suddenly found a mille-franc plaque under somebody's chair, sat down immediately at the big table, and in the course of a few hours won a vast fortune amid an envious crowd of onlookers. The dreams varied in superficial detail, but the climax was always the same.

A polo-playing friend of Ruby's lent us ponies and we rode them daily up and down the sands, borrowed riding-breeches spoiling for me a little the dashing picture I made. 'Noel Coward enjoying a brisk morning canter on the beach at Deauville,' seemed a nice caption for my mind's eye, but I suffered, when we dismounted for the morning *apéritif* from the consciousness that my seat was sagging behind me like the elephant's child.

Sir James Dunn arrived one day on a yacht with Lady Queensberry (now Lady Dunn), his daughter Mona, Diana and Duff Cooper, and several others. Large dinners were given nightly in the Casino, and certain private social dramas among the party enlivened the hours until dawn. I felt that I was seeing a side of life which should by rights be glamorous to eyes unfamiliar with it; all the correct adjuncts were there: champagne, beautifully-gowned women, high-powered gambling, obsequious *maîtres d'hôtel*, moonlit terraces – a perfectly arranged production with all the parts well cast according to type. I think, perhaps, that there must have been something wrong with the dialogue. The author must have had a common mind, because soon I became irritated and bored and wanted to go home. The leading lady, as far as I was concerned, was Ruby. She was good all through. Her wit saved the more tedious scenes and her performance was gallant to the last.

Jimmy Dunn took a sudden interest in me at about four o'clock one morning and informed me, to my immense surprise, that I was a genius! My astonishment was natural, owing to the fact that up till that moment he had paid no attention to me whatever. However, I concluded rightly that Ruby had been trying to do me a good turn on the side and that it was up to me to take advantage of it; so I interrupted him with no more than a routine smile of self-deprecation, while he went on to say that I obviously had a great career ahead of me, and that as he had been given to understand that I was oppressed by money worries, it would give him great pleasure to finance me for the next five years. I should like to say here that no one could have more personal charm than Jimmy Dunn, when he likes to turn it on. He can be gentle, kind, humorous and sympathetic all at the same moment, and before that little interview was over I believed that all my troubles were ended, and that all I had to do was to go back to England and write what I wanted to write in comfort, with the certain knowledge that on the first day of every month, for the next five years, a cheque for a hundred pounds was going to drop into the letter-box.

The next day I felt a trifle damped when he practically cut me dead at lunch, but in the evening his enthusiasm was reborn and he asked me, charmingly, to sing to him and Irene Queensberry in the deserted dining-room of the Royal Hotel, which was where the only available piano happened to be. It was a strange setting: piled-up tables, shuttered windows, a dust-sheet pushed half off the piano and a few palms in pots looking, under the sharp electric light, as though they were going to be sick. I felt somehow that I was singing for my life. Jimmy Dunn's personality was strong, and I expect the atmosphere of the whole place had nurtured in me a reverence for riches which, even in my most poverty-stricken moments, I had not been aware of before. They talked animatedly during my songs, but appeared to be quite carried away with appreciation at the finish and, when I went with them to the Casino and actually won forty-eight francs at *boule*, I felt that my star had definitely risen for good.

On my return to England, Gladys was the first person, and I think the last, to whom I broke my glorious news. It wasn't so much that she poured cold water on the idea; she submerged it in a sea of icy disapproval. She pointed out that having got so far in my career unaided, it was idiotic to lose faith in myself at a critical moment which, when analysed, was critical only because I happened to have a slight overdraft and no immediate prospects. I had been in far worse straits before and managed to come out unscathed, and that to contemplate tying myself up for five years to a strange financier was sheer lunacy. Worse than lunacy, it was craven cowardice, a mean clutching at expedience, an abysmal admission of defeat! Faced with this unexpected vehemence I was forced to take stock of the situation all over again from a different angle. The contract between Jimmy Dunn and me was to be drawn up on his return to London on the following lines: that he guaranteed to pay me twelve hundred pounds a year for five years, on the understanding that he was to take twenty per cent of anything I happened to earn during that period. This arrangement had seemed fair enough to me in Deauville, but in the cold light of Gladys's reasoning the glow of philanthropy faded from it. It seemed less munificent and more like a business deal than I had hitherto imagined it, and after discussion I decided, with a deep secret sense of relief, that she was unquestionably right.

Having made this decision I nourished for quite a while a resentful anger against Jimmy Dunn. I can only suppose that my conscience was uneasy. I was ashamed somewhere inside because I had so nearly allowed myself to be made a fool of, not by him, but by myself through him. His charm, personality, perception and generosity changed, in my mind, into sinister sheep's clothing, and it wasn't until much later that I was able to see him as he really was: a man of blustering tempers, kind impulses and excellent business acumen.

12

In looking back now on those months, August, September and October, 1924, I can detect a glow of nostalgia upon them. They mark in my life such a definite end to a chapter. The weather was fine and clear, and nothing seemed to be happening. Whether or not I felt frustrated I cannot remember, but for that little while I was undoubtedly suspended – irritably, I expect – in a sort of vacuum. Several plays were written and ready for production, but nobody was interested enough to wish to produce them. My position was equivocal. As far as the theatre world was concerned I was well known and moderately popular. I was not yet 'unspoiled by my great success,' but in danger of being distinctly spoiled by the lack of it. The Press regarded me as 'promising' and were waiting, without any undue signs of impatience, for the day when they could tie on me a less ambiguous label. The general public, on the whole, were ignorant of my existence. Meanwhile the leaves fluttered down from the trees in Dockenfield, mist lay along the meadows in the evening, and London managers announced lists of interesting plays for the autumn, not one of them by me. Yes, the nostalgia is there all right, I can feel it strongly. It is like a sensation that every traveller knows when his ship steams away from a place to which he is sure he will never return. Not perhaps that he wants to. Not perhaps that he has been particularly happy there, but he feels a pang as the land slips down below the horizon. The little café where he used to have coffee. That boring walk along by the sea and back. The view from the balcony. The conversations with the barman. The hotel wallpaper. All part of living Time, never to be known again, the closing of a phase.

PART SIX

I

The Everyman Theatre, Hampstead, was, in its infancy, a Drill Hall, but by the time I knew it all military flavour had departed, and it was firmly and almost defiantly a theatre. Under the management of Norman Macdermott it had achieved an excellent reputation, and several plays had been successfully launched there, later to slide down the hill into the West End.

The theatre itself was small, intimate and draughty. Its auditorium, foyer and corridors were carpeted austerely with coconut matting, and there was a subtle but determined aroma of artistic endeavour pervading the whole place.

Norman Macdermott was a short, affable man with nice eyes and a faintly unreliable expression. He invited me to go to see him after he had read *Hay Fever* and *The Vortex*, and announced, to my joy, that he would produce one of them, but that he had not quite decided which would stand the greater chance of success. He had a slight bias towards *Hay Fever*, but as there was no good part for me in that, I managed to sheer him over to *The Vortex*.

Casting was even more difficult than usual owing to the rule of the Everyman Theatre that all actors appearing there must agree to do so, regardless of their position, at a fixed salary of five pounds a week. Naturally if the play was successful enough to be transferred to a West-End Theatre, they reverted to their normal London salaries. This was actually an admirable arrangement, but it limited our choice to actors who were sporting enough to take a chance. We finally collected a cast headed by Kate Cutler and myself, which included Helen Spencer, Mary Robson, Millie Sim, Bromley Davenport, Kinsey Peile, George Merrit, and Alan Hollis.

Macdermott, after a little argument, agreed that Gladys Calthrop should design the scenery and dresses, and it wasn't until all the contracts were signed and we were about to start rehearsals that he called me to his office and told me that he was sorry to say that he couldn't do the play at all, as he hadn't enough money, and that unless two hundred pounds were procured immediately the whole thing would have to be abandoned.

This was the first of many horrible setbacks attending that production. I was in despair, and spent a black twenty-four hours racking my brains to think of someone whom I could ask for the money. Ned Lathom was out of the question, as I felt that I had already sponged on him enough. I scurried miserably through my address-book, marking with crosses the names of my richer acquaintances and later discarding them all on the fairly accurate assumption that, being rich, they wouldn't be good for more than a fiver, if that. Suddenly, on turning back at the beginning of the book again, I lighted on the name Michael Arlen. I had not seen him for a year or so, and during that time *The Green Hat* had been published and was a triumphant Best Seller. I remembered our casual meetings during the last few years. I remembered our occasional heart-to-heart talks sometimes in corners at parties, sometimes in his little flat in Shepherd Market. He knew all about being poor. He knew all the makeshifts of a struggling author. He also must have known, many times, the predicament I was in at the moment, that dismal resentment of being forced by circumstances into the position of being under obligation to people. He was the one to approach all right. Success was still new to him, and the odour of recent shabbiness must still be lingering in his nostrils. I telephoned to him straight away and he asked me to dine with him that night at the Embassy.

It was a smart evening at the beginning of the winter season. We had cocktails in the newly-decorated bar and smiled with affable contempt upon the newly-decorated clientele. Half-way through dinner I blurted out my troubles, and without even questioning me about the play or making any cautious stipulations about repayment, he called for a cheque form and wrote out a cheque for two hundred pounds immediately. After that the evening seemed even more charming than it had been in the beginning.

Rehearsals started and all went well for a few days. Then Helen Spencer developed diphtheria, and despair set in again. This was a bitter disappointment. However, Mollie Kerr was engaged to take over the part and played it excellently.

Our next obstacle appeared to be insurmountable and reared itself up in the most unexpected quarter. Kate Cutler, for whom I had written the part of 'Florence,' suddenly refused flatly to go on rehearsing. I have never quite known to this day what strange devil got into her. We were close friends and she had been my strongest and wisest ally through all the vicissitudes of *I'll Leave it to You* and *The Young Idea*. At all events she became surprisingly angry because, upon realising that the last act was too short, I had rewritten it, enlarging my own part considerably in the process. It was a painful and, I still think, unreasonable quarrel. Norman Macdermott was away for the week-end, and there was no one to whom we could appeal for arbitration. After a violent scene in which Kate and I both held our ground sturdily and refused to give way an inch, Kate left the theatre, and there I was, a week away from production, faced with two alternatives. I could either stick to my guns, in which case I should have to find a new leading lady immediately and rehearse her from the beginning, even supposing that I could persuade any first-rate actress to undertake such a task at such short notice. Or I could surrender to Kate by reverting to the original last act which I knew to be too short and lacking the correct emotional balance in the conflict between the mother and son. The fact that Kate seemed to imagine that I had rewritten it only in order to give myself better material as an actor made me extremely angry. I remember roaring out several grandiloquent phrases about my 'literary integrity,' etc., which, although pompous, were certainly justifiable in the circumstances.

Gladys and I drove back to Ebury Street in my red car, much too fast and sizzling with indignation. When all rage was spent and blood had resumed its normal circulation, I decided, quite firmly and without passion, that neither then nor at any time in my life would I allow myself to be dictated to in the old-age battle between actor and author: a resolution, I am proud to say, that I have kept more or less shining and unsullied to this day.

In the meantime a new mother had to be found, and all through that night a grotesque ballet of middle-aged actresses whirled through my dreams. The next morning, having been forced to discard, for various reasons, all those who were even remotely suitable to the part, I decided to work from another angle and make a list of actresses as far removed from the type of 'Florence' as possible. this list was headed by Lilian Braithwaite. She was tall and dark. Florence should be small and fair. She was well-bred and serene. Florence should be flamboyant and neurotic. Lilian Braithwaite had been associated in the public mind for some years with silver teapots in Haymarket comedies. She was almost inextricably wedged in a groove of gentle, understanding motherhood. Her moral position was clearly defined, and her virtue unassailable. Even in *Mr Wu* a few years back, when by a hair's breadth she had, nightly for over a year, escaped dishonour at the hands of a Chinaman, she had still managed to maintain an air of well-bred integrity, all of which went to prove the foolish incongruity of casting her for Florence. On the other hand, there was the finally important fact that she happened to be a first-rate actress. And so, waiving aside all obvious objections, I telephoned to her and about twenty minutes later was sitting in her drawing-room in Pelham Crescent reading the play to her.

Before starting, I had explained the Kate Cutler situation and told her that before anything definite could be decided, Kate must be given one more chance to say either yes or no. Lilian also told me that she was about to start rehearsals for a new play, *Orange Blossoms*, in which her part was bad but her salary extremely good. She added, however, with a slight glint of her eye, that she had not yet signed the contract.

That being such a portentous interview, I am sorry that I cannot remember more details of it. I recall that the room was dimly green, and that there were well-arranged flowers and several silver photograph frames; I remember Gladys's hat, which was brown and perky; also her rather screwed-up position in an armchair. Lilian wore a far-away expression during the reading; she was looking out of the window beyond the trees of the Crescent, at herself in a blond wig, rather *outré* clothes, with perhaps a long cigarette-holder. I knew by the occasional nods she gave that she was liking the play and recognising the value of the part. At the end, without any quibbling, she said that if Kate refused finally, she would play it. I explained about the regulation salary being only five pounds a week at the Everyman, and that unless the play were successful enough to be transferred to the West End the engagement would only be for a fortnight; to which she replied that she was willing to take the chance providing that we let her know definitely within a few hours. It was a nice clean morning's work. There were no blandishments and no superlatives, no time wasted on inessentials. Gladys and I gulped down some sherry, dashed out of the house and drove straight off to see Kate. It was only a short way, but to our strung-up minds it seemed miles. By that time we had bolstered ourselves into the belief that Lilian was absolutely ideal casting for the part and must play it at all costs. This was actually unfair to Kate, but it provided us with a certain necessary impetus. We burst in on Kate and found her still angry and still adamant. This was, of course, a relief superficially, but I felt horrid and sad inside as though I were playing her a dirty trick by allowing her, and at this moment definitely encouraging her, to throw away one of the best opportunities of her life. But there it was. It had to be done. I told her that, after careful reflection, I had decided to keep the play exactly as I had rewritten it, and that I wished her to say finally whether or not she would play it. She said 'No, no, no,' with rising inflections, and that was that. Gladys and I left the house, thankful that the scene was over, and went back to Lilian for another glass of sherry.

Before the Monday morning rehearsal I had a stormy interview with Norman Macdermott, who, furious that an important decision had been made while his back was turned, struck the desk firmly with his clenched fist and said that Lilian Braithwaite was utterly wrong for the part, and would ruin the play, and that if she played it he would wash his hands of the entire production.

I tried to reason with him and was at length forced to remind him that as I had scraped up a good deal of the backing, the production was no longer his, anyway, and leaving him to his hand-washing, I went down on to the stage to rehearse Lilian.

That week was almost entirely beastly, and I should hate to live through it again. The weather was icy, damp and foggy. The roads were so slippery that driving to and from Hampstead was a nightmare. Gladys worked like a slave over the scenery and dresses, assisted by Mrs Doddington, 'Doddie,' the housekeeper at the Everyman. Doddie was a darling; fat and warm and dressed in untidy black. It was she who kept the fire going downstairs in the subterranean cavern where we all dressed. The dressing-rooms were little more than cubicles with a passage running between them which opened out into a small draughty space in front of the fireplace on either side of which were two frowsy, comfortable settees. Here, at any time of the day or night, Doddie brought us cups of strong tea.

Lilian learned her part in two days and devoted the rest of the time to developing and polishing her performance, with a dry, down-to-earth efficiency which was fascinating to watch. It was the only brightness in those cold, hurrying days. I knew, after her second rehearsal, that she was going to be superb, but in addition to all the extraneous details I had to attend to I was dreadfully worried about my own performance. The play as a whole I had, of course, never seen, as I was on the stage myself most of the time. I had no way of telling whether I was overplaying or underplaying, or whether my emotion was real or forced. Gladys emerged seldom from the basement, and as Macdermott remained up in his office, there was nobody out front to give me the faintest indication as to whether I was going to be good, bad or indifferent. Lilian remained a rock and allowed me to dash my miseries and hopes and fears and exaltations against her. Over and over that last act we went when everyone else had gone and the lights were reduced to one working lamp on the stage. That memory is vivid enough, anyway. Those blank rows of empty seats in the foggy auditorium; Lilian and I wrapped up in coats and tearing ourselves to pieces. 'That speech was bad – let's go back' – 'I must start crying later, if I start too soon the scene's gone' – back again – then suddenly an uninterrupted flow for a while – 'it's coming this time' – triumph! – then back again just once more, to set it – no life – no flow – despair! So on and so forth until gradually there began to grow into the scene the shape and reality we had been working for. Gladys came up one night towards the end of the week and saw it through. She was clearly excited by it, and we all went downstairs exhausted and drank tea by the fire.

The dress rehearsal staunchly upheld theatrical tradition by being gloomy and depressing to the point of suicide. The acting was nervous and unbalanced. The dresses looked awful, and the lighting was sharply unbecoming. The theatre cat made a mess in the middle of the stage, which everybody said was lucky, but which, to me, seemed to be nothing so much as a sound criticism of the entire performance.

An incident occurred which was remarkable only because it marked the first and last time that I have ever seen Gladys shed a tear over a production. At the end of the second act she appeared suddenly in my dressing-room trembling with rage and clutching a proof of the programme. The cause of her rage was a little paragraph which announced that the scenery of Act One and Act Three had been designed by G. E. Calthrop, and that of Act Two by Norman Macdermott. Considering that the whole essence of Gladys's scheme of *décor* lay in the contrast she had made between the highly-coloured modernism of the first and last acts and the oak-and-plaster simplicity of the country house in Act Two, her anger was understandable. True, Macdermott had contributed an idea for the construction of the fireplace, but apart from this the whole structure, colour and conception of the set had been Gladys's. We immediately went up into the stalls and tackled him about it, whereupon he said blandly that the complete set had been designed by him and that the programme must remain as it was. We then left him and went straight upstairs to his office, where we ransacked his desk and finally unearthed Gladys's original sketch with Macdermott's 'O.K.' scribbled across it in his own handwriting. We took it down to him triumphantly and he was very cross, and became crosser still when I said that I would not rehearse any further until the programme was changed. He ultimately gave in, however, and ordered his personal fireplace to be hacked out of the scene. This was done, and we were left with no fireplace at all for the opening night.

The next day Gladys was at the theatre early in the morning with the carpenter and George Carr, our stage manager, and by about seven in the evening, an hour before the play was due to begin, the set was fixed satisfactorily.

Meanwhile I was having a spirited duel with the Lord Chamberlain (Lord Cromer) in his office in St James's. He had at first refused point-blank to grant a licence for the play because of the unpleasantness of its theme, and it was only after a long-drawn-out argument, during which, I must say, he was charming and sympathetic, that I persuaded him that the play was little more than a moral tract. With a whimsical and rather weary smile he finally granted the licence, and with this last and most agitating of all obstacles safely surmounted, I jumped into my car and drove up to Hampstead to help Gladys with the set.

We spent a couple of hours with hammer and nails hanging pictures and tacking bits of material on to the last act furniture, and at seven o'clock allowed ourselves a quarter of an hour to rush over the road and have some tomato soup, which, for the first time in the history of that particular café, happened to be so scorching hot that we were almost unable to drink it. Then back to the theatre again. Gladys changed into evening dress in my dressing-room while I made up. The call-boy called 'Half an Hour,' then 'Quarter of an Hour,' then 'Beginners.'

The stage was reached by a spiral iron staircase; I can feel the ring of it now under my feet as I went up, my heart pounding, to see that everything was in order and to listen, with a sort of dead resignation, to the scufflings and murmurings of the audience at the other side of the curtain. Gladys, with a tightened expression about her mouth, moved about the set arranging flower-vases and cigarette-boxes on small tables. George Carr made a few little jokes and animal noises in order to make us giggle and forget for a moment the lifts going up and down in our insides. Lilian appeared resplendent in pillar-box-red and a blond wig, wearing her 'emu' face, a particular and individual expression of outward calm masking inward turmoil. She was apparently placid – as cool as a cucumber. First nights were nothing to her, she had known too many of them! But yet there was a little twitch that occurred ever so often at the side of her jaw, as though she were biting very hard on something to prevent herself from screaming. Presently Kinsey Peile, Mary Robson, Millie Sim and Alan Hollis came on to the stage in various stages of alert misery. George Carr glanced at his watch and said 'Clear, please,' very softly, as if he were scared that we might all rush madly out into the street. Gladys gave one last hopeless look at the set. We all cleared to the side of the stage and, amid a sickening silence, the curtain rose on the first act.

That evening was altogether an extraordinary experience. There was a certain feeling of expectancy in the air, an acceptance almost that the play would be a success. The audience looked distressingly near owing to there being no orchestra pit and no footlights. Familiar faces suddenly jumped out of the darkness and accosted us in the middle of a scene. Lilian was cool and steady and played beautifully. I was all over the place but gave, on the whole, one of those effective, nerve-strung *tour-de-force* performances, technically unstable, but vital enough to sweep people into enthusiasm.

At the end of the play the applause was terrific. I happened to cut a vein in my wrist when, towards the end of the last act, I had to sweep all the cosmetics and bottles off the dressing-table. I bound it up with my handkerchief during the curtain calls, but it bled effectively through my author's speech.

The first person to clutch my hand afterwards was Michael Arlen. His face was white with excitement and he said: 'I'd be so proud, so *very* proud if I had written it.'

After him came the deluge. And a very gratifying deluge it was too. There was little or no empty politeness about it. People had obviously been genuinely moved and Lilian and I held court for a long time until finally the last visitor went away and we could relax.

There it was real and complete, my first big moment. I don't remember exactly how I felt. I do know that I was tired. We were all tired. I know also that I recognised a solidity underlying all the excitement; this time I really had done it. The cheering and applause had been no louder than it had been for *I'll Leave it to You* and *The Young Idea*. If anything it had been a trifle less, owing to the smallness of the Everyman Theatre. The back-stage enthusiasts had used the same phrases; their superlatives were still in my ears; the same superlatives as before; the same 'divines,' 'darlings,' 'brilliants,' and 'marvellouses.' The same fervent embraces and handshakes; the same glistening eyes. But this time there was a subtle difference. Lilian said wearily: 'Do you think we are all right?' And I knew, and she knew that I knew, that the question was merely rhetorical, a routine gesture of diffidence. We were all right, more than all right. We were a smash hit.

2

The Press notices the next day were, on the whole, enthusiastic, although most of the critics deplored the fact that the characters of the play were 'unwholesome,' which, of course, was perfectly true. Their insistence, however, on the cocktail-drinking, decadence and general smart-settishness of the play was good for the box office, and we played to packed houses.

Those two weeks at the Everyman were exciting. Bit by bit I improved my performance technically; controlling my emotion, holding tears in reserve until the right moment. Different scenes took shape and became more complete. Never in my life had I looked forward so much to getting down to the theatre at night. Lilian and I discussed, sharpened and polished our last act until it became almost as good as people said it was.

Meanwhile there was the anxiety of wondering which management would take us over in the West End. Finally Alban Limpus and Charles Kenyon offered us the best terms and the Royalty Theatre was decided upon.

Our last night at the Everyman was almost as exciting as our first. There was more cheering and speech-making and we felt sentimental and sad to be leaving that draughty, uncomfortable and loving little theatre. Doddie cried copiously and deluged us with tea and Gladys and I drove away down the hill for the last time, waving valedictions to our various landmarks: the pillar-box that we had run into after the dress rehearsal, the private gateway where we had had to leave the car all night in a pea-soup fog, the corner just by Lord's Cricket Ground where we had once missed a lorry by inches. Those drives from Ebury Street to Hampstead and from Hampstead to Ebury Street, so fraught with agitations and emotions, were now just part of the past, along with all the early rehearsals, the snatched meals at the café opposite the stage door, the arguments, the agonies, the crises. It was again the nostalgia of leaving a familiar shore. Several weeks of fever-pitch, strung-up heavens and hells, hours of desperate concentration, slipping away behind us as the road was slipping away behind us into the mist. I remember saying dolefully to Gladys: 'And now what?' But, oddly enough, I cannot recall her reply.

3

Success altered the face of London for me. Just for a little the atmosphere felt lighter. I'm not sure whether or not the people who passed me in the street appeared to be more smiling and gay than they had been hitherto, but I expect they did. I do know that very soon life began to feel overcrowded. Every minute of the day was occupied and I relaxed, rather indiscriminately, into a welter of publicity. No Press interviewer, photographer, or gossip-writer had to fight in order to see me, I was wide open to them all; smiling and burbling bright witticisms, giving my views on this and that, discussing such problems as whether or not the modern girl would make a good mother, or what would be my ideal in a wife, etc. My opinion was asked for, and given, on current books and plays. I made a few adequately witty jokes which were immediately misquoted or twisted round the wrong way, thereby denuding them of any humour they might originally have had. I was photographed in every conceivable position. Not only was *I* photographed, but my dressing-room was photographed, my car was photographed, my rooms in Ebury Street were photographed. It was only by an oversight, I am sure, that our lodgers escaped the camera.

I took to wearing coloured turtle-necked jerseys, actually more for comfort than for effect, and soon I was informed by my evening paper that I had started a fashion. I believe that to a certain extent this was really true; at any rate, during the ensuing months I noticed more and more of our seedier West-End chorus boys parading about London in them.

I found people difficult to cope with in my new circumstances. Their attitude to me altered so swiftly and so completely. Naturally my intimates and the few friends I happened to know well remained the same, but ordinary acquaintances to whom I had nodded and spoken casually for years, gummed strong affection to me like fly-paper and assumed tacit proprietary rights. Apparently they had always known that I was clever, talented, brilliant and destined for great things. 'How does it feel,' they cried, 'to be a genius?' To reply to this sort of remark without either complacency or offensive modesty was impossible, and so I chose the latter as being the less troublesome course and wore a permanent blush of self-deprecation for quite a long while. I can indeed still call it into use if necessary. Sometimes I became so carried away by my performance that I alluded to my success as luck! This monumental insincerity was received with acclaim. People were actually willing and eager to believe that I could throw out of my mind all memories of heart-breaks, struggles, disillusionments, bitter disappointments, and work, and dismiss my hard-earned victory as luck. Just glorious chance; an encouraging pat on the back from kindly Fate. I can only imagine that this easy belief in a fundamental schism in my scale of values must have been a comfort to them, an implication that such a thing might happen to anybody.

The legend of my modesty grew and grew. I became extraordinarily unspoiled by my great success. As a matter of fact, I still am. I have frequently been known to help old friends in distress and, odd as it may seem, I have actually so far forgotten my glory as to give occasional jobs to first-rate actors whom I knew in my poorer days. Gestures such as these cause widespread astonishment. The general illusion that success automatically transforms ordinary human beings into monsters of egotism has, in my case, been shattered. I am neither conceited, overbearing, rude, nor insulting to waiters. People often refer to me as being 'simple' and 'surprisingly human.' All of which is superficially gratifying but, on closer analysis, quite idiotic. Conceit is more often than not an outward manifestation of an inward sense of inferiority. Stupid people are frequently conceited because they are subconsciously frightened of being found out; scared that some perceptive eye will pierce through their façade and discover the timid confusion behind it. As a general rule the most uppish people I have met have been those who have never achieved anything whatsoever.

I am neither stupid nor scared, and my sense of my own importance to the world is relatively small. On the other hand, my sense of my own importance to myself is tremendous. I am all I have, to work with, to play with, to suffer and to enjoy. It is not the eyes of others that I am wary of, but my own. I do not intend to let myself down more than I can possibly help, and I find that the fewer illusions that I have about me or the world around me, the better company I am for myself.

Naturally in 1925 my reasoning on myself was not as clear as it is now, but the nucleus was fortunately there. I opened my arms a little too wide to everything that came, and enjoyed it. Later on, just a little while later – three years, to be exact – circumstances showed me that my acceptance has been a thought too credulous. The 'darling' of the London Theatre received what can only be described as a sharp kick in the pants. And while my over-trusting behind was still smarting, I took the opportunity to do a little hard thinking.

Perhaps, after all, in the above paragraphs I have been a little stingy with my gratitude. I hereby render deep thanks to those booing hysterical galleryites and those exultant, unkind critics and journalists for doing me more constructive good than any of their cheers or their praises have ever done.

As all this, however, belongs to a later part of the book, I will stop digressing and return to the Royalty Theatre in December, 1924.

4

The Vortex opened at the Royalty Theatre on December 16th, 1924. The first performance felt to all of us a little dull after the intimate excitement of the Everyman. The audience, although much larger, was further away, separated from us by an orchestra pit and footlights; also the nervous strain was lacking. We knew from our Press notices and from the advance sale that we were already an established success. The audience seemed to be conscious of this too, and so we just played the play as well as we could, and they appreciated it as well as they could, and despite the fact that many of them were obviously suffering from bronchial catarrh during the first two acts, they overcame their wheezings and coughings and cheered quite lustily at the end.

My dressing-room was large and comfortable, and there I sat nightly at the end of the play receiving people and giving them drinks and cigarettes and listening to praise. So much praise. So many various ways of expressing it. It was fascinating. Some would come in sodden with emotion and break down and have to be soothed. Others would appear to be rendered speechless for a few minutes and just sit nodding at me. The majority were voluble. There had apparently never been such acting or such a play in the history of the theatre. Many of them had friends who were the exact prototypes of Florence and Nicky. It was extraordinary, they said, how I had managed to hit off so-and-so with such cruel accuracy. No amount of protesting on my part that my characters were imaginary and that I barely knew the person in question convinced them in the least.

I arranged a series of code signals with Waugh, my dresser, by which means we contrived to get rid of visitors when the delight of their presence was wearing thin. He would vanish and reappear again with urgent telephone messages, and on one occasion became so carried away by his own virtuosity that he announced in ringing tones that Lady Biddle's car was waiting for me. I must have appeared rather over-excited at this news because in order to control my laughter I was forced to embark upon a sea of explanations relating to my lifelong connection with the Biddle family. However, it all passed off quite successfully, and from then onwards Lady Biddle and her car were used *ad nauseam*.

It must not be imagined that I was blasé and lacking in proper gratitude towards all those kind people who said so many charming things to me. I loved it all, but I had learned from experience that dressing-room opinions, unless based on sound theatrical knowledge, are actually worth little beyond the amiable impulse that prompts them. When fellow-actors or authors came backstage to see me it was quite different. It is deeply gratifying to be praised by one's peers, to know that that little bit of business by the window in Act One and that crushing out of the cigarette in Act Two was not only noticed, but appreciated and remembered. Laymen cannot be expected to note these small subtleties; indeed, it would be disconcerting if they did, but never let it be said that their appreciation, however untechnical, is unwelcome; far from it. It is warming and delightful and most comforting. It is only occasionally, after the performance of a strenuous part, that an actor may feel a little tired, a little hungry and a little anxious to get his make-up off and get out of the theatre to have supper.

The supper routine during the run of *The Vortex* is one of my pleasantest memories. There were two clubs flourishing at that time, clubs where it was not necessary to dress and where one could eat the kind of food one wanted to eat in comparative peace and quiet. The Gargoyle was practically next door to the Royalty Theatre and specialised in sausages and bacon and a small dance band consisting of a pianist and a trap-drummer who caressed, tenderly, the latest tunes, without imposing the slightest strain either upon the ears or the digestive tract.

The Fifty-Fifty was rather more flamboyant but equally theatrical in atmosphere. It was run by Constance Collier and Ivor Novello and catered exclusively to 'Us.' I put 'Us' in inverted commas advisedly, for although 'Us' were happy and contented with it at the beginning because we really could come in after the show in sweaters and old clothes without being stared at, this congenial state of affairs lasted only a little while. All too soon the news got around and various social liaison officers began to appear with representative groups, and the small-part actors, who were the basic reason for the club's existence, were seen to be shrinking away into the shadowy corners of the room until finally they no longer came at all. Personally I mourn to this day the loss of the Fifty-Fifty Club. I spent so many happy hours there. Constance, of course, was the spirit of it. Her table was enchantingly insular; the island of theatre, washed only occasionally, by wavelets from the outer sea. Conversation was amusing and gay and bound together by old understanding. Memories of early days suddenly took life again for a little. No one can talk theatre like Constance. There is a percentage of her tinsel quality in her book of memoirs, but inevitably only a small percentage. Anecdotes, particularly theatrical anecdotes, lose charm in print. Stage reminiscence needs a close intimate audience of stage people; people for whom it is not necessary to translate jargon; people from whom the mention of Crewe Station or Ackers Street, Manchester, will bring forth appropriate chuckles of recognition. Constance's principal asset as a raconteuse was self-laughter. Her humour rippled as lightly over tragic years as over gay ones. She was, I often suspected, an outrageous liar, and yet I found more truth in her than in many people. She has always epitomised for me the theatre world that I love and honour, and she will always have for me, like the glow of footlights on a red plush curtain, a deep and lasting glamour.

5

The house in Ebury Street blossomed perceptibly with the success of *The Vortex*. The feet of the lodgers on the high steep stairs trod more lightly. The water became more swiftly hot in the taps, and even the depressing little lobby separating the bungalow from the hall acquired a sheen of complacency.

I ordered new chintz covers for my sitting-room and had my bedroom done over in pillar-box scarlet, a decision which I afterwards regretted. Gladys set her seal on this by painting, out of the goodness of her heart and the deeps of her erotic imagination, a few murals to brighten up the room in case the scarlet paint became too monotonous. There were two pink nudes over the fireplace, and a third doing its languid best to disguise what was quite obviously a po cupboard. It was in the midst of this misguided splendour that I was unwise enough to be photographed in bed wearing a Chinese dressing-gown and an expression of advanced degeneracy. This last was accidental and was caused by blinking at the flashlight, but it emblazoned my unquestionable decadence firmly on to the minds of all who saw it. It even brought forth a letter of indignant protest from a retired Brigadier-General in Gloucestershire.

Lorn, who had been my secretary intermittently for two years since the death of our much-loved Meggie Albanesi, for whom she had officiated before, was now established permanently. Every morning she arrived with my breakfast tray and sat on the side of the bed while we smoked, drank coffee and transacted what we were pleased to call the business of the day.

Later on, another room in the house was taken over and transformed into an office. We had two letter files, known as 'Poppy' and 'Queen Anne' respectively, and a sinister cardboard-box labelled 'Shortly,' into which we put all the letters we felt incapable of answering at the moment. About once in every month or so it overflowed and we had to concentrate, finding, to our delight, that lapse of time had made unnecessary to answer at all at least three-quarters of its contents. This admirable system, founded far back in 1924, we still employ with success. Of course there is occasionally a slip up, and I am attacked by some irate acquaintance whose urgent invitation to do something or other has been completely ignored, but, on the whole, our percentage of failure is small.

I indulged immediately a long-suppressed desire for silk shirts, pyjamas and underclothes. I opened up accounts at various shops, happy to be able to order things without that inward fear that I might never be able to pay for them. I wasted a lot of money this way, but it was worth it. My clothes certainly began to improve, but I was still inclined to ruin a correct ensemble by some flashy error of taste.

I went to a lot of lunch parties in the most charming houses which, in retrospect, appear all to be exactly the same. This may be a trick that Time has played upon me, but I have a uniform memory of pickled oak, modern paintings, green walls, a strong aroma of recently burned 'Tantivy' from 'Floris,' and eggs, mushrooms, cutlets, sausages and bacon sizzling in casserole dishes. The conversation, I am sure, was distinguished, but that too has become lost in transit. I only remember that I felt happy and confident and very pleased to be eating such nice food with such nice people. I loved answering the questions put to me by eminent politicians. I loved noting that fleeting look of pleased surprise in people's eyes when it was suddenly brought to their attention that, in spite of theatrical success and excessive publicity, I was really quite pleasant and unaffected. This, of course, was all nonsense, but I was at least no more affected than anyone else. A social intermingling of comparative strangers automatically imposes a certain strain, an extra politeness which is not entirely real. This, I think, may be described simply as good manners. I had been brought up by Mother in the tradition of good manners, and so had they, therefore everybody was extremely agreeable to everybody else. I think possibly what surprised them was that I could play the game as well as they could, but then, after all I had learned many different parts by heart long before I had ever met them.

6

Soon after the opening of *The Vortex* I started work on a revue for Cochran. This had been tentatively discussed before. There had been an interview with C. B. in his office in Old Bond Street in course of which we bickered for about two hours because he wanted me only to write the book of the revue, and I wished to compose the entire score as well. Finally his armour of evasive politeness cracked, and he was forced to say that he was very sorry, but he frankly did not consider my music good enough to carry a whole show, and that he intended to engage Philip Braham as composer. That settled it for the time being, and I retired, vanquished, to concentrate on ideas for sketches and burlesques.

The ideas came swiftly and, oddly enough, nearly every idea carried with it its accompanying song. In my planning of the show almost every scene led up to a number, and so when the revue was complete it was discovered, to the embarrassment of everyone but me, that with the exception of three numbers by Philip Braham for which I had written the lyrics, a few odd pieces of classical music for use in ballets, etc., and one interpolated song for Delysia, the whole score, book and lyrics were mine. A few days before we were due to open in Manchester I tackled Cochran and asked him to raise my percentage, which was for the book and lyrics alone. He explained painstakingly, with great charm but implacable obstinacy, that he could not in any circumstances ask his backers for any more money, but that I was to leave it to his discretion to decide upon some additional reward for me if the show happened to be a success.

In the face of his confidential gentleness and impressed by his financial dilemma which he outlined so clearly to me, I felt that there was nothing for it but to give in. It was altogether an exasperating interview and took place in a rehearsal room in the Helvetia Club. For the benefit of the untheatrical public I would like to describe here, briefly, the general horror of rehearsal rooms. There are several crops of them all over London, and they are a necessary evil, particularly in big musical productions. Stages are not always available, and even when they are it is usually only during the last week of rehearsals that they are occupied by the entire company. Until then a show is rehearsed in bits, dialogue scenes in one place, dance numbers in another and vocal numbers in another. This frequently necessitates members of a company scudding miserably from one side of the West End to the other. Touring companies are rehearsed almost exclusively in rehearsal rooms, seldom achieving the dignity of a stage at all until a hurried run through on the day of the opening night.

Cochran productions alternate monotonously between the Poland Rooms and the Helvetia Club. There is little to distinguish between the two except that the Poland Rooms are slightly larger. Both places are equally dusty and dreary. Each room in each place contains a tinny piano, too many chairs, a few mottled looking-glasses, sometimes a practice bar and always a pervasive smell of last week's cooking. Here rows of chorus girls in practice dress beat out laboriously the rhythms dictated by the dance producer. The chairs all round the room are festooned with handbags, hats, coats, sandwiches, apples, oranges, shoes, stockings and bits of fur. It is all very depressing, especially at night in the harsh glare of unshaded electric bulbs.

My interview with Cochran occurred during a morning rehearsal to the accompaniment of 'Cosmopolitan Lady,' which Delysia was rather irritably running through with the chorus. The general din was no aid to coherent thought, and I remember my attention being constantly distracted by wrong notes and sharp cries from the dance producer. I tried hard to remain adamant and business-like, but Cochran and the atmosphere and a certain bored weariness got the better of me, and the whole question was shelved.

We all travelled to Manchester on the following Sunday for the orchestra rehearsal, dress rehearsal and opening night. I had arranged to stay off for the Monday and Tuesday performances of *The Vortex* and allow my understudy to play for me. I would never behave so casually to the public nowadays, but then I was new to stardom and unencumbered by any particular sense of responsibility.

Incidentally, my understudy happened to be a keen young actor named John Gielgud, so in the light of later events the public were not really being cheated at all.

On With the Dance, which was the title finally selected for the revue, was lavish to a degree and very good in spots. There were two ballets created and danced by Leonide Massine and an excellent cast including Douglas Byng, Nigel Bruce, Hermione Baddeley, Ernest Thesiger and several others. The star of course was Delysia. Everything she did she did well, with a satisfying authority and assurance. She was occasionally temperamental and flew into a few continental rages, but to me she was always easy to work with and extremely agreeable.

Those three days in Manchester were on the whole unpleasant, although fraught with incident. In the first place I discovered soon after my arrival that my name was not on the bills at all. The show was labelled 'Charles B. Cochran's Revue,' which, considering that I had done three-quarters of the score, all the lyrics, all of the book, and directed all the dialogue scenes, and several of the numbers, seemed to be a slight overstatement. I went roaring back from the theatre to the Midland Hotel and attacked Cockie in his bathroom. I'm not at all sure that I didn't deprive him of his towel while I shrieked at him over the noise of the water gurgling down the plug-hole. I will say, however, that he retained his dignity magnificently, far more than I, and in due course calmed me down and gave me some sherry. It is odd that in all the years I have since worked with Cockie, that show was the only one over which we have ever quarrelled. I think the psychological explanation must be that then, in those early days of our association, we had neither of us estimated accurately enough our respective egos. And a couple of tougher ones it would be difficult to find.

The dress rehearsal started at ten o'clock on Monday morning and continued without a break until lunch-time on Tuesday. I can never quite put out of my mind the picture of that large auditorium in the early hours of the morning. The limp exhausted bodies of chorus girls and boys strewn all over the stalls, some lying in the aisles, small miserable groups of people huddled in corners drinking coffee out of thick cups and trying to digest even thicker sandwiches. Meanwhile Frank Collins, Cochran's most admirable of Admirable Crichtons, dealt calmly with lighting men, property men, carpenters, and stage hands, never raising his voice and preserving to the end an expression of unrelieved gloom and an unquenchable sense of humour. Cockie himself sat in the front row of the dress circle supervising operations, with a grey felt hat at a rakish angle on the back of his head and a large cigar jutting truculently out of his mouth.

Cockie and I had still one more battle, this time over 'Poor Little Rich Girl,' which he considered too dreary and wished to take out of the show. I fought like a steer, backed up by Delysia, and fortunately for all concerned we won, as it turned out to be the big song hit of the revue.

Sibyl Cholmondeley travelled from London for the first night, and she and Mother and Gladys and I sat tremulously in a stage box. The dress rehearsal had ended only a few hours before, and we were taut with nerves and weariness. Cockie in his box was suave and calm. I know his first-night face now so well, but then it was new to me, and I must say that all my small angers and resentments were immediately swamped by admiration of his courage. There he sat with a beaming smile, occasionally waving a welcome to some acquaintance in the stalls, as though everything were smooth and in the best of order. Nobody could possibly have guessed from his bland expression that hardly one scene had gone through without a hitch at the dress rehearsal, that it was probable that every quick change in the show would last twenty minutes instead of thirty seconds, that the lighting men knew little or nothing about the running order of the scenes, that the stage hands and the company were dropping from exhaustion, and that Delysia was liable to lose her voice completely on the least provocation. Cockie continued to smile as he always does in a crisis, and also, as usually happens with a Cochran production, his smile was justified. The show went through without any noticeable accidents. There were spontaneous bursts of applause and cheering at frequent intervals during the evening, and a great deal of enthusiastic hullabaloo at the end. Cockie made a speech and led Delysia forward and me forward, and we all bowed and grinned over baskets of flowers. There was a festive party at the Midland afterwards, where all rancours and harsh thoughts were submerged in champagne, and a great many photographs were taken of everybody for the *Daily Mail*. Not only was all anger forgotten, but I may add, the possibility of my getting a larger percentage of the gross was also completely forgotten.

7

Almost simultaneously with the production of *On With the Dance* in Manchester, came the rehearsals of *Fallen Angels* in London. This play had at last been bought by Anthony Prinsep as a vehicle for Margaret Bannerman. Edna Best was engaged to play opposite her, and the producer was my old friend Stanley Bell. Bunny Bannerman, one of the kindest-hearted and least troublesome leading ladies I know, was dead tired and heading for a nervous breakdown, having played a series of long parts at the Globe, none of which, with the exception of *Our Betters*, had been successful enough to enable her to relax. She tried bravely to remember her words, but every day they receded further and further away from her. This, not unnaturally, made her more and more hysterical and nervous until finally, four days before production, she had a brain storm and said that she couldn't play it at all. We had advanced too far to be able to call the whole thing off, which might have happened if her breakdown had occurred earlier. Edna, as usual, was word-perfect and calm, and we were faced with the necessity of finding someone at once with a name of more or less equal drawing power. Once more that endless weighing of names in the balance. So-and-so was too old, So-and-so too young, So-and-so far too common, and So-and-so just about to have a baby. Finally, after a brief telephone conversation with Tony Prinsep and a slightly longer one with me, Tallulah Bankhead came flying into the theatre. Her vitality has always been remarkable, but on that occasion it was little short of fantastic. She took that exceedingly long part at a run. She tore off her hat, flipped her furs into a corner, kissed Edna, Stanley, me and anyone else who happened to be within reach and talking incessantly about *Rain*, which Maugham had just refused to allow her to play, she embarked on the first act. In two days she knew the whole part perfectly, and on the first night gave a brilliant and completely assured performance. It was a *tour de force* of vitality, magnetism and spontaneous combustion.

Edna pursued an orderly course of accurate timing and almost contemptuous restraint and skated knowledgeably over the holes in the script.

There was no sense of struggle between the two leading ladies. Their team work was excellent. They also remained entirely friendly towards each other all through the run which, considering that their parts were about equal and that they had to play the whole second act alone together, was definitely a strategic triumph.

The Press notices for *Fallen Angels* were vituperative to the point of incoherence. No epithet was spared. It was described as vulgar, disgusting, shocking, nauseating, vile, obscene, degenerate, etc., etc. The idea of two gently nurtured young women playing a drinking scene together was apparently too degrading a spectacle for even the most hardened and worldly critics. The *Daily Express* even went so far as to allude to these two wayward creatures as 'suburban sluts.'

All this was capital for the box-office and the play ran for several months. It had one disagreeable effect, however, which was to unleash upon me a mass of insulting letters from all parts of the country. This was the first time I had ever experienced such a strange pathological avalanche, and I was quite startled. In the years that followed, of course, I became completely accustomed to anonymous letters dropping into the letter-box. They have come in their hundreds, crammed with abuse and frequently embellished with pornographic drawings. Then I was still ingenuous enough to be amazed to think that there were so many people in the world with so much time to waste.

With *Fallen Angels*, *On With the Dance*, and *The Vortex* all running at once, I was in an enviable position. Everyone but Somerset Maugham said that I was a second Somerset Maugham, with the exception of a few who preferred to describe me as a second Sacha Guitry.

On With the Dance had opened at the London Pavilion and was a big success. 'Poor Little Rich Girl' was being played in all the restaurants and night clubs. I went to too many parties and met too many people. I made a great many new and intimate friends, several of whom have actually lasted. My old ones were still nearly all with me, with the exception of Stoj whom I saw only every now and then. She had married, had a baby, published two or three novels and embraced Christian Science with tremendous ardour. This depressed me but apparently gave her a great deal of pleasure, a pleasure, I may add, that was not entirely free from superciliousness. To this day we still meet occasionally and have a good time, but the paths back into the past are long and tortuous, and new faiths, like new policemen, are over-zealous in obstructing traffic.

The Vortex, having moved from the Royalty to the Comedy, was transferred once more, this time to the Little Theatre where I had made my first appearance in *The Goldfish* in 1910. This was the fourth theatre in which we had played it; a quiet intimate house peopled for me with ghostly hordes of small children dressed as fish. It was a far cry from 'Prince Mussel' in *The Goldfish* to 'Nicky Lancaster' in *The Vortex*. I sometimes imagined how the fond matrons of 1910, blissfully regarding the antics of their progeny, would have shuddered could they have visualised the podgy little boy with the throbbing treble voice, posturing on that same stage fifteen years later as a twisted, neurotic drug addict.

The theatre was so small that we were able to jog along for ages to adequate business. Our routine was set and, although the last act was a slight strain when we were tired after a matinée, we managed to uphold a pretty good standard of performance. On one occasion Seymour Hicks, that most generous of actors, came to a matinée, and stood up on his seat at the end, cheering wildly. This was thrilling to us because we had been long resigned to rather dim audiences and no 'bravos' had rung in our ears for many months. On another occasion Madge Titheradge came and fainted afterwards in Lilian's dressing-room which was equally gratifying.

One night in May a young man in the front row of the stalls caught our attention early in the first act. His rapt absorption in the play inspired Lilian and me to renewed efforts, and at the final curtain we both conceded him a gracious bow all for himself. This situation frequently occurs when actors have been playing a play for a long run. The routine has become dull, the repetition of the same words night after night has become so monotonous as to be almost automatic, when suddenly, out of the gloom of the auditorium, a single face emerges. Just for a fleeting second you note the attitude of intense interest, the gleam of enthusiasm in the eye, and if you are a conscientious actor, you refrain from looking again except only occasionally, and even then obliquely as though you are not looking at all. But the difference it can make to your performance is extraordinary. You play exclusively in your mind to that one stranger, and by the end you find that your most boring scenes have passed in a flash, and that you have probably played better than you have played for weeks. There are many unknown people in the world to whom I shall always be grateful because on some night in some play in some theatre somewhere or other, their little extra interest caught my eye and set a spur to my imagination, causing me to give a fresh and vital performance of a part which I had played and played until my nerves were sick and tired of it.

1. Aged about five years

2. Cornwall, 1907

3. As Slightly in *Peter Pan*, 1913

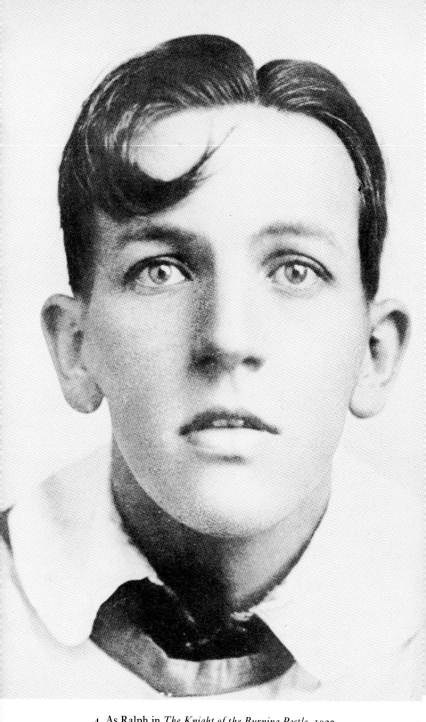

4. As Ralph in *The Knight of the Burning Pestle*, 1920

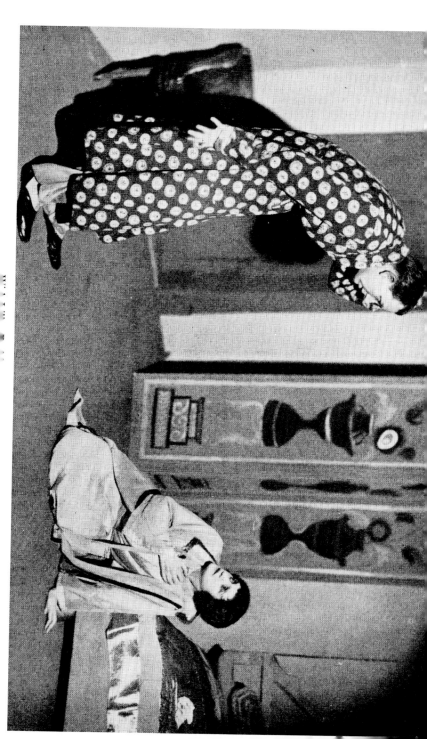

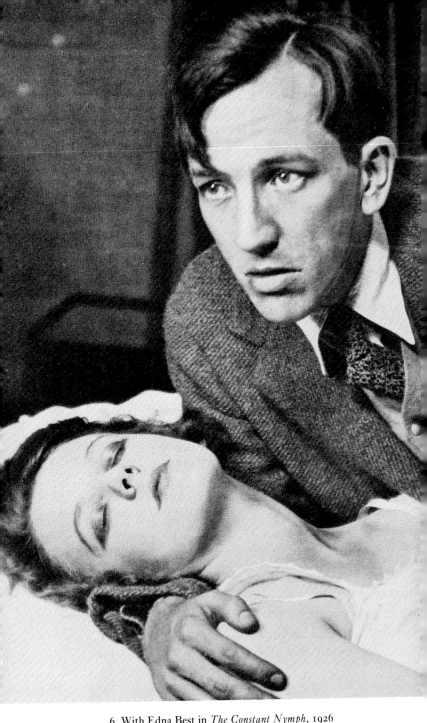

6. With Edna Best in *The Constant Nymph*, 1926

7. With Gertrude Lawrence in *Private Lives*, 1930

8. In *Private Lives*, 1930

On that particular night in the Little Theatre the young man responded nobly to our bow, by applauding even more loudly. I remember remarking to Lilian that he must be an American because he was wearing a turn-down collar with his dinner-jacket. A few days later, a mutual friend told me that he knew a young American who was very anxious to meet me, and could he bring him round to my dressing-room one night, and the next evening Jack Wilson walked nervously, and with slightly overdone truculence, into my life.

Gladys was in my dressing-room and we both considered him amiable enough but rather uppish. He left after a drink and a little commonplace conversation, having asked me to lunch with him in New York when I came over with the play. We promptly forgot all about him, no clairvoyant being present to tell us that my trio of closest, most intimate friends, Gladys, Jeffery and Lorn, were fated, in those few minutes, to become a quartette. We should, I think, have laughed at the idea that that almost defiantly American stockbroker would become so much part of our lives that scarcely any decision could be made without him. That, however, is what ultimately happened.

8

My final efforts of that full season were concentrated upon *Hay Fever*, which, having mouldered sadly in a drawer for months, was suddenly taken out, dusted off and put into rehearsal at the Ambassadors Theatre.

This all came about because Alban Limpus and Charles Kenyon wanted a play for Marie Tempest, who was no longer under her own management but under theirs. I told them that I didn't think she would do it as she had already turned it down once. They insisted, however, that it would be a good idea for her to read it again. This she did, and, much to my surprise, said that she was delighted with it and that I must produce it. This scared me somewhat because, although my opinion of my own talents was reasonably high, I hardly, even in my most bumptious moments, visualised myself showing Marie Tempest how to act. Nevertheless I agreed and arrived at the first rehearsal probably more nervous than I have ever been in my life.

Actually I needn't have worried; moreover, I should have known that an artist as fine and experienced as Marie Tempest automatically takes direction with more graciousness and docility than a dozen small-part actresses rolled into one. She stamped her foot at me early in rehearsals and said sharply with the utmost decision: 'Come up here, Noel, and play this scene for me. You wrote it and you know it, I didn't write it and don't!' I clambered obediently on to the stage and played the scene as well as I could, whereupon she kissed me and said: 'Excellent, my dear, you've shown me exactly where I was wrong. Let's go back.'

She touched me, thrilled me, and enchanted me all through those rehearsals, and she has touched, thrilled and enchanted me ever since. I have seen her on occasion snappy and bad-tempered, particularly with actors whose lack of talent or casualness in the theatre exasperated her. She has a personal imperiousness that demands good behaviour in others, but if you give in to her too much she'll bully the life out of you. She is lovable as a person and unique as an artist, and her charm is ageless. And if it were not that my intention in this book is to write about me, I should probably continue indefinitely to write about her. In any event she is bound to appear again, for even the most impersonal book dealing with the theatre could not avoid frequent reference to the first lady of it.

We gave an invitation dress rehearsal of *Hay Fever* to which all the actors in London came. They greeted it with hilarious enthusiasm although the general consensus of opinion was that the play was fundamentally too theatrical in flavour and too thin in plot ever to be a success with the public. On the first night I remember dear Eddie Marsh, that Dean of first-nighters, wobbling his head sorrowfully at me and saying: 'Not this time, Noel. Not this time.' He was fortunately wrong. And I went on at the end in response to the calls for 'Author' with a slightly less modest demeanour than usual. I was still smarting from the insults I had received over *Fallen Angels*, and I announced, with some tartness, after I had correctly thanked Marie Tempest and the company, that although the audience and the critics may have found the play a trifle dull, they would at least have to admit that it was as clean as a whistle. This called forth delighted laughter and was later alluded to in the Press as being amusing and witty, thereby proving that my stock that winter was still obstinately high.

The bulk of the notices referred to the play variously as being dull, amusing, thin, slight, tedious, witty and brittle. It ran to excellent business for over a year.

Since *The Vortex* had opened in November I had received several offers from different American managements who wished to present it in New York. For a long while I was undecided which to accept and also, which way to do the play. Either with an all American cast and an American star to play 'Florence,' or else with Lilian and the principals from the English cast. I had a shrewd suspicion that, all personal feelings aside, it would have to be a very fine actress indeed, star or no star, to give a better, or even as good a performance as Lilian. Also the thought of rehearsing from the beginning and playing that heavy last act with somebody else depressed me, and so finally I arranged with Basil Dean that he should take over the play and produce it in New York under the auspices of Charles B. Dillingham and Erlanger. This seemed really to be the most satisfactory arrangement. I knew Basil well and admired his work, and I didn't want to carry the burden of producing the play myself as well as acting in it.

It was ultimately agreed between Basil and me, after a lot of dogged haggling over percentages in course of which Basil became more and more business-like, and I became more and more vaguely artistic, until I finally won from sheer dreamy stubbornness, that we would take with us, in addition to *The Vortex*, *Easy Virtue* and *Nadya*. (This was later re-titled *The Queen was in the Parlour*.) *The Vortex* was to open first with Lilian, Mollie Kerr, Alan Hollis and me and new people for the other parts, and the other two plays were to come later. September the 7th was set for our try-out week in Washington, and as it was now only June I set about making plans for a holiday. I was certainly in need of one, and I persuaded Alban Limpus to let me leave the cast of *The Vortex* and go away. John Gielgud took over my part and played it beautifully, and the play continued for a considerable while after I left. Lilian, I need hardly add, stood staunchly to her post and never missed one performance.

9

I sailed for New York on the *Majestic* in the middle of August. It was a gay, nervous voyage and far from peaceful. In addition to Lilian, Alan Hollis, Basil Dean, Mercy (his wife), Mother, Gladys and me, there were on board, Leslie Howard, Ruth Chatterton, Laura Hope-Crews, Mercédès de Acosta and Eva Le Gallienne. Laura was delightful, and we seemed to know each other well at once. Ruth Chatterton was still and reticent, and it wasn't until long afterwards that I grew to know her as a devoted friend. Eva I had known before. She and Mercédès had been in Paris presenting, rather disastrously, Mercédès' play on Joan of Arc. I think they were sad about it, at any rate they alternated between intellectual gloom and feverish gaiety and wore black, indiscriminately, for both moods. Leslie was vague and amiable and spread his own particular brand of elusive charm over every gathering. The whole trip consisted of gatherings. We had bathing parties, cocktail parties, dinner parties and poker parties. We discussed the theatre exhaustively and from every angle. We were all anxiously looking forward to the autumn season. Leslie was going to play *The Green Hat* with Katherine Cornell. Laura was to do *Hay Fever*, Eva had plans for a few Ibsen revivals. Ruth was going to do *The Man With a Load of Mischief*, Basil and Gladys and I were twittering with our own projects. The sea was calm and the weather fine, but the air on that ship felt definitely electric.

New York looked more beautiful than ever in the early hours of the morning, but by the time we docked most of the colour had been drained away by the full glare of noon. We went to the Plaza for the first few days, and then moved to a singularly inappropriate apartment in East 54th Street, which seemed to have been designed exclusively for the blonde plaything of a tired business man. It was dainty to the point of nausea; however, we saw very little of it, as rehearsals started almost immediately, and there were lots of things to be done. Gladys and I left Mother to deal with the intricacies of American housekeeping, and she shopped, mastered the Frigidaire and engaged coloured maids without turning a hair.

Those first few days were overcrowded and breathlessly hot. I was received with genial kindliness by Charlie Dillingham, who lent me his car and sent us masses of flowers. Everyone we met welcomed us with the utmost enthusiasm and seemed cheerfully convinced that *The Vortex*, although most of them had never seen it, could be nothing but a tumultuous success. Nevertheless, in spite of all this encouragement, an unpleasantness happened very soon. Charles Dillingham and Abe Erlanger were to present the play in conjunction with Basil Dean, and in due course, a conference was called in the Erlanger offices. This was my first meeting with Mr Erlanger, and I had not been in the room five minutes before he informed me that the play could not open in New York until I had rewritten the last act. Although he never removed his feet from his desk throughout the entire interview, he was patient and fatherly with me, explaining that mother-love in America was a real and universally recognised ideal, and that the public would assuredly rise as one man and leave the theatre at the spectacle of a son so vilely abusing the woman who gave him birth. He added, gently, that the little question of reconstruction would not be difficult as he could come to rehearsals and tell me what to do.

He talked for a considerable time. I regarded the over-furnished office, his perspiring form leaning back in shirt-sleeves with a cigar stub in one hand and a lily cup of ice water in the other; the dusty beams of sunlight slanting through the open windows catching refractory gleams from a gargantuan spittoon in the middle of the floor; the 'We must be tactful at all costs' expression on the faces of Basil Dean and Charlie Dillingham; and my spirit revolted.

I remembered that *The Vortex* had been turned down cold by many managers in London and New York, and that I had had finally to borrow money from Michael Arlen to get it produced at all. I remembered the obstacles we had had to overcome during rehearsals. The difficulties, the disappointemnts, the battles and the despairs., I remembered also the impact of that last act upon the first-night audience. And here was this theatrical magnate, soggy with commercial enterprise, prattling smugly to me about the ideal of mother-love, and imagining that I would agree to rewrite my play at his dictation. I knew, in that moment, that I would far rather go back to England the next day and not do the play in America at all, than submit to such insolence.

I must say, to my credit, that I controlled any outward display of temper and waited, politely, until he had finished. Then, ignoring Dillingham's frantic grimaces, I said quite calmly that I intended to play the play exactly as it was, and that, far from listening to any of his suggestions for the altering of the script, I would not even allow him inside the theatre while I was rehearsing. With which I made a swift exit. Not too swift, however, to miss a gratifying roseate suffusion of Mr Erlanger's face and neck. I was overtaken by Basil and Charlie Dillingham in the passage, where they assured me that I had been over-hasty, and that they would guarantee that Erlanger wouldn't worry me at all during rehearsals, and that, with a little tact, he was perfectly easy to manage.

I replied that I had not travelled three thousand miles to manage Mr Erlanger, but for him to manage me, and left them to go back to the office and be as tactful as they liked. The upshot of the whole thing was that Sam Harris and Irving

Berlin took over the play, and Erlanger and Dillingham absolved themselves, misguidedly, from any connection with it.

The important additions to our New York cast were Leo Carril as 'Pawnie' and Auriol Lee as 'Helen.' Auriol was an old friend. She had a witty mind and gave a fine performance.

We had been fortunate in getting the Henry Miller Theatre. It was one of the nicest theatres in New York and perfect, both in size and atmosphere, for the play.

Henry Miller himself was extremely hospitable, and on the first day turned over his private office to me. It was well furnished and comfortable, and had its own shower-bath and dressing-room, and I looked forward to cooling myself luxuriously in it after tiring rehearsals. A few days later, however, Henry Miller went away, and from then onwards the office was inexorably locked, and all my protestations to the house manager were unavailing. He said that there was only one key, and *that* Mr Miller had taken away with him. This seemed to be rather eccentric of Mr Miller, but I remained deeply appreciative of his initial gesture.

Gladys had only two weeks in which to collect all the furniture and get the scenery built, and so we seldom met until evening. She disappeared early each morning into the maw of New York in search of scene-painters and standard lamps and sofas and chairs. It will always be a mystery to me how she managed to get everything done in time, but she did, and with apparent ease.

During the first week of rehearsals I had a letter from Jack Wilson asking me to lunch. Flushed with pride at having even remembered his name, I dictated a letter of acceptance and waited, in a mounting rage, for three-quarters of an hour on the day specified, and finally was forced to lunch alone in a cafeteria. It later transpired that my secretary had never posted the letter.

10

In later years I have travelled extensively. I have sweated through the Red Sea with a following wind and a sky like burnished steel. I have sweated through steamy tropical forests and across arid burning deserts, but never yet, in any Equatorial hell, have I sweated as I sweated in Washington in September 1925. The city felt as though it were dying. There was no breeze, no air, not even much sun. Just a dull haze of breathless discomfort through which the noble buildings could be discerned, gasping, like nude old gentlemen in a steam room. The pavements felt like grey nougat and the least exertion soaked one to the skin.

We floundered through a dress rehearsal on the Sunday night with the make-up streaking down our faces, every extra dab of powder creating gloomy little rice puddings round the corners of our nostrils, and every word we uttered crackling in our throats like brown paper. We prayed ardently for a thunderstorm, prayers to which the Almighty responded with unparalleled thoroughness, granting us not just one thunderstorm during the day to cool the air, but one every night of the week without cooling the air. The first one was timed, with perfect accuracy, to burst in the middle of the second act on the opening night, and from then onwards, in spite of our frantic shrieks, not one word of the play was heard. On the second night the storm broke at the beginning of the last act, and so on throughout the week with monotonous regularity, until we were forced to conclude that God shared Mr Erlanger's views on the sanctity of mother-love and that by offending one I had obviously offended the other.

The only coolness in that unpleasant week was supplied by the Press. The notices referred to the play as unwholesome, dull and mediocre. One critic even went so far as to say that if, as he had heard on good authority, I was considered to be the white hope of the English theatre, God help the English theatre.

We played on the week to a little over six thousand dollars and returned to New York on the Sunday miserably prepared for certain failure. Lilian, I believe, actually had the forethought to make tentative steamship reservations.

We were due to open on the Wednesday night, and Mother and Gladys and I occupied those agonising days by going to plays and moving into a new apartment.

The apartment we had taken was in the Hôtel des Artistes on West 67th Street, and belonged to Miss Mae Murray. Its assets were that it was spacious and high up, and commanded a grand view over Central Park. Its defects were that it was exceedingly expensive and rather trying to the eye. The main studio was Italian Gothic in intent but papier-mâché in reality. There were two elaborately wrought-iron gates which flew away lightly at a touch, and a set of really wrought-iron chairs which were quite immovable. There was a stained-glass window depicting a ship at sea, which lit up at night unless we were careful. Also a tall Renaissance chair with a red velvet cushion under which lived an electric victrola.

In the dining-room there was a wooden trellis over which clambered festoons of tin ivy. I remember looking at it abstractedly as I tried to eat a light meal at six o'clock on the evening of September the sixteenth, 1925.

11

I remember driving from West 67th Street through Central Park and down Sixth Avenue trying, with all the will-power I could exert, to coax myself into a more detached frame of mind. The play was going to be a failure, of that I was convinced. It would be a horrible evening, tense and depressing; certain people I knew would come backstage afterwards and be as sympathetic and comforting as they could, saying, with almost defiant enthusiasm, that I had given a wonderful performance and that they had liked the play anyhow. I knew that behind their kindness I should be able to detect the truth, and have to steel myself to the additional strain of putting up a good show for them; not letting them know that I knew; accepting their politeness with as good a grace as possible; betraying, neither by bitterness nor over-jocularity, that my heart was sick inside me.

I strove vainly to project my mind a few weeks ahead when I should be able to view this dreadful night in perspective, set in its right proportions. After all, it didn't matter as much as all that. My whole career was not going to be blasted by one failure in New York. I had written other plays and intended to write still more. The fact of failure would not, in this instance, necessarily mean that the play was bad; it had been a proven success in London and dealing, as it did, with an extremely small and typically English social group, there was no earthly reason why a New York audience should recognise its values at all; the dialogue, to them, would be nothing but an alien jargon; Washington, by all accounts the most cosmopolitan of cities, had regarded it with blank distaste; the New York reaction would be just so much blanker and, after some bad notices and a week or two of bad business, the show would close, and that would be that.

In this mood of dreary resignation I arrived at the theatre and went in to talk to Lilian for a little while. She was making up lethargically with a white cloth tied round her head, looking remarkably like an early photograph I had seen of her as the Madonna in *The Miracle*, but wearing an expression that was less tranquil and a good deal more pessimistic. 'We can only do our best,' she said, slapping her face viciously with a powder puff, 'and if they don't like it they can do the other thing!'

Both our dressing-rooms were crowded with boxes of flowers and there was a pile of about a hundred and fifty telegrams on my table; many of them from total strangers. All the managers, all the stars, everyone, it seemed, connected with the American theatre, wanted me and the play to be a success. It was my first professional experience of the tremendous warmth and kindness that New York people extend to strangers, and I was touched by it almost beyond endurance. There was a lot of time, far too much time, and I made up slowly and methodically, opening fresh batches of telegrams as they came, and occasionally wandering round the room looking gloomily at the cards on the flowers. Mother and Gladys arrived in due course, dressed up and scented and looking as though they might break if anyone touched them. Basil appeared too, in an opera hat that was a little too small for him. His manner was pathetically breezy, and he slapped me on the back rather harder than he meant to and made me choke. Eventually the 'Five Minutes' was called, and they all went round to the front of the house.

My dressing-room was on the stage level, and I heard the curtain rise. A few minutes later I heard, to my astonishment, a laugh from the audience; then, almost immediately, a bigger one. I could only conclude that either Leo Carril or Auriol Lee had fallen flat on their faces. A little while later there was a prolonged round of applause. That was Lilian's entrance. I got up then and after a final dab at my face and the usual nervous gesture to discover if my fly-buttons were properly done up, I went on to the stage. Lilian was playing her scene at the telephone; I noted a certain strain in her voice, but she was timing beautifully and getting laugh after laugh. Remembering the damp unresponsiveness of Washington I could hardly believe it. I paced up and down gingerly on the strip of coconut matting at the side of the stage and was told by the theatre fireman to put out my cigarette. At last it was near my time to go on, and I stood holding the door knob with a clammy hand, frowning in an effort to keep my face from twitching. My cue came and I made my entrance. There was a second's silence, and then a terrific burst of applause which seemed to me to last for ever. Fortunately the first thing I had to do was to embrace Lilian, which I did with such fervour that her bones cracked. The applause continued, and there we stood locked in each other's arms until I felt her give me a little reassuring pat on the back, and I broke out of the clinch and managed, in a strangulated voice, to speak my first line.

Never before or since in all my experience have I received such a direct personal stimulus from an audience. First nights are always over-strung and nerve-racking. There is always a certain tension and, for leading actors, always a reception on their first entrance. This comes to be regarded less as a tribute than as an inevitable part of a first performance. Some actors like it and say so, some like it and pretend they don't, some really hate it. I belong to the first contingent. To me a round of applause, even though it may interfere for a moment with the action of the play, even though it be conventional rather than spontaneous, almost always sets my performance off on the right foot. On that particular night, however, it did more than that, it saved me. I had expected a little clapping – after all even Washington had accorded me that – but this sound was of such a different quality, and the genuine ring of it uprooted my deep-set conviction of failure and substituted for it a much stronger conviction of success.

There was no false modesty in my astonishment at such an ovation. I had never appeared in New York before. They had no reason to make the smallest demonstration until the end of the evening when they could decide whether or not I merited it. As it was, they made me feel as though I were one of their most beloved and established stars, and I tried with everything I had in me to deserve it. I do know, to my lasting satisfaction, that I gave the best performance that night that I have ever given in my life.

In *The Vortex* we had made it a rule not to take any curtain calls until the end of the play. This was not a new idea in America, although in London, where the public were inured to watching a row of actors bowing and smiling after every act, it was considered to be quite an innovation. It is now, I am thankful to say, usual in both countries. On that first night in New York the play ran more smoothly than it had ever run. Everyone in the cast seemed to be inspired, and when the curtain fell after the piano-playing scene at the end of the second act, there was prolonged cheering, so prolonged, indeed, that we could still hear it while we were changing in our dressing-rooms.

We had now only the last act to be got through, but it was technically the most difficult of all, and we enjoined each other urgently to keep clear and cool, and to hold everything in reserve until the last few minutes.

We played it with the utmost wariness, feeling the audience completely with us. There wasn't a fidget or a sneeze or a noseblow, or even a cough. The whole act was received in absorbed silence. The curtain fell and rose again on the final picture of me kneeling with my head buried in Lilian's lap while she mechanically stroked my hair, still in dead silence, until, just as it fell for the second time, the cheering broke over us, and we struggled trembling to our feet.

I had rehearsed a polite little speech in my mind in case it should be called for, but when the time came for me to say it, my throat was so constricted that I was able only to mumble a few incoherent words of thanks and clench my hands tightly to prevent myself from breaking down.

We stood in our dressing-rooms afterwards for over an hour receiving. A few faces in that procession stand out in my mind: Mother's, very pink and powdered over tear-stains; Gladys's aloof and almost expressionless except for a triumphant glint in the eye; Jeanne Eagels's, with little rivulets of mascara trickling down her cheeks. I was hugged and kissed and crowned with glory, and that night is set apart in my memory, supreme and unspoilt, gratefully and for ever.

12

The Press notices the next day were enthusiastic and the advance sale tremendous. Ticket speculators bought up seats and sold them, sometimes on the side-walk outside the theatre, for as much as twenty and twenty-five dollars a pair. It was obviously a violent and glittering success, and I became, extremely happily, the talk of the town. I was photographed and caricatured and interviewed and publicised with even more thoroughness than in London. I was the guest of honour in all directions and made brief speeches at immense ladies' luncheons. I was invited to restful week-ends in large houses on Long Island, but these I had to give up very soon, as they were far too strenuous, and I was too tired after such clamorous relaxation to be able to give a good performance on Monday evenings.

Jack Wilson appeared at the stage door of the Henry Miller after the first matinée. He had been to a cocktail party where he had drunk enough to give him enough courage to come and attack me for not having answered his invitation to lunch. Fortunately I remembered his face and after a moment's scurried thinking, his name, which mollified him somewhat and after a few high words in the alley, I took him back to dine at the studio where Gladys, with royal thoroughness, also remembered him at once, so that his outraged feelings were soon smoothed out.

From then onwards we became close friends, and a few months later he gave up being a stockbroker in order to be my personal manager, in which capacity he has bullied me firmly ever since.

The Vortex being safely launched I had to start work immediately on *Hay Fever*.

There had been a considerable muddle over the casting owing to the eccentric behaviour of the Shuberts, who were given to engaging people recklessly without even a cursory knowledge of the types required by the script.

On the morning of the first rehearsal I walked on to the stage of the Broadhurst Theatre and was startled to find a company of over thirty which, for a comedy of nine characters, seemed excessive. I weeded them out gradually, but one lady gave me a great deal of trouble. She was a brassy blonde in a *décolleté* afternoon dress of black lace, and was lying on her back on a wooden bench chewing gum with an expression of studied languor. At first she replied to my questioning laconically, but even in her monosyllables it was not difficult to detect a strong Brooklyn accent. I asked her what part Mr Shubert had promised her and, shifting the gum from one side of her mouth to the other, she replied, 'Myra,' and turned her head away wearily as though the whole interview were distasteful to her. Out of the corner of my eye I observed Laura Hope-Crews at the prompt table convulsed with laughter. I persevered, with as much tact as I could manage, and said that I was extremely sorry, but that Myra was such a typically English character she could obviously not be played with such a thorough-going American accent; whereupon the blonde rose in a sudden fury, spat her gum neatly into a chiffon handkerchief, said: 'Accent Hell! I've got a contract,' and flounced off the stage.

The fact that she had indeed got a contract cost me many wasteful hours in the Shubert office later.

Eventually after days of argument the cast was set – never, I must say, to my satisfaction – but I was at a loss in New York, and had, more or less, to accept actors on other people's recommendation.

Hay Fever played a trial week in Brooklyn, and opened in New York at the Maxine Elliot Theatre to a specially invited audience on a Sunday night.

I had decided, with careless optimism, to give a large party at my studio after the show, to celebrate its success, and I sat, during the performance, wishing with all my heart that I hadn't. It was, without exception, one of the most acutely uncomfortable evenings I have ever spent in the theatre. Everyone of artistic importance in New York was there. All the stars, all the writers, and all the critics. Not only were they there in the theatre, but most of them were coming to the party afterwards, and I, being in a box with Mother and Gladys and Jack, had an uninterrupted view of their faces as the play proceeded majestically, and with measured tread towards complete failure. The cast, never inspired at best, seemed utterly crushed by the splendour of the audience, all of them, that is, excepting Laura, who, in a praiseworthy but misguided effort to lift the play and her fellow-actors out of the lethargy in which they were rapidly congealing, gave a performance of such unparalleled vivacity that it completely overbalanced everything.

The critics tore her to pieces the next day for over-acting, which indeed she did, but what they didn't realise, and what I realised fully, was that in the circumstances it was certainly excusable. She lost her head a bit and hit too hard, but she was surrounded by a cast who were lying down and not hitting at all.

The applause at the end was polite, and the atmosphere in Laura's dressing-room strained. She knew, and I knew, and everybody knew, that the play was a flop; however, there was the party to be got through, and Laura gallantly agreed to come to it in spite of everything.

Many of the guests had already arrived by the time I got back to the studio, having left the theatre as quickly as they could in order to evade backstage condolences. Apprehensive social smiles seemed to be glued on to the face of everyone, and the preliminary gaiety was forced, to say the least of it. Looking back at it, that party was hilarious; at the time, however, it was pretty dreadful, especially for the first hour or so before the dampness of the play had been dispelled by liquor. Laura's social performance was superb; this time she didn't overact a fraction; she was gay and gracious and accepted guarded compliments with the most genuine of smiles.

The Press notices the next day were extremely depressing and the advance sale non-existent, and the play, having played to rapidly diminishing business for about six weeks, gently expired.

13

Christmas came and went with its attendant festivities, and owing to a throat infection, my voice went with it, and I was forced to stay out of the cast for a whole week. My understudy was a boy called Allen Vincent, who played the piano excellently.

Basil Dean was busy producing John Van Druten's first play, *Young Woodley*, and when that had been successfully launched we devoted ourselves to Jane Cowl and *Easy Virtue*.

Although Jane Cowl has been described with amusing malice by Mr Joseph Reed in his book *The Curtain Falls*, I should like to have a slap at her too; my slap, however, will be more in the nature of a loving pat, as I found her, both in spite of and because of her temperament and capriciousness, a most enchanting personality. To begin with, she is everything a famous theatrical star is expected to be; beautiful, effective, gracious, large-hearted, shrewd in everything but business, foolishly generous, infinitely kind to lesser people of the theatre, extremely annoying on many small points, and over and above everything else, a fine actress. She and Basil inaccurately measured each other's quality early on, and proceeded firmly to misunderstand each other on every possible occasion.

The production of *Easy Virtue* was tricky, especially the dance scene in the last act which Basil, with his usual passion for detail, polished within an inch of its life. The cast, on the whole, was excellent, and the play opened, after a trial week in Newark, at the Empire Theatre where it was received with only moderate acclaim. Jane's performance was smooth and touching, but she always played the big scene at the end of the second act too dramatically, thereby jerking the play too far back into the Pineroism from which it had originally sprung. My object in writing it had been primarily to adapt a story, intrinsically Pinero in theme and structure, to present-day behaviour; to compare the *déclassée* woman of to-day with the more flamboyant *demi-mondaine* of the nineties. The line that was intended to establish the play on a basis of comedy rather than tragedy, comes at the end of the second act when Larita, the heroine, irritated beyond endurance by the smug attitude of her 'in-laws,' argues them out of the room and collapses on to the sofa where, suddenly catching sight of a statuette of the Venus de Milo on a pedestal, she shies a book at it and says: 'I always hated that damned thing!'

Jane invariably delivered this line in a voice strangled with sobs and brought the curtain down to tremendous applause. If, however, she had said it and played the scene leading up to it with less emotion and more exasperation, I don't think that the play would have received quite so much criticism on the score of being old-fashioned. On the other hand there would probably not have been so much applause, and so I expect that Jane, from her point of view, if not from the play's, was quite right.

At all events she made an enormous personal success, and if I had to bear the gleeful laughter of Alexander Woollcott and a few stinging comments from the other critics, I had, at least, the satisfaction of knowing that Jane was filling the theatre to virtual capacity, and that the play would certainly run for months.

14

I remember drinking-in the year 1926 alone with Mother. We had a bottle of champagne all to ourselves, and stood at the window looking out over Central Park. There had been a heavy fall of snow, but the night was clear and starry; the traffic far below us looked like a procession of toys illuminated for some gigantic children's party, and when we opened the window the noise of it sounded muffled and unreal.

All along upper Fifth Avenue and West 59th Street the buildings glittered with lights; it was a beautiful sight, but so alien to us that it made us homesick. We both sighed for the gentle familiarity of London. Mother kept on saying: 'I wonder what Eric and Arthur and Vida are doing,' and refraining from the obvious surmise that they were probably bickering like mad, I allowed the sentimentality of the moment to have its fling, and pictured the Ebury Street house *en fête*, left-over Christmas decorations looped from the ceiling of the bungalow and festooned over Grandfather's sword; Father sipping inferior port and cracking nuts, and Eric and Auntie Vida wearing firemen's hats and laughing immoderately.

We stood with our glasses correctly poised while the ice-cold air blew over us through the open window; syrens were blowing and bells were ringing, and a wave of depression engulfed us. I knew, from the trembling of Mother's lip, that she was remembering too much, but my own thoughts were occupied more with the future than with the past. I think I realised in that moment how warily I should have to go; how infinitely more dangerous the achievement of ambition was than the struggle to achieve it. Here we were, Mother and I, having survived many despairs, at last safe, financially safe at any rate, for quite a while, providing we weren't too foolishly extravagant and providing that my grip on my talents didn't become loosened with too much success. How dreadful it would be, having got so far, to sink slowly back; not perhaps this year, nor even the next year, but later, when praise and publicity and 'stage centre' had insidiously become necessary to me, too necessary to be discarded without heart-break. The picture of a one-time white-headed boy advancing bitterly into middle age with yesterday's Press headlines yellowing in a scrap-book, and only an occasional Sunday night performance by the Stage Society to remind him of past glories, seemed far from improbable and almost too depressing to be borne. Perhaps I was over-tired. Perhaps I was wiser than I knew, but instead of welcoming that new year with a grin of triumph, which in the circumstances I had every right to do, I greeted it suspiciously, with guarded politeness, like a newly-crowned King receiving the leader of the Socialist Party at his first levée.

However, natural resilience and another glass of champagne dissipated the mood, and we both began to giggle at the spectacle of ourselves, hovering on the verge of sentimental tears in a Metro-Goldwyn-Mayer mausoleum. We retired to bed early in a gale of hiccups, and the next morning 1926 seemed happily indistinguishable from 1925.

15

By this time I had whittled down my large circle of New York acquaintances to the small group of people I really liked. I had for some weeks been gradually eliminating big parties, finding them tiring and almost always disappointing. Before, I had accepted every invitation with a little thrill of anticipation; So-and-so was going to be there, and also Such-and-such, and it would sure to be gay, and I should probably meet someone new and exciting. It didn't take me long to realise that there was little or no novelty in any large party; people looked the same and talked the same and sang the same songs and made the same jokes. Only very occasionally, for a brief hour or two, generally round about three in the morning when most of the guests had gone, a certain magic occurred, and the few who were left really relaxed and enjoyed themselves; but these moments were rare, and you could never be sure that the various elements were really going to fuse successfully. Even if they did, awareness that there was a rehearsal the next morning, or a matinée to be played the next afternoon, made the dreary hours of waiting hardly worth while.

Frances Wellman, whom I had known since my first visit to New York, administered, like Elsa Maxwell in Paris and Sibyl Colefax in London, the best social mixtures. At the crack of her whip Park Avenue clapped Broadway on the back, and Broadway generously went through its hoops for Park Avenue. I soon discovered, however, that Park Avenue, like Mayfair, had not yet acquired the estimable habit of keeping quiet when someone was entertaining them. It appeared that life was too swift for them, too crowded with excitement and endeavour, to permit them to sit still and listen to some fine musician such as George Gershwin or Vincent Youmans or Richard Rodgers, without breaking the spell by whispering shrilly, or demanding, over-loudly, the few songs they happened to know. It was on account of this odd restlessness that one had to wait so long for most parties to become good. However, Frances organised well as a rule, and professionals were allowed to show off to their hearts' content, without too much competition from amateurs.

My own entertaining was usually confined to small suppers after the show, when nobody was expected to dress, and music and conversation were possible without strain.

16

After a run of just over five months *The Vortex* closed in New York, and we went off on a short road tour. Mollie Kerr returned home to England and an excellent actress, Rose Hobart, took over the part of 'Bunty.' With this exception, the cast remained the same.

I cannot say that I look back on that tour with any pleasure. The business was good for the first few weeks, but I was too tired of playing that heavy part night after night to care much. It was then that I made a vow that never again in any circumstances would I play a play for longer than six months, preferably three months in London and three months in New York. For an actor alone, this decision would seem to be rather high-handed, but I was a writer too, and the routine of eight performances a week, with all the attendant obligations, precluded any chance of concentration on new ideas. Nobody but an actor knows the vitality that has to be expended during a single performance; even after months of playing, when you move through the play automatically and without nerves, you still have to be strung up to a certain extent in order to get yourself on to the stage at all. In *The Vortex* there was always the last act hanging over me; the interminable physical strain of lashing myself, on cue, into the requisite frenzy. There were bad nights when the tears wouldn't come at the right moment, or when they came too soon and dried up completely just before they were really wanted. There were scarifying moments when suddenly my mind went blank, and I had no idea what came next or what had gone before. This happens to many actors when they play long runs. The displacement of a chair; the ticking of a clock; a sudden unexpected sound, either backstage or in the front of the house, or a new intonation on one of the other actor's lines is quite enough to dry them up dead. It is a horrible sickening sensation and leaves you shaken and insecure, not only for the rest of the evening, but for several performances afterwards.

Audiences, too, after the first month or so, begin to deteriorate in quality, and whereas during the first part of a run you can count on at least five good audiences a week, later, the percentage gets lower and lower until every performance seems drearier than the last, and it is only very rarely that you feel, on your first entrance, that blessed electric tension in the front of the house which means that for once you won't have to pump the words over the footlights, and nurse and coddle every line until your nerves ache with boredom.

The Mecca of our tour was Chicago. The company reminded each other at frequent intervals of the delights of that city. 'Wait,' they said, ignoring the kindly enthusiasm of Newark, Brooklyn and Cincinnati, 'wait until we get to Chicago. There, they'll really appreciate the play. There they'll eat it up!'

We arrived in Chicago having been advertised to play a six-weeks' season, but reserving smugly to oursleves the right to prolong this indefinitely. Mother was with me and Jack; Gladys wasn't, as she was on tour with Eva Le Gallienne working with her on plans for the formation of the famous Civic Repertory Company for which she, Gladys, was to be art director. On the advice of Mary Garden we had reserved an expensive suite at the Lake Shore Drive Hotel, in addition to which I had ordered my car to come from New York and be there to greet us when we arrived. The car had been, at the outset, a wild extravagance. It was a vintage Rolls-Royce with a shining new Brewster body which successfully concealed from the casual eye the aged dilapidation of its engines. Ravished by its appearance, I had bought it against all unprejudiced advice. After all it was a Rolls-Royce, and Rolls-Royces were well known to last for ever, also the drive was on the right-hand side, which would be very useful in England. The fact that I had often stepped in to it outside the stage door and been forced to step out on the other side into a taxi, I merely ascribed to the inadequacy of the chauffeur. At all events, it looked marvellous, and although in the long run it cost me as much as three new Bentleys, I am still grateful to it for the many plutocratic thrills it gave me.

It managed to reach Chicago all right, and met us at the station, and we drove out to the Lake Shore Drive, none too impressed with the atmosphere of the town, but determined to enjoy our stay there as much as we could.

Mary Garden had lovingly and generously written a squib for the papers – 'My divine breezy city, you have with you four words that spell "Genius": Noel Coward, *The Vortex*!' – and we opened to a packed house at the Selwyn Theatre on the night of George Washington's birthday.

They seemed unappreciative of the comedy in the first act, but we struggled manfully across the damp patches where the laughs should have been, deciding in our minds that they were a dramatic audience rather than a comedy one. In this we were wrong. They were essentially out for comedy, and they got their first big belly-laugh at the curtain of the second act. This struck me like a blow on the head. With every audience I had ever played it to, I had always been able to rely on complete absorption at the particular moment; it was really the most tragic scene of the play, when the son plays jazz more and more feverishly in order to drown the sound and sight of his mother abasing herself before her young lover. Chicago, however, saw it only as supremely comic, and Lilian and I retired to our dressing-rooms with prolonged laughter instead of prolonged cheers ringing in our ears. I was trembling with rage; I wanted to go out before the curtain and inform that gay holiday-spirited audience that this was the first and last time that I would ever appear in their divine, breezy city, and that to save themselves and me further trouble they could go back to their dance-halls and speak-easies immediately as there was not going to be any last act at all. Lilian restrained me by gripping me by the shoulders and hissing in my face: 'Remember you are English! Remember you are English!'

The last act was worse than I could ever have imagined it to be. The sight of me in pyjamas and dressing-gown started them off happily, and from then onwards they laughed without ceasing. Never, since *Charley's Aunt* on a Saturday night in Blackpool, have I heard such uproarious mirth in a theatre. The curtain fell to considerable applause, and I even had to make a speech, which, remembering that I was English, was a model of grateful restraint.

I have regretted ever since that I didn't tell them what I thought of them; it wouldn't have made any difference, as the play was a dead failure, and it would, at least, have given me a little satisfaction.

The two principal critics of the town wrote two such diverse notices that they nullified each other. Ashton Stevens said that the play was great and fine and subtle and tragic, while his confrère, whose name I forget, said it was cheap and comic and stupid and dull. Unfortunately we couldn't close at once because there was no other attraction ready to come into the theatre. Pauline Lord was playing next door in *They Knew What They Wanted*, and came popping in as often as she could to cheer us up, but apart from her my theatrical career in Chicago was miserable.

Socially, however, everyone was extremely kind. I was made a member of the Riding Club, and rode every morning with Diana Cooper and Iris Tree, who were playing *The Miracle* at the Auditorium. There were gay supper parties given almost every night, and when they weren't, we gave impromptu ones in our hotel and ran up and downstairs between each other's kitchenettes bearing bacon and cheese and ginger-ale.

Diana and Iris and Rudolph Kommer were at the Lake Shore Drive; Pauline

Lord, Helen Hayes and Judith Anderson were not far away, and apart from the horrible hours I had to spend in the theatre, I had quite a good time.

Before leaving the Selwyn Theatre, Chicago, I wrote on the wall of my dressing-room in indelible pencil, 'Noel Coward died here,' and when I visited Clifton Webb in the same room years later, I was delighted to see that the inscription was still there.

Cleveland received us kindly, and we finished our tour to good business. I don't ever remember feeling so relieved and happy as I did on that last night. I had played the part over four hundred and fifty times, and although during the tour I had forced myself to write a play, it had been a tremendous strain, and I felt that many months of creative impulse had been frustrated. The play I wrote was called *Semi-Monde*, and the whole action of it took place in the public rooms of the Ritz Hotel in Paris over a period of three years. It was well constructed and, on the whole, well written; its production in London or New York seemed unlikely as some of the characters, owing to lightly suggested abnormalities, would certainly be deleted by the censor; Max Reinhardt, however, was enthusiastic about it, and it was translated into German by Rudolph Kommer and taken in due course to Berlin, where for years it escaped production by a hair's breadth until eventually Vicky Baum wrote *Grand Hotel*, and *Semi-Monde*, being too closely similar in theme, faded gently into oblivion.

Mother and I had reservations on the *Olympic* which didn't sail for two weeks, and so I left her in New York and went to Palm Beach to stay with my old friends, Florence and John Magee. It was an uneventful but lovely holiday. The air was soft and the sea blue, and I bathed and lay in the sun. There were dinner parties, lunch parties and picnic parties. Perhaps they were dull, perhaps they weren't; I only know that I enjoyed every minute of them. I was out of prison; free! Not for as long as I liked would I again have to be in any theatre every night at a certain time. I could have a nice strong cocktail before dinner with a clear conscience, and no fears that it might spoil my performance. Of course it was conceivable that too strong a cocktail might spoil my performance at dinner, but I don't think it ever did, and I returned to New York decently tanned and feeling a great deal better.

17

Jack, having already wisely invested a lot of my money in American securities, and having convinced his family that a career as my business manager would ultimately prove more lucrative than that of a stockbroker, was sailing to England with Mother and me. We had drawn up an elaborate contract in a lawyer's office, bristling with legal technicalities, options and percentages, so that in the event of sudden unforeseen mutual hatred, we could still continue to work together, however dourly, on a business basis.

Happily that situation has not, to date, occurred and as during the last ten years we have weathered more storm and stress than the average business association has to combat in a lifetime, I think it can safely be said that our original summing up of each other's characters was fairly shrewd. During that voyage home I remember feeling a little apprehensive over Lorn. I wondered how she would welcome the introduction into our slap-dash business lives of a hard-headed and extremely uncompromising American. Fortunately, however, my fears were groundless, as they took to each other on sight; in fact, the only scenes that have ever taken place since have been the result of both of them, for some reason or other, basely combining against me.

18

The Rolls-Royce was brought over to London at great expense, and on the rare occasions when it was not being overhauled at Derby, I drove about in it with considerable satisfaction and found that the streets of London, although retaining their well-worn familiarity, took on a new sheen viewed through Rolls-Royce windows. Bouncing along on gracious, buff-coloured upholstery, I noted with a thrill of conscious pleasure various landmarks of my still very recent past. Garrick Street, Bedford Street, Leicester Square, Shaftesbury Avenue, St Martin's Lane, looking in the warm May sunlight so exactly the same, still, in the mornings, thronged with actors hurrying in and out of agents' offices, stage doors, and rehearsal rooms. Even the chocolates and cakes in the windows of the Corner House seemed unchanged except for the difference that now I no longer yearned for them. It felt strange after months in America to be back again as an established star. True, I had been that when I left, but now Time had allowed the sediment of novelty to settle a bit, and I could accept the situation more tranquilly. The success in New York seemed to have added assurance to my position. This was all right, concrete. The sense of unreality had faded, and I no longer felt as though I were flying faster and faster through a nervous dream.

Easy Virtue was playing its last weeks in New York, and Basil had arranged to present it in London with Jane and practically the same cast in June. Meanwhile there was nothing much to do, and so I went off for a trip to the South of France, Sicily and Tunis. While in Palermo I wrote a new comedy called *This Was a Man*. It was primarily satirical and on the whole rather dull; the bulk of its dullness lay in the second act which was an attenuated duologue between two excessively irritating characters. The fact that the characters were intended to be irritating in no way mitigated the general boredom, and this vital error in construction ultimately cost the play its life.

On my return to London I showed it to Basil, who thought it excellent, and so we sent it to Lord Cromer for a licence with the intention of producing it immediately after *Easy Virtue*. The licence, however, was refused, principally, I think, because of a scene in the last act when the husband, on being told that his annoying wife had committed adultery with his still more annoying best friend, bursts out laughing. The fact that the circumstances of the story made this behaviour more than permissible weighed not a jot with the board of censors, who like the commandments broken solemnly or not at all; and so, after a little gleeful publicity in the Press, the play was shelved for later production in America.

Jane arrived three days before we were due to open *Easy Virtue*, and we travelled up to Manchester. The Manchester Watch Committee, for some strange reason known only to itself, refused to allow us to use the title *Easy Virtue*, and so it was announced merely as *A New Play in Three Acts*. At the cinema next door to the theatre a film entitled *Flames of Passion* was complacently advertised for the whole week: perhaps, however, the vigilance of the Watch Committee did not extend to mere celluloid. *A New Play in Three Acts* was a big success, and Jane made a gracious first-night speech, explaining that she was a stranger and rather scared, but that she already felt absolutely at home in dear Manchester. She was appropriately mobbed by the gallery girls at the stage door and conveyed in triumph to the Midland.

London fell into Jane's lap like a ripe plum. She made a tumultuous success and was immediately adored. She still played the end of the second act too emotionally, and the dramatic impact she gave to it still brought forth terrific cheering. The bulk of the critics sniffed superciliously at the play, but I was prepared for this and didn't mind much. The business was excellent, and everybody rightly felt that the London Theatre was the richer by the presence of a new and glamorous star.

19

Almost immediately after the production of *Easy Virtue*, *The Queen was in the Parlour* went into rehearsal at the St Martin's Theatre. The cast, headed by Madge Titheradge, included Herbert Marshall, Francis Lister, C. M. Hallard, Ada King and Lady Tree. The rehearsals were remarkable for the fact that Madge and Basil worked together in complete peace and harmony. By this time, having worked with Basil a good deal, I had grown to know him very well, not only as a producer but as a person. The two were in no way synonymous. As a man he was pleasant, occasionally gay with an almost childish abandon, and in his more relaxed moments exceedingly good company. As a producer he could be and frequently was a fiend. It was not that he meant to be in the least, but his genuine passion for perfection of detail, his technical thoroughness, and his tireless energy as a rule completely shut him off from any personal contact with his companies. He often blinked at me in amazement when I told him how bitterly he had offended So-and-so, or how unnecessarily cruel he had been when poor Miss Such-and-such had been unable to get the right intonation. I don't think it ever occurred to him that actors' feelings are notoriously nearer to the surface than average people's; if they weren't they wouldn't be good actors. Every good surgeon knows that no operation, however swift and brilliant, can ultimately be considered a complete success if sensitive membranes and organs and viscera have been handled carelessly in the process. A first-rate theatrical producer should learn early on in his career that most actors wear their intestines on their sleeves. Basil's only real failing in the theatre was lack of psychological perceptiveness. His actors on the whole were terrified of him; frequently even stars of big reputation quailed before him. True, their fear took various forms, but it was there all right, under their blusterings and ragings and tearful refusals to do this or that. His knowledge and efficiency were undeniable and his personality was strong, but generally, rehearsals under Basil were nerve-racking. Jane, who had fought him stubbornly step by step, finally won hands down, slightly at the expense of the play. Madge never fought him at all. She took his direction with enthusiasm automatically changing anything she didn't approve of, but with such expert technique that I don't believe he ever noticed. She agreed wtih everything he said and emerged triumphantly at the end of it unruffled by anything but her own temperament. Her performance of *The Queen was in the Parlour* was flawless both in its comedy values and its moments of tragedy. She gave to the play more reality and pathos than it actually deserved, and although as an experiment in Ruritanian romanticism it wasn't so bad, it was Madge, I am sure, aided by a brilliant cast and production, who made it the success it was.

20

We gave up the little house in Dockenfield and set to work to find somewhere less cramped and villa-ish and in deeper country than Surrey. There were many kindly memories attached to it: the first day when it had risen out of a thick fog to welcome us; long spring evenings when we had made toffee on its inadequate stove and listened to the rain dripping through the bathroom ceiling into a tin basin; lovely summer nights when we had driven down late from London, tearing much too fast over the long straight stretch of the Hog's Back, whirling through Farnham with only a few lights winking at us from the sleeping houses, finally arriving at that kind, silly little villa squatting on its haunches in a field.

I wanted, if possible, to be near the sea, and I naturally turned towards Kent where we had been so happy before. We stared at advertisements of houses to let in the *Kentish Times* until our eyes ached. None of them were any good. They were either too old and falling to pieces, or so new that they were horrible. Finally we were on the verge of fixing upon a more or less passable-looking red-brick house at Stone near Rye, when we had a letter from Mr Body, our one-time neighbour at St Mary's. He wanted to let his farmhouse at Aldington and move into one that he had just built on the Marsh. Mother went down and saw it first and said it was all right, but rather poky; I went down a little later on and agreed with her, but as the rent was only fifty pounds a year and it had six acres of ground, electric light and a garage, it seemed a good idea to take it for a year or so, still keeping a lookout for something better. It was called, floridly enough, 'Goldenhurst Farm.' There was the house proper which was lop-sided and had a Victorian air; jammed up against this was the 'new wing,' a square edifice wearing perkily a pink corrugated tin roof and looking as though it had just dropped in on the way to the races. There was a muddy yard enclosed by thatched barns which were falling to pieces, there were two small ponds, five poplars, a ramshackle garden consisting almost entirely of hedges, and an ancient, deeply green orchard with thick grass and low-growing apple-trees. At the end of the garden the land sloped away to the Military Canal and one could see across miles of marshes to Dymchurch and the sea-wall. Beyond this the sea looked high as though it were painted on the sky; on clear nights the lights on the French coast glimmered along the horizon.

The house itself was indeed poky and quite hideous, made up into dark little rooms and passages, but there was a certain atmosphere about the place that felt soothing and somehow right, and so we decided to move in the moment the Bodys moved out in October.

21

Easy Virtue and *The Queen was in the Parlour* ran along together for a little, and when *Easy Virtue* closed because Jane had to go back to America, *The Queen was in the Parlour* was transferred from the St Martin's to the Duke of York's. In the meantime Basil was planning *The Constant Nymph* and suggested that I should play Lewis Dodd for the first month of the run. I wasn't at all keen, as it was a heavy part and I was feeling exceedingly tired, also it meant postponing until November our production of *This was a Man* in New York. However, Edna Best was to play Tessa, and after a good deal of argument both she and Basil prevailed upon me and we started rehearsals.

It was a crowded play and Basil tore himself and us to shreds over the production of it. As an actor it was excellent experience for me, being utterly unlike anything I had ever played before. Basil adamantly refused to allow me to use any of myself in it at all. I wasn't even permitted to smoke cigarettes, but had, with bitter distaste, to manoeuvre a pipe. I had grown my hair long and put no grease on it for a month, consequently it was dry and fluffy and sparks from the pipe frequently blew up and set fire to it. In addition to the pipe, I wore purposely ill-fitting suits, and spectacles through which I peered short-sightedly; altogether I don't remember ever having been so thoroughly uncomfortable on the stage in my life. I hated Lewis Dodd whole-heartedly from the first rehearsal onwards. In the book his character was clearly defined and understandable; in the play he seemed to me to be a clumsy insensitive oaf with little to recommend him over and above the fact that he was supposed to be a musical genius. I say 'supposed to be', because, beyond a few modern piano chords and a burlesque opera in the first act and a little Scarlatti and a doggerel rhyme in the second, he betrayed no marked talent whatsoever. I was told, even by my most uncompromising critics, that I gave a fine and convincing performance, which still comforts me, as I was under the impression then, and am still, that I was awful.

Edna gave a tender, exquisite portrayal of Tessa and was so gallant and moving in the death-scene at the end that she almost made me forget my own dreariness.

The whole production, with its multitude of small parts, ensemble scenes and minute details, was magnificently done; the doing of it, however, was gruelling work. The party scene was Basil's pet, and we went over and over it endlessly until, whatever spontaneity there might have been at the beginning, set like cement in our joints, and we were unable even to remember our words. There was also a supper scene in the first act to which he was extremely attached. It had more props in it than *Ben Hur*: plates, mugs, knives, forks, spoons, bread, jam, cheese, biscuits, ham, all of which had to be manipulated on cue. Wooden benches and tables and chairs had to be moved on to their correct marks for the opera scene immediately following it. Owing to there being so many of us, there were no consecutive sentences lasting for more than a few lines, and so we had to listen like hawks and spear our cues out of the general chaos like fish from a boiling cauldron. The effect from the front was, of course, masterly, but the strain on the stage was unbelievable.

In the second act alone I had three two-minute changes: lounge suit to tails, back to lounge suit, and back to tails again; these changes were achieved frenziedly at the side of the stage, usually in the pitch dark. Before the death scene I had only one minute in a black-out in which to change completely from evening clothes to flannel trousers, shirt, tie, thick socks, shoes, hat and coat, with the result that I generally shot on to the stage like a rabbit with no breath at all. It was worse than revue because once on, the scenes were long and difficult, whereas in revue nothing lasts longer than a few minutes.

That rehearsal period was a bad time for my unfortunate intimates. Lorn and Jack bore most of the brunt of it. I gave up the part publicly on Mondays, Wednesdays, and Saturdays, and privately every night of the week. Basil, impervious to my wailings, kept my nose firmly to the grindstone, and I know whatever good there was in my performance was entirely due to him. Margaret Kennedy, the authoress, twittered in and out endeavouring, with sudden bursts of the most obvious tact, to persuade me how good I was going to be, although I am certain that she had an unshakable conviction that I was as much like her beloved Lewis Dodd as the Queen of Sheba.

Mrs Patrick Campbell rang me up on the day of the last dress rehearsal and implored me to allow her to come, explaining at length that she was a poor unwanted old woman and couldn't afford seats for the first night. She arrived rather late, bearing in her arms a Pekinese which yapped insistently through the quieter scenes. The next morning, the actual day of production, she rang me up again. Her voice sounded sympathetic over the telephone; she said that she had enjoyed the play very much and that the little fair girl (Edna) was quite good, but that, why, oh why, had I ever consented to play the part? 'You're the wrong *type!*' she moaned. 'You have no glamour and you should wear a beard!'

The play opened and was an immediate smashing success. I moved through the opening performance in a dull coma of depression. Jack appeared in my dressing-room after the second act and told me that everyone was saying how marvellous I was; this I took to be a well-intentioned but transparent lie, and asked him gloomily to go away and leave me alone, which, to my considerable irritation, he did. I played Lewis Dodd for just over three weeks, and then my nerves, resenting at last the strain that had been imposed upon them for the past two years, finally snapped and I went through one whole performance weeping for no reason whatever, to the bewilderment, not only of the audience but of the cast as well. Edna guided and upheld me as well as she could, and at the end I subsided on the floor of my dressing-room, where I remained until my doctor arrived and gave me a strychnine injection and put me to bed.

I stayed in bed for a week without seeing anybody, and then, feeling slightly rested, insisted, against the doctor's advice, on sailing for New York.

I was certainly in no condition to enjoy the rehearsals of *This was a Man*; indeed, even if I had been as radiant with health as a Phosferine advertisement, I doubt if I could have derived much pleasure from that dreariest of dreary productions.

My withdrawal from the cast of *The Constant Nymph* made no more difference to the business than if an aunt of Margaret Kennedy's had died in Scotland. John Gielgud took over Lewis Dodd and played it successfully for a year, pipe and all.

22

My first serious play, *The Rat Trap*, was produced at the Everyman Theatre while I was on the *Olympic* bound for New York, and so I never saw it; however, from what I gathered later from eye-witnesses, I didn't miss much.

The leading parts were played by Robert Harris, Joyce Kennedy and Mary Robson, and the smaller ones by Adrianne Allen, Elizabeth Pollock and Raymond Massey. But in spite of the effulgence of the cast, the play fizzled out at the end of its regulation two weeks. I was not particularly depressed about this; *The Rat Trap* was a dead love. Seven years had passed since I wrote it with so much ardour, and during those years its glory had been eclipsed by more balanced and mature work. It had achieved publication at least, and I could read it in my first volume of *Three Plays* with indulgent cluckings of the tongue at its youthful gaucheries. The two big scenes were still good, but the first act with its strained epigrams and laboured exposition of character, and the last act in which the heroine bravely admits that she is going to have a baby, thereby tying up the plot with a bow on the top, made me shudder, nostalgically, but with definite embarrassment. It was neither good enough nor bad enough to merit a West-End run, and it was perhaps a mistake to have allowed it to be produced at all; however no harm was done, and I am sure that it was admirable exercise for the actors.

On arrival in New York we set to work to find an attractive star to play the extremely unattractive part of Carol in *This was a Man*. This was difficult, and it was only after considerable blandishments that we persuaded Francine Larrimore to do it. As a type she was miscast, but her name was a draw and she was a first-rate actress. The other principals were Auriol Lee, Nigel Bruce and A. E. Matthews

The rehearsals were slow and uncomfortable and the tension increased by the fact that Basil's effect on Nigel Bruce was much the same as that of a python on a rabbit. Like so many large, bluff and hearty actors, Nigel was acutely sensitive and tremulous with nerves. He knew his lines perfectly until he stepped on to the stage, when, confronted by the menacing figure of Basil in the stalls, his moral legs became like spaghetti, his tongue clove to the roof of his mouth and all coherence was lost in a flurry of agonised stammering. Francine was calm and doggedly efficient, although occasionally tearful; A. E. Matthews ambled through the play like a charming retriever who has buried a bone somewhere and can't remember where, and Auriol Lee snapped in and out like a jack-knife.

The first night was fashionable to a degree. Everybody who was anybody was there, that is, they were there up till the end of the second act, after which they weren't there any more. Jack and Gladys and I sat with neatly arranged first-night faces in a box and watched the theatre slowly emptying until the stall floor was almost deserted except for a few huddled groups of the faithful. We had the feeling that even they were only staying because the theatre was warm.

I must say that Basil had not done his best with the play; if the writing of it was slow, the production was practically stationary. The second-act dinner scene between Francine Larrimore and Nigel Bruce made *Parsifal* in its entirety seem like a quick-fire vaudeville sketch. The scene between Nigel Bruce and A. E. Matthews in the last act might have livened things up a little if A. E. Matthews had not elected to say the majority of his lines backwards; however, it didn't really matter, for by then the play was down the drain, anyhow. Gladys and Jack and I, after a few jocular condolences with the company, went back to the Ritz where we lapped up neat brandy in order to prepare ourselves for the inevitable party which was being given by Schuyler Parsons ostensibly in my honour.

It turned out to be a highly successful party where fortunately the glaring failure of the play was quickly dimmed by the arrival of the Queen of Roumania. We all had some more brandy, and recent agonies receded farther and farther away until suddenly George Jean Nathan appeared from behind somebody, shook me warmly by the hand and said that he thought the play was excellent and had enjoyed it thoroughly. This was so unmistakably the crack of doom that I gave up even pretending to be cheerful and went disconsolately home to bed.

That two months' sojourn in America was altogether unsatisfactory. I felt far from well and lacking in energy when I arrived, and soon my nerves began to get really bad again. For so many hours of each day I felt all right and then, suddenly without warning, melancholia enveloped me like a thick cloud, blotting out the pleasure and colour from everything. It was a difficult malady to explain; a bursting head that didn't exactly ache but felt as though it were packed tightly with hot cotton-wool; a vague, indefinable pain in my limbs when I lay down to rest, a metallic discomfort as though liquid tin had somehow got mixed up with my blood-stream, making sleep impossible and setting my teeth on edge.

I went off for two weeks to White Sulphur Springs with Jack in order to get fresh air and rest. I was unused to being in anything but the best of health, and was irritable and unhappy. We got up early every morning and rode peaceful horses up and down the mountain trails until lunch. There was nothing to do in the afternoons but lie about and read or write, and so I of course wrote.

I really should have rested completely, but I had promised Marie Tempest that I would write a comedy for her, and as an idea had been kicking about inside me for some time, I huffed and puffed and poured out nervous energy which I should have been conserving, and finally completed a pleasant little eighteenth-century joke called *The Marquise*. The last act was a bit weak, but I thought on the whole it would make a good evening's entertainment.

When it was finished I sent it to England and came back to New York in time to attend, with resigned lassitude, the last performance of *This was a Man*.

There was no reason for me to stay any longer in America, and I didn't feel equal to going back to the cold and damp of London and facing the casting and rehearsing of *The Marquise*. I felt suddenly sick of the theatre and everything to do with it, sick of cities and high buildings and people and screeching traffic. I decided that the time had come for me to go away, right away from everyone I knew and everything that was familiar, so I procured hurriedly, before my determination cooled, passport visas, typhoid inoculations, some new suitcases and a ticket for Hong Kong.

This sudden drastic decision jumped me for a little out of my nervous depression, and I set off across the continent with Jack, who, disapproving of the whole idea, insisted at least upon coming as far as San Francisco with me. He was right to disapprove because I was actually too tired and out of condition to make such a long trip all by myself, but I argued and insisted and finally convinced him that it was a case of kill or cure. If I didn't make a clean break and let a little new air into myself I should probably, within a few months, subside into some gloomy mental nursing-home in a state of complete nervous collapse. By going boldly out into the blue the very adventure of the thing would uphold me for a little while, and although I was fully prepared for days, perhaps weeks of acute loneliness, Time in the long run, together with new sights and sounds and climates, would be sure to cobble up the rapidly widening holes in my nervous fabric.

Finally, on Christmas Day, in the evening, I sailed for Hong Kong on the *President Pierce*. It was foggy and cold and, up to date, the wretchedest and most forlorn moment of my life. Syrens were blowing and a brassy band was playing. The air was filled with loud, sharp noises, and coloured-paper streamers fluttered and stretched between the ship and the dock.

I watched Jack, my last link with familiar life, disappearing down the gangway wearing my fur coat which he was taking back to New York. He turned and waved once, with a very forced, gay smile, then as I couldn't see any more I went below to my cabin.

PART SEVEN

I

The reconstruction of despair is difficult. I find that now it is only with the utmost concentration that I can catch for a moment or two a clear memory of the profound unhappiness I suffered during those seven days on the *President Pierce* between San Francisco and Honolulu. It is grey and nebulous in my mind like the cloudiness on an X-ray photograph that marks a diseased area.

I can remember a few hours when I emerged from my cabin and, with almost hysterical vehemence, endeavoured to fling my miseries over the rail and into the past. But I was too tired and weak to sustain the gesture and back came the hosts of darkness, crowding me down into my cabin again, twitching my nerves with sharp fears for my sanity and clouding the future with the most dismal forebodings.

Too much had happened to me in too short a time. I had written too much, acted too much and lived far too strenuously. This was the pay-off; possibly, I thought, the full stop to my creative ability which I had strained and overworked beyond its strength. My talent or flair for formulating ideas and dressing them up with words was squeezed dry and I felt convinced that I should never be able to write again. To add to my troubles, sleep evaded me and I spent many hours of every night trudging round the deserted decks until finally I persuaded the ship's doctor to give me some sort of sedative.

He was an amiable man but obtuse and offered me, in addition to the sedative, some kindly meant but irrelevant words of comfort. He seemed to be obsessed with the idea that lack of money was the only vital ill that the flesh was heir to, and regaled me with sad little stories about the engineer who only got so much a month and had three children, and the stoker who got even less and had five children and a wife with diabetes.

If my illness had been of the variety that profits from a counter-irritant, that foolish man would undoubtedly have effected a complete cure. As it was, his dullness and lack of understanding only served to emphasise my loneliness. I do not know if there were any amusing people on board, because I rarely came on deck except at night when everyone was asleep. I had a couple of radios from Gladys and Jack, whose intent to cheer made me almost suicidal, with a temperature of a hundred and three, and a black loathing for the *President Pierce*, the ship's doctor, my Chinese room steward, the entire Dollar Line and everything connected with it.

Florence Magee had telegraphed to her friends the Walter Dillinghams, who lived in Honolulu, asking them to entertain me, and I was met on the dock by a smart Japanese chauffeur, who placed a *lei* of sweet-smelling flowers round my neck and informed me that Mrs Dillingham was expecting me at the Peninsular. I of course had no idea where the Peninsular was, and he omitted to tell me that it was twenty miles away. We drove out through the town and into the country. I noted feverishly and without particular enthusiasm the luxuriant foliage and bright new colours. Bananas, palms, sugar canes, Flame-in-the-Forest, poinsettias and hibiscus flashed by, and the air was soft and cool, for it was still early. I wondered what Mrs Dillingham would be like and whether she would think I was drunk when I fell flat on my face at her feet. I had definitely decided not to continue my journey in the *President Pierce*, but I doubted whether I could hold out long enough to explain coherently that I was ill and wanted to go to bed.

We arrived at a Japanese house in a Japanese garden and Louise Dillingham came flying out, surrounded by dogs and children. She was a woman of abundant vitality, charming-looking and smartly dressed, and almost before I had finished my halting explanations she had bundled me back into the car together with herself, the dogs and the children, and back we went at a great rate to the town I had just left. She expressed a hope en route that I was not too ill to come to the lunch party she had arranged for me; she said that the people she had invited were all absolutely delightful, and that I couldn't possibly fail to adore every one of them. After lunch, she added, we would see about getting me a comfortable room in the hotel, unless of course I preferred to come and stay with her. I gave a hurried glance at the dogs and the children and said in a weak voice but with a firm intonation that I would rather go to the hotel.

We whirled through the town and along a coast road fringed with gigantic palms until we reached 'La Pietra,' the Dillingham home on Diamond Head. Even ill as I was I couldn't fail to notice the loveliness of that cool, pink house with its terraces and *patios* and tinkling fountains. The children and dogs disappeared miraculously the moment we arrived and I was left alone on the terrace with a strong whisky and soda, while Louise Dillingham changed her dress to receive the lunch guests. I lay in a swing chair under a 'Hau' tree looking out over a green valley to the deep blue sea; the town was in the middle distance and purple mountains lay along the horizon. The whisky went to my head at once, and I could hardly stand up to receive the first guest, who happened to be a doctor. His name was Withington and sensing sympathy in his manner, I explained quickly how dreadful I felt, and he promised to keep his eye on me. Then other people arrived and I have only a vague recollection of summer dresses, small talk and hot little sausages on sticks.

We went into lunch and sat down at a shiny table. I concentrated on my plate because, whenever I looked up, people's faces seemed to rush close to me and then recede again like a badly cut film. About half-way through the meal I happened to see through the window the car turn into the drive and, suddenly realising that I could bear it all no longer, I got up from the table with a mumbled apology to Louise Dillingham, rushed downstairs and, jumping into the car, directed the chauffeur to drive to the boat. There I dismissed him and staggered on board and down to my cabin. The boat was deserted, and there was nobody to help me, but I managed by degrees to pack everything, collect a couple of deck hands and get my luggage off and into the Customs House. I had to wait for about half an hour because another ship had just arrived, so I sat down on the ground with my back against a trunk until the officials were ready to deal with my bags. When they had passed them I had them piled on to a taxi and drove off to the Moana Hotel. By then I think my fever must have mounted still higher, because there were strange noises inside my head and I could hardly see. However, I contrived by a great effort of will to register my name at the desk and send a cable to Jack explaining my change of plans; after that I don't remember any more until I woke up in bed. Paul Withington, the doctor I had met at lunch, was in the room. He was calm, reasonable and wonderfully quiet; everything about him was quiet – face, movements and voice. He explained to me gently that I had a slight fever that was nothing to worry about and which would go down soon, and that he had given me a strong sleeping draught and something to make me sweat.

Of the two concoctions, the 'something to make me sweat' won easily. I woke up soaked every hour or so during the night and had to rub myself down and change beds.

The din outside on the beach and in the streets was terrific owing to it being New Year's Eve; it seemed as though the entire Chinese population of Honolulu had chosen the immediate vicinity of the Moana Hotel to blow their squeakers and let off their fire-crackers.

The next morning, and several times a day for a week, Paul Withington appeared bringing me books and more sedatives and bunches of vivid tropical flowers from Dillinghams' garden. My fever gradually subsided and towards the end of the week I was able to sit up for a few hours a day and watch from the window the beach boys riding the surf. They came flying in over the rollers like animated bronze statuettes; and marvelling at their grace and agility, I wondered miserably whether I should ever be able to lift a hand or a foot again without gasping with exhaustion.

Paul Withington gave me a meticulously thorough examination when I was strong enough to get to his surgery. Everything about me was tested in order to discover the cause of my fever, for which there seemed to be no apparent reason whatever. Finally, in the X-ray photographs, he pounced on the long-since-healed tubercular scar on my lung and announced with clinical triumph, but strange lack of psychological consideration, that I had T.B.

This I didn't really believe for a moment, but it was an unpleasant possibility to go to bed with. Fortunately my earlier T.B. experiences at Dr Etlinger's sanatorium and with Ned Lathom at Davos reassured me a good deal. As far as I could see I had none of the symptoms. I had lost only a little weight from the fever and now that it had gone I didn't sweat at night at all; my breathing was sound and I had no cough. All the same, my imagination worked overtime for a few days, visualising the future years as an attenuated procession from sanatorium to sanatorium surrounded by the well-known T.B. paraphernalia: doctors, nurses, lung inflations, sputum cups, and chill beds on snow-covered verandas. It was not a cheerful vision, but it gave me something definite to fight and, oddly enough, stimulated my nerves. I decided that however long it took I would lie in the sun and fresh air until all possibility of such horror should be completely eliminated.

The Dillinghams, with infinite kindness, told me that their ranch at Mokuleia on the other side of the island was at my disposal for as long as I liked. A French caretaker and his wife lived near by and would cook meals for me; apart from them nobody would speak to me or worry me and I had nothing to do but sleep and relax and get well.

I accepted gratefully and a day or two later Paul Withington drove me there, with a suitcase and a few books packed into the back of his car.

There are some places in the world that charm the spirit on sight; Mokuleia was one of them. A soothing graciousness seemed to emanate from it.

The ranch itself lay at the foot of a high mountain and was built on three sides of a square. The middle part was one big room opening on to a veranda; the bedrooms were on either side. At the back, an avenue of enormous royal palms led to the foot of the mountain. In the front was a sweep of grass, a tall eucalyptus tree and then a banana and sugar plantation, through which a little road led to a small copse of pines and then the sea. Although it was over a mile away, you could hear from the veranda the noise of the surf pounding ceaselessly on the reef like muffled thunder. The beach itself was a semi-circle of gleaming white sand that shelved steeply into deep water and in which it was perfectly safe to bathe because the reef was a protection against barracudas and sharks.

We arrived in the evening, just after sundown. Madame Thevenin, the caretaker's wife, greeted us with an omelette and coffee and freshly baked bread. She was a round little woman with a kind, comfortable face.

The twilight changed swiftly to darkness and then the moon came up as suddenly as though someone were jerking it through the sky on a string. After supper we drove down to the sea; the pinewood was ghostly with shadows but the beach was almost as light as day and we took off our clothes and swam out through the warm surf into deep water.

Presently it was time for Paul Withington to go back to Honolulu, so he dropped me at the ranch and drove off. I watched the tail lights of his car disappearing down the road and when the noise of it had died away I stayed for a little, sitting on the veranda rail and listening to all the various unfamiliar sounds of the night. There were tree-frogs and cicadas and lizards and some strange hooting little bird in a tree not far off. The air was heavy with the sweet scent of night-blooming cereus, and presently, fearing that the spell might be broken by a sudden attack of scare or loneliness, I went to bed and slept deeply and dreamlessly for the first time in weeks.

2

I stayed at Mokuleia for several weeks. Occasionally Paul and Constance Withington, his wife, drove out to visit me, and we had picnics on the veranda or on the beach; apart from them I saw no one but the Thevenins. Their house was at the end of the garden, and I had all my meals with them; breakfast at six-thirty, lunch at one and dinner at seven. Although their English was reasonably good, we spoke mostly in French. Monsieur Thevenin had a fine face, white hair and piercing blue eyes which flashed cold fire whenever he was propounding his extremely violent political opinions; and as this was practically all the time, they flashed a good deal. My French was not fluent enough for me to be able to argue really satisfactorily, and so I filled in agreeably with enough '*ouis*' and '*c'est vrais*' to make him feel that his eloquence was not being entirely wasted.

There was a ferocious bull-terrier chained up in the yard who bared his teeth and snarled whenever anyone went near him. The Thevenins assured me that he was dangerous, but I had a feeling that he was bluffing and so one day I boldly offered him my hand to bite. This embarrassed him horribly, and he seemed at a loss to know what to do with it. Finally, he licked it apologetically and from then onwards he spent most of his time with me, accompanying me down to the beach every morning, sleeping on my chest during my afternoon siesta on the veranda, and walking with me through the planatations in the cool of the evening.

The big moment of every morning was eleven o'clock, when one train a day rattled across the little wooden bridge just behind the beach, and disappeared into the hills. 'Owgooste' always heard it before I did and started barking, whereupon I sprang up from the sand and raced to the top of a dune in time to wave my towel, forgetting in the excitement of the moment that I was stark naked. This, the Dillinghams told me later, shocked immeasurably many of the native passengers and also the engine-driver.

Frequently, during the early part of my time there, I had bad hours when the peaceful charm of the place turned suddenly sour and I felt neglected and far away. These black patches were usually caused by the arrival of a cable from Mother or Gladys or Jack asking how I was and when I planned to return. In the instant of reading them peace slipped away from me and a troubled restlessness took its place. My mind's eye blinked resentfully at the vivid colours all round me and ached for the gentle greens and greys of Kentish marshes, the familiar procession of red buses trundling down Piccadilly, or the garish lights of Broadway at night. A longing to be within reach of the things and people I knew tugged at my heart-strings, robbing me of my appetite and making me irritable and snappy with the Thevenins.

I could, of course, go back quite easily. There was nothing to hold me there except my own private vow not to budge until I felt, beyond doubt, that I was completely cured.

There were many things to be adjusted before I could consider myself really fit to plunge once more into the strenuous life that had so nearly wrecked me. Not only my physical health – that was coming along beautifully; I was already burnt black by the sun and sleeping and eating well – but my mind needed a great deal more solitude and a great deal more time before it could safely be guaranteed to function as I intended it to function. I meant to take no more chances. Never again would I allow myself to sink into that pit of unreasoning dreads and despairs. I had scrambled out by the skin of my teeth and intended to stay out for the rest of my life. In those long hours alone, lying on the hot sand with the noise of the sea in my ears, or on the veranda, rocking gently in the swing chair, or wandering along the dark roads in the evening, I had had time to round up an imposing array of past mistakes. It seemed that I had not only burnt the candle at both ends, but in the middle as well, and with too strong a flame. From now onwards there was going to be very little energy wasted, and very little vitality spilled unnecessarily.

People, I decided, were the danger. People were greedy and predatory, and if you gave them the chance, they would steal unscrupulously the heart and soul out of you without really wanting to or even meaning to. A little extra personality; a publicised name; a little entertainment value above the average; and there they were, snatching and grabbing, clamorous in their demands, draining your strength to add a little fuel to their social bonfires. Then when the time came when you were tired, no longer quite so resilient, you were pushed back into the shadows, consigned to the dust and left to moulder in the box-room like a once smart hat that is no longer fashionable.

I remembered the *chic*, crowded first night of *This was a Man* in New York. Three-quarters of the people present I knew personally. They had swamped me, in the past, with their superlatives and facile appreciations. I had played and sung to them at their parties, allowing them to use me with pride as a new lion who roared amenably. I remembered how hurriedly they left the theatre the moment they realised that the play wasn't quite coming up to their expectations; unable, even in the cause of good manners, to face only for an hour or so the possibility of being bored. True, there was no reason why they should stay. They had paid for their seats, most of them, and they were under no obligation to me or the management. I felt no bitterness towards them, no bitterness, that is, beyond a realisation of their quality, a forewarning of what to expect if I continued to fail.

I sorted them out, those names and the chinchilla wraps and piqué evening shirts, and stacked them neatly along the rail at the end of the veranda. On the other side, a few more dimensional individuals sat at ease. These were a little cleverer, more reliable, and could be counted on for certain hours of pleasant companionship providing one didn't ask too much or allow the burden of acquaintanceship to weigh too heavily on their shoulders. In the centre of the lawn, against the shadow of the eucalyptus tree, half a dozen figures moved into the light moonshine. These were my friends and I was glad that there were so many.

3

I firmly resisted the temptation to work during those weeks. This was difficult, as I had soon got through most of the books in the ranch that were readable, and there was nothing whatever to do in the evenings.

A tune certainly did slip through the barricade one day while I was on the beach and, between waking and dozing in the sun, I lazily fitted words to it. It lay forgotten at the back of my mind for many months until it emerged, nearly a year later, as 'A Room with a View.'

Apart from this, my vegetation was complete, until one day the urge to return home became too insistent to disregard any longer, and I went back to Honolulu to make plans for sailing.

At last, on a still, crystal-clear evening, I sailed on a stumpy little ship called the *Wilhelmina*. Few passengers were on board, but those were nice, particularly the Paepckes, a young American couple whom I had already met with the Dillinghams. Lots of people came down to see us off and we were loaded with *leis* of every flower imaginable.

The *Wilhelmina* sailed out of the harbour to the strains of 'Aloha,' played and sung by a band of Hawaiians on the dock; the coloured streamers snapped and broke, and the plaintive music followed us out over a sea that looked like grey oiled silk. There was so little breeze that the tall palms on Waikiki could only wave languidly as we passed.

I stayed on deck looking out through the gathering dusk until Diamond Head loomed over the port bow. I could see lights in the Dillingham' house and others springing up along the coast.

There is a superstition in Hawaii that travellers who are sailing away, and wish to return to the islands, must drop the flower *leis* that have been given them into the wake of the ship.

I remembered Mokuleia, the little road winding down through the plantations, 'Owgooste,' the light shining from the cosy sitting-room of the Thevenins' house and making shadows across the lawn, the pine wood and the thunder of the surf on the reef, and with a nostalgia that a few weeks ago I could not have believed possible, I dropped my *leis* one by one into the sea.

PART EIGHT

During the ensuing year the realisation that my nervous disorders, fevers and despairs, culminating in those rejuvenating weeks in Honolulu, had come at a very opportune moment, was brought, forcibly home to me. I discovered that I had need of every ounce of the moral and nervous stamina that the rest had stored up in me.

My various reunions went off satisfactorily. Jack and Gladys met me in New York, both looking much younger and nicer than when I had left them. The *Olympic*, in which Jack and I sailed to England, had been repainted. Lorn was gay and in the best of spirits, Mother was well and delighted with Goldenhurst, and *The Marquise* had opened at the Criterion Theatre and was a big success. I went to it on the night of my arrival. It was beautifully played by Marie Tempest, W. Graham Browne and Frank Cellier; and William Nicholson had designed an accurate and charming setting.

The spring and summer passed agreeably and without agitation. To begin with, Jack and I discovered during the first week-end we spent at Goldenhurst that, beneath its tiled fireplaces and hideous wallpapers, it was really a fine old seventeenth-century farm-house groaning with oak beams which a surveyor from Folkestone told us were free from dry-rot and in perfect condition. We immediately bought the house and grounds freehold at a ridiculously small price and set to work to make improvements.

We knocked walls down right and left and banished all family horrors of sentimental value into Mother's and Auntie Vida's bedrooms, substituting for them solid oak furniture from every antique shop within a radius of fifty miles.

Mother and Auntie Vida wailed a good deal at first, but we overrode their protests; later on they admitted that they were very proud and pleased that we had.

In the late spring Jack and I went to Vienna to see the first performance of *The Marquise* at the Volkstheater. It was played by a celebrated German actor named Albert Bassermann, who, I believe, only consented to play it because the Marie Tempest part provided a fine opportunity for Frau Bassermann, his wife. She, I gathered from current gossip, was not quite such a public idol as he was.

The whole thing was rather bewildering. We arrived only an hour before curtain time, dressed hurriedly at the Bristol Hotel, and were escorted to a stage box by several directors and the translator, who, in the scramble, had omitted to explain to me that he had taken the liberty of transposing the period of the play from the eighteenth century to the present day.

My lack of knowledge of German prevented me from discovering this until about ten minutes after the beginning of the first act; up to then I had been under the impression that we were watching a curtain-raiser. When finally I caught the word 'Eloise,' which was the heroine's name, and observed Frau Bassermann enter in a red leather-motor coat, the truth dawned upon me and I laughed so much that I nearly fell out of the box.

I gathered from Albert Bassermann's performance that he was primarily a tragedian, as his idea of comedy consisted of little beyond sudden bull-like roarings and noisy slappings of his own face. Frau Bassermann, on the other hand, was going to be a comedienne or die. This, apparently, was her big opportunity to establish herself once and for all as a light soubrette, and it was clear that she intended to leave not a stone unturned. Unfortunately, her stage experience, like her husband's, had obviously been hitherto confined to heavier rôles and her comic resources were limited to a repeated wrinkling of the nose as though she were going to sneeze, and an incessant giggle.

There was, however, an utterly delightful performance of the *ingénue* part by a comparatively unknown young actress named Paula Wessely, who, I am gratified to know, is now one of the greatest stars in her own country.

At the end of the play I was called on to the stage and, hand-in-hand with the Bassermanns, took endless curtain calls. Finally a group of students clambered over the footlights with a zeal that I could not but feel was out of proportion to the merits of either the play or the performance, and we all signed autographs, thereby setting the seal of success upon what had been, for me at any rate, a thoroughly hilarious evening.

2

During the summer I wrote a comedy called *Home Chat*. It had some excellent lines and a reasonably funny situation, but I was not entirely pleased with it. However, I read it to Madge Titheradge, for whom I had visualised the leading part, and she liked it, and as Basil also thought it good, we settled to do it in the early autumn.

Gladys came back from America with a hard black hat and mumps, having severed finally her connection with the Civic Repertory Company.

Lynn and Alfred appeared too, later on in the summer and came down to Goldenhurst. They had just finished playing S. N. Behrman's comedy *The Second Man* for the Guild, and were extremely enthusiastic about it as a play for me. A cast of only four characters made it comparatively simple for them to play the whole thing through for me in the drawing-room, which they did immediately. A certain amount of argument sprang up between them, and Alfred forgot one of the most important scenes and burst into tears, but I gathered enough inspiration from their performance to set about getting hold of the rights of the play at once.

I discovered that Macleod and Mayer held the English rights and were planning to do it in the late autumn, but I managed to persuade them to wait for me and do it in January instead.

Basil had for a long while been anxious to produce *Sirocco*, the play I had written in New York in 1921, and after we had had a series of discussion about it, I rewrote a great deal of it and we decided to put it into rehearsal directly after we had launched *Home Chat*.

Having thus light-heartedly sealed my doom, I spent a charming holiday with the Cole Porters in Venice and returned home fairly crackling with health and optimism to start work. The cast of *Home Chat* was good and rehearsals proceeded with sinister smoothness.

On the first night I suspected, early, with growing certainty, that we were in for a bad failure. The audience was restless, particularly in the cheaper parts, and I recognised danger in their whisperings and scufflings. Basil had not been insistent enough on *tempo* during rehearsals, with the result that the play moved with admirable realism, but too slowly. Poor Nina Boucicault, who was playing Madge's mother, and had not acted for some time, was horribly nervous and dried up on several of her lines, thereby causing long pauses which, in addition to those that Basil had put in purposely, brought the action frequently to a standstill. I writhed about on my chair in the box, sniffing disaster and seeing no way of averting it. Madge, with her unfailing ear, did her best to quicken things up, but it was of no avail, and at the final curtain there was booing from the gallery and the pit.

I dashed through the pass door and on to the stage as quickly as I could, feeling that it was unfair for the company to bear the brunt all by themselves. Basil was nowhere to be seen and the stage manager was in a panic.

The moment I appeared the booing became a good deal louder and then subsided as I advanced to the footlights. My intention was to ignore all hostility, thank the audience briefly but insincerely for their kind reception, and get the curtain down as quickly as possible, but just as I was about to speak, a voice yelled 'Rotten!' from the pit and another one shouted from the gallery: 'We expected a better play!' whereupon I snapped back that I expected better manners, and the curtain fell amid considerable tumult.

The notices the next day were all bad. Some contented themselves with supercilious patronage while the rest were frankly abusive and the business, needless to say, did not profit by them.

3

The two principal parts in *Sirocco* were played by Ivor Novello and Frances Doble, and the only theatre available was Daly's, which had housed nothing but musical comedies for many years.

Basil took infinite pains over the production, and although the *festa* scene in the second act was considered by some to be over-elaborate, I personally thought it a superb piece of ensemble work.

Ivor was a difficult proposition. Although his looks were marvellous for the part, and his name, owing to film successes, was a big draw, his acting experience in those days was negligible. I must say, however, that he worked like a slave and endeavoured, to the best of his ability, to do everything that Basil told him. Unlike Nigel Bruce, he was not in the least fussed or nerve-stricken and, although Basil at various times brought up all his artillery, gentle sarcasm, withering contempt, sharp irascibility, and occasionally full-throated roaring, Ivor remained unimpressed, behaving on the whole gaily, as though he were at a party.

Frances Doble was frankly terrified from beginning to end. She looked lovely, but, like Ivor, lacked technique. On the whole she gave a good performance, although it ultimately transpired that neither she nor Ivor had at that time strength or knowledge enough to carry those two very difficult parts. The play, I think, was fairly good. The characterisation was clear, and although the story was a trifle thin in texture, it seemed to me that it should be strong enough to hold.

On the evening of the first performance Mother, Gladys, Jack and I, elaborately dressed and twittering with nerves, dined at the Ivy. Abel, the proprietor, stood us champagne cocktails, and we drove to the theatre in good time to go backstage and wish everybody success.

When we went into the box I noticed, over the squeaking and scraping of the refined quintet in the orchestra pit, the familiar sound of restlessness in the upper parts of the house. The gallery was jammed – mostly, I suspected, with Ivor's film fans. The atmosphere in the theatre was certainly uneasy, and when the house lights went down, my heart went down with them.

4

Probably nobody not connected with the theatre could appreciate fully the tension and strain of that dreadful evening. The first night of any play is uncomfortable enough for those who are intimately concerned with it.

And in the case of *Sirocco* it was a losing battle from the word 'Go!'

The first act was received dully. Ivor got a big reception from the gallery when he came on; apart from that there was nothing but oppressive stillness, broken, only very occasionally, by two or three half-hearted titters on certain comedy lines.

The curtain fell to scattered applause, and in the orchestra pit a quintet, with almost shocking vivacity, struck up the Henry the VIII dances. G. B. Stern came to my box and said that she was sitting at the back of the stalls close to the pit, and that there was going to be trouble.

Jack's face assumed a slightly greenish tinge, Gladys's chin shot up so high that I was afraid she would rick her neck. Mother, unaware of impending disaster, waved to Madame Novello Davies at the opposite side of the theatre, and the second act started.

The storm broke during Ivor's love scene with Bunny Doble. The gallery shrieked with mirth and made sucking sounds when he kissed her, and from then onwards proceeded to punctuate every line with catcalls and various other animal noises.

The last act was chaos from beginning to end. The gallery, upper circle and pit hooted and yelled, while the stalls, boxes and dress circle whispered and shushed. Most of the lines weren't heard at all. Ivor and Bunny and the rest of the cast struggled on doggedly, trying to shut their ears to the noise and get the torture done with as quickly as possible.

The curtain finally fell amid a bedlam of sound, and even Mother, who was slightly deaf, was forced to realise that all was not quite as it should be. I remember her turning to me in the darkness and saying wistfully: 'Is it a failure?'

I replied, without quibbling, that it was probably the bloodiest failure in the history of English theatre, and rushed through the pass door on to the stage.

During the first act I had felt utterly miserable. The sense of hostility was strong in the house and I knew it was directed against me. The second-act commotion jumped me from misery into angry, and by the last act I was in a white-hot fury. I don't ever remember being so profoundly enraged in my whole life. I could think of no way to account for this violent change of public feeling towards me. The failure of *Home Chat* had not been important enough to cause it, and *Sirocco* as a play, although far from perfect, was at least superior in quality and entertainment value to many plays running successfully in London at the moment.

Whether or not the demonstration was organised by personal enemies I neither knew nor cared; I was conscious only of an overwhelming desire to come to grips in some way or other with that vulgar, ill-manner rabble. When I reached the side of the stage, Basil, who never attended first nights of his own productions, and had been quietly dining somewhere, was standing in the prompt corner smiling and ringing the curtain up and down. From where we stood, the tumult in the front of the house might conceivably be mistaken for cheering and he, having no idea of the horrors of the evening, was happily convinced that it was.

I quickly disillusioned him and walked on to the stage. Without once looking at the audience I went along the frightened line of the company to the centre, shook hands with Ivor, kissed Bunny Doble's hand, presenting my behind to the public as I did so, and walked off again.

This, as I expected, increased the booing ten thousandfold. I whispered hurriedly to Basil that I was going on again and that he was to take the curtain up and keep it up until I gave him the signal. If we were to have a failure I was determined that it should be a full-blooded one.

I went on again and stood in the centre, a little in front of Bunny and Ivor, bowing and smiling my grateful thanks to the angriest uproar I have ever heard in a theatre. They yelled abuse at me, booed, made what is known in theatrical terms as 'raspberries,' hissed and shrieked. People stood up in the stalls and shouted protests, and altogether the din was indescribable.

It was definitely one of the most interesting experiences of my life and, my anger and contempt having reduced me to a cold numbness, I was able almost to enjoy it.

I stood there actually for about seven minutes until their larynxes became raw and their breath failed and the row abated a little. Then someone started yelling 'Frances Doble'; it was taken up, and she stepped forward, the tears from her recent emotional scene still drying on her face and in the sudden silence following what had been the first friendly applause throughout the whole evening, said in a voice tremulous with nerves: 'Ladies and gentlemen, this is the happiest moment of my life.'

I heard Ivor give a gurgle behind me and I broke into laughter, which started a fresh outburst of booing and catcalls. Bunny stepped back, scarlet in the face, and I signalled to Basil to bring the curtain down.

Ivor's behaviour all through was remarkable. He had played a long and strenuous part in the face of dreadful odds without betraying for an instant that he was even conscious of them, and at the end, with full realisation that all his trouble and hard work had gone for less than nothing, his sense of humour was still clear and strong enough to enable him to make a joke of the whole thing. Nor was he apparently in the least ruffled by the inevitable Press blast the next day. He made no complaints, attached no blame or responsibilities to anyone, and accepted failure with the same grace with which he has always accepted success.

The evening for me, however, was not quite over. The fireman sent a message to me in Ivor's dressing-room where we were all drinking champagne in a state of dazed hysteria, to say that there was a hostile crowd outside the stage door and that it would be wiser for me to leave by the front of the house. This information refuelled my rage and I went immediately up to the stage door. The alley was thronged with people who yelled when I appeared. I surveyed them for a moment from the steps, wearing what I hoped was an expression of utter contempt, and then pushed my way through to the car. Several of them spat at me as I passed, and the next day I had to send my evening coat to the cleaners.

5

The next morning Lorn appeared early in my bedroom and peered at me sympathetically over an armful of newspapers. 'This time, my darling,' she said, 'we have undoubtedly bought it!'

I read carefully through every notice and was interested to discover that in not one of them was there so much as a kindly word. I noted also, however, that the notices themselves were much longer than those usually accorded to failures.

There was an unmistakable note of glee discernible in most of them. It seemed that all along, for the past three years, since *The Vortex*, the bulk of the critics had known that my success was ephemeral, merely a foolish whim of the public's and based upon little merit beyond a superficial facility for writing amusing lines. There was little or no surprise that a play of mine should be so appallingly bad, for, in their minds at least, I had never been anything but a flash in the pan, a playboy whose meteoric rise could only result in an equally meteoric fall into swift oblivion. In fact, so general was the conviction that I was done for, that several journalists announced it in so many words.

There were, however, two notable exceptions. One was St John Ervine, who wrote an impartial, careful criticism of the play with no malice, and even a certain amount of praise, and the other was Edgar Wallace who, although we had never met, took the trouble to write a long article in my defence, warning the gentlemen of the Press that their announcements, in his opinion at any rate, were not only unsporting but distinctly premature; this heartened me a great deal.

We certainly passed a gloomy enough morning; Lorn, Jack, Gladys and I, sitting round in my bedroom, drinking coffee and deciding what was best to be done. Even the comfort of knowing that the house was sold out for three days was denied us, for when we rang up the box office we were told that more than half the seats already booked had been returned.

My first instinct was to leave England immediately, but this seemed too craven a move and also too gratifying to my enemies, whose numbers by then had swollen in our minds to practically the entire population of the British Isles.

We finally came to the conclusion that the best plan was for me to brazen things out for a week, to be seen everywhere, and to try, as convincingly as possible, to make light of the whole fiasco. After that it seemed best to go away, preferably to America, writing first, of course, to Macleod and Mayer asking them to release me from my *Second Man* contract, and also to Cochran, for whom I had agreed to write a new revue.

It seemed absurd to embark on further theatrical enterprise in London with the Press and the public so obviously against me. An absence of a year or so would give them time to forget and enable me to make a come-back with a more reasonable chance of success.

Having decided upon this, we strapped on our armour, let down our visors and went to the Ivy for lunch.

The Ivy looked much the same as usual. Perhaps it was our overwrought nerves that sensed a sinister quality in the atmosphere. So often, after success, we had filed in triumphantly to our usual table in the corner, just to the right of the door; receiving congratulations modestly and trying not to allow too much cocksureness to colour our jokes. This time our task was more difficult. A line had to be drawn between what we felt and what we wanted people to think we felt. It wasn't unfriendliness exactly that we had to combat. Most of the Ivy's clientele were essentially well disposed towards us; indeed, on this occasion, kindly sympathy was all too apparent in every eye.

This had to be accepted with tempered gratitude. Condolences were harder to handle than congratulations, particularly as we felt them to be more whole-heartedly sincere.

Our table was in no way isolated. We were not ostracised for a moment, in fact the rush was quite flattering. Expressions of shocked horror, revilings of the shameful manners of first-nighters, scornful recriminations of the Press, rattled on to our plates and splashed into our dry Martinis. If I had expected even the most embittered character actresses to rise up and spit at me, I was doomed to disappointment. In fact the whole thing, after the first few difficult moments, went with a swing.

Realising that the eyes of Lorn and Gladys and Jack were set upon me with an almost clinical watchfulness, I was constantly wary that no undue bitterness should sully my replies, nor, on the other hand, any overdone jocularity either. A too casual attitude would be obviously false and recognised at once, whereas any indication of the real anger and humiliation I felt would not be in keeping with the gay, cynical, playboy-of-the-theatre tradition which had proved such a useful façade for so long. Also, I considered, without rancour, that my real feelings were nobody's business but my own.

Doubtless the reader will wonder why, in the circumstances, we went to the Ivy at all. Why, in addition to the strain and anxiety of the night before, and in the face of such thorough-going disaster, we elected to make ourselves the target for possibly still further slings and arrows. The reader will also probably say to himself or herself: 'How foolish, how unnecessary and, above all, how conceited to imagine that the mere failure of a play was of such importance. To believe, for an instant, that the Press and the public were really interested enough in so small an event as to feel exultant.'

In this the reader would be completely justified. Even at the time we realised in our hearts that the bulk of the public knew nothing about *Sirocco* and cared less. The theatre world, however, was different, and it was with the theatre world that we had to deal. We went to the Ivy that day as a gesture – not to our friends, nor our acquaintances, nor our enemies, but to ourselves. Nor was it entirely a gesture of defiance. To hang our heads in private and not be seen about anywhere would only make our ultimate emergence more embarrassing, and it seemed much more sensible to take the bull, however fetid its breath, by the horns at the outset.

Ivor, we were delighted to see, had decided upon the same course, and was sitting, surrounded by his coterie, at a large table just opposite to us. His gaiety seemed, even to me, to be genuine, and we all joined up for coffee and discussed the miseries of the night before with growing hilarity, and it wasn't until we had separated and gone our different ways that I realised that, on the whole, I had enjoyed myself.

6

After an unpleasant week in London, a week of lunches and dinners and suppers during which *Sirocco* was discussed interminably, by me with an air of semi-humourous resignation, nicely adjusted and not too semi-humorous, and by everyone else with various degrees of anger, conjecture, pleasure, wit, shocked astonishment and sympathy, I went to Paris, where Jack and I stayed with Edward Molyneux in Neuilly for a while before going on to St Moritz for Christmas.

Macleod and Mayer had gallantly refused to release me from my contract for *The Second Man* and Cochran had almost laughed at me for wishing to postpone doing his revue. He said, with a kindly wisdom born of many years of battling with success and failure, that in a few weeks' time any hubbub over *Sirocco* would be entirely forgotten and that he was quite sure that the revue would turn out to be a triumphant one in the eye for the lot of them.

I was grateful to him for this. His faith in me was so genuinely unimpaired, and although I wouldn't have blamed him if it hadn't been, I was extremely glad. It was altogether a sentimental interview, sentimental in the best sense of the word. He, more than most people, perceived beneath my business-like nonchalance, a certain vague scurry of apprehensions. I was scared inside, scared that perhaps, after all, the Press were right, that I was really nothing better than the flash-in-the-pan, the over-bright little star they had so caustically described. These fears were far from concrete, and received from me, even in my dimmest moments, no actual recognition. But, on looking back, I know they were there, swimming about in my subconscious, trying to clamber out and shake themselves like beetles striving to escape from a bath-tub. I rescued them later, quite a while later, and, after scrutinising them thoroughly, squashed them with murderous satisfaction.

Then, however, I needed outside manifestations of confidence in my ability, and Cockie bolstered me generously. No gleam in his eye indicated that he remembered my past shrill quarrel with him, no suggestion of veiled patronage. It was, as I said before, a thoroughly sentimental interview because, above all things, Cockie's sentiment rises supreme in failure. It is, I am sure, through his failures that he has made his friends. No other theatrical manager that I have ever known can rally adherents so swiftly in catastrophe. Temperamental stars demand to be allowed to pawn off their jewellery for him. Chorus girls, stage managers, members of his office staff eagerly offer him their services indefinitely for nothing. Even hard-boiled backers rush through the flames with their cheque-books over their mouths to aid him, regardless of the fact that the flames are probably consuming many of their own investments.

We discussed some of my already formulated ideas for the revue. This time there was no question raised as to the advisability of anyone else having anything to do with it. The whole show was to be mine: music, book, lyrics and supervision of production. The cast was to be headed by Maisie Gay, Jessie Matthews, Sonnie Hale and a Viennese dancer called Tilly Losch, whom Cockie had seen with Reinhardt and considered brilliant.

I remember leaving his office much cheered and with a new tune whirling round in my head, a tune to which the words 'Dance, Dance, Dance, Little Lady' had resolutely set themselves even before I got home to the piano.

I fear, however, that Jack and Edward had a bad time with me in Paris, as for many hours of the day I was what is known as 'a prey to melancholy.' My moods of depression were in no way mitigated by the English papers, which can be obtained far too easily in that gayest of gay cities.

In everyone I chanced to look at, daily or weekly, I was confronted by either unpleasantly veiled or direct allusions to my recent débâcle. I should, of course, far from being upset, have congratulated myself on the stringy persistence of my news value; no other dramatist that I could remember, with the exception of Bernard Shaw, having been the object of such a sustained attack for many years. However, I was upset, exceedingly upset. It seemed strange that the various editors should permit such redundant flogging of a dead donkey, unless perhaps they had a suspicion that after all the donkey might not be quite dead, and wished to make sure. At all events I formed a vicious little resolution then and there that in the future, however many triumphs I might achieve, I would never again, in any circumstances, give an interview to the London Press.

Never again should their readers be gratified by my opinion of 'The Modern Girl.' Henceforward my views on Birth Control, Television, Long Skirts, D. H. Lawrence, Free Love and Bicycling Waitresses should be locked in my own bosom and, strange as it may seem, good resolutions as a rule being so frequently trodden into the dust by the march of Time, I have adhered to that vow ever since.

With the passing of the years, of course, even the memory of my disgust has evaporated and my feelings towards the Press are friendly in the extreme and I hope will remain so. But the resolution still holds firmly and gratefully, for the simple reason that it saves me an incalculable amount of time.

Edward's quiet, lovely little house in Neuilly presently began to soothe me down a bit. It had been at one time a royal pavilion attached to the French Court, and there was enveloping it an atmosphere of departed glory. The high trees in the garden bowed sadly in the winter wind; they seemed tremendously dignified and long since resigned to the shock of a revolution which had swept away all familiar charm and elegance, a revolution, I could not help reflecting, whose impact on world history had on the whole been more serious than the screeching of a few gallery girls in a London theatre.

7

The Second Man was a witty comedy, with only four characters in it and my part, Clark Storey, a cynical, intelligent dilettante, was the pivot around which the play revolved. It was, in consequence, extremely long and, owing to the author's unrestrained passion for the *Oxford Dictionary*, very difficult to learn. There was, however, much wisdom and charm in the lines, and by devoting a few hours of every day to it in St Moritz, I managed to learn it by the time rehearsals started.

The other three parts in the play were played by Zena Dare, Ursula Jeans and Raymond Massey. Basil Dean produced with commendable gentleness which was only occasionally ruffled into irritability by the fact that Zena Dare was constantly bathed in tears.

This happened to be one of her peculiarities and really reflected very little on his directorial manner. She was the victim of a desperate inferiority complex, which was enhanced rather than minimised by a strong sense of humour directed principally against herself, with the result that every time she cried, she laughed at herself for crying, becoming in the process more and more hysterical until eventually rehearsals were brought to a standstill. Owing to early and arduous training in musical comedy, her first ingrained instinct was to smile, this smile often persisting even while the tears were cascading down her face. I think one of the most entrancing spectacles I know was Zena's expression when something untoward occurred on the stage, or when she lost a line and knew that she hadn't the remotest idea what to say next. On would flash the smile immediately, stretching into a mirthless grimace; meanwhile her eyes, in deathly panic, searched wildly the ceiling, the floor and the furniture for inspiration. Still smiling, she would hiss out of the corner of her mouth: 'For God's sake, dear, agony dear, what do I say, dear?'

At rehearsals, of course, such contretemps were the signal for tears; in actual performance, however, the trouper spirit was too strong in her to permit collapse, and she persevered gamely until, the danger over, her smile changed from macabre ferocity to relief and wafted her off the stage. She was a darling in the theatre and we all adored her.

Raymond Massey was another slight thorn in Basil's side, owing to his eccentric habit of behaving like a windmill whenever he dried up on a speech. Horrified at the outset by the fact that I was practically word-perfect, he lashed himself into a frenzy several times a day, tearing at one particular long-suffering lock of hair and rending the air with incoherent Canadian curses, not at me, which would have been understandable, but at himself. There is nothing so irritating as rehearsing scenes with someone who already knows them, and I was fully conscious that my unethical slickness was putting him off. I apologised profusely, explaining that the reason I had played such a dirty trick on him was that my part was long and I wanted to get the actual learning of it out of the way in order to give myself time to polish.

He moaned at me wretchedly, alluding to his obtuseness and slowness with a wealth of invective that was nothing less than masochistic; the fact that he was giving one of the most expert performances of his career never occurred to him, and he continued to wallow. However, long before the dress rehearsal he vanquished his troubles and became word-perfect, which was, in a way, disappointing, as the picture of that tall, gyrating figure with arms and legs waving had grown dear to me.

Ursula Jeans was the fourth member of the cast. She was ebullient, quick and only occasionally flustered. She rushed at her scenes as though she were about to vault over a high gate, but eventually, the first exuberance over, she simmered down into a charming performance.

Altogether, it was well acted. I was happy with my part and I think I was good in it; at all events, when Sam Behrman, the author, arrived from America, he said that he was delighted with all of us. I trembled at his arrival even more than the others did, realising that he had known the inestimable pleasure of seeing the play acted by Alfred and Lynn. I didn't want him to say that I was better than Alfred; if he had, I should not only have disliked him for saying so, but not believed him. However, I needn't have worried; Sam Behrman was tactful and kind to a degree. He insisted that there was no comparison between the two performances, that they were completely different both in approach and technique; and if in his secret heart he considered Alfred better than I in certain scenes and me better than Alfred in certain other scenes, I am convinced that no amount of cajoling would ever have got it out of him.

He was encouraging and charming to us all and instead of hating him coming to rehearsals, which we had all been doing in anticipation, our hearts sank whenever we looked out and noticed that his shining bald head and quizzically gleaming spectacles were missing.

8

The first night of *The Second Man* should by rights have been particularly nerve-racking for me, but somehow or other it wasn't.

To begin with, I had so often, during the past two months, visualised the horror of it, that when it arrived I was conscious of little beyond a steely hatred of the first-night audience even before they came into the theatre. I wondered dispassionately whether they would shriek anything offensive at me on my first entrance, or just sit in sullenness, daring me to be good. As a matter of fact they did neither. They applauded me politely when I came on and I judged, from an early laugh or two, that they were quite willing to be amused.

By the middle of the second act I knew the play was a success. There was a pleasant tension in the house and considerable laughter and applause. No hitches occurred. The champagne bottle opened with a good resounding pop (ginger-ale professionally bottled for us by Messrs Mumm), and Raymond's revolver in the last act went off without any of those abortive clickings which are often so mortifying to an actor. In fact everything was smooth and satisfactory and the cheering at the end would have been undoubtedly gratifying if, through it, I had not been listening ironically to crueller noises.

The notices were good and there were many sly suggestions to the effect that there was in reality no such person as S. N. Behrman, as the play had obviously been written by me under a pseudonym, apparently in the craven hope that it would thus be received more favourably.

Several writers even went so far as to assert that they had discerned definite examples of my wit in many of the lines. They were palpably delighted to have uncovered such a juicy secret, and it seemed almost unkind to have to undermine such proud assurance, but although Sam and I both acknowledged to each other how sincerely flattered we were, truth *was* truth and it had to be stated that there wasn't even one phrase or word of mine in the whole play.

9

Rehearsals for the revue started almost immediately after the opening of *The Second Man*, beginning as usual with a week or so of auditions for the chorus and small parts.

Daily, morning and afternoon, we sat in the dust-sheet enshrouded gloom of the London Pavilion, Lorn, Jack, Gladys, Frank Collins and me, while Elsie April, perched on the stage at an upright piano, pounded out accompaniments and drank endless cups of tea. With us also in the stalls was Cissie Sewell, the ballet mistress for all Cochran productions, her job being to remember accurately all dance movements originated by me or Max Rivers, the dance producer, and rehearse the girls apart at different hours of the day. Cissie was red-haired, smart, nice-looking, and efficient. Her memory was fantastic, and enabled her to catch the most fleeting movement of the leg or shoulder or hand and reproduce it later in the rehearsal room with precision. She possessed, in addition to her other virtues, an outspoken critical faculty allied to the kindest heart imaginable. This combination frequently set up a considerable conflict within her during the audition period. She knew, from years of experience, most of the aspirants who appeared before us. She knew whether they were kept or not kept, whether they needed the job or merely looked on the stage as a side-line, whether they were good workers or bad workers.

She and Elsie, who were bosom friends, had a series of code signals which they exchanged whenever one of their particular favourites or *bêtes noires* appeared. Elsie, with one swift twiddle round of the piano stool, would shoot a knowing look at Cissie in the stalls. If genuine talent was imminent she would give a satisfied little nod; if, on the other hand, some poor inexpert creature of old repute came on, she would shrug her shoulders and fling her eyes up to heaven with an expression of such untold resignation, that we knew, long before the poor thing started, what to expect.

They were usually pretty accurate in their judgments, although occasionally, owing to private knowledge of some girl's sad circumstances, they would argue tooth and nail to get her the job, even if her talents were not quite up to scratch. These kindly, sentimental efforts were generally frustrated by Frank Collins, who also knew a thing or two, but as a rule, it worked both ways, for he too had his special loves and hates, and auditions were often greatly enlivened thereby.

The atmosphere of those dim auditoriums; the dust-sheets, the large brass pot for cigarette ends, the bars of chocolate contributed by Lorn, are indelibly stained on to my memory. I will always remember the weariness at the end of a long day when Elsie finally clambered down from the piano to join us in the stalls, while we added up the odd hundred people we had seen and selected dispiritedly about three possible ones. So tired were we as a rule that the effort of getting up and going home seemed too much for us, and we sat around lethargically, gossiping a little, wondering whether Phyl would be strong enough for such and such a part or whether Vera – 'You remember, dear, the one that sang "Love, Here is my Heart," and did a buck and wing' – would be, although less pretty, more reliable.

Cockie himself seldom attended these general hurly-burly auditions, preferring to wait for the later ones at which, having weeded out most of the drearies, we recalled those whom we thought were really worthy of his consideration. Naturally nobody could be definitely engaged without his O.K. and we were often on tenterhooks lest our selected pets should appear less talented than we thought, and let down our faith in them.

The finding of a title for the revue caused us all many racked hours of the day and many sleepless nights. We sat round with pencils and papers flogging our brains and shooting forth anything we thought of, however inappropriate, in the hope that the very fatuity of our suggestion might inspire somebody else with an idea. All the ideal revue titles seemed to have been done: *Vanity Fair, Bric-à-Brac, London, Paris and New York, Odds and Ends*, etc., etc. Finally Lorn said *This Year of Grace*, and we instantly knew that we were all right. *This Year of Grace* it was, and I still think it one of the best revue titles I have ever heard.

The show opened, as usual, in Manchester, This time I did not stay off and allow my understudy to play for me, but I went up all the same for the Sunday dress rehearsal, which went on, as was expected, all through the night but was not, on the whole, nearly as depressing as *On With the Dance* had been.

Arnold Bennett was with us, I cannot at the moment remember why, and appeared to be enchanted with the whole thing, enjoying keenly with detached amusement every hitch and every hold-up. It was nice having him there, because he cheered up our blacker moments with a joke or two, and generally emanated good will from every pore.

This Year of Grace opened at the London Pavilion in March, and was an immediate success. I was still playing *The Second Man*, but as this didn't begin until just before nine, and the revue, on the first night, rang up at eight, I was able to watch, from the back of the dress circle, the first three-quarters of an hour of it.

Quite early in the first half came my series of short one-line parodies on current plays, the final one of the series being announced as 'Any Noel Coward Play,' and I was particularly anxious to see the effect of this on the first-night audience. The scene consisted merely of a row of people, with an author in the centre, bowing, until at a given moment the leading lady stepped forward and, with tears in her voice, said – 'Ladies and gentlemen, this is the happiest moment of my life!' whereupon she burst into sobs and the entire orchestra and any of us in the audience who happened to be in the know, booed and raspberried with the utmost fervour.

The response of the first-nighters to this was interesting. There was first of all dead silence, then a titter of shocked amazement and then a full-bellied roar of laughter.

That night the performance of *The Second Man* must have been exceedingly bewildering to the audience. The management had kindly agreed to cut the intervals down to half, and I had primed Ray and Zena and Ursula to play as quickly as they could, in order that I might get back to the Pavilion in time for the finale.

I don't suppose that a play has ever been performed with such speed without losing coherence. We all four rattled through it like express trains and it was not until nearly the end of the last act that I was suddenly conscious-smitten by the sight of a poor old gentleman in the front row of the stalls, leaning forward with a strained expression and his ear cupped in his hand.

I slowed down for the last few minutes, but we all managed to get to the Pavilion, still in make-up, for part of the second half of the revue.

Everything in the show went well. Tilly Losch made a huge success. Maisie Gay triumphed with 'The Bus Rush' and her Channel-swimmer song, 'Up, Girls, and At 'Em.' Sonnie Hale and Jessie Matthews were charming in 'A Room with a View' and 'Try to Learn to Love,' and Sonnie brought down the house with 'Dance, Little Lady,' which he did with Laurie Devine against a group of glittering, macabre figures wearing Oliver Messel masks.

A great sensation was caused by Jack Holland and Jean Barry, who danced

'The Blue Danube' in the finale of the first half and a Spanish dance in the second half. They were certainly magnificent, swift, graceful and handsome to look at. Everybody fared well, and the notices were ecstatic. It appeared, from reading them, that I was the most brilliant man of the theatre that England had ever known, and the delightful audacity of parodying my own recent failure shook journalistic admirers of the sporting instinct to the marrow. In fact, far from creeping back into favour I was shot into it with the drum accompaniment and velocity of a Star Trap Act.

10

The idea of *Bitter Sweet* was born in the early summer of that year, 1928. It appeared quite unexpectedly and with no other motivation beyond the fact that I had vaguely discussed with Gladys the possibilities of writing a romantic Operette. She and I were staying with Ronald Peake, her family solicitor, in Surrey, and an hour or so before we were due to leave, Mr Peake happened to play to us on the gramophone a new German orchestral record of 'Die Fledermaus.' Immediately a confused picture of uniforms, bustles, chandeliers and gas-lit cafés formed in my mind, and later, when we were driving over Wimbledon Common, we drew the car to a standstill by the roadside, and in the shade of a giant horse-chestnut tree mapped out roughly the story of Sari Linden.

The uniforms, bustles, chandeliers and gas-lit café all fell into place eagerly, as though they had been waiting in the limbo for just this cue to enter.

There had been little or no sentiment on the London musical stage for a long while. The Daly's operettas, with their crashing second-act finales in which the heroines dissolved in tears, or danced with the footman, had given place to an endless succession of slick American 'Vo do deo do' musical farces in which the speed was fast, the action complicated, and the sentimental value negligible.

It seemed high time for a little romantic renaissance, and very soon, a few of the preliminary melodies began to form in my head. However, the whole idea had to be shelved for a while owing to the urgency of other plans.

The Second Man had finished its run, and Cockie and Archie Selwyn were trying to persuade me to play in *This Year of Grace* in New York in the autumn. The idea was for me to rewrite certain of Sonnie Hale's material to suit my own talents and to co-star with Beatrice Lillie, who was to use the bulk of Maisie's numbers and sketches. There would, of course, have to be an entirely new cast, as Cockie wisely and resolutely refused to break up the London company, which was playing to capacity.

I was not particularly keen on the project at first, but presently the idea of dancing, singing again and playing a series of different rôles during an evening instead of only one, began to seem more attractive, and finally I decided to do it, and signed my contract.

In July Cockie and I travelled over to New York for a couple of weeks, a little outing that we both agreed should come under the heading of 'Managerial Expenses,' considering that the object of our visit was to discover fresh talent and discuss with Archie various arrangements for theatres, try-outs, etc.

As a matter of fact, we didn't find much talent beyond George Fontana and Marjorie Moss, whom we had both known for years, and one girl who could do side splits and walk on her hands with an air of social nonchalance that was exceedingly fetching. But we had a pleasant time.

We stayed at the Ritz and went out constantly to theatres and parties. Constance Collier was in New York, staying at the Algonquin in her usual slightly rusty splendour, surrounded by cats, dogs, monkeys, parrots and coffee percolators. She had become close friends with the new phenomenon of Broadway, Jed Harris, who had produced already, in rapid succession, several sure-fire successes.

He was an extraordinary creature, with an authentic flair for the theatre. He talked brilliantly, and turned on, whenever he considered it worth while, a personal charm that was impossible to resist. He had made a large fortune, but beyond a shining Packard car, the evidence of it lay only in his conversation, and then only occasionally. His was one of the most interesting self-devouring egos I had ever met, and I found him enchanting company. Now and then he suggested to my mind that strangely ruthless insect, the Praying Mantis. I couldn't help wondering how long it would be before Jed's ego, prompted by sheer passion, ate up every scrap of him. We went to his production of *Coquette* in which Helen Hayes gave an agonisingly perfect performance and tore our emotions to shreds. We saw *Funnyface*, in which Fred and Adele Astaire were more electric than ever, and also the Guild production of the negro play *Porgy*, which Cockie immediately bought for London.

In fact, theatrically speaking, that was one of the richest two weeks I have ever spent.

As all the ships were crowded, on the voyage home Cockie and I were forced to share a cabin on the *Berengaria*. Although we had both viewed this prospect with slight apprehension, it turned out to be extremely cosy. Neither of us snored, apparently, and conversation after lights out was stimulating.

During that voyage I wrote, roughly, the first act of *Bitter Sweet*, and when I read it to Cockie and explained to him the story of the rest of it, he became at once enthusiastic. One of his greatest qualities is his amazing flair for visualising a play completely from the barest outline, and he decided then and there that he would do it, providing that I could finish it in the time, in the spring of the following year, 1929.

11

Meanwhile at home the family fortunes continued to pursue an upward course. We had sold the lease of the Ebury Street house, although as I had recently had my rooms done up at great expense I decided to keep them on.

Father, at last free from the burden of lodgers, tax-collectors, window-cleaners, etc., was installed at Goldenhurst, where he gardened to his heart's content, dealing with the wider landscape problems, while Auntie Vida had charge of the bulbs, potting and flower beds. With this arrangement, of course, a certain amount of friction was inevitable, and high words frequently winged their way across the velvet lawns.

Mother drove recklessly about the countryside in a new car. She drove well, but with an unchristian spirit of truculence towards any other vehicles that happened to be on the road. Her mishaps, on the whole, were few. She once upset the Vicar of St Mary's and his wife into a ditch in a fog, and on another occasion, owing to mistimed acceleration, she advanced triumphantly through the plate-glass window of Pearks' grovers' shop in Ashford, remaining at the wheel in a state of splendid calm, while pots of blackcurrant jam, light plum, dark plum, strawberry and Golden Shred marmalade ricochetted gaily off the wind-screen on to the radiator. Her rage over this incident simmered for days and was not soothed by the fact that the local Ashford paper grudgingly awarded her only a paragraph or two instead of the full column she had expected.

My brother Eric, then aged twenty-three, was rather at a loose end. He had had two or three jobs, in none of which he had been particularly happy. I felt, and I know that he felt too, that to be the brother of anyone as spectacular as myself was far from comfortable. True, there were certain perquisites accruing from it, but, on the whole, I fear that my shadow lay heavily upon him.

If he had possessed any outstanding marketable talent it would, of course, have been different, but alas, apart from a genuine passion for music and sufficient ability to play it quite well on the piano, his assets were little above the average.

We discussed his prospects at length, and eventually, as he had a keen desire to see something of the world, we arranged for him to go out to Ceylon in the autumn as a tea-planter.

It was about this time that the great Barn Battle took place. This campaign, started quite unintentionally by Jack and me, flared up violently and showed every indication of continuing with all the futile persistence of the Hundred Years' War.

The beginning of it was simple. There was an old barn near to the house which we had left intact, feeling that later on it might be useful to us.

In the early spring of 1928, realising that for all of us, Mother, Father, Eric, Auntie Vida and me, supplemented frequently by Lorn, Father, Jack or Jeffery, to live together in one small house was really asking too much of human forbearance, Jack had evolved a plan for rebuilding the interior of the barn and transforming the whole into a home for the family, while I took over the house. The view from the barn was much lovelier than from the house and, with bathroom, dining-room, bedrooms, living-room, etc., we considered that it ought to be the acme of comfort.

At this suggestion the family rose to a man, alternatively furious, outraged, martyred, hurt, and bitterly resigned. The basis of the trouble was apparently a deeply embedded conviction that I had grown to be ashamed of my loved ones and wished to banish them beyond sight and sound of my new-found 'grand' friends, for whom I obviously considered them not good enough.

As my new-found 'grand' friends that year had consisted solely of Bobbie Andrews, who had come down for a couple of weekends, this argument seemed unjust. Jack and I, terrified by the storm we had created, surrendered, but as it seemed a shame that all our elaborate schemes for the expansion of Goldenhurst should be grounded on the shoals of family pride, we set to work, and with the aid of builders and plumbers from Folkestone, made over the barn and cottage into an establishment for my exclusive use.

When ultimately finished, the family were enraptured with it, and, to this day, use it a great deal in my absence, for entertaining their new-found 'grand' friends.

12

My determination that in this narrative the reader shall take the rough with the smooth impels me to relate that, two days before rehearsals for the American production of *This Year of Grace* were due to begin, I was operated on for piles.

This meant postponing everything for two weeks, during which I lay, in bad pain and a worse temper, in a nursing home.

The newspapers described the affair with light-hearted reticence as 'a minor operation,' and I couldn't help reflecting that if that were a minor operation, I should have been far happier with a Caesarian.

The night before I was to go under the knife, having been respectfully shaved and offered some barley sugar, I was left dejectedly alone in a small bed in a minute white room. Realising that after the anaesthetic I should probably have all, if not more, sleep than I was usually accustomed to, I passed the long hours until dawn pleasantly enough by writing the second act of *Bitter Sweet*, and in the morning conscious that I had accomplished a considerable job of work upheld me throughout the routine indignities that I had to endure.

The nursing home was conservative to a degree, and so nineteenth century in atmosphere that I fully expected the nurses to come in in crinolines.

There was one bathroom on the fourth floor which contained, in addition to the usual offices, a forbidding geyser. This snarled angrily at those patients who were strong enough to survive a long, frightening ascent in a lift which, I imagine, must assuredly have been the pride of the Arts and Crafts Exhibition at Earl's Court in 1842.

I had several visitors during my convalescence, all of whom were kind and sympathetic, and seldom referred, except obliquely, to the mortifying nature of my complaint.

Marie Tempest was the exception. She came a lot to see me, and we discussed every detail with enthusiasm, and I need hardly say that her visits were far and away the most welcome of all.

It was my first experience of nursing-home life, and once the acuter discomforts were over I settled down to enjoy it. There was, first and foremost, a pleasant sense of timelessness. The moment the early morning washing and prinking were done with I could sink back in clean pyjamas on to a freshly made bed with the heavenly sensation that there was no hurry and no necessity to do anything whatever.

There came a beaten-up egg in milk at eleven, and possibly a visit from the Surgeon at twelve; apart from these minor interruptions the hours stretched lazily ahead towards lunch, my afternoon snooze, one or two amiable visitors, an early supper and then the night.

The nights were the nicest of all. When the bed had been remade, the curtains drawn, the dark green shade put over the light, and the night nurse had whisked out of the room, a different kind of peace descended. There was no obligation to sleep. I had rested a lot during the day and could rest more on the following day. A gentle dimness enveloped me, a detachment from affairs. The life outside seemed incredibly remote.

Occasionally a taxi drew up on the other side of the road. I could hear the screech of the tyres, the sound of the door opening and shutting, a murmur of voices, a sharp little ting as the driver reset the fare meter, then the grinding of gears and a diminishing hum until there was silence again. I pictured, without envy, those strangers letting themselves into their houses, switching on the lights in the dining-room and finding the usual decanter, siphon, glasses and sandwiches curling slightly at the edges in spite of having been covered with a plate.

I imagined problems for them: jealousy perhaps, suspicions of infidelity, a business crisis to be dealt with the next day, a brief to be prepared, or a political speech. Sleep was essential to them; they must get to bed and sleep because Time was whirling them along too fast. Not for them the luxury of lying still and making faces out of the shadows on the ceiling. Not for them the delight of a sudden cup of tea at three in the morning with a couple of Marie biscuits and one chocolate one. They had to be active and energetic and get things done, as I should have to in a week or so, but in the meantime I could relax, comfortably aware that I was not imprisoned by a long illness and that I should be up and about again before this delicious enforced rest had had time to become tedious.

13

We rehearsed the American production of *This Year of Grace* on the Pavilion stage and in the Poland Rooms. I had, during the summer, taken the precaution of going for six weeks to a dancing school in order to get limbered up, a necessary but painful procedure, for although I was not called upon to dance much, I had to be reasonably agile.

The show was unchanged except for the interpolation of two single numbers for Beattie, 'World Weary' and 'I Can't Think' (an imitation of Gertrude Lawrence); two duets which we did together: 'Lilac Time,' an *opéra bouffe* burlesque, and 'Love, Life and Laughter,' a sketch and song of Paris night life in the eighties, which had originally been created by Maisie Gay in one of the Charlot revues.

The cast was surprisingly good considering how difficult it always is to duplicate an entire production, and we all sailed off to America to play a try-out week in Baltimore, before coming to the Selwyn Theatre in New York.

The Lunts, who happened to be playing in the next-door theatre to us in Baltimore, came to our Sunday rehearsal and assured me that I was going to be fine, but I was depressed and perfectly certain that I was going to be nothing of the sort. In 'Lilac Time,' 'Love, Life and Laughter' and 'Dance, Little Lady,' which latter I did with Florence Desmond, I was all right, but in 'A Room with a View' with Madeleine Gibson, and in the ballet announcement, I wasn't half as effective as Sonnie had been, and in most of the other things I had to do in the show I felt myself to be only adequate.

Beattie was good all through, but being, like all of us, in a bad state of nerves and fright, she contrived to be completely and utterly devilish throughout the whole week. Before I continue further, I should like to say that she was then, and is now, a much-loved friend. The fact that she was an uppish, temperamental, tiresome, disagreeable, inconsiderate, insufferable friend during that one week of her life in no way sullies my steadfast love for her. It may have temporarily dimmed it to the extent of my wishing ardently to wring her neck, but once we had opened in New York all rancour disappeared, as the mist on a glass disappears with the application of a damp rag, the damp rag in that instance being the re-emergence of Beattie's real character. Whether it was the stimulus of the triumphant success she made, or a letter from her son at home, or the General Election, I don't know. I do know, however, that the moment the first night was over she changed miraculously back to her old self, just as though some magician had whacked her sharply over the head with a wand, and became, what I had always expected her to be, one of the most generous and delightful partners it had ever been my privilege to work with.

There was even more than the usual first-night excitement going on when we opened in New York. Everyone was running in and out of everyone else's dressing-rooms, the passages were stacked high with boxes of flowers, Frank Collins and Dan O'Neil were conducting a gloomy little conference with the heads of departments on the bare stage.

I felt as though I were in a sort of coma. The outlook was so black, the past week had been so gruelling, and although I was sure that the scenery was bound to fall down, the lights go wrong all through and the audience walk out on us, I was really too exhausted to care.

We went through the first half in a trance, more and more astounded, as each scene concluded, that no hitches had occurred. The second half went, if possible, even more smoothly than the first. Not a light was wrong (Frank Collins had stationed himself in the limelight box in the front of the house), not a property was out of place, and the cast, stimulated by the responsiveness of the audience, played magnificently. Altogether it was a triumphant evening, and Beattie and I fell into each other's arms sobbing with relief at the end.

From then onwards Beattie and I co-starred not only theatrically but socially in all directions. We appeared together everywhere. At large Charity Balls where we sang 'Lilac Time,' at select Ladies' Clubs where we sang 'Lilac Time,' at fashionable night-clubs where our entrance was the signal for an immediate flood of requests for us to sing 'Lilac Time,' and at small convivial theatrical parties to which we were invited on the strict understanding that in no circumstances would we sing 'Lilac Time.'

A week or so after the opening of the revue we gave a midnight performance which theatrical New York attended *en masse*, and which completely unbalanced our performance for several days afterwards. However good the audience were following that midnight show, they inevitably seemed flat and uninspiring.

In order to chasten our spirits and bring us down from our high altitude with a bump, Archie Selwyn had arranged that the next night should be a 'Benefit.' This benefit business is a custom in America, and although from the point of view of the charity concerned it is unquestionably profitable, from the point of view of the actors concerned it is Hell.

One of the most remunerative and popular means of raising funds for a pet cause is the buying out of the house for a performance of a successful play. Once bought and paid for, the tickets are resold at fabulous prices to the supporters of the charity in question. this, of course, is not effective unless the show is new and the demand for seats high.

The managements obviously have no objection to the arrangement, as it ensures the house being sold out at box-office prices, which is as much, if not more than they can ordinarily expect. For the actors, however, it is miserable in the extreme. A 'Benefit' night means, as a rule, an audience of such soul-shattering dreariness that it is as much as one can do to give even the semblance of a good performance.

The reason of this is difficult to discover. Whether the fact that they have all paid far too much for their seats, and are consequently in a mood of sullen resentment to start with, accounts for their behaviour, I do not know. But I do know that whether I have been warned beforehand that it is a charity audience, or whether I haven't, I can tell the first moment I step on to the stage.

To begin with, the stalls are usually half empty during the first act, and one is continually distracted by the noisy arrival of late comers, who churn down the aisles, generally in parties, and discuss loudly, with complete disregard for the performers or those already present, who is to sit next to whom. Once seated they scan the house anxiously with opera-glasses to discover whether or not their dearest enemies have better seats than they have. Their response to the play is apathetic, to say the least of it. Lines which, with an ordinary audience, always get big laughs, are unrewarded by so much as a twitter, and the play proceeds with almost as little reaction as if one were playing a dress rehearsal in an empty theatre.

Generally, in one of the intervals, a lady arrives back-stage covered with pearls, sables and orchids, to make a speech before the curtain, appealing for funds, which invariably enshrouds the house in still deeper gloom, so that the effort to re-establish the mood of the play afterwards is similar in sensation to remounting a horse immediately after you have fallen off it and broken three ribs.

During the last act there is a certain awakening of activity as people rise and leave in chattering groups in order to get to their cars before the rush begins. At the final curtain there is a general exodus, and the cast is lucky if it gets one curtain call.

14

This Year of Grace continued to play to packed houses. I had originally contracted to play it only for three months, but in the face of the business and Archie Selwyn's persuasions, I agreed to carry on for longer. During that winter Alec Woollcott inaugurated his Sunday morning breakfast parties. These peculiar functions, starting at nine a.m. and continuing until three or four in the afternoon, were adorned by a varied mixture of personalities ranging from Ethel Barrymore and Harpo Marx to lady novelists, osteopaths, *soi-disant* foreign princesses, cub-journalists, and grey university professors.

Alec, although lacking the essential grace and fragility of an eighteenth-century marquise, being as a rule unshaven and clad in insecure egg-stained pyjamas, managed in his own harum-scarum way to evoke a certain 'salon' spirit.

There was always a din of voices augmented by the crash of crockery and the rattle of dice and backgammon men, above which Alec could sometimes be heard crooning to himself in ghastly baby language – 'Evwy night my pwayers I say, I learn my lessons EVWY day' – until his opponent happened to throw double sixes, whereupon he would scream shrilly – 'Bitch delivered of a Drab' in tones of such, apparently, ungovernable fury that any strangers present who were unaccustomed to his particular brand of badinage would hastily brush the breakfast crumbs from their laps and edge, nervously, towards the door.

In addition to Dorothy Parker, Ben Hecht, Charlie MacArthur, Herbert Swope, George and Beatrice Kaufman, Alice Duer Miller, and Marc Connelly, you would be almost certain to find the Lunts, Margalo Gillmore, Thornton Wilder, twittering gently in a corner, Kathleen Norris, in majestic black satin and pearls with a rowdy look in her eye, and, if she and Alec happened to be on speaking terms, Edna Ferber.

It was at one of these strange galaxies that I met William Bolitho. His name I knew from his book *Murder for Profit* and his articles in the *New York World*, and the first thing that struck me about him was his intensity. It was not an obvious intensity, in fact his manner was on the whole singularly detached. He looked, if anything, a little irritated, as if the close proximity of so many people irked him and made him uneasy. He was tall and fair with blue eyes and a biggish nose, which he had a trick of whacking with his finger when he wished to emphasise some particular point. I liked him immediately, and when he invited me to dine the following evening before the show, I accepted with pleasure.

We dined at the Plaza: he, Sybil (his wife), and me. We talked incessantly, frequently all three of us at once. It was as though we were together again after a long absence; a reunion of close friends rather than an introductory meeting.

They lived near Avignon at Montfavet. Their house, they said, was surrounded by trees and there was a swimming-pool that William was very proud of, and several fruit trees and a vegetable garden of which he was still prouder. They spent six months of every year there and were returning quite soon.

I told them to expect me some time during the summer, and left them in a rush, having allowed myself only a bare ten minutes in which to get to the theatre.

15

During that winter, January and February, 1929, I finished *Bitter Sweet*, on which I had been working intermittently for the last few months. The book had been completed long since, but the score had been causing me trouble, until one day, when I was in a taxi on my way back to the apartment after a matinée, the 'I'll See You Again' waltz dropped into my mind, whole and complete, during a twenty minutes' traffic block. After that everything went smoothly, and I cabled to Cockie in London suggesting that he start making preliminary arrangements regarding theatre, opening date, etc.

My first choice for Sari had been Gertie Lawrence, but when the score was almost done, she and I both realised that her voice, although light and charming, was not strong enough to carry such a heavy singing rôle. She was naturally disappointed and I promised that the next play I wrote would be especially for her.

In the meantime a leading lady who could sing beautifully, look lovely and act well, had to be found. Evelyn Laye was the obvious choice in London, but she, unfortunately, owing to various previous contracts, was unobtainable.

One afternoon, in the lobby of the Algonquin Hotel, I ran into Peggy Wood. She had just come in from the country and was wearing a raincoat, an unbecoming rubbery hat on the back of her head, and horn-rimmed glasses, and she looked as far removed from my vision of Sari Linden as Mrs Wiggs of the Cabbage Patch.

I had known her on and off for several years, in fact ever since my first visit to New York in 1921, but oddly enough, in all that time I had never once seen her on the stage. I had, of course, heard on all sides enthusiastic accounts of her acting and her looks and the loveliness of her voice, but never having been able to judge for myself, and confronted by that rubber hat, that face devoid of make-up and those horn-rimmed glasses, it was with some trepidation that I heard myself asking her if she would care to come over to London and do an operetta.

She replied that she'd love to, but that hadn't I better hear her sing first? And so we rushed off immediately to my studio in the Hôtel des Artistes. On arrival, Peggy realised that she hadn't any music, and so she darted out and down the street where, fortunately, her music teacher happened to live, and returned in a few minutes with the score of *Manon*.

She sat down at once and started to sing, but had to stop owing to lack of breath.

After she had rested a little and had a glass of water she started again, and the first few bars she sang assured me that here was the ideal Sari.

I was impressed by her surprising lack of 'star' manner. With a long list of distinguished successes behind her she behaved as though she were being offered a good part for the first time. She was enthusiastic over the music I played to her. I knew from that moment that she would be a delight to work with, and I was right. In due course Cockie cabled a contract to Peggy, and with that primary difficulty settled, I continued to add finishing touches to the score and lyrics, until the whole show was complete.

16

Bitter Sweet went into rehearsal at the Scala Theatre at the end of May. We were ultimately bound for His Majesty's, but the Guitrys were at the moment in possession of it, and as the show was booked for a three weeks' try-out in Manchester, it was more convenient to rehearse in an empty theatre, where we could set up our scenery and work at nights as well as in the mornings and afternoons.

From the beginning *Bitter Sweet* went smoothly. Cockie and I, having taken an arduous trip to Berlin and Vienna in an effort to find a foreign tenor to play 'Carl,' had returned to London empty-handed and engaged George Metaxa, who had been available all the time. Ivy St Helier, for whom I had written the rôle of 'Manon La Crevette,' was already engaged, and the rest of the cast fell into our laps with hardly any trouble on our part at all.

We had had the usual auditions, and the chorus we had engaged sang well and looked pleasant. The scenery was well under way, the first and last acts having been designed by Gladys and the middle act by Ernst Stern. Peggy Wood arrived in good time from America and proceeded slowly but surely to build her distinguished performance. In fact, I reflected, with everything going so marvellously, the play, according to all theatrical tenets, couldn't escape being the gravest fiasco.

Cockie, who had tactfully left the production entirely to Gladys and me, came to the last rehearsal before the dress rehearsal. Before he arrived I made a little speech to the company through my microphone which I had had installed in the dress circle, imploring them to play up for all they were worth. The scenery was up but there was no orchestra, so Elsie officiated at the piano at the side of the stage. The company wore their ordinary day clothes and the lights consisted merely of a few battens and the footlights. In fact it was a thorough-going working rehearsal.

In due course Cockie arrived and he, Lorn, Jack, Frank, Cissie, Gladys and I took our places in the front row of the dress circle and waited apprehensively while Elsie scampered through the overture.

Of all the performances I ever saw of *Bitter Sweet* that rehearsal was far and away the most exciting. Each and every member of that always fine company, from Peggy down to the smallest walk-on in the café scene, was perfect. There were no dry-ups, no muddles in the dance routine and no undue waits between the scenes. Dan O'Neil, even with a skeleton staff, was, like everyone else backstage, inspired.

At the end Cockie thanked the company through the microphone in a voice husky with emotion and added that he wouldn't part with his rights in the play for a million pounds.

It was an unforgettable, glorious three hours and the dress parade the next day, according to the law of compensations, was correspondingly ghastly.

Many of the dresses had not been finished in time, and several of those that were, didn't fit. Half the shoes were missing. The stage was littered with squabbling dressmakers, shoemakers, wigmakers, fitters, and resentful chorus girls who hated their wigs and their bonnets, complained about their feet, and said they couldn't sing unless their collars were loosened. Several of them appeared with their bustles on back to front, and the smart uniforms of the Austrian officers looked as if they had only recently evacuated the front-line trenches.

Peggy sailed on and off in a series of lovely gowns, causing no trouble and minding her own business. Ivy, on the other hand, carried on like fifty prima donnas in one. She loathed her dresses, refused to wear her wigs, tried to insist on silk stockings which for the period would have been quite inappropriate, wept and wailed and entreated, until Gladys and I sprang at her like tigers and nearly murdered her.

At the dress rehearsal in Manchester she cheered up a bit, and after the opening night when she had given a splendid performance and had made a triumphant success, she changed back, like Beattie in New York, into her old gay, humorous self.

The Manchester first night was riotous. Peggy made a gracious speech and so did Cockie, in which he touchingly and generously handed me the credit for the whole production which, I may say, without his enthusiasm, his lavishness, and his unwavering trust in me, could never have been possible. The Press notices the next day were almost incoherent with praise, and the house was immediately sold out for the entire three weeks.

I think that of all the shows I have ever done *Bitter Sweet* gave me the greatest personal pleasure. My favourite moments were: the finale of the first act when Carl and Sari elope; the café scene when the curtain slowly falls on Carl's death, in a silence broken only by Manon's sobs; the entrance of Madame Sari Linden in her exquisite white dress of the nineties and, above all, the final moment of the play, when, to the last crashing chords of 'I'll See You Again,' Sari, as an old woman, straightens herself with a gesture of indomitable pride and gallantly walks off the stage. That gesture was entirely Peggy's idea, and the inspired dramatic simplicity of it set her for ever in my memory as a superb actress.

The London first night was definitely an anti-climax after Manchester. The audience were tremendously fashionable, and, for the first part of the play, almost as responsive as so many cornflour blancmanges.

Later on they warmed up a little, and at the end the upper parts of the house cheered. I sat with Gladys at the end in the dome of the auditorium where the spotlights were housed. It was pleasant to look down upon the audience unobserved. None of them seemed anxious to leave their seats and go home, from which I gathered that they were waiting for me to appear to make a speech. But my speech-making days were over, I did not appear, and when an hour or so later I was hailed at the stage door by a mob of vociferous gallery girls who demanded why I had not come out in response to their calls for me, I replied, with genuine irritation, that I only came on when they booed.

The Press notices the next day and on the Sunday following were remarkable for their tone of rather grudging patronage. It seemed as though the critics were ashamed of their recent outburst of enthusiasm over *This Year of Grace* and wished to retrench themselves behind a barricade of non-committal clichés. It would be too bad, after all, if I were encouraged to believe that there was anything remarkable in writing, composing and producing a complete operetta. I might become uppish again and this was an excellent opportunity of putting me gently but firmly in my place. Some praised the book, but dismissed the music as being reminiscent and of no consequence. Some liked the music, but were horrified by the commonplace sentimentality of the book. The lyrics were hardly mentioned, and although the acting and *décor* were favourably received, the general consensus of opinion was that the play would probably run for six weeks or, at the most, three months.

17

Cockie, already occupied with plans for an American production of *Bitter Sweet* in the autumn, had persuaded Evelyn Laye to play 'Sari.' This settled, he and Gladys and I went to France to start off again on the discouraging search for a tenor to play 'Carl.' This time, in addition to a tenor we had to find a soubrette to play 'Manon.'

Paris was hot and uncomfortable. We were surrounded by active theatrical agents who produced tenors and soubrettes by the score, until we were dizzy. None of them seemed anywhere near good enough.

Finally we engaged a little French comedienne called Mireille for 'Manon.' She was actually a bit young for the part, but her English was good and she sang well.

We were still without a 'Carl,' and were becoming more and more disheartened, when a handsome young Roman appeared with a letter of introduction from Princess Jane San Faustino. He had a good voice, long eyelashes, short legs, no stage experience and a violin, and although at the moment he couldn't speak a word of English, he swore with fervour that he would learn it in two months if we would only give him the part. We all felt a little dubious, but he seemed the likeliest possibility so far and so, after a certain amount of weary discussion, we engaged him.

This achieved, Gladys went back to London to devote herself to scenic problems, and I went to Avignon to stay with the Bolithos.

There was nothing to do at Montfavet but swim in the pool, lie in the garden, and occasionally drive into Avignon. William was just completing his book *Twelve Against the Gods* and was seldom visible before lunch.

The house was indeed thickly surrounded by trees, and might have been gloomy had anyone but the Bolithos been occupying it. As it was, the atmosphere was gay enough and indescribably peaceful. The food was plain and good, and we drank a sourly delicious *vin du pays* with every meal. Also with every meal William talked, and Time being serenely unimportant in that house, we often sat on for hours arguing and discussing and shouting at one another. He talked with fire and grace and beauty, and with apparently a profound knowledge of every subject under the sun. His vocabulary was brilliant and varied. He was often violent but never didactic, and he never appeared to monopolise the conversation or to show off or to try for too long to hold the floor.

Of all the minds I have ever encountered, his, I think, was the richest and the most loving. Those all too brief ten days I spent in his company turned me inside out, stimulated the best of my ambitions, readjusted several of my uneasy values, and banished many meretricious ones, I hope, for ever; and I went back to London strongly elated and bursting with gratitude to him for the strange new pride I found in myself.

18

The rehearsals for the American production of *Bitter Sweet* also took place at the Scala, and whereas with the original company everything had been easy, with this one it was exactly the opposite. The stimulus of building something new, watching the play grow, fill out and develop day by day, was naturally lacking. Everything was set, the formula was laid down, and with no excitement and no sense of discovery, it was all dreary to a degree.

Evelyn was delightful to work with, and the one bright spot in the whole business.

Jack, Gladys, Frank, Danny, Evelyn and I travelled over on the *Mauretania*, while the company followed on a slower boat. Cockie, much to our dismay, was unable to come at all, which meant that I was nominally in charge, and had to deal with Selwyn and Ziegfeld. If I had realised at the time the exasperation that this entailed, I should have insisted on Cockie's coming, even if it had meant shanghai-ing him. The voyage was comparatively uneventful. Ina Claire and John Gilbert, who had been staying with me at Goldenhurst in the course of a rather strained honeymoon, were on board, and enlivened the trip to a certain extent by their conjugal infelicities, quarrelling and making up and quarrelling and making up again unceasingly, all the way from Southampton to the Statue of Liberty.

Eventually we arrived in Boston for our two weeks' try-out, and embarked on a full Sunday-night rehearsal with orchestra in the Colonial Theatre.

It was at that rehearsal that we realised once and for all that our Roman tenor could never open without doing incalculable harm to the play. We had been buoying ourselves up with the hope that his English, over which he had been slaving, would improve sufficiently for him to be understood, but it was no good; up against the orchestra he was not only unintelligible but inaudible as well, also his lack of acting experience was so apparent, that even if he could have been heard, his important scenes would have gone for nothing. I felt desperately sorry for him. He had worked hard and done his best, but Evelyn and the play had to be considered, and so I told him that he couldn't appear. It was a painful scene, as those scenes always are, but there was no time to waste, and I left Dan O'Neil to comfort him and devoted my attention to Gerald Nodin, whom I had decided to put in his place. Nodin had originally sung 'Tokay' in the London production, and although quite wrong in type for 'Carl,' he had the advantage of knowing the show thoroughly, and was ambitious enough to make the utmost of himself.

All that night and all the next day he worked. Evelyn played her scenes with him over and over again, encouraging him and helping him in every way she could think of. Watching her and knowing how tired and nervous she was, I found it easy to understand why she was so adored by every company she had ever worked with.

On the day of production Ziegfeld asked me to lunch and told me in course of it that, as I had so resolutely refused his offer of a smarter male chorus and twelve ravishing show-girls (an offer, incidentally, which had been made daily since our arrival in America), he was going to refrain from any undue display over the New York first night and, contrary to his usual custom, was not even going to raise the prices. I received this dispiriting announcement apathetically, being far too exhausted to care whether he gave the seats away with a packet of chewing-gum.

The show, however, was an enormous success in Boston, and by the time the New York first night arrived, it had been so publicised that a special cordon of police had to be called out to control the traffic in Sixth Avenue. Floodlighting was used to illuminate the gratified audience as they came into the theatre. Flashlight photographs were taken of every celebrity that entered the lobby, and seats on the orchestra floor were sold by speculators for as much as two hundred and fifty dollars a pair. Ziegfeld, whom I now addressed affectionately as 'Flo,' had placed his office and private box at the disposal of Gladys, Jack and me. He had generously stacked it with flowers, caviare and champagne, and whenever, during the performance, we found a certain scene too wearisome to be borne, we retired to it and had a drink, with the result that by the end of the evening we were merrily unconcerned as to whether the show was a success or not. As a matter of fact, it was. The company, although I never felt them to be up to their London equivalents, played, on the whole, remarkably well. But it was Evelyn who turned the scale. It was Evelyn's night from first to last. She played as though she were enchanted. Never before at any of the rehearsals or at any of the performances in Boston had she given a quarter of the grace and charm and assurance that she gave that night. Early on in the ballroom scene she conquered the audience completely by singing the quick waltz song, 'Tell Me, What is Love?' so brilliantly, and with such a quality of excitement, that the next few minutes of the play were entirely lost in one of the most prolonged outbursts of cheering I have ever heard in a theatre.

Her performance was magnificent all through, and she fully deserved every superlative that the Press lavished upon her the next day. It would, of course, have been impossible for her to play with such inspiration at every subsequent performance, and I don't suppose for a moment that she either could or did, but it was she, and she alone, who put the play over that night.

PART NINE

I sailed from San Francisco in one of the Dollar Line ships, the *President Garfield*, at four p.m. on the 29th of November, 1929.

The day was grey and chilly, and an angry wind swept through the Golden Gate, whipping the harbour into waves and tearing the smoke out of the ship's funnel in a straight black line.

The important fact that this holiday was an escape that I had been planning for a long while dwindled under a general sense of futility. Jeffery, who had given up his job on the *New York World* in the spring and gone off in a freight boat to the South Seas and Australia, had arranged to meet me on the 23rd of December in the Imperial Hotel, Tokio. We had sat in the garden at Goldenhurst with a globe between us on the grass planning the places we were going to, picturing (inaccurately) the Temple of Heaven in Peking, the Ruins of Angkor, vivid tropical jungles and the road to Mandalay, flying-fish and all. Then, with soft Kentish greens all around us and grey Kentish sheep punctuating our imaginative flights with gentle bleats, the whole scheme seemed glamorous beyond words; now, however, in the grip of inevitable 'boat-departure' anti-climax, I was lonely and depressed, and felt that I should have been far wiser to have stayed at home and read a travel book.

I looked dismally at the packages of fruit and flowers and books which various friends had sent me, and even more dismally at a map hanging by the purser's office. Far over in the corner of it, among a welter of greens and browns, I could discern a minute reddish speck which was England and with the aid of the pin from my tie I fixed approximately the spot where, probably at this very moment, Auntie Vida was battling through the weather with a trowel to attack the weeds in the orchard.

After dinner – an interlude of polite conversation at the captain's table – I sat on deck for a while. It was getting dark, and far away astern a few lights were shimmering on the coast. The weather was clearing and the sea calm.

It was a good moment for retrospection, so I put my feet up on the rail and relaxed, aware suddenly that time was no longer exigent. I had nothing to do, hours stretched before me into the future, hundreds and thousands of hours. No more rehearsals, no more first nights, no more leading ladies to be cajoled, no more theatrical anxieties, arguments and irritations. My dramatic sense saw me picturesquely languid, wearier than I really was, and a self-conscious peace descended upon me as I lay there looking up at the stars.

I journeyed back into the past without any particular aim or direction, allowing events of the past few months to hobnob with more elderly memories. I saw myself in a sailor suit singing 'Come Along with Me to the Zoo, Dear'; in a tail-suit singing, 'Dance, Little Lady'; in a sweat-stained dressing-gown in New York pounding out short stories on my typewriter; in baggy riding-breeches riding along the sands at Deauville. I heard, dimly, the cheers for *The Vortex* and, less dimly, the catcalls for *Sirocco*. I heard orchestras tuning-up and fateful, shuffling sounds of curtains rising. People, too, popped up briefly out of the limbo and then sank back again like the little white letters in vermicelli soup when you churn it with your spoon. Gwen Kelly singing 'Every Morn I Bring Thee Violets'; Mary Garden singing 'Vissi D'Arte'; Mother in grey satin and a feather boa smiling exultantly over an ice-cream soda in Selfridge's – Mother again, hot and tired, cooking in the Ebury Street kitchen; Charles Hawtrey patting me on the back; Robert Courtneidge saying: 'You're not only a very young actor but a very bad actor!'; Stoj in a white knitted coat and skirt riding along suburban roads on a bicycle; John Ekins buying vivid artificial silk socks with me for two shillings a pair in the Berwick Market. I suddenly remembered William Bolitho talking to me just before I left New York. I had told him of a novel I intended to write, rather a neurotic novel about a man who committed suicide because he was bored. William whacked his nose with his finger and said, almost sharply: 'Be careful about Death, it's a serious business, big and important. You can't go sauntering towards Death with a cigarette hanging from your mouth!'

I didn't know then that those were the last words he would ever speak to me, and he effaced himself along with the others to make room for some clamorous new friends I had found in Hollywood.

Looking back over my ten days in Hollywood made me gasp a bit and wish for a little neat brandy. I felt as though I had been whirled through all the side-shows of some gigantic Pleasure Park at breakneck speed. My spiritual legs were wobbly and my impressions confused. Blue-ridged cardboard mountains, painted skies, elaborate grottoes peopled with familiar figures: animated figures that moved their arms and legs, got up and sat down and spoke with remembered voices.

The houses I had visited became indistinguishable in my mind from the built interiors I had seen in the studios. I couldn't remember clearly whether the walls of Jack Gilbert's dining room had actually risen to a conventional ceiling or whether they had been sawn off half-way up to make room for scaffolding and spluttering blue arc-lamps.

I remembered an evening with Charlie Chaplin when at one point he played an accordion and at another a pipe-organ, and then suddenly became almost pathologically morose and discussed Sadism, Masochism, Shakespeare and the Infinite.

I remembered a motor drive along flat, straight boulevards with Gloria Swanson, during which we discussed, almost exclusively, dentistry.

I remembered, chaotically, a series of dinner parties, lunch parties, cocktail parties and even breakfast parties. I remembered also playing a game of tennis with Charlie MacArthur somewhere at two in the morning, with wire racquets, in a blaze of artificial moonlight and watching him, immediately afterwards, plunge fully clothed into an illuminated swimming-pool.

I remembered Laura Hope-Crews appearing unexpectedly from behind a fountain and whispering gently: 'Don't be frightened, dear – this – THIS – is Hollywood!'

I had been received with the utmost kindness and hospitality, and I enjoyed every minute of it; it was only now, in quietness, that it seemed unreal and inconclusive, as though it hadn't happened at all.

It occurred to me that I had been living in a crowd for too long; not only a crowd of friends, enemies and acquaintances, but a crowd of events: events that had followed each other so swiftly that the value of them, their causes and effects, their significance, had escaped me. My nervous energy, always excessive, had carried me so far. My determination, ambition and almost hysterical industry had been rewarded generously, perhaps too generously. I remembered driving with Gladys down the long road from Hampstead after the first night of *The Vortex* – 'And now what?'

Then there had been no time to answer; success had to be dealt with, adjustments had to be made to my new circumstances, more money, more people, more noise, more diffusion of experience, new attitudes to be acquired, a thousand new tricks to be learned. And now, after only five years, here was that offensive little query bobbing up again. The acquired attitudes were no longer new, I could slip them on and off with ease to suit every occasion. The social tricks, then so fresh and shiny, were now creaking mechanically. There were the demands I had made, miraculously granted, looking a bit smug. Most of my gift horses seemed to have bad teeth – and now what?

I comforted myself with the thought that perhaps this uneasiness, this vague sense of dissatisfaction was a good sign. If I was as superficial as so many people apparently thought – a subtle whip this, always guaranteed to raise a weal – if my mind was so shallow, if the characters I had written were so meretricious and unreal, if my achievements fell so far short of the first-rate, surely this moment of all moments, this relaxed contemplation of recent triumphs should fairly swaddle me in complacency. I should be able to smile, a smooth, detached smile – 'People say – what do they say? – let them say!' I should be able to boast, not loudly but with a quiet satisfaction – 'at least I have done this and that in a remarkably short space of time.' I should be able to defy the envious, the jealous, and the unkind – come on, if you're so critical – come on and do better! I should be serene, content with my light-weight crown, without a headache and without doubts.

On the other hand, however, I felt no conviction that this reasoning was in the least accurate. It seemed arbitrary to assume that a superficial mind was necessarily invulnerable. Perhaps my uneasiness was the true indication of my worth, the inevitable shadow thrown by thin facility; a deeper mind might suffer more, win less spectacular laurels and in the long run stake a richer claim.

There seemed no criterion by which I could judge my quality, or rather so many criteria that they nullified each other.

How, from all the written and spoken praise, blame, admiration, envy, prejudice, malice, kindness and contempt that these last few years had brought me, could I abstract a little of what was really true? Which of all those critical minds had been the most unbiased – nearest to hitting the nail on the head? How much had the precipitate flamboyance of my success prejudiced not only those who criticised my work, but the work itself? In fact, where was I and what was I? Had I done what I thought I'd done or what others thought I had done? Was my talent real, deeply flowing, capable of steady growth and ultimate maturity? Or was it the evanescent sleight-of-hand that many believed it to be; an amusing, drawing-room flair, adroit enough to skim a certain immediate acclaim from the surface of life but with no roots in experience and no potentialities?

Among all the thousands of people I knew I searched vainly in my mind to find one who could give me an answer or, at any rate, a comment accurate and honest enough to restore my sense of direction. The simple single track of earlier years seemed far away. There had been no necessity to look either to the right or to the left then, success was the goal – 'Noël Coward' in electric lights. Now I found the electric lights so dazzling that I couldn't see beyond them. It was no use asking for help, jogging policemen's elbows and enquiring the way. The lights blinding me would probably be blinding the policeman too. Solutions and answers would fall into place in time. Nobody, however well-intentioned, could find my own truths for me, and only very few could even help me to look for them. In moments of private chaos it is better to be alone; loving advice merely increases the chaos. At all events I could congratulate myself whole-heartedly on one count: I had realised, I hoped not too late, the necessity for space, and had deliberately broken away. Perhaps the next few months would answer a few of my questions for me; perhaps new countries, sights, sounds and smells, the complete cessation of familiar routines, this strange sense of timelessness would release from the caverns of my mind the most gratifying profundities. It would be enjoyable to return to my startled friends with, in addition to the usual traveller's souvenirs, a Strindbergian soul. I remember leaving the sea and the sky and the stars in charge of my problems and going below to my cabin chuckling a little at my incorrigible superficiality.

2

We arrived at Honolulu at six a.m. on a calm opalescent sea. I looked out of my port-hole as we passed Diamond Head towering above the palm trees; perched half-way up it I could see the Dillinghams' house where I hoped, at that very moment, breakfast was being prepared for me.

It all looked so gay and different from that horrible morning three years before when I had arrived and collapsed in the Moana Hotel. Then, seen through a haze of fever and unhappiness, everything had seemed too bright and highly-coloured and somehow unfriendly. But now it was enchanting.

Walter Dillingham's secretary met me at the dock and we drove off past the outlying buildings of the town, along that lovely road with the palm-fringed surf on one side and the mountains rising, clear-cut, out of the plains on the other.

Louise was unfortunately away visiting her eldest son in the States, so Walter and I had breakfast by ourselves, sitting on the terrace and looking out over descending green lawns to the town in the distance. The wide sweep of the sea outside the reef was deep blue, but inside near the shore the water was streaked with jade green. I could hear distinctly in the stillness the cries of the beach boys riding the surf at Waikiki, although they were nearly two miles away. A freighter with a jaunty red-and-black funnel was trundling across the bay, rolling so lackadaisically in the slight swell that I almost expected it to yawn.

Walter gave a dinner party for me that night, and while we dined a small Hawaiian orchestra played and sang softly outside. After dinner we all went out on to the moon-flooded patio and laying long chairs drinking coffee and liqueurs, listening to further music and gazing up at Diamond Head above us.

The four days in Honolulu passed swiftly. I motored over to Mokuleia and bathed from that beach where before I had spent so many homesick hours. I re-trod the road from the ranch through bananas and sugar-canes where the white dust had formerly been furrowed by my tears of self-pity. I walked through the pine trees, with the roar of the surf growing louder and louder in my ears until I came out on to the sand and saw the enormous waves advancing endlessly like rolls of blue velvet, unfrilled and unruffled until they broke in thunder on the reef, sending smaller editions of themselves to splay the beach with foam. I went out at night on a fish-spearing expedition and wandered about the reef waist-deep in water, making ineffectual dabs with my spear whenever I saw anything move in the light cast by the torches until finally, in triumph, I transfixed a wriggling pink octopus and handed it graciously to the natives to kill, which they did by biting its eyes out.

I visited the Thevenins who had left Mokuleia and were living in a small house just outside the town, and learned to my sorrow that poor 'Owgooste' had had to be destroyed owing to an outburst of indescribable savagery in which he had bitten the behind of a Filipino coolie.

Finally, a trifle exhausted but warmed by Hawaiian sunshine and hospitality, and conscious that I had laid for ever a number of personal ghosts, I sailed on the *Tenyo Maru*, a distinctly *passé* vessel of the N. Y. K. Line, for Yokohama.

3

The eight days on the *Tenyo* were more or less uneventful, except that we completely lost a whole Saturday, which worried me rather.

I worked hard on my novel *Julian Kane*, but became increasingly discouraged by its obvious dullness, until I finally decided that if it continued as it was going the future readers of it would commit suicide from boredom long before the hero ever reached that point of defeat, and so discarding it I proceeded to concentrate on finding an idea for a play.

Gertie Lawrence, the night before I had left New York, had given a farewell party for me and, as a going-away present, a little gold book from Cartiers's which when opened and placed on the writing-table in my cabin disclosed a clock, calendar and thermometer on one side, and an extremely pensive photograph of Gertie herself on the other. This rich gift, although I am sure prompted by the least ulterior of motives, certainly served as a delicate reminder that I had promised to write a play for us both, and I gazed daily, often with irritation, at that anxious *retroussé* face while my mind voyaged barrenly through eighteenth-century salons, Second Empire drawing-rooms and modern cocktail bars in search of some inspiring echo, some slight thread of plot that might suitably unite us in either comedy, tragedy or sentiment.

However, nothing happened. I was aware of a complete emptiness. The Pacific Ocean, bland and calm, swished by with the perpetual off-stage effect of rice in a sieve; flying-fish skittered away from the bows, skimming along the surface for a while and disappearing with little plops; my fellow-passengers paraded round and round the deck providing me with nothing beyond a few irrelevant and purposeless conjectures, until I finally gave up. This was a holiday after all, and I refused to allow my writer's conscience to agitate it any further. I also resolved never again to make any promises that implicated my creative ability. They were limiting and tiresome and imposed too great a strain. I would write whatever the spirit moved me to write, regardless of whether the subject matter was suitable to Gertie Lawrence, Mrs Patrick Campbell or Grock, and in the meantime, feeling no particular urge to write anything at all, I closed Gertie's clock with a snap and read a book.

4

At about five o'clock on a bitter December afternoon the *Tenyo Maru* came to a standstill in the bay of Yokohama. There was a blizzard raging and, through it, I could see from the smoking-room window the quarantine launch approaching like an asthmatical old lady fussing through bead curtains.

Shapes of land appeared at intervals through the driving sleet; strange nobbly mountains dotted here and there with white specks which I gathered were lighthouses.

The drive from Yokohama to Tokio takes as a rule about fifty minutes, but mine took longer as a wheel came off the taxi when we were half-way. I sat inside in a pool of water watching, in the downpour, several excited Japanese put it on again and feeling, on the whole, discouraged by my first view of the 'Glamorous Orient.'

The Imperial Hotel was grand and comfortable, and was renowned for having stood firm during the big earthquake. A wire was handed me from Jeffery saying that he had missed a boat in Shanghai and wouldn't be with me for three days which, although disappointing, was a relief, as I had begun to think I was never going to hear from him at all.

The night before he arrived I went to bed early as I wanted to greet him as brightly as possible at seven in the morning, but the moment I switched out the lights, Gertie appeared in a white Molyneux dress on a terrace in the South of France and refused to go again until four a.m., by which time *Private Lives*, title and all, had constructed itself.

In 1923 the play would have been written and typed within a few days of my thinking of it, but in 1929 I had learned the wisdom of not welcoming a new idea too ardently, so I forced it into the back of my mind, trusting to its own integrity to emerge again later on, when it had become sufficiently set and matured.

We found Tokio flat and painfully ugly: a sad scrap-heap of a city, rather like Wembley in the process of demolition. The streets were all muddy and everything appeared to be in course of reconstruction owing, we supposed, to perpetual earthquakes and an excess of zeal in the way of Western improvements. Fortunately, however, Tokio is far from being representative of Japan. Nikko is only four hours away with its snow-capped mountains and gurgling streams, and its temples and shrines peacefully sheltered in groves of trees.

We spent a couple of days there in a neat, shiny little hotel with paper walls, a few back numbers of *Woman and Home* and excellent food.

After three weeks in Japan we crossed the Yellow Sea to Fusan, and travelled by train up through Korea to Mukden in Manchuria where we were met, at six in the morning, by a gentleman in furs who turned out to be not only the British Consul, but the brother of Frank Tours, the musical director of *Bitter Sweet* in New York.

He gave us a delicious, thoroughly English breakfast and a hot bath, after which we went out in rickshaws to see the town; but we soon came back with tears of agony running down our faces, as the wind happened to be blowing from Siberia that morning, and the temperature was thirty below zero.

That evening we spent a pleasant hour or two in the English Club. The English and American residents, of which there were few, had organised a fancy-dress dance to celebrate the passing of 1929. It was a strange party and, beneath its gaiety, exceedingly touching. Pierrots, Columbines, Clowns, red rep Cardinals and butter-muslin Juliets, all pulling crackers, drinking punch and crossing hands to sing together 'Should auld acquaintance be forgot,' while outside the wind blew like ice over the Manchurian wastes and the snow piled high on the window-sills. If they had not all been so kind and hospitable to us we might have had time to feel a little guilty. We were only passing through. We were free to go where we pleased, whereas the bulk of the people present were condemned to stay in that grim, remote place perhaps for years.

I will spare the reader a detailed description of a twenty-four-hour journey to Peking in an unheated train in which we sat, wrapped in fur coats, in a wooden compartment trying unsuccessfully to conquer intestinal chills by eating nothing at all and drinking a bottle of brandy each, while the frozen Chinese countryside struggled bleakly by the windows.

Lady Lampson, the wife of Sir Miles Lampson, the British Minister, was particularly charming to us in Peking. She showed us the incredible beauties of the city; organised our shopping expeditions, and took pains to prevent us from buying soapstone instead of jade, and plaster instead of Ming pottery.

We travelled as far as Shanghai with her and her little boy, who was going home to school in England. A few days later we heard that she had been taken seriously ill with spinal meningitis on her arrival in Hong Kong and, a little later still, that she was dead. This saddened us horribly. We had only known her for a few weeks, but during that time she had been so hospitable and kind that we felt we had lost a much older friend.

5

A bout of influenza laid me low in Shanghai, and I lay, sweating gloomily, in my bedroom in the Cathay Hotel for several days. The ensuing convalescence, however, was productive, for I utilised it by writing *Private Lives*. The idea by now seemed ripe enough to have a shot at, so I started it, propped up in bed with a writing-block and an Eversharp pencil, and completed it, roughly, in four days. It came easily, and with the exception of a few of the usual 'blood and tears' moments, I enjoyed writing it. I thought it a shrewd and witty comedy, well constructed on the whole, but psychologically unstable; however, its entertainment value seemed obvious enough, and its acting opportunities for Gertie and me admirable, so I cabled to her immediately in New York telling her to keep herself free for the autumn, and put the whole thing aside for a few weeks before typing and revising it.

With influenza and *Private Lives* both behind me I entered the social whirl of Shanghai with zest. There were lots of parties and Chinese dinners and general cosmopolitan junketings, which, while putting a slight strain on our lingual abilities, in no way dampened our spirits. We found some charming new friends, notably Madame Birt and her twin daughters who, apart from being extremely attractive, could quarrel with each other in six different languages without even realising that they were not sticking to one; and three English naval officers, Ascherson, Bushell and Guerrier, with whom we visited many of the lower and gayer haunts of the city and sailed as their guests on our first but, as far as I was concerned, not my last voyage in one of His Majesty's ships.

Ever since then I have become increasingly indebted to the Navy. To me, the life of a guest in a warship is deeply satisfactory. I have passed some of the happiest hours of my life in various ward-rooms. The secret of naval good manners is hard to define; perhaps discipline has a lot to do with it and prolonged contact with the sea; perhaps a permanent background of such dignity makes for simplicity of mind.

Perhaps all this is an illusion, perhaps it is merely the complete change of atmosphere that so englamours me; if so I shall certainly take good care never to outstay my welcome long enough to break it.

Ascherson, Bushell and Guerrier, having firmly inoculated me with the naval bug, obtained permission from their captain, Captain Arbuthnot, for us both to travel as far as Hong Kong with them, and we sailed down the river from Shanghai in the H.M.S. *Suffolk* on a cold sunny morning in February. The warships of other nations, American, French and Italian, saluted as we moved down-stream. Jeffery and I, well placed out of everyone's way on the gun deck, stood, uncertain whether to keep our hats on or off, knowing only that we mustn't smoke and must wait there, however cold, until fetched into the ward-room for a drink. We watched the busy water-front slide away. The air was sharp and clear, and the blue of the coolies' coats on the bund took from the sun such vivid brightness that, in the distance, it looked as though the river had climbed up into the streets and was swirling among the houses.

The voyage took five days, as we stopped every now and then on the way for various exercises. I think we behaved adequately well on the whole. We learnt, and remembered, various little lessons in naval etiquette and jargon as we went along. We had a comfortable cabin each, and the captain allowed us the use of his bathroom. There is a permanent humming noise in a warship which is soothing to the nerves, and a clean, efficient smell, impossible to describe, but quite unique. No one paid much attention to us and we were free to wander about and observe the life of the ship, and a very cheerful and energetic life it seemed to be. There was an incessant orgy of polishing and swabbing and scrubbing from the moment we left Shanghai to the moment we arrived in Hong Kong. There was also a great deal of bugle-blowing and fast running, crabwise, up and down narrow iron ladders. At night we dressed for dinner and sat round the shiny ward-room table while the marine band fought its way gallantly through the intricacies of *Bitter Sweet* and *This Year of Grace*, the parts of which the bandmaster had hurriedly bought in Shanghai when he heard that I was to be a passenger.

The ship changed for dinner, too. It changed its personality entirely, becoming silent, purposeful and almost sinister. There was no activity and hardly any noise except for the humming of the engines. We usually went up on the bridge for a little while before going to bed, and put the final seal upon the drinks we had drunk in the ward-room by swallowing a mug of ship's cocoa with the officer of the watch. Then, of all moments, we were most conscious of the good old layman's romantic 'thrill of the Navy.' The ship slid quietly through the darkness and we felt the pulse of her strength beneath our feet. The water cut away from the bows and swished and gurgled alongside, occasionally streaked with phosphorus, while overhead strange and larger stars appeared. There was a slight panic one night because Guerrier, who happened to have the middle watch, sent a frantic message down to the ward-room to say that he'd mislaid an island and did anyone know where it was! A good deal of agitation ensued, and it was finally located several miles off the port bow. This joke lasted everyone for quite a while.

Finally, on the fifth evening, Hong Kong sprang abruptly at us out of a fog. The sun was just setting, and the island against a suddenly clear sky was a fantastically beautiful sight, but at that moment sad and unwelcome for us both because it meant that we had to go ashore.

We loitered on board as long as we could. Long after the captain had left in his launch, long after night had fallen, we were still standing about in the ward-room accepting with gracious melancholy 'gimlet' after 'gimlet' until finally we clattered unsteadily down the ladder behind our luggage and went bouncing off across the harbour to the Peninsula Hotel at Kowloon, where we ate some caviare and drank still more gin. Jeffery indeed was so sunk in depression that he signed the hotel register 'Mackintosh' without my noticing, a slip of the pen which caused us considerable trouble later on.

We stayed a week in Hong Kong. I spent most of it sitting in my hotel bedroom typing and revising *Private Lives*. When it was completed I sent copies of it to Gertie and Jack in New York, and told them to cable me in Singapore what they thought about it.

The night before we left we gave a farewell dinner to all the officers of the *Suffolk*. They were going to sea early next morning and that evening, although tinged with regret, was, to say the least of it, a success.

We rose with cracking heads to watch from our windows the *Suffolk* sail away. We felt very proud to know her as she steamed with slow dignity out of the harbour, and also so low that we ordered a bottle of champagne then and there, a drink that we both detest, and drank it to the last drop sitting miserably in a hot bath.

We embarked that same afternoon on one of the filthiest little freight boats I have ever encountered. We were bound for Haiphong in Indo-China, and there were no other boats available. This one, whose name I will withhold owing to the laws of libel, was French-owned, and manned by a crew of murderous-looking

Annamites and three French officers with singularly untidy personalities. Our cabin contained two cast-iron bunks and a tin basin, and we shared it with hordes of cockroaches, bed bugs and fleas, and a dead mouse which we buried at sea as soon as the tragedy was discovered.

We were immured in that God-forsaken tub, with a cargo of copra and salt fish, for five days and nights.

On arrival at Haiphong we hired a car and drove to Hanoi, which is the capital of Tonkin. Here we were not allowed out of the hotel as there was a revolution in progress; however, Monsieur Pasquier, the Governor-General, to whom we had a letter of introduction, sent his A.D.C. and car to fetch us, and we spent a strange evening in the Government Palace with Monsieur Pasquier, two Generals, an Admiral and the A.D.C. Outside the revolution was in full swing, and there was occasionally the sound of gun-fire. Inside all was peaceful and well-ordered. The dinner was delicious, the wine excellent, and Monsieur Pasquier the most delightful host.

We hired a car and a driver and set off the next day down the length of Indo-China to Saigon. The journey took the best part of a week, the scenery alternating violently between the steepest of steep mountains and the flattest of flat plains, with a little jungle thrown in every now and then, and a never-ending series of rivers across which we were ferried on creaking, insecure barges. We were deeply impressed by the admirable French colonisation which enabled us to procure excellent coffee and rolls in the remotest villages.

The night before we were due to arrive in Saigon we stopped at a small village called Nah Trang. The rest-house was clean but primitive, and we went to bed early as we were getting up at dawn to make the last lap of our journey. At about a quarter to five, before it was light, I was wakened by Jeffery demanding, in a shaky dry voice, a thermometer. I struggled out from under my mosquito net, lit a candle and took his temperature which, to my horror, was nearly a hundred and four. I disguised the truth from him and told him it was just on a hundred and, having roused our driver and dressed as quickly as we could, we set off, hell for leather, for Saigon. It was a hideous journey – our driver, none too good at any time, became demoniac when urged to drive fast. We slaughtered countless chickens and ducks, two dogs, a snake and a cat. Jeffery was delirious part of the time, and I watched him anxiously for symptoms of coma, because my mind all the while was haunted by the memory of Lady Lampson and spinal meningitis.

We arrived in Saigon in the full glare of midday. Every blind was down and there wasn't a creature moving. The streets were white with heat, and Jeffery by then was almost unconscious. I got him into a room in the hotel and set off in a rickshaw, the hotel porter having directed me to a clinic, where I managed to persuade a pompous little doctor to rouse himself from his siesta and come with me.

The result of all this was that Jeffery was moved into the clinic, with what the French doctor hilariously diagnosed as *'mal au foie – rien que mal au foie.'* He was given a few injections and some vegetable soup immediately, and why he didn't die I shall never know, because several weeks later when he was properly examined in Singapore he was found to be suffering from amoebic dysentery.

However, he lay in the clinic in Saigon for close on a month, and finally emerged looking more like a hat-pin than a human being, but pronounced fit enough to continue our journey up through Angkor and into Siam. In the meantime I spent those four weeks in isolated splendour in the Grand Hotel. Saigon is very small and is referred to proudly by the French as the Paris of the Orient. This, I need hardly say, is an over-statement. It is a well-arranged little town and it has several cafés and a municipal opera house, but it is *not* very like Paris.

I visited Jeffery twice a day and discovered a pleasant little café and brothel combined which catered mostly for the lower-class mercantile marines and a floating clientele of tarts of all nations; apart from these distractions I spent most of my time sitting on a cane chair outside the Grand Hotel watching the *beau monde* bouncing up and down the Rue Catinat in rickshaws. The hotel orchestra played selections from *Tosca*, *Madame Butterfly* and the tinkling French operettas of the nineties every evening, and for a little while the scene took on a certain forlorn charm. But even this faded after the first few days, because it took only a very short while to know every single person that passed by sight.

When Jeffery so strangely recovered from the ministrations of that doctor we set off to Angkor, where we stayed for ten days. We wandered through queer magnificent ruins; we watched the temple dancers in the vast courtyard of Angkor Vat, swaying and stamping to harsh music in the flickering light of torches and coloured flares; we drove through the jungle roads, coming upon villages still in the process of excavation, still in the grip of the jungle, houses with strong trees growing right up through them and grey monkeys chattering on the crumbling roofs.

From Angkor we motored to Aranya Pradesa, the Siamese frontier, over the most appalling road I have ever encountered; from there, after a night in a surprisingly German rest-house, we took a train to Bangkok, where we stayed for two weeks. The Phya Tai Palace, which had once belonged to the Royal Family, was now a hotel, cool, spacious and reasonably comfortable, although I must admit that I once woke up from my after-lunch siesta to find a majestic procession of red ants making a forced march from one side of the mattress to the other, by way of my stomach.

We saw all the sights the city had to offer, and they were many and varied, ranging from an emerald Buddha the size of a football to the Pasteur Institute, where they extracted the venom from snakes by the apparently casual method of seizing them by the neck and making them bite little parchment saucers.

6

During that holiday, I think my spirits reached their lowest ebb on the first evening I spent in Singapore . I sat on the veranda of the hotel, sipping a gin-sling and staring at the muddy sea. There was a thunderstorm brewing and the airless heat pressed down on my head. I felt as though I were inside a hot cardboard box which was growing rapidly smaller and smaller, until soon I should have to give up all hope of breathing and die of suffocation.

My state of mind was not solely due to the climate. Jeffery had been taken badly ill again in the little Danish freighter which had brought us from Siam, and I had just left him in the hospital, looking like death and waiting to be diagnosed. My imagination was busy wording, as gently as possible, the fatal telegram to his mother. I pictured her receiving it in the cool quietness of her Wilton Crescent drawing-room while I, in this God-forsaken hole, dealt sadly but efficiently with grisly funereal details; in fact, by the time my second gin-sling was brought to me Jeffery was dead and buried.

Presently the thunderstorm broke and raged violently for about an hour. It was the most thorough-going storm I had ever seen. The sky split in two; the sea lost its smooth, oily temper and rushed at the hotel as though it wanted to swallow it up, and then the rain came. I recognised it as rain only because I knew it couldn't possibly be anything else; it certainly bore no resemblance to any rain I had ever met before. It fell like a steel curtain, and its impact on the roof of the veranda was terrific. Then, abruptly, the whole performance stopped. The sea relaxed, the skies cleared, the stars came out, and in the cooler air my imagination became less fevered. I drove up to the hospital after dinner and found Jeffery enjoying a cigarette and an animated conversation with the night nurse.

The next day the doctors said that he had dysentery and would be able to leave the hospital in about a month if all went well. Once resigned to this enforced pause in our travels we both felt better, and while Jeffery concentrated on his discomforts and treatments, I set out to discover what Singapore had to offer in the way of distractions.

The first and principal distraction I found was an English theatrical touring company called 'The Quaints.' They were appearing at the Victoria Theatre and their repertory was almost shockingly varied. They played, with a certain light-hearted abandon, *Hamlet*, *Mr Cinders*, *Anthony and Cleopatra*, *The Girl Friend*, *When Knights Were Bold*, and *Journey's End*. I was taken to their opening performance of *Mr Cinders* by the manager of the theatre and from then onwards I never left them. My chief friends among them were Betty Hare and John Mills, both of whom have worked with me a great deal since, and the general major-domo of the whole enterprise, Jimmy Grant Anderson. Jimmy was rich in quality; he was 'of the dust the theatre bore, shaped, made aware,' his blood was the best grease-paint. I had met him before in a thousand people, but never so concentrated, never such triple distilled essence. His mind was a prop hamper crammed to the lid with theatre finery. To him the sea and the sky were only painted on canvas, and not any too well painted at that. Behind the immediate Singapore act drop there were other scenes being set, there always had been and there always would be. I had the feeling that even after his own death he would merely retire, to some celestial dressing-room and take off his make-up.

There were other Quaints, a dozen of them. *En masse* we went to supper parties and swimming parties after the show at night. Some of the more refined social lights of Singapore looked obliquely at us, as though we were not quite the thing, a little too rowdy perhaps, on the common side. I'm sure they were right. Actors always laugh more loudly than other people when they're enjoying themselves, and we laughed most of the time.

Intoxicated by so many heady draughts of familiar vintage theatre, I allowed myself to be persuaded by Jimmy to appear as 'Stanhope' in *Journey's End* for three performances. The Singapore Press displayed gratifying excitement and my name glittered proudly in blue bulbs across the front of the Victoria Theatre. I learnt the part in two days and had three rehearsals. The *élite* of Singapore assembled in white ducks and flowered chiffons and politely watched me take a fine part in a fine play and throw it into the alley. The only cause for pride I had over the whole business was that I didn't dry-up on any of the lines. True, I became slightly lost during the second performance in a maze of military instructions, and commanded a surprised sergeant-major to take number eight 'platoolian' into the back trenches; and I was never actually certain which scene I was playing, and how long it was going to last, but Bob Sherriff's lines remained, on the whole, intact, although I spoke the majority of them with such over-emphasis that it might have been better if they hadn't. John Mills, as 'Raleigh,' gave the finest performance I have ever seen given to that part, and Jimmy Grant Anderson was excellent as 'Trotter.' The whole company was good and the production admirable. The outstanding failure was undoubtedly me. Of course there were many excuses: only two days to learn it, insufficient rehearsals, etc., etc.; all the same I should have been ashamed of myself for attempting anything as important as *Journey's End* in such circumstances. In discussing it beforehand it had seemed a lark, great fun, an amusing experiment; it wasn't until I got on to the stage in a temperature of about 115 in the shade, with the sweat rolling off me, that I began to be aware of my folly, and it wasn't, mercifully, until the three performances were over that I relaxed enough to realise my impertinence.

The third performance was a little better than the first two, and probably with a few weeks of hard work I might ultimately have played it properly. If it had been a bad play I should have accepted the lark at its surface value and been content that I had, at least, amused The Quaints; as it was, however, my retrospective embarrassment afterwards was mortifying and I have never quite forgiven myself.

Singapore's behaviour to me was beyond reproach, with the exception of one of the gentlemen of the Press, who was indelicate enough to hint that I was not quite as good as the man he had seen play it before. I saluted him, wanly, for his honesty.

7

I have often thought I should like to write a travel book. Not the *Through Tibet on a Bicycle* variety, nor yet the Richard Haliburton formula with pictures of myself swimming unswimmable rivers and straddling ancient statuary. Rather a casual travel book, in which the essence and charm of every strange place I visited would be captured in a few apt and telling phrases; in which I could devote pages and pages to gentle introspection; sketching lightly my opinions of Life, Love, Art and Letters on to incongruous backgrounds of mountains and deserts and shrill tropical vegetation.

My body has certainly wandered a good deal, but I have an uneasy suspicion that my mind has not wandered nearly enough. It is a well-trained mind, disciplined to observe, record and store up impressions without any particular wear and tear or exhaustive effort. It is capable of functioning quickly, and making rapid and usually intelligent decisions. It is at its best when dealing with people, and at its worst when dealing with the inanimate. Its photographic propensities are good, but something goes wrong with the developing, because the pictures it takes of landscapes and seascapes fade too easily. Faces, events and tunes remain clear, fragments of past conversations also, and the sudden stinging memory of long-dead emotions. But visual experience, that glorious view when you reach the top of the hill, that moment in the Acropolis just before sunset, those pale dawns at sea, all these become smudged and half-rubbed out until, frequently, not even an outline remains.

My travel book would be difficult to write, for in addition to these defects, my mind resents certain kinds of information; it cannot or will not accept history for history's sake. Remote foreign churches, carved, sculpted and decorated by remote foreign monks centuries ago; ruins, museums and cathedrals, unless for some specific reason they happen to catch my imagination, leave no imprint whatsoever. In fact, many of the world's noblest antiquities have definitely irritated me. Perhaps the sheen on them of so many hundreds of years' intensive appreciation makes them smug. I feel that they bridle when I look at them. Once, in Ceylon, I saw an enormous sacred elephant sit up and beg for a banana; I don't believe it really wanted the banana, it merely knew what was expected of it. I have also seen the Pyramids give a little self-deprecatory simper at the sight of a Kodak. I have not, as yet, seen the Taj Mahal at all, but I feel that when I do it will probably lie down in a consciously alluring attitude and pretend to be asleep.

I freely admit that this blindness is perverse; perhaps it's a repressed complex.

perhaps I was frightened by a Bellini Madonna when I was a tiny child, but there it is, complex or not, a permanent obstacle to a respectable travel book. On the other hand, although insensitive to history for history's sake, I am keenly responsive to travel for travel's sake. I love to go and I love to have been, but best of all I love the intervals between arrivals and departures, the days and nights of steady, incessant movement, when the horizon is empty and time completely changes its rhythm. Then I can sleep, wake, write, read and think in peace. It is in these hours I feel that, after all, there may be a chance for me, less likelihood of opportunities missed, less intolerable distraction. It is probably a temperamental defect in me that I can only catch this elusive quietness when moving, a maladjustment of my nervous system, but it is certainly the reason above all others that I go away, not to get anywhere, not even to return, just to go.

Jeffery emerged from the hospital in Singapore more emaciated than ever, but definitely on the way to recovery. We lingered on a little. The Quaints left for Hong Kong and we celebrated their going with a party, waving them hazily into a small P. and O. at two in the morning. We went to a few dinners, picnics and cocktail parties, and finally went on to Ceylon by way of Kuala Lumpur and Penang. From Penang to Colombo we travelled in a Prince Line freighter; an enchanting few days, most of which we spent lying in a canvas swimming tank rigged up on the fo'c'sle.

At Colombo we were met by my brother Eric, in shorts and a sola-topee. We stayed with him in his bungalow in the hills for a few days, and then came down again to the Galle Face Hotel, where there was a jazz orchestra, curry, Cingalese waiters with elaborate combs in their hair and, surprisingly enough, Cole and Linda Porter. They were on their way from Java and Bali, and looked splendidly immaculate. The climate did its best to flurry Linda's coolness, but without success; she remained serene and smooth, and bought a lot of emeralds. Meanwhile, a tremendous telegraphic bickering was taking place between me and Gertie Lawrence in New York. She had cabled me in Singapore, rather casually, I thought, saying that she had read *Private Lives* and that there was nothing wrong in it that couldn't be fixed. I had wired back curtly that the only thing that was going to be fixed was her performance. Now cables were arriving at all hours of the day and night, with a typical disregard of expense, saying that she had foolishly committed herself to Charlot for a new revue – could we open in January instead of September – could I appear in the revue with her, just to fill in – could I wire to Charlot to release her from her contract – that it wasn't a contract at all, merely a moral obligation – that it wasn't a moral obligation at all, but a cabled contract – that her lawyers were working day and night to get her out of it – that she would rather do *Private Lives* than anything in the world – that she couldn't do *Private Lives* at all? In her last telegram she remembered to give me her cable address which, had she done so sooner, would have saved me about forty pounds. I finally lost patience and cabled that I intended to do the play with someone else, and I heard nothing further until I arrived back in England.

8

Our journey from Ceylon to Marseilles was accomplished in one of the older P. and O. ships, in fact so old was she that we expected her to hoist enormous bellying sails when a light wind sprang up in the Red Sea. The voyage started badly for me; I was awakened from a deep sleep at eight o'clock on the first morning out by the games organiser, who walked peremptorily into my cabin and told me that I was to play shuffle-board with Mrs Harrison at eleven, and deck-quoits with Miss Phillips at ten-fifteen. I replied that I intended to pass most of the day in the lavatory and that if Mrs Harrison and Miss Phillips felt like a little Russian bank or backgammon, he could tell them where to find me.

Owing to this reasonable outburst of irritation, both Jeffery and I were considered snobbish and exclusive by our fellow-passengers and were, mercifully, excluded from most of the ship's social activities, with the exception of the fancy-dress ball at which I was invited to give the prizes. Here I disgraced myself again by giving the first prize to a woman who had been ignored by most of the ladies on board, apparently because they suspected her of coloured blood. Had I known this, I should have given her the first prize, even if she had been a Zulu.

During that voyage I wrote an angry little vilification of war called *Post-Mortem*; my mind was strongly affected by *Journey's End*, and I had read several current war novels one after the other. I wrote *Post-Mortem* with the utmost sincerity; this, I think, must be fairly obvious to anyone who reads it. In fact I tore my emotions to shreds over it. The result was similar to my performance as 'Stanhope': confused, under-rehearsed and hysterical. Unlike my performance as 'Stanhope,' however, it had some very fine moments. There is, I believe, some of the best writing I have ever done in it, also some of the worst. I have no deep regrets over it, as I know my intentions to have been of the purest. I passionately believed in the truth of what I was writing; too passionately. The truths I snarled out in that hot, uncomfortable little cabin were all too true and mostly too shallow. Through lack of detachment and lack of real experience of my subject, I muddled the issues of the play. I might have done better had I given more time to it and less vehemence. However, it helped to purge my system of certain accumulated acids.

9

Back in London again, the Far East receded swiftly. Once the various presents had been doled out and the principal anecdotes related, all memories fused in a highly-coloured jumble.

I sat in the garden at Goldenhurst in the sunset, worrying about pneumonia rather than malaria; I no longer shook my bedroom slippers to see if there were any scorpions inside them, although I must admit I was badly frightened one night by a daddy-long-legs falling on to my face. Jungles, mountains and seas looked up at me from snapshots. Yes, I had been there and there and there – there was Saigon, that suffocating little Paris of the Orient – in the right-hand corner was the hotel terrace where I sat interminably night after night – the little orchestra – *Tosca, Bohème, Véronique* – the rickshaws passing back and forth – podgy French business men in creased, tropical suits, clambering in and out – Jeffery in the clinic, lying yellow and wretched under a mosquito-net. There was the Tartar Gate in Peking – I'd been through that – ice-cold winds blowing across from the Gobi Desert – clouds of stinging grey dust. Hong Kong harbour, unrecognisable in the photograph, just a view, no suggestion of its reality – that gigantic island rising out of the sea – the peak with white veils of cloud round it, as though it had been washing its head – at night the millions of lights – the little ferry-boats chugging to and fro across the harbour. There was the *Suffolk* looking glossy and prim and over-posed – there was the scuttle through which I stared at the China Sea – the cross marks my bedroom window. Indo-China – Siam – monks in faded yellow robes – temples and palaces with porcelain roofs – emerald Buddhas – silver mesh floors – cobras hooded and angry, snapping at bits of parchment – ships of all shapes and sizes – freighters, P. and O.s, Dollar Line, N.Y.K., sampans, junks – Singapore – a thunderstorm like the breaking of the sixth seal – straight, flat streets lined with coloured shops – palms, flame-in-the-forest, hibiscus, poinsettias – the Victoria Theatre, with large electric punkahs eternally scuffling round and round, while I sweated and ranted in a British warm and full trench equipment – Kuala Lumpur, Penang, Colombo, Kandy, Aden, Suez – names on a map no longer, but places that I had been to; I – me – sitting here in a familiar garden – I had walked along those streets, eaten and drunk, gone to sleep and wakened up in those strange hotel rooms; crossed those wide seas; bumped over those faraway roads, and here I was again; the world was round all right, one small circle had been completed, perhaps Time was round, too. I remember going indoors, twirling the globe and looking towards future journeys.

10

We played a short provincial tour of *Private Lives* before bringing it to London. Gertie had arrived back in England in gay spirits and, by hook, crook, love and money, managed to extricate herself from her moral, legal and financial obligations to Charlot. She seemed happily unaware that there had ever been any question of her not playing *Private Lives*. All the cables and muddles and complications hadn't existed. Here she was, eager, enthusiastic and looking lovely; the play was perfect, nothing had to be fixed at all. Gertie has an astounding sense of the complete reality of the moment, and her moments, dictated by the extreme variability of her moods, change so swiftly that it is frequently difficult to discover what, apart from eating, sleeping and acting, is true of her at all. I know her well, better, I believe, than most people. The early years of our friendship set her strongly in my mind. I knew her then to have quick humour, insane generosity and a loving heart, and those things seldom change. I see her now, ages away from her ringlets and black velvet military cap, sometimes a simple, wide-eyed child, sometimes a glamorous *femme du monde*, at some moments a rather boisterous 'good sort,' at others a weary, disillusioned woman battered by life but gallant to the last. There are many other grades also between these extremes. She appropriated beauty to herself quite early, along with all the tricks and mannerisms that go with it. In adolescence she was barely pretty. Now, without apparent effort, she gives the impression of sheer loveliness. Her grace in movement is exquisite, and her voice charming. To disentangle Gertie herself from this mutability is baffling, rather like delving for your grandmother's gold locket at the bottom of an overflowing jewel-case.

Her talent is equally kaleidoscopic. On the stage she is potentially capable of anything and everything. She can be gay, sad, witty, tragic, funny and touching. She can play a scene one night with perfect subtlety and restraint, and the next with such obviousness and over-emphasis that your senses reel. She has, in abundance, every theatrical essential but one: critical faculty. She can watch a great actor and be stirred to the depths, her emotional response is immediate and genuine. She can watch a bad actor and be stirred to the depths, the response is equally immediate and equally genuine. But for this tantalising lack of discrimination she could, I believe, be the greatest actress alive in the theatre to-day.

Adrianne Allen (Mrs Raymond Massey) played 'Sibyl' in *Private Lives*, and Laurence Olivier, 'Victor.' The whole tour was swathed in luxury. Adrianne travelled in a car, so did Gertie and so did I, the touring days of the past belonged to another world. Assurance of success seemed to be emblazoned on the play from the first, we had few qualms, played to capacity business and enjoyed ourselves thoroughly. We felt, I think rightly, that there was a shine on us.

In London we opened in a new theatre, the Phoenix. We were an immediate hit, and our three months' limited engagement was sold out during the first week. It was an interesting play to play, naturally more interesting for Gertie and me than it was for Larry and Adrianne. We had the parts, or rather, the part, as 'Elyot' and 'Amanda' are practically synonymous. The play's fabric was light and required light handling. Gertie was brilliant. Everything she had been in my mind when I originally conceived the idea in Tokio came to life on the stage: the witty, quick-silver delivery of lines; the romantic quality, tender and alluring; the swift, brittle rages; even the white Molyneux dress. Adrianne played 'Sibyl' with a subtle tiresomeness and a perfect sense of character, more character actually than the part really had. Larry managed, with determination and much personal charm, to invest the wooden 'Victor' with enough reality to make him plausible. I frequently felt conscience-stricken over them both, playing so gallantly on such palpably second-strings. Gertie and I certainly had most of the fun and, with it, most of the responsibility. Our duologue second act, when, for some reason or other, we were not feeling quite on the crest of the wave, was terribly exhausting. We both knew that if we let it sag for a moment it would die on us. On the other hand, when it flowed, when the audience was gay and appreciative, when our spirits were tuned to the right key, it was so exhilarating that we felt deflated when it was over.

We closed, at the end of our scheduled three months, with the gratifying knowledge that we could easily have run on for another six. This arbitrary three months' limit of mine brought me a certain amount of criticism. 'It was a sin,' people said, 'to close a play when it was doing so well.' Some even prophesied, darkly, future catastrophes: 'A day will come,' they said, 'when you will bitterly regret this.' I am told that even Sir Cedric Hardwicke sprang into print about it. However, I remained convinced that that policy, for me, was right. Perhaps a day will come, as the Cassandras foretold; perhaps in later years, when I'm looking for a job, I shall indeed regret those lost grosses, but I don't really think that I will. I consider myself a writer first and an actor second. I love acting, and it is only during the last few years that I have become good, although, as yet, limited in scope. If I play the same part over and over again for a long run, I become bored and frustrated and my performance deteriorates; in addition to this, I have no time to write. Ideas occur to me and then retreat again because, with eight performances a week to be got through, there is no time to develop them. For me, three months in London and three months in New York once in every two years is an ideal arrangement. It is, of course, more than possible that I might write and appear in a play that wouldn't run three weeks. In that bleak moment, age permitting, I shall turn gratefully to a revival of *Private Lives*.

I spent Christmas at Goldenhurst before sailing for America. Goldenhurst was growing; bedrooms and bathrooms were multiplying rapidly, so also was acreage. I could now walk proudly for quite a long way over my own land. Goldenhurst was a continual pleasure. Even then, in 1930, it was unrecognisable from what it had been a few years before. Now, of course, at the moment of writing, it has almost over-reached itself. It has completed its metamorphosis from a tumbledown farmhouse to a country estate. To do it justice, it hasn't got a self-made look. It has no vulgar '*nouveau-riche*' mannerisms, it doesn't eat peas with its knife, but I am beginning to feel a little awed by it, especially when I come across its photographs in the smarter illustrated weeklies.

I employed that Christmas week by writing some numbers for a revue that Cochran was preparing. Two of them, 'Any Little Fish' and 'Half-caste Woman,' were reasonably successful, although the revue – which I never saw – wasn't.

11

During the London run of *Private Lives*, I discussed with Cochran the idea of doing a big spectacular production at the Coliseum. I felt an urge to test my producing powers on a large scale. My mind's eye visualised a series of tremendous mob scenes – the storming of the Bastille – the massacre of the Huguenots – I believe even the Decline and Fall of the Roman Empire flirted with me for a little. Soon my imagination became overcrowded, and I began to simplify. These mass effects were all very well, but they couldn't sustain a whole evening; they should be, at best, a background for a strong story; at worst, padding for a weak one.

Cockie was enthusiastic and settled himself blandly to wait until I delivered him a more concrete proposition; meanwhile history continued to parade through my mind, usually at night, when I was tired and wanted to go to sleep. Events, grand and portentous, battles, sieges, earthquakes, revolutions and shipwrecks, but no story, not the shadow of a theme. The Second Empire was the most tenacious of all; gaslight – chandeliers – richly apparelled courtesans driving in the Bois – Englishmen in deer-stalker caps climbing out of smoky trains at the Gare du Nord – the Empress herself, haughty, beautiful, crinolined; somehow a little synthetic – the whole scene a little synthetic – Winterhalter figures moving to Offenbach tunes. At the time perhaps a trifle shabby, but now, set in retrospect, charming. A sentimental, daguerreotype sort of charm, belonging to the past, but not too far away.

However, as an idea for the Coliseum it seemed too pale, too lacking in action; so away it went with the chariot-races and carmagnoles and blood-and-thunder, and I continued the search, until one day I happened to buy, at Foyle's in the Charing Cross Road, some ancient bound volumes of *Black and White* and the *Illustrated London News*. This was chance, and extremely happy chance. In the first volume I opened there was a full-page picture of a troop-ship leaving for the Boer War, and the moment I saw it I knew that I had found what I wanted. I can't explain why it rang the bell so sharply, I only know that it did. The tunes came into my mind first, tunes belonging to my very earliest childhood; 'Dolly Gray,' 'The Absent-minded Beggar,' 'Soldiers of the Queen,' 'Bluebell' (later this, but I neither knew nor cared). I played them on the piano immediately. G. B. Stern, who was coming to tea, found me in a state of high excitement; by then I had progressed, musically, quite a long way through the years; I'm not sure, but I think she entered to the tune of 'Tipperary.'

The emotional basis of *Cavalcade* was undoubtedly music. The whole story was threaded on to a string of popular melodies. This ultimately was a big contributing factor to its success. Popular tunes probe the memory more swiftly than anything else, and *Cavalcade*, whatever else it did, certainly awakened many echoes.

That afternoon in my studio, Peter (Stern) tottered a bit under the full impact of my enthusiasm, but she rallied after a while and, renouncing any personal problems she might have wished to discuss, obligingly retired with me to the beginning of the century. She remembered Mafeking Night, the Relief of Ladysmith, 'Dirty old Kruger,' One-armed Giffard, and newsboys – particularly newsboys – shrill Cockney voices shouting victories and defeats along London streets; cooks and housemaids running up foggy area steps to buy halfpenny papers; elderly gentlemen in evening capes stopping hansoms in order to read of 'Bob's' latest exploits. Then the illness of the Queen – newsboys again – the Queen's sinking – latest bulletin. She remembered vividly, graphically, and became as excited as I was. Later on I dedicated the published play to her in gratitude for those two hours.

My original story was different from what finally emerged, but the shape was the same, New Year's Eve 1899 to New Year's Eve 1930. Events took precedence first in my mind, and against them I moved a group of people – the bright young people of the nineties, the play was to finish with their children – the same eager emptiness, but a different jargon. After a while, I realised that the play should be bigger than that. I had flogged the bright young people enough, my vehemence against them had congealed, they were now no more than damp squibs, my Poor Little Rich Girls and Dance, Little Ladies. Thirty years of English life seen through their eyes would be uninspired, to say the least of it. Presently my real characters appeared in two classes: 'the Marryots,' and 'Ellen' and 'Bridges.' 'Jane Marryot' displayed a greater fecundity in my original conception, there were several more children than just 'Edward' and 'Joe;' however, these fell away, still-born, into oblivion, discouraged by my firm determination to keep the whole thing as simple and uncomplicated as possible, and gradually the whole story completed itself in my mind.

I knew I couldn't attempt the actual writing of it until I had finished with *Private Lives* in New York. It would obviously require a lot of time, concentration and research, so I outlined it, in brief, to Cockie and promised it vaguely for the following year.

12

Private Lives was as gratifyingly successful in New York as it had been in London. Adrianne Allen was unable to come, and so Jill Esmond (Laurence Olivier's wife) played 'Sibyl' excellently, in a blond wig. The New York critics resented the thinness of the play less than the London critics, and enjoyed the lightness of it more; in fact, many of them came to see it several times. I think we retained, on the whole, the shine that we had started with; at all events, we strained every nerve to justify the almost overwhelming praise that was most generously lavished upon us.

I lived in a little penthouse on West 58th Street, with a lot of rather 'Ye Olde Teashoppe' furniture, a French cook and an uninterrupted view of the Empire State building. Here, with the extremely twentieth-century sounds of New York in my ears, I embarked on my researches for *Cavalcade*. I had brought stacks of books with me from London, even the faithful bound volumes of the *Illustrated London News*. I started at an earlier date than 1899, feeling that to work slowly through the seventies, eighties and nineties would give my people a more solid background than if I just let them appear, untouched by any past experience whatever, in leg-of-mutton sleeves. For some of the later scenes of the play I could, of course, draw on my own memory.

The 1910 seaside scene – Uncle George and his Merrie Men from Bognor would be useful there – the war scenes – 'We don't want to lose you, but we think you ought to go,' 'On Sunday I walk out with a soldier.' I could remember Gwennie Brogden singing that in *The Passing Show* at the Palace. The Victoria Station scene – hospital trains coming in, leave trains going out – I remember that clearly – walking home from the theatre at night after the show, a sinister air-raid consciousness in the air – hardly any lights anywhere, the Mall ghostly and almost deserted. I often walked through Victoria Station, it was practically on my way, and there was always activity going on. It seems, looking back on it, more dramatic than I expect it actually was. In those days everybody was quite used to that interminable anti-climax. Khaki everywhere. Tommies laden with trench equipment. Tired officers in thinner khaki and Sam Browne belts – movable canteens on wheels – movable Red Cross stations, too – nurses, V.A.D.s, chaplains, R.A.M.C. corporals, military police with red bands round their arms – groups of anxious civilians and always, always the tarts mincing about on high heels, with their white fox furs and neat navy blues and checks – permanent grimaces at our national morality – hoping to squeeze a little profit from a few last drunken moments of leave.

Armistice night – I could certainly remember that – thousands and thousands of human beings gone mad – very effective on a revolving stage – yelling, dancing, fighting, singing, blowing squeakers. Then – later on – a night club; a gigantic noisy brassy night club – Dance, Little Lady again – Twentieth-century Blues – a comment accurate enough and empty enough.

'Jane Marryot' took shape in my mind quite early. She seemed real to me and still does, a bit of my own mother and millions of others, too; ordinary, kind, and unobtrusively brave; capable of deep suffering and incapable of cheap complaint. I was proud of 'Jane Marryot' from the first.

In March I had a cable from Cockie saying that we couldn't have the Coliseum, but that we could have Drury Lane if I could guarantee him an opening date. This flurried me a bit, I have always loathed working to set time-limits; however, I made a few rapid mental adjustments, bade a sad adieu to the revolving stage and cabled back that I would have the play completed and ready to open at the end of September.

Gertie got ill towards the end of our three months' run, so we closed the theatre for two weeks. This naturally put a little additional time on to the end of the run, and I arrived back in England to start on *Cavalcade* at the beginning of May.

13

It was a long time before I could settle down to the actual writing of the play. Mother was taken ill with appendicitis, and an anxious time ensued, during which concentration was impossible. It was then discovered, after a series of scenic conferences at Drury Lane, that certain structural alterations would have to be made, and a lot of new lighting equipment installed. Frank Collins, Dan O'Neil, William Abingdon, the Lane stage manager, all the heads of departments, the Strand Electric Company, Gladys and I, spent hours on end trying to solve, on paper, a mass of complicated technical problems. We planned the production so that there should be never more than thirty seconds' wait between any of its twenty-three scenes. The stage was divided into six hydraulic lifts. These had to be timed to sink and rise on light cues from the prompt corner; at the same moment, other light cues would cause the hanging parts of the scenery to be whisked up into the flies and simultaneously replaced. We installed a row of automatic lights along the front of the second balcony. These had five changes of colour and could be regulated by the electricians from the stage. The footlights were reconstructed so that they could silently disappear altogether for the big scenes, and rise into place again for the small interiors when needed. When all the estimates were passed and the work under way, Gladys and I retired to Goldenhurst and set ourselves to a rigid daily routine, until every word of the play and every scene design were completed. We worked from eight in the morning until five in the afternoon, with an hour's break for lunch, Gladys downstairs in the library, I upstairs in my bedroom. We passed through every emotional phase: the height of exhilaration, the depths of despair and all the intermediate grades between. Fortunately, our moods were, as a rule, mutual. On gay, successful days, when everything had gone well, we drove into Folkestone in the evening, relaxed and happy, and went to the pictures. At other times, when everything had creaked and stuck, when there had been no flow, we sat miserably in the garden, hardly speaking, convinced that we had bitten off a great deal more than we could chew, and sick to death of chewing.

At last it was finished; the dialogue all written and typed, the sets designed and coloured, the changes approximately timed, the dresses and uniforms sketched, individually for the principals, in blocks for the crowd.

While the scenery was being built, we took a short breather in the South of France, but the holiday, although outwardly peaceful, lacked inner tranquillity.

The sun was hot; the sea blue. We drank a lot of Pernod, and watched brightly-dressed crowds passing to and fro. They looked care-free and irresponsible, no recalcitrant hydraulic lifts haunted their sleep; no obstinate, unautomatic, automatic lights bedevilled them. The Alpes Maritimes, the smooth Mediterranean, the coloured houses, the harbours, the beaches, seemed to us to be only so many act drops, liable to rise at any moment and disclose a vast stage, dimly lit and crowded with odds and ends of furniture and mumbling actors. Most of the cast had been engaged before we left London, and on our return we dealt with the crowd auditions. This was a depressing business. We needed about four hundred, and over a thousand applied. Hour after hour we sat on the stage at a long table set against the lowered safety-curtain, while an endless stream of 'out-of-works' passed by us – all of them professional actors or actresses, every one of them so in need of a job that the chance of being engaged as a super for thirty shillings a week was worth queueing up for. Many of them, at some time or other, had been comparatively successful; in fact, we had several in our crowd who had actually played important parts on that very stage. The old ones were naturally more pathetic than the young; little thin old women, rather dressy, terrified of not being engaged, but quibbling a bit at the salary, asking time to think it over, then giving in suddenly – 'Very well, I'll take it.' Pride was all very well, but times were hard, almost too hard to be borne.

They were tragic, those auditions, and they lay heavily on my conscience for a long while. I felt sentimentally ashamed at having succeeded so quickly, faced with those old lives who had worked all their years and never succeeded at all. I knew that thirty shillings a week was hopelessly inadequate, but the production was budgeted down to the last penny, and couldn't be put on at all if the crowd were paid any more.

I discovered, to my horror, that Cockie, in past moments of expansiveness, had promised three stage-struck society girls walk-ons in the show. There they stood, rather nervously, wearing excellently-cut clothes, good furs and discreet jewellery. One of them whispered sweetly to me that she believed I knew her aunt. I told them, all three, that they were not the types I wanted, but Cockie intervened and insisted on engaging them. After a long argument, I finally gave in on condition that for each of them I engaged two extra for the ranks of those who really needed the work.

In September rehearsals started. The carpenters and electricians were still in possession of the stage, and so I worked with the principals in the bar for the first ten days, getting all the dialogue scenes learnt and polished before I dealt with the crowd. As with *Bitter Sweet*, I felt a direct enthusiastic response from the cast. Everyone seemed to know their lines almost immediately, nobody was obtuse, tiresome or temperamental. I had lots of old friends with me: Moya Nugent, always efficient, gentle and utterly reliable; Maidie Andrews, Phyllis Harding, Betty Hare, John Mills, and several others. The newcomers seemed imbued with the same spirit; in fact, the amount of work achieved in those first ten days was remarkable. Mary Clare played 'Jane' with simplicity, tenderness and complete reality. Irene Browne was stylish and effective as 'Margeret.' Una O'Connor and Fred Groves, as 'Ellen' and 'Bridges,' set themselves securely in the framework of the play from the first. Everybody was admirable, and the smaller parts were as expertly handled as the bigger ones. I woke up on the morning of my first crowd rehearsal frankly terrified. All night long a shouting mob of four hundred people had shared my bed, pushing and clamouring and asking me what I wanted them to do. I was in a bad panic, but the dreadful day had to be faced, so off we went, Lorn, Jack, Gladys and I, to the theatre.

I had decided to break the ice with the seaside scene, and it sat on the stage, complete in every detail, lowering forbiddingly at us as we filed into the front row of the dress circle. Below us, in the stalls, was the full strength of the company, chattering and whispering. There was an extra buzz of expectancy when we came in, and then silence. I had thought out, in advance, a plan for handling such large numbers of people which, as it saved us endless trouble and time, I will explain. I had divided, on paper, the entire cast into groups of twenty. For each group there had been made a set of large plaques in different colours and numbered from one to twenty. Number one in each group was the captain, and was virtually in charge of the other nineteen. Each captain was responsible for his group having their plaques tied on before rehearsal started, and was also empowered to collect them at the end of the day and deliver them to the property master. This scheme, after a little preliminary confusion, worked splendidly. I could direct, through my microphone in the dress circle, without the strain of trying to memorise people's names, entirely by numbers and colours: 'Would number seven red kindly go over and shake hands with number fifteen yellow-and-black stripe?' etc.

At that first rehearsal it naturally took a long time to get everybody correctly numbered and sorted. Finally, however, it was done, and there they stood, serried ranks of them, waiting for what was to appear next. That was the moment that I nearly broke. I had an insane desire to say, quite gently, into the microphone: 'Thank you very much, everybody, I shan't be wanting you any more at all' – and rush madly from the theatre. Fortunately, I conquered this impulse and gave them a brief explanation of the scene. I told them that it was a seaside resort in the year 1910, and that when I blew a whistle I wished them all to walk about and talk and behave as though they really were at the seaside. There was the parade (number two hydraulic lift), the beach, the steps leading down, the small stage for Uncle George's Concert Party, sand-castles for the children, bathing-machine and the bandstand. All they had to do was to use their imaginations and circulate until I told them to stop. I gave them full permission to use any by-play and bits of business that they could think of, with the proviso that any undue overacting would be discouraged. Then I arranged Uncle George's Concert Party round their small stage, commending my soul to Heaven, blew the whistle. The effect was fantastic – immediately the scene came to life, whole and complete. People laughed and talked, promenaded to and fro along the esplanade, children patted their property sand-castles, Uncle George besought the crowd to listen to his concert. It was a most thrilling and satisfying moment, and from then onwards I had no more fears.

We did the scene over again several times, until it was set. Little bits of excellent business crept in; a child burst its balloon and screamed, and its mother smacked it; an old lady collapsed in a deck-chair, and one young woman shut herself up in her parasol when she heard the noise of an aeroplane. The by-play was prodigious and hardly any of it overdone. I was considerably praised later on for my little touches of sheer genius in that scene, and few believed me when I replied that the only genius I had displayed was in blowing a whistle!

Scene after scene was accomplished in that way, and rehearsals progressed rapidly. There were several comic interludes and a few tragic ones. In time we grew to know the names of nearly everyone, numbered or not. One of our lighter diversions was the 'Shy Bride.' This was the locomotive in the Victoria Station scene. All it had to do was to advance, amid clouds of steam, for a few yards, on rollers, and stop at the buffers. This it resolutely refused to do. It went backwards, it went sideways, it tangled itself in the black velvets and the fog gauzes, but never, until almost the last dress rehearsal, did it come in on cue.

We had a full week of dress rehearsals which, although chaotic at first, gradually righted themselves. The whole thing was the most thrilling theatrical adventure I could ever have imagined. The play grew and lived just a little bit more each day. The first time the Queen Victoria funeral scene went without a hitch, we found ourselves crying. Suddenly, unexpectedly, the emotional content of the play caught us unawares; once set, of course, and rehearsed over and over again, the scenes became familiar and lost their sting, but there were always certain moments in *Cavalcade* that touched me however often I saw them.

Cockie came to rehearsals during the last weeks, and encouraged everybody, as he always did, with just the right amount of praise and criticism. Frank Collins and Dan O'Neil achieved miracles of stage management. Elsie April pounded the piano, sorted band parts and evolved brilliant ideas for the blending of the popular tunes; in fact, everybody concerned with the production worked with untiring diligence and enthusiasm.

Gladys remained calm throughout. She had designed and ordered the entire scenic part of the production; sketched, planned and chosen about three thousand seven hundred costumes; selected and hired every stick of furniture, and managed to be at my side through almost every rehearsal. Without undue modesty, I can truthfully and most gratefully say that *Cavalcade*, apart from its original moment of conception, was as much hers as mine.

14

The first night of *Cavalcade* will remain for ever in my memory as the most agonising three hours I have ever spent in a theatre. This, I am sure, will appear to be an over-statement to any reader who happened to be present at it. But nobody in that audience, excepting Cockie and a few who had been concerned with the production, had the remotest idea how near we came to bringing the curtain down after the third scene and sending the public home.

The evening started triumphantly. The atmosphere in the auditorium while the orchestra was tuning-up was tense with excitement. Many people had been waiting for the gallery and pit for three days and nights. Gradually the stalls and dress-circle filled; Reginald Burston, the musical director, took his place. I came into my box with Mother, Jack, Gladys and Jeffery, and received a big ovation. The overture started and we settled ourselves to wait, while the house-lights slowly faded. The first scene went smoothly. Mary was nervous, but played with experienced poise. The troop-ship, with our military band and real guardsmen, brought forth a burst of cheering. The third scene – inside the house again – went without a hitch. Half the strength of the orchestra crept out during this to take their place on the lower hydraulic lift, on which they played for the theatre scene.

It was a very complicated change. The second two lifts had to rise so many feet to make the stage. The first lift had to sink and rise again with the orchestra in place on it. The preceding interior had to be taken up into the flies, and the furniture taken off at the sides. Two enormous built side-wings, with two tiers of boxes filled with people, had to slide into place on rollers, when the first lift had risen to its mark. All this was timed to take place in just over thirty seconds, and had gone perfectly smoothly at the dress rehearsals.

We sat in the box on the first night with our eyes glued on to the conductor's desk, waiting for the little blue warning light to show us that the scene was set. We waited in vain. The conductor played the waltz through again – then again – people began to look up at us from the stalls; the gallery became restless and started to clap. Neither Gladys nor I dared to move, there were too many eyes on us, and we didn't want to betray, more than we could help, that anything was wrong. I hissed at Jack out of the corner of my mouth, and he slipped out of the box and went down on to the stage. In a few moments he returned and said, in a dead voice: 'The downstage lift has stuck, and they think it will take two hours to fix it.'

Gladys and I talked without looking at each other, our eyes still set on where the blue light should appear. She said, very quietly: 'I think you'll have to make an announcement,' and I said: 'I'll give it another two minutes.' Still the orchestra continued to grind out the 'Mirabelle' waltz, there seemed to be a note of frenzy creeping into it. I longed passionately for it to play something else – anything else in the world. The audience became more restless, until suddenly, just as I was about to leave the box and walk on to the stage, the blue light came on, the black curtain rose and the scene started.

From then onwards there wasn't a moment's peace for us. The effect of the hitch on Dan O'Neil and the stage staff had obviously been shattering. The company caught panic too, and the performance for the rest of the evening lost its grip. I don't think this was noticed by the audience, but we knew it all right. That unfortunate accident took the fine edge off the play, and although the applause at the end was tremendous, we were heart-broken. I appeared at the end against my will, but in response to frantic signals from Cockie in the box opposite. It was one of the few occasions of my life that I have ever walked on to a stage not knowing what I was going to say. However, standing there, blinded by my own automatic lights, and nerve-stricken by the torment I had endured in course of the evening, I managed to make a rather incoherent little speech which finished with the phrase: 'I hope that this play has made you feel that, in spite of the troublous times we are living in, it is still pretty exciting to be English.' This brought a violent outburst of cheering, and the orchestra, frantic with indecision as to whether to play my waltz or 'God Save the King,' effected an unhappy compromise by playing them both at once. The curtain fell, missing my head by a fraction, and that was that.

15

Lorn came in the next morning and plumped all the papers down on my bed. 'I think,' she said, 'that our little piece is a success!' We read the notices through carefully. Mounting paeans of praise – not a discordant note. Jack and Gladys appeared presently, and we had lunch at the Ivy, where our reception was most satisfactory. Abel gave us all cocktails and drank to us solemnly, trembling a little with kind, friendly emotion. Congratulations bombarded the table. Our little piece was a success. Such a success, indeed, that I knew the moment had come for me to disappear. It seemed to me that there was danger in the air – a private, personal danger. I was happy enough, more than happy, delighted, but somehow, somewhere, not quite comfortable. Everybody seemed to be more concerned with *Cavalcade* as a patriotic appeal than as a play. This attitude I realised had been enhanced by my first-night speech – 'A pretty exciting thing to be English' – quite true, quite sincere; I felt it strongly, but I rather wished I hadn't said it, hadn't popped it on to the top of *Cavalcade* like a paper-cap. I hadn't written the play as a dashing patriotic appeal at all. There was certainly love of England in it, a certain natural pride in some of our very typical characteristics, but primarily it was the story of thirty years in the life of a family. I saw where my acute sense of the moment had very nearly cheapened it. The Union Jack stretched across the back of the stage – theatrically effective jingoism. 'It's pretty exciting to be English' – awareness of the moment, not quite first-rate, a nervous grab at success at any price. Fortunately the essence of the play was clear. A comment mostly, emotional at moments but, on the whole, detached enough. The irony of the war scenes had been missed by the critics – naturally, they couldn't be expected to see it in a time of national unrest with a General Election looming in the immediate future. The Queen Victoria funeral was good – dignified, reticent and touching – the *Titanic* scene excellent, too, in a different way – the 1914 outbreak of war was again touching, but there was irony here, the beginning of bitterness. 'My world isn't very big.' The Trafalgar Square scene, obvious, not quite psychologically accurate, but undeniably effective, all that noise and movement against 'Land of Hope and Glory.' Best of all the Toast speech – 'Let's couple the Future of England with the Past of England. The glories and victories and triumphs that are over, and the sorrows that are over, too. Let's drink to our sons who made part of the pattern and to our hearts that died with them. Let's drink to the spirit of gallantry and courage that made a strange Heaven out of unbelievable Hell, and let's drink to the hope that one day this country of ours, which we love so much, will find dignity and greatness and peace again.'

That was all right. That was deeply sincere and as true as I could make it. I do hope, profoundly hope, that this country will find dignity, greatness and peace again – no cheapness there, that came from the heart, or rather perhaps, from the roots – twisted sentimental roots, stretching a long way down and a long way back, too deep to be unearthed by intelligence or pacific reason or even contempt, there, embedded for life.

With reasoning I felt better; better for myself, but sadder for poor *Cavalcade*. It was already becoming distorted and would, in time, be more so. 'A message to the youth of the Nation.' 'A Call to Arms.' 'A shrill blare on a trumpet,' blowing my decent, simple characters into further chaos. I could stay in England and cash-in if I wanted to, cash-in on all the tin-pot glory, but I felt that it would be better for me, and much better for my future work, if I went away.

16

On the twenty-ninth of October, 1931, Jeffery and I left for South America. It was a casual departure, without the strained courtesy of long farewells; in fact, there weren't any farewells at all. England slipped away into the mist behind us without waving a single handkerchief. A slightly complacent England, basking in pale sunlight and the ambiguous security of a vast National Government majority. I compared her in my mind to a gallant, unimaginative old lady convalescing after an abdominal operation, unaware of the nature and danger of her disease, and happy in the belief that it could never possibly recur, because all the doctors had told her so.

Seagulls followed the boat for a little way, screeching with what may well have been national pride, and as we rounded the harbour jetty we could see the whole of Folkestone greyly spreading over the hills. Small figures promenaded along the Leas, invalids probably, sad, flat women and rheumaticky old gentlemen in Bath chairs. There were nursemaids sitting in the shelters, easily distinguishable by the perambulators drawn up before them; other figures, too, huddled on iron chairs, seeking protection from the sharp wind in the shadow of the empty bandstand.

Far and away to starboard, Dungeness point crept into the sea from the marshes, and nearer, dominating the picture, just before the cliff dipped towards Sandgate, rose proudly the Grand Hotel and the Metropole Hotel, sisters in impressiveness and flushed with gentility.

We were catching a small German-Spanish ship at Boulogne, for Rio de Janeiro – seventeen days of the Atlantic were ahead of us, not our well-known Atlantic of violence, wind and icebergs, but a gentle ocean growing hourly gentler, later becoming warm and phosphorescent under new stars.

We planned to be away about nine months. We had no itinerary. After Rio we intended to drift in whatever direction the spirit moved us; our anticipatory flights included jungles, orchids, lianas, turgid tropical rivers, squawking, coloured parakeets, vast mountains, Inca ruins, deserts and languorous Latin-American cities with white houses, green jalousies and dark-eyed, attractive people sipping cool drinks on palm-shaded patios. Most of these things, we knew, would drop into place, modified a little, perhaps, by actuality, but glamorous enough on the whole. England receded a little farther, and only a few gulls remained with us.

The whole world seemed remarkably empty to me, probably because the last weeks had been so full. From the first night of *Cavalcade*, until this moment, I had been unable to put myself down at all. The tempo of everything had increased alarmingly. If I had been working all these years merely for the outward trappings of success, I had certainly achieved my destiny, and there was nothing left for me to do but hop over the side of the ship and triumphantly drown.

I was almost surprised that my incorrigible sense of the right moment didn't force me to do it. I had had a lot of this 'right moment' business dinned into me just lately. There seemed to be a set conviction in many people's minds that I had dashed off *Cavalcade* in a few days, merely to help the General Election and snatch for myself a little timely national kudos. The rumour was fairly general that I had written it with my tongue in my cheek, in bed, probably, wearing a silk dressing-gown and shaking with cynical laughter. This I knew was partly my own fault – that good old Union Jack – 'Land of Hope and Glory' – my redundant theatre sense over-stepping the mark a bit. But still, there it was – a louder success than I had ever dreamed – vulgarised a bit, but real and satisfactory within its limits. The apex had been reached the night before I sailed, the night immediately following the election results, when Their Majesties, the King and Queen, and the entire Royal Family had come to the play. A thrilling, emotional event, everything in its place. Sitting in our box, exactly opposite the Royal Box, Gladys, Jack, Lorn and I had heard the roar outside the theatre as the Royal Party arrived. The house was crammed to the roof, the dress circle presented an unbroken line of diadems, tiaras, sunbursts and orders – people sat on the steps and stood in the aisles. When the Royal Family came into the box, the whole audience stood and the orchestra played 'God Save the King.' We stood rigidly to attention. I remember trying not to cry, trying not to let the emotional force of the moment prevent me from discovering what it was that was so deeply touching. I didn't succeed, the force was too strong.

The play started and went smoothly from the first; everybody played perfectly; none of the effects failed; even the 'Shy Bride' steamed in eagerly on time.

After the second act, Cockie and I were received in the ante-room behind the Royal Box. Six Royal bows, one after the other, were rather agitating, but we were kindly and graciously put at our ease. I repressed a nervous desire to describe to Their Majesties the extreme squalor of that very ante-room in the early hours of the morning during our first lighting rehearsal, when Gladys and I had used it as a sort of combined rest-room and snack-bar. My mind's eye could still see curling ham-sandwiches in greasy paper – crumbling Banbury cakes and bottles of gin and tonic littering that smooth, correct table. I think Their Majesties were pleased with the play, and the Prince of Wales asked me several searching questions. I was a little too nervous entirely to enjoy the conversation, but I hope I acquitted myself favourably; at all events, it was a proud moment for me, and I set it gratefully in my memory.

The end of the evening was even more exciting than the beginning. When Mary Clare spoke the Toast speech, there was such a terrific burst of cheering that I feared the chandeliers would fall into the stalls. At the final tableau the audience rose again, and sang 'God Save the King' with the Company. The curtain fell, and the Royal Family left the box, but the cheering persisted wth increasing volume until, after a while, they came back.

Of all emotional moments in that very emotional evening, that, somehow, was the most moving; the Queen drew back a little, leaving His Majesty in the front of the box to take the ovation alone. He stood there bowing, looking a little tired, and epitomising that quality which English people have always deeply valued: unassailable dignity.

It had been a tremendous night for me; a gratifying theatrical flourish to my twenty-one years of theatre.

Twenty-one years since I had sung 'Liza Ann' unaccompanied to Lila Field, in a small bare room off Baker Street – a rich, full, and exciting twenty-one years – 'Jam yesterday; jam to-morrow, but never jam to-day!' wasn't quite true of me. I had enjoyed a lot of immediate jam, perhaps a little too much. I didn't want it to cloy, I didn't want to lose the taste for it, but I comforted myself with the assurance that there were lots of different varieties. This was another holiday, another escape, another change of rhythm. In the months before me, I should have a little breathing-space in which to weigh values, reassemble experience, analyse motives, and endeavour to balance the past and present against the future. I waved a loving *au revoir* to Mother, Gladys, Lorn and Jack, to my family and to my friends, and went below to have a drink with Jeffery. When we came up on deck, there was no England left. Nothing but sea and sky!

Past Conditional

PAST CONDITIONAL: 1931-1933

WRITTEN: 1965-67
HITHERTO UNPUBLISHED

Having already written two autobiographies *Present Indicative* and *Future Indefinite* I feel that the moment has come for me to write a third, and possibly, later on, a fourth. To pretend that my life has not been varied, interesting and extremely successful would be both affected and unconvincing. It has brought me in contact with a number of diverse and fascinating people and carried me to many strange and far off places. It has taught me several lessons from which I hope I have profited and also inculcated in me an insatiable and profound interest in the behaviour of my fellow creatures. The impulse to put on record the events and encounters, the achievements and failures and some of the unlikely adventures that have befallen me in the course of my sixty-five years is a fairly reasonable one, also, taking into account the amount that has already been written about me by other people, it is not I think arrogant to suppose that when I have gone far away into the silent land, there will be a great deal more. If only for the sake of anyone who in future years feels that I might be a suitable subject for a 'revealing' biography, a statement of the facts of my career might at least give them something to go on. I am aware of course that these facts might conceivably be disregarded or misinterpreted or even wilfully distorted, but that contingency is obviously beyond my control. I am not now and never have been very preoccupied with the verdict of posterity. It would be agreeable of course to feel that some of my work might be remembered with pleasure, but if on the other hand it fades swiftly into oblivion, there will be nothing then that I can do about it.

In any case the urge to write this particular book has been growing in my mind for some time, ever since, in fact, I realised that eight vital years of my earlier life have never been recorded at all. *Present Indicative* began with my birth and ended in November 1931, while *Future Indefinite* only covered my experiences during the war years, beginning in 1939 and ending in 1945. Therefore there are two gaps to be filled. The eight years from late 1931 to mid–1939 and all the years from 1945 onwards. These I feel will have to wait until I have dealt with the 'Thirties'. I cannot any longer allow those, for me, most important years, to slip further and further into the limbo, even as it is I am bound to find some details of them elusive for although I am gifted with a good memory, I never began to keep any sort of diary or 'journal' until 1940. Lorn Loraine, my beloved secretary, managed to keep a sort of office diary which dealt with dates of opening nights and times and places of Actor's Orphanage meetings and the names of the committee members etc. Beyond these stark and only temporarily relevant facts, her entries are far from stimulating. It is tantalizing, when racking the memory for details, to find; 'Feb. 27th Noël went abroad,' and, several pages later; 'May 17th Noël came back. Met him at Southampton.' Perhaps Lorn's ingrained and stubborn insularity made even the scribbling down of foreign places obnoxious to her, at any rate Feb. 27th until May 17th have to be gouged out of the past somehow or other. Where did I go on that fateful day Feb. 27th? Was I alone? Had I a planned itinerary? Did I go to America, China or Heligoland? And if so for what reason? These sort of questions have teased my mind considerably throughout the months that I have been compiling the notes for this book. Some of the riddles I have finally managed to solve and others I have just had to guess at and pray that some unexpected spur to memory will suddenly arrive out of the blue. A quarter of a century has passed since I wove my hectic course through the Thirties, and a fairly turbulent quarter of a century at that, however I hope and suspect that the perspective provided by those twenty-five years will aid me in selecting events that were really important to me and save me from encumbering my narrative with too many casual and insignificant details.

2

In November 1931 Jeffery Amherst and I embarked on the second of our long journeys together. The first had begun in 1929 and finished in 1930 and had covered Japan, Korea, Northern Manchuria, Southern China, Siam, Malaya, Indo-China and Ceylon. This time we were headed for South America. We intended to start at Rio de Janeiro, get into the interior of Brazil and work our way down one of the tributaries of the Amazon until we reached the Argentine, then go on from there either South, East or West as the spirit moved us.

On a grey day we set off from Folkestone on the ordinary boat and arrived at Boulogne in time to get on board the *Antonio Delfino* a fair to middling little ship belonging to the Hamburg-Süd-Amerikanische line. Its personnel was mainly German; its passenger list also. Our cabins were clean and comfortable and the food was good. The weather, after the first few days, became steadily warmer and gentler until soon we were lying about on deck in shorts and sunglasses watching flying fish and feeling the damp of England drying out of our bones. It was an agreeable, uneventful voyage. We fraternized to a certain degree with our fellow passengers but no lasting friendships were formed. We played 'Russian Bank' endlessly, a game which when played in its double form, can be one of the most irritating in the world. We read books. I remember trudging manfully through H. G. Wells' *History of the World*, Green's *History of England*, several light novels and a number of execrably written travel books about Latin America. I also had a portable gramophone and a set of Linguaphone records in Spanish which I listened to assiduously for an hour every day and even now there is little about La Familia Fernandez that I could not tell you straight off the bat. As things turned out it was lucky that I forced upon myself this burden of self-education, because with the aid of those reports, plus a brief course at the Berlitz School some years before, I managed to acquire a reasonably fluent vocabulary and an excellent accent which rapidly became debauched when I reached the Argentine. The Argentine accent in Spanish is soft and alluring and very confusing if you have already happened to learn the more gutteral intonations of 'Castiliano Puro', lisp and all.

Meanwhile behind us in England God seemed to be, politically at least, firmly ensconced in his Conservative heaven and all was right with the world. There was a feeling of hope in the air and a sort of rebirth of honest, homely patriotism. *Cavalcade* was playing to capacity at the Theatre Royal Drury Lane and I had been assured on all sides that I had done a great service for England by writing it and producing it at such a timely moment. I suppose I believed all this? Looking back so far from now to then it is difficult to believe that I did. But perhaps the laurels rested comfortably enough on my head and I accepted the tributes without irony. I can realise even now that it gave to those who saw it, or to the majority of them at least, a nostalgia for the more dignified past, a sense of English pride. I know that it made many people cry and gave to some of them a feeling of hope for England's future, so perhaps I did do them a service after all, for it is better to hope than to despair. In any event either emotion may turn out to be illusory and a waste of time. I remember clearly however that it gave me personally a tremendous and most gratifying sense of achievement. It was a vast production and I was proud of it. There were certain specific scenes in the play of which I was proud also. The Queen Victoria Funeral scene dialogue, and the outbreak of the 1914–1918 War particularly. It was written with sincerity and as much truth as I knew. I couldn't have been expected to have known then what I know now thirty-four years later when I am thirty-four years older.

Curiously enough with all the violent changes that have taken place in our world since 1931, my basic feelings about my country, those that inspired me to write *Cavalcade* have not altered and are still, to me, valid. *Cavalcade* was hailed as a patriotic fanfare, an expert bit of Jingoistic flag-waving, cunningly put on the stage at exactly the right political moment. In point of actual fact, it was a great deal more than that. I had no idea about the accuracy of the political moment because I was far too busy in the theatre, nor had I any conscious intention of Jingoistic flag-waving. It merely occurred to me, as an Englishman of thirty-one years old, who was observant, fairly well-read and more travelled than the average, that I belonged to a most remarkable race. In later years I have seen no reason to revise this opinion. I am quite aware of our shortcomings, perhaps even more so than more impartial observers because I have suffered from them personally. I despise our national docility, the silliness of some of our laws, our meek acquiescence to circumstances which, with a little extra work on our part, could be twisted to our favour rather than allowed, through our mental and physical laziness, to dominate us. I also detest the climate except for sudden, unforgettable days of magic which, alas, are all too rare. However so much as I may loathe this and that and the other, it is what I love that really counts, and what I love about my country is really quite simple. I love its basic integrity, an integrity formed over hundreds of years by indigenous humour, courage and common-sense.

Love of country, of our own territory, is more deeply ingrained in the human animal than the shrill anti-nationalist, anti-patriotic, citizen-of-the-world pamphleteers and orators would have us believe. It is useless to try to dismiss this inherent pride in the land of our roots as facile patriotism, as nothing more than a convenient banner to be waved by unscrupulous politicians and newspaper Barons when a commercial trade agreement is at stake or a war is in the offing. For the human animal as for the primates from whom he descended millions of years ago, there is nearly always a war in the offing. And, as scientists have incontrovertibly proved, the instinct for protection of territory in millions of varieties of mammals, reptiles, birds, insects and fish, is far stronger than the urge for food, sex or self-preservation.

In the year 1956 when I decided, for carefully considered financial reasons, to give up my English residence and become domiciled abroad, I was reviled and execrated by the majority of the British Press for being unpatriotic and failing in my duties as an Englishman. The force of these accusations is liable to fade a little under a modicum of intelligent scrutiny. In the first place, patriotism is an emotional instinct compounded of love of country and pride in that country's achievements and inherited characteristics. In my own case at any rate it most emphatically does not embrace the various Governments under which I have laboured, nor many of the laws that they have seen fit to pass. In the second place, I feel it to be the primary duty of a creative and talented Englishman, or indeed a creative and talented Chinaman for the matter of that, to continue with his work wherever he sees fit and, by doing so, contribute perhaps a little to the sum total of his country's proud artistic record. I cannot feel that my obdurate refusal to pay taxes which I consider to be both exorbitant and unjust, need in any way prevent me being of value to my country whether I decide to live in Switzerland, the Galapagos Islands or Kathmandu. It does not seem to have occurred to my self-righteous, journalistic attackers, in whose attitude may I say I detect a tiny streak of envy, that I may prefer to live out of England, taxes or no taxes. As a matter of fact, however, that happens to be the truth. I do. And for further information on this point it may be of interest to note that I have not *lived* in England for more than two or three months a years since 1948 when I built my house in Jamaica. My course has wobbled variously across the world mainly between America, France, England and Jamaica, with a number of other foreign countries thrown in. I happen to have an insatiable wanderlust, a personal eccentricity which I should think should by now be fairly widely recognized. In any event, in those far off days when I was rolling serenely across the South Atlantic in search of new adventures, my patriotic reputation in my damp but lovable homeland had reached dizzy heights. I was the hero of the hour, a fairly brief hour I may add in the stately progress of recorded time, but at the moment, a little startling and entirely gratifying. The gentlemen of the Press outdid themselves in praise of my skill and talent and, above all, my political acumen. There were a few faintly dissentient voices heard chirping reprovingly in some of the more intellectual weeklies, and one very loud voice indeed, emanating from none other than the late Sean O'Casey, who was seeking refuge from Irish discomforts in the Devonshire dales. For some reason, best known to himself, he decided that *Cavalcade* was beneath contempt. So violent were his diatribes that the late James Agate sprang articulately to my defence either in the *Sunday Times* or the *New Statesman*, I forget which, and the controversy raged for some weeks. As I never met Mr Sean O'Casey and had never to my knowledge, done anything to rouse his ire, I can only conclude that his loathing of me, which continued briskly until his death, must have been inspired by some curious mental obsession. On the other hand of course he may merely have seen a photograph of me in the papers. In any case I am bound to admit that the disagreeable old *embusqué* wrote at least a couple of very good plays.

3

Our first view of the harbour of Rio de Janeiro was as sensational as we had expected it to be. The Sugar-Loaf mountain climbed up into the sky and the other mountains behind it emerged from the morning mist, shedding their clouds gracefully and looking a little self-conscious as though they had been caught washing their hair. After an hour or so in a suffocatingly hot customs house we drove off, bag and baggage, to the luxurious Copacabana Hotel where we had reserved a suite.

It is not my intention, even were my memory capable of it, to stun my readers with a blow by blow account of every incident that occurred, of every person we met and every scenic marvel we gazed at during those long-ago, erratic wanderings across the sub-continent of Latin America. It is inevitable in the course of my narrative that a scenic marvel or two will pop up now and again and that a few outstanding characters will emerge, but they will be severely rationed for, as the Genie succinctly remarked at the end of the first act of *Where The Rainbow Ends*, "Time is short and we have far to travel".

The first outstanding character to appear in Rio was Mr Edwin Morgan, the American Ambassador, who called on us the afternoon of the day we arrived and invited us to a sumptuous party which was to be given that evening. After fourteen days spent in the company of our relentlessly Teutonic fellow-passengers, the idea of a slap-up Brazilian social soirée appealed to us immediately, and we accepted with enthusiasm. The party fulfilled out highest expectations. It was indeed sumptuous and glittering and gay and, thanks to dear Edwin Morgan for taking us to it, we were able to meet all the crème de la crème of Rio society at one fell swoop. From then onwards we never looked back. There were bathing parties, barbecues, formal ambassadorial receptions and informal moonlight picnics to say nothing of fancy dress balls and a couple of treasure hunts. An English Major with a black patch over one eye took us riding up a perpendicular mountain on sturdy but resentful Brazilian ponies. Later on, this kind and most hearty man, took me aside and, flushed with manly embarrassment, handed me a bundle of poems that he had been working on secretly for years. He stood over me anxiously while I read them. I can still remember the last two lines of the first one. "Oh simple shepherd praise thy God – That thou art nothing but a sod."

Two life-long friends emerged from those dizzy three weeks in Rio. One was 'Baby' Guinle (now Mrs Richard Pendar) a strikingly beautiful Argentine who reappeared in my life in Paris during the first weeks of World War Two and managed, with glamorous efficiency, to find me a charming flat in the Place Vendome. The other was Daan Hubrecht, the son of the Dutch Ambassador. He was twenty-one, tall, handsome and dashing, he spoke several languages perfectly, and he only needed side-whiskers and a moustache to have been a credit to Ouida. He was, at the moment, embroiled in a rather perilous love affair with an Englishwoman married to a Brazilian and so when, a little later on, Jeff and I asked his parents if they would allow him to come with us on our expedition into the interior, they agreed with ill-concealed alacrity.

The Maté Langeiras Company, for some obscure reason that I have never been able to fathom, most generously invited us to make our projected journey to the Iguassú Falls via the Paraná river, as their guests, even going so far as to provide us with a private coach on the train, cook and all, for the three days journey from Sao Paulo to the railhead at a place called Presidente Epistacio. From here we were transported, still as privileged guests, down the river to La Guaira on a curious contraption consisting of three boats lashed together. Jeff and Daan and I occupied the middle one while the two on either side carried the captain and crew respectively. It was a mysterious and enchanting experience floating endlessly downstream on that wide, beige-coloured river in the middle of the Brazilian jungle. Occasionally we would tie up alongside a rickety wooden pier and go ashore for a while to stretch our legs in some primitive little Indian fishing village. I remember that I celebrated my thirty-second birthday on the Rio Paraná. The birthday feast consisted of two small tins of caviar and a great deal of luke warm Vodka on which we all three got hilariously drunk. In the evenings we sometimes asked the Captain to shut off the engine for an hour or so and we would drift along silently through the brief tropical twilight, watching strange animals come down to the waterside to drink and listening to the eerie sounds of the jungle preparing for the night. As the light swiftly faded from the sky it seemed to be caught and held for a few extra moments on the surface of the water so that the whole stretch of the river before and behind us looked like luminous glass. It was romantically awe-inspiring to reflect that the dense, matted jungle on the right bank extended for two thousand miles across the vast continent to the mountains of Bolivia and Peru; two thousand miles of mainly unexplored virgin forest in which one could become hopelessly lost only a few hundred yards inland from the shore. Those remote, still evenings on the Rio Paraná, even now in 1965, stay clearly in my mind. It is such moments that explain my wanderlust and justify my eternal restlessness. They are rare of course, extensive travel does not automatically provide an inexhaustible supply of glowing memories, very often it can be arduous, uncomfortable and disillusioning, but when all the discomforts and setbacks and irritations can suddenly add up to an hour or so of untarnished enchantment, then, to me, they are all more than worth while. I have never yet, in all my years, outgrown the childish and perhaps egocentric pleasure of being able to say: This is I, myself, sitting on top of this alien mountain; in this ferry boat chugging across Hong Kong harbour; staring out through coco-palms at this coral sea. I, myself, who in my earlier days knew the grey drabness of provincial lodging-houses, the oppressive gentility of English suburbia, who so often trod hot, unyielding London pavements between various theatrical agents' offices in my midsummer search for an autumn engagement. Look at me now! My spirit crows, lying on the deck of a swaying ship gazing up at the crowded, tropical stars. Look at me now! I cry, even at this very moment, sitting on my high-up Jamaican verandah, watching the changing shadows on the sea, my full grown, scarlet tulip trees which I planted only eight years ago, glowing in the hot sunlight, and, over and beyond the diminishing headlands, the jagged range of Blue Mountain peaks standing against the sky.

I trust that the reader will not be too embarrassed at this sudden outburst of self-congratulatory enthusiasm. It is only that whenever I reflect with what alarming rapidity I am trundling towards old age and the dusty grave, I find it comforting to count my blessings. And although the future, like the late Mrs Fiske, is heavily veiled, my blessings, up to date, have certainly been considerable.

4

Guaira, where we finally disembarked from our three-fold river craft, was a settlement inhabited by three hundred thousand Indians and one white Resident and his wife. He was a husky-looking Argentine attired in 'bombachos', elaborately ornamented leather boots and a rather skittish beige hat. He spoke no English but greeted us politely and led us to a guest house on a spick and span and faintly irrelevant boulevard lined with trees. Beyond the boulevard, in fact all round the township, the jungle was waiting to pounce and it took a good deal more than seven maids with seven mops daily to keep it at bay. The town itself was clean as a whistle and even boasted a railway station for a train which ran exactly two hundred and fifty kilometres and came to an abrupt stop in a jungle clearing. The guest house was also as clean as a whistle which was more than we were. On the boat we had emptied buckets of water over each other at stated intervals but we had none of us had a bath or a shower for several days. We drew lots as to who should have the first go at the bath and I won and within a few minutes I was lying blissfully in tepid fresh water gazing up at the wooden ceiling.

Here I must digress for a moment to explain that before we left Sao Paulo we had paid a visit to the snake farm in order to become acquainted with some of the perilous reptiles and insects we might possibly encounter on our expedition. A delightful man called Doctor Almeira took us round and cheerfully showed us a number of the more deadly hazards in store for us. He also presented me at parting with a tiny and exquisitely coloured coral snake (harmless) which lived happily in my breast pocket for several days until Jeff, unbeknownst to me, gave it a few sips of his dry martini which killed it instantly. Among the various lethal creatures Doctor Almeira introduced us to was a peculiar deadly type of tarantula which, apart from its instantaneous death-dealing capacities, was so repellent to look at that we shuddered and turned away. Its body was about the size and shape of a small bun the colour of red lacquer and covered with bright ginger hairs. It had a beastly little beak and a multitude of long legs also hairy. The memory of this hideous example of nature's tastelessness haunted me for some days. It was while I was lying in that longed-for ecstatic bath in the guest house at Guaira that my memories of it were revived with ghastly suddenness. I noticed, on the wooden ceiling above my head, a slight movement, after a second look I was out of that bath and screaming down the passage in a split second. Eventually the house-boy appeared with an O-Cedar mop and killed it in the bath where it had dropped, presumably a moment after I had vacated it. Both Jeffery and Daan rallied me with warm gin and, when their turns came, approached the bathroom with the utmost caution. I do not know the exact genus of this unattractive insect but I do know that if it bites you you are dead within ten minutes and that if it only sees fit to crawl across any area of your exposed flesh, that area is liable to be paralysed for ten days. I retailed my gruesome little adventure to Señora and Señor Rhode after dinner in halting Spanish, and they rocked with laughter.

The scenic marvels of Guaira being limited to a sedentary ride in the train and a tiring walk through the jungle to look at some sparse remains of a derelict seventeeth-century Jesuit village, we left after two days and pressed on towards the main object of our trip which was to see the famous Iguassú falls. This necessitated going on down the river in whatever steamers were available until we reached a disembarkation point near to Iguassú which was some way inland. I think the place we finally got to was Encarnación, or it might have been Piray or Posados. Whichever it was there was nowhhere to spend the night except on board an ancient, long discarded pleasure steamer which had a sinister, 'Outward Bound' atmosphere and contained a few cockroach infested cabins, a vast, dark dining-saloon and a mad steward dressed in a greyish-white bum-freezer, ominously stained blue trousers and multi-coloured carpet slippers. He had two complete rows of brilliantly gold teeth and, as it was his habit to go into gales of high-pitched laughter whenever we asked him for anything, we were almost blinded. Apart from him and us and the cockroaches, the only other living creature on board that macabre vessel was an incredibly old mongrel which had no teeth at all, gold or otherwise. Its name was Peppo. The food, needless to say, was disgusting, but fortunately we happened to carry our own liquor with us and managed to make ourselves a nauseating but potent brew of gin, boiled water, lemon-juice and brown sugar. After our nasty meal we sat out on the deck in the pitch dark listening to the river muttering by and chain-smoking cigarettes to discourage the insects. Later on in the evening Peppo made a determined effort to get into bed with me but I succeeded in repelling his advances and he finally retired wheezing down the dark corridor.

I would like to be able to describe the magnificence of the Iguassú falls. I am sure that they were as vast, impressive and awe-inspiring as they were claimed to be. Unhappily however we were unable to see them very clearly. Owing possibly to the time of the year or to some freak of Nature, the entire area was densely clouded with large black mosquitoes. We wore grubby cotton gloves, hastily borrowed from the waiter at the delapidated rest-house where we lunched, and straw hats from which hung thick green veils which we were obliged to tuck into our shirts. Luckily our ankles were protected because we were all three wearing jodhpurs and boots. We were ushered into a curious squarish-shaped boat by a loquacious, half-naked young man whose *désinvolte* attitude towards the mosquitoes fascinated us. He chattered away merrily while they settled on his brown sweating body in swarms making his skin look like some new and outlandish material designed by Schiaparelli. What fascinated us less was the fact that, still talking, he steered us practically to the lip of the main falls, nonchalantly arresting our progress from time by time by leaning over the side and seizing hold of passing weeds. The roar of the waters hurtling into the abyss was deafening, and the heat, under our hats and veils, intolerable. When finally, in what seemed to be to be the nick of time, we turned back, soaked to the skin with sweat and spray and dry-mouthed with terror, he helped us ashore and led us, at a stumbling trot through a 'rain forest' which ultimately led to a narrow, slippery ledge on which he forced us to crouch and peer down through large ferns and our green veils, at a churning tumult of waters several hundred feet below us. Admittedly there were a couple of rainbows scintillating in the humid air, and a few harebrained birds whizzing about, but we were too exhausted and uncomfortable to do more than acknowledge them briefly and stagger back to the rest-house as quickly as possible.

With this dramatic but agitating adventure behind us we made our way back to the main river again and proceeded in a leisurely manner downstream in a small trading steamer until we arrived at Corrientes. Here we embarked on a pseudo-de-luxe passenger boat for the last lap of our journey to Buenos Aires. There are few things more agreeable than a bout of luxury after a prolonged period of roughing it and we were looking forward eagerly to soft beds, clean sheets, hot baths and all the other amenities of expensively civilized travel. A greater power than we could contradict however thwarted our intentions, the greater power being invested in the Captain and personnel of that pseudo-de-luxe floating monstrosity. We went on board in the later afternoon, and having washed and showered and tidied ourselves in our genuinely luxurious cabins we made our way to the bar to have a drink before dinner. The first blow fell when the barman refused contemptuously to serve us. We then sent for the Chief Steward who informed us, not over politely, that we were not suitably dressed to be served in either the bar or the dining-saloon, nor would we be permitted to enjoy any of the privileges of the first class accommodation unless we wore coats and ties. Considering that (a) we were all three tired from having travelled fairly ruggedly for a long time; (b) we were spotlessly clean in our khaki open-necked shirts and jodhpurs and (c) that we had paid the maximum for our first class tickets, it was not surprising that we all three lost our tempers immediately, and the row was on. It was really quite a good row as rows go and attracted a gratifyingly large crowd of our more correctly attired fellow passengers. The Purser was sent for and finally, the Captain himself. He was a tubby, red-faced little man with a slight squint. He was also pompous, obdurate and entirely bloody-minded. By that time of course it had occurred to all of us that we *had* got coats and ties packed away in our suit-cases and it would perhaps have been both time- and trouble-saving to have given in. But our blood was up. It had by then become a question of principle and the idea of surrendering to their pettifogging little rules and regulations could not be entertained for a moment. The steamer had already sailed so it was impossible for the Captain to order us ashore. Finally, after the battle had been raging for some time, I raised my hand, and my voice, to silence the general hubbub and announced icily that, having seen the first class accommodation and the type of people that occupied it, I felt that we should be more comfortable if we spent our three days' voyage with the crew. With this we all stalked majestically away to our cabins where we broke into giggles and drank our own gin from tooth mugs. The net result of the whole absurd fracas was, that after sending a radiogram to the British Consul in Buenos Aires protesting against our treatment, we removed ourselves, with the help of the Purser in whose eye we detected a sympathetic gleam, to three cabins below the water-line. The cabins were hot and stuffy, but three electric fans were produced. Meals were served to us on a trestle table set up in the wide passage outside our cabins and we appropriated a minute space on the after deck where we reclined, on mattresses during the daylight hours, with no clothes on at all. News of the imbroglio had spread through the ship and the stewards and the members of the crew we happened to encounter, were all on our side. We organized little community singing groups in the evenings and, on the whole, enjoyed ourselves very much.

Upon arrival at Buenos Aires three days later we were met by the British Consul, a friendly man called Gudgeon. Needless to say we emerged, at a carefully chosen moment when all the first class passengers were milling about preparatory to going ashore, impeccably turned out in white tropical suits and ties which the stewards had gleefully pressed for us the evening before. Mr Gudgeon made a formal complaint to the Captain and forced him to apologize to us, which he did with obvious reluctance. We accepted his apology with stately dignity and I, as spokesman, delivered a short homily in which I suggested that the next time an Ambassador's son, an eminent English writer and a British Peer of the Realm set foot on board his ship, they should be treated with the courtesy due to them no matter if they happened to be clad in nothing but jockstraps. I forget now what word I used in Spanish for jockstraps but I remember that I had looked it up in the dictionary and managed to arrive at some sort of approximation. I don't think however that it could have been a very accurate approximation because the Captain stared at me in blank astonishment.

Mr Gudgeon, who had evidently enjoyed the whole situation, drove us into the city and deposited us at the Plaza Hotel where we were received most affably by the manager who ushered us into the bridal suite. Jeffery and Daan got on with the unpacking while I gave a few press interviews in a mixture of Spanish, French and English. After this we ordered a bottle of pink champagne, drank it, and went happily down to lunch.

5

Our social career in the Argentine was launched initially by the British Ambassador and Ambassadress, Sir Ronald and Lady MacCleay. They were tremendously hospitable and kind and, under their aegis we sailed through three weeks of almost continual entertaining. In my own country I only rarely attend large-scale receptions and dinner parties and dances, mainly I suppose because I am usually working too hard to have the time to enjoy them. In a strange foreign city however it is different and in any case it provided a marked contrast to our wanderings through the jungle. Sir Ronald MacCleay's reception of us was also a marked contrast to our encounter with our Ambassador (or Minister, I forget which) in Rio, who, ten days after we had dutifully signed our names in the book had invited us to tea. He greeted us vaguely and with conspicuous lack of enthusiasm. At tea, we sat, in comparative silence, watching him devour, with the utmost concentration, two boiled eggs, after which we went away.

Shortly after our arrival in Buenos Aires Sir Ronald took me aside and asked me tentatively whether or not I would mind being 'used' as a celebrity every now and again during my visit. He explained that the only Britisher of any eminence who had come out during the last few years was Philip Guardella, who had given some brilliant lectures and gone away. Since then the Prince of Wales and Prince George had paused there for a while during their South American tour and had been an enormous success with the Argentines to whom the Prince of Wales talked Spanish with immense brio and considerable personal satisfaction. The Royal visitors, according to Sir Ronald, had not apparently paid quite enough attention to the English residents thereby causing a certain feeling of resentment. In fairness to the Princes I had to admit that I rather saw their point. It is obviously more important during an official tour to devote yourself to your foreign hosts rather than to any of your own countrymen who happen to be about. However be that as it may I was naturally flattered to be told that by opening an art exhibition, a flower show and making speeches at one or two clubs, I could in any way enhance the prestige of my country, so I agreed. My official appearances were brief and quite painless and as a matter of fact I rather enjoyed them.

A few days before the end of our stay in the Argentine Daan left us to return to Rio. We missed him sadly because he had been gay and charming company. Shortly after this we made a series of good-bye visits to all our newly found friends, and departed ourselves, in a very hot train, for Patagonia. I cannot honestly recommend to any travel-lover, however enthusiastic, a three days' and two nights' railway journey across the Argentine Pampas in a midsummer dust storm. However we emerged from it gritty but unscathed and spent an enchanting week with Carlos and Leonora Basualdo at a place called Nahuel Huapi. Leonora was an old friend and we had first met when she had been the Leonora Hughes, dancing partner of the famous 'Maurice'. She looked as lovely as ever and Carlos, her husband, and the whole Basualdo family entertained us so sweetly that I shall never forget them. It was a strange and fascinating house, 'rough luxury' at its best, glorious beds, marble bathrooms and every conceivable modern convenience set in the middle of wild, untamed country verging on the Chilean lakes. We bathed and sailed and explored the lake in a speed-boat. We also rode for miles on well-mannered horses equipped with Mexican saddles which I had never tried before and found extremely comfortable. Somebody once wrote a book called *The Horse as Comrade and Friend,* a title which has tantalized me for years, perhaps because I have never had either the time or the opportunity to cultivate such a relationship. Being an inveterate animal-lover I am quite fond of horses although, unlike many of my countrymen, I do not idolize them. I have ridden a certain amount in the earlier years of my life but with neither style, grace nor technique. Curiously enough, although I have frequently been bolted with, I have never either fallen off or been thrown which, in one way, stamps me as a bad rider I suppose. All experienced horsemen are constantly flung from their steeds as a matter of course. The horse, to me, has always been an unpredictable and slightly hysterical animal. I have encountered placid ones, spirited ones, fiendish ones and even sentimental ones but none of them has ever quite qualified for the status of Comrade and Friend. I think perhaps that the only thing that has saved me from being rolled on and trampled to death years ago is the fact that I am not afraid of them. Fear, I am told, exudes a certain unmistakable odour which is immediately recognizable by our four-footed Comrades and Friends. I can only conclude therefore that in this respect I am odourless.

In Nahuel Huapi the horses were models of good behaviour and there was one, called Carmencita, with whom I achieved, as near as no matter, a true homo-equine affinity. Lolling on her broad back in my comfortable Mexican saddle and encouraging her occasionally with a friendly pat or a honeyed word, I cantered about the countryside for hours at a time and, apart from feeling a little stiff in the evenings, was all the better for it. Eventually we bade good-bye to our delightful hosts and all the horses and set forth across a series of lakes to reach the Chilean frontier. Carlos Basualdo had organized the first part of our trip in advance, for which we had good reason to be grateful to him because it turned out to be a fairly complicated procedure. A series of lakes had to be crossed in various ramshackle little steamers and over the frequently mountainous tracts or territory separating them we were conveyed, with all our luggage, on even more ramshackle little mules. This experience precluded once and for all any possibility of my writing a book called *The Mule as Comrade and Friend.* We were assured by our Indian guides that these disagreeable animals were instinctively intelligent and sure-footed but I am bound to confess that those that I bestrode betrayed no signs of either of these excellent qualities. In fact the last one I hoisted myself onto seemed to have only one idea in its horrid little mind which was to 'un-mule' me as soon as it possibly could. It lurched and stumbled and frequently lay down without warning, preferably on the edge of a ravine and I was constantly having to yell to Jeffery and the Indians who turned back perilously down the jagged path and with oaths and blows forced it to stagger to its feet again. When, at long last, we came down to the shore of the final lake, I tried, magnanimously, to pat it good-bye, but it merely bared its hideous yellow teeth and plunged at me. Happily, being more sure-footed than it was, I managed to dodge aside, kick it as it passed, and retire hurriedly to the boat.

Our journey from then on to the railhead where we were to entrain for Valparaiso, was relatively uneventful. All I can remember of it is a gloomy rest-house at a place called Tronador in which we ate a greasy and unpalatable dinner and were later subjected to a plague of large white flying ants which successfully kept us awake until dawn.

We spent the early hours of that morning sitting in the station waiting-room waiting for our train which was late, sleepily playing 'Russian Bank' on the top of a suit-case and glancing occasionally at our fellow-passengers who sounded as if they were conducting a full-scale revolutionary meeting, but were actually merely discussing the weather and the crops. They were a picturesque group consisting of one enormously fat old Priest who mopped his face continually; several dusty looking nuns; a young man and a girl, possibly a honeymoon couple, dressed to the nines and sweating profusely; a few working types; two hirsute and tiny sailors; and a florid lady with a basket in which were three hens and a baby. Every now and then the baby shrieked whereupon she disentangled it from the hens and jammed its face irritably against a vast yellowish gas globe which she produced from inside her bodice.

When the train finally arrived we managed to get a first class compartment to ourselves, stretch ourselves out and go to sleep. The journey was interminable and hot and monotonous, a monotony which was rudely shattered by a sudden grinding of brakes and a dreadful scream. I looked out of the window and saw, before I had time to turn away, the bleeding torso and head of a young man who had been cut completely in half by the wheels. Even now, after all these years, that ghastly sight is imprinted indelibly on my memory. The train was halted for an hour or so in the blazing midday heat, a crowd of officials appeared and some of the poor boy's relatives who were apparently travelling in the train. One of them, presumably his mother, flung herself onto his remains and had to be dragged away shrieking. The general clamour was so excruciating that finally Jeff and I retired to the lavatory where we sat, sickened and shuddering, until the train started again.

We arrived late in the evening at Valparaiso, installed ourselves in a comfortable modern hotel and, after a delicious dinner for which we had little appetite, we retired to bed and slept for twelve hours.

6

The few days we spent in Valparaiso were enlivened for us by the Royal Navy. There was a light cruiser accompanied by two destroyers in the harbour and it wasn't long before we met some of the officers either in the bar of the hotel or at somebody or other's cocktail party. From then on we were swiftly whirled through a number of enjoyable Naval occasions including a whole day of gunnery practice some fifty miles out to sea; a couple of fairly libidinous 'guest nights' and various other marine junketings.

This was one of the very early stages of my long and proud association with the inaccurately termed "Silent Service" and consolidated the opinion I had formed a few years before when Jeff and I had travelled from Shanghai to Hong Kong in H.M.S. Suffolk, which was that the officers and men of the Royal Navy, apart from being gay and delightful company, have the best manners in the world. In those early days of the Thirties, halfway between World War One and World War Two when the illusion of Peace in our Time was firmly imbedded in the ostrich minds of our Western Governments, the activities of our fleets, both at home and abroad, were little more than perfunctory. The disciplinary morale was of course upheld by a series of battle exercises, target practices, occasional mock invasions and various other prescient operations, while, behind the scenes, the backroom boys were secretly preparing future scientific miracles. The outward aspects however were fair and untroubled and the international seas appeared to be as calm as millponds. One of the principal functions of His Majesty's ships at that time was merely to 'show the flag' which meant sailing the smiling oceans in 'Battle's magnificently stern array' with no ulterior motive beyond the perhaps naive assumption that 'To impress the Natives' was 'A Good Thing'. In my experience, which is considerable, the Royal Navy invariably executed this task with triumphant style and dignity. In my time I have visited a great many foreign ports as a guest in our warships and I have never once known the performance to fail. I would like to add however that these successes were by no means so casually achieved as they appeared to be. Nonchalant 'panache', like expert high comedy acting, can only be acquired after meticulous rehearsal. The luncheon and dinner parties on board for local dignitaries, the receptions, both formal and informal, the cocktail parties and the inevitable dances on the Quarter Deck englamoured by flags, bunting, coloured lights and the cynical radiance of alien stars, were all organized down to the minutest detail. Even over the lighter entertainments unobtrusive tradition presided, benign but watchful, like an insular English 'Nanny' at a possibly unpredictable children's party.

I am glad to say that even in this grubbier era the disciplined grace of Naval manners still persists. Only a short while ago when I was passing through Hong Kong I was telephoned by a Flag Lieutenant and invited to lunch on board the flagship with an Admiral Scatchard. I naturally accepted with pleasure and, during my voyage across the harbour in the Admiral's barge which had been sent for me, I racked my brains to remember where in the past, in what circumstances and in which ship I had met Admiral Scatchard before. It was only when he greeted me on deck that I recognized, through the lines that years and the weather had lightly etched on his face, the cherubic countenance of a young midshipman I had known over a quarter of a century before, who had brought me cups of ship's cocoa up to the bridge and called me 'sir' with such relentless persistence that I had felt like clouting him. It was now my turn to call him 'sir' and, after we had lunched in his comfortable cabin and I had been taken to the wardroom to be introduced to the rest of the ship's officers, he saw me over the side. As I bounced across the glittering water of the harbour, sitting in the stern of the barge, I looked back at the grey ship set against the multi-coloured panorama of the island peak, and happily reflected that I had been infected all over again by the Navy's, to me, imperishable magic.

In Valparaiso, our principal host was a Captain Vivian, who, many years later, I encountered during the war when he was Admiral-in-Charge of The King Alfred Training Establishment in Hove. He invited me to a guest night to witness a number of young cadets 'pass out', not, I hasten to add, in the alcoholic sense. Their 'passing out' was a joyful ritual, a longed for milestone in their young careers, a celebration of the fact that their months of shore training had been successfully accomplished and they could now look forward to the very near future, when they would go to sea for the first time. I remember being driven back to London by Admiral Vivian through the rainy, blacked-out countryside and wondering, in the intervals of pleasant reminiscence about our long-ago days in Valparaiso, how many of those eager, cheerful young men would survive the dark years ahead.

7

In Santiago we spent a halcyon week with the British Ambassador, Sir Henry Chilton, his wife and their two daughters. I must apologize to the reader if the pages of this narrative up to date seem to have been overloaded with Ambassadors, but he must realise that in those days Englishmen of the mildest repute travelling abroad gravitated automatically to their country's nearest and highest representatives. Not invariably of course. There has always been a percentage of the more hard-bitten, before-the-mast, work-your-own-passage, types of travellers who, for various reasons, deliberately eschew all social contacts above a certain level and ardently pursue discomforts even when they are not strictly necessary. I am naturally not referring to those whose means preclude them from luxuries and whose true spirit of adventure impels them to travel on the cheap rather than not travel at all. For these I have nothing but admiration. But I have, in my day, run across certain characters who, although they could perfectly well afford comfortable hotels wherever they were available, deliberately, and perhaps a trifle self-consciously, head for the nearest waterside doss house. It is unnecessary to state that I do not belong in this category. I am prepared to accept cheerfully any hardships that happen to come my way when I am travelling, providing that they are unavoidable, but I see little sense in seeking them out.

Nor need it be assumed from the above that I make a habit of staying in Embassies, Residences and Government Houses on my journeys. On the contrary, as a general rule, I avoid them. To my mind there is a good deal more to be said against official hospitality than there is for it. In the first place, unless your particular host and hostess happen to be old friends with whom you can kick off your shoes and giggle after the last more transient guest has departed, the strain of continual 'best behaviour' is apt to become intolerable. It has fortunately not often been my lot to find myself, for some reason or other, an official guest of a Governor and Governor's lady whom I have never met before and who are pompous and stiff-necked into the bargain, and even on these rare occasions I have usually managed, with a calculated performance of modest, unspoiled-by-my-great-success simplicity to puncture, after a little while, their pro-consular reserve. These tactics I find tiring and frankly not worth the trouble, and I would infinitely rather exert my winning ways to charm hotel managers, floor-waiters and chambermaids from whom I can hope to get more appreciable rewards.

In any case I find, as a general rule, that I would rather stay at an hotel than in other people's houses, official or otherwise, unless of course they happen to belong to close friends with whom I can relax. I do not care for the obligation of having to be considerate to other people's servants, nor do I care to experiment with other people's ideas of comfort which are so often widely dissimilar from my own. In an hotel I can ring the bell or raise the telephone and protest if there aren't enough pillows or the bedside lamp doesn't function properly. In a private house I cannot. In an hotel room I can put a 'Don't Disturb' sign on the door and sleep for as long as I like and capriciously demand a poached egg and a cup of tea at three o'clock in the afternoon, if I feel so disposed, without feeling that I am shattering an established routine and possibly causing my hostess's cook to give notice. To me the very idea of a round of country-house visits is anathema, although many of my more social-minded friends take this curious practice as a matter of course. Whenever I hear one of them announce with every sign of pleasurable enthusiasm; 'I am spending from Tuesday until Friday with darling Ronnie and May at Cratchley, then the week-end with poor Walter and his ghastly new wife, then for the whole of the following week I shall be in Dumfries with the MacRattigans before going to Michael at Snurbdridge for Easter' I shudder with dismay. I am also given to wonder whether darling Ronnie and May, Walter, the MacRattigans and Michael are equally enraptured at the prospect. Possibly they are, but I am fairly certain that I wouldn't be. I am apt to find professional guests almost as tedious as professional hosts.

To the dear Chiltons in Santiago, Chile, however, none of the above strictures apply. They were un-ambassadorial to a degree and the word pomposity was not in their vocabulary. While we were staying with them a large package of long delayed English mail caught up with us, and I remember sitting in the garden with Jeff in the shade of some unpronounceable tree reading the news from home. There was a good deal of it one way and another; long letters from Lorn, Gladys and Joyce and Binkie (see footnotes, if any) explaining who was doing what and with whom. There was a lot of enjoyable theatrical gossip but nothing of any special significance. What was of considerable significance however was a cable from Alfred Lunt and Lynn Fontanne in New York saying tersely; 'Darling, our contract with the Theatre Guild up in June, what about it?' This shocked me into the sudden realisation that floating down strange rivers, clambering up far away mountains on mules and basking in tropical sunshine was all very well in its way, but that life was real, life was earnest and that the world was too much with me late and soon. Indeed the theatre world to which the major part of my life had been dedicated had almost vanished from my consciousness. 'What about it?' was the operative phrase in the cable and I knew what it meant only too well. I also knew that although the call of the wild might charm my ears for a brief while, the call of the Lunts had a stronger resonance. There was no rush, no urgency, no immediate necessity to plunge back into the hurly-burly, but from that moment onwards, my South American wanderings, although they were to continue for some months longer, lost a little of their initially carefree abandon.

In the summer of 1921 when Lynn, Alfred and I were all in New York together, they in lodgings on West 73rd Street and I in a small, lent apartment on Washington Square, we had made a mutual pact that when we had all three achieved individual stardom in our own rights, I should write a play and that the three of us would play it together. In thos suffocatingly hot days eleven years away from the shady coolness of the Chilton's garden, the idea had seemed to be little more than a far-fetched and over-ambitious pipe-dream. But a lot can happen in eleven years and, to Lynn, Alfred and me, a lot had. For one thing we had achieved the first part of the pipe-dream, we were all three established stars in our own rights. The first move towards fulfilling the second part of the dream was now obviously over to me. The play had to be written and, what was more, written before June. I couldn't expect the Lunts, much as they loved me, to wait about indefinitely once their rather irksome Theatre Guild contract came to an end. Also, once it became known that they were at long last available and free to pick and choose, every management and playwright in America would be deluging them with scripts. I remember going to bed that night in a fairly pensive state of mind.

I would like to explain here and now that to sit down and write an effective vehicle for one talented personality in the theatre is none too easy, to attempt to write one for three, particularly three of such equal status as Lynn, Alfred and me, seemed to me then, as indeed it seems to me now, an exceedingly tricky assignment. It was also of course one of the most stimulating challenges I have ever faced in my life. In any event from the moment that cable arrived my casual 'Traveller's Joy' was abandoned; not with gloom but with a sense of restlessness and urgency. We still had a long way to go before our self-imposed itinerary was completed; there were still many experiences and adventures to enjoy and still many wonders to see but for me there was a slight withdrawal of concentration. I was not unduly haunted or worried because I knew from experience that once I could snatch out of the air the right idea for a play, the actual writing of it would not take long. Once the basic theme of a play has been worked out in my mind, I have always written quickly. It's getting the basic theme that takes the time. And of course as I was so intent on getting a plot for the three of us, my own eagerness defeated itself.

We battled our way through jungles and over mountains; we met diverse characters and had a number of bizarre travelling adventures, some enjoyable, some maddening and all of them, with a few rare exceptions, interesting. We visited Cuzco high up in the Andes and Alleantitambo, the source of the Amazon where the great river gurgles out from under some small stones. We encountered strange birds and beasts including a herd of carpinchos which are of the guinea pig family and the size of Shetland ponies. They are also riddled with lice and extemely friendly. We travelled for hundreds of miles in an auto-carrill, a small Ford car attached to the railway tracks which, whenever there was the danger of meeting an express train head-on, was shunted into a siding.

It was an extraordinary journey, as clear in my memory as if it had happened only last week. I recall a moment of particular enchantment when we stopped in bright moonlight to stretch our legs and eat some sandwiches. An enormous valley spread all round us encircled by snow-capped mountains under a sky blazing with myriads of stars. The silence was awe-inspiring and broken only by an occasional raucous cough from a herd of llamas grazing nearby. We felt that we were on the roof of the world and it was with the utmost reluctance that we finally climbed back into our bizarre vehicle and continued our journey to Arequipa where we arrived at two in the morning and drew up before the Quinta Bates.

The Quinta Bates was a hotel and rest-house, and we were greeted by Tia Bates, the redoubtable lady who ran it, who was waiting up for us in a red merino dressing gown. She was an eccentric and delightful character, long since dead, with wild grey hair, a humorous glint in her eye and an air of ineffable distinction. A mixture of cosy landlady and Grand Duchess, whom we loved immediately. I had the luck to see her once again in later years when she suddenly appeared in my dressing room after a matinée of *Design for Living* in New York. We stayed with her gratefully for ten days before going on to La Paz and Lima where, all in one day, there was a revolution and an earthquake. The former left us unmoved but the latter knocked us off our stools in the bar where we were having a drink before lunch and caused me to crack my head against a heavy brass spittoon.

After this, having mutually agreed that Peru was a trifle restless, we flew to Panama where we relaxed for a few days in lovely tropical heat. It was in Panama, or rather Colon, which is the Atlantic end of the Canal, that our journey ended. Jeff had to go back to England and I discovered a Norwegian freight-boat called – why, I shall never know – the *Toronto*, in which I was able to reserve the Owner's Suite for myself. It was a small ship and I was the only passenger. I took my meals with the Captain who was a Joseph Conrad character; clear-eyed, humorous and a militant atheist. Occasionally in the evenings after dinner which was served at six o'clock sharp, I used to join the crew in the fo'c'sle for drinks and a sing-song. The drinks were potent and the sing-songs remarkable for their complete lack of musical talent. I should like to be able to state nostalgically that rich tenor and baritone voices echoed out into the darkness and mingled with the eternal murmur of the sea and the sighing of the wind through the rigging, creating an atmosphere of sublime nautical magic, but to do so would be, alas, sadly inaccurate. Their voices echoed out into the darkness all right but with such violence that only a cyclone sighing through the rigging could have been heard above them. Those raucous evenings however were sufficiently charged with maritime romanticism to remain for ever in my memory. One of the crew members, a strapping bearded young Viking clad in the briefest pair of shorts I have ever seen, not only played a guitar but actually wore a single gold earring. I remember reflecting at the time how much better it would have been if he had been content to allow his spectacular appearance to strike the romantic note and left his guitar at home.

The ten days I spent in that small cargo ship creeping slowly up the Pacific coast of America were among the most enjoyable I have ever known. I was only slightly weary after the ardours and adventures of Latin America. I had no fellow passengers to fascinate, bore or repel me. There was nothing to do from dawn until dawn. As a concession to the Captain I wore shorts and a shirt for meals, for the rest of the time until the night closed down I wore nothing at all. I had, as always, a suitcase full of books. I also had my typewriter on which, with no urgency, no consciousness of Time's winged chariot at my back, I began and completed *Design for Living*. The idea slipped into my mind, with neither prayer nor supplication, on the first evening out of Panama. I wrote it morning after morning almost effortlessly, with none of the routine moments of unbalanced exultance or black despair. It was a painless confinement and no instruments were required to ease the birth beyond an extra typewriter ribbon, which I happened to have with me. I finished it tidily two days before we were due to dock in Los Angeles and celebrated the occasion by having a royal piss-up with the crew, in which even the Captain, briefly shedding a little of his Nordic austerity, joined with enthusiasm. The ship, curious to relate, remained on an even keel and in due course, about twenty-eight hours later, deposited me in a blaze of early morning sunshine onto the dockside of Los Angeles harbour where Jack, in a state of contolled hysteria, met me. What had caused his hysteria was that none of the port officials had ever heard of the *Toronto*, and he had spent a frantic hour rushing from shipping office to shipping office trying to locate it. Jack of course was unaccustomed to meet any craft of lesser tonnage than the *Queen Mary* and when he finally appeared, breathless in my cabin, had to be soothed by gin in a toothglass.

8

The next ten days were in direct contrast to those I had passed on board that tranquil little ship. I have been assured by many of my friends that life in Hollywood can be as calm and uneventful as in an English Cathedral town. This may be so for those who live there but for those who visit it as I did, for a brief spell, it is hectic in the extreme. When ultimately I fell into my bed on the Super Chief at Pasadena I was so exhausted that I slept almost continually until the train got to Chicago. I had enjoyed myself immensely but the pace had been killing. Dinner parties, supper parties, brunches, hours spent in driving over mountains and through valleys to get to and from the various houses of hospitable friends. I had forgotten the vast distance it is necessary to travel to get from one gracious home to another. I had also forgotten how curiously similar they seem to be once you have arrived in them. All luxuriously comfortable, all with swimming pools and every one of them the pride and joy of its owner. The food I ate in them seemed to have been cooked by the same expert chef. True the cocktail canapés or 'Appetizers' varied a bit in different houses; in some the little rounds of toast with meltingly succulent cheese might be discarded in favour of little rounds of toast with little rounds of bacon wrapped round little hot prunes but the main gastronomic delights were, or seemed to have been, identical. I had downed so many endless slices of rare roast beef, so many thousand perfectly roasted potatoes and fields of tender green broccoli submerged under yellow seas of sauce Hollandaise that when in the dining car of the Super Chief I was faced with a tough railway steak and some pressure-cooked tasteless vegetables, I fell on them with a sigh of relief.

Then of course I realised, as the train gathered speed, that for the next three days I would also not have to keep awake until the small hours staring at a movie screen. In those days in Hollywood no private dinner party was complete without a full length epic beginning before you had gulped down your coffee. It was all done with the greatest style and comfort. The guests settled themselves in vast arm-chairs with drinks on small tables at their elbows. A screen either rose noiselessly from the floor or came down from the ceiling or swung into view on hinged bookshelves and there you were luxuriously stuck for a minimum of two hours. If you happened to have seen that particular movie before it was just too bad, but in fairness it must be admitted that this contingency seldom arose. The film exhibited was invariably brand new and usually starred your hostess which was all very well if you enjoyed it but embarrassing if you didn't. Happily for me the majority of my hostesses were good actresses and most of the movies excellent but there is no denying that those sybaritic evenings were conversationally arid. In addition to these nocturnal distractions there was the daily dose of celluloid to be digested. I never set foot in a studio without being led almost immediately to a projection room where I was installed in the usual vast arm-chair with a drink at my elbow and shown whole films, half films, rough-cuts and rushes. It was in one of these projection rooms that I first saw Norma Shearer and Robert Montgomery in *Private Lives*. I remember that just as the lights went out Bob, who was sitting next to me, slipped into my hand an expensive watch with my initials on it. 'This,' he hissed, 'is to prevent you from saying what you really think of my performance!' It didn't, because I thought his and Norma's performance charming and was not required to dissemble. At all events it was a beguiling and typical gesture.

So much has been written about Hollywood both in praise and dispraise that I feel it would be redundant to add my own view to the swollen flood; however I cannot resist making a few comments, not on the basis of the brief ten days described above but because since then I have revisited it several times and on one occasion actually worked there. Not in a movie, but in a television 'Spectacular' of *Blithe Spirit* with Claudette Colbert, Lauren Bacall, Mildred Natwick and myself in the four leading parts. I rented a small attractive house on the side of a hill and for six weeks lived a regular Hollywood life. Regular is the operative word, for anyone who works professionally, even for a short time, in that curious environment realises very quickly that discipline, and fairly rigid discipline at that, is the keynote of existence. For those readers of movie magazines who imagine that life in that unique Never Never Land is an endless round of glamorous parties and star-spangled orgies, the truth would be sadly disillusioning. Perhaps in its earlier years when fascinating silent stars galloped about on mettlesome horses, indulged in over-publicised marriages and divorces and flung themselves in and out of each other's swimming pools life was less real and less earnest. Now, at any rate, it is so controlled and ordered as to be almost humdrum. True, on Saturday nights with a work-free Sabbath just ahead, there are occasional social and even sexual junketings, but on the other six evenings of the week most of the big box-office stars are usually in bed by ten with Ovaltine rather than champagne and scripts rather than lovers. Film-making, contrary to much popular belief, is a demanding and exhausting business. The working hours alone preclude many opportunities for casual dalliance. During the shooting period of any movie not only the floor crews and the studio operators but the directors and extras and actors have to be ready and on the set by eight o'clock in the morning. For those performers who happen to be playing characters necessitating an elaborate make-up, the call is still earlier. This, taking into account the time getting to the studio from wherever you happen to be living, means being torn from sleep at about five-thirty A.M. When I was making my first picture *The Scoundrel* in 1936 at the Paramount Astoria Studios in Brooklyn, I remember driving over the 59th Street Bridge every morning for weeks and watching the dawn come up. In Hollywood of course, owing to the climate for one thing, conditions are more agreeable than in New York in mid-winter. To watch the sun rise over majestic mountains and the Pacific Ocean is pleasanter than watching it rise over skyscrapers and blocks of dirty ice drifting down the East River.

Another dismaying facet of 'Movie' life in Hollywood – and alas elsewhere – is the soul-destroying tradition of 'conferences'. I don't know when this ghastly innovation first came into being but I do know from personal experience that it is the most monumental, ego-strutting time-waster in the business. A film confer-ence, ideally speaking, should be a brief discussion between the director and heads of departments concerning ways and means, general procedure and time schedules. What it usually is is nothing of the sort. A large group of people, many of them redundant, sits around a table in somebody's office with pads and pencils and sometimes a jug of water and a few glasses in front of them, and talk a great deal.

I must here state parenthetically that I am temperamentally allergic to confer-ences or committee meetings of any kind. During my twenty years tenure of office as President of the Actor's Orphanage I incurred much criticism for cutting them down to the minimum. We are all aware that the egos of most human beings are frustrated in some way for some reason or other, and, so far as I have observed, committee meetings of any sort provide baleful opportunities for these egos to puff themselves up and waste their own time and everybody else's. I am convinced that the frequent recurrence of Board Meetings in all big businesses can mostly be accounted for by the fact that the majority of the members present welcome a chance to show off which their wives deny them at home. When a committee is formed by actors and actresses whose egos are overdeveloped anyhow, the result is more often than not, chaotic.

I remember once, at one of the first Orphanage meetings at which I presided, a famous actor who shall be nameless, stood up and delivered an impassioned speech in defence of a former administrator of the funds whom I had sacked for gross incompetence. The actor, with blazing eyes, fulminated against me for dismissing this saintly character who had lovingly devoted thirty years of his life to the dear children. (The actor was unaware that the saintly character had not only been more than adequately paid for his lifelong devotion but was rumoured to have handled the funds of the charity a trifle whimsically.) When he had finished his tirade and sat down, deeply moved by his own eloquence, I asked him civilly whether he had ever been to the Orphanage and if he knew where it was. He was forced to admit, as I suspected, that he hadn't and didn't. My lawyer, whom I had wisely invited to be present, then produced documents proving conclusively that the financial affairs of the Orphange had been consist-ently mismanaged for many years; that many important decisions had been made in committee lacking the adequate quorum and that the administration had been so lax for so many years that many of the committee members present might be liable to criminal prosecution. This, not unnaturally, caused a profound sensation and I was feverishly elected President for five years.

The first film conference I ever attended took place in Hollywood three days after I had landed from my South American travels, in an office on the Fox lot. As I entered the room my heart sank at the familiar spectacle. There was the shiny table, there were the pads and pencils and the jugs of water. On this occasion however it was not Child Welfare that was to be discussed but the movie version of *Cavalcade*. Also present was a collection of people, many of whom I had never seen before and have never seen since. What their particular functions were and why they were present I had as little idea then as I have now. In due course, after various introductions had been made, we all sat down. I was placed on the right of the Chairman whose name unfortunately eludes me. He was exceedingly courteous and had one of those affable grey faces that one immediately forgets. An anonymous script writer – not Reginald Berkely, who ultimately did a fine script – was invited by the Chairman to start the ball rolling by giving us his ideas. There was a slight pause while he put on his glasses and assembled a sheaf of typewritten sheets of paper before him. He then cleared his throat and began, with admirable assurance, to speak.

'The opening of the picture as I see it should be as follows.' He paused, consulted his notes for a moment and then went on. 'After the credits, which should rise slowly up the screen from the bottom to the top against a panorama of moving clouds, we see the branch of a tree in winter. The branch is flecked with snow, and on it is perched a little bird, just one little bird, looking lonely and forlorn. As we look at the little bird the background music swells and it is suddenly Spring. The tree is covered with tender young leaves and the original bird has been joined by hundreds of other birds, fluttering and chirrupping and building their nests.' He sat back in his chair and regarded us with a complacent smile. Whether he expected us to give a round of applause or cry in unison that we did believe in fairies I shall never know because, seized with a violent inward fury, I rose to my feet. I think it was that smile as much as anything else that exasperated me. I looked around the table at all those vacuous faces waiting so attentively for further treacly symbolism and realised with dreadful clarity that all the worst stories I had heard about the Hollywood mentality must have been, if anything, understated. I also knew that if I stayed at that table one minute longer I should probably lose my temper and be very rude indeed and that to make an ugly scene at such an early stage of the proceedings would do more harm than good. So, forcing my lips into an apologetic smile, I said that I had completely forgotten an appointment of pressing urgency at the Beverly Wilshire Hotel and left the conference room never to return.

The sale of the *Cavalcade* movie rights had occurred long after the play opened, actually only a few weeks before it closed. I thought, in common with everyone else connected with the production, that of all the plays I had ever written *Cavalcade* was the most likely to be snapped up immediately by the movie boys. It had a stirring story, good parts, lots of opportunity for spectacle and as it had originally been written in a series of short scenes it could, with the minimum of effort, have been adapted for the screen practically as it was. The cinema Moguls however thought otherwise. *Cavalcade* was relentlessly turned down by all the major studios in Hollywood and in England. It was ultimately bought by the flimsiest of coincidences.

A certain Mrs Tinker, to whom I have every reason to be grateful – as indeed have numberless other people – happened to be in London during the last weeks of the run of *Cavalcade* and went with a friend to Drury Lane Theatre. She was so impressed by the play that, on returning to her hotel, she immediately sent a cable to Mr Tinker, urging him to acquire the film rights at all costs. Mr Tinker had recently been elected as one of the Directors of the Fox Studios and, obviously aware that he had married a remarkably intelligent woman, put her suggestion before the Board. Not having been present I cannot vouch for the accuracy of what I have been told took place. Apparently Mr Tinker was swiftly snubbed for his pains and the suggestion arbitrarily dismissed. However dear Mr Tinker, whom sad to say I never met, was obviously not the type of man who cares to have his opinions summarily ignored; in addition to which he was very rich, and it was thanks to his financial intervention that Fox Studios had evaded bankruptcy by the skin of their perfectly capped teeth. I like to imagine that there was a strong dramatic Galsworthian scene in course of which Mr Tinker, purple in the face, delivered a blistering tirade, hammered the desk with his clenched fist and finally by sheer force of Right over Might won his point and sank down in his chair mopping his face with a bandana handkerchief, but I fear that the reality was more prosaic.

At all events he did win his point and, bitterly against its will, Fox Films capitulated. A week or so later, evidently having decided that they might as well be hung for a sheep as for a lamb, they sent over to London a posse of cameramen and cameras and assistant directors and production managers and, possibly, clapper boys to film the play as it was presented on stage. (Actually a very sensible procedure and I could only wish that other Hollywood studios would adopt it.) This resulted in three days intensive work and my beloved company earning a lot of extra money. Having gone this far Fox considered that it had done enough, Tinkers or no Tinkers, and beyond engaging an English director called Frank Lloyd, who I believe had been wandering unemployed through the Hollywood limbo for some time, they washed their hands of the whole affair and turned their dangerous attention to more important matters.

This of course was the greatest luck of all. Had they been enthusiastic about *Cavalcade* it would inevitably have been ruined. Millions would have been spent; scads of script-writers would have been engaged to change the play beyond all recognition; stars of grotesque unsuitability would have been asked to play the leading parts; Ace directors would have been hired and fired left and right and the result would have been an epic Hollywood shambles. As it was, their sulky withdrawal from the situation enabled Frank Lloyd, who was a brilliant director, to carry on with his job without indeed much encouragement but also without interference. He proceeded to engage an excellent cast headed by Diana Wynyard, Clive Brook, Frank Lawton, Ursula Jeans, Una O'Connor and Irene Browne (the latter two actresses having played in the London production), none of whom could be described as top-flight Hollywood stars and all of whom were first rate actors. The picture was shot within a reasonable time and I believe stayed more or less within its financial budget. It was also shot in almost cloistered seclusion. Few if any top executives' wives and sweethearts and friends were invited onto the set to stand about and gape and get in everyone's way, although it would delight me to think that Mr and Mrs Tinker had been granted full access at all times and been provided with canvas chairs with their names emblazoned on them in gold.

It was only I believe when the picture was in its last days of shooting that word got around that it was liable to be fairly sensational and all the little Foxes scurried out of their embossed leather holes and began to sniff around and clamber onto the bandwagon. When at last it had been titled and dubbed and shown secretly in Foxy projection rooms, the jig was up. Rumour has it that a very bright young man who had ardently supported the film at one of the initial conferences and been immediately fired was hurriedly re-engaged with an astronomical rise in salary. I devoutly hope that this is true but fear it is apochryphal.

As far as I can remember *Cavalcade* opened more or less simultaneously in Hollywood and New York and was acclaimed on all sides as one of the greatest pictures ever made which, at that time, I honestly think it was. A little later it repeated its triumph in London and throughout the world. All of which was highly gratifying for the authors, actors, the director and all concerned, and absolutely lovely for Mr and Mrs Tinker.

9

Upon arrival in New York I read *Design for Living* to Lynn and Alfred who were even more enthusiastic than I had hoped they would be. Like many people, myself included, neither of them really enjoy being read to. They much prefer to have the script to themselves and concentrate on it without the distraction of having to listen to someone else's voice and intonations. I, however, while agreeing with them entirely, have my own ego to think about. Much as I dislike being read aloud to, I very much enjoy reading aloud, and the Lunts with loving indulgence resigned themselves to the inevitable. They sat like beautifully behaved mice, nobody sighed or yawned or coughed and Alfred mixed stimulating little drinks between each act. It was a very happy occasion. So often in our profession, as indeed in many others, dreams are dreamed which are never realised and hopeful plans made which ultimately come to dust. This was a long established dream for all three of us and that first reading was the moment when it actually came true. Fortunately later on it didn't let us down, the play was an enormous success and all was well, but that was the moment of magic. I am aware that my worst friends could not accuse me of diffidence. I am and always have been self-assured, on the surface at any rate, but no good writer, even when exultant at having finished a new work, is ever quite quite sure, just as no actors, or at least very few, can step on the stage on an opening night without being nervous. A few pretend to be immune to this occupational disease and a few are strong willed enough to convince themselves that this immunity is genuine but I for one find it hard to believe. Admittedly when I was a child in the theatre I bounced on without a qualm and thoroughly enjoyed myself, but a child – even a child star which I was not – is too young to feel the weight of responsibility which comes when a certain status has been achieved. It is only natural I think that established stars should become more and more prone to stage fright as the years stack up behind them. They have gradually, in course of their careers, unconsciously set their own standards, and it is not fear of the audience or terror that they might forget their lines that makes them tremble; it is the dread that those self-imposed standards may not, for once, be upheld. I do not believe this to be a conscious thought process but I do believe that it is the fundamental reason underlying our first-night miseries. I have little patience however with those who indulge their nervousness to the extent of spoiling their performances. I have seen this happen on occasion and been aware of irritation rather than professional sympathy. If an actor is undisciplined enough to allow his own self-consciousness to intervene between himself and his talent he should leave the theatrical profession and devote himself to some less agitating occupation.

First-night nerves are inevitable and have to be taken into consideration as one of the hazards of the game. It is no use hoping to banish them entirely so therefore the obvious thing is to utilise them. To be able to do this successfully requires humour, technique and a strong will. Fortunately very few first rate actors lack these requirements. On they go with trembling hands and dry mouths, longing to be anywhere else but where they are and praying for the stage to open and pitch them into oblivion. Then, when the applause which greets their first entrance dies away like a volley of musket fire on a battlefield and they discover, astonishingly, that they are still alive, the stage magic begins. They hear their voices saying the lines and identify gratefully (sometimes) the misty faces of their fellow actors and suddenly, sometimes gradually, they begin almost to enjoy themselves. The sooner they do this the better it is for the audience and the author and certainly for themselves.

The Lunts were so pleased with the play and we were all three in such a state of happy excitement that we longed to cast it and go into rehearsal right away, but circumstances and common sense restrained us. It would be the height of folly to open a new play in New York at the beginning of summer when all but the biggest hits are about to fold up. Also I had a contract with C. B. Cochran to do a revue at the Adelphi Theatre in London, so we agreed, reluctantly, to postpone the production of *Design for Living* until early in the following year.

Before I left for London however a few important decisions had to be made. The first and most important of these was which management to select to present the play. On the face of it this statement appears to be insufferably smug, but it must be remembered that in 1931 Lynn and Alfred and I were individually ace-high box office attractions. (To pursue smugness still further, we still are in 1967, although we may be getting a little brown at the edges.) Had any of us decided to star in any given play we could have been pretty certain of success, always provided that the given play was a reasonable one. Few stars, however popular, can triumph over a bad script. The combination of the three of us therefore, in the eyes of all the commercial managements, was 'a consummation devoutly to be wished', even though we had stipulated a limited run. I found myself in a very enviable situation, and it would be hypocritical to pretend that I didn't enjoy it very much indeed. I was overwhelmed by vast bouquets of flowers and cases of champagne, whisky, gin and brandy from most of the leading New York managements. On the cards accompanying these gifts no mention of my new play was made, they were apparently just friendly, motiveless gestures of welcome. I enjoyed receiving them immensely although my hotel room became as stuffy and overcrowded as the Orchid House in Kew Gardens.

The only manager extant who didn't send so much as a box of chocolate peppermints was Max Gordon, possibly because at that particular moment of his career he couldn't afford to. Instead he appeared a few days after my arrival and announced dramatically that if I didn't allow him to present *Design for Living* he would cut his throat then and there. I cherished then and still do a warm affection for Max Gordon. His passionate love of the Theatre illuminates his whole personality like a travelling spotlight. No dedicated crusader, no valiant knight of King Arthur's Court could have pursued the Holy Grail with a quarter of the ecstatic adoration that Max pursues the Drama. When, in response to his threat of immediate suicide, I replied nonchalantly that of course he could present the play, he went into such convulsions of gibbering ecstasy that I had to give him some water in the tooth mug from my bathroom. It was a highly gratifying moment for both of us. For Max, because he had, during the last few seasons, fallen from grace as a successful producer by putting on a series of flops, for me because it enabled me to pay off a debt that I had owed him for a long time. It was not a financial debt but a moral one.

In 1930 when Gertie and I were playing *Private Lives* at the Phoenix (Adrianne Allen and a young actor called Laurence Olivier were also in the cast), Max Gordon had come to see the play and burst into my dressing-room after the performance like a fire-cracker. Never have I been drenched by such a flood of articulate praise. He ranted and roared and bounced up and down and the air glittered with superlatives. It was not until he had exhausted himself (not me) that his theatrical integrity over-rode his professional tact and he blurted out, almost shockingly in the golden glow he had created, a home truth which endeared him to me for ever. 'Why the hell did you ruin the effect of your whole performance by mugging and overplaying the breakfast scene in the last act?' The smile of delighted but modest deprecation that I always assume when receiving extravagant praise was wiped away as abruptly as if he had suddenly emptied a jug of iced water over my head. I was, for a split second, completely flabbergasted. Disregarding my pained astonishment and carried away by his own conviction, he proceeded to press his point home with deadly determination. To see an actor of my quality and experience descend to the depths of cheap vaudeville hamming in the last act of a play after playing the first two with unparalleled taste and brilliance (better) was one of the most miserable experiences he had ever had in the theatre. It was not only an insult to the audience but to my own talent and, he continued, so outraged was he that if he had not happened to be sitting in the middle of a row he would have got up and left the theatre. He went on in this vein for several minutes until suddenly seized by the suspicion that he might be going too far, he struck his forehead a resounding blow and faltered to a stop.

Dear Max, I can clearly remember his expression of guilty dismay until this day. There was, so far as I can recall, a moment or two of fraught silence, which I shattered by bursting out laughing. It was quite genuine laughter although I must admit that quite a lot of it was on the wrong side of my face. Sometime later when the success of *Design For Living* had rocketed him back to his rightful place as a leading New York producer he came, rather coyly, to visit me. I received him sitting up in bed in my hotel bedroom. I don't remember that I was ill, merely sitting up in bed. Max bumbled about the room for a while until he finally sat down and looking almost sheepish, he made me a proposition. The proposition was that from that moment onwards he wished me to have first refusal of the English rights of every play he produced. Not unnaturally I was touched by this most generous gesture and accepted it with alacrity. We shook hands solemnly on the deal and that was that.

He was of course true to his word, and, as a result of this sentimental little episode, I received, wherever I happened to be, every new script that was bought by the Gordon Office. For one reason or other I was compelled to turn them all down until one day there arrived the script of *Born Yesterday*. The play, which I had not seen, was a smash hit in New York, and when I read it I clearly understood why. Written by Garson Kanin, an old friend of mine, it was witty and well constructed and obviously a pretty sound commercial proposition for London or anywhere else. Delighted that I could at last avail myself of Max's initial gesture, I cabled to him immediately and said I was prepared to direct the play myself under the Tennent Management in London within the next few months. Shortly afterwards, when I had discussed it with Hugh Beaumont and we were tentatively casting in in our minds, a further cable arrived from Max, and a very agonised cable it was, explaining that after all I couldn't have the English rights because, unbeknown to him, Garson had already promised them to Larry Olivier who was then in management at the St James's Theatre. This naturally was a disappointment but as all concerned were personal friends of mine, my only course was to bow myself gracefully out of the picture, so I cabled Max at once renouncing my promised rights and wishing everybody good luck. When the play was ultimately produced in London it ran for a year, and a few weeks after it had finally closed, I received a cheque from Max Gordon for all his personal royalties. It was a fairly large cheque, and certainly a very large gesture.

10

In the spring of 1932 I sailed from New York to England in the *Bremen* or the *Europa*, I forget which, because the Germans with their usual low cunning had designed both their principal Atlantic liners to look exactly the same. I presume that there must have been some minor difference but to the casual eye they were identical. The same ornate decor in the main saloons and private cabins; the same expensive but rather sickly colour scheme in curtains and upholstery; and the same, faintly guilty obsequiousness of the personnel. I may of course have imagined this because of my own suppressed guilt in travelling in a German ship. The 1914–18 war was long over and done with, but it had cast a heavy shadow over my adolescence and although in the nineteen-thirties the international skies were apparently cloudless and Europe was just one big cosy happy family, I was perceptive enough to realize that none of it quite rang true. Later, as the decade progressed towards the holocaust of 1939, my sense of inward insecurity proved to have been dismally prophetic. With a few individual exceptions the German people have always been antipathetic to me. There is something about the Teutonic mentality that grates on my nerves and although in the twenties and thirties I had been received by them with the utmost courtesy and hospitality and although their appreciation of me as a writer has been unstintingly generous there remains in the depth of my mind an area of resistance, an inherent feeling of distrust. On the surface this can easily be accounted for by the two World Wars, but actually I think it is something more, possibly their fundamental lack of humour. No nation with a grain of genuine humour could have accepted seriously the grotesque rantings and roarings of Adolf Hitler. His physical appearance alone should have been sufficient for a belly laugh. I find it almost impossible to believe now as I found it impossible to believe at the time that a man with those stumpy female little legs, those rounded hips and that comedic moustache could subjugate a nation of several millions. I remember that even during the gloomiest days of the war I was unable to look at him on a cinema screen without giggling. Mussolini with his vast head and pop eyes was admittedly fairly silly-looking but at least he had a certain masculine virility and compared with the Führer he was an Adonis.

In the summer of 1938 I happened to be in Rome on my way either to or from Capri. I lingered for a few days because Rome has for me much charm, particularly in the summer. I have spent many happy hours sitting at a café table on the Via Veneto and watching the crowds stroll by. I find this an enjoyable occupation in whatever city I happen to be in, except London of course where one can't do it at all, but Rome is my favourite. That long sloping promenade from the gates of the Farnese gardens to the Excelsior Hotel, and the slow-moving, ceaseless procession of summer-clad individuals of all shapes and sizes and nationalities, fascinates me for hours on end. When in 1938 I decided one sunny afternoon to renounce the pleasures of the Via Veneto and go to a rally in the Stadium in order to see Mussolini in the all too solid flesh, it was with considerable reluctance. However my curiosity to see The Duce at close quarters overcame my midsummer lassitude and, having procured an aisle seat on the third row from the hotel concierge, I drove off through the parched terracotta streets to have a look at Italy's saviour.

It was a long time before he appeared and I sat sweating on a skittish little wooden chair that wobbled dangerously if I made the slightest movement, while hundreds and hundreds of Fascist youths marched up and down and back and forth shining with zeal and drilling themselves to a lather. They were on the whole a handsome lot but the expression of dedicated fanaticism on their moist young faces was fairly irritating. A few weeks previously I had spent a week-end in Kent with Anthony and Beatrice Eden. Anthony, just returned from summit conference or other, had given me a blow by blow description of Mussolini at an official lunch party given in Anthony's honour. Apparently the harmony of the occasion had been unwittingly shattered by Anthony himself at the very outset. The guests, I think about twenty of them, were standing about sipping their cocktails and making polite conversation when the large double doors were flung open and luncheon was announced. The Duce, with an imperial gesture motioned Anthony to come with him into the dining-room but Anthony, with his customary good manners, hung back and said, 'What about the gals?' This apparently so infuriated Mussolini that he marched angrily into the dining-room himself leaving Anthony and the rest of the party to follow as best they might. I don't know why but I have always treasured this little vignette; I suppose it is the conflict between dictatorial flamboyance and unyielding British public school rectitude that makes it so funny. Anthony had also told me that The Duce, at close quarters, had a trick of whirling his tiny brown eyes round and round like catherine wheels. I suspected at the time that Anthony had invented this fascinating accomplishment, but I learned later from other impeccably reliable sources that it was absolutely true.

So it was not without pleasurable anticipation that I wriggled on my uncomfortable little chair on that blazing summer afternoon in 1938. At long, long last the interminable drilling came to an end and after a pause during which the vast audience chanted 'Duce-Duce-Duce' at the top of its lungs, he, himself, the cocky little big-shot strutted into the arena. Prepared as I was to be discreetly amused, as I always am when faced with blatantly organised rabble-rousing, I was not prepared for the actual close-up of the hero when he appeared. He had, most unwisely, squeezed his squat little figure into a dazzling white uniform; his face, bursting out of the top of it looked like an enormous, purple-red Victoria plum surmounted by a black and gold tasselled forage-cap several sizes too small. In addition to all this his expression, as he stood acknowledging the shrieks of the crowd and shooting his right arm out and back like a clockwork doll, was so ludicrously pompous and self-important that I burst into uncontrollable laughter. Realising that in the circumstances this was not only tactless but downright dangerous, I tried, not entirely successfully, to disguise it as a coughing fit and, with my handkerchief pressed against my face I stumbled up the steep wooden steps and out of the Stadium, hailed a taxi and collapsed on the back seat of it. This was the only time in my life I have experienced a full, hundred per cent, knockout *fou rire* all by myself. I have endured many a bout of hysteria in the company of sympathetic friends and have had to be lead, sobbing convulsively, from theatres, churches and opera houses, but never before entirely alone in alien surroundings. I can remember now the bewildered expression of the taxi driver as he watched me in his driving mirror writhing and groaning in the back of his cab. On reflection I can only thank God that I never attended one of Hitler's free-for-alls in Munich or Berlin. I have a feeling that the Germans might have been quicker on the draw than the volatile Italians and that I should have found myself in very serious trouble indeed.

I I

During the run of *Design For Living* there had been much cable communication between Cochran and me regarding the revue I had undertaken to write for him. This revue, after various titles had been suggested and discarded, was ultimately called *Words and Music* and was presented by C. B. Cochran at the Opera House Manchester on August 25th 1932. On September 16th it opened at the Adelphi in London where it ran for several months, not, as I had hoped, for two years. It was a good revue on the whole and received excellent notices but what it lacked was a big star, or better still, two big stars. The cast included Ivy St Helier, Joyce Barbour, John Mills, Romney Brent and Doris Hare, all of whom were expert performers but none of whom at this time had that indisputable star quality which commands queues at the box office. Later it was produced in New York under the title *Set To Music* with Beatrice Lillie and Richard Haydn. Nobody could question the 'star' status of Beatrice Lillie but even with her name over the marquee the show, after three months capacity business, lingered on for a further month or so and then closed. All of which, I am reluctantly forced to admit, proves that the revue itself wasn't quite as good as it should have been. It had some good songs in it, notably "Mad Dogs and Englishmen" and "Mad About the Boy" and a hilarious first act finale, "The Midnight Matinée", in which Beatrice was inimitably funny as the amateur lady organizer, but it didn't hit the jackpot and that was that.

When I was a very little boy my beloved housemaid-cum-nurse, Emma, used to admonish me by saying, 'Don't be too sharp or you'll cut yourself!' This I think, on looking back, was what was wrong with *Words and Music*. It was too clever by half. It contained too much satire and too little glamour to attract the masses. However as it didn't exactly flop humiliatingly in either London or New York I can quite happily chalk it up as a near miss and remember it with affection. I am also grateful to it for giving me one of the most fascinating experiences of my life.

During the Manchester try-out the Musical Director was suddenly taken ill and I, at two hours' notice, decided to conduct the orchestra myself. This, considering that I could neither read nor write music, was a fairly impertinent decision. I have never been embarrassed by my technical ignorance. Many of the most successful composers of light music are unable to transcribe a note of it. Being gifted with an impeccable ear I can distinguish a wrong note in a symphony orchestra providing that the symphony orchestra happens to be playing one of my own compositions. This 'Musical Ear' is far from being unique and I am proud to share it with Irving Berlin and the late Jerome D. Kern to name only two. Even George Gershwin before he devoted four years of intensive study to counter-point and harmony was unable to write down his music unaided, although he had already been responsible for several Broadway musicals loaded with song hits. Irving Berlin, who I suppose has composed more lilting popular melodies than any man alive, cannot even play his own tunes effectively on the piano. He hammers them out, without brio, in the key of C Major which (for the benefit of the uninitiated) is the only key on the piano that has none of those tiresome black notes in it. Many years ago another haphazard composer, George M. Cohan, was generous enough to send me a specially designed upright on which the key could be changed by turning a handle. It was a fearsome instrument and the tone was ghastly but I was able to strum away on it in my own favourite key – E Flat – with no danger of imperilling my vocal range. Later, impelled by a guilty feeling that I was somehow cheating, I discarded it and forced my reluctant fingers into dreadful keys bristling with unsympathetic sharps but I soon gave up the struggle and reverted to my own true love. Over the years my untutored piano playing has improved considerably but still today when I have heard a tune in some musical or other that I wish to recapture, E Flat is my first instinctive choice. Later, with blood and sweat, I may succeed in transposing it but the effort involved is seldom worth the trouble.

Although a composer of popular music can afford to be as key-bound as he likes, a conductor of an orchestra most certainly can't. He must be able to recognise accurately every confusing little squiggle on the manuscript and issue instructions to his instrumentalists in the complicated jargon that they alone can understand. As I was abysmally incapable of any of this it was with considerable trepidation that I walked into the band-room of the Opera House Manchester a quarter of an hour before the overture and announced to the startled gentlemen of the orchestra that I was going to conduct that evening's performance. I had taken the precaution of rehearsing for two hours in my suite at the Midland Hotel during which Elsie April, my staunch musical adviser, patiently explained to me the changes of rhythm I should be required to beat out in course of the evening. When finally I arrived, more dead than alive, in the orchestra pit itself, I placed her on the ground at my feet just below the podium where she crouched like a gnome with the open score on her knees. When I appeared, the front of the house limelight operator, whom I could willingly have garrotted, flung a dazzling pink and amber spotlight onto me and I was forced to acknowledge a cheerful round of applause. Then, a trifle theatrically I fear, I held out my arms commandingly, whereupon there was a loud roll on the drums. I jumped as if I'd been shot and hissed to Elsie out of the corner of my mouth. 'What the hell's that? It isn't in the score.' 'Don't be silly dear,' she replied calmly. 'It's the National Anthem. Just a straight four-four all through. Take it nice and slowly.' There was nothing to do but obey her instructions, so I chopped my right arm in a firm down-beat and a wave of deafening sound enveloped me through which I could hear the scuffling noise of the audience rising to its feet behind me. Then, after a short pause out went my arms again and I began to beat out the first number of the overture which incidentally I had never heard before owing to being occupied with the company back-stage while it was being rehearsed. I went on doggedly while Elsie, at my feet, kept up a running commentary. 'That's right dear – just go on like that for thirty-two bars – look out here comes a modulation into three-four – that's right you're doing fine, nothing to worry about now until you get to the six-eight, just two in a bar dear nice and steady.' By the end of the overture I had begun to feel my oats and managed to beat my way more or less successfully through the whole show. For the rather complicated ballet music I surrendered the baton to Spike Hughes who had orchestrated it.

Taken all in all those were two of the most alarming and enjoyable hours I have ever spent. The next morning I was unable to move my right arm but after having it massaged several times during the day I was able to conduct the show again in the evening. I conducted every performance for two weeks, and it wasn't until Hyam Greenbaum, whom Cockie had himself engaged in London, arrived in Manchester that I was forced to relinquish that lovely little white stick with the knob on the end. Only three more times in later years was I able to enjoy the exacting, ego-boosting experience. Once was during the run of *Operette* in Manchester, when more or less the same sort of crisis occurred. This time the cast was headed by Peggy Wood and Fritzi Massary. Fritzi Massary, who had been the greatest operatic star in Germany for many years until the advent of the Nazis in 1933 forced her to leave the country, had been, during her resplendent and glamorous career, accustomed to the best conductors and composers in Europe including Leo Fall and Franz Lehár, several of whose operettas she had created in Berlin. I fully expected an ugly but justified display of temperament when she found herself on the stage faced by an amateur who couldn't even read a page of sheet music, let alone an orchestral score. But I needn't have worried. She was too great an artiste and too wise a woman to waste time in an emergency. She gave me such professional, whole-hearted co-operation that, when it came to her big *Wiener Valse* number in the last act, the applause was overwhelming and held up the show for several minutes. Later on when *Operette* had opened in London at His Majesty's Theatre and she had scored a personal triumph, it became an understood thing between us that, on gala occasions when visiting celebrities or members of the Royal Family were present, I would slip into the orchestra pit to conduct that particular number especially for her. I am bound to admit however that she tore the place up with it at every performance whether I was there or not, but I can also assert, without undue modesty, that a little extra magic occurred when she looked down and saw me poised, with my arms out, red carnation and all. Fritzi Massary was one of the most important artists I have ever been privileged to work with and I shall never cease to be grateful to her.

The third and last time I waved a baton was on the quarterdeck of H.M.S. Arethusa. The ship, in which I was the guest of Admiral Wells and Captain (then) Philip Vian, was lying in a tranquil bay off one of the Greek Islands. On a Sunday evening the ship's band gave a concert and I was invited by the Bandmaster to conduct a selection of *Bitter Sweet*. After a moment of panic I agreed and managed to get through it all right, principally because the bandsmen knew it by heart and were wise enough to pay scant attention to me. Naval good manners, as usual, saved the occasion and I received a tumultuous but ill-merited ovation. The setting was perfect to begin with. There was a full moon and a sky blazing with stars. The quarterdeck was illuminated by festoons of little coloured lights, and the sea, flat calm and almost motionless, glimmered with streaks of phosphorous. The officers sat in a wide, semi-circle with the rest of the ship's company behind them, some clinging to the rigging and all in their tropical 'whites', which seemed to gleam in the darkness. That evening remains in my mind as one of the most visually romantic memories of my life.

12

The end of the three-weeks' try-out of *Words and Music* in Manchester coincided with the return of my brother Eric from Ceylon, where he had been a tea planter on the hills of Naralia. A year or two previously Jeffery and I had visited him on his plantation, and he had, with inordinate pride, taken us over every acre of it. I think my relationship with Eric requires a little explanation, principally because he played such a small part in my life that many people would have been surprised to know that I had a brother at all. He was five years my junior, having been born in Sutton, Surrey, in 1905. I was reasonably fond of him but I cannot honestly say that we were ever very close until perhaps the last sad months of his life. Perhaps this five year difference in our ages was either too long or too short. At all events I have to admit, a trifle guiltily perhaps, that I never found him very interesting. It is possible that I might have been subconsciously jealous of him and resented his intrusion into the cosseted 'only son' pattern of my life, but in fairness to myself I don't think that this was so. I tolerated him, was occasionally irritated by him and, engrossed as I was by my crowded and exciting career as a boy actor, paid very little attention to him. He was there, an accepted member of my immediate family circle, but no real intimacy between us was ever established.

When in the autumn of 1932 he was sent home to England on sick leave my first sight of him was a profound shock. He seemed to have shrunk to half his normal size, his face was gaunt and drawn and it was obvious that he was very seriously ill. I immediately appealed to that remarkable woman Almina Carnarvon, whose well-known efficiency was only equalled by her kindness, and he was installed in her nursing home in Portland Place the very next day. After Lord Moynihan had made a thorough examination he sent for me and told me that Eric was suffering from a lethal form of cancer and could not be expected to live more than six months. Realising that Eric was anxiously waiting for a medical verdict and that he was also desperately frightened I asked Almina to think up quickly some ultimately curable disease that I could convince him he was suffering from, something preferably that he could verify in a medical dictionary if he had a mind to. After some thought and hurried research we decided on "Hyperplasia of the Abdominal Glands" and armed with this dubious but necessary fabrication I returned, with a sinking heart, to his room. He accepted my explanation suspiciously at first but after a while I managed to convince him. I told him, truly enough, that there was no necessity for him to stay in the nursing home longer than a few more days and that I would arrange for him to go down to Goldenhurst, my home in Kent, where he could slowly convalesce with a nurse. I also, in a moment of inspiration, told him that he could repay me by making an accurate and detailed index of all my gramophone records. He perked up considerably at this and I left him and drove back to Gerald Road for a couple of hours' rest before attacking my next miserable assignment which was the breaking of the news to my father and mother. This ghastly interview, organised with consummate tact and sympathy by Lady Carnarvon, took place in her private sitting-room in the nursing home at four-thirty on the same afternoon. I do not wish to enlarge on it because even after so many years I find the memory of it intolerable.

13

Lynn, Alfred and I opened in *Design For Living* on January 2nd at the Hanna Theatre in Cleveland, after which we played Pittsburgh and Washington. On January 22nd, two days before we were due to open at the Ethel Barrymore Theatre in New York I received a cable from mother saying that Eric had died peacefully in his sleep at Goldenhurst. I immediately telephoned to her and arranged for her and Aunt Vida to come out to New York, and ten days later they arrived. I was living in a rented apartment, 1 Beekman Place, and I managed to get reservations for them in the Beekman Tower which was just around the corner from me. Although *Design For Living* was a smash hit, which was of course immensely comforting from the professional point of view, achieving, as it did, an ambition which we had all three cherished for years, it was an unhappy and difficult period of my private life. Alfred and Lynn, I need hardly say, were marvellous to me and continued, with loving shrewdness, to be consoling and sympathetic, without overdoing it. I remember Alred coming into my flat one morning and saying, with rather obviously simulated anger, 'Noëlie – you've been crying again!' A few days after Mother arrived, the strain of the whole dismal business went to my throat and I lost my voice on a Saturday morning. I telephoned to the Lunts and huskily explained that I couldn't possibly play the matinée. Alfred was round in a flash. 'You've *got* to play', he said. 'If you don't we shall close the theatre.' This seemed to me to be over-dramatic, as I had a competent understudy engaged on his special recommendation. I argued vainly that if I could stay off just for that day, I could rest through Sunday and be perfectly all right by Monday but he would have none of it. 'Neither Lynnie nor I would dream of playing a single performance of this play without you,' he said, 'and that's final.' He then added, more gently, that if I would only make the effort and appear he would say as many of my lines as he could. Irritated by his stubbornness, I gave in and dragged myself to the theatre, feeling really dreadful and unable to make a sound. When I came on, shaking, for my first entrance Alfred confronted me with a blank stare and dried up dead. This so enraged me that I prompted him in a stentorian voice that Chaliapin would have envied and played through both performances without so much as a croak. All of which goes to prove that the Theatre is a remarkable profession, and Mrs Baker Eddy definitely had a point when she opined that Actors are very curious animals.

In the nineteen twenties, when I had played *The Vortex* in England and America for two years and finished up with a nervous breakdown, I made a decision that I have never regretted. The decision was that I would never henceforth play a play, however successful it might be, for more than three months. This was not quite so arrogant as it appears. If I were simply an actor, I would be grateful for the opportunity of playing a long run, but I am primarily a writer and I have found from experience that it is too much of a strain to be creative while playing eight performances a week. Acting a long part night after night requires maximum vitality and there is none left over for any other kind of work. It can be done of course in an emergency but as a steady routine it is impossible. Because of the special circumstances of *Design For Living* and Alfred and Lynn, I gladly broke my rule to the extent of two extra months. I rented a little cottage in the woods at Sneden's Landing on the banks of the Hudson. It was remote, utterly peaceful and only a thirty-five minutes' drive from the stage door. I had always loved Sneden's and had stayed there on and off for years with Kit Cornell and Guthrie McClintic. My cottage was small and primitive but well heated, the view through the trees to the river was enchanting and I was looked after by a round coloured servant called Henry who, in earlier days of glory, had played a Eunuch in *Aida*. His voice was, understandably, very high indeed and he fussed over me, cooked for me, cossetted me and, only very occasionally, sang.

My mother and aunt returned to England in May, and at the beginning of June we closed *Design For Living* in a blaze of triumph; in fact so great were the crowds during the last week that extra police had to be called to control them. During the run of the play a kidnapping scare swept America, touched off by the unspeakably horrible abduction and murder of the Lindbergh Baby. There were other abductions and hold-ups as well and, having received several threatening anonymous letters, I engaged, on the advice of my local Chief of Police, a private detective called Tommy Webber, who accompanied me back and forth between Sneden's and New York and sat at the side of the stage nightly bulging with armaments. He was a delightful character and shadowed me faithfully right up to the moment when I stepped on board the ship for Bermuda. He was present in fact at the farewell cocktail party I gave in my cabin and poked me cheerfully in the ribs with a gun before vanishing down the gangway.

14

The vessel that took me to Bermuda was a cruise-ship crammed to the gunwales with Mid-Western tourists who throughout three whole days and nights drank themselves silly, although I suspect the majority of them were fairly silly to start with, and made such a hideous noise that I was forced to spend most of the time locked in my stateroom. The locking of the door was a necessary precaution because it was frequently banged on in the middle of the night by groups of drunken ladies wearing paper caps. I think those dreadful three days were responsible for my later satirical musical *Sail Away*. In course of my extensive wandering across the world I have formed a strong aversion to tourists *en masse*. I am aware that this attitude could be criticised as being selfish and perhaps snobbish. I know that, ideally speaking, it is a 'good' thing that people who have never before set foot outside their own back yards should be able to enjoy the wonders of the world and I chide myself with fanciful visions of sad little old ladies receiving unexpected legacies and gallantly spending them on adventurous travel. Unfortunately however very few of the old ladies I have encountered on cruise ships have been either sad or little. On the contrary, most of them have been aggressive, full-bosomed, strident and altogether intolerable. My fellow passengers on board the ship to Bermuda were no exception. They drank and shrieked and made such noisy vulgar beasts of themselves that if I hadn't had the forethought to provide myself with earplugs I should either have run amok and kicked them in the teeth or thrown myself overboard.

I have always detested crowds. The very idea of a vast number of human beings herded together fills me with dismay, except of course when I happen to be separated from them by a row of footlights. This personal antipathy to crowds has prevented me from enjoying all street processions and public parades of any sort. Even in England where the tradition of pageantry is more decorously organised than anywhere else in the world I shut myself indoors or flee to the country rather than become involved. Nowadays of course since the invention of television the problem for me has ceased to exist. If any famous personage is being hailed or crowned or buried I can sit cosily at home and watch the proceedings without being either pushed or buffetted or frozen or suffocated. In the United States unfortunately the mania for public parades has reached almost lunatic proportions, what with the Shriners, the Rotarians, the Kiwanis and countless other esoteric organisations, not to mention the Irish, whose frenetic celebration of St Patrick's Day annually reduces the city of New York to chaos. The ordinary citizen whose principal concern is to get on with his job and earn his living is reduced to a state of gibbering frustration. Many a time when I have been driving from my apartment on the East Side to play a matinée on Broadway I have had to hop out of the taxi and fight my way on foot across town, arriving at the theatre breathless a few minutes before curtain time looking and feeling as if I had been involved in a lynching, and all because a number of frisky old gentlemen wish to make figures of fun of themselves by staggering along Fifth Avenue in funny hats. I am sure that this irritable outburst will bring down on my head an avalanche of furious letters saying 'Who do you think you are?' and 'Go home Limey', in which case I will merely stick them into my 'N. C. Abuse Scrapbook', which is growing ominously thicker as the years roll by, and read them over on long winter evenings with a comfortable retrospective snarl.

The object of my voyage to Bermuda was to join a British light cruiser, H.M.S. *Dragon*, in which I had been invited to make a cruise of the Caribbean. My host on this occasion was the Ship's 'Number One' Lieutenant John Temple. My other hosts were Admiral Wells, whose flagship it was, Captain Philip Vian and the ship itself. Philip, or to me 'Joe', Vian was tall with piercing blue eyes and extremely aggressive eyebrows. Soon after World War Two broke out six years later, he achieved fame (which he detested) as the Hero of the *Altmark*. It was he in fact who spoke the now legendary phrase, 'The Navy's Here'. Having delivered this warning statement he proceeded first to rescue a number of British sailors who were imprisoned below decks, and then blow the hell out of the *Altmark*. On my first introduction to him on the quarterdeck he wagged his eyebrows ferociously and said 'What the hell are you doing on board this ship?' I replied cringingly that I was exhausted, over-worked and on the verge of a nervous breakdown and had joined the ship in order to be nursed back to health and strength and waited on hand and foot. Whereupon he gave me some gin in his cabin and sent me back, a trifle unsteadily, to the wardroom. Since that day I have been his guest in many different ships from Scapa Flow to the China Seas, and at the risk of infuriating him by my theatrical sentimentality I must flatly admit that I am very fond of him indeed.

That particular cruise in H.M.S. *Dragon*, of all my cheerful gallivantings with the Royal Navy, was one of the happiest. I actually was fairly exhausted after the run of *Design For Living* and to be at sea again, with nothing to do but lie about and enjoy myself in the best possible company, was the most reviving tonic I could have wished for. I insisted at the outset on being made an honorary member of the Wardroom, which meant that I could sign for loads of drinks myself instead of monotonously letting others do it. Naval hospitality being what it is I had to fight tooth and claw for this privilege but I won the battle and was able to relax.

I was supposed to leave the ship at Colon, but I dumped my luggage overboard onto a motor launch and sailed in her through the canal. Unfortunately no-one had informed me that she was heading straight out into the Pacific without stopping at Panama, and I finally had to clamber down a rope ladder onto the pilot boat. It was a perilous exit because as I got to the end of the ladder the pilot boat, unheeding, hooted and turned to go back to shore. Frantic signals were made to the Captain while I dangled over the waves to the delight of the ship's company which was lining the rails. They were still more delighted when the boat finally came back and I flung myself onto the deck in a heap. They cheered vociferously and my heart was heavy as I watched the water widening between us.

After a few days of sitting about in the shady garden of the hotel in Colon watching the ships slide in and out of the Canal and feeling a little flat after my naval engagements, I sailed in the *Colombie* for Trinidad. The *Colombie* was one of the latest Messageries Maritime ships, and the local representative of the line who accompanied me on board and lavished on me the full V.I.P. treatment was as volubly proud of her as if he had laid her keel with his own chubby hands. He insisted on showing me over every inch of the ship including the engine-rooms after which we retired to the Captain's Cabin and had sweet champagne and chocolate biscuits. The three days' voyage was pleasant and uneventful and I passed most of it undisturbed in my cabin reading and sleeping. On the very early morning of the third day the mountains of Trinidad appeared on the horizon, and as we drew nearer to shore over a pale mauve motionless sea they seemed to change their positions as though they were gracefully moving themselves into the correct formations for greeting us. They also, as the sun climbed higher in the sky, began to glow with brilliant colour; every conceivable variety of green picked out with splashes of scarlet and pink and mauve when the Flamboyants, Flame-in-the-Forest and Jacarandas caught the early light. I have never, in all my travels, lost the thrill of arriving at a foreign port. From the moment that land is first sighted until the ship ties up alongside the dock I am aware of an inner excitement, a sense of new adventure. Even the long-familiar sight of the New York sky scrapers rising out of the morning mist enchants me as much to-day as on that summer morning in 1921 when I first saw it.

Of course there have been setbacks; my habitual delight at arriving at strange places has invariably been dampened from time to time: Shanghai in a thick wet fog; Liverpool in a driving blizzard; and the forbidding approach to San Pedro, Los Angeles with its forest of oil derricks and cranes depresses my spirit either in rain or shine. Now that I come to think of it our own dear Newcastle-upon-Tyne, even on a radiant summer day, is hardly likely to quicken the pulses of the most romantic-minded traveller. The glamour-seeker however must be prepared to take the rough with the smooth, and if, like me, he happens to be a genuine addict, the very fact of arrival provides enough of it.

Just off the coast of Trinidad there is a small island called Point Baleine. Having heard it enthusiastically described by various Trinidadians, I decided to have a look at it, so I hired a motor launch and on a cloudless shining morning set out over a flat sea accompanied for most of the way by a Homeric escort of dolphins, who plunged and curvetted round the bows occasionally flinging themselves bodily out of the water, as though unable to control their exuberant joy of living. I hope and believe that dolphins have as good a time as they appear to. To me they are the most beguiling and enchanting creatures, and I am ready to swear that this group that accompanied me to Point Baleine were in continual fits of laughter. It has been explained to me that all that uninhibited diving and leaping merely means that they are hungry and in grim pursuit of flying fish and other prey that saunter near the surface. I prefer however to hold on to the illusion that their laughter is genuine and that if only they were able to speak they would prove to be the gayest and wittiest company in the world.

The hotel on Point Baleine was owned and run by an ex-sailor and his wife to both of whom I took an immediate liking. The hotel was primitive according to Hilton standards but perfectly comfortable. It was, as far as I can remember a two-storied wooden building surrounded by a few single-room bungalows, one of which I inhabited. The food, mostly fish, was well-cooked and abundant and the whole atmosphere of the place enchanted me. Meals were eaten in the main house but my breakfast was brought to my private verandah, the mainland was only a very short way away and a little motor launch chugged back and forth several times a day. In later years I tried, not entirely successfully, to reconstruct the atmosphere of the place in my play, *Point Valaine*. It was a peaceful and lovely spot and only at weekends, when groups of visitors came over from the mainland, was its charm temporarily diminished.

From Trinidad I sailed back to England in another Messageries Maritime ship, *the Flandre*. It lacked the spit and polish of the *Colombie* but the food, as usual in French ships, was excellent and the passengers unobstrusive. The *Flandre* was far from being a Blue Ribbon record breaker but she had the same kind of peculiar, for me, nostalgic charm of a fat comfortable old concierge who sits day after day in a stuffy ground floor room with a bell on the door. I had a feeling that if I dived over the side I should find, instead of a keel, a pair of thick black stockings and faded red bedroom slippers. She chugged unhurriedly across the Atlantic, no capricious storms impeded her dogged progress and her bow wave was practically non-existent. Other ships of all shapes and kinds, including a fishing boat under sail, overtook and passed her effortlessly. In some of these the crews lined the decks and encouragingly cheered her on.

By the time she had arrived complacently in Plymouth Sound I had completed the libretto of *Conversation Piece*. The idea of it had come to me when we were two days out of New York and I had happened to read a delightful book by Dormer Creston called *The Regent and His Daughter*. Up until then the Regency as a period had never attracted me. The dramatic appeal of the late eighteenth century and the gas-lit glamour of the latter decades of the nineteenth had established prior claims on my imagination. In spite of Jane Austen, whose sly wit I am sure would have been equally enchanting in any period from the Ancient Britons to the present day, the years from the end of the French Revolution until the crinolines and chandeliers of the Second Empire, were for me undiscovered territory. Napoleon to me seemed to be the antithesis of glamour. His short legs and strutting didacticism aroused in me no ardour. In later years I need hardly say I have revised this superficial opinion, but I still feel that a few extra inches would have enhanced his legend considerably. I remember when I was a child a very short verger in St Alban's Church Teddington for some reason or other roused my father's ire. He disposed of him in one terse phrase. 'His brains are too near his bottom.' It must not be imagined, being five feet eleven and a half inches tall myself, that I automatically deprecate those of lesser stature, indeed several of my most delightful friends barely reach my ear-lobes, but world-conquering demagogues and leaders of men should be, ideally speaking, taller than their fellow men. Alas, they seldom are. Few of the world's heroes have exceeded five feet eleven.

Future Indefinite

FUTURE INDEFINITE: 1939-1945

WRITTEN: 1947-53
FIRST PUBLISHED: 1954

PART ONE

Present Indicative was the story of my life from birth until the age of thirty-one. It finished just after the production of *Cavalcade* when I embarked on a voyage to South America. The last line of the book was: – 'When we came up on deck there was no England left. Nothing but sea and sky.'

That was November 1931. It is now April 1948 and I am sitting looking out at a blue sea and sky, both far removed from the choppy, grey-green waves of the English Channel. Here there is no shadowy outline of the coast of France appearing out of the mist; there are no sea-gulls flying in thin, watery sunshine; instead there are buzzards; little banana-birds with yellow bodies and pink heads; humming-birds, and strange black creatures with long tails that dive for fish. I can no longer hear the noise of waves tearing away at the shingle, but in the distance there is the more muffled sound of surf breaking on the reef. This is the island of Jamaica and it seems to me to be a good place to start writing a book. When and where the book will be finished there is no knowing, but at the moment anyhow there is enough peace for me to begin it.

It took me four years to write *Present Indicative*, but then I worked on it spasmodically whenever there was enough time. It was something that I could only return to when circumstances allowed and my circumstances during those pre-war years were restless. I was writing plays, acting plays, directing plays, writing lyrics, composing music, making gramophone records, broadcasting and travelling. I was a highly publicised, irritatingly successful figure and much in demand.

Present Indicative was greeted kindly by the critics and was a success both in England and the United States. I read it through the other day and was pleased to find that it was better written than I expected it to be. The style is sometimes convulsive, there are too many qualifying adjectives, it is technically insecure and there are several repetitive passages which slow up the narrative, but on the whole there is little in it that I regret having said: from it there emerges enough of my true character to make it valid within the limits of its intention, which was to record the factual truth about myself in relation to the world I lived in, the people I met and the rewards I worked for and often won. Well, there it is, written and published and done with. For as long as it is in print or obtainable from second-hand book shops there will be people, possibly in diminishing numbers, who will be fascinated or repelled, charmed or unimpressed by the story of an alert little boy who was talented and determined and grew up to attain many of his heart's desires and who, throughout his childhood, youth, adolescence and ten of his adult years, remained consistently fond of his mother. This fact inspired many hundreds of people to write to me in glowing terms. It apparently proved to doubting minds that in spite of success and adulation, and beneath a glittering veneer of wit and vintage playboyishness, I had managed, with extraordinary strength of character, to retain a few normal human instincts. I must admit that I resent the basic assumption that the first gesture of any young man who makes good is to kick his mother in the teeth, but alas it is one of the most annoying disenchantments of success to be praised for the wrong things.

Readers who liked *Present Indicative* and expect this to be a straight sequel to it will, perhaps, be disappointed. For whereas *Present Indicative* covered thirty-one years this book will be concerned only with the years between 1939 and 1945. Not that those pre-war years were lacking in interest and variety. On the contrary they were rich in incident and I enjoyed living them. And I cannot agree with contemporary social commentators that they were so appallingly decadent and degraded. It is true that there was a certain flush discernible on the face of High Society – High Society in the Long Island, Paris, Riviera sense – but on the whole those poor maligned years were not nearly so bad as they are now made out to have been. There were worse things going on in the twenties and thirties than casual amorality in the South of France and ostentatious parties at the Ritz. The Lido contributed less to future chaos than Geneva, and the propaganda of the Comintern throughout the modern world swayed our destinies far more than the perfumes of Chanel.

The temperature and tempo of millions of lives rose and increased in August 1939, but for me the pre-war past died on the day when Mr Neville Chamberlain returned with such gay insouciance from Munich in 1938.

In the December of that year I produced a revue in America called *Set to Music* with Beatrice Lillie as the star. In February 1939 I went to Honolulu with the express purpose of writing a play for myself but wrote some short stories instead. These were later published under the title of *To Step Aside*. In March, feeling that another crisis was imminent, I returned to England. During April and May I stayed in my house in the country and wrote two plays: *Present Laughter* and *This Happy Breed*. I planned to appear in both of these myself in the autumn, acting them on alternate nights with the same company. They both turned out well in spite of the fact that while I was writing them I was aware that they would in all probability never be produced, at least not at the time that I intended them to be. This dismal clairvoyance was ultimately justified. However, bathed, as we all were at that time, in a glow of Governmental optimism and complacency, it would have been churlish to take too gloomy a view of the future and so I persevered, finished them, cast them, presided at our annual Theatrical Garden Party for the Actors' Orphanage, of which I am president, and found myself in the middle of June with six weeks free before I started rehearsals in August. In more ordinary times I would have gone directly to the South of France or Venice or somewhere where I could relax and lie in the sun, but I was oppressed by my own views of the general situation. My mind was uneasy and I had an urge to see for myself a little of what was going on in Europe. I discussed this with Robert Vansittart at the Foreign Office, who was wise and helpful, and a few days later I set forth on a flying trip to Warsaw, Danzig, Moscow, Leningrad, Helsinki, Stockholm, Oslo and Copenhagen.

2

The flight from Heston took about six hours with a brief halt in Berlin. I arrived at Warsaw at six o'clock in the evening, where I was met by Mrs Clifford Norton, the wife of the British Chargé d'Affaires, a representative of the British Council, and several Press reporters and photographers. Mrs Norton drove me in her car with a newspaper man who fired a series of questions at me all the way from the airport to the city. The theatrical ones I answered as concisely as I could; the political ones I evaded. I had always imagined Warsaw, I can't think why, as a grey-stoned, medieval town clambering up a hill; a town of dark alleys and narrow, crowded, twisted streets. And here it was, flat as a pancake, widely spaced, and predominantly yellowish in colour. This last was largely the effect of the evening sunlight and the dust, for it had been a stifling day with no rain to cool the air.

Mrs Norton left me at the Europski Hotel, where I gave a couple more Press interviews, ordered myself a dry martini and looked out of the windows of my room at the city. It appeared calm and secure in the dusk. Immediately before me was a large square, and beyond that the Foreign Office, an impressive white building guarded by sentries. Lights were coming up all over the town and from just below in the hotel terrace café rose the chatter of many voices to the accompaniment of a string orchestra playing a selection from *La Tosca*. There seemed to be a feeling in the air, indescribable really but quite definite, that all this was artifice expertly contrived, an admirable façade behind which the real issues were being decided.

In course of the next few days I explored the city and talked to many people, at least those who could speak either French or English, and most of them could. I met musicians, artists, writers, actors, soldiers, airmen and politicians, in all of whom I detected the same fatalistic conviction that war was not only inevitable but imminent. In none of them did I observe the faintest fear or doubt as to the ultimate outcome. They had complete faith in their Army, their Air Force, their leaders, and their own indomitable spirit of resistance. They were cheered and encouraged by their alliance with Great Britain but the wiser ones doubted that any practical aid we could give them would arrive in time.

There were many gay incidents, adventures and experiences, many pleasant personal contacts and parties and fun in those two weeks. Warsaw had much to give to the casual traveller. It was a light and charming city. The Painted Square is now, I believe, in ruins, but at least I have a memory of its coloured houses, the baroque charm of its florid, faded designs, its twisted porticos and crooked steps. The ageing and ageless sense of the turbulent past brooded over it and gave me the impression that it was hanging there, suspended in time, like an ancient tapestry draped over the shining, clean walls of a modern museum.

Then there was a week-end I spent in the castle of Lancut, the home of Count Alfred Potocki and his mother, Countess Betka. She was a remarkable woman; exquisitely gowned, fluent in several languages, shrewd, efficient, and with the most thorough-going feudal point of view I have ever encountered. The whole atmosphere of Lancut was feudalism rampant. Myriads of servants; a private theatre; a private orchestra composed of about fifty stable boys and grooms, which played the house party into church on Sunday morning and out again in time for lunch. Before this it gave a few brassy selections in the vast courtyard. On the Sunday morning that I arrived it played 'God Save the King' in my honour and I had to stand to rigid attention, touched by the gesture, but nevertheless in desperate fear that I might burst out laughing, not from any patriotic irreverence, but because one of the trombones was about half a tone off key, and I knew from the bandmaster's expression that he as well as I was painfully aware of it.

After dinner that night the house-party assembled in the theatre to watch a film made up chronologically of some of the famous people who had visited the castle in the past. We saw the Archduke Franz Ferdinand walking very quickly along a garden path only a few weeks before his assassination at Sarajevo; the Kaiser, jerky and jocular, at a shooting party; the Baronne Eugene de Rothschild, then the Countess Schonborn, wearing what appeared to be a white night-gown, and acting with considerable verve in an impromptu mystery drama got up a little too obviously on the spur of the moment during some gay, vanished house-party in the early nineteen-twenties. There were many other famous people and crowned heads and statesmen, driving coaches or having picnics or sipping tea on smooth terraces. There was a certain Family Album nostalgia about the whole film. Those animated, swiftly-moving figures, many of whom were long since dead, making silent jokes, laughing soundlessly, lighting cigarettes, sitting down and getting up, nodding and beckoning and calling noiselessly to each other across the lawns and through the trees, gave me a sense of finality, almost of doom, and yet a doom that seemed to hover perilously near the ridiculous. Whatever sentimental reveries may have been stirring the hearts of my fellow guests, they were sharply interrupted when suddenly the late Queen Marie of Roumania flickered at immense speed across the screen in a barouche, and the Roumanian Ambassadress, who was sitting next to me, burst into tears and had to be led out.

Early the next morning I left with Prince Carol Radziwell to drive to Cracow. He was a charming young man serving in the Polish Air Force, and he drove with an abandon that either betokened nerves of steel or complete lack of imagination. He held strongly developed anti-Semitic views, about which I argued with him whenever we hit a straight piece of road. The country through which we drove for several hours was beautiful, although the small towns and villages seemed dilapidated and poverty-stricken. We certainly did pass a lot of Jews of the biblical sort with dusty caftans and matted black beards, who, although they looked harmless enough to me, if a trifle untidy, were commented upon by my companion with a rising flood of invective in both English and French. I realised quickly that any efforts of mine to convince him that in my experience there were a great many Jews extant who were intelligent, sensitive, generous and kind, and a great many Christians who were the exact opposite, were doomed to failure at the outset, so I gave up the whole thing and led the conversation, whenever possible, to less controversial topics.

Upon arrival in Cracow we explored the sombre, haunted medieval parts of the city for a couple of hours before driving out to the Radziwill castle a few miles away. The sky was overcast and there was a light, thin rain falling. I was aware of a gentle melancholy in the air as we turned into the drive; the trees rustled mournfully and the house seemed to be waiting for us with polite resignation. It was as far removed from Lancut in size, design and atmosphere as the Petit Trianon is from the Kremlin. Carol's father, a handsome, greying man in riding clothes, met us in the hall with several enormous dogs. I was shown into a dim, red-tapestried room on the ground floor with a bathroom adjoining, so that I could have a bath and a rest before dinner, both of which, after that dusty and agitating drive, I badly needed.

That whole evening remains in my memory as charming and strange and unreal as though I had dreamt it. The house was lit by lamps. Everybody was in black because a relative had recently been killed in an air crash. The food at dinner was simple and exquisitely cooked; candlelight flickered over the dining-table, and the conversation, in French, murmured on quietly to the accompaniment of the rain, which by then had developed into a downpour and was beating insistently against the windows. After dinner we went into the drawing-room, where tea was served with little cakes. Inevitably the approaching war was discussed, and again I was aware of that fatalism, that resigned determination to accept whatever was to come, and do the best they could about it. I remember Prince Radziwill saying that it wasn't so much the Germans he feared as the Russians, and looking at him, the typical, high-bred, courteous, urbane and so much hated aristocrat, I sadly saw his point. Later, some time after the fall of Poland, I heard that the Russians had shot him, but in the early months of nineteen-forty Carol appeared in Paris, having escaped from a concentration camp in Roumania, and told me that his father and family were still alive but had been turned out of their house and were living in the servants' lodge on a few roubles a month.

At about eleven o'clock that evening Carol drove me into Cracow to catch the midnight train to Warsaw. He waved cheerfully to me as the train moved out of the station, a dashing figure in his Air Force uniform, and I waved back with equal cheerfulness, but I felt depressed.

On my return to Warsaw I received a message from the Foreign Office to say that Colonel Beck would receive me at six o'clock on the following evening. Anthony Eden had given me a letter of introduction to him the day before I left London, which had been duly handed, by the Nortons, to one of the Foreign Office secretaries. I had been warned tactfully that it would be much appreciated by His Excellency if the international situation was *not* discussed. This I found damping, as my principle object in wishing to see him was to discover as much as I could of what he thought and felt about the imminence of war. However, I rose above my disappointment and presented myself obediently at the Foreign Office the next evening with a few carefully rehearsed conversational gambits ready in my mind, ranging from the Lunts' performance in *Amphitryon 38* to Eve Curie's biography of her mother. I had been told by Anthony Eden that the Colonel spoke no English at all and that his French, though fluent, was guttural and difficult to understand, and so it was with slight trepidation that I finally arrived in his office. However, within the first few minutes all my fears evaporated. True, his French was guttural and a little hard to understand, but his personal charm was clear. He had a compelling eye, a polished manner, his navy-blue pin-stripe was soigné to the last degree, and he chain-smoked incessantly. Also the gay informality with which he plunged immediately into a detailed discussion of the international situation was extremely interesting. I had no opportunity of heading him off even if I had wished to, and the Lunts' performance in *Amphitryon 38* remained, as far as he was concerned, as though it had never been. He spoke rapidly and nervously; his face, strictly speaking, was ugly and arresting; his figure was taut and spare and he had a habit of twitching the corner of his mouth when he spoke. His attitude was tinged with the same 'Do or Die' bravado that I had noted elsewhere, but with the subtle difference that in him I didn't quite believe it. It was not that there was any lack of conviction in what he said, on the contrary he was more vehement in his assertions of the Polish powers of resistance than anyone I had yet talked to, but all the same I sensed a certain cynical realism behind his words not entirely consistent with what he was saying. It was a most entertaining hour that I spent with him. His humour was infectious, the range of his knowledge and experience wide-spread, and his manner, even when talking most seriously, was devoid of the smallest trace of ministerial pomposity. He told me that in his opinion Poland would hold out against Germany for at least three months, and that even if by that time Britain had been unable to get sufficient aid to her, her resistance to the brunt of the first German attack would have provided England and France with enough time to prepare a smashing offensive. He went on to say that although in the interim Warsaw and other Polish cities would inevitably be laid waste, the spirit of the people would not fail, and if necessary they would retreat into the vast forests and plains of the

hinterland and entrench themselves until the German invasion, however successful it might be at the beginning, fizzled out into inconclusive anti-climax. All this
was most cheering, and I left him feeling that perhaps after all I had been over-
dramatising my sense of foreboding. In the light of later events I have often
recalled that meeting. I have heard sinister rumours of Colonel Beck's hurried
retreat into Roumania in the heat of the crisis; reports of treachery, intrigue and
cowardice. Whether they are true or not I haven't the faintest idea, but if they are
I am very surprised. Possibly after all his French *was* too guttural and hard for me
to understand, for he certainly didn't strike me as being a cowardly man. Ruthless
and unscrupulous perhaps, but not a renegade. I shall continue to hope that my
estimation of him was right.

Before leaving Poland I had one commission to execute, and that was to
deliver a private letter to Professor Carl Burckhardt, the High Commissioner of
Danzig. This project bristled with difficulties and had a certain E. Phillips
Oppenheim tang to it owing to the fact that it *was* a private letter and I was
unable to divulge to anyone in authority who it was from. Danzig, ironically
designated at that time as a 'Free' City, was difficult to get to. The train service
between Warsaw and Gdynia was suspended and the only means of transportation
was an aeroplane which sometimes took off to schedule but mostly didn't. I
hopefully booked a seat on it and telephoned, with some perseverance, to
Professor Burckhardt to say that I was coming on the following Sunday morning
to spend the day with him. It was necessary to have a special permit to pass from
Gdynia across the line into the 'Free' territory, and this I had not got and was
unable to persuade the Polish authorities to give me. As a matter of fact I doubt
actually if they could have, as I was not going on official business.

The only hope of evading a possible sojourn in a Nazi jail was that the High
Commissioner's car would meet me at the airport and whisk me across the lines
in such an aura of officialdom that the sentries would be too impressed to halt
and question me. Fortunately this happened. The car did meet me and whirl me
swiftly across the frontier, and what is more the sentries smartly saluted me,
which flurried me rather, as I had flung my hat on to the floor of the car and had
nothing to take off and bow with in response; however, I waved and left them,
still at attention, staring after me in some perplexity. Professor Burckhardt was a
Swiss. He was a distinguished man and had, among other things, written an
excellent life of Cardinal Richelieu. His French was neither guttural nor hard to
understand, being pure Parisian without a trace of accent. His position as
High Commissioner was obviously no sinecure and was growing rapidly more
uncomfortable every day. He was fully aware, he told me, that he might have to
duck and run at any moment. After I had delivered the letter, we talked for an
hour or so before going for a walk in the town. In the course of talk he told me of
three recent interviews he had had with Hitler, at one of which the Fuehrer had
really lost control and shrieked the place down. I asked him if he hadn't wanted

to laugh. And he said not until afterwards, because at the time it really was too alarming.

We walked through the beautiful old town and he pointed out its architectural and historical splendours to me; he also bought me a bottle of liqueur with flecks of gold floating about in it. It was a Sunday and so the streets were crowded. There were Nazi soldiers and officers stamping about, looking quite insufferably pleased with themselves. The ordinary citizens, I thought, looked less pleased, there was an air of furtiveness and apprehension about them. I had a feeling that if there were a tyre-burst or any other sudden, loud noise they would panic at once and disappear into their houses. We lunched with Burckhardt's family and soon afterwards I had to leave to catch my plane, which left Gdynia at four-thirty. I got across the frontier again without mishap and caught the plane all right, but I have seldom endured such an uncomfortable and frightening flight. We ran into an electric storm immediately after leaving the airport, whereupon the pilot, misguidedly I am sure, decided to fly home at an altitude of about fifty feet. We bumped and banged and rattled, frequently missing the tops of trees by inches, and I descended at Warsaw, bright green in the face, with a splitting headache and reflecting bitterly that if the military pilots of Poland were anything like the civil ones the war was lost before it started.

My last few days in Warsaw were uneventful although sociably agreeable. With the Nortons and others I lunched and dined in open-air restaurants, devoured thousands of red river crayfish, listened to little string orchestras in cafés and under the trees, drank thick, sweet mead made of honey in a dark tavern in the Painted Square, consumed a formidable amount of vodka and generally enjoyed myself immensely. There were other, grander junketings as well, notably a resplendent dinner-party given by Anthony Biddle, the American Ambassador, and his wife. The house was lovely and the garden even more so, and the whole party was a glittering success. I believe that it was the last one they gave before the war crashed into the land and destroyed for ever that house and garden together with so much more that was graceful and charming. Finally, on an airless, sultry night, I was conveyed affectionately to the station by several of my newly-acquired friends and seen into the train for Moscow. Once more I waved with a cheerfulness that I was far from feeling. Once more that sense of valediction and doom descended upon me. The figures of my friends on the platform dwindled into the distance as the train bore me away. I think only one of them is alive today.

3

My train arrived at the Russian frontier at six o'clock in the evening. It was breathlessly hot and the flat countryside was bathed in golden light, but stretching across the sky was a belt of ominous, black storm-clouds.

I had had no time to procure a Russian visa before leaving London, and for the last two weeks the British Embassy in Warsaw had been working hard to get one for me and had, at the last minute, succeeded. There was no possibility of getting a diplomatic stamp or a *laisser-passer* as I was not a member of the diplomatic corps and had no official reason for wishing to enter the country. Nor was I coming in under the aegis of the Intourist agency or the Vox, which is a cultural relations organisation which officially sees to it that any aliens visiting the Soviet Union are shown exactly what the State wishes them to be shown and nothing more. I was making my entrance alone, unheralded, unprotected, and with the added stigma that the destination marked on my entry form was the British Embassy in Moscow. This, although I was unaware of it at the time, was unfortunate. Nobody had told me that not only the British Embassy but all the Foreign embassies in Russia were regarded with the utmost suspicion, and that anyone attached to them, or even visiting them, was, to the simple-minded Russians, inevitably a secret agent. This naif misapprehension caused me a great deal of inconvenience. Luckily, however, I have travelled enough to be immune to the vagaries of Customs men and passport officials. A detached defence mechanism begins to function automatically in me the instant I set foot in a frontier station. I resign myself quite cheerfully to hours of inactivity, to waiting about, being questioned and having my baggage ransacked. I sit down whenever I can, usually with a book; I smoke if I am allowed to; if not, I rise above it, having learned long ago that any display of temperament, any fussing or fuming or resentment, merely makes matters far worse and prolongs the whole tedious business. On entering Russia, however, this philosophic detachment was strained almost to breaking point. For four hours I was questioned, stared at, whispered about and sent ricochetting back and forth from office to office and from official to official. My passport was scrutinised all ends up. My bags were unpacked to the last sock and every garment minutely examined. My dressing-case, which is my own special design and contains enough of the little necessities of travel to last me for a year, is fitted, among other things, with a small medicine chest containing band aid, iodine, aspirin, etc., a hypodermic, various pain-alleviating drugs, castor oil in capsule form, and a small phial of anti-tetanus serum. This outfit, although I have used it comparatively little, has been a great comfort to me on my journeys through tropical jungles and the more out of the way parts of the world. The Russians were so intrigued with it that they forced me to explain slowly, and in detail, the whys and wherefores of every drug and every bottle. This necessitated a lot of expressive pantomime and after a while I began to enjoy myself. I had a fair success with my performance of an anti-tetanus injection, but my great triumph was a graphic impression of the effect of the castor oil capsules. This, to use a theatrical phrase, had them in the aisles! In fact two of my inquisitors laughed until they cried. Finally, after answering all their questions and acceding affably to all their demands, which stopped short only at a request for a specimen of my urine, I was allowed to re-pack my bags, under surveillance, and get into the Moscow express.

The wagon-lit was one of those spacious, old-fashioned models that I could imagine in its heyday conveying the late King Edward the Seventh to Baden-Baden. With the years it had accumulated not only an inconceivable amount of dirt, but a creaking, swaying gait, which gave me the insecure feeling that it might bounce off the tracks at any moment and roll majestically down the embankment. The restaurant car, in which for the first time in my life I was handed a plate with *enough* caviar on it, was of the same Edwardian vintage. The windows were wider and larger than any I have seen in any other train, and the whole coach gave me the impression that I was in a vast glass coffin. Outside, in the black night, the ominous clouds which I had noted earlier had launched themselves into a thunderstorm of demoniac violence, the noise of which, crashing against all those windows, was scarifying. I drank enough vodka to banish the 'Breaking of the Sixth Seal', 'Book of Revelation' sense of doom that had descended upon me, and staggered back to my wagon-lit, where, thinking it wiser not to undress and place myself between those grey, unalluring sheets, I lay down on the creaking bed and, after a while, went to sleep.

Early the next morning the train arrived, to my mind miraculously, in Moscow. Not only did it arrive but it got in only about an hour late, which, someone later informed me, was quite unprecedented. Gordon Vereker, the First Counsellor of the British Embassy, most kindly came to meet me and told me that he had arranged for me to stay in his house because there was a carnival week in progress and all the hotels were full. He was a cheerful, very typical Englishman, wearing a Palm Beach suit and no hat, for the weather was very hot. We piled my suitcases into his car and off we went. My first impression of the city as we drove out of the station was spectacularly unlike what I had imagined it would be. Once more there were wide streets instead of the narrow twisted ones that I had imagined. Again there was strong, hot sunlight, but whereas Warsaw, although dusty, had at least looked cared for, Moscow looked as though the streets hadn't been cleaned for years, which in all probability they hadn't. There were crowds of people drifting along the pavements, doubtless an extra number because it was carnival week. They were poorly clad the men without shirts or ties and the women mostly without stockings. This did not surprise me, for I had hardly expected to find the Russian proletariat parading about in silk hats and morning coats, and black satin and pearls, but what did surprise me was their appearance of aimlessness. Nobody seemed to want to get anywhere. I noticed no giggling, chattering young girls; no flash young men; not one expression on any face that could, by the wildest stretch of imagination, be described as gay. There was not much traffic apart from a few antiquated taxis, trams and bicycles. The surface of the road was bumpy and uneven and spattered with garbage and bits of paper, and the whole effect was depressing. Perhaps I was disgruntled owing to my none too comfortable night in the train. Perhaps my sub-conscious had built up such a wall of preconceived prejudices that I was unable to see over the top of it. Perhaps all these people were happy and vital and having a glorious time, but if they were, prejudice or no prejudice, their way of showing it was unconvincing.

By the time we reached the Red Square and the Kremlin came into view with its photographically familiar minarets and bulbous towers, the scene brightened a little but not enough. There were still fragments of orange peel and cabbage stalks and dirty bits of paper swirling about in the gutters, and there was still that drab, uniform mass of humanity moving along to and fro, quietly and lethargically as though one direction were as good as another, and in any case it couldn't matter less whether they got to where they had originally planned or whether they didn't. I thought of Blackpool or Margate during a carnival week – the bustle and noise; children playing 'tag' up and down the pavements and dodging in and out of the crowds; young men and women arm-in-arm wearing grotesque paper hats and blowing squeakers; bands and barrel organs blaring; ice-cream vendors and sellers of pink 'Rock' yelling their wares; the cheerfulness, the kindly, warm vitality of the English public on parade when it is really out to enjoy itself – and my heart was sad for these poor, bewildered, dreary-looking people drifting through their carnival week at such a slow tempo. Surely in the earlier days, with all their injustices and terrors, even the Russians must have had some lighter moments? Must every now and then have walked gaily through the streets to meet their lovers, or to say their prayers, or to go to a party? The carnival spirit is not and never has been solely the prerogative of capitalists and the aristocracy. On the contrary, in most of the countries I have visited, it is generally the poorer people who seem to have the real capacity for enjoying themselves; the rich are usually too bored and the middle classes too prim. I know it is an accepted theory that the English take their pleasures sadly, but as far as I could see the Soviets didn't take them at all, or perhaps there weren't any to take. At all events I have seldom been conscious of such a mass effect of general lethargy.

Gordon Vereker's house was cool and comfortable, and after we had had some coffee we went along to the Embassy, where I met Sir William Seeds, the Ambassador. He looked frail and strained, for he had recently been ill and also, for a long time, had had the unenviable task of dealing with the complex Russian mentality, and trying to thread his way through a labyrinth of inconclusive, quasi-oriental dialectic to find some indication of what their war policy was likely to be. The view across the river of the Kremlin was dramatic. Somewhere in the fantastic, architecturally tortured building was Stalin, the wily, all powerful, unpredictable enigma who, to date, seemed to have evaded every foreign issue, blocked every diplomatic approach and shown no indication whatever of whether he intended to side with the British or the Nazis, or if indeed he intended to side with either. The general opinion among the diplomatic corps was that he would remain on the fence until the last possible moment, but this was obviously only a guess, for few of them had even clapped eyes on him. At that time, of course, his ironic pact with Hitler was still veiled by the future, and nobody whom I talked to seemed to suspect that such an unpleasant surprise lay in store for us.

In the afternoon Gordon Vereker drove me out to the Stadium to see a football match. We arrived early and for an hour or so we watched a gymnastic display by groups of the Moscow Youth, both male and female. It was very similar to most other gymnastic displays, with the difference that the crowds seemed to be less demonstrative. Perhaps I was spoiled by a visit I had paid to the Stadium in Rome a year before when Mussolini had been present, looking like an over-ripe plum squeezed into a white uniform, and where each twist, turn and gyration of the contestants had been greeted with shrieks of rapturous approbation. There were few shrieks at the Moscow performance, but the general routine was identical except that the Italian Youth had looked a trifle cleaner. Here, row after row of muscular girls in shirts and shorts did handsprings and ran races; young men in singlets and shorter shorts flung themselves over hurdles, threw heavy poles into the air, and drilled, not very tidily, in various formations.

At last the football match began and I was delighted to see that they played with a red ball. The crowd cheered up a bit as the game progressed and it was a distinct relief to see them leaning forward on their benches and actually showing interest in something. Every now and then they applauded and I even heard a few cheers.

It was stiflingly hot and the stone bench on which we were seated was hard, and so after we had watched the match for about three quarters of an hour we decided that we had had enough and got up to go. At this moment a strange man and woman accosted me. They spoke perfect English and were representatives of the Vox Cultural Relations Organisation. They said that they would very much like to take me for a tour of the chief sights of Moscow the next morning. I accepted politely, noticing with interest that they neither looked nor spoke to Gordon Vereker at all. He explained to me later that it was very dangerous for Russians to be seen speaking to foreigners unless they had a specific reason for doing so. The Ogpu spies were everywhere and people who transgressed this rule frequently disappeared, presumably to Siberia, and were seldom seen again. He also told me that all members of the Embassy staff, including himself, were spied on and followed wherever they went, and that undoubtedly I would be too. I asked if the constant feeling of being watched didn't get on his nerves, and he replied airily that he was completely used to it and often handed the spy on guard outside his house a drink through the window.

That evening we drove out into the near country to dine with the Military Attaché and his family. On the way we had to draw into the side of the road and stop twice because a Commissar's car happened to be passing. The house was typically 'Tchekov' and was set in a grove of mournful trees. After dinner we sat on the veranda and talked and smoked cigarettes, and the atmosphere, in the long summer twilight, became even more familiar. The house, before the revolution, had belonged to some well-to-do family long since banished or murdered, and I had the feeling that their ghosts were still wandering among the trees and through the rooms, straightening an ikon on the wall, or pulling a curtain aside to look vaguely out at the lights of the city. It was so perfect a setting for anything Russian that I have ever read or seen that I fully expected Nazimova to appear at any moment in a dark dress and announce that she was absolutely sick of everything.

My hostess was an enthusiastic theatre-goer and she bewailed the fact, as also did I, that I wouldn't have an opportunity of seeing anything of the Russian theatre, as all the companies were on tour during the summer months. This was a bitter disappointment to me. So many people whose judgement I admired and repsected had given me glowing accounts of the brilliance and efficiency of Russian acting and production. Lynn and Alfred Lunt had returned, a few years before, from a three weeks' holiday to Moscow, bursting with articulate and technical enthusiasm. They led me, both talking at once, through every production they had seen. My impressions afterwards were confused, but I gathered beyond a shadow of doubt that as far as lighting, team-work, under-playing, and psychological subtlety were concerned, the Russians had left us a long way behind. In addition to the genuine pleasures they had derived from watching their beloved *Theatre* handled with such taste and imagination, Lynn and Alfred had been entertained by all the leading actors and producers and treated with much honour, as indeed they fully deserved to be. But all that, as I said before, was some years ago, and also they had come to the country respectably and correctly, and not, as I had, crept in inquisitively under the fence. At a cocktail-party given some days later by Gordon Vereker, the Russian correspondent of the *Daily Telegraph* delivered to me some gracious and welcoming messages from some of the principal Muscovite stars, together with the regret that owing to one thing and another they would be unable to receive me. I questioned him about this and he explained that, much as they would have liked to invite me to their houses, in the present circumstances, and without official sanction, it would be exceedingly dangerous for them. This was disappointing, but there was nothing to be done about it beyond reflecting sadly that in a state-controlled workers' heaven the Arts had to toe the line just as much as everything else.

On the morning following my dinner-party in the Tchekov villa, the Vox lady who had accosted me at the football match appeared in a dusty limousine to take me for a good-will tour of Moscow. Gordon Vereker, who had for some reason or other not been working at the Embassy that morning, asked if he might come too, but was politely refused. This put me into a bad temper to start with and I clambered into the limousine scowling. My lady guide, whose manner was sullenly affable, wore – unwisely, I thought – a short cotton dress which was none too clean and exposed, to an alarming degree, her short, hairy legs. She also smelt strongly of stale soup. We drove slowly through the hot streets of the city while she recited what she had been trained to recite, about the glories of the Five Year Plan, and the crèches where working mothers could deposit their tots for the day and collect them in the evening, and how, in so many years, everyone, thanks to the far-seeing and brilliant administration of the Soviet State, would be healthy and wealthy and wise and happy as larks. Every time we passed a scaffolding, which was far too often, she explained in detail just what the building under construction was going to look like and what it was for. Finally, as a sort of *bonne bouche* to finish off a morning of exquisite boredom, she took me for a ride in the Underground railway. Over this she really came to life; her eyes sparkled with enthusiasm, and her conversation lost some of its parrot-like monotony. We ran up and down steps, forced our way into one train, rode through a couple of stations and then forced our way out and into another. She chattered and laughed with all the naïve excitement of a young girl being taken on the roller coasters at Coney Island for the first time. The trains were very high and glassy and there were only six stations in all – I think I am right about this, but I may be exaggerating – at all events they were each built in different styles of architecture and decorated with different shades of marble, and the total effect as we whisked through them was of a series of ornate gentlemen's lavatories. Finally we emerged into the sunshine, by which time the limousine had disappeared. I was hot and thirsty and suggested innocently enough that we might have a cooling drink of some sort. She at once assumed an air of stern disapproval and said 'No' with the utmost firmness. We walked along the crowded pavement for a little until, mercifully, I spotted a taxi and hailed it. This seemed to shock her even more, but by this time I had the bit between my teeth and was too irritable and sticky to care what she thought. I asked her, without much fervour, if I could drop her anywhere, and again she said 'No,' this time with a furtive look over her shoulder, and I realised, by that one look, that the poor beast was terrified out of her wits. Obviously the limousine having disappeared had disorganised the whole performance, and here she was walking down a crowded street, not marked in the itinerary, with a dangerous foreigner. I also became aware that the taxi man was regarding us both with some suspicion, and so, realising that the longer I stayed talking to her, the nearer it would bring her to the salt mines of Siberia, I wrung her hand warmly, asked her to give the driver my address, jumped in and drove off leaving her standing on the kerb staring after me. She didn't wave.

Nothing of particular interest occurred during the rest of my stay in Moscow. I walked about the city, without official guidance, and tried to visualise it as it had been in the past, but without much success. It was too difficult to imagine Dostoevski and Tolstoy countesses, wrapped in heavy sables, driving in their droshkys through those hot dusty streets – perhaps they never visited Moscow in the summer months anyhow – at all events there was no imprint of their ghosts on the atmosphere, in fact there seemed to be very little atmosphere. The buildings in the Red Square were disfigured by enormous garish posters of various Commissars; there were a number of aggressively modern apartment houses, on every identical floor of which I presumed jolly proletarian families were living in crowded, communal bliss. There were lots of cinemas and advertisement hoardings, and everywhere masses and masses of people moving slowly along the pavements. The shop windows were filled mostly with strictly utilitarian merchandise and there seemed to be a glut of electrical fittings, radio equipment, pots, pans, kettles and brooms. Some of the big stores had made a slight bid for glamour by displaying wax models wearing rather curious under-clothes, and in one window I noted an actual evening dress, but the wax model wearing it looked so ashamed that I hurried by with my head averted in order not to embarrass her further.

In all these lonely peregrinations about the city I was fully aware that I was being followed and watched assiduously, and occasionally I amused myself by going into a big store by one door, darting through it and nipping out by another. Also on one occasion I suddenly broke into a brisk trot and cantered up and down several side streets, but it was too hot to do it for long, and nobody seemed to pay the faintest attention anyhow. I only once identified one of my shadowers, an innocuous little man with a green velour hat; I had noticed him several times standing a little way away from me when I was looking in the shop windows. Finally, after I had doubled on my tracks once or twice and made quite sure that he was still near-by, I rushed up to him, shook him enthusiastically by the hand, and said I hadn't seen him for ages and how were Anna and the children? He looked very startled, mumbled something unintelligible, backed away from me, and I never saw him again. Whether or not he spoke English or understood a word I was saying I shall never know.

A few nights later Gordon Vereker saw me into the midnight train for Leningrad and, without regret, I waved good-bye to glorious Moscow.

4

The Leningrad express was a more modern and altogether more comfortable train than the one that had brought me from the frontier to Moscow. My sleeper also seemed to be reasonably clean and I was able, without dismay, to undress and get into bed. I lay awake for an hour or so meditating on the defects in my character that made it so difficult for me to feel enthusiasm and sympathy for this great economic and social experiment that I was seeing, briefly, at first hand. 'Briefly', of course, was the operative word. I was being far too swift and flippant and superficial over the whole business. I should have stayed longer – perhaps taken a small grey flat, and asked many more searching and more intelligent questions. I should have tried to learn a little Russian and plunged into the lives of the people, and gone to live on a collectivist farm for a few weeks before daring to criticise a vital revolutionary movement of which so many intelligent minds in England thought very highly. True, comparatively few of them had been to Russia even for so short a time as I had, but they had obviously read a lot and taken a great deal of trouble and gone into the matter thoroughly. I remembered, some time before, seeing photographs of Lady Astor and George Bernard Shaw in the papers on their return from a brisk tour of the Soviet Union. I forget exactly what they had said to interviewers, but the impression I got was that they were brimming with admiration and enthusiasm. I remembered also talking to Walter Duranty in New York, who spoke glowingly of the charms and Communist-Social delights of life in the USSR. I have heard that in later years his enthusiasm had cooled somewhat, but this may be merely hearsay. At any rate it was evident that there was something sadly lacking in me, some missing core of human understanding, that debarred me from sharing, with so many intelligent and thoughtful people, the belief that Communism, as practised by the Russians, was progressive and hopeful for the future of mankind. As far as I could see, the Communism propaganded by the Comintern in other countries was widely different from that which existed in Russia itself. Here, in this vast territory through which my train was carrying me, there seemed to be no semblance of freedom for the ordinary citizen. He was spied upon, regimented and punished, frequently without even being aware that he had committed a crime. He was kept arbitrarily in ignorance of what took place in other countries, and risked prison or deportation to Siberia if he spoke freely to any alien visitor who might enlighten him. His working days and his holidays were alike ordered by the State and, cruellest of all, he could have no trust in his heart for his fellow men, any one of whom might be a police spy and betray him for saying a careless word or making a foolish joke at a party.

Personally I have always believed more in quality than quantity, and nothing will convince me that the levelling of class and rank distinctions, and the contemptuous dismissal of breeding as an important factor of life, can lead to anything but a dismal mediocrity. I have frequently seen on the newsreels informatory documentary films about animal life which dealt with the cross-breeding of cattle and showed proud and noble pigs and prize bulls and race-horses being sent abroad, having fetched enormous prices, to compete with lesser alien breeds. I have observed the immense care with which professional greyhounds are weaned and cosseted and trained, great importance being given to who their mothers and fathers were and to the classy, impeccability of their ancestral line, and I cannot help feeling that it is retrogressive rather than progressive to rate the human race at a lower level than their money-making four-footed friends.

I was met on the platform at Leningrad by a lady who seemed to have stepped directly out of the film of *Maedchen in Uniform*. She wore her hair scragged back behind her ears, a black coat and skirt, and large boots. She fixed me with a compelling eye and I knew immediately that there was no trifling with her. She announced that she represented Vox and that everything had been arranged for me, and, after organising my baggage out of the train and into a waiting car, she drove me briskly to the Astoria Hotel. The Astoria Hotel in past days of lighter social significance had obviously been well run, well furnished and luxurious.

Now, however, it appeared to have wilted a bit. A marked divergence of taste was apparent in the decoration and furnishing. Whereas originally the curtains had probably been quiet and unobstrusive and the lamp-shades designed to fit discreetly into the general décor, now all was changed. I suspected that some artistic Commissar's wife had been given the job of re-doing the whole thing and had attacked it with enthusiasm but a defective colour sense. The loose covers and curtains in my dusty suite were so noisy that I almost had to stop up my ears. The wall-paper came under the heading of 'Le Jazz' and had obviously been copied from a railway hotel in Northern France in the early nineteen-twenties. My 'Maedchen in Uniform' left me alone to unpack and I rang for the floor-waiter, feeling that some strong black coffee might alleviate my claustrophobia. Presently he arrived wearing a bottle-green black coat and greyish-white trousers. Fortunately he spoke a little French and so when I had given my order I began to question him casually about life in Leningrad. He immediately became embarrassed and kept on shooting hunted looks at the telephone on the desk and, following his eyes, I observed that the receiver was neatly balanced just off the hook, a trick that I remembered clearly from the 'Nick Carter' detective series that I used to read in the Union Jack library when I was eight years old. Ignoring the poor waiter's pleading expression I sat down at the desk and went on with the conversation, speaking slowly and distinctly. I asked him why everyone in Russia looked so depressed and why the Commissars drove about in large cars while the ordinary people had to fight their way into crowded buses and trams. I asked him if the early days of the glorious revolution had been fun, and whether or not he had got any personal satisfaction from persecuting the hated bourgeosie, or if he had merely stayed quietly at home hoping that the excitement would soon be over. I gave him a glowing account of the Midland Hotel in Manchester and said that, in many ways, it was comparable to this one except that there was a slight shortage of vodka and the décor was brighter. After a little while I realised that the strain was telling on him and so I let him go. As the door closed behind him I lifted the telephone receiver and said: 'That will be all for the moment. Thank you so much,' and hung up. Later, while I was unpacking, I became panic-stricken and wished that I hadn't been so flippant. I was haunted by visions of sinister Ogpu agents appearing suddenly and leading me off to a Russian jail. About an hour later another, much more taciturn, waiter brought my coffee. He had a wary gleam in his eye and looked at me coldly. I suspected that the first one was, at that moment, bumping along in the train on his way to Siberia. Presently, when I had finished unpacking and had my coffee, I decided to shave and have a bath. The bathroom was large and encrusted with marble; the rusty shower refused to work and so I turned on the bath tap marked 'Hot' and was startled to see a tadpole come out of it and vanish down the plughole. Later on, when I had dressed and gone downstairs, I spoke to the manager about it. I explained, as politely as I could, that although he might consider what I was saying to be alien propaganda, in England when we turned on a hot tap, as a general rule, hot water came out of it, whereas if on the other hand we wished for a hot tadpole, we turned on a tap marked 'Hot Tadpole' and, owing to the efficiency of our Capitalist State, a hot tadpole usually appeared. The manager received this gentle reprimand with the utmost courtesy and I walked out into the streets of Leningrad. I hadn't, however, got more than a few yards when my Maedchen in Uniform came up behind me and struck me sharply on the shoulder, which frightened me dreadfully. 'You will be wishing a guide,' she said firmly. I replied with equal firmness that I wasn't wishing any such thing and that I wanted to wander about on my own and gather my impressions of the city without instruction. She looked at me balefully, thought for a moment, and then said: 'There will be a guide for you this afternoon. She is a very fine guide. She will be awaiting you outside the hotel with a car at two-thirty.' With this she turned abruptly and left me. I walked on aimlessly, enjoying the sunshine and the feeling of the city, and wondering idly how many wretched little men in green hats were being hurriedly detailed to follow me. There were mercifully few people about compared with the teeming crowds of Moscow and those that were seemed to be gayer and cleaner and less lethargic. Perhaps the atmosphere had something to do with it, for here the atmosphere was clear and definite. Here it was possible to envisage the romantic past without stubbing your toes too sharply against the aggressive present; here there seemed still to be room for a few ghosts to walk along the pavements without being elbowed off into the gutter. I had never realised how beautiful Leningrad was nor with what exquisite taste it had been ordered and designed. The painted houses along the banks of the Neva, in the old days embassies and legations, were faded now and their light colours were peeling, but they still retained an air, a memory of former dignity. There was spaciousness and charm in the streets and squares, and the superb façade of the Winter Palace stared with grey serenity at the roof-tops and spires of the city. Here all the characters of Russian fiction could come to life easily: the countesses in their sables and droshlkys that I had so missed in Moscow; the dashing young cavalry officers in bright uniforms, in their way to assignations with witty mistresses, who would give them scented tea from samovars and discuss the heresies of Anatole France and the latest opera or ballet. Here too the furtive anarchist with the smoking bomb, and the eternally oppressed masses glowering with hate and envy at all the glitter and extravagance. At least, I couldn't help reflecting, then, unlike now, they had something to glower at.

The dining-room of the Astoria Hotel was cool and dim and the tablecloths were filthy. I asked for caviar, which was not on the menu, and got it, doubtless because Vox, having arbitrarily taken my situation in hand, were determined that I should have no cause for criticism. I was glad of this, because it was large and grey and delicious. The chicken that followed it was also large and grey, but less delicious. The waiters who served it were small and grey, and their suits, which had originally set out to be white, were very grey indeed and looked as though they had been slept in. A string orchestra, with a heartless disregard for proletarian feelings, played a selection from *The Dollar Princess*.

After lunch I went into the lobby of the hotel and there was my old Maedchen again waiting for me. With her was a timid, pretty young woman with wide-set blue eyes and a charming smile. This, I realised thankfully, was to be my guide. When she had introduced us, Maedchen issued a series of hissing, last-minute instructions in Russian and escorted us outside to the car. I looked back at her standing rather forlornly on the pavement and suddenly felt sorry for her. Perhaps under that hard, laced-in bosom there beat a romantic heart. Perhaps, when released from the exigencies of her job, she was as merry as a grig and kept her whole family in stitches with her gay stories and bawdy jokes. At any rate I was grateful to her for not assigning to me a hirsute monster like the one in Moscow. My present guide, to whom I will allude from now on as Natasha, that being as Russian and as appropriate a name as any, was palpably nervous at first, but after a while she relaxed a little and even allowed herself to giggle occasionally. She began with the usual routine of carefully rehearsed propaganda and shied away when I said anything not relevant to the subject in hand. Gradually, however, I wore her down and persuaded her to speak about herself, her husband, who worked in a radio factory, and her child, who was eight years old and went to a State school and liked drawing animals. She had a nice voice and a pleasant manner and, when relaxed, seemed to be intelligent. Her English was extraordinarily good and she spoke with hardly any accent. Among other things she pointed out to me the Youssupof Palace where young Prince Felix, a gifted singer with guitar, had lured Rasputin with the promise that he would sing him some of the convulsive Russian gypsy songs that he loved so well. I looked at the house with interest, remembering the graphic account the Grand Duke Dimitri had given me in London several years ago of that macabre and confused episode. It was difficult to imagine a crime of such amiable surrounding. The house loked pleasant and primly aristocratic; there seemed to be no aura of dark horror about it and if there ever were it must have faded many years ago. I fully expected to see an ivory old lady come out of it, followed by her maid carrying a plaid rug, and step into a high electric brougham. I wondered if Rasputin, on arrival, had gone to the front entrance or the back, and whether or not he had the faintest premonition of what was going to happen to him as he stepped across the fatal threshold. I also wondered, still remembering Dimitri's story, how he could possibly have eaten so many cakes crammed with cyanide of potassium without twigging that there was something peculiar about them. In the end, of course, the cakes having proved to be ineffective, they had to shoot him over and over again. They had also had to shoot Dimitri's favourite dog (although what he was doing at the party I shall never know) to provide a reasonable explanation of so much gunfire in the middle of the night. They were then forced to drag the almost dead body of their obstinate guest into a car, drive it to the Neva and throw it over the bridge on to the ice, where it lay accusingly, like a black sprawling shadow in the moonlight.

I asked Natasha if we were allowed to go into the house and see the cellars where the preliminary gambits of the murder had taken place. She said 'No,' disapprovingly, and so we drove on.

During the ensuing days Natasha showed me many of the sights of the city: palaces, factories, boulevards, the inevitable crèches and several churches. When I asked her if it were true, in spite of State-issued instructions and a salutary massacring of the clergy in the early days, that religion still maintained a grip on the hearts of many people, she admitted, under pressure, that it was. I tried to get her to shed further light on this subject, but she began to look scared, and so out of consideration for her feelings I desisted. I tried also to talk to her, without undue emphasis, about our ways of life in the democratic countries as compared with those I had already noted in Soviet Russia. She listened politely enough but made no comment whatsoever, and I gathered from her strained silence that this subject also was taboo; that she had certainly been trained rigorously to barricade her mind against any conversation that smacked even faintly of enemy propaganda. Again for her sake I desisted because she was an intelligent, well-mannered woman and I had no wish to involve her in any trouble, but I had a sudden sensation of despair, of utter hopelessness for the future of the world in which a political experiment of apparently immense significance should, in order to achieve its obscure ends, have to be based primarily upon enforced ignorance; the denial of personal freedom, even of thought; and the organised debarring of an entire race from the slightest contact with any ideas of life other than those arbitrarily imposed upon it by a self-constituted minority.

On the day before I left Russia, vowing never, never to return if I could possibly help it, Natasha drove me out to Tsarskoe-Selo where the famous Palace built by the Great Catherine still stood among its trees and lakes, kept, doubtless, as a reminder to the vast numbers of people who visited it that the dissolute crimes of riches and Royal extravagance did not pay, and that here all that was left of their former tyrants and oppressors was the gaudy shell in which they lived. If pointing this moral was really the idea underlying the State's decision to leave the Caterina Palace more or less as it was in the past, I cannot feel that it was an unqualified success. Walking, with Natasha and several hundred others, through the exquisitely proportioned, sumtuously furnished private apartments, State apartments, dining-halls, ballrooms and galleries, I could not help noticing the rapt, fascinated expressions on the faces of my fellow sight-seers. The impact on them of so much beauty of design, so much colour, such unfamiliar grace and spaciousness, was quite startling. They whispered excitedly among themselves, pointed various *objets d'art* out to each other with little sighs of pleasure, and altogether displayed more mass animation than I had observed since my arrival in Russia. True, they didn't cheer, as the Moscow crowds had at the football match, but they certainly seemed to me to be happier and more alive. The moral implications of the spectacle appeared to be going by the board completely. I think the several professional guides who escorted them must have been aware of this, for their voices became shrill, and they flung themselves into frenzies of invective in a vain effort to lash their audience into the right mood of loathing and contempt. On our way out we passed through the main hall of the Palace and I noticed on one of the walls a large, garishly painted picture. It portrayed, with photographic realism, the terrible disaster that had occurred on the night of the coronation of the late Tsar and Tsarina when the grand stands, erected in a public park for the festivities, had collapsed, resulting in a wild panic and the death of many thousands. I remember reading somewhere that on that stifling summer evening the Tsar and Tsarina had sat in their private apartments, wretched and horror-stricken, listening to the carts, piled high with the bodies of the dead, rumbling by below their windows.

There was a large crowd collected in front of the picture and, haranguing them, a little man with a professionally fanatical expression and untidy hair. Occasionally his voice rose to a scream and he pounded his fist vehemently into the palm of his hand. I asked Natasha what he was saying and she replied, reluctantly, that he was explaining to his gaping listeners that the entire tragic accident had been planned and organised by the Tsar and Tsarina for political reasons! I walked out on to the sunlit terrace and down the steps feeling a little sick and extremely angry. In the car driving home I mastered my rage sufficiently to ask her whether or not she believed such nonsense. She blushed and said in a frightened whisper that frankly she didn't, but that she supposed that sometimes it was necessary to misrepresent facts in order to prove to the people how much better off they were now than they had been before. I restrained the torrent of furious argument that was bubbling up inside me and we drove home to the Astoria Hotel in silence. Maedchen met us in the lobby wearing her usual forbidding and suspicious expression and her black boots. I said good-bye to them both politely but with a certain brusqueness, explaining that I was leaving the next morning and thanking them for having done so much to make my stay in Leningrad pleasant. I then went upstairs, ordered some vodka, and packed my bags with feverish efficiency.

5

The journey from Leningrad to the Finnish frontier takes only an hour, and my relief when the train finally pulled out of the station was considerable. I felt exactly as though I had been let out of prison after serving a long term, and I wouldn't have been in the least surprised if a kindly chaplain had suddenly appeared and given me a change of clothes, five pounds, and a few exhortations to lead a better life in the future.

In 1939 the railway bridge crossing the river that separates Russia from Finland was painted half red and half white. I presume that now it is entirely red. The station on the Russian side was dirty and uncomfortable and swarming with small officials, some in uniform and some not and all inquisitive and suspicious. My luggage was again examined, but less meticulously than before; I was again questioned and cross-questioned, and made to wait about interminably while a yellowish gentleman with a cropped head and a spectacular wart on his chin thumbed through my passport and handed it in turn to several of his colleagues. Finally I was permitted to get back on to the train and sat there for an hour waiting for it to start. It was an unpleasant hour because I was ill at ease and beset with fears. I really had the sensation that I was escaping by the skin of my teeth and might at any moment be hauled out of the train and sent back to Leningrad for further interrogation. I cursed myself for having made foolish jokes; for having complained about the tadpole; for having asked too many questions, and for having, by my manner, made it too obvious that I had been unimpressed by what I had seen of Soviet life and activities. I envisaged gloomily the headlines in the English newspapers if I were detained in the Soviet Union on some trumped-up charge of espionage, and also the inevitable questions that would be asked by Mr Shinwell in the House of Commons. Mr Shinwell had already, on several occasions, displayed a flattering interest in my career, and was for ever popping up and enquiring sarcastically why I was doing this or that, and whether or not his honourable friends were aware that Mr Coward, at infinite cost to the British tax-payer, was being conveyed hither and thither in ships of the Royal Navy. I foresaw with dismal clarity that if the Russians decided to be unpleasant to me Mr Shinwell would have a field day. I looked out on to the platform and noticed a small group of officials in green uniforms, talking excitedly and pointing in my direction, and I was just about to slink along the corridor and lock myself into the lavatory when, at long long last, the train shuddered and grunted and began to move. I lit a cigarette with trembling nonchalance and left the Soviet Union, I hope, for ever.

The Finnish frontier station was most beautiful in my eyes; most beautiful and gay and clean. The officials were smiling and courteous, and one of them even seemed to like my passport photograph. The Customs men, god-like creatures with blond hair and gleaming teeth, marked my baggage without even looking at it, and I was ushered into the buffet, where a waitress, who was a cross between Marlene Dietrich and Lady Diana Cooper, brought me some ambrosial bacon and eggs and a bottle of Lea and Perrin's Worcestershire sauce. My fellow passengers – most of whom were Finns – appeared to be as sensitive to the change of atmosphere as I was. They chattered and laughed and made jokes with the waitresses and there was a holiday feeling in the air. There was a lovely smell too, compounded of roasting coffee, frying bacon, the geraniums in the window-boxes and the heady, intoxicating scent of freedom.

After lunch the train strolled on to Helsinki and I looked out of the window at soft summer hills and the glistening sun.

Sadly enough I have little to say about Finland beyond the fact that I found it enchanting and its people hospitable and kind. I say 'Sadly enough' because it is a dreary comment on human nature that recorded pleasure inevitably makes duller reading than recorded irritation and criticism. I found nothing to criticise in Finland and much to admire. I stayed in a comfortable, well-run hotel. I visited a charming country house belonging to the Baroness Vrede, in which there was some lovely furniture and several large tiled stoves. The food was simple and good and so was the conversation, in fact life itself there seemed to be simple and good and marred by only one discordancy: the threat of Russian invasion. Madame Vrede discussed this, as Prince Radziwill had done, with detached resignation, as though she had steeled herself against what was to come and had prepared her mind to accept the inevitable with fortitude. A year later I saw the opening performance in New York of Robert Sherwood's *There Shall Be No Night*. This moving tragedy, as originally written and played, dealt with the conquest of Finland by the Nazis. Later, when the Lunts performed it in London, the locale was changed to Greece, for by then the drama of Finland was over and done with, and its sad destiny no longer of dramatic interest; also it had not been invaded by the wicked Nazis but by the friendly and efficient Russians, a fact which at that time would have limited considerably the play's popular appeal. However, on opening night in New York as I watched Lynn Fontanne grimly and quietly loading a gun, and explaining as she did so exactly what she proposed to do when the invaders approached the house, my mind went back for a moment to Madame Vrede talking to me in the twilight of a summer evening only a short year ago. I remembered her gently ironic smile when I said, admittedly not with much conviction, that perhaps after all a Russian invasion might not be quite so bad as a German invasion. I remembered her sitting there on the terrace with her hands folded patiently in her lap and her eyes looking out over the wooded valley, and saying: 'They will come. We have no means of preventing them. And when they do, it will be all over.'

During my stay in Helsinki someone suggested that I should pay a call on Sibelius, who, although he lived a life of the utmost quiet and seclusion, would, I was assured, be more than delighted to receive me. This, later, proved to be an overstatement. However, encouraged by the mental picture of the great Master being practically unable to contain himself at the thought of meeting face to face the man who had composed 'A Room with a View' and 'Mad Dogs and Englishmen', I drove out graciously to call upon him. His house was a few miles away in the country and my guide-interpreter and I arrived there about noon. We were received by a startled, bald-headed gentleman whom I took to be an aged family retainer. He led us, without any marked signs of enthusiasm, on to a small, trellis-enclosed veranda, and left us alone. We conversed in low, reverent voices and offered each other cigarettes and waited with rising nervous tension for the Master to appear. I remembered regretting bitterly my casual approach to classical music and trying frantically in my mind to disentangle the works of Sibelius from those of Delius. After about a quarter of an hour the bald-headed man reappeared carrying a tray upon which was a decanter of wine and a plate of biscuits. He put this on the table and then, to my surprise, sat down and looked at us. The silence became almost unbearable, and my friend muttered something in Finnish to which the bald-headed gentleman replied with an exasperated nod. It then dawned upon me that this was the great man himself, and furthermore that he hadn't the faintest idea who I was, who my escort was, or what we were doing there at all. Feeling embarrassed and extremely silly I smiled vacuously and offered him a cigarette, which he refused. My friend then rose, I thought a trifle officiously, and poured out three glasses of wine. We then proceeded to toast each other politely but in the same oppressive silence. I asked my friend if Mr Sibelius could speak English or French and he said 'No'. I then asked him to explain to him how very much I admired his music and what an honour it was for me to meet him personally. This was translated, upon which Sibelius rose abruptly to his feet and offered me a biscuit. I accepted it with rather overdone gratitude, and then down came the silence again, and I looked forlornly past Sibelius's head through a gap in the trellis at the road. Finally, realising that unless I did something decisive we should probably stay there until sundown, I got up and asked my friend – whom I could willingly have garrotted – to thank Mr Sibelius for receiving me and to explain once again how honoured I was to meet him, and that I hoped he would forgive us for leaving so soon but we had an appointment at the hotel for lunch. Upon this being communicated to him, Sibelius smiled for the first time and we shook hands with enthusiasm. He escorted us to the gate and waved happily as we drove away. My friend, whose name I am not withholding for any secret reasons but merely because I cannot remember it, seemed oblivious of the fact that the interview had not been a glittering success. Perhaps, being a rising journalist, he had already achieved immunity to the subtler nuances of social embarrassment. At all events he dismissed my reproaches quite airily. Mr Sibelius, he said, was well known to be both shy and unapproachable. I replied bitterly that in that case it had been most inconsiderate to all parties concerned to have arranged the interview in the first place, for although I was neither shy nor unapproachable, I was acutely sensitive to atmosphere and resented being placed in a false position possibly as much as Mr Sibelius did. We wrangled on in this strain until we reached the hotel, where we parted with a certain frigidity. Later, troubled by conscience, I wrote a brief note of apology to Sibelius, who, despite the fact that his seclusion had been invaded and the peace of his morning disrupted, had at least received me with courtesy and given me a biscuit.

There were several other, less constricted, social occasions during the remainder of the time I spent in Finland that I enjoyed immensely. The people I met were uneffusive and genuine; they took me sailing along the coast, and we picnicked in the small bays and inlets and swam in cool, clear water. There was a little night life too, but nothing spectacular. I remembered a cabaret where a lady sang 'Deep Purple' in French and a gentleman gave a spirited rendition of 'I'll See You Again' on a xylophone. Altogether it was a gay holiday and only very occasionally, for a few brief moments, the shadow of the future lay across the conversation, and I was allowed to feel, as I had felt in Poland, the imminence of change and dissolution.

6

Stockholm in July 1939 had not only changed its clothes for the summer but had changed its atmosphere too. Perhaps my view of it was jaundiced by my growing conviction that the whole of Europe was headed for imminent catastrophe, and my imagination prejudiced by the sinister portents I had observed in Poland, Russia and Finland. There seemed to me to be a leaden wariness in the air. The people I met and talked to were outwardly friendly and hospitable as usual, but I sensed a hidden uneasiness in their attitude to me as a visiting Englishman, as though my presence among them, while not being immediately embarrassing, might through some incident, some change of circumstance, prove to be very embarrassing indeed. There were of course many Germans in the city, more, it seemed to me, than there had been when I was there before. There was a group of them at the next table to me in the dining-room of the Grand Hotel. They might have been high-ranking military strategists in civilian clothes, travelling salesmen, minor officials attached to the German Legation, or merely ordinary tourists. Whatever they were, I was convinced that they were all secret agents. I looked at them with cold eyes and an expression of superior aloofness that I hoped would convince them that I knew accurately and to the last detail all there was to know about their subversive activities. This apparently was a failure, as one of them winked affably at me, which forced me to turn my head away and look grandly out of the window at nothing.

The British Minister, knowing that I was going on to Norway, asked me if I would mind taking the 'Bag' with me on the night train to Oslo, and so, imbued with a sense of political importance, and carrying a courier's passport covered with imposing red seals, I boarded the train and locked myself into my sleeper. The early hours of the night were disturbed for me by visions of masked spies with skeleton keys forcing their way in, wresting the secret documents from my defenceless grasp, and leaving me weltering in a pool of blood. However, nothing happened at all and I delivered the 'Bag' to a vague gentleman in a bowler hat on the platform at Oslo the next morning. I spent only a few days in Norway because by this time I was becoming bored with darting from capital to capital when I might have been lying in the warm Mediterranean sunshine, probably for the last time for many years. The curiosity that had prompted me to embark on these journeys in the first place had been abundantly satisfied. There were no longer any doubts in my mind about the imminence of war and chaos and destruction. The atmosphere of every place I had visited was heavy with it. At home in the House of Commons Mr Chamberlain, goaded to exasperation by some of the younger members suggesting that in the face of growing European tension it might be a good idea to forgo the usual summer recess, had petulantly moved for a vote of confidence in the Government. This political curl-tossing had won the day and our Parliament was on holiday. The Prime Minister himself, I suspected, was probably at this very moment fishing in some quiet English stream, wearing a curious tweed hat, and dreaming happily of his inevitable niche in posterity. The man of peace who had saved the world. I remembered gloomily a witticism attributed to the late Lord Birkenhead: 'The most we can hope for from dear Neville is that he should be a good Lord Mayor of Birmingham in a lean year.' This was a lean year all right and showed every indication of becoming a great deal leaner. Mr Chamberlain however was not Lord Mayor of Birmingham, but the Prime Minister of England.

In Copenhagen, in spite of warm Danish hospitality and the charms of the Tivoli Gardens in summer, my nostalgic yearning for the South of France crystallised into a firm resolve to have just one more look at it, even if only for a week, and so I got myself on to a plane and flew, via Paris and Marseilles, to Cannes. I arrived in the evening, in time to look out of the window of my suite in the Carlton Hotel at the lights coming up along the Croisette. From the balcony of my suite I could see the whole sweep of the coast, far away to the right the Estoril mountains, smoky-grey in the moonlight, and to the left, over the glittering lights of the Palm Beach casino on the point, the dark shape of Cap d'Antibes crouching in the sea. Conflicting strains of music rose from the little bars along the Croisette, and below me, from the terrace of the hotel, came the steady buzz of voices broken occasionally by sudden laughter and the clinking of ice in glasses. The air was cool and gentle after the heat of the day and the sense of leaden foreboding that had oppressed me for the last few weeks evaporated. I felt that it would be somehow discourteous to tarnish the tinsel enchantment of that familiar playground with premonitions of death and destruction. It would be like a fortune-teller at a gay party announcing to a young woman flushed with happiness and vitality that she was to die of cancer within the year. Perhaps, after all, the imminent madness, cruelty and futility of war were not as inevitable as I thought. Perhaps there was still time for some miracle to happen; for some superman with strength and courage and common sense to cut through the vacillations of frightened politicians and stand up to the loud-mouthed braggarts who were bent on plunging the world into chaos. Perhaps even they, the Dictators, would suddenly, at the last moment have a change of heart; realise in a blinding flash of revelation that war was no solution, that it never had been, and never could be, and that the course they had set themselves must, in the long run, only lead them to ignominy and death. Then, with sudden desolation, I knew that there were no perhapses; that the destiny of the human race was shaped by neither politicians nor dictators, but by its own inadequacy, superstition, avarice, envy, cruelty, and silliness, and that it had no right whatever to demand

and expect peace on earth until it had proved itself to be deserving of it. Saddened but not defeated by this reflection, I went down to dinner.

The preliminary tour of *This Happy Breed* and *Present Laughter* was scheduled to begin in Manchester on September the 11th and so I had only a week to bask in the irresponsible sunshine before rehearsals started. The sets and dresses were under way, and the cast all engaged and straining at the leash, so there was nothing but the destruction of civilisation to worry about. Leonora Corbett and Joyce Carey, my two leading ladies, were staying at Antibes, covered in Elizabeth Arden sun-tan oil and anxiously studying their scripts. Gladys was nearby on a private yacht. Somerset Maugham was in his villa on Cap Ferrat; Arthur Macrae, Marlene Dietrich, Alan Webb, Charlotte Boisselvain, Barry Dirks, Eric Sawyer, and countless other friends were available to lunch with, dine with, drink with, and swim with, and there were picnics on the islands with *langoustes* cooked in garlic, and crisp French bread and vin rosé; motor trips to Nice and Monte Carlo and San Tropez; occasional dressy evenings in the Casino enlivened by elaborate gambling systems, which usually resulted in anxious whispered calculations followed by quick dashes to the 'caisse' to change more traveller's cheques. There was also a very fast speed-boat which I hired recklessly at a fabulous price, feeling that at that particular moment any extravagance was justified. On the evening before I left for London I went off in the boat to say good-bye to Maxine Elliott in her lovely villa, the Château de l'Horizon. I landed at her little private jetty below the swimming pool and walked up the twisting path, shaded by oleanders, to the house. There was no house-party because Maxine was very ill, and the terrace and the pool, in the past invariably thronged with people, wore an air of sadness. Maxine Elliott was wise and kind and good; her supreme selfishness, of which she frequently accused herself, lay in the indulgence of her own generosity. She entertained lavishly and with exquisite taste, and to stay in that house, which she had designed and built so lovingly, was a special pleasure.

I went upstairs into Maxine's bedroom. She was in bed, bitterly against her will, and looking more beautiful than I had ever seen her. She joked about her illness and said that she was a cat with nine lives, eight of which had been lived to the full; the next attack, she said in her charming deep voice, would be the grand finale. She grumbled a good deal about being forced to stay in bed, and railed against the doctor and Fanny, her beloved maid, for refusing to allow her to get up and walk about and play games and go for drives. I stayed gossiping with her for about an hour, and then, noticing a tired look in her eyes, I kissed her and went away. I stepped into my speed-boat at the jetty and it started, as usual, with a roar. When it was a little way from the shore I turned and looked back at the house, and there was Maxine, leaning against one of the supports of her balcony and waving a white handkerchief. Her white hair, her white night-gown, and the handkerchief were tinged with pink from the setting sun. I waved back and then the lovely picture became blurred, because I knew, in that moment, that I should never see her again, and my eyes were filled with tears.

The next morning Gladys and I flew back to England.

7

The next three weeks were devoted to rehearsing morning, noon and night. The cast was quick and enthusiastic and learned their lines; the plays began to take shape; there were no quarrels and no hitches; the sets arrived in the theatre ahead of time and were put up and everyone concerned seemed to be making an extra effort; to be inspired with a special urgency; like people in a tropical country who, hearing the wind rising, close and bolt the shutters and busy themselves assiduously with household tasks, hoping against hope that it may not after all be the dreaded hurricane.

The dreaded hurricane, however, was drawing nearer and nearer with horrible swiftness. All over the country hope was dying. Young men began to appear on the streets in uniform, looking proud and a little self-conscious. There was the usual crop of people in the know; people whose friends' friends had husbands working for the Government and who knew, on impeccable authority, that Hitler was bluffing; that the Germans were even less prepared for war than we were; that London was going to be destroyed completely on the coming Tuesday; that Mr Chamberlain was going to pop off in still another aeroplane and persuade everybody to kiss and be friends; and that Hitler had cancer of the throat and couldn't possibly live through the winter. So many people knew so much and the words and phrases and rumours with which they tried to comfort their listeners and themselves were so often belied by the growing fear in their eyes.

On the Sunday morning following the first week of rehearsals I was sitting in the garden of Goldenhurst with Jack and Natasha Wilson and Joyce. We had driven down the night before, elated with the progress of the plays, and trying to keep at bay the growing suspicions in all our minds that the war would come before we could open. It was a lovely morning bathed in peace and security. There was a heat haze on the marsh and the sun glinted on the sea in the distance. Joyce, I remember, was engrossed in the *Sunday Times* Crossword and we were all shooting facetious suggestions at her, when Cole came out of the house and said that Sir Campbell Stuart wished to speak to me on the telephone. As, I regret to say, I had never heard of Sir Campbell Stuart, I told Cole to say that I was out. He returned a little later to say that Sir Campbell would ring up again in an hour's time and that it was urgent. Upon being questioned he admitted that Sir Campbell had a peculiar voice and that the whole thing sounded rather fishy. Just before lunch Sir Campbell rang up again and I answered the telephone myself, and that was the beginning of one of the most violent detours my life has ever made. He certainly had a peculiar voice, but what he said was more peculiar still. He began by announcing abruptly that he could only speak to me for three minutes as he had to rush off to 10 Downing Street; that he had a matter of extreme urgency to discuss with me and wished to see me that night. I replied that that was impossible as this was my only day in the country and that I should not be driving up to London until very late. This didn't discourage him in the least, and he said that he would come to my studio in Gerald Road at midnight precisely, and did I like Paris? Slightly bewildered by this apparent irrelevance I said, with remote dignity, that I was devoted to Paris but it would really be more convenient if we could meet at some other time. 'It's very important,' he said. 'To-night at midnight,' and rang off. Irritated by this peremptoriness I rejoined the others, and when Robert Boothby arrived for lunch I asked him if he could shed any light on this strange character who had telephoned me out of the blue. He roared with laughter and explained that Sir Campbell Stuart was a director of *The Times*; that he had been a protégé of the late Lord Northcliffe and had worked successfully on propaganda in the last war. He added that he was an unusual man, not enormously popular in political circles, but that he had power and a great deal of drive. I would like to say here that the question of what exactly I was going to do in the event of war had been perplexing me for some time. Owing to my affiliation with the Navy through the Royal Naval Film Corporation which Lord Louis Mountbatten had organised in 1937, I knew that it was tacitly assumed by the Admiralty that I would be willing to work as a sort of welfare officer and organise entertainments for the troops both in shore establishments and at sea whenever possible. This, of course, would have been an easy solution of my problem, so easy indeed that I distrusted it. For many years past I had been privileged to be a guest of the Royal Navy in all parts of the world, and in every type of ship, ranging from the battlewagons to submarines. This will always be to me a subtle and most important honour. I am primarily a writer and a man of the theatre, and the major portion of my working life has naturally lain in capital cities. Realising a long while ago that, for a writer particularly, too much urbanity is limiting, I determined to travel as much and as far as I could, and mix with all sorts and kinds of people whose ways of living and views of life were as far removed from mine as possible. This was a deliberate policy and I had pursued it, whenever opportunity offered, since I was twenty. The slogan 'Join the Navy and See the World' had for me a special significance. I joined the Navy for the first time in Shanghai in 1930 when I was invited to take passage in H.M.S. *Suffolk* to Hong Kong. Since then I had joined the Navy and seen the world whenever I could possibly wangle an invitation.

Thus it was fairly obvious that if war came the simplest course for me would be to join the Navy again, in whatever capacity that was suggested, do what I was told as efficiently as I could and be done with further argument. I should be living and working among people whom I trusted and liked in an atmosphere with which I was pleasantly familiar. The state of war would of course change it to a certain degree, but the essentials would remain the same. Everything, including my personal inclinations, seemed to point in the same direction but for one formidable obstacle, which was my conscience. Perhaps, on looking back, it was nothing after all but my ego and not my conscience at all, but I felt at the time, and I still feel that I was right, that my mental attributes and my creative talent would be of more service to my country than my theatrical experience in organising entertainments. I know a number of people who could do this as well as, if not better than, I. I also felt, arrogantly perhaps that for me to spend the duration of the war sitting in offices in various shore establishments, dressed as a Lieutenant-Commander R.N.V.R. and arranging which artists should precede which, would be a waste both of my time and my capacities.

It was obvious that Sir Campbell Stuart was going to offer me a job connected in some way with intelligence or propaganda. It was also obvious, as he had asked me so pointedly if I liked Paris, that it would have some contact with France and the French. This fact prejudiced me in favour of the idea even before I knew specifically what it was. I have always liked France and the French people, and I spoke the French language with reasonable fluency, although with only a bowing acquaintance with its grammar. However, with a little concentration that could soon be remedied. Bob Boothby, who was driving up to London in the afternoon and dining at Chartwell, en route, with Winston Churchill, suggested that I should go with him and get Mr Churchill's advice before taking steps in any direction. This seemed to me to be a wise plan and so we telephoned, I was duly invited, and off we went. I had known Winston Churchill for several years but never very well. We had met from time to time, with Anthony and Beatrice Eden, with Diana and Duff Cooper, at Maxine's villa in the South of France, and I had been once or twice to Chartwell, where he had lectured me firmly but kindly about painting in oils instead of dabbing away at water-colours. He had always been courteous and agreeable to me, although I had a gnawing suspicion that there was something about me that he didn't like. This of course worried me, because the thought of there being anything about me that anybody doesn't like invariably worries me, and, naturally, the possible disapproval of Winston Churchill, whom I so admired and respected, ceased to be a mere worry and inflated itself into a major disaster. However, I determined not to allow these hypothetical doubts to impair my natural poise and make me uneasy in his presence. After dinner I played and sang to him some of my lighter songs which he has always liked, 'Mad Dogs and Englishmen' being his favourite with 'Don't Put Your Daughter on the Stage, Mrs Worthington' as a close runner-up. Altogether the evening might have been written off as an unqualified success but for the fact that the purpose of my visit was lurking in the shadows, and my instincts told me that whatever questions I wanted to ask him about my proposed war service should have been asked before dinner, and not afterwards, when the atmosphere was gay and relaxed.

However, time was passing and I had to get to London by midnight for my mysterious assignation with Sir Campbell Stuart, so I finally rose reluctantly from the piano and asked Mr Churchill if he would give me ten minutes of his time, as I was in a state of indecision and in need of his considered advice. He led me into another room and we sat down with a whisky and soda each, and I proceeded to explain, as concisely as I could, my situation with regard to the Navy; the problematical offer from Sir Campbell, and my own feelings as to the best service I could give to the country if it came to the point of war. It was, on the whole, an unsuccessful little interview. I was aware throughout that he was misunderstanding my motives and had got it firmly into his mind that I wished to be a glamorous secret service agent. I tried vainly to disabuse him of this by assuring him that nothing was further from my thoughts, and that even if my heart were set on such a course, the very fact of my celebrity value would prove an insuperable obstacle. I emphasised repeatedly my firm conviction that my brain and creative intelligence could be of more service to the Government than my theatrical ability. I think the word 'intelligence' must have been the monkey wrench, because at the mere mention of it he said irascibly, 'You'd be no good in the intelligence service.' I endeavoured, with growing inward irritation, to explain that I didn't mean 'The Intelligence' in inverted commas, but my own personal intelligence, which was not in inverted commas. He would have none of it, however, and went off at a great tangent about the Navy (which in any event was preaching to the already converted). Finally, warming to his subject, he waved his hand with a bravura gesture and said dramatically: 'Get into a warship and see some action! Go and sing to them when the guns are firing – that's your job!' With, I think, commendable restraint, I bit back the retort that if the morale of the Royal Navy was at such low ebb that the troops were unable to go into action without my singing 'Mad Dogs and Englishmen' to them, we were in trouble at the outset and that, although theoretically 'Singing when the guns are firing' sounds extremely gallant, it is, in reality, impracticable, because during a naval battle all ship's companies are at action stations, and the only place for me to sing would be in the ward-room by myself. At last, realising that little had been gained, and a great deal of my hard-won popularity at the piano lost, I thanked him for his advice and went sadly away. On the drive up to London I re-enacted the whole interview in my mind and came to several conclusions, one of which was that my facility for light entertaining, although I am grateful for it, can on occasions be a serious disadvantage. I saw Mr Churchill's point clearly. In his view I was primarily an entertainer, a singer of gay songs, and that, come rain or shine, peace or war, victory, defeat or bloody chaos, that was what I should remain. I knew also that his admiration for me in this capacity was wholehearted and sincere. But what he failed to realise was that I didn't sing and play nearly as well as he thought I did, and that I could do one or two things a good deal better.

There would obviously be countless opportunities in the coming years for me to sing to troops, and I was resolved to do it gladly whenever the circumstances demanded, but I could not and would not take a palpable line of least resistance when I knew in my innermost heart that if I were intelligently used by the Government, preferably in the field of propaganda, where my creative ability, experience of broadcasting and knowledge of people could be employed, I could probably do something really constructive instead of wasting the Government's time and my own energy in some set, time-serving routine. I do not think that my conviction over this was either extravagant or conceited, but even if it was, the motive underlying it was sincere. I was thirty-nine years old, and in the last war, when I was yanked into the Army at the age of eighteen, I had distinguished myself by falling on my head; resenting bitterly the Army, the war and everything to do with it; and finally ending my inglorious career as a soldier in an advanced state of neurasthenia in the Colchester Military Hospital. Psycho-analysts, after reading my account of this period of my life in *Present Indicative*, have advanced the theory that this neurasthenia was self-engendered and the outward manifestation of inner conflict; that the concussion and coma resulting from my fall on returning from musketry drill was in reality a form of hysteria induced by a subconscious escapism, a compelling urge to break away from the rigours of unfamiliar Army routine. This theory is probably correct except in one detail. My longing to escape was far from being subconscious. I would have done anything in my power to escape from the routine and regimentation which crushed me down to a level of despair that I had never experienced before and have never experienced since. The fall on my head was motivated by an unsubconscious wooden slat which tripped me up. The ensuing concussion and coma which lasted for three days I cannot vouch for, as I have no recollection of it. I only know that when ultimately I was discharged from His Majesty's service (with, I hasten to add, a small pension, which proves that someone must have blundered) it was the happiest day of my life. All that was in October 1918, and now, in August, 1939, I could look back over the intervening years and reflect gratefully that Fate had been prodigiously kind. With all their ups and downs and victories and defeats, they had been wonderful years and lived to the full. I had worked and played all over the world; achieved many of my ambitions and, above all, acquired a few friendships that could never die, and which would uphold me in whatever circumstances I might find myself, regardless of wars and changing worlds, until the end of my life. Now was the moment of all moments to think clearly and unemotionally, and to face facts honestly. If I bungled this moment, and by doing so betrayed my own code of morals, I should never be comfortable with myself again and, what is more, whatever books or plays I lived to write in the future would be inevitably and irrevocably tainted by the fact that I had allowed to slip through my fingers the opportunity to prove my own integrity to myself. That was how I felt in 1939. That was how I reasoned with myself, and that was what I sincerely believed.

The first step therefore was to decide what I wanted to do and then go ahead and do it. I arrived home on that fairly fateful evening just before midnight, and at twelve o'clock precisely Sir Campbell Stuart appeared. The ensuing interview lasted for about three hours and was highly enjoyable. The keynote of it was professional charm. We both worked hard and succeeded in charming each other to a standstill. Oddly enough, although it was such a set piece, that mutual charm session formed a very pleasant basis which has remained firm through many vicissitudes. Sir Campbell's appearance surprised me considerably because, having been told by Bob Boothby that he was a Canadian, I expected him to be broad-shouldered, breezy and rather tough. Instead, however, I was confronted by a tall, very thin gentleman with a ragged moustache, slightly projecting teeth and kindly, grey eyes. He wore a dark suit and, like my Maedchen in Uniform in Leningrad, large black boots. Unlike her, however, he had an irrepressible sense of humour and proceeded, in the first few minutes, to flatter me so outrageously that if it had not been for the twinkle in his eye I think I would have asked him to leave. He said, among other extravagances, that the reason he wished me to represent him in Paris was that he knew, on excellent authority, that I was revered and adored by the French nation; that my brilliance and wit was a byword from one end of France to the other; that Monsieur Jean Giraudoux, who at the moment was about to become the French Minister of Information, would take it as a personal compliment if I agreed to work on propaganda in Paris, and that my appointment as representative of Sir Campbell Stuart would do much to consolidate the 'Entente Cordiale'.

Fascinated by this news of my, hitherto unsuspected, importance to the French nation and relieved that Sir Campbell had not suggested that I should go immediately to the Maginot Line and sing a translation of 'Mad Dogs and Englishmen' to bolster up the morale of the *poilus*, I relaxed in a warm glow of self-satisfaction, and allowed further cascades of comforting flattery to wash over me. Presently, when the softening process had obviously begun to take effect, and Sir Campbell realised that I was about ready for the kill, he became suddenly practical and outlined clearly and articulately exactly what he wanted me to do. This was to go to Paris immediately on the declaration of war and set up, in his name, a Bureau of Propaganda in friendly cooperation with the French Commissariat d'Information. The propaganda was to be directed exclusively into Germany and Sir Campbell, from his secret headquarters in the English country, would supply me with directives and ideas, which I, in turn, would be required to discuss with the French. He informed me that as far as the English side of the business was concerned the whole organisation was complete and ready to operate immediately. He also told me that he would give me a Chief of Staff and whatever secretaries I needed, and that the Chief of Staff in question would be David Strathallan, the son of Lord Perth. He added that Strathallan, being a Viscount, would also impress the French very favourably. I remember remarking that if the French were so Debrett-minded, it would be better to get a marquis or even a young duke if there were any available. Sir Campbell rose above this with an indulgent laugh and continued to paint, in increasingly glowing colours, the picture of myself in the French capital, suave and brilliant, conducting the propaganda bureau with matchless efficiency and, by so doing, making an important personal contribution to ultimate victory. All this was gratifying, but I wasn't entirely convinced. To begin with, I felt that to deal with propaganda exclusively directed into Germany while other organisations were handling the neutral countries might lead to overlapping and confusion. It seemed to me that all propaganda should be under one head. Sir Campbell gaily agreed but said that unfortunately it wasn't feasible. We talked on and on and I told him of my tacit commitment to the Admiralty. This he also rose above with nonchalance. A great friend of his, he said, was a certain Admiral who, being the head of the Secret Service, could wield unearthly powers and could whip me out of my commitment without any hard feelings in any direction. He then told me that, if I agreed to work for him, I would receive no salary but that all my expenses would be paid; that I should have to start being briefed right away, which, in view of the fact that I was rehearsing during the day, would mean a couple of hours' concentration every night, and that the whole business would have to be conducted with the utmost secrecy. I was to tell nobody, not even my closest friends, and that if the Press should get an inkling of what I was up to it would be disastrous. I remember thinking at the time that this was perhaps a little excessive, but I did not realise then, although I certainly realised it later, that Sir Campbell had a romantic passion for secrecy. I think really that this was an amiable form of self-dramatisation. Whatever it was, it was destined to cause me a great deal of inconvenience in the future. At all events when he left at about 4 a.m. and got into his car, with a controlled furtiveness that the late Sir Henry Irving would have envied, I retired to bed in a state of considerable confusion. Sleep was out of the question for a long while and I lay in the dark trying to sort things out. In the main the idea seemed a good one, stripped of Sir Campbell's rococo compliments and viewed with a practical eye. It was a job that with hard work and concentration I might be able to do well. It would at least give me an opportunity to use my mind and my imagination, and it would also be utilising my position as a writer, for the French, unlike the English, had a wholesome respect for literary talent and actually considered artists to be people of importance. Balanced against these obvious advantages were many doubts that tormented my mind. I was not sure of Sir Campbell Stuart. I had never clapped eyes on him before in my life, and although he had been most courteous to me I was in no way certain as to how far he could be trusted. For all I knew he might not have been Sir Campbell Stuart at all and the whole thing turn out to be an elaborate hoax. And yet as he had put it to me it had seemed sensible enough. I was a well-known British Writer. I was fairly popular in France. Propaganda was, or should be, primarily a writer's job. I finally went to sleep worried and undecided and dreamt that I was appearing as a clown in the Cirque Medrano and that Winston Churchill was in a box applauding vociferously.

The next morning I missed rehearsal and went to see Robert Vansittart at the Foreign Office. As a man whose wisdom and knowledge I respected and whose friendship I valued he seemed to me the most likely source of impartial information regarding Sir Campbell Stuart. I explained my situation to him and the offer that had been made to me and, rather to my surprise, he seemed to think it would be a good idea for me to accept it. He said, as Bob Boothby had said, that although Sir Campbell Stuart had many enemies in political circles, he also had many influential friends and was a man of energy and considerable ability. He added that if, after a month or so, I found that I was unhappy in the job, it would always be possible to resign from it and try something else. Fortified by this advice I went across to the Admiralty to see the Second Sea Lord, Admiral Pridham-Wippell. He received me with a pleasant but rather rueful smile and the first thing he said was: 'I hear you have been whisked away from us!' This, I must admit, startled me; it also impressed me with the fact that Sir Campbell was certainly not one to let the grass grow under his black boots. I told the Admiral, with the utmost sincerity, how sorry I was in one way not to be working for the Navy, but that in the face of the offer I had had I really felt that I ought to accept it. He agreed without rancour and wished me the best of luck. I left him, feeling rather miserable but at the same time relieved that I had anyhow made a definite decision.

The next two weeks were strenuous. I rehearsed the plays in the mornings, afternoons and evenings, finishing as a rule about ten-thirty, and went home to my studio. Then, sometime between eleven o'clock and midnight, Campbell Stuart himself would arrive or Colonel Dallas Brooks, Royal Marines, his second-in-command. Together or separately they briefed me on the details of what was expected of me and explained the intricacies of the organisation in England, all of which, I need hardly say, were of the utmost secrecy. The headquarters of Sir Campbell and his merry men lay sequestered in the depths of the English countryside, where I should have thought it would have been fairly easy to find by any German agent with the faintest enterprise. However there it was, secret as the grave and buzzing with hidden activities. Colonel Brooks was as charming as Campbell Stuart but in an entirely different way. He was large and good-looking and impeccably dressed in a blue pin-stripe suit. He had won a D.S.O. for conspicuous gallantry at Zeebrugge in the last war, and was a typical Royal Marine officer, which means that he was efficient, sentimental and had perfect manners. His delivery was measured and he seemed to have as great a passion for secrecy as Sir Campbell. Whenever I asked him any question which seemed to him to verge on the indiscreet, he would assume a veiled, quizzical expression and tap his nose with his forefinger. I liked him at once and he taught me a secret code which I was to use in moments of supreme urgency. It was a naïve little code and consisted mainly of calling people by different names. These names he wrote down on bits of paper and when I asked him if, after learning them by heart, I should chew them up and swallow them, he smiled dimly and said that that would not be necessary.

On August the 30th and 31st we had rough dress-rehearsals of *This Happy Breed* and *Present Laughter*, and both plays went through with remarkable smoothness considering that we were still over a week away from production. On Friday September the 1st the Germans invaded Poland and it was obvious that it would only be a question of days, or perhaps hours, before we were at war. It was a miserable company that assembled that morning on the stage of the Phoenix Theatre. They had all known, of course, that if war came we should not be able to open, but, like everybody else, they had been hoping all along for a miracle to happen. Now it was too late for any further hoping and we all said good-bye to each other and made cheerfully false prophecies for the future. Everyone behaved beautifully and there were only a few tears. Joyce and Gladys and Jack and I lunched at The Ivy as usual, and we were over-bright and jocular and made little jokes to tide us over.

On Sunday morning David Strathallan arrived at my studio, for we were to drive down to the Hush-Hush headquarters for our final briefing. Together we listened to Mr Chamberlain's lachrymose announcement that a state of war had been declared between England and Germany. Then we got into my car and drove off. David was intelligent and gentle, and I suspected that his obvious integrity would soon override French disappointment at his being a mere viscount. At any rate it was a great relief to me, knowing that we were to work together in the closest co-operation, to discover that he had humour and was not the type to be easily flurried by anything or anybody. We got as far as Lord's cricket ground when the air-raid sirens started wailing. It was a curious sensation, because although we had heard that particularly dismal sound before when the sirens had been tried out for practice purposes, now it was the real thing and for the first time I experienced that sudden coldness in the heart, that automatic tensing of the muscles that later on was to become so habitual that one hardly noticed it. A zealous A.R.P. warden appeared from nowhere and waved us to take cover immediately. We were ushered into a large apartment building and led down into the basement, which was rapidly becoming overcrowded. Everyone was calm, but one lady carrying a baby was in tears. I remember wondering whether this was going to be a real knock-out blow, a carefully prepared surprise attack by Hitler within the first hour of war being declared. It was an unpleasant thought and well within the bounds of possibility. More and more people came hurrying down, and I decided that if I had to die I would rather die in the open and not suffocate slowly with a lot of strangers at the bottom of a lift shaft. I hissed this to David, who agreed, and so we forced our way up the stairs and into the hall. Here, to my surprise, we found Morris Angel, the famous theatrical costumier, who said, ignoring the disapproval of the A.R.P. gentleman who was trying to force him down the stairs: 'I think this calls for a bottle of Bubbly!' He then led us up to his flat on the third floor, introduced us to his wife, who was very cross because the electricity had been cut off and her Sunday joint was ruined, and opened a bottle of excellent champagne. With this we toasted the King, each other, and a speedy victory for the Allies.

Hush-Hush headquarters was in Bedfordshire. Some kindly villagers in their Sunday best directed us to it, seemingly unaware that they were indulging in careless talk of the most dangerous kind. One man even offered to come with us on the footboard in case we missed a turning in the lane. We finally arrived at a gate festooned wth barbed wire from which some very young sentries sprang at us with loud cries. We pacified them by showing passes and went on through an impressive park to the next line of defences, where the same process was repeated. At last, after we had been passed through an office, questioned, cross-questioned and, I think, finger-printed, we were escorted to Sir Campbell's private establishment, which was a mock Tudor villa some way away from the main buildings. It had an air of suburban peace about it, which was very soothing after the perils of the latter part of our journey, and we relaxed gratefully and had an excellent lunch. When this was finished Campbell took us on a personally conducted tour of the whole outfit, and most impressive it was. We were introduced to various heads of departments and a great many intricate operations were explained to us, very few of which I grasped. David, being more serious-minded than I, nodded his head wisely, made appropriate clucking noises, and gave every indication that he understood perfectly. I was much comforted by this, for it gave me an opportunity to study Campbell's technique in dealing with his staff. It really was an admirable performance. He was jocose, serious, gay and shrewd in turn; his personal approach to each individual was perfectly attuned to his psychological knowledge of them. He over-decorated occasionally, and was perhaps a little too ebullient, but the whole business was a superb exhibition of personality and kindly egocentricity. I could see clearly why he had good friends as well as powerful enemies. I could also see why he might very easily be distrusted in political circles. There was a childishness about him, his phraseology was too extravagant, and he seemed too eager to impress. In spite of and because of all this, however, my heart warmed to him and has remained warm to him ever since.

David and I, crammed with secret and confusing information, drove back through the summer twilight to London. We were to leave on the following Thursday for Paris. David was going by train and boat with the luggage. I was to be flown across in a special plane with 'The Papers'. It all sounded very dashing and a trifle alarming. I dined quietly and went to bed early; and thus ended, for me, the first day of the war.

8

On the morning of September 7th I flew to France in a Vega Gull. There was only room in the plane for the pilot, the observer and myself. I wore a dark suit and a bowler hat and carried a gas mask in addition to various contrivances that had been hooked on to me: a parachute and a sort of inflatable belt for keeping me afloat in the Channel. I also carried a brief-case containing 'The Papers', most of which were marked 'Secret', and all of which were dull. It was a clear, lovely morning; the light was strong and the countryside, as it slipped away beneath us, had a shiny, model look as though it were not real at all but had been accurately reproduced in coloured papier mâché. The roofs of the houses were too red and the pine trees too green, and I felt that the traffic on the roads and the trains running along their lines might all suddenly stop dead if someone pulled a switch. The sky was a light, sharp blue with exactly the right amount of woolly clouds, and the whole idea of war, and the fact that my life was so violently altering its course, seemed quite inconceivable.

Apart from a couple of camouflaged planes that came up to have a look at us there was no sign anywhere that everything wasn't perfectly normal. A flight to Paris in a private plane; lunch on arrival, probably at Larue's or somewhere in the Bois, an afternoon of shopping or just wandering about, then dinner and a theatre. I had known many such gay, unsignificant arrivals in the past. I had always enjoyed arriving in Paris more than any other city in the world from the very early days when I had little money and used to go via Newhaven and Dieppe, first class on the boat, second class on the trains, sitting up with my head wobbling against the harsh lace antimacassars, and occasionally pulling aside the blind to peer out at the brightly-lit stations. Then later the ineffable pleasure of walking out of the smoky station into early morning; driving through the empty streets in a taxi; watching chairs being unstacked outside the cafés, and smelling that indefinable, pungent smell that belongs to no other city. This arrival would certainly be unlike all the others. The lightness in the air would be less, perhaps there would be none left at all. War had come again, and not only Paris but the whole world was changing, and there was no time to be wasted in irrelevant nostalgia. The snows of yesteryear had better melt as quickly as possible even from one's memory. We flew out over the Channel. The sea was flat calm and utterly deserted; it wasn't until we had almost reached the French coast that I noticed one self-conscious-looking freighter, which must have been going very slowly for there was hardly any wake at all. I looked back at England, still clear in the distance, and wondered dispassionately whether or not I should ever see it again. At that moment it seemed quite possible that I shouldn't. Paris was even less prepared for defence against air attack than London, and it was conceivable that the Germans might decide to start the war with a bang and bomb it to hell. I had been through all this before in my mind of course. I had spent many hours trying, not always successfully, to get myself into the right attitude of mind, but there had been difficult moments. A great deal had happened in the last few weeks and far too quickly. And now here I was, embarking on a new phase of life which was certain to be utterly different from anything I had known before. I would have to be painstaking and efficient, and force myself to tolerate routine and dullness, for I wasn't naïf enough to imagine that running an 'Enemy Propaganda Office' in Paris was going to be breathlessly exciting. I hoped, however, for a few interesting and dramatic moments, and these hopes, I am glad to say, were not entirely unrewarded.

As the plane approached Tréport the pilot looked ruefully over his shoulder at me and said that he had to fire off a gun with coloured rockets; that there was a different identifying colour for each day of the week, and he had forgotten which was today's. He added cheerfully that the French might quite possibly shoot us down. I suggested that he fire off all the colours at once and see what happened. He did so and the effect was very pretty. Presently two planes came up and forced us to land. Then there ensued a lot of light-hearted explanation, the burden of which fell on me as neither the pilot nor the observer could speak French. Finally we were allowed to take to the air again and set out on the last lap to Paris. We plodded along at an altitude of a thousand feet without further incident. It wasn't very bumpy, so I was able to doze a little and go back in my mind over the last few days. They had been difficult days and I was glad they were over and that I was finally away. The worst had been a horrid drive down to Goldenhurst in the black-out to say good-bye to Mother and Jack and Natasha, who were waiting there until they could get a passage home to America. Joyce Carey came with me for company and Gladys Calthrop drove on ahead in her own car because she was taking some things down to her Mill. We caught up with her at the point just before Ashford where she turns off, stopped both cars, lit cigarettes and had a little light conversation. We were rather high and full of jokes about driving in the blackout, which was then, of course, new to us. I remembered Gladys flicking her cigarette into the ditch, making a cloud of sparks, which I pointed out was a direct invitation to the German Air Force to drop everything they had on to us. Joyce and I drove on. Ashford was dark and the streets were crowded, so we had to go slowly. There were no signs of life at Goldenhurst from the outside. When we got out of the car there was a lot of scuffling, and Jack appeared with a carefully shielded torch and led us proudly into the big room to show us his handiwork, which I must say was shattering. He had been very conscientious indeed. There were blue bulbs in most of the lamps; two bicycles leaning against the bookshelves, the windows were thickly veiled in black material; all very right and proper and indescribably depressing. The library was better because the curtains were naturally thick, and there were no blue bulbs. We hurriedly had a drink and became more cheerful. Natasha, looking lovely and business-like in dark blue trousers and a white shirt, was knitting a most extraordinary boot. She had christened it 'Horsey', and to this day I don't believe it ever had a companion. I went up and talked to Mother in her room. She inveighed spiritedly against Jack's zeal in making the house look so dreadful. 'A lot of nonsense,' she said, 'I can't see my hand before my face, I nearly fell down the stairs, and the whole thing's idiotic!' We had food in the dining room, which was deeply shrouded, with only candles on the table. There was an unreal, nightmare atmosphere which was funny in a way, but our hearts were heavy. A little later all the good-byes were said and, with Joyce by my side dutifully prepared to light cigarettes for me, I drove away along the drive, up the hill to Aldington past The Walnut Tree; along the twisting bit of road to Smeeth station and the main road. On arrival at the corner where I had so often waited in the Ford luggage wagon to meet friends who had driven from London and guide them home, I remembered wondering, not too sentimentally, but with a remote, affectionate detachment, if I should ever see Goldenhurst again. It had been important in my life for many years and I had done a great deal of work there. I had also done a great deal of work in other places. Goldenhurst was not essential by any means, nevertheless I should certainly miss its comfort. I should miss the early breakfasts downstairs in the library before a blazing wood fire; working all the morning staring out over the marshes to the sea; the evening drives to Gladys's mill with perhaps a complete act to read to her and Patience Erskine, and then driving back along the winding marsh roads in the late dusk with the headlights making patterns on the hedgerows. I should miss finally arriving home, leaving the car in the garage and walking across to the house, sometimes along the straight bit of drive from which I could see the light flashing at Dungeness, and sometimes by the crazy-paving path between the pond and the tennis court. I should miss the welcoming fire in the big room, and popping up to say good-night to Mother, if it wasn't too late, and then perhaps playing the piano for a little or sitting down with a whisky and soda and planning tomorrow's work. Happy days all right. Happy and productive and good. Then, driving away with Joyce through the black-out, it was part of the past already, but now, suspended between the French countryside and the sky, a different life, a different world. 'To remember with tears'? Perhaps. To remember anyhow with gratitude.

PART TWO

Paris, during the first weeks of September 1939, was dusty and deserted. Most of the main shops, restaurants, hotels, theatres and cinemas were closed; the streets, compared with normal times, were virtually empty and there was an arid mournfulness enveloping the whole city. Criss-crosses of paper disfigured many of the windows; the boulevards were lined with acres of vacant chairs and tables; the few people who were about looked furtive and worried, and there was no lightness in the air; in fact there seemed to be very little air, for the heat was oppressive and lay over the abandoned quais, squares and avenues like an absorbent grey blanket sucking up all moisture and leaving the atmosphere stale and devitalised. The Ritz, gallant to the last, was open – at least the Place Vendôme side was; the Rue Cambon side, however, had thrown up the sponge and lay shuttered and dark at the end of its long passage lined with empty show-cases. One of the few relics of pre-war light-heartedness that remained open was Maxim's, and it was there that I dined on the night of my arrival with Captain 'Hookie' Holland, the Naval Attaché, who had left a note at the Ritz to greet me, bidding me to dine, and offering to help me with my job, whatever it might be, in any way he could. David Strathallan, who arrived in due course with our luggage, came too, and we ate caviar and *filet Mignon* and drank pink champagne just as though life in Paris was as gay and care-free as it so often had been. Albert, the *maître d'hôtel*, hovered and smiled and bowed as he had hovered and smiled and bowed for many years. Had we but known it, he was destined to continue to do so throughout the Occupation, for Air Marshal Goering later adopted Maxim's as his favourite restaurant. On this evening, however, such a far-fetched contingency naturally didn't occur to us; the degrading fate that France was to suffer during the next five years was still in the dark future, and the question of defeat and enemy occupation was beyond the bounds of possibility. Some difficult times might lie ahead perhaps; there might be a few air raids and discomforts and anxieties, but on the other hand no war lasted for ever, and there was after all and above all the Maginot Line.

Hookie, apart from his office in the Embassy and a secret hideout in the country where he hobnobbed with various French Naval executives, had the use of an office in the Ministère de la Marine just across the road. This, he explained, I could use whenever I wanted to make an urgent telephone call to England, for it had a direct line to the Admiralty from which I could be connected to Dallas Brooks at Electra House. Both David and I were delighted, for at that time apparently the only direct telephone line to London was from the Embassy and that, in our as yet ambiguous position, we obviously would not be permitted to use. To have achieved, through Hookie's kind co-operation, telephonic communication with our Chiefs on our very first night in Paris seemed to us a fabulous piece of luck and would, we hoped, be regarded as a striking proof of our speed and efficiency. True, Hookie told us that we should have to be careful what we said on the line because it was tapped continually, but, remembering my secret code, I was able to reassure him: 'That will be all right,' I said with a suave smile.

Our initial efforts to establish a smooth-running propaganda organisation in close and friendly co-operation with our French allies were not remarkably successful. The day after we arrived we called, as we had been told to do, upon a Captain of Marines who, Dallas had explained, had a shrewd, capable mind and, despite a somewhat unprepossessing appearance, was smart as a whip and thoroughly *au courant* with everything that was going on. We finally ran him to earth in the Hotel Danou, where he was sitting up in bed sipping milk and bismuth because he was suffering from stomach ulcers. He seemed depressed and not quite as brilliantly *au courant* with everything that was going on as we had been led to expect. We suggested that our first step must obviously be to contact Jean Giraudoux, who was the Minister of Information, and André Maurois, who, I had been informed, was his right hand. The Captain gave a small, defeated belch and shaking his head gloomily said that he didn't think it would be possible to see Giraudoux or Maurois just yet, and that we had better look round a bit first and get our bearings; he added that in any event he didn't know either of them. He then expatiated at some length on the perfidy and folly of the French as a race, and spoke bitterly of some abortive interviews he had had with certain officials in the Commissariat d'Information. From the way he pronounced their names I gained the impression that his knowledge of the French language was still in the preliminary stage. Finally we persuaded him to rise from his bed of pain and take us to see an elderly Admiral at the Invalides, who apparently was the only Frenchmen to date who had evinced any interest whatsoever in the Campbell Stuart Propaganda Bureau.

Admiral Fernet, to our immense relief, was intelligent and helpful. He was also short and stocky, had twinkling grey eyes and had known Proust quite well. Our interview with him was at least agreeable and we left the Invalides feeling a little more hopeful.

In the afternoon I telephoned to Jean Giraudoux and was immediately invited to dine with him that night.

The dinner with the Giraudouxs was delightful. I picked them up at their *appartement* on the Quai d'Orsay and we all piled into a car – there were several other guests – and went to a 'Bistro' in Montparnasse where the food was delicious. Madame Giraudoux was charming. Jean-Pierre Giraudoux, her son, was charming, and Jean Giraudoux himself was charming as always. The other guests were gay and vivacious. We discussed the French Theatre, the English Theatre and the American Theatre; we talked of Jouvet, the Lunts, Helen Hayes, John Gielgud, Edith Evans, Yvonne Printemps, and Pierre Fresnay, who it appeared, had plunged Yvonne into despair by suddenly becoming a *zouave* and retiring into the secret fastness of the Maginot Line. We also discussed, naturally enough, Jean Giraudoux, Noël Coward, Henri Bernstein, Marcel Achard, Edouard Bourdet and the Comédie Française, which Bourdet had reorganised entirely, some said brilliantly, some said indifferently. A subject, however, that was not mentioned at all was Propaganda into enemy territory. I tried once or twice to get the conversation round to it, but each time I was frustrated and so I finally desisted and gave myself up to the pleasure of the evening.

A few nights later I dined with André Maurois, who, Campbell Stuart had told me, was to occupy the position of my 'Opposite Number'. André Maurois in his exquisite house in Neuilly seemed unaware of this peculiar distinction. We discussed French literature, English literature and American literature. We also discussed mutual friends and reminisced cheerfully about the various occasions on which we had met in the past, when there was no war or even threat of war and the glittering decadence of the 'twenties and the 'thirties was at its height. There was no one else present beside André and his wife, and so after dinner I thought it was time to get down to business. I took the plunge and told them firmly about Campbell Stuart and my position as his representative; I emphasised the importance of establishing, as soon as possible, a clear liaison with the Commissariat d'Information so that we might pool our mutual ideas about Propaganda-into-Germany, and tabulate concisely for our mutual benefit the directive policies of our respective Governments. Maurois laughed pleasantly, although I thought a trifle cynically, and said that it all sounded very easy and effective as I had put it but that he feared it might not be quite so simple to organise as I had hoped. He also said, what I had felt from the first, that propaganda into enemy territory as a separate operation was liable to overlap propaganda into neutral countries, thereby causing a great deal of confusion and waste of time. He explained various political intricacies concerning the Commissariat d'Information and Giraudoux's rather invidious appointment as Minister. He obviously thought highly of Giraudoux as an artist and a playwright but seemed sceptical of his administrative capacities. As far as he himself was concerned he was vague. Officially he was attached to Giraudoux, but the exact scope of his activities had not yet been defined. He implied fairly firmly that he did not think he would remain in this equivocal position for very long because, being bi-lingual, he felt that he would be more useful as a Military Liaison officer. He concluded by assuring me that he would do everything in his power to help me, and that if I was in the slightest doubt about anything I was to telephone him immediately. As at that moment I was in the gravest doubt about almost everything, it was as much as I could do to restrain myself from asking him the way to the nearest call-box. Realising, however, that such a display of flippancy might be undiplomatic I switched the conversation to lighter topics and, a little while later, warmed by his kindness, but chilled by the foggy indefiniteness of the whole situation, I drove back to the hotel, where I had a brief, discouraged talk with David, and went to bed.

By the end of our first week in Paris we had achieved a little, but not so much as we should have liked. After some telephonic bullying by me, Jean Giraudoux arranged for us to meet Professor Tonnelat, Monsieur Vermeil and a tiny, rather cross Colonel called Schul in the Commissariat d'Information, which, in gayer days, had been the Hotel Continental. All three of these gentlemen had been connected with propaganda during the 1914–1918 war. Professor Tonnelat was harassed but kindly, Monsieur Vermeil was less harassed but equally well disposed, and Colonel Schul was crochety from the outset. I gathered that he had little affection for 'Perfide Albion' and viewed David and me with considerable suspicion, in which I had to admit I saw his point. David, who for secret purposes of State had been created a bogus Captain of an unspecified regiment, looked exceedingly nice in his uniform but lacked military deportment. I was impeccably dressed in morning clothes and looked as if I might be on my way either to the Foreign Office or the Theatrical Garden Party. We were staying at the Ritz, which was undoubtedly a frivolous address, and no one in the Commissariat d'Information had ever heard of Sir Campbell Stuart. However, we pressed on and arranged to have meetings twice a week to discuss 'Directives'. As far as I knew, the 'Directive' of His Majesty's Government propaganda policy at that period was the drafting and dropping of leaflets in tens of thousands on to Germany. The R.A.F. unenthusiastically did the dropping, and the leaflets were closely printed admonishments translated from speeches by Mr Chamberlain and Lord Halifax. Their subject matter was concerned mainly with the fact that war was wicked and peace was good and that the Nazis had better beware because the Allies were very strong indeed and prepared to fight to the death to defend the democratic way of life. All of which was admirable, though a trifle inaccurate and more than a trifle verbose. Some time later I wrote in a memorandum that if the policy of His Majesty's Government was to bore the Germans to death I didn't think we had enough time. For this I was reprimanded. The Germans meanwhile were flooding France with lurid and most effective cartoons depicting carnal British officers raping French ladies in looted châteaux; and baths of blood into which grinning English Tommies were pushing French *poilus*. We had no way of knowing what teasing leaflets our own Government was having dropped over neutral countries, but we suspected gloomily that they were long-winded, moral and ineffective.

I went to the British Embassy to call on Sir Eric Phipps, whom I had known for several years, taking with me a letter from Sir Campbell Stuart. The letter was in an envelope marked 'Very Secret', which was enclosed in a larger envelope marked 'Secret and Confidential'. The Ambassador opened it with a quizzical expression, which turned out to be fully justified, for it was merely a letter of introduction explaining in general terms how charming I was, and how Sir Campbell hoped that Sir Eric would receive me with kindness and give me every consideration. Perhaps galvanised by this, Sir Eric gave me a dry martini and a very good dinner, during which he tried with wily diplomatic suavity to coax my secrets from me. I think he said 'What the hell are you up to?' but I may be misquoting him. At all events I was forced to admit that I hadn't the remotest idea. However, he kindly said that either David or I or both of us could attend the daily Ministry of Information meetings, which took place from twelve to one in a gilded room on the ground floor, and that if we wanted any help in any way the Embassy was always at our disposal. I was touched by this and also soothed, because I was beginning to feel fairly silly.

Perhaps here I had better warn the reader against condemning too hastily my flippancy in describing many of these incidents. Actually it is only now, over ten years later, that I can see those months in Paris in their proper perspective and laugh at them and at myself without bitterness. I am proud to say that even at the time my sense of humour did not entirely desert me, but I was deeply in earnest, and although I could not avoid realising quite early on that the job I had undertaken was neither so serious nor so important as I had been led to believe, I still felt that it had potentialities, and I was utterly determined to make a success of it within or without its limitations. David was equally determined and never for a moment allowed absurdities and discouragements to deflect him. My gratitude to him was then, and is still, profound. At all events we persevered doggedly and managed, after two weeks of cajoling, coaxing, writing and telephoning to Chefs-du-Cabinet, and insisting on interviews with any officials whom we considered might be useful to us, to get at least some idea of the obstacles we would have to overcome and the varying degrees of *laisser-faire* we would have to override before we could rent an office, set up shop and really start work.

During those two hectic and exasperating weeks I decided to avail myself of Hookie Holland's kind offer, and telephone to Dallas Brooks from the Ministère de la Marine to report progress. Feeling suitably mysterious, but without any noticeable disguise, I arrived at the Ministère after seven o'clock in the evening as Hookie had told me to do. No suspicious sentries challenged me and the whole operation was a good deal simpler than going into the Galeries Lafayette. There was a French P.O. in the outer office, to whom I said *'Bon soir'* graciously; he replied with a grunt and made no attempt to prevent me from going into the inner office. I gave the special number to the telephone operator, upon which I heard a shrill scream of laughter and, to my intense surprise, was put through to the British Admiralty immediately. Whether or not the operator was laughing at my accent or at a book she was reading I shall never know. I was put through in a few seconds to Electra House, where Dallas Brooks answered the telephone himself. I at once embarked laboriously on the code he had given me. 'This is Diplomat speaking,' I said. (Diplomat was my code name.) To this he replied rather irascibly, 'Who?' 'Diplomat,' I said again slowly and clearly, and then went on with a rush to explain that I had interviewed 'Lion' (Sir Eric) and established successful contact with 'Glory' (Giraudoux), but had not yet been able to get into touch with 'Triumph' (Daladier), although I had had a charming interview with his Chef-du-Cabinet, whose name I was unable to divulge as we hadn't got a code word for it—— He interrupted me at this point by saying: 'What the bloody hell are you talking about?' Repressing my rising irritation I started from the beginning again, articulating very, very slowly as though I were talking to an idiot child. There was a pause and he said wearily: 'It's no good, old boy, I can't understand a word.' At this I really lost patience and explained to him the code, word for word. This foolhardy betrayal of an important secret must have shocked him immeasurably, because there was a moment of silence and then he hung up. I returned fuming to the hotel, where I typed out the whole thing in a letter which I marked 'Secret, Confidential and Dull'.

He explained some weeks later verbally that he had been asleep when I rang up and thought I was Reggie! An unsatisfactory explanation if ever I heard one. However, he tried to atone for his obtuseness by teaching me another code which really was a code. I think he must have known I should never be able to master it in a thousand years. It consisted entirely of numbers which had to be subtracted and added and multiplied, and as I was then, and still am, incapable of adding up a bezique score, no good ever came of it, and if ever I had been captured by the Gestapo they would certainly have had a tough time getting me to betray it. At the end of the first week of oppressive heat and anti-climax I decided to fly back to England, to explain verbally to Sir Campbell and Dallas Brooks our various difficulties, and to offer a few suggestions for surmounting them.

A number of planes flew to and fro daily, and, provided one had the slightest claim to officialdom, it was easy to get a passage.

David came to Le Bourget with me and saluted self-consciously as the plane took off. The heatwave was over; the weather was sharp and clear and, apart from the strange emptiness of the Channel, the outward aspects of the flight seemed to be much the same as usual; inside the plane of course the atmosphere was different from pre-war days: there were no women wearing mink coats and carrying jewel cases and hat-boxes, no stewards or stewardesses, and no clamorous children. Most of my fellow passengers were in uniform, and the few who were not looked inscrutable and, like me, carried brief-cases and gas-masks.

We landed at Hendon, where I managed to find an Admiralty car which drove me and two others to our destinations.

Upon arrival at Gerald Road I was greeted by Lorn (my secretary) with the gratifying enthusiasm usually accorded to a warrior returning home after several months in the trenches. Jack and Natasha were in London and, having at last succeeded in procuring a passage to America, were due to sail in a few days' time.

After telephoning to Mother at Goldenhurst to let her know that I was so far unscathed, I rushed off to Electra House, where Dallas Brooks and Campbell

Stuart were waiting, without any visible signs of impatience, for hot news from the Propaganda Front. I fear that, as usual, my articulateness overrode my discretion; I talked a great deal and very quickly, outlining the frustrations, obstructions and general apathy that David and I had been grappling with, and pleading earnestly that our position in Paris should be clarified, not only to the French, but to the British Embassy and all concerned. I explained, with some bitterness, that the air of mystery and secrecy surrounding our endeavours was making us appear both pretentious and silly, and was also quite unnecessary because, in actual fact, nothing we were preparing to do was either mysterious or secret. I suggested that a Bureau of Propaganda was a normal institution in war-time and that although later on, when firmly established, it might conceivably be utilised as a cover for less open activities, at the moment of its inception it must be and could be nothing but what it was: an organisation for the dissemination of propaganda into enemy territory. They listened to my tirade indulgently and took me out to dinner at the Carlton Grill.

During the week-end I was invited out to 'Hush-Hush' headquarters and treated by Sir Campbell, as usual, with the utmost charm.

On the Monday I flew back to Paris, having extracted from him a promise to come over himself as soon as possible and assess the various difficulties of the situation at first hand.

A week or so later he kept his promise and arrived, radiating vitality, accompanied by Major Tony Gishford, his secretary, and Dallas Brooks. David and I met them at Le Bourget with a hired car and whirled them in state to the Crillon. During the few days they spent in Paris I watched with interest Campbell's dynamic personality working at full blast. It was a remarkable performance. He flew from office to office and minister to minister; names were scattered through the air like confetti; projects of far-reaching magnitude were discussed, blown up like gas balloons, and exploded painlessly. Bewildered French officials were invited to lunches and dinners, charmed and flattered by his inadequate French but more than adequate persuasiveness, and although, at the end of it, both they and I were still hazy as to what it was all about, the immediate effect was impressive.

On the third day of the visit the same hired car drove us all to Arras to lunch with Colonel Mason-Macfarlane, the Director of Military Intelligence. The luncheon took place in the Hotel de l'Univers. The D.M.I., tall, grey-haired and a trifle bent, had a twinkle in his eye; he had also an individual, almost pedantic way of speaking, and a passion for light verse. I liked him at once and, later on in the war, when he was Governor of Gibraltar, I stayed with him frequently. His second-in-command, Major Gerald Templer, had a swift mind and was extremely nice, but I felt instinctively at the outset that they both viewed Campbell with suspicion. Under their polite, cold gaze, his lively affability seemed to wilt a little; his flattering implications splintered against their flinty disapproval, and even his personal charm took on a rococo quality. I was reminded suddenly of a comedian

I had seen many years before giving an audition to a group of unsmiling managers and agents: in the face of their dreadful unresponsivenes his jokes fell flat, his antics became increasingly strained, and his whole performance, bereft of the laughter which alone could give it life, died coldly on the bare stage. Whether or not Campbell was aware that he was not being quite so easily victorious as usual, I don't know, but I suspect that he sensed the nip in the air.

Dallas remained bland and amiable throughout the meal; David looked slightly uneasy, and I, spurred on by an over-developed social conscience, wore myself out.

After lunch we all assembled in Mason-Macfarlane's office to discuss the intricacies of front-line propaganda and if, when, and how it could be co-ordinated with our less specialised, more general policies. It was finally decided that either David or I should visit the D.M.I. once a fortnight in order to exchange ideas and, by working together in happy liaison, eliminate, as much as possible, the prevailing confusion.

During the four-hour drive back to Paris Campbell was in the highest spirits. We had, he assured us, in an incredibly short space of time, formed a basis of solidarity between the front line and our organisation which, in the ordinary course of events, might have taken weeks or even months to achieve. 'There is nothing so essential in matters of this kind,' he added enthusiastically, 'as the Personal Approach.'

From then on things began to move. David and I were empowered to rent an office as soon as possible, and engage a carefully vetted, tri-lingual secretary. It was also suggested that I find a flat in a conveniently central position in which to entertain not only Mason-Macfarlane when he came to Paris but any other eminent gentlemen, either military or civil, who might be useful to us. Before leaving Le Bourget in a flurry of white snow and black boots, Campbell assured me with the most winning sincerity that not only was he pleased with my work, but absolutely astounded by the swiftness with which I had acquired a complete grip of the whole situation. 'You are doing,' he said firmly as he stepped into the plane, 'a more vital and important job for your country than either you or anyone else realise.'

Reflecting that only the last part of his sentence was accurate, I waved him away into the grey sky and drove back into Paris with David.

2

By the end of October quite a lot had happened. In the first place, Paris, having recovered from the initial scare of being bombed, had begun to come to life again: theatres, cinemas and restaurants opened timidly at staggered hours and staggered days of the week; more people and traffic appeared in the streets; the war clouds receded and banked themselves on the far side of the Maginot Line, and the autumn sun shone with all its might.

David and I obediently rented an office at Number 18 Place de la Madeleine, in which we installed some office furniture and a newly-found secretary, Miss Cameron. Miss Cameron was, from first to last, our greatest asset: she had a dry, Scottish sense of humour, her secretarial efficiency was beyond criticism, she could speak German, French and Spanish fluently, and her political morals, carefully vetted by the Deuxième Bureau, were impeccable. A tall Dutchman with a Scottish title, Lord Reay, was added to our staff. He was most agreeable and ploughed through the reams of secret 'bumph', which was sent to us daily, with a sort of sleepy diligence. Cole, my personal servant, was despatched to me from England by Dallas Brooks, and settled down at once to learn French, which he contrived to speak and read with surprising fluency in a very short space of time. Cole had come to me originally as cook-valet when I was playing *Tonight at Eight-Thirty*, in 1936; since then he had become an integral member of the household, and, after many years and many vicissitudes, he still is. The quality of his mind evinced itself early and Lorn and I soon realised that he was far better read than either of us. At the present moment of writing he has moved up to being my secretary, while Lorn has become my 'representative', a state of affairs that bewilders everybody but us.

With the aid of an old friend of mine whom I had originally met in Rio de Janeiro in 1931, Madame Guinle, I found a flat in the Place Vendôme. It was not large but it was light and gay and very convenient, being in the centre of Paris, and only a short walk from my office. In due course Cole and I moved into it, having bought some fairly expensive furniture at the Samaritaine de Luxe, and taken over the services of the *femme de ménage* Yvonne, who had worked for the previous owners. She was a voluble Lyonnaise, she saturated everything with garlic, and was very good for Cole's French.

About this time it was borne home to me that, although I could speak it fairly fluently, my own knowledge of the French language left a lot to be desired; I decided therefore to take lessons in grammar, and proceeded to look around for someone suitable to give them to me. Subsequently, on the the advice of Louis Jouvet, I interviewed a lady named Blanche Prenez, who agreed to come, either to the flat or to the office, on three afternoons a week, and try to force into my brain the intricacies of French syntax. I warned her in advance that this would be a difficult task, for she would almost certainly discover that she had to teach me English grammar at the same time. She light-heartedly accepted the challenge, and the lessons began then and there and continued until I left Paris finally in April, 1940. Blanche Prenez, apart from being an experienced teacher, was a most endearing character. Her age was somewhere in the late forties; she was dumpy, with twinkling blue eyes and hair that had been dyed several different shades on several different occasions and had at last achieved a variegated permanence. She was fiercely patriotic; she adored the Theatre and her criticisms both of acting and playwriting were shrewd and frequently witty. In addition to all this she contrived, by alternately bullying and cajoling, to instil into me a great deal more grammatical knowledge in a few months than anyone else would have been able to do in so many years. She kept after me remorselessly; she forced me to write pages of subjunctives, one of which was; '*Il faut que vous ne me guillotinassiez pas!*' She made me tell her long stories, during which she corrected me and interrupted me on every line until I could have throttled her; she made me read aloud *David Copperfield*, and translate it into French as I went along and, worst of all, she insisted that, in between lessons, I did homework. I fought like a steer against this but she overruled me, and I was compelled to spend miserable hours in bed, wrestling with the damned subjunctives, declining hideously irregular verbs, and composing bright, informative little essays about the events of the day, which she would gleefully tear to pieces the next time she appeared. Just before I left France I arranged for her to translate my book of short stories, *To Step Aside*, and, I am thankful to say, paid her for the whole job in advance; I have hoped ever since that the money was of some comfort to her, for I never saw her again. In England, in 1944, I received an anonymous message which said she had died of tuberculosis in Nantes; later on I heard rumours that, some while before her death, she had been arrested and tortured by the Gestapo. I have no proof of this, but, knowing her vituperative hatred of the Germans and her fanatical love of her own country, I have a dreadful suspicion that it may be true. I owe so much to her patience, her firmness, and her deep affection, and I should have been so proud if she could have seen me acting in Paris, in French with a French company, in 1948. I can only hope that she would have been proud too, but I rather doubt it. It is strange to recall that, during those gay lessons, we had a recurrent joke which concerned an English lady who spoke French so affectedly that she pronounced 'Dunquerke' 'Doonque-querker!' – an ominous, tragic word on which to base a joke.

Shortly after we had established ourselves in the Place de la Madeleine, I discovered a pleasant-looking, bogus Squadron Leader loitering in the annexe of the British Embassy. His bogusness lay in the fact that he had never been in an aeroplane in his life; the explanation of his uniform was that he was a radio expert and spoke French perfectly; and he was loitering in the Embassy annexe because he required an office to work in and there wasn't one available. Upon learning this I offered him accommodation in our office, which he accepted with grateful alacrity, and moved in immediately. Once installed, he proceeded to wreck, for all time, our one and only radio in the short space of half an hour. From then on he was known affectionately as the Squadron Wrecker. His name was Bill Wilson; he was tall and thin and had a French wife, and a slightly professorial manner which was entirely misleading. He led his own life in our office, where he had technical conferences from time to time with curious gentlemen from the B.B.C., and occasionally disappeared abruptly into the hinterlands of France, from which he assaulted us with highly-coloured post-cards in verse.

Another addition to our personnel was Paul Willert, who was large, articulate and ready to argue heatedly on any given subject. He had a knowledgeable and bitter contempt for international politics; he spoke German and French, and lived with his wife Brenda and a small white poodle in the Place Dauphine. Their apartment was enchanting, and I often lunched or dined there, while the Seine flowed gently by under the windows and we discussed, frequently with considerable violence, the incompetence, negligence and stupidity of those in authority over us. Paul's gift for invective was highly developed and although he occasionally betrayed a certain facile intellectual defeatism slightly tainted with Bloomsbury, and was often madly irritating, I never had a dull moment in his company. In our office he represented the, by then, more furtive side of our activities. His function was to establish private liaison between us (Sir Campbell Inc.) and various reputable and disreputable refugees with whom it might have been indiscreet for the office to have direct contact. Often he would vanish for a while and reappear later wearing an expression of sinister prescience that was hard to bear.

Our staff was now complete except for Peter Milward, an irreverent and cheerful friend of Edward Molyneux's, who volunteered his services and was subsequently installed as a Press Scavenger. His job consisted of wading doggedly through all the French daily newspapers, from which he picked out anything equivocal, subversive or informative, and, having translated it and commented upon it, placed it on my desk. With this expanding *état-majeur* it was not surprising that we became rather cramped and were forced to move to a larger suite of offices on a higher floor.

By November the social life of Paris was in full swing again. Lady Mendl entertained in her famous Villa Trianon in Versailles; the Duke and Duchess of Windsor entertained in their house on the Boulevard Suchet; there were lunch-parties, supper-parties, dinner-parties, cocktail-parties, private views, opening nights; in fact all the clamorous paraphernalia of peace-time existence, with the one difference that we were at war. This embarrassing actuality brooded lightly over the festivities and was seldom obtrusive: the fact of its existence, however, inevitably affected some of the superficial aspects of society. It was considered 'chic', for instance, not to wear evening dress, except in the presence of the Duke of Windsor, who had announced in no uncertain terms that he liked *le smoking*; fortunately there were only a very few mutterings of rebellion against this edict and a soignée time was had by all. There also appeared on the face of *la vie Parisienne* an unpleasant rash of functions and entertainments in aid of war charities. As yet, of course, there had been scarcely enough war to justify them, but they provided a form of occupational therapy for those of Le Gratin whose nerves had been cruelly jolted by the events of the last eighteen months. However, behind this gaily-painted social drop-curtain there was naturally a great deal going on. Droves of cabinet ministers and high-ranking staff officers flew back and forth between London and Paris, and were photographed, singly and in groups, looking appropriately grave. Conferences of far-reaching significance took place daily in the War Office, the Invalides, the Commissariat d'Information, the Quai d'Orsay, the Ministère de la Marine, and Maxim's.

My conferences, on a lower scale, were held twice a week, alternately in my office and in Professor Tonnelat's office in the Hotel Continental. They were, on the whole, fairly dreary. Occasionally Mason-Macfarlane with Ewan Butler or Gerald Templer appeared and enlivened proceedings a bit, but even so I cannot believe that much was achieved beyond the exchange of a few ideas which were seldom put into execution.

On January 1st, 1940, I began, for the first time in my life, to keep a day-to-day diary and, although it is neither detailed nor comprehensive and consists usually of little more than a small page of scribbled telegraphic sentences recording the events of the day, it has been of value to me in writing this book. To any reader other than myself I fear that it would appear fatuous to the point of idiocy. Few memorable aphorisms adorn its pages, and as it is written the last thing at night when I am tired and sleepy, it is slap-dash, repetitious, and frequently illegible. Nevertheless, it serves its purpose as an aid to memory, and despite the fact that it has less literary value than a railway time-table, for me, and for me alone, it is evocative and, every now and then, curiously touching. So often when I open it at random I come upon a phrase, written in the long vanished heat of the moment, that sends my mind hurtling back to stare in dismay at the picture of myself sitting up in some strange bed in some strange hotel or tent or ship, writing down the day's frustrations with an indelible pencil and a desolate heart. The Paris entries in this journal are, however, less poignant than some that came later on in the war, and I find, on re-reading them, that the deepest emotion they arouse is irritation. It was certainly a period of anti-climax, and although there was a tremulousness in the air, a sense of unease, it was too vague to weigh heavily on people's spirits; in fact it is questionable whether or not the large majority was even conscious of it. I believe, or rather I like to believe, that I was, but I am not sure. It is so easy, when reconstructing the past, to endow oneself with superior foresight. Of course I should like to feel that, however blind and obtuse others may have been, I was one of the few who really sensed impending disaster. It seems incredible now, in the lurid glare of later events, that I lived through those months without a twinge of premonition, but perhaps I did; perhaps, with so many of the people I knew, I averted my gaze from the sinister horizon and assumed that somehow or other everything was going to be all right. My diary, I am bound to admit, records no specific flashes of clairvoyance: it records annoyances; books read; lunches and dinners eaten; occasional diatribes against the incompetence of officialdom; convivial evenings with the D.M.I.; quiet evenings with Edward Molyneux. It also records the hectic arrivals and departures of Campbell Stuart and his entourage; some fairly acrid descriptions of 'Policy' conferences, and a few sidelights on characters and personalities; but nowhere in its pages can I find, alas, a nice meaty example of true prophetic instinct. I have searched through it meticulously hoping against hope to discover some illuminating phrase such as: 'Saw Daladier today – He says definitely, that France will be invaded, defeated and occupied in the early summer – Oh dear!' But no, the numbered days are void of prescience.

3

Gallantly determined to overcome my inherent detestation of fixed routine, I arrived resolutely at the office every morning between nine and nine-thirty and sat, swathed in supreme authority, at my desk. Miss Cameron bashed away at the typewriter in the next room, from which I gathered that she must have an extensive circle of acquaintances; large trays of papers were brought to me daily – the papers were mostly mimeographed copies of the B.B.C. Monitoring Service, which was efficient but verbose, and they were marked 'Secret', although any interesting information they contained had usually appeared in the Continental *Daily Mail* three days before. During our first weeks in the Place de la Madeleine, buoyed up by a grinding sense of duty, I read them through page by page, marking with a red pencil any items that might be of interest to our organisation, and passed them on to David, who marked what he thought might be useful to us with a green pencil. After this, as far as I can recall, they were never seen again. By noon the office was generally a hive of activity. Peter would appear brandishing a scurrilous attack on somebody or other in one of the French 'dailies'; Paul would put his head round the door and say, in a voice choked with sinister implication: 'I've got to meet someone at Weber's – I may be quite a long time!' – and disappear; David would burst in, white with rage over a letter from London H.Q. which had completely disregarded an urgent question he had written a week previously. Reay, who shared David's office, typed laboriously and interminably, although to this day I have not the faintest idea what he could have been typing. Occasionally odd people would come to see me; among them a madwoman who arrived one morning in a red hat, and announced that her husband had been killed in the 1914–1918 war and that because of this she had nourished ever since an undying hatred for the Germans. I nodded sympathetically and said that I saw her point. She then said, with a certain peremptoriness, that she wished me to arrange for her to be sent immediately to Frankfurt, that her cousin had married a metallurgical engineer there in 1932 and that this fact would provide good cover for her. I explained gently that the dispatching of secret agents to Germany was not my department, and suggested that she go to the Deuxième Bureau, where they specialised in that sort of thing. She asked me whom she should interview there, which flummoxed me for a moment, but I rallied quickly and said: 'General Poincingy-Duclos, and say that I sent you.' With this I asked David, who was purple in the face, to show her out.

Our big moment in the office occurred two or three times a week: this was the arrival of 'The Bag' from London. 'The Bag' was heavily sealed and contained, in addition to the inevitable wads of B.B.C. monitoring papers, our personal letters. It was always opened with ritualistic solemnity, and occasionally I spoke a brief incantation over it before the seals were broken. When we had all grabbed our private mail the intensive business of the office subsided until we had read them. My own letters were usually from Mother, Lorn, Joyce or Gladys, and occasionally a verse from Winifred (Clemence Dane). I found it nostalgic, immured in my Parisian vacuum to read titbits of gossip and news from my other life, which, it seemed, was going on very nicely without me: plays were opening and closing; so-and-so had fallen down in the black-out and bruised her knee; there had been a blazing row at the Actors' Orphanage between the matron and the headmaster; The Ivy was more crowded than ever at lunch-time; James Agate had said something disagreeable to Lilian Braithwaite, who had retaliated; the clock still stood at ten to three and there was honey still for tea. Frequently when too oppressed by these echoes from dear green England, I was compelled to leave the office abruptly and have a very good lunch. Of course I flew home to dear green England whenever opportunity offered, and this occurred on an average about once a month. I usually managed to arrive on a Friday, discuss whatever had to be discussed with Campbell or Dallas, and spend the rest of the weekend with my loved ones. They were happy interludes and I looked forward to them eagerly.

My first evening in London was almost always spent in Clemence Dane's rickety little house in Tavistock Street, Covent Garden. There we all foregathered: Gladys, Lorn, Joyce, Dick Addinsell, Olwen (Winifred's secretary), Winifred herself, and Ben (her neurotic fox terrier). Winifred is large in every way, and her capacity for friendship is without limits; apart from her recognised fame as a writer she is a brilliant sculptress and painter, and her vitality is inexhaustible. From 1930 onwards, whenever I have returned from abroad, or even from the wilds of Manchester, I have always winged my way, like a homing pigeon, to that cosy, friendly, long-suffering room on the first floor overlooking the market. I say 'long-suffering' because the poor place has to put up with a great deal: its pictures are changed constantly; it is often flecked with paint and spattered with clay; it has been deafened for years by discussions, play-readings, piano-playing and film conferences; it has been barked in, sung in, shouted in, eaten in, and, occasionally, slept in; it has had to endure sudden, unpredictable onslaughts of tidying, which ill become it, and its walls are sodden with argument. It has also had to stand firm, not only against enemy bombing, but against the impact of violent personalities both alive and dead: Queen Elizabeth, Nelson and Shakespeare are constant habitués, together with Sybil Thorndike, Alexander Korda, Alfred Lunt, Lynn Fontanne, Katharine Cornell, Mary Martin, etc., etc., not to mention Winifred herself. If its walls have ears, I can only hope that they had the sense to plug them with cotton-wool many years ago.

Back in Paris after these brief excursions, life continued its routine course. It would be unfair to emphasise too heavily its monotony because there was always something going on to agitate us mildly and keep us on our toes, but, on the whole, I felt then, and I feel now, that our work was sadly lacking in importance. This was neither Campbell's fault nor ours; we did our best with the material at our disposal, and he did his best to encourage and help us in every way possible, but I suspect, although I have no actual proof of it, that he was considerably more ham-strung by bureaucratic intrigue than he cared to admit.

That there was an overlapping of policies and directives there can be no doubt, both in France and England. There was no supreme head of Propaganda appointed in either country. Had there been, the various groups and organisations which were all working away so industriously and so separately might have been successfully co-ordinated; as it was, everything seemed to be in a tangle, and there was nobody with enough power and authority to unravel it. Certainly, in my opinion, there was far too much importance attached to secrecy. Hardly a missive arrived in our office that was not stamped either 'Secret' or 'Confidential', and in nine cases out of ten anything contained in them could have been read aloud in the Reichstag without menacing Allied security in the least.

Naturally enough the words, 'Secret Service' and 'Intelligence' have a melo-dramatic ring about them: there is always a certain fascination, not only for the thriller-trained layman, but for many of those actually engaged in Intelligence work, in the fact of knowing something that many other people don't know; in being privy to information which, if it leaked out, might seriously effect the trend of great events. This is understandable and perfectly valid when the information concerned genuinely is secret, but when nearly all official papers, regardless of their contents are religiously stamped 'Secret and Confidential' it becomes both tedious and confusing. I came to the conclusion early on in the war that there were far too many adult, sometimes elderly, men in official positions who had never outgrown their schooldays; a great number of them still retained a perennial 'boyishness' which was particularly noticable in intelligence matters. In some of my later contacts with such men I remember often feeling surprised that they didn't suggest that we crouch down under the desk and play Indians.

The Secret Service virus was epidemic in Paris in 1940. Everybody was up to something, especially, of course, those who were up to nothing. The most unexpected people would arrive suddenly from London, wrapped in mystery and wearing strange, secretive smiles; indeed one young man whom I had known slightly for years came out into the open and announced to me firmly, with his habitual stammer: 'I am h-h-here on a t-t-t-terribly s-s-s-secret m-m-m-m-mission!' To many of my acquaintances, both in Paris and London, it was a foregone conclusion that I was involved in espionage up to the eyebrows, and it was quite useless for me to protest against their implications, because whenever I did so they merely smiled knowingly and ostentatiously changed the subject. Finally I was forced to give up the struggle and look as mysterious as everybody else.

Shortly after Squadron-Wrecker Wilson joined us in the Place de la Madeleine I asked him to explain to me, as simply as possible, the technicalities of radio, warning him at the same time that my obtuseness in such matters was appalling. I have tried at various times of my life to grasp the rudiments of inventions such as the telephone, the camera, the wireless telegraphy, and even the ordinary motor-car, but without success. My mind, when faced with such, to me, miraculous phenomena, becomes a blank, and I am ashamed to admit that a ten-year-old boy of average intelligence has a far clearer conception of the marvels among which we live than I could ever hope to achieve.

I have driven cars of all shapes and sizes efficiently for thirty years, but if any piece of their mechanism happens to require the simplest adjustment I am utterly confounded and have to walk to the nearest garage. I have even flown an aeroplane without disgracing either myself or my instructor, but no one has yet been able to make me understand why or how it takes off, flies through the air, and comes down again. Television, of course, and Radar and Atomic Energy are so far beyond my comprehension that my brain shudders at the very idea of them and scurries for cover like a primitive tribesman confronted for the first time with a Dunhill cigarette-lighter.

When depressed by these vast fissures in my intelligence I comfort myself, defiantly, with the reflection that as there are quite a number of important things that I do know about, I had better content myself with these and waste neither my time nor my energy endeavouring to acquire knowledge which my brain resolutely refuses to accept. In 1940, however, I was still foolhardy enough to hope that, if I really concentrated, really willed my mind into a state of receptiveness, I could learn at least some of the basic principles of White Man's Magic, and by doing so increase my efficiency in my job. Bill Wilson persevered and after a while I could talk fairly glibly, although without profound conviction, about 'Alternating wave-lengths,' 'Cross-bearings', 'Jamming', etc. This stubbornly learned but, alas, ephemeral knowledge nevertheless stayed long enough in my mind to enable me to accomplish at least one job of relative importance, actually the only achievement during the whole of my time in Paris upon which I can look back with real pride; a pride that is in no way lessened by the fact that the entire affair was quite outside my province and none of my business.

It had been agreed between the French and the English in August 1939, that in the event of hostilities all radio activities in France should be centralised, all transmissions controlled and restricted to certain wave-lengths, and all independent, commercial and unofficial stations shut down immediately. One morning towards the end of October, Bill, pale with anger, burst into my office with the announcement that although 'Radio Normandie' had obediently closed down according to decree, a small commercial station at Fécamp, only a few kilometres distant from it, was blasting away merrily by night and by day. It was obvious, even to me, that this station, situated where it was, could provide cross-bearings for enemy aircraft on their way down the Channel to bomb Portsmouth, Southampton, and other towns on the south coast of England. From that moment, egged on by Bill Wilson, Douglas Colyer, the Air Attaché, and later by other R.A.F. officers, I started a determined campaign to get Fécamp closed down, and finally, on January the 4th, two months later, it was.

During those two months, however, I learned a lot. I learnt, for instance, that men of apparent integrity, occupying positions of considerable responsibility can when financial interests are involved, behave with shoddy evasiveness. I learnt that graft, corruption and petty intrigue, far from diminishing in time of national emergency, seemed to gain from it an added impetus; all of which of course I should have known before, but at that time, on the threshold of middle age, I was still naif enough to be shocked. It is to this day a matter of surprise to me that I worked myself into such a state over that damned radio station, and although, as things ultimately turned out, I am glad that I did, I am still faintly puzzled that I should have fought so doggedly over it and minded so much. I can only assume that, at the moment when Bill first mentioned it to me, I must have been going through one of my periods of frustrated zeal.

First of all I flew to London and explained the situation to Campbell Stuart and Dallas Brooks, both of whom expressed appropriate concern and, having agreed that it was a disgraceful breach of security, presumably wiped it from their minds. Next I tackled Lord Chatfield, the Minister for Co-ordination of Defence, who, being an old friend, saw me immediately and listened carefully and seriously to what I had to say. When I had finished my story he told me not to worry any more, because a minute had been signed by the War Cabinet two weeks previously ordering the Fécamp radio station to shut down at once. I received this reassurance with scepticism and asked him if he had a radio handy; he replied that he had, and led me to it, whereupon, with a beating heart, I fiddled inexpertly with the controls for a few moments until suddenly, to my mixed fury and relief, there it was: 'Radio Fécamp broadcasting a programme of recorded dance music.' Lord Chatfield was genuinely astonished and very angry indeed, and, after thanking me for bringing it to his notice, ushered me out.

I returned to Paris glowing with the consciousness that I had been instrumental in getting a dangerous wrong righted, and feeling that at least I had made a small but bona-fide contribution to the war effort. However, my glow faded swiftly a few weeks later when I discovered that not only was Fécamp still operating as usual but that it had never closed down for a split second.

By this time my blood was up and I proceeded to unearth a number of disturbing facts. One of these was that fairly eminent French politicians were financially concerned in the enterprise.

At about this time Winston Churchill was making one of his periodic visits to Paris and so, nothing daunted, I telephoned Duncan Sandys, his son-in-law, who was accompanying him, and asked if Mr Churchill could see me for ten minutes as I had something of considerable urgency to bring to his notice. I was not in the least surprised when Duncan replied that an interview with Mr Churchill was out of the question as he was occupied every moment of the day; however, he went on to say that if I cared to pop round to the Ritz and explain to him what my urgent business was, he would pass it on to his father-in-law if an opportunity presented itself.

After a quick check-up with Bill on the technical aspects of the situation, and praying that I should be able to explain briefly and concisely the one all-important fact that danger threatened our south coastal towns from any transmitting station in the Normandy area, I hurried off to the Ritz, where Duncan Sandys was waiting for me in the foyer.

We sat down in two heavily brocaded chairs and I proceeded, as intelligibly as I could, to put the facts before him. Perhaps I was over-eager, too emphatic; perhaps my sense of drama over-coloured and over-weighted my argument, because I felt, while I talked, that my words were falling on stony ground. He was polite and attentive and listened indulgently, but there was something in his manner that gave me the impression that he was humouring me, like a benevolent uncle who nods understandingly when his small nephew announces shrilly that he has just seen three full-blooded pirates in the back garden. After the interview, when I rose to go, he smiled charmingly and said what a good idea it would be if only I could write a gay, morale-lifting war song, something on the lines of 'Mad Dogs and Englishmen'. I knew then how dismally I had failed, and with a sad heart left him, reflecting on my way back to the office that the Churchill family's passion for 'Mad Dogs and Englishmen' verged on the pathological.

A few days later, by which time my determination had become almost fanatical, I called upon one of the eminent French politicians who was interested financially in Radio Fécamp. The E.F.P. received me graciously and spent about twenty minutes explaining how passionately devoted he was to the Arts, and that all he had ever really wanted to do in his life was either to write or paint or compose music. I gathered from his conversation that his admiration for me was unbounded, and that if he only had one tenth of my glorious talent he would have renounced the drab world of politics years ago and been a far happier man. I listened to all this with becoming modesty and waited for the pay-off. This came when presumably he considered that I was sufficiently soaked with flattery to accept it.

Abruptly, and with a marked change of manner, he said that he had heard that

I had been concerning myself with the question of whether or not a certain radio station at Fécamp should continue to operate. I smiled ingenuously and admitted that I had heard the subject discussed at various times, but that as my knowledge of such matters was virtually non-existent I was not really qualified to give an opinion either way. I here interpolated a self-deprecatory giggle, as one artist to another, implying that he could speak freely without there being much danger of my being able to understand more than the simplest aspects of the situation. The giggle must have reassured him, for he launched forth immediately into a lengthy refutation of all the arguments against Fécamp and explained, with slightly overdone emphasis, that the whole matter had been gone into by experts, and that although there were certain scaremongers who feared that transmissions from that area might provide enemy aircraft with cross-bearings on their target, such fears were unfounded and nonsensical, for the simple reason that all radio stations shut down automatically the moment an Alert was sounded.

I listened to this rationalisation with what I hoped was the right degree of puzzled attentiveness, and had the sense not to remind him that the crux of the whole argument lay in the fact that Fécamp could provide guidance for enemy aircraft long *before* they were identified and the Alert sounded. Encouraged by my docile acceptance of his explanation, he produced a typewritten brochure setting forth all the arguments in detail. I looked at it wistfully, wondering what possible wiles I could employ to induce him to let me take it away with me. I knew that if only I could get it to my office, have it translated into English, and give copies to the various air authorities concerned, it might be possible to get any specious statements it contained officially refuted. I glanced at it casually while he stared at me and drummed his fingers on the desk, then I handed it back to him with a light laugh and a shrug of the shoulders saying that it was far too long and involved to be taken in at a sitting, I would take his word for it. This indication that my interest in the affair was obviously superficial seemed to relieve his mind and, after a moment's thought, he handed it back to me again and said that he would hate me to have any misapprehensions about the situation and that I could take it home with me and study it, on the strict understanding that I show it to no one else and would promise to return it to him by special messenger the following morning. Still protesting that I probably wouldn't be able to understand a word of it, I placed it in my pocket and switched the conversation back to Art. He was an urbane and affable man and we parted in a shimmering haze of mutual compliments.

The next morning I had the brochure returned to him by special messenger, having had it copied, translated and sent to the Air Attaché. After that nothing happened for a while, until one morning Air-Marshal Barratt called me up from Rouen and said that Fécamp was still functioning in spite of all orders to the contrary, and that the moment had come for pressure to be brought to bear on Monsieur Daladier and General Gamelin. I protested that I knew neither Daladier nor Gamelin personally and that, although I fully realised the seriousness of the situation and was willing to do anything in my power to help, actually it was none of my business, and should be handled by the British Ambassador. The conversation ended with him urging me, in the event of non-co-operation from the Ambassador, to do the best I could. Startled, and of course flattered, by his confidence in my powers, I contacted Douglas Colyer, the Air Attaché, immediately, and we went to the Embassy to call on Sir Ronald Campbell, who had only recently replaced Sir Eric Phipps. Sir Ronald listened to what we had to say and agreed that something should be done, but I could sense from his manner that he felt it to be more a Service problem than a diplomatic one and, I suspected, was understandably wary of involving himself in what might turn out to be an unpleasant and complex imbroglio. At all events he said that he would make enquiries and do what he could.

A day or two later, as nothing had transpired, I embarked on a course of action which was slightly dishonest but, on the whole, enjoyable. I went to call on Jean Giraudoux wearing an expression of dreadful urgency, and told him, in the strictest confidence, that I had heard, on impeccable authority, that a scandal of horrifying dimensions was about to burst regarding Radio Fécamp. I told him that the Press were all standing by ready, and that the resulting repercussions would not only cause grave inter-Allied disunity, but would almost certainly unseat the Government. He appeared to be considerably disturbed by this information, particularly as he himself, quite unwittingly, had authorised a message of Christmas cheer over Radio Fécamp only a week or so previously. He was a dear man and I felt a twinge of conscience at upsetting him, but I also felt that the end might justify the means. I insisted that he procure for me an interview with Daladier's Chef-du-Cabinet immediately so that I could place the whole matter before him myself. He agreed to this and rang up then and there for an appointment.

About a quarter of an hour later Monsieur Genebrier received me, and I went through my whole act again, implying a close personal liaison with both the English and French Press which was entirely imaginary. Monsieur Genebrier, looking as startled as poor Giraudoux, assured me that he would approach the Prime Minister that afternoon and telephone me the result at five o'clock. I said firmly that on no account was he to do any such thing; that my connection with the matter was unofficial and my warning confidential. I then left him with the assurance that I would communicate privately with the Air Attaché, who would be awaiting his telephone call punctually at five o'clock.

At five thirty that afternoon Douglas Colyer called me up triumphantly to say that he had received a notification that Fécamp would be shut down finally at midnight. As a matter of actual fact it wasn't shut down until forty-eight hours later, but the battle was won, and I felt quite light-headed with relief and extremely pleased with myself. The whole affair had been an obsession with me for weeks, and whether or not my conviction of its importance was exaggerated, it seemed to me then, as it does now, that for financial interests to be permitted to override security measures in time of war was both sinister and disgraceful.

Perhaps I made a cracking fool of myself. Perhaps my dramatic sense over-egged the pudding and inflated it out of all proportion to its actual significance. Certainly, by poking my nose into what was officially none of my business, I made a few powerful enemies. At all events it was done; the piddling little radio station was closed down, and Bill Wilson, Douglas Colyer and I celebrated the occasion by giving ourselves an excellent dinner and then going on to hear Edith Piaf sing in her night-club.

As far as I was concerned the affair had one very agreeable repercussion. At the beginning of April I was invited by Air Marshal Playfair, who was the Air Officer Commanding in France, to visit him at his headquarters in Rheims. I took a long week-end off from Paris and duly arrived on the morning of April the 6th. I was met by a cheerful Squadron Leader called Hamilton whom I had known before, and for three days, either in a camouflaged car or in a small reconnaissance plane, I was driven and flown to our Advanced Striking Force stations, and discovered many old friends that I had known at Lympne and Singapore and other parts of the globe before the war. Back in Rheims I was wined and dined and made much of. It was a gay and exciting interlude and I shall always be grateful for it.

4

From the beginning to the end of my time in Paris I was victimised, even more than usual, by my own publicity value. Certain sections of the English Press were irritated, I suppose naturally enough, because they had been given no information about the job I was doing. As a matter of fact it would have been perfectly simple to have issued a statement at the outset explaining that I was working for the Government as the official representative of Sir Campbell Stuart, but this was not done and as I had been told by both Campbell and Dallas that on no account was I to give any newspaper interviews, nor discuss my activities with anyone beyond those who already knew, my status was never clearly defined, and I had to press on in exasperated silence against a rising tide of absurd mis-statements and far-fetched rumours, one of which, at least, caused me much personal annoyance and, I suspect, a certain amount of public harm.

Sometime in early 1940 a paragraph appeared in the 'Peterborough' column of the *Daily Telegraph*, announcing that I had been seen 'sauntering along the Rue Royale in naval uniform'. Hookie Holland was temporarily in London, and I immediately got through to him at the Admiralty and asked him to have the statement officially denied. I know that he did his best, but whether he succeeded I never discovered. In any case it was too late; the damage was done, and a short while afterwards the *Sunday Pictorial* came out with a two-page attack on me, shrilly demanding, on behalf of the British Public, why a well-known theatrical 'Playboy' should be allowed to don, at will, the uniform of one of the Fighting Services. This sanctimonious article, written in the usual oleaginous journalese, brought forth a flood of letters from strangers, some anonymous, some signed; some insulting or downright abusive, and some merely sorrowful or contemptuous. I found this hard to bear, but what annoyed me most was the thought that such shameless and bland inaccuracy should be read, believed and commented on by many thousands of my countrymen whose affection and respect I had striven to gain through all my professional years.

Actually, of course, it wouldn't have mattered so very much if it had been true. Many men of unquestioned integrity accepted honorary rank in the Services during the war when the exigencies of their jobs, or the area in which they worked, made it more convenient. Indeed the question of whether or not I should wear some sort of uniform had been discussed by Campbell and Dallas and me in the early days of my appointment. They both seemed to think it a good idea as a means of facilitating any journeys I might have to make through military zones. I held out against it on the grounds that I thought I could be more effective as an independent civilian; the same argument I had used in 1939 when I had been offered the honorary rank of Lieutenant-Commander R.N.V.R. after my participation with Lord Louis Mountbatten in the forming of the Royal Naval Film Corporation. I hated having to refuse the honour because for me it would have been a most gratifying accolade, but I sincerely felt that considering many of my naval friends were commanders and captains – indeed some of them were admirals and commanders-in-chief – it might be embarrassing for them to see me come bouncing on board their ships, glittering with unearned gold braid, and compelled to salute them whenever they spoke to me.

I believe, had it been really necessary to my job in 1939, that Their Lordships of the Admiralty might have been induced to renew their offer, but it was not really necessary.

And I felt strongly that my name, my reputation, and my friends would get me wherever I wanted to go within reason, an assumption which I am proud to say was abundantly justified during the later years of the war.

Another, more light-hearted, Press episode occurred in early December. Douglas Colyer, who was then still a Group Captain, telephoned me one morning in great glee to say that he had been made an Air Commodore and had a very fetching brass hat. I told him to come round at once and show it to us. This he did and the staff saluted and curtseyed with proper deference. We had nothing to celebrate with except some not very good sherry and a glass jar of boiled sweets from Boissier's which we couldn't open. When we had drunk some of the sherry I presented him officially with the sweets, and he promised that he would get one of his minions to open the jar and would send some back to us in an envelope marked 'Secret'. A few minutes later when I was in the lobby seeing him out, I said, in a sharp, peremptory tone, 'Please see about that Boissier business as soon as possible.' Assuming an air of meek subservience, he said: 'Aye, aye, Sir,' saluted, and disappeared into the lift.

It was then I noticed a strange young man who had evidently secreted himself behind the door when I opened it. Realising that further concealment was impossible he stepped forward and said that he had been sent by the *Daily Express* and would I give him an interview? I replied that I was very sorry but my orders were to give no Press interviews in any circumstances. Unrebuffed, he advanced closer to me and peered inquisitively past me through the open door into my office. 'My Editor wishes to know,' he said, 'just exactly what war work you are engaged in.' Aware that it would be impolitic to lose my temper I explained to him gently that I perfectly saw both his and his Editor's point, and that although I was not at liberty to discuss my work, I could at least assure him that it was a routine job; that there was nothing mysterious about it, and that I would be sincerely grateful if he would take my word for this and do me the honour of regarding me, for the duration of the war, as an ordinary civilian and not as a theatrical celebrity. I then rang for the lift, ushered him into it, and away he went.

The next morning I was called up by the censorship department of the British Embassy. 'We have just had to censor a startling article about you,' said a voice with a slight giggle in it. 'It states, among other things, that "Mr Noël Coward, in impeccable civilian attire, sits all day behind a vast desk in a luxury office in the Place de la Madeleine, issuing orders to officers of the highest rank"!'

That was one of the few occasions in my life when I have been profoundly grateful for censorship.

In November I was asked by the Military Attaché to appear at an Anglo-French troop concert in the theatre at Arras, and to persuade Maurice Chevalier to appear too. Maurice, after a little coaxing, agreed, and in due course we set off along that interminable road on a bitterly cold Saturday afternoon. There were to be two performances on Sunday and Monday evenings respectively, and a full dress-rehearsal on the Sunday afternoon.

The first performance was attended by the Duke of Gloucester, Anthony Eden and a group of Dominions V.I.P.s who were making an official tour of the area. Among these was a good-looking Australian of middle height with a forceful personality and rather bushy eyebrows. His name was Richard Casey, and on the Monday morning, just before he left with the others for Paris, we had a drink and a brief discussion of the shape of things to come, in course of which he told me firmly, for there was nothing equivocal either in his speech or his manner, that I owed it to myself to visit Australia. He spoke lovingly and with humour of his own land, and I liked him so much that I found myself agreeing that, whenever opportunity offered, I would fly straight to the Antipodes. The significance of that encounter was not apparent at the time and we parted as casually as we had met.

By March, 1940, I began to get restless. My initial patriotic fervour had evaporated in a haze of anti-climax and, apart from my gratuitous interference over Radio Fécamp, it seemed to me that I had achieved very little. My position remained ambiguous officially, and although both Campbell Stuart and Dallas Brooks assured me that I was doing a useful job, I was becoming increasingly aware that actually I was doing nothing at all beyond presiding at meetings, at which much was discussed but little achieved; giving diplomatic dinners and lunches occasionally to various Big Shots passing through Paris; and generally providing a pleasantly social façade, behind which a great deal should be happening, whereas in point of fact nothing was.

When Campbell and Dallas and entourage descended on us for brief visits the tempo increased and the temperature rose. We gave two large lunch-parties in a private room at Larue's for Campbell to meet certain eminent members of the French Governmental hierarchy with whom we were supposed to be in constant and breathless contact. The first one was more or less work-a-day, with the dear professors and others from the Commissariat d'Information, interspersed with prominent journalists such as de Kerillis, 'Pertinax', Buré, etc. The second one, however, was sensational and included among others our own British Minister, Oliver Harvey, all three Service Attachés, Hookie Holland, Douglas Colyer and Willie Collier, and, as a political *bonne bouche*, Paul Reynaud and Georges Mandel, whom I placed on either side of Campbell with myself opposite so that I could keep one ear cocked and be ready to intervene in the event of any lingual emergencies. Campbell behaved beautifully until the end, when he inadvertently lost a good deal of the ground his charm had gained by announcing that he had to leave immediately for an appointment with General Gamelin. Before I could stop him he had risen, shaken hands briskly with Reynaud and Mandel, and vanished like a dancing dervish. Whether or not he actually had an appointment with General Gamelin was beside the point. What really mattered was that even supposing he had an appointment with the King, Churchill or the Dalai Lama, he had commited a grievous offence against the laws of protocol by leaving before two eminent French Ministers. I watched Paul turn scarlet and David turn pale, and the three of us launched ourselves upon the rapidly stiffening guests of honour with such a spate of gay, flattering conversation that they had no time to take more than inward umbrage. Finally they left, mollified I hope, if a trifle confused.

An air of misty indecision enveloped our propaganda activities. Every now and then, during our conferences, somebody would give birth to a fairly good idea and for a while we would all enlarge upon it eagerly, but by the time it had been referred to the High-Ups in the Commissariat d'Information and to our own headquarters in England, and various modifications had been suggested and argued about, whatever effectiveness the original idea might have had was dissipated and it disappeared into the limbo never to be heard of again. Personally I contributed one sound suggestion, but nothing came of that either. The Germans at that time were boasting that the R.A.F. had never flown over

Germany. As we knew perfectly well that night flights were frequently made over Berlin in order to drop the usual turgid pamphlets, which were immediately collected by the police and disposed of before dawn, I recommended that, instead of dropping leaflets which were of a size easily discernible on the darkest night, we should deluge the city with specially made sticky confetti, each scrap of which should have the Union Jack on one side and the Tricolor on the other. I contended that if bags of this were scattered from a great height, the confetti would stick to the roofs and pavements and window-sills, thereby convincing the sceptical Berliners that the R.A.F. could reach their town easily, and have the added attraction of driving the police agents mad. This idea was ultimately turned down on the grounds that it was too frivolous. Under such cutting criticism my creative impulse withered and I settled back to listen politely to other, less provocative and more seemly suggestions.

The office was running smoothly. There were Cabinet crises and reshufflings. The days and weeks went by.

On looking back now on those strange, frustrating months, I find it difficult to believe that I ever lived them at all. They seem in my memory to be, not exactly vague, but irrelevant, almost as though I had dreamed them.

9. As Captain (D) in *In Which We Serve*

10. With Judy Campbell in *Blithe Spirit*

11. With Judy Campbell in *Present Laughter*

12. As Frank Gibbons in *This Happy Breed*

13. With the R.A.F., Middle East, 1943

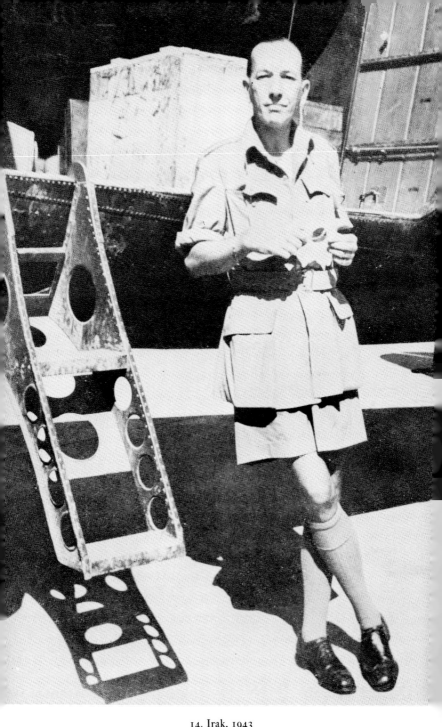

14. Irak, 1943

15. Alderley Street, Cape Town

16. With American troops, Assam

PART THREE

I

On the evening of Thursday, April the 18th, I left Paris. David, Paul, Peter, Bill and Cole saw me off at the Gare de Lyon. The station was dimly lit owing to the 'blue-out', but apart from this the departure seemed to be much the same as usual; grey women in overalls were wheeling trolleys festooned with pillows, trolleys with magazines and papers, and trolleys with ham rolls, chocolate, fruit, biscuits, and bottles of wine. There was the usual smoky, railway-station smell and the usual din. I leaned out of the window of my sleeper talking and laughing with my see-ers-off as I had done so often in the past; the familiarity of the scene was intoxicating and nostalgic at the same time. I might have been off on a holiday to St Moritz, Cannes or Venice: the hour was the same, the place was the same, even the train looked almost the same although perhaps a little less clean than it used to be. I shouted parting instructions, drank everyone's health from a small, flat bottle of cognac that Bill had given me, and implored them all to press on valiantly, to be good and noble and true and, above all, to see to it that Number 18 Place de la Madeleine upheld its world-wide reputation of being the most efficiently organised, smoothly run and vital weapon of political warfare in existence. The train began to move, they laughed and waved, and Paris slid away from me for five years.

I settled back on the hard, dusty, blue upholstery, took another swig of cognac and relaxed. I felt light-hearted, more so than I had felt for months: I was off on my travels again and although I was bound neither for St Moritz, Cannes nor Venice, it was even so, in many respects, a holiday. Six weeks would pass quickly, but in their passing they would let a lot of fresh air into me, and the monotony of office routine and all those depressing meetings would perhaps feel less oppressive when I returned in June. The wagon-lits attendant in familiar brown uniform came in to collect my ticket and passport; the usual urgent little man passed along the corridor ringing a bell and shouting 'Première Service'; the train, gathering speed, rattled and swayed through echoing suburban stations until presently the rhythm became steady and set and there was nothing to be seen from the window but my own reflection mirrored in blackness.

Early in March, during one of my flying visits to London, I had dined with Campbell and explained that I was becoming oppressed and irritated by the Paris routine and by the growing conviction, despite his encouraging assurances to the contrary, that I was achieving very little. In the early days when we were establishing the office, forming liaisons and seeking contacts, my celebrity value, allied to my theatre training in organisation, had been useful, but now, when everything was running smoothly and all necessary contacts had long since been consolidated, I sincerely felt that I was becoming increasingly stale and ineffective; David ran the office far more efficiently than I ever could; everything was under control, there was no longer any need for improvisation, bluff or show-off, no further necessity for making snap decisions and cutting through bureaucratic pomposities and red tape; there were no longer any crises, excitements and sudden urgencies, and no more hurdles to jump. I am sure that Campbell, who was no mean psychologist, recognised in all this, plausible as my arguments were, that the real truth lay deeper. It was, in fact, my same old trouble: the gnawing, irrepressible restlessness, the longing for change, the stubborn resistance to routine that had conditioned all my years in the Theatre and out of it.

Campbell, whose swift ear discerned, behind my arguments and explanations, the frenzied beating of wings, looked at me with a quizzical twinkle in his eye and said that I could take six weeks' leave in April. Later on, the matter was further discussed and both he and Dallas decided that if I took my six weeks in the United States, which was what I wanted to do, it might turn out to be very useful from several angles. They said, with truth, that I could, at least, travel about a bit, listen to what was being said, talk to leading newspaper owners and editors, etc., and obtain a certain amount of first-hand information on the general attitude of mind. I asked Dallas if he would like me to send him a weekly resumé of my observations in a code to be selected by him, but he shuddered and said 'No.'

I dispatched a cable to Jack, hinting that he might expect to see me in April, and settled down impatiently for the time to pass. I arranged to sail on the S.S. *Washington* from Genoa on April the 20th, although both Campbell and Dallas seemed to think, taking into account my Press reputation as an international naval spy, that it might be risky for me to travel alone and unprotected through Italy. I don't believe that they seriously envisaged any actual danger, but they did point out that if by any chance any trouble should occur, it would be difficult to extricate me from a neutral country.

If anyone had told me at that time that I was high up on the Nazi black list, I should have laughed and told him not to talk nonsense. In this, however, I should have been wrong, for, as it ultimately transpired, I was. In 1945, when the Nazi list of people marked down for immediate liquidation was unearthed and published in the Press, there was my name. I remember that Rebecca West, who was one of the many who shared this honour with me, sent me a telegram which read: – 'My dear – the people we should have been seen dead with.'

When the Germans invaded Norway and Denmark, the atmosphere in Paris changed completely overnight: to say that it lightened would be inaccurate, but it certainly became more alive. The moribund lassitude of the last few months vanished, there was a nervous excitement in the air and I felt, walking down the Boulevard des Italiens, as though the voices of everyone had been raised a full tone. It was of course the same, irrational, 'Something is going to happen at last' sense of relief that I had felt in England when, after so much dread and anticipation, war was finally declared. The Commissariat d'Information was full of unaccustomed bustle and fuss and tremulous with surmise. Our own office reacted differently but definitely. David became paler than ever and looked grave; Paul wandered in and out with an 'I told you so' expression on his face; Bill looked resigned and tried repeatedly to get through to the B.B.C. Peter kept on appearing and re-appearing with news bulletins from the Press; only Lord Reay and Miss Cameron remained apparently unmoved and continued to type. I too was infected by the 'Something is going to happen at last' contagion, but the realisation that this would almost certainly cancel my trip to America depressed me. A little later, after the first excitement had died down, and after Mr Chamberlain had announced roguishly that Hitler had 'missed the bus', I flew to London to see Campbell.

To my surprise he said that in the present circumstances he thought it was even more important that I should go to the States than it had been before. The reaction of the Americans to the sudden break-up of what they themselves had christened the 'Phoney War' would be interesting to observe at close quarters, and any personal reports I sent back to him on the subject might be extremely useful. This was a relief in one way, but I felt reluctant to leave the office and the staff and the job just as things were beginning to be exciting. At all events it was finally decided beyond further equivocation that I was to leave Paris as arranged on April the 18th, get myself on board the ship the moment I arrived in Genoa and remain locked in my cabin until it sailed. On looking back, this over-cautiousness appears to be fairly idiotic, but I suppose, at the time, it was quite sensible. In any case I was forced to disregard it, for upon reaching Genoa in the afternoon of the 19th I discovered that, even if it were possible for me to get on board the ship twenty-four hours before sailing time, which was doubtful, I should not be able to take my luggage with me and could expect neither food nor service.

Not fancying the idea of spending the night locked in a stuffy cabin with neither pyjamas, tooth-brush, food nor drink, I gallantly snapped my fingers at peril and went to the best hotel, where I engaged a comfortable room with bath. Later on, further emboldened by an excellent dinner and a half-bottle of Chianti, I walked recklessly out into the crowded streets without even pulling my hat over my eyes. I wandered about through the arcades, sat outside various cafés, sipped Drambuie, watched the people, and bought a large packet of nougat. Just before midnight I arrived back at the hotel unmolested and went peacefully to bed, reflecting that either the great Gestapo scheme for luring me into Germany and extracting from me, on the rack, the secrets of Number 18 Place de la Madeleine had gone badly awry, or that the Nazis just didn't care.

I got myself and my luggage on board the *Washington* the next day without incident. The sun was shining, the dock was crowded, and people were screaming and yelling and throwing paper streamers as though there were no war anywhere and nothing but gaiety, cheerfulness and good fellowship from one end of the world to the other.

The Captain invited me to sit at his table and also to have a drink with him in his cabin. His name was Harry Manning, and he was typically American in the best sense: tough, humorous, and easy-going. He was an ex-flyer and had flown a great deal with Amelia Earhart. In course of conversation I remember asking him whether or not, in the event of a German submarine stopping the ship in mid-Atlantic and demanding my body, he would hand me over. 'Sure,' he said. 'Why the hell shouldn't I?' I took an immediate liking to him.

The voyage was without incident. I relaxed and read and slept and prepared my mind for the inevitable impact of New York, an impact which had always, even in times of peace, been strong and over-stimulating and which, in present circumstances, might put a severe strain on my self-control. The American attitude to the European war during the period of apparent anti-climax between September, 1939, and April, 1940, had been growing more and more irritating to those immediately concerned with it. The Isolationists' – 'Let 'em get on with it – it's none of our business' – viewpoint had been clearly expressed in various American newspapers and magazines and I had noted, in several of the correspondents and other visitors from the States, a determination to regard the existing stalemate as a comforting proof that nothing further was going to happen. There was also the line, taken by many, that America, having once pulled England's chestnuts out of the fire and won the last war for her, was not going to be so easily fooled a second time, and even supposing that the war flared up into a conflagration that destroyed the whole of Europe, she, America, would remain neutral and unscathed, swish aside her skirts from the dust of conflict, rise above the entire abortive situation and, by so doing, fulfil her rightful destiny as the one inviolable sanctuary of Democracy in Western Civilisation.

Even my experienced and loving affection for America suffered a slight setback in the face of such naïve and shrill whistling in the dark. Admittedly, what small knowledge of international affairs I had was very recently acquired, but, even so, it seemed to me that for adult citizens of a great country so blatantly to pull the wool over their eyes was a frightening proof of the human capacity for self-deception.

Having for many years regarded America as my second home, I was naturally more concerned by all this than many of my countrymen who, less fortunate than I, had never enjoyed American hospitality, never experienced that welcoming, ardent kindliness and had no personal ties and memories and affections over the water.

Crossing the ocean again in an American ship, my mind was troubled with apprehensions. I was longing to see New York once more, to see my friends, to go to theatres, to look from high windows at the lights of that fabulous city. I looked forward also to American trains, to sandwiches in drugstores, to weekends in Connecticut with Jack and Natasha, and the view from my little bedroom on the top floor, across the sound to Long Island. There was so much of America that I knew well and loved and respected, and now, owing to war, and heightened temperatures and fears released, it might be difficult, less welcoming, it might indeed be infuriating.

2

My determined efforts to steel myself against the impact of arrival turned out to be a waste of nervous energy, for this instance proved to be in no way different from countless other arrivals. The Press reporters and photographers came on board at Quarantine and were as friendly to me as they had always been in the past; nobody snarled any virulent isolationism in my face; there were no tasteless witticisms about the 'sit-down war'. There was the usual queuing up for the Immigration authorities; the usual rushing about and noise and chaos, while the city of New York glided by in the morning mist, the ferry boats hooted, and the small, stocky tugs nuzzled and shoved the ship alongside the dock. Jack and Natasha were waiting at the foot of the gangway.

Not having much luggage I got through the Customs swiftly and was soon driving across town to the St Regis. When the first spate of *non-sequitur* and mutual gossip had exhausted itself and we had had cocktails and lunch at Twenty One, Paris, England and the war had receded so far that I wouldn't have been surprised if Jack had suddenly informed me that rehearsals started on Monday, and that the opening date had been changed from Wilmington on the 23rd to New Haven on the 27th.

The air was quivering with theatrical tension because Lynn and Alfred were opening that very night in the new Robert Sherwood play, *There Shall Be No Night*. After lunch we went along to the theatre, where we found Alfred in the throes of last-minute lighting. After a little while Lynn appeared, having been leaving flowers for me at the St Regis, and we sat in the empty theatre all talking at once while the stage lights went up and down and on and off. Then, for a sudden moment, surrounded by my old friends, I was stricken with a dreadful homesickness for the past, a sickening longing to be part of it all again instead of just a visitor from another world on six weeks' leave.

At six-thirty, Neysa McMein, another of my very dear ones, appeared at the hotel and we talked while I finished dressing. Neysa was one of the rare people in the world whose genius for friendship could pierce through all façades, surmount all defences and find its way immediately and unerringly to the secret heart. This exquisite sensitivity she preserved untarnished until the day of her death in 1949. Never, in all the years I knew and loved her, did I see her foolish or flurried or mistaken. The quality of her own truth was so wise and sure and so rich in humour that it gave grace to everyone who knew her, which was a prodigal output, for her friendship embraced all sorts and kinds and classes of people. In case I should be accused of over-idealisation, of praising her too highly, of allowing my own affection for her to blind me utterly to her defects, I will add that her clothes were erratic, her political views frequently unsound, her spelling appalling, and her luck at games of chance maddening. At all events, when she arrived at the St Regis that evening, her instinct told her at once that beneath my joy at seeing her and in spite of the fun and excitement of being in New York again, there was a core of uneasiness, an area of discontent somewhere that had to be dealt with. While I was dashing in and out of the bathroom, putting cuff-links into my shirt and grappling with my tie, she proceeded to deal with it so thoroughly and so effectively that by the time we had joined Jack and Natasha for dinner my fears had vanished and I was in such a mood of wise, kindly, international tolerance that if anyone had rushed up to me brandishing the Stars and Stripes and screamed, 'England is done for and the British Empire stinks!', I should merely have smiled sweetly and said, 'God bless you.'

The first few days passed in a whirl as the first few days in New York invariably do. It always takes me at least a week to become acclimatised, to be able to put myself down, to be able to sleep for more than five hours a night. Reunions with old friends, theatres, suppers, Press interviews: all, or nearly all, pleasurable and stimulating, and all, or nearly all, cheerfully insignificant. Jack and Natasha were deeply involved in the organisation of a Gargantuan Allied Relief Ball which was to be held at the Hotel Astor on May the 10th. Jack was running a cabaret in a private room, and so I immediately became involved too, and spent a great deal of time rushing from theatre to theatre and dressing-room to dressing-room persuading glamorous stars to promise to appear.

On the Saturday afternoon I drove out to Jack's house in Fairfield, Conn., with Hope Williams. We purred along the wide interminable boulevards of the Bronx; past the familiar rash of lunch-counters, gas-stations, vacant lots and immense blocks of apartment buildings in course of construction. Further on, in the hinterland of Connecticut, where there are small hills and valleys, orchards and twisting roads, it is possible for a fleeting moment, every now and then, to imagine that you are in England, Buckinghamshire perhaps, somewhere between Fulmer and Gerrards Cross, or Kent, on the road from Canterbury to Maidstone before it joins the main by-pass; but the illusion is transient, for the quality of the land is different, less trodden down by the centuries, less secure, and far less gentle. I always feel that in America the land itself, however smooth and well cultivated it may be outwardly, has no inward acquiescence; it is as though it were not yet quite broken in, still half-tamed and a bit skittish; as though it still had hopes of winning in the long run. On the main highways, of course, it is so tame that it sits up and begs; shackled by intersected parkways, made foolish by hoardings, drive-ins, road-houses and hamburger heavens, it knows it is beaten and can only retaliate mildly by effacing itself to such an extent that it has no resemblance to country at all. I often feel when driving along the Merrit Parkway, for instance, that I might just as well be indoors.

Hope Williams another of the enduring bonds that bind me to America, I had first known in the 'twenties in the full flush of her brilliant but disappointingly brief stage career. A curious shyness, a certain detached spiritual independence prevented her from enjoying completely her success in the theatre. She had a charming speaking voice and delivered lines in a special way of her own, with a sort of beguiling tonelessness. She always looked well-groomed and her clothes were as much a part of her personality as her cropped blond hair and quizzical blue eyes. She was slangy without being vulgar, modern without being brash, and her gaucheries of movement had a peculiar grace. Her popularity was considerable; her name flared up in lights for a little, and then, suddenly, it wasn't there any more. Her nervousness and diffidence and lack of ego lured her away to gentler pleasures and, ever since, she has lived contentedly for a large part of each year on a ranch in Wyoming. She, like Neysa, had her own brand of quiet wisdom and, driving along in the car that day, not having seen her for at least two years, there was no need to explain anything; I could just talk at random, generally or intimately, without the faintest likelihood of being misunderstood.

Jack's house stands on a ridge overlooking a golf course and the Sound. At night a lighthouse flashes, and in day-time in the summer white-sailed yachts form a little corps de ballet in the distant harbour. None of it had changed since I had last seen it in 1938. In the spring of 1940 it felt enviably peaceful. I looked out of the window at the view while I was changing for dinner. Dusk had fallen, the lighthouse was already on the job, there were no ominous undertones, no fears nor dreads nearer than three thousand miles; serenity lay over the scene, indeed, I felt it lay over the whole continent of America, like a cellophane wrapping, keeping out all the dangerous germs and viruses of war and disruption, preserving every vitamin intact. I tried to envisage a squadron of Messerschmitts flying in low over the darkening water, the bombs curvetting down and tearing ragged craters on the golf course, ripping through the wooden frame houses, leaving flame and smoke curling up into the sky. I listened with my mind's ear to the harsh staccato splutter of machine-gun fire, to the wail of sirens; but I could neither see nor hear any of it, it was too far-fetched, too absurdly beyond the bounds of possiblity.

Alfred and Lynn came down on the Sunday and we discussed the play and the notices, and the war and me and Paris, and the invasion of Norway and the play and the notices.

The next morning I flew to Washington. I felt, having promised Campbell a report on my personal observations of the general situation, that Washington would be the best place to start observing. Paul Willert, who was an old friend of Mrs Roosevelt's, had given me a letter of introduction to her, and so, when I had settled myself in the Carlton Hotel, I sent it round to the White House by special messenger. This done, I went to lunch at the British Embassy, where I sat next to the wife of the Australian Minister, who told me that her husband, Richard Casey, had met me in France and very much wanted to see me again. This was a pleasant piece of luck, and we agreed to get together at Walter Lippmann's on the following evening and make a date. She was gay and intelligent and there obviously was no nonsense about her, and one more link was forged in the chain that was to lead me across the world.

In the evening I dined with Joe Alsop. The evening was hot, so we dined in the garden and no word of the conversation, which was largely political, could have rasped the nerves of the most vulnerable Englishman. The dinner-party was select and consisted of Felix Frankfurter, Senator Murphy and Senator Byrnes. They talked sensibly; their opinions seemed to me to be the result of careful consideration and were neither swayed by bias nor tainted by wishful thinking. I also felt instinctively that, courteous and pleasant as they were, they were none of them likely to soft-pedal their views merely because there was an English visitor present. They appeared to accept as inevitable America's ultimate participation in the war, and to face a truth which so many Americans were reluctant to admit: that the present conflict, although still confined to Europe, was not merely a squabble between far-away decaying nationalisms, that could safely be allowed to burn itself out in a splutter of remote gunfire, but was a world issue far transcending the predatory, racial wars of the past, on the outcome of which depended the survival of Western Civilisation. The conversation, however, was not exclusively devoted to such grave matters. There were jokes as well and lightness of touch and delicious food and wine. Altogether it was a well-mannered, adult evening, and I returned to my hotel a great deal the better for it.

The next day a note arrived from Mrs Roosevelt inviting me to dine that night. This flung me into a slight dilemma, for I had already arranged to dine with Walter and Helen Lippmann, but I rang them up and explained truthfully how anxious I was to meet the President and Mrs Roosevelt and that probably such an opportunity would not occur again, whereupon they gracefully forgave me and I promised to join them at eleven-thirty.

Upon arrival at the White House I was led, much to my surprise, directly to the President's study, where he received me alone and we talked, uninterrupted, for quite a while. So much has been written about Franklin D. Roosevelt, so much love, hate, praise, blame, vilification, prejudice, abuse and hero worship have been poured over his memory, that one more personal impression of him cannot matter either way. I never knew him well although we met subsequently on two occasions. I knew nothing of his alleged perfidies, his political treacheries, his reckless expenditures, his double-faced diplomatic betrayals and his unscrupulous egomania. I know nothing of them now. All I knew of him then and later was that he had kindness, courage and humour. Even discounting his personal charm, which was impressive, these qualities seemed to me to be perfectly clear in him. Perhaps his immediate friendliness to me, his utter lack of pomposity, his apparently effortless manner of putting me at my ease, blinded and flattered me to such an extent that my critical perceptions atrophied. Perhaps it was all a professional trick; perhaps such facile conquests were second nature to him and the whole performance was a habitual façade behind which he was regarding me with cynical contempt. If this were so I can only say that he went to a lot of trouble to deceive me, and for motives which must remain for ever unexplained.

His study was typical of him, I think. It was furnished unpretentiously and in quiet taste: there were a number of personal knick-knacks and books and models of ships; his desk was solid and business-like, although at the moment it had banished affairs of state for the day and given itself up to frivolity, for it was littered with an elaborate paraphernalia of cocktail implements. There were bottles, glasses of different sizes for short and long drinks, dishes of olives and nuts and cheese straws, also an ice bucket, a plate of lemons with a squeezer, a bowl of brown sugar, two kinds of Bitters and an imposing silver shaker. Among all these the President's hands moved swiftly and surely; they were flexible hands and never erred, whether he happened to be looking at what he was doing or not. He was evidently proud of his prowess as a barman, as indeed he had every reason to be, for the whisky-sour he finally handed me was perfect.

Throughout the whole operation he talked incessantly. He commented guardedly on Neville Chamberlain, glowingly on Winston Churchill and casually on international affairs. He jumped lightly from subject to subject, occasionally firing a question at me and suspending cocktail-mixing for a moment while he waited for my reply. He even told me a few funny stories, at which my heart sank, for as a rule I resent and despise funny stories, but he told them briefly and well.

Presently Mrs Roosevelt came in with Miss le Hand and Mr and Mrs Henry Morgenthau. The President proceeded to mix a fresh brew of whisky-sours and the conversation became general. The first thing that struck me about Mrs Roosevelt was her grace of movement; the second, that she was as warm and approachable as her husband. Never having seen her before I was surprised to observe how discourteous cameras had always been to her: they had shown merely a heavy face with a too large mouth; their inaccurate lenses had transformed her wide friendly smile into a grin and ignored the expression of her eyes, which was gentle and slyly humorous; they had also ignored her quality of distinction, which, in its essence, was curiously Victorian; I could imagine her driving through the nineteenth-century English countryside to take tea with Mrs Gaskell.

When dinner was announced she ushered us all out of the room first and the President remained behind. When we were settled in the dining-room he was wheeled in by his valet, who transferred him from his invalid chair to his ordinary chair at the head of the table. This operation was effected smoothly, without fuss, and without the faintest suggestion of spurious gallantry. This good-looking man, bursting with energy and vitality, bearing so lightly the heavy responsibilities of his position, just happened to be paralysed from the waist down and that was that; it seemed to be the most natural thing in the world and cried for no pity.

It is an established rule that no liquor may be served in the White House and so, fortified by the illicit Presidential whisky-sours, we settled down to pleasant food and delicious iced water.

After dinner I obliged with a few songs at the piano, and noted with a pang of dismay the President's marked partiality for 'Mad Dogs and Englishmen', which he made me sing twice. It could now only be a matter of time, I thought, before I received an official request from him to go to Norfolk, Virginia, and sing it to the naval cadets. Happily, however, this idea didn't occur to him, and after a little while the party broke up and he asked me back to his study for a night-cap. This time he talked specifically about the war and America's, as yet, confused attitude towards it. He explained, candidly and without prejudice, the point of view of the Isolationists and the various political, emotional and religious elements underlying it. He had, I felt, a personal admiration and affection for England, but he, rightly, seemed to consider that it was unnecessary to stress this and spoke of our problems and policies and statesmanship realistically rather than sentimentally. When finally I rose to go he asked me to come and see him again before I returned to Europe, and I left the White House with the conviction that it was fortunate, not only for Great Britain, but for all the democratic peoples of the world, that the man in command of the vast resources, potentialities and power of the United States of America possessed both vision and common sense.

By the time I arrived at the Lippmanns' house most of the party had left, but Richard Casey and his wife were still there and we sat out on the porch where it was cooler and talked about Australia, or rather they did. As I had noticed when I first met him in Arras, Casey's whole personality lit up when he talked of his native land; Maie, his wife, shared his enthusiasm, and when finally I had left them and retired to bed in the Carlton, my mind was so stimulated that I couldn't close my eyes, and I lay in the darkness while a procession of Koala bears, kangaroos, sheep and wallabies, occasionally shepherded by Marie Burke, whirled through my brain together with a series of confused visions of stately eucalyptus trees, mountains, valleys, deserts and limitless sandy beaches. I ultimately fell into a deep sleep troubled by regret that Mother and Father had not had the sense to emigrate with me in 1905, instead of merely moving to Lenham Road, Sutton, Surrey.

The next day I flew back to New York and spent the afternoon listening to Moss Hart read me his new musical play, which was to be called *Lady in the Dark*, and was destined for Gertrude Lawrence. Although I had not heard the score, the book seemed to have the authentic ring of success. Gertie, as usual, was undecided, she wouldn't say 'Yes', she wouldn't say 'No'; Moss, treading for the first time this well-worn path of anxiety and frustration, implored me, almost tearfully, to reason with her. He seemed to be so agitated, so obviously heading for a nervous breakdown, that I agreed to coax her, or failing this, bash her into definite acceptance. Consequently, a few days later, I took her out to lunch and wagged an authoritative finger in her face as I had so often done in the past. She shilly-shallied a bit, took refuge in irrelevancies, giggled and finally gave in. All things considered, it was a profitable little lecture, for *Lady in the Dark* proved to be one of the greatest triumphs of her career.

Many months later, in March 1941, when I was passing through New York on my way back from New Zealand, I saw her in it and watched, spell-bound, the brilliant assurance with which she wove her way through the intricacies of that varied and difficult part. The play had not then been running very long and her performance was still fresh and exciting. Gertrude Lawrence, of all the actresses I know, could, when she was playing true, give me the most pleasure. Having worked with her a great deal and known her all my theatrical life, it was doubly fascinating to sit in a crowded theatre and observe what she did with words and music that had not been written by me; with scenes that I had not directed or even seen rehearsed. I remember her on the opening nights of *Oh Kay* and *Nymph Errant* sweeping, with her rich talent, the whole audience into frenzies of applause. Watching her in *Lady in the Dark* with a loving but critical eye, I saw her do it again. Except for two scenes in the psycho-analyst's office when she over-dramatised, her performance was magnificent, no one else could have done it, I, who knew by heart every trick, mannerism, intonation and turn of her head, was as completely enslaved as if I were an enthusiastic layman seeing her for the first time. Later on, I believe, she slipped a bit and began to embroider and over-emphasise, but this I never saw. All I saw was Gertrude Lawrence at her very best, which, to me, means a great artiste.

On the evening of May 9th, 1940, the night before the great Allied Relief Ball, I went over to Werba's Theatre in Brooklyn to see Katharine Cornell play *No Time for Comedy*. After the performance Neysa and I went back with her, Guthrie McClintic, Gert Macey and Margalo Gilmore to supper in Beekman Place. Every evening I have ever spent in that quiet house, overlooking the East River, has had its own special enchantment.

It was late when I left and I walked back across town to the St Regis through the nearly empty streets, reflecting happily how much I was enjoying myself and how comforting it was to be back again for a little in my own 'world', which, although esoteric and generally deaf to the clamour of international affairs, can give much to those who really belong to it. I had no regrets, beyond a little superficial nostalgia, about leaving it temporarily, because I knew that when the war was over I should be back in it, casting, arguing, rehearsing, slapping on the Max Factor, exhorting some people not to over-act, imploring others to put more into it; thanking and blessing audiences for their wonderful receptiveness; cursing them under my breath for being a lot of wooden-headed clods. I should know again all the stresses and strains, the fussings and fumings; the gloomy conferences and inedible meals in provincial hotels, the awful final dress-rehearsals in provincial cities; above all, the feverish concentration, the elimination of the outside world and all that was going on in it, when a new scene had to be written or one of the cast fired and replaced. All this I missed sorely and when I compared it in my mind with the Paris office, the policy meetings, the lunches and dinners clanking with axes to grind, I shuddered and my heart sank. It sank still further a few minutes later when the elevator boy at the St Regis told me with dramatic glee that Germany had invaded Holland. I let myself in to my suite, sat down and lit a cigarette: sleep was out of the question, and there didn't seem to be anything else to do.

The next day was horrible, horrible and interminable. Headlines screamed from all the papers; radio programmes were interupted constantly by 'Flash' announcements; there was a note of hysteria in the voices of the announcers: some were vibrant with melodramatic implication, some heavy with doom. I was surprised to find that I definitely missed the maddening suavity of the dear B.B.C. boys. I went round to Jack's flat early and we crouched over the radio, Natasha in tears and me with lead in the pit of my stomach. Jack was quiet, miserable and exasperated. I think his exasperation was due to a subconscious awareness that the fact of his being an American separated him from Natasha and me. To a certain superficial extent this was true. Natasha, as usual in times of stress, spoke mostly in French: we were both so ineradicably European and this was, all too obviously, the beginning of the end for Europe. It was worse for Natasha than for me. Being an Englishman, I was more insular, a little more detached than she. I had then, and preserved all through the grim years to come, a strange, deep-rooted conviction that, whatever happened on the other side of the Channel, my own country would somehow survive. She, although Russian-born, was, to all intents and purposes, French. Most of her youth, and all her adult life until she married Jack in 1937, had been spent in France. France was the home of her loves and memories and allegiance. Here in New York, married to an American, she still felt herself to be an alien and I knew, much as she loved Jack, that she was suddenly lonely with that bleak, desolate loneliness which only foreigners in strange lands can ever really experience. Naturally, on that bright spring morning in New York, neither she nor I could foresee with what appalling swiftness the French 'débacle' was approaching: there was still room for hope; still reason for believing, with the British Expeditionary Force intact on French soil, that combined Allied resistance might succeed in beating the Germans back. There was still indeed the Maginot Line.

Added to our sick feeling of dread was the minor but unpleasant realisation that we had the Allied Relief Ball to get through. Obviously, postponement was out of the question and the only thing to do was to put on bright faces and endure it as best we could. The very idea of dressing up, being gay, dancing and singing songs, seemed, in that beastly moment, to be macabre. However, it had to be faced and so we pulled ourselves together and concentrated for the rest of the day on dealing with last-minute details. I had immediately sent cables to Campbell, Dallas and David saying that I wished to return, but I couldn't hope for a reply until the following day.

The Ball that evening was a great success and our private cabaret a triumph, in spite of the fact that there were far too many people, and there was the usual clamour of all the stars wanting to go on at the same moment. Gertie Lawrence was tireless and no trouble at all: she merely looked lovely, did everything she was asked to do, and worked unflaggingly.

At seven o'clock in the morning, Jack, Natasha, Joe Moon, my accompanist, and I had breakfast in Child's Restaurant on Broadway, blinking in the light of day and far too exhausted to feel any emotion at all. The headlines in the morning papers screamed louder than ever, but we shut our eyes and ears to them and went wearily home to bed.

A cable in reply to mine arrived from Campbell Stuart, also one from David in Paris. The tenor of them both was the same: they both stressed the point that although the war situation had taken a grave turn for the worse, everything was under control as far as our organisation was concerned, and my return would not affect matters either way. Campbell's indeed told me specifically to stay where I was until I heard from him. Accepting this as a veiled reminder that I had agreed to utilise at least a part of my leave in making out a private report for him on what I had heard and observed, I decided, without much enthusiasm, to carry on with my plans as arranged. These included visits to Chicago, Los Angeles, San Francisco, Salt Lake City, Omaha, Cincinnati and Cleveland. On Monday the 13th, therefore, I boarded the train for Chicago..

It is difficult to recapture now, so many years later, my feverish discontent during these few weeks in the States. All the amenities, the material comforts, of American life that I had so much looked forward to were there to be enjoyed, but somehow, somewhere there was a catch in it. The over-luxurious journey from New York to Chicago in the 'Twentieth Century'; the red carpet laid across the platform; the obsequious coloured porters in their white coats; the deep arm-chair in the club car; the superlatively dry dry martini before dinner; the dinner itself, perfectly served and of such infinite variety, so far removed from the sullen table d'hôtes of our own dear Southern Railway; the wide commodious bed stacked with pillows, the efficient, hygienic private lavatory; the celestial iced water with which I could slake nocturnal thirst by merely turning on a special tap. All these unspiritual but positive delights were there in abundance as usual, but my sybaritic pleasure in them had evaporated; the fearful winds of war and change and disruption had blown it away. Instead of soothing me, pouring balm on my exacerbated nerves, these triumphant symbols of man's progress from the straw pallet, the ox cart and the outside privy merely irritated me: I felt perversely and, I am sure, wrongly that I should have welcomed the ox cart and the outside privy and slept more tranquilly on a straw pallet after a dinner of herbs and a nice glass of mead.

My dry martini was spoiled for me by the conversation of two commercial gentlemen sitting opposite me: they both wore garish neck-ties and were abusing, at the top of their lungs, President Roosevelt, Mrs Roosevelt and everything they either of them said or did. The edge was taken off my appetite at dinner by a repellent small boy at the next table across the aisle, who was accompanied by a stout, doughy-looking woman, presumably his mother. The boy, in the intervals of shovelling food into his mouth, was explaining, in a monotonous nasal whine, the abysmal inanities of some comic strip he had been reading. The din he made was abominable, but nobody made the faintest effort to control him, indeed several of the other diners clucked and smiled indulgently, which, of course, encouraged the horrid little extrovert to further transports of exhibitionism. The peace of my wide, luxurious bed was destroyed for me by an article I read in one of the magazines I had bought at the station. The article, purporting to be written by an authority on international affairs, was unsigned, and so charged with hysteria, pseudo-religious pacifism and anti-British bias that it flung me into a passion, and I spent wakeful hours tossing and turning and planning in my mind crushing replies to it. None of them were ever written or even thought of again, but the composing of them lulled me eventually to sleep.

Chicago was stimulating theatrically but politically unrewarding. I was there too briefly to have time to contact strangers, and the town was full of old friends. Clifton Webb was playing *The Man Who Came to Dinner* at the Selwyn: Tallulah Bankhead was in *The Little Foxes* at the Sam Harris next door, and Katie Hepburn was drifting huskily and enchantingly through *The Philadelphia Story* at the Blackstone. We had supper-parties at the Ambassador East, during which arguments about the world situation flared up with histrionic ferocity. Tallulah was garrulous and frequently sound in her opinions, although the violence with which she stated them proved them to be based on emotion rather than 'high reason and the love of good and ill'. Katie's comments were sensible, to the point, and generally designed to curb the ebullience of Van Heflin, her leading man, who, either from genuine conviction or from a mischievous pleasure in taking the opposite side, repeatedly threw pinkish monkey wrenches into the works, thereby drawing explosions of Southern wrath from Tallulah, acid reproofs from me and a few scandalised ejaculations from Clifton.

Present on the first of these occasions was a Chicago lawyer named Tom Underwood. I watched him sitting quietly with a Scotch highball in his hand and a twinkle in his eye while the spate of words frothed and foamed around him. He seldom gave an opinion on any of the world-shaking issues under discussion, unless directly appealed to, but when he did, he spoke with such authority and was so evidently well informed that I resolved to talk to him alone. On my second morning in Chicago I therefore called him up, and we had a quiet lunch, during which he confirmed the impression I had gathered the night before: that he was well informed, that he spoke with authority because he knew what he was talking about, and that his was one more name to write down on my private list of Americans who, in spite of being so far removed geographically from the war, refused to allow their minds to be deflected by Isolationist propaganda and realised, without panic or prejudice, the full implications of what was taking place. These implications we discussed at lunch and his understanding and acceptance of them reassured me on several counts, the most important of which was the fact that despite many indications to the contrary, such as the magazine gurglings of muddled sentimentalists, the scared fulminations of ill-informed senators and the flagrant anti-British diatribes in the Hearst Press, there were, in every major city of the United States, a number of men at least who were capable of independent thought and who, in the dangerous times ahead, could be relied upon to preserve their integrity and stand firm on the most essential premise of all, which was that England and America should stick together in sickness or in health, in peace or war, profit or loss, for ever and ever, Amen. It is incredible to me that any adult of reasonable intelligence could deny this obvious truth for a moment, but many doubted it then and many doubt it still. Today, with the wind rising again and the skies darkening, the asses are still braying, the saboteurs are still busy, not only the paid ones, the professional trouble makers whose appointed job it is to reduce civilisation to anarchy, but the silly men, the little men, the bigots, the fanatics and the fools. It is a desolate spectacle, as depressing now as it was then. Tom Underwood, if he should ever read this book, will doubtless be surprised that he made so lasting an impression on me. I have never seen him since and he could never have guessed, on such a fleeting acquaintance, how eagerly and gratefully I welcomed that, on the whole, unremarkable conversation.

I left Chicago on the night plane for Los Angeles, seen off, in a blinding rainstorm, at one o'clock in the morning, by Clifton, Katie and Tallulah. It was an elaborate plane with every modern convenience; I had a bunk to sleep in and, happily, no magazines to read.

Cary Grant met me at the airport and drove me to his small house by the sea in Santa Monica. He was friendly and cheerful as usual; the house was comfortable; he gave me a car and chauffeur and a valet of my own so that I should be in no way dependent on his comings and goings and could drive about, elegantly pressed and groomed, to visit the studios and call upon my friends. He and Randolph Scott shared the house, which was on the beach, and we lay in the sun, swam in the redundant pool, with the Pacific pounding away a few yards from us, relaxed and gossiped and, for a little, the war turned away and allowed me to have a good time. Hollywood is lavish to its visitors, particularly if the visitors have any claim to celebrity. In my case I had it both ways. Leaving aside the harassing but flattering attentions of Press photographers, radio agents, newspaper columnists, etc., I had a number of friends, some of long standing, whom I was eager to see. In the course of those very few days it seemed to me that I saw them all, and more. There was hardly a dull moment, or even time for introspection, except on the rare occasions when I found myself alone in my car driving from somebody's house to somebody else's house. There were cocktail-parties, dinner-parties, studio luncheons, interludes in projection rooms looking at unfinished movies, and longer interludes looking at completely finished ones. There was also an impressive banquet given by Darryl Zanuck for Winthrop Aldrich, the Head of the Red Cross. The keynote of the occasion was patriotism and a number of English actors present made moving speeches. I sat gripping Madeleine Carroll's hand under the table and feeling rather out of it.

Meanwhile the war news got worse and worse. I had a small radio in my bedroom to which I listened each morning while I was having breakfast. Outside, the ocean glittered and the famous Californian sunshine gave monotonously the best performance of its career; the mountains stood about idly like benevolent Nannies keeping a protective eye on their infant charges playing in the park. Behind and beyond them were two thousand miles of deserts and plains and flourishing, populous cities reaching to the Eastern Seaboard; beyond this were a further three thousand miles of grey sea stretching to the shores of Europe, breaking on the edge of that cruelly darkling plain 'where ignorant armies clashed by night'. They clashed by night and they clashed by day: along the once peaceful roads German tanks were advancing relentlessly; German aeroplanes were filling the once quiet air with hideous sound and scattering the earth with death. The British Expeditionary Force was trapped. It was unlikely that more than a few thousand English soliders would be able to escape. England was waiting, calmly of course, but with the dreadful, controlled calm of someone who knows that catastrophe is imminent and is yet powerless to avert it. Englishwomen were running their houses, queuing up for their groceries, serving in canteens, driving cars, working in factories, offices, theatres, cinemas, hospitals and ministries, with, all the time, the growing realisation that hope was fading, that only a miracle could save their sons and husbands and brothers and lovers from annihilation. The minor miracle that did occur – the fabulous victorious defeat of Dunkirk – was still nearly a week away.

I, eating scrambled eggs and crisp Beechnut bacon in a bedroom overlooking the Pacific, was five thousand miles away, and I suddenly knew that I couldn't bear it and that I must leave at once. I telephoned and got a reservation and then drove out to Fritzi Massary's house to lunch. Fritzi was sitting on the terrace when I arrived; by her was a radio, and the tears were running down her face. Liesl and Bruno Franck, her daughter and son-in-law, were sitting together in a hammock-seat staring at the bright garden while the announcer's voice stabbed out the latest bulletins. Fritzi switched off the radio when I appeared and flung her arms round me; Ella, her maid, flew out of the house and embraced me too, and after a while, with the radio silenced and with the aid of a strong bourbon and ginger-ale the atmosphere became less tremulous and I relaxed and we laughed and talked of other things.

Later on that day, after I had packed, and after a hurriedly organised farewell cocktail-party at Cary's, Marlene Dietrich drove me away in her car. It had been an understood thing between us for years that she should always see me off at airports and stations and docks whenever she happened to be in the vicinity, and here we were again bowling along in her black Packard as we had done so often before. We didn't talk much, beyond a few local Hollywood superficialities, but she knew that I was feeling low and I knew that she knew and it wasn't necessary to go on about it.

Afterwards I reflected how curious it was that, in a moment of intense patriotic unhappiness, the people who had comforted me most were, by birth and breeding, completely Teutonic.

Upon arriving in New York I found cables from Campbell Stuart and Dallas Brooks explaining that under the new National Government Duff Cooper had been appointed Minister of Information and that he was taking over our organisation. Knowing that Winston Churchill had never been a fervent admirer of Campbell Stuart, I gathered, rightly, that he was out of a job, for the time being at any rate. I had no way of knowing to what extent this would affect our Paris office and whether it would continue to function as it was or be reorganised or disbanded; I therefore cabled to Duff Cooper suggesting that I return at once either to Paris or London, whichever he thought best. On the following day I received an ambiguous reply from him saying that he thought I could be of more use in America, but that I must use my own judgment as to whether I returned or not. Although I had no illusions about my importance to the Paris office, where I had been little more than a figure-head for several months, I did feel strongly, having founded it and weaned and nursed it into health and strength, that if it were to be disbanded, I should be back in time for the finale. Also the suggestion that I could be of more use in America, although possibly true, was too vague to be accepted without further definition and discussion. Maybe I could indeed be of considerable value in America if I were appointed to some specific job, but, without official backing, without being attached either to the Embassy, the British Information Service, or any other British organisation sanctioned by the Government, I would be in an invidious position and unable to achieve anything at all.

Realising that Duff, of whose friendship I was assured and whom I had known well for many years, was probably too engrossed in the arduous business of taking over the Ministry to give much time to my affairs for the moment, I excused his courteous vagueness, restrained the impulse to send back a caustic reply and merely cabled him that I *had* used my own judgement and was flying to London as soon as I could get a reservation. This was a good deal easier said than done and the next few days were maddeningly frustrating. There was apparently no possibility of getting on to a plane for Europe for at least a month. However, finally by argument, persuasion and string-pulling, I managed to procure a reservation on the Clipper scheduled to leave on June the 8th. There was no ship sailing that would have got me home any sooner and so I resigned myself to waiting as patiently as I could. During those interminable ten days, with the news growing steadily worse and the emotional tension in New York rising, I tried really hard to keep outwardly calm and not to allow the prevailing hysteria of the Press and radio to get me down. I also tried repeatedly to analyse my emotions coldly and clearly; to still my anxieties by segregating them, by separating the sheep from the goats. How much, for instance, of this general desolation I felt was really true? How much of it was based on facile sentimentalism? I remember looking up the word 'patriot' in the Oxford Dictionary: 'Patriot. One who defends or is zealous for his country's freedom or rights. Hence, Patriotic, adjective; Patriotically, adverb; and Patriotism, noun'. It was accurate enough as far as it went and there was almost comfort in its flat brevity. I wondered how truly zealous I was for my country's freedom or rights, or if whatever zeal I had was merely superficial; the result of middle-class upbringing, naval influence, and having read Kipling and written *Cavalcade*. True, I had not intended *Cavalcade* to be so Jingoistic, so True Blue Conservative in tone as many people imagined, nor, as many people also imagined, had I dashed it off with cunning political foresight to coincide with the fall of the Labour Government. I had merely decided to write an episodic play depicting thirty years of English life, and it had emerged as my instincts and talent had dictated. However, there it was; in essence definitely patriotic (adjective); a fairly durable proof of my own personal patriotism (noun); and here was I, nine years later, beleaguered in a neutral country at a time of infinite peril to England, weeping patriotically (adverb).

I found it difficult to prove to myself that this patriotic sentimentalism was merely a veneer, superimposed on my real mind by circumstances, by people I had met, by a too easy acceptance of values and traditions that I had not taken the trouble to analyse. Surely, fundamentally, I was too sensible and also too egocentric to permit such outmoded nonsense to sway me? My fears for my personal friends, the people I loved, were easy to understand; also my irrational, but quite natural, desire to be with them in time of trouble rather than comfortably ensconced on the other side of the Atlantic. But England itself? That damp, weather-sodden little island from which for many years I had escaped at the first opportunity? How could I, face to face with myself, admit solemnly and truthfully that I minded so much: By straining thus to coax myself into a mood of cynical detachment, to apply to my quivering nerves a little cool, intellectual balm, I actually wasted a great deal of time, because all that emerged finally from it was the realisation that I was entirely incapable of an intellectual approach to anything; that I had no cynical detachment where my emotions were concerned, and that I was a flagrant, unabashed sentimentalist and likely to remain so until the end of my days. I did love England and all it stood for. I loved its follies and apathies and curious streaks of genius; I loved standing to attention for 'God Save the King'; I loved British courage, British humour, and British understatement; I loved the justice, efficiency and even the dullness of British Colonial Administration. I loved the people – the ordinary, the extraordinary, the good, the bad, the indifferent, and what is more I belonged to that exasperating, weather-sodden little island with its uninspired cooking, its muddled thinking and its unregenerate pride, and it belonged to me whether it liked it or not. There was no escape, no getting round it, that was my personal truth and in facing up to it, once and for all, I experienced a strong relief. From that moment onwards, 2 a.m., in my bedroom at the St Regis Hotel in New York, on Thursday the 30th of May, 1940, one part of my mind at least remained at peace until the end of the war.

I was fortunate that I was able so firmly to consolidate my feelings about my country so early in the war, because in the months and years to come it handed me a few unpleasant surprises.

A few days after this soul-searching took place I was invited again to the White House, and I arrived at Washington in the full blaze of a June afternoon. A car from the White House met me at the airport and conveyed me, sweating profoundly, through the airless streets. There is something unique about Washington in the grip of a heatwave; I know nothing to compare with it excepting perhaps Calcutta just before the monsoons, and there, at least, the heat is expected and familiar, so everyone is prepared for it. Summer always seems to catch Washington unawares, to break over it like an awesome seventh wave, flooding it with sudden, sweltering discomfort. There is air-conditioning, of course, and there are iced drinks and sun-blinds and electric fans, but even those fail to dispel, for me at any rate, a feeling that such breathless oppressiveness must herald a cosmic disaster, that some feckless star has changed its course and we are all about to frizzle, curl up and die.

The President received me in his private office. He was sitting at his desk in his shirt-sleeves, mopping his face with a handkerchief and looking utterly exhausted. He wearily motioned me to a chair and asked his secretary to bring two large Coca-Colas with lots of ice. We talked for about an hour, solemnly this time and without jokes. The evacuation of Dunkirk evidently had moved him profoundly and he spoke of it at length, enlarging, without sentimentality, on the epic quality of the whole operation; this quality, he said, lay deep in the British character and was compounded of diverse ingredients: stubbornness, gallantry, refusal to envisage the possibility of failure, lack of imagination, vision and an inherent genius for improvisation. None but the British, he said with a faint smile, could transform a full-scale military defeat into a shining spiritual victory. Later on he asked me if I thought there was a possibility of the Germans successfully invading England. I replied 'No' immediately, and he said gently that although my vehemence did me credit he wondered how much of it was based on logical reasoning and how much on blind faith. I then explained as clearly as I could that my absolute conviction that England would never be conquered was based neither on logical reasoning nor on blindness, and that its strength lay in the fact that it was shared unquestioningly by well over forty million of my fellow countrymen. All of us, I said, were aware that our defences were inadequate, that our Air Force was outnumbered and that we were in for a very bad time; and all, or nearly all, of us realised that the situation was grim in the extreme, but even so, even in the face of every glaring indication to the contrary, we knew, beyond all logic and reason, that England would not be beaten. 'If that isn't blind faith,' said the President dryly, 'I should like to know what is.'

Later on I wondered, a little irritably, if I had appeared foolish in Roosevelt's eyes: if my bland assertion of faith in England's survival had sounded naïve, silly, or even spurious. I felt uneasy and almost ashamed, as though I had drunk too much at a party and wakened the next morning with the vague awareness that I had been showing off, talking out of turn, making an ass of myself. However, by the time I had finished dressing I had arrived at the comforting conclusion that, whatever he thought of me, I had only said what I believed to be true, and although he might consider me ill-informed and possibly hysterical, he was too astute not to recognise my sincerity. When I joined him in his study for a cocktail I was relieved to see that there was no apparent change in his manner towards me; he offered me a dry martini without contempt.

After dinner the President disappeared and, discovering that Mrs Roosevelt had to make an appearance at an Agricultural Students' dance at the Mayflower Hotel, I offered to accompany her. My admiration for her increased when I observed how simply and how kindly she handled the affair. First of all there was the official reception, which took place in the lobby of the hotel. A red-faced gentleman in a white dinner-jacket made a speech of welcome and a young girl dashed forward in a startled manner and handed her a bouquet. Then we were ushered into the ballroom, where the agricultural students were assembled in a vast semi-circle. Mrs Roosevelt, followed sheepishly and anonymously by me, started off from the left and worked her way doggedly to the right shaking hands and saying something appropriate to each one. I shook hands firmly too, and when they mumbled their names at me I mumbled mine back without any sign of mutual recognition; some of the handshakes were so agricultural that I winced, and everyone looked very hot. When this was over we were escorted to a raised dais, where we sat down, were offered a drink and invited to watch a square dance. I had only seen a square dance once before, years ago, in Genesee Depot, Wisconsin, with Lynn and Alfred. Then everybody had arrived muffled to the ears and there was deep snow outside and an atmosphere of country frowstiness inside. This occasion was more elaborate and, although equally noisy, more formal. It was fascinating to see the fierce concentration of all those moist, healthy young faces; they 'dipped for the oyster' and 'dug for the clam' as though their lives depended on it. The setting, of course, was entirely incongruous, but my mind's eye dismissed the modern hotel décor, the immaculate dance band, the careful evening dresses and the chandeliers, and substituted for them paper decorations, oil lamps, wooden benches round the walls, gingham and organdies and a fiddle and an upright cottage piano; then the whole thing fell into place and became genuinely gay and touching and accurate.

When it finished Mrs Roosevelt made a brief speech and we were led back through the lobby by the reception committee and tucked into the car. On the way back to the White House Mrs Roosevelt said that she would like to show me the Lincoln Memorial by moonlight, and so we made a slight detour and presently drew up before that austerely beautiful monument reflected in the water. The air had cooled a little and the dark sky was without a cloud. There was the muted noise of an aeroplane revving up on the airfield in the distance and, further away still, the plaintive whistle of a train; that typical, for ever American sound that always, when I hear it in movies, fills me with nostalgia; a sort of second home-sickness. Our own English trains have a shriller, more purposeful note; they always seem to be whistling for a very good reason, either because they are approaching a level-crossing, or going into a tunnel, or coming out of a tunnel, or whirling round a curve. The American whistle is less definite and has a more mournful quality; it conjures up higher mountains, deeper valleys and vaster distances; its implications are more timeless and strangely devoid of urgency.

President Lincoln looked out quietly at the glittering lights of the spread-out city that he had known so well in its younger, smaller days; at the flashing Coca-Cola signs, at the illuminated names of movie stars scurrying along the marquees or cinemas; at the Capitol, rising like a dignified, flood-lit blanc-mange; and perhaps at Mrs Roosevelt and me sitting in a shiny black car drawn into the side of the wide parkway. I wondered how he would have reacted to the present dangerous, misunderstood world situation: 'I intend no modification of my oft expressed personal wish that all men everywhere could be free' ' – and that government of the people, by the people and for the people, shall not perish from the earth.'

3

On Sunday, June the 9th, I drove out to La Guardia airfield with Jack and Natasha. The Clipper, which according to schedule should have left the day before, was sitting complacently on the quiet water like a large prehistoric bird. The airport was buzzing with the usual rumours: there would be three hours delay, there would be six hours delay, there was engine trouble, the plane was not going to take off at all. We stood about and sat about talking brightly. Natasha's manner was tremendously gay and I knew that she was near to tears. Several people had come to see me off: Lynn and Alfred, Ruth Chatterton, Constance Collier, Eleonora von Mendelssohn, Neysa, Tallulah and Clifton. Madeleine Carroll and Simon Elwes were to be my travelling companions and there was a great deal of Press photography, and the atmosphere, beneath the thin veneer of cheerful behaviour, was sad. My own spirits were fairly low; it seemed more than probable that I should not see Jack, Natasha, Alfred and Lynn nor any of my other American friends again for a long time, perhaps never. The large prehistoric bird was about to take Madeleine, Simon and me, together with nine depressed-looking gentlemen of mixed nationalities, away from peace, security, abundant food and bright lights, and plump us down in a world where there were bombs, black-outs, food rationing and many fears; a shadowed world, ennobled perhaps by suffering, redeemed by fortitude and courage, but quite definitely damned uncomfortable.

At long last the final good-byes were said and we were herded into a launch which conveyed us to the Clipper. As I climbed on board I turned and waved, but my friends were already too far away to be distinguishable.

The flight, from the material point of view, was the acme of comfort. We had cocktails and a good dinner; the weather was clear and our passage through the upper air was so smooth that there was no sensation of moving at all; we might just as well have been sitting in a well-appointed bus that had become somehow embedded in the sky. There were several Frenchmen on board who sat staring straight in front of them with misery in their eyes; occasionally they spoke to each other and they cheered up a bit after a couple of cocktails, but they were profoundly unhappy men and I felt very sorry for them. Presently, even before the cocktails, the poignancy of the last good-byes faded in my mind and was replaced by a detached sense of excitement. Madeleine and Simon, I think, felt this too and we became extremely cheerful, perhaps irritatingly so from the point of view of our fellow passengers. Simon was returning to England. Madeleine was determined to get, via Lisbon, to the South of France, where her fiancé and her family were. I had my train reservations for Paris on the Sud-Express which left Lisbon on the morning after we were due to arrive. Lisbon was our point of departure. From there we would all three shoot off in our separate directions and deal with our own separate private problems; meanwhile here we were whirling through space with nothing to do but to enjoy the situation and get the best we could from each other. In this I must say we succeeded triumphantly. None of the three of us knew each other well. We had met on and off over a number of years, but only casually, without significance and, strangely enough, we have only met casually since. But that journey established an intimacy between us which, as far as I am concerned, will always remain. We talked without ceasing and laughed immoderately; the uncertainty into which we were flying at such high speed, combined with the fact that we were the only British passengers on the plane, set us apart in our own company, gave wings to our conversation and brought us closer than we could ever possibly have been in less specialised circumstances.

The next day, when we were somewhere between the Azores and Lisbon, the pilot sent word back that Italy had entered the war. This galvanised our fellow passengers into a state of frantic volubility and for a while the noise was considerable. We arrived at Lisbon at 7.30 p.m.

Early the next morning I was rung up from the Embassy and told that the Ambassador wished to see me and would I come at once and have breakfast with him. I hurriedly packed my overnight bag so as to be ready to catch the train, which left at twelve-thirty, and drove in a taxi to the Embassy. The Ambassador, Sir Walford Selby, whom I had never met before, received me kindly and proceeded, unknown to him and to me, to save my life. The upshot of his conversation was that he felt it his duty to forbid me to go to France, as the

Embassy had been unable to establish any communications with Paris for the last ten days and the situation was growing steadily worse. I explained that my reservations were made and that I was anxious to get to Paris as soon as possible if only to help in evacuating my office staff. He then told me to cancel my reservations and that he would guarantee me priority on a plane direct to England within the next few days. From there, he added, I could fly across to Paris in a couple of hours if circumstances permitted it, but that if I persisted in travelling overland as arranged he would have to put it on record that it was entirely against his official advice. Impressed by the urgency of his tone and the common sense of his words, I agreed, and we sat down to breakfast. The Sud-Express left that morning without me and arrived, presumably, in Paris on the morning of the 13th, twenty-four hours before Hitler. Had I been on it I should have only discovered my flat empty and the office evacuated and abandoned; I should also have discovered that every avenue of escape was closed and, in due course, been arrested, imprisoned, and possibly shot. I owe indeed a great debt of gratitude to Sir Walford Selby.

The few days I spent in Lisbon were strained but uneventful. Madeleine managed, by the expenditure of a great deal of personal charm, and determination, to get herself flown to Madrid, whence she intended to make her way to Hendaye and over the border into France.

Simon was due to leave on the 14th, in the same plane with me. The Ambassador asked me to speak at the British Club the day before I left, which filled me with inward dismay because I loathe making impromptu speeches and there was no time to prepare one. However, he had been more than kind to me and the least I could do was consent. It was a stag luncheon and consisted of about seventy-five club members and a few journalists. As usual on such occasions, I was nervous and picked at the food without enthusiasm, wishing myself anywhere else in the world but where I was. However, once the secretary had introduced me and I was on my feet I felt better. I started by reading them a fine piece of writing from the *New York Times* on Dunkirk, then I spoke firmly about Anglo-American relations, reiterated my conviction that in spite of all alarms and portents England would survive, and finished up, rather theatrically, with the Toast from *Cavalcade*. They were a receptive audience and my nerves vanished when I began speaking. It was no moment to indulge in personal nervous flurries, anyhow. They were all British except two of the journalists; I was a transient British visitor, our home was in danger and we were far away. I, luckier than they, was going back. Even if I had muffed every word and made a stammering fool of myself they would have understood and been sympathetic and would, I think, rather have listened to me than not. As it was, I didn't do badly and I hope that at least I cheered them a little.

The flight from Lisbon to London was smooth. The plane left at nine o'clock in the morning of June the 14th. There were only a few passengers, among them the Portuguese Ambassador, who sat opposite to Simon and me and talked incessantly: words poured from him in an endless stream punctuated by staccato barks of mirthless laughter. This interminable, agitated monologue combined with the rhythmical roaring of the engine had such a soporific effect on me that my eyes ached and I had to bite my lips and dig my nails into the palms of my hands to prevent myself from falling into a deep sleep. Fortunately, just as I was about to give up the struggle and sink into a coma, the hypnotic spell was broken by the plane landing at Bordeaux. Simon and I staggered out into the sunshine and went straight to the airport café, where we revived ourselves with black coffee heavily laced with cognac. The place was crammed with people; the noise was deafening and the atmosphere quivered with hysteria. News had come through that the Germans had entered Paris that morning. We sat squashed against the wall at a corner table and watched the crowd milling about. Many people, both men and women, were in tears. Others looked grey, defeated and without hope. I felt rather sick and after a while we went outside.

Our plane was standing on the runway with a cordon of gendarmes round it to prevent refugees from attempting to stow away on board. I think, but I am not sure, that it was the last civilian aircraft to touch down in France for five years. I remember feeling a sudden, irrational urge to jump into a taxi, drive to the station and get into the first train for Paris: nothing could be easier of course, because the trains would be empty. I longed to see what was happening; whether the city was shuttered up and deserted, or whether there was fighting in the streets, and whether or not Cole and David and the office had got away in time. With a pang I conjured up a picture of my light, cheerful flat in the Place Vendôme; the cool quiet of the entrance hall after the bright heat of the Place; the rickety little *ascenseur* with its flapping glass-panelled doors and open top, creaking slowly up to the fifth floor on its oily steel pole; the familiar unforgettable smell of floor polish, dusty stair carpets and other people's cooking which, quite inoffensively, permeated the whole rambling building. My flat had its own particular smell; there was cooking mixed up with this too, but it was not predominant; what was predominant was wood-smoke: even if we had not lit the fire in the salon for days the acrid, smoky odour of it still lingered. I wondered if Yvonne had stayed on in the flat and was at this moment sitting in the kitchen, or if she had packed up as much as she could and abandoned it to its fate. I wondered also about my French friends; which of them had managed to escape and which of them had remained: Blanche Prenez in her tiny flat in the Avenue Victoire, sitting behind bolted doors, seething with anti-German fury; Yvonne Printemps in her sunny house at Neuilly; Jean Cocteau, Maurice Chevalier, Genevieve Tabouis, Denise and Edouard Bourdet, Henri Bernstein, Eve Curie, Bébé Bérard, Marie-Louise Bousquet etc., etc., and again etc. There were so many that I knew and liked and had fun with, more than I had realised, now, suddenly, with appalling swiftness, quarantined in defeat, out of my reach perhaps for years, possibly for ever. The thought of the Nazis swaggering through the streets of Paris, as, only a year before, I had watched them swaggering through the streets of Danzig, was unbearable. I discovered, standing there on the airfield at Bordeaux, that my affection for Paris was deeper and stronger than I knew; that its fall and surrender affected me personally much more than I imagined it could, almost as though I belonged to it. Simon, noticing, I think, that I was looking miserable, suggested that we expend the francs we had over on some champagne, a couple of bottles for the pilot and his assistant and one for ourselves. I agreed to this with the proviso that we gave it to them after we landed at Hendon. We just managed to get the three bottles in time before we were ordered back to the aircraft. Upon boarding it we noted, to our relief, that the voluble Ambassador had found some friends and moved to the forward end of the plane. Every seat was now occupied. In the two places on the other side of the aisle from us were a youngish man and woman; she was polishing her nails violently with a chamois leather buffer that she had taken from her bag; he had his head down and was staring at a book on his lap; I noticed two tears splash on to the open pages. In the two seats opposite us, one of which had been vacated by the Ambassador, were two nuns. They sat quietly with their hands folded, wearing expressions of complete blankness. Remembering that Simon was an ardent Catholic I restrained the impulse to hiss at him that two nuns travelling together were well known to be terribly unlucky in planes, trains or ships, and that we were practically bound to crash on the take-off. Presently the aircraft gave a shudder as though it shared my superstition and began to lumber uneasily along the runway. One of the nuns crossed herself with a quick surreptitiousness that endeared her to me; the plane came to a halt, turned slowly into the wind, revved up its engines with such violence that our cheeks wobbled like jellies, and it finally took off. I pressed my forehead against the small glass window and watched France sink away into the summer haze. A little later we managed, with the help of the steward, to open our bottle of champagne, and when we had drunk most of it out of plastic mugs, we felt cheerful again.

The plane flew low over the Channel Islands, we could see fishing boats rocking in the harbours and children playing on the beaches, and then, lower still, we flew across the Hampshire coast and on towards London. The countryside was bathed in golden, late afternoon sunlight; trees and telegraph-poles made black shadows across the roads and fields and we could distinguish cattle standing about in the lush meadows. The impression of calm and peace, of remoteness from war, was extraordinary. There it lay, the English land, waiting gently for the dusk that follows a long summer day.

PART FOUR

I

On Sunday, July 21st, I sailed from Liverpool for New York on the *Britannic*. The ship, crammed to the gunwales, had been lying in the Mersey for twenty-four hours with several other large vessels until the convoy escort was ready to usher it on to the bosom of the Atlantic. Many of the passengers lived in their lifebelts and we queued up for everything; meals were staggered because there were too many of us to be served at one sitting. We queued up not only for lunch and dinner but for baths, lavatories and even lifeboat drill. The ship was overrun by children ranging from babies a few months old to cheerful little boys of twelve and thirteen who wore neat grey flannel suits, scampered up and down the decks chattering to each other in clear, treble English voices, and treated the whole voyage as high adventure, which indeed it might have been. There were several play-pens put up on the promenade deck in which anxious mothers could deposit their younger offspring and snatch a few hours of comparative peace. Fortunately the weather was calm, so there was no seasickness to contend with. However, from dawn to dusk the noise was earsplitting. Only after dinner in the smoking-room, when the young had been stowed away in their bunks, was it possible to be quiet and make believe for a little that it was an ordinary voyage without urgency and the underlying dread of sudden disaster. I spent a good deal of time in my cabin trying to review the last five weeks as objectively as possible.

My day-to-day diary offered me little but a series of flat statements, occasionally enlivened by a sudden outburst of frustrated rage. I seemed to have been tied into a strait-jacket of Frustration since the moment I had set foot on English ground in June. I found it difficult to believe that that hopeful, happy landing was only five weeks ago; it seemed years away, years of decisions, counter-decisions, plans, hopes, disappointments and interviews. Above all, interviews. My friends in high places had been amiable, understanding and patient, they had also been very, very busy. I had telephoned them, waylaid them, written to them, forced my way into their offices and homes and nagged at them to give me a job that I considered worth while. This, of course, was the stumbling-block, because what I considered worth while differed radically from what they considered worth while. I could have obtained some minor position in the Ministry of Information; I could have organised entertainments at shore establishments anywhere from John o' Groats to Land's End in spite of the fact that hundreds of other people were doing exactly that, both in uniform and out of it. I could have become, with a little string-pulling, a Welfare Officer in the R.N.V.R., which would have been an excellent solution of my problem within its limits, but it seemed to me then, as indeed it had seemed before, that the limits would have been too limiting. One clear fact only emerged from all the blather, and that was my conviction that wherever I went and whatever I did my celebrity value should be utilised to its fullest extent. This obviously was sound sense, and after much discussion with influential friends, non-influential friends, loved ones and casual acquaintances, I finally decided to follow the advice Duff Cooper had given me at the outset, which was to go back to the United States, where, he assured me, I could be far more useful than in England. So here I was setting forth on my travels again with a Ministry of Information ticket and a private letter from Duff Cooper to Lord Lothian in Washington. I had, of course, a fairly clear idea of the recommendations contained in the letter, but I had not actually read it. My feelings were mixed, because I had so recently spent six weeks in America and had no wish to return so soon; the mission I was embarking upon was hazy and unspecified and one that the British Ambassador might be unwilling to recognise. Also I was leaving behind a great many people I was fond of and a great many things that mattered to me. In addition to frustrations, irritations and perplexities, there had been an intricate problem to deal with during those five weeks. This was the question of whether or not we should evacuate the children of the Actors' Orphanage to Canada or America for the duration of the war. My committee and I were much concerned about this and the discussions of it were long and many, and complicated by the fact that all of us, being actors and highly articulate, talked at once. Finally it had been decided that all the children under the age of fifteen should be transferred to America. A Hollywood committee of British actors and actresses was hurriedly formed under the aegis of Dame May Whitty and it was ultimately arranged, thanks to the generosity of the Gould Foundation in the Bronx, that our orphans should be taken in, educated and cared for. The whole business was further complicated by the fact that only a few of them were actually orphans; many had one parent living and in some cases both. This entailed, of course, getting permission from the various parents and relatives concerned. When I sailed on the *Britannic* this was still under discussion; the Hollywood committee was arguing with itself and, by cable, with us whether the children should be settled in California among the oranges and sunshine where there wasn't anywhere for them to live, or in New York without the oranges and sunshine where there was. All this I had guaranteed to deal with on arrival in New York.

Meanwhile the grey ships of the convoy steamed on across the Atlantic with alert little destroyers rounding them up and barking at their heels. Happily no submarines appeared and the voyage was uneventful. Upon arrival in New York I was met by a hot and flustered gentleman from the British Information Service, who implored me breathlessly to tell the Press that I was arriving unofficially on my own theatrical business. This irritated me and I explained to him that the Press, as usual, had met me at Quarantine, but that he need not worry for I had been the soul of discretion. New York was hotter than hell and Washington even hotter, and I rocketed back and forth between the two cities, interviewing, persuading, arguing and cajoling, all without the faintest effect. Lord Lothian was sceptical about the Duff Cooper plan, but assured me that I could be of considerable service if I travelled about the States for a while and talked to key citizens, notably news editors and tycoons in the various cities, about England and the British war effort, so off I went by train and plane and talked at every possible opportunity. In each city I visited the hospitality was, as always, unfailing. People I had never met in my life gave dinner-parties, cocktail-parties, lunches, week-end parties; during which I made speeches, sang songs and generally tried to make myself as attractive as possible. I received much genuine kindness and, naturally enough, a good deal of 'lionising'. Only occasionally I ran into trouble and had to bare my teeth in a snarl; once when a purple-faced business magnate, at a dinner in Salt Lake City, announced with fatuous conviction that Britain was done for and that I could be god-damn sure that America, having won the 1914–18 war, was not going to be played for a sucker a second time. This of course was routine Isolationist stuff and I dealt with it accordingly. It was not a notable victory, because after I had withered and insulted him well beyond the bounds of social behaviour, he seemed to forget entirely what the argument was about, and, placing a pudgy beringed hand on my shoulder, asked me if I played golf. Another maddening occasion was a brief interview with ex-President Hoover in Palo Alto, California. He delivered a tirade against England and the perfidies of the British Government which went on for about a quarter of an hour, during which I sat with Paul Smith, the editor of the *San Francisco Chronicle*, smoking a cigarette and watching Mr Hoover's small eyes suffusing in his large, square face. On this occasion I refrained from any comment whatsoever, because he seemed so dangerously cross that even the lightest verbal pin-prick might have given him a stroke. I discovered later that the reason of his outburst was that he had been prevented by the British from going over to occupied Belgium and France and delivering food to the starving populations. Similar excursions apparently had earned him spectacular acclaim in the last war; and although it had been explained to him that any food taken by him to occupied countries would immediately be appropriated by the Nazis, and therefore be of no assistance to anyone but the enemy, the craze to do publicised good had obviously driven common sense from his mind, and there he stood, a humanitarian *manqué*, and hopping mad into the bargain. There were, in addition to these, a few minor tussles, but on the whole my self-imposed Odyssey was rewarded by much more sympathetic understanding than I had anticipated. It also cost me a great deal of money, for I was travelling unofficially and paying my own expenses out of my private bank account in New York. The fact that by doing this I was breaking the law and making myself liable to heavy fines and imprisonment had been tactfully withheld from me both by the Minister of Information and the British Ambassador. I pressed on therefore in cheerful ignorance, upheld by the thought that I was at least spending my own hard-earned money in my country's cause. The total amount expended was, in English currency, approximately £11,000.

I returned to New York. I returned to Washington. I reported what I had heard and observed and what, if anything, I had deduced from it. Lord Lothian was flattering and grateful, but President Roosevelt and Harry Hopkins was definitely more interested. In the meantime the orphans arrived from England; and were installed in the Gould Foundation, where they were welcomed enthusiastically and made a great deal more comfortable than they had ever been in their lives. They splashed about in a swimming pool; learned baseball; were wrapped in hygiene and psychiatry and surfeited with the Grade A milk of human kindness. The generosity of the American welfare officials, indeed the generosity of everybody concerned, officials or not, was so heart-warming and so unstinting that it could never be adequately repaid and, I hope, never forgotten. The fact that when the children ultimately returned to England many of them were exceedingly difficult to manage was nobody's fault. The immediate amenities of living in modern America are greatly in advance of those of war-scarred England and it was tricky trying to persuade the adolescents, particularly the girls, that life was real, life was earnest, and that lipsticks, motor rides, summer camping and chocolate Malteds were *not* the goal. Some of them settled down all right and a few, with praiseworthy determination, returned to the States when they were old enough and married. The smaller ones, of course, missed their luxury cots only briefly and accepted their greyer surroundings without lasting regrets.

2

During my voyage across the Atlantic in the *Britannic* I met a man whom I had known slightly before called Ingram Fraser. He was nice-looking, suave, spoke impeccable French and was, to me, quite palpably involved in some form of cloak and dagger business. It was difficult then, as indeed it still is, to distinguish between those who were genuinely engaged in some branch of the Intelligence services and those who were merely shooting a line and pretending to be. There was a saying, much quoted in the war years, that if an Englishman told you he was a secret agent it was a lie, and that if an American told you the same thing it was true. Ingram, however, was English, or rather Scottish, and we walked round each other warily for days. Finally, on the last night of the trip, we sneaked out of the smoking-room with our whiskies and sodas and went into the ladies' writing-room, which was not used in the evenings and was unlighted because of the black-out. Here, in the eerie darkness lit only by the glow of our cigarettes, we exchanged mutual confidences. No desperate secrets inimical to the security of our troops on land or sea emerged from the conversation, but a few small kittens were let out of a few small bags and were allowed to frolic for a little before we popped them back and returned to the smoking-room. The upshot of it was that shortly after my arrival in New York Ingram took me to visit a man who was to have a considerable influence on the next few years of my life. His name was William (now Sir William) Stephenson, and he was known colloquially as Little Bill. Little Bill received me in a chintz-covered room in the Hampshire House. He was small, quietly affable and talked very little. He gave me two strong 'Cuba Libres' one after the other, and waited politely for me to talk a great deal. I obliged, up to a point, and was asked to return a few evenings later. He did not make the psychological mistake of swearing me to secrecy. He never mentioned secrecy at all. That impressed me, because by that time I was of course perfectly aware that whatever his exact occupation was, it was very secret indeed. It is not my business here to discuss his activities except when those activities impinged upon my own life, which from time to time they did. This, for me, momentous meeting took place at the end of July, 1940, and from then until the end of the war the realisation that Little Bill completely trusted my integrity, had faith in my discretion and understanding of my motives, was a great comfort to me. That suite in the Hampshire House with the outside chintz flowers crawling over the walls became pleasantly familiar to me, and in later years, when he moved into equally luxurious but more aesthetically austere surroundings, I mourned it.

Another casual acquaintanceship that had begun in the Hotel de l'Univers at Arras in November, 1939, and been renewed in May, now became significant. During one of my frequent visits to Washington, Richard Casey, the Australian Minister, invited me to lunch and asked me if I would like to go out to the Antipodes as a guest of the Australian Government to make broadcasts about the British war effort and give concerts for troops in training and for the Australian Red Cross. He showed me cables he had received from Robert Menzies, the Prime Minister, and Sir Keith Murdoch, the Minister of Information, assuring me of a wonderful welcome. This, being the first concrete offer I had had to do anything constructive since Campbell Stuart had asked me to go to Paris in August 1939, cheered me up considerably. I went to ask Lord Lothian's advice, which was definite and, I thought, almost over-enthusiastic. I suspected from the glint of incredulous relief in his eye that the possibility of my being removed to the other side of the world was the best news he had heard since Science and Health. Not that he betrayed this in any undiplomatic manner; he merely slapped me on the back and asked me to stay to lunch, after which he graciously ushered me out and, a trifle prematurely, wished me 'Bon Voyage'. Poor Lord Lothian. He was a kindly man and I fear my constant re-appearance in his Embassy must have irritated him exceedingly. He promised to wire his approval of the Australian visit to Duff Cooper. I also cabled to Duff, and then returned to New York to discuss the project with Little Bill, who thought it a good idea provided I got back in the following March, when, he said, he would have something of great importance to discuss with me. Encouraged by these two approvals and without waiting for Duff's reply (which was just as well, for neither he nor anyone in the

M. of I. even acknowledged my cable), I wired to Robert Menzies in Canberra accepting his invitation and received a confirmatory cable by return. After a series of detailed advices, recommendations and projected itineraries had flown between Washington and Canberra, it was decided that I should leave by ship, rather than by plane, to give myself time to prepare a dozen broadcasts and read up as much information about Australian history as I could cram into my brain. Finally, on October the 16th, I sailed from San Pedro, California.

3

The *Monterey*, one of the ships of the Matson Line, was comfortable and half-empty. The voyage lasted for three weeks. We stopped for a day in Honolulu, where the ukeleles played 'Aloha', leis were hung round my neck and the well-remembered harbour obligingly produced all its familiar glamour. The native boys dived for nickels and dimes while the music came wafting over the blue water as we drew alongside. Diamond Head rose, plum-coloured, in the sunlight, and if there was a war being waged anywhere one felt that it couldn't even be so near as the other side of the world; that it must be on another star.

Later on in the war, when my journeys were by air and less relaxed, I often looked back on the curious, detached peace of that voyage to Australia, while the *Monterey* steamed across the, as yet, un-blooded Pacific. Soon after we left Honolulu we were told that our course would be deflected, because orders had come through to the Captain that instead of calling at Fiji and Pago-Pago, and arriving ultimately in Fremantle, we would go via Japan and the China Sea and arrive in Sydney. There was a good deal of anxious surmise and discussion among the passengers. As far as I was concerned, I didn't mind one way or the other. The detour would give me a few more days to work on my broadcasts and prepare myself for my impact on Australia and Australia's impact on me. Also I was delighted at the idea of visiting Yokohama and Tokyo again, and also Shanghai, where, in the February of 1930, I had written *Private Lives*.

The ten days and nights separating Honolulu from Yokohama followed each other demurely and without incident. As we neared the Japanese coast the weather became colder and there were no more flying fish. At last, one windy, rainy morning, I looked out at the bay of Yokohama, at the miniature hills and cliffs, bright green under a heavy sky. We were approaching the docks and so I spruced myself up to go ashore. However, I needn't have troubled, because none of the few English passengers were given permission to land. I asked the Japanese Immigration Officer for an explanation of this, but he merely looked at me with an expression of cold dislike and turned his back on me. I controlled an overwhelming urge to kick him across the smoking-room and went to see the Captain, who said that nothing could be done, so I resigned myself to a day of irritated solitude in an empty ship and retired to my cabin with a book.

To be confined to a ship in harbour was dismally frustrating. There, lying just near, was the alien town with its shops, streets and cafés to be explored. Here was I, having planned to drive to Tokyo, do some shopping, have a drink at the Imperial Hotel and a Sukiyaki dinner in some recherché Japanese restaurant, imprisoned either in my cabin or the smoking room, or leaning on the deck rail looking wistfully at the activities of the port. By dinner-time I had worked myself into a rage. I asked my table steward if he was going ashore. He said 'Yes', with a slight leer, and added that about a dozen of the crew always made up a party when the ship was in Yokohama, where the night-life was even gayer than in Tokyo. This later proved to be a gross over-statement; however, I bribed him to wangle me a crew pass and spent the next hours disguising myself as a tough American seaman. My bedroom steward entered into the spirit of the thing and produced a cap and a duffle coat. I emptied my pockets of anything that might identify me and also left behind my watch and identity bracelet. In due course I was conducted below and introduced to 'the boys', and off we went. We were lightly searched by an official at the harbour gate, during which I gave a performance of slightly drunken resentment which delighted 'the boys'. After this initial excitement, I regret to say the evening was rather dull. We went from bar to bar and brothel to brothel; a few tattered-looking geishas appeared from time to time and led some of 'the boys' away for a little while. They returned to us later, looking, I thought, far from refreshed. By 2 a.m. some of us were drunk, some of us were irritable and all of us were sleepy. Actually the only thing that interested me in our progress from bar to bar was the preponderance of Germans. In every place we visited there were numbers of them, drinking gallons of musty beer and occasionally heiling Hitler. One of them, a second officer on an oil tanker, came and sat next to me. His English was fairly good but not nearly as good as my American. Our conversation was fatuous to the point of imbecility but it convulsed 'the boys'. At long last my table steward and I rounded up as many of our companions as we could find and reeled back to the ship. The evening fortunately had passed without incident and there were no repercussions, although I reproached myself afterwards for my silliness, for had I by chance been caught I might have found myself in serious trouble. There might even have been more questions asked about me in the House of Commons.

A few days later we sailed up the Whang-Po river and slid alongside the Shanghai Bund. The city looked unchanged, and, except for a few observation posts drooped with barbed wire at the corners of certain streets, there was no outward indication of war. The traffic and noise and general hubbub of the waterfront was the same as before, bicycles and rickshaws weaved in and out between the larger vehicles and 'Coolie' blue was, as usual, the predominant colour. It is a wonderful blue and was the first thing to attract my eye, when, years before, I arrived in Shanghai for the first time.

The *Monterey* stayed in Shanghai for two whole days, so I packed a suitcase and went to the Cathay Hotel, where I was received with enthusiasm and given a large suite filled with managerial flowers. Although there was no actual plaque announcing that I had written *Private Lives* there, the management, despite the rigours of war and occupation, had obviously remembered the fact with pride, which touched me. I enjoyed those two days; it was a relief to be on land again and there were several old friends to visit and much to remember. I was determined to call on Madame Birt (Mamita) although advised on all sides not to because both her daughters, Tita and Margot, were married to Italians and her husband, Dr Birt, was apparently an ardent Nazi. This, though disconcerting, I decided to ignore. Mamita had been hospitable to me in the past; she was a remarkable old lady and I was fond of her, and so, with some difficulty, because she had changed her address, I ran her to earth in a small, dark flat in an apartment building. She received me with surprise, and then, after some strained, formal conversation, burst into tears. After that the tension lessened and we talked of old days and vanished pleasures in a less tormented world. It was, on the whole, a sad little reunion, but I was glad I went, for I think my visit cheered her. In addition to this I did a broadcast, defiantly anti-Japanese in tone; visited another old friend, Oke Hartman, in a lacquered Chinese house where I ate a delicious but interminable Chinese dinner; bought two vast tins of caviar and several bottles of vodka from a Russian restaurant proprietor, and finally returned to the ship.

Between Shanghai and Manila the weather changed and became tropical again; the flying fish reappeared and broke the oily surface of the sea in vast shoals, skittering along until the hot sun dried their wings and they plopped back into the water. I spent most of each day either reading or banging away at my typewriter. The broadcasts were not easy to write, as I had no idea of what the Australian public would or wouldn't like. I persevered, however, on the assumption that lack of pomposity and simplicity of style were the two key rules to follow when writing for any public. I tried to inject a little humour into them here and there whenever an opportunity offered, and hoped for the best. When finished they were innocuous and, I fear, a trifle dull. However, when I eventually spoke them into the microphone they apparently satisfied the listeners, for I received many letters from people in out-of-the-way places, saying how comforting it had been to hear news of home at first hand. These broadcasts were later published in booklet form in aid of the Australian Red Cross, and, later still, Heinemann's published them in England.

The ship paused in Manila for one night. I gave a Press interview, made a short impromptu broadcast and then dined with the American High Commissioner. The news had just come through that Roosevelt had been re-elected, and I remembered the last time I had seen him, sitting up in bed in the White House having his breakfast. He was in a very cheerful mood because he had at last managed to get Congress to agree to allow Great Britain to have the fifty destroyers about which there had been such a hullabaloo. When I asked him point-blank what he thought his chances were of winning the election, he said briefly, with a twinkle in his eye, 'Willkie will talk and I won't.'

From Manila to Sydney the *Monterey* was crammed with American service wives and children. The pandemonium was deafening, the dining-saloon like Bedlam, and the stewards run ragged. I emerged from my cabin very seldom, generally at dead of night when the decks were deserted. There were a number of cocktail-parties given daily in different cabins; these often ended in tears and, on one occasion, in a rousing, hair-pulling, face-slapping free-for-all, which assumed such serious proportions that the Captain had to be sent for. Judging from the eye-witness account given me by my bedroom steward it had been a remarkable spectacle involving, all told, about twenty people. The origin of the fracas remained obscure, but apparently it began with a slight argument between two naval wives about their respective children. Mother love, particularly in America, is a highly-respected and much-publicised emotion and, when exacerbated by gin and bourbon, it can become extremely formidable. On this occasion it burst all bounds and the ship rocked with the repercussions for several days.

Meanwhile the islands of the East Indies slipped by; there was a series of spectacular dawns and sunsets and at night the stars grew larger and larger. At home the blitzes had lessened, and England, grim but undismayed after its first baptism of fire, was settling down to the rigours of the first real war-time winter.

I had lots of time to think during those long sweltering days and nights. Now, looking back across so many years, I find it difficult to recapture the curious, over-comfortable, nightmare quality of that voyage. Perhaps nightmare is too dramatic a word to use; it was only really nightmarish at moments when imagined horrors took advantage of a few hours' imsomnia and pounced on to my nerves. Most of the time I managed, as far as I can remember, to be fairly detached and to concentrate on my forthcoming tour of Australia.

Now, in the early 1950s, those alarms and despondencies and desperate moments are over and done with, endured and dealt with more than ten years ago. Even then, in November, 1940, in my cabin in the *Monterey*, the agitations of a few weeks back had faded and lost their reality. If only one could train oneself to remember in moments of crisis or despair how swiftly the passage of time, even a comparatively little time, can relax tension and deaden pain. Gay episodes I find easier to recall. I can enjoy retrospective laughter again and again, but retrospective tears never. The eyes remain dry.

4

The *Monterey* arrived in Sydney harbour at mid-day on November the 16th. The rain and mist that had enveloped us all the morning cleared by the time the ship drew alongside, and I was able to get a bird's-eye view from the upper deck rail of my reception committee. There seemed to be a great many of them and I was shattered for a few seconds by an attack of 'First Night' nerves. I felt panic-stricken, under-rehearsed and desperately unsure of my lines. My heart sank still further when I saw a radio van and newsreel cameras. I am not very good at making impromptu speeches, although in later years I have improved. I was entirely alone with no supporting cast and not even an assistant stage-manager to cue me. My brain felt woolly and clogged with fear and I knew with dreadful certainty that when the microphone was shoved under my nose I should make a complete fool of myself.

Fortunately by the time the Press men had come on board and photographed me and fired questions at me, my nervousness had diminished enough to enable me to step ashore with outward certainty at least. I was greeted by a bewildering number of officials, who rushed me immediately to the dreaded microphone; the news cameras clicked; flash-bulbs blinded me and I managed to stammer out a few stereotyped phrases without utterly disgracing myself. However, I was unable to prevent my mind's eye envisaging thousands of disgruntled Australians, in far-away townships and sheep farms, crouching eagerly over their radios in expectation of a gay flood of Mayfair witticisms, only to be fobbed off with a strangulated, disembodied voice, saying 'Hullo, Australia – I am very happy to be here.' When this unimpressive performance was over there were more introductions and hand-shakings and I was hustled into a car and driven to the Australia Hotel. People in the streets waved as I passed, and I waved back and smiled until my face muscles ached. Upon arrival at the hotel I was plumped straight into a Press reception. Now to me there is nothing in the world so nerve racking as a Press reception. It isn't that newspaper men and women individually are so very different from anyone else; it isn't that they are universally malign and ill-disposed and determined to strip their shivering victims of every shred of dignity and charm. On the contrary, most of them, with a few exceptions, are human, kindly and interested. *En masse*, however, the atmosphere they create is uneasy and sticky with prejudice. This prejudice is, I am sure, quite unintentional in most cases and, on the whole, understandable. Newspaper reporting, either of events or people, depends for its effectiveness on superficial observation and snap judgments; speed and brevity are essential and there is rarely time for subtle analysis or true assessment of character. Usually, in the case of a celebrity, the label has been fixed and the clichés set for years. Sometime in the past, when they stepped into contemporary fame for the first time, some reporter coined a phrase, some interviewer emphasised a peculiarity, some incident occurred that stamped their personalities indelibly on to the journalistic mind. From then on they are typed once and for all and the prejudice is formed. In my particular case the die was cast in 1924, when *The Vortex* was produced in London and I was rocketed overnight into a blaze of publicity. *The Vortex* was a social drama of the 1920s, satirising a small group of wealthy, decadent people. I played the part of a neurotic misfit who took drugs, made sharp, witty remarks and was desolately unhappy. There was my label, ready to hand and glaringly printed. Nicky

Lancaster was twenty-four, well groomed, witty and decadent. Noël Coward, who played him, also was twenty-four and presumably well groomed, witty and decadent. Whether or not he was a drug addict was never accurately proved, although it was frequently suspected; his underlying desolate unhappiness, although suspected, was never proved either, but none of that was important. All that was important for monotonous future reference was the created image – the talented, neurotic sophisticated playboy. In later years this imaginary, rather tiresome figure, suffered occasional eclipses but they were of short duration. *Cavalcade, Bitter Sweet, This Happy Breed, Brief Encounter* and *In Which We Serve* scratched a little gloss off the legend, but not enough to damage it irreparably. It still exists today in 1952, with the slight modification that I am now an ageing playboy, still witty, still brittle and still sophisticated, although the sophistication is, alas, no longer up-to-date, no longer valid. It is a depressing thought, to be a shrill relic at the age of fifty-two, but there is still a little time left, and I may yet snap out of it. 1940, however, was twelve years ago and the journalistic synthesis of me, owing to continual repetition, was flourishing like a green bay tree. For instance, apropos of the fracas in the House of Commons about my American trip, the *Sunday Express* had stated: 'In any event, Mr Coward is not the man for the job. His flippant England – Cocktails, Countesses, Caviare – has gone. A man of the people more in tune with the new mood of Britain would be a better proposition for America.' The *Daily Mirror*, not to be outdone, made the following pronouncement: – 'Mister Coward, with his stilted mannerisms, his clipped accents and his vast experience of the useless froth of society, may be making contacts with the American equivalents . . . but as a representative for democracy he's like a plate of caviar in a carmen's pull-up.' These sinister references to caviar – once with an E and once without – struck at my conscience like a dagger when I remembered the two large tins I had bought in Shanghai, also there were my stilted mannerisms and my clipped accents, to say nothing of those legions of countesses I had left behind, presumably in a series of Mayfair luxury-flats.

It was not to be wondered at that this publicised sybarite, this mannered exotic, flicking the useless froth of society from his blue pin-stripe, was a trifle apprehensive. There was a great deal of prejudice to be overcome when I walked into that crowded room in the Australia Hotel, Sydney, and I was definitely aware of it even if they themselves were not. The effort to be friendly was not difficult. I am prepared to be friendly if people are friendly to me, and the atmosphere, although charged with alert expectation, was in no way unkind. The strain, however, lay in resisting the temptation to play up to their pre-conceived notion of me and give the performance they were subconsciously demanding. A few irreverent flippancies and witticisms and the serious implications of my visit would be undermined. I had no exaggerated idea of the importance of my mission and no illusions that my visit to Australia was fraught with any particular significance. All I wanted to do was to let the Australians know a little about what was happening in England, help to raise money for their Red Cross and sing to as many of their soldiers, sailors and airmen in training camps as wished to listen to me. This initial meeting with the Press obviously was of immense importance to the whole enterprise. The impression I made on them would immediately be relayed over the length and breadth of the continent, and I was determined that that impression should be of my genuine character and not of my superficial legend. After the first quarter of an hour or so I felt the tension relax and my own nervousness relax with it. There were some anxious moments; a few yawning abysses opened at my feet; there were one or two important and malicious questions fired at me, notably from those reporters whose papers were in opposition to Robert Menzies and the Government whose guest I was; but, taken all in all, disaster was avoided and I was led to my suite for ten minutes breathing space before making another broadcast.

When this was over I was hurried off to a reception given for me by Mr P. C. Spender, the War Minister. The reception was a large one and I shook hands with several hundred people. I had no time to say anything particular to anyone beyond the usual 'How do you do' and 'How happy I am to be here', but I was conscious of much warmth and kindliness.

At six o'clock I rushed off to pay my official call on Lord Gowrie, the Governor-General. He was a tall, handsome man with white hair and twinkling blue eyes; there was something in his manner, an emanation of kindness and common sense, that put me at ease, and he assured me that he would support me in any way he could during my tour but warned me, as Richard Casey had done, that it would be arduous.

After this I had just time to get back to the hotel, bathe and change and get to Prue Dickson's house for dinner. Prue Dickson was the daughter of Violet Vanbrugh and Arthur Bourchier, and we had first met in *Peter Pan* in 1914, when she played Curly, and I, Slightly. The dinner-party was mercifully small and I ate Sydney oysters for the first time. I think I ate two and a half dozen. The dinner-party, however, was but a brief prelude to the Red Cross Ball given in my honour at the Town Hall. This was a concert as well as a ball, and several famous Australian artists had consented to appear and sing my music. It was my first public appearance and the crowds in the streets and in the Town Hall itself were enormous. I heard afterwards that owing to the high price of admission the attendance was not quite as great as had been hoped. If this was so I can only say that I was very thankful. To me there seemed to be quite enough. When I drove up in the car with Prue there was a guard of honour of V.A.s (Voluntary Aids) and W.A.N.S. (Women's Australian Nursing Society), each about a hundred strong, waiting for me on the steps. I was received by the Lord Mayor and Lady Mayoress. I walked up and down the rows of attractive, uniformed Australian girls, shaking hands with each one. Inside the hall I stood with my host and hostess while people filed by and were introduced to me one by one, all of which took a long time. At last the concert began and I was able to sit down and enjoy myself. The orchestra was good and Marie Bremner sang 'I'll See You Again' and 'I'll Follow My Secret Heart' beautifully. Inevitably I had to climb on to the stage and make a speech. Whether or not I sang any songs I forget, but I believe I dashed off 'Marvellous Party' and 'Mad Dogs and Englishmen' in sheer desperation. This function ended just before midnight and I made a tour of various nightclubs until 2 a.m. Not, I hasten to say, for pleasure but because I had to find a good accompanist for my troop concerts.

I can sing certain songs to my own accompaniment, but I am far happier and more at ease when there is someone to play for me. I find that I can command more authority over my audience when I am standing up; also, when chained to the piano, half my attention is devoted to my playing with the result that the projection of the lyrics is more difficult and often less effective.

My search, that first night in Sydney, was finally rewarded at Romano's, where I found an excellent pianist who agreed to come and rehearse with me early the next morning, and play for me in the afternoon at my first troop concert at Ingleburn Camp, which was about seventy miles away.

At two-thirty I went to bed, took three aspirin and went to sleep. That was the end of my first day, or rather half day, in Australia and those that followed were exhaustingly similar.

My tour lasted seven weeks and was, to me, both strenuous and rewarding. The Red Cross made a profit of approximately twelve thousand pounds from my appearances in different cities. My broadcasts, judging by the letters I received, gave pleasure to many people in out-of-the-way places who were unable to come to any of my performances. The newspapers and magazines, with only two exceptions, helped me enormously by publicising me with courtesy and kindness.

The two exceptions were *Smith's Weekly* and *Truth*, both of which were in opposition to the Government. These gleefully reprinted anything derogatory they could find in the English Press, which offered them a wide, though not varied, choice. When they couldn't quote they invented and on the whole, wasted a vast amount of energy and printer's ink with little effect. Only on one occasion did they achieve a brief triumph when I was faced at a training camp outside Melbourne with an audience of 'Diggers', who proceeded to shout me down before I had even started to sing to them. This unexpected hostility startled me for a moment and horrified my poor accompanist, Sefton Daly, who was not so inured to the vagaries of troop audiences as I was. I let them get on with their whistling and catcalls for a little and then announced, with some firmness, through the microphone, that I intended to sing steadily for three quarters of an hour whether they liked it or not. This dreadful threat silenced them for a moment and gave me a chance to bawl out, 'Don't Put Your Daughter on the Stage, Mrs Worthington', which drew from them a few grudging titters, after which I was allowed to get on with the rest of my programme. At the end they applauded and cheered vociferously, and carried me out of the hut on their shoulders, which was uncomfortable but gratifying. A half an hour later I gave another show in the same hut, which was not quite big enough to accommodate the whole camp. The word must have got round that I was more 'dinkum' than had been anticipated, because this time, although they were rather slow in the uptake, there was no overt hostility.

When both these curious performances were over and I was having a cup of tea with the Commanding Officer, he explained that *Smith's Weekly and Truth* were the only papers his chaps ever read and that they had been, naturally enough, prejudiced against me. I asked him why he hadn't warned me about this before I went on, to which he replied that he didn't want to upset me. Bewildered by this reasoning I asked him if, in warfare, he would prefer to be warned of an enemy ambush awaiting for him just around the corner, or would rather be left in happy ignorance and allowed to walk straight into it. At this he laughed superciliously and said it wasn't quite the same thing, was it! After that the subject was dropped.

To offset this disconcerting episode, all the other troops concerts went smoothly from start to finish. The public performances were all successful and the audiences wonderful.

Dick Casey, in a note he wrote to me just before I sailed, said: 'If I were you I'd tell the people who are in charge of you that (A) you'll work like a black for five days a week, but (B) you can't make any appointment before 11 a.m. and (C) you have to have two days a week without any appointments at all. If you don't make some such stipulation they'll run the legs off you. However, if you want to break these rules yourself to meet people you like the look of – well, you have only yourself to blame.' Well, I had only myself to blame, I suppose, because I made no stipulations at all and cursed myself later for having been so sure of my own endurance. The itinerary handed to me was certainly formidable, but not unmanageable. If, at the outset, I had begun cancelling engagements and saying I couldn't do this or that, it would have caused disappointment, given rise to a number of complications and created a bad impression. The Government had appointed me an A.D.C. called Monte Lake, an efficient secretary, Mavis Gully and Jim Wilcox, a fair, tough young man, who was excellent company and my Press representative. For the first few weeks an amiable man called Mackenna was the sort of major-domo of my entourage; later, however, he was withdrawn from the band-wagon and Myles Cox took over. Myles had a saturnine appearance and a most unsaturnine temperament. He kept me in order with infinite tact. We were a gay little troop and on the few occasions when we could all get together and relax we had a very good time. Such occasions were rare, and after the first couple of weeks Mavis had to be supplied with an assistant.

The routine was as follows. Myles supervised all arrangements and organised transport and plane tickets, time sheets, etc.; Monte appeared in the morning and briefed me on the day's doings, and Mavis appeared for an hour or so every day and stood over me while I autographed photographs, letters and books. Jim looked after the newspaper men, photographers and interviewers and nipped them into my presence whenever there were a few minutes available. Monte accompanied me everywhere and whisked me in and out of functions; he also had to get me in and out of cars, which was sometimes more complicated. The police were cheerfully co-operative and supplied me with a bodyguard for those occasions when we feared the crowds might get out of hand. The pianist I found at Romano's played for me once at my first troop concert at Inglebourne. Actually he played only three songs, was taken ill and staggered from the stage, whereupon I had to take off my jacket and fend for myself. Finally, after a series of auditions and much trial and error, Marie Burke sent me Sefton Daly, a young New Zealander, who had played for her frequently. He was a good pianist and a fine natural musician, but he couldn't read at sight. This was a serious defect, but I so very much preferred his playing to those I had heard who could read from sight that I engaged him and set him to learn the whole of my repertoire, song by song. Luckily there was a good deal of time every day when I was going over factories, visiting airfields, opening and closing bazaars and making interminable speeches, when I had no need of music. During these excursions he sat at home in the hotel slogging away until, in a remarkably short while, he had really mastered most of my principal numbers and was starting on the more obscure ones. Those early concerts must have been nerve-racking for him, but he never betrayed it and never let me down by so much as a B flat. He was also, later, when he had time, a great addition to our travelling circus and enlivened many a civic reception by giggling at the wrong moment.

Sydney, Melbourne, Adelaide, Perth, Fremantle, Canberra, Brisbane, Launceston, Hobart. Back and forth and up and down I went until I was dizzy. By the time I reached Brisbane I had, most reluctantly, to cancel my projected visit to Cairns and Darwin because I was so exhausted that I could hardly speak. But after three days in a small hotel on the Queensland coast I returned to the attack, if not bursting with energy, at least refreshed.

Wherever I went I was received with heart-warming friendliness. I had been warned beforehand that Australians were inclined to be touchy and quick to take offence. If they are, I can only say that I didn't notice it. I found them cheerful, unpretentious and without guile. The only touchiness I observed every now and then lay in their intense, perhaps over-intense, civic pride. Each city I visited was quite obviously convinced that it was better in every way than any of the other cities. This exaggerated spirit of internecine rivalry only occasionally exceeded the bounds of courtesy – once when I was attacked in Sydney because I happened to say something in praise of Melbourne and once in Melbourne when I happened to say something in praise of Sydney.

Apart from this inter-state rivalry I found little to criticise in Australia and much to admire. I would have liked, had time permitted it, to visit a sheep farm and see some of the real country at close quarters rather than from several thousand feet in the air. I would have liked to have driven through the hinterland of Victoria, New South Wales and Queensland and had the leisure to observe Australian life away from the big cities. Perhaps some day I will. At all events, the places I did see and the people I did meet made me anxious to return quietly one day without publicity and without an official itinerary.

My farewell performance in Sydney, which closed my tour, was a special matinée given in aid of the bombed-out victims of the London blitzes. Lord Gowrie drove in a hundred miles from the country to support it and all the leading artists of Australia appeared willingly and gladly as theatre people always do. It was a tremendous success and, with the help of generous donations, a total of two thousand pounds was raised. I presume that this was sent to the Lord Mayor of London, but I do not know for certain for I never received any acknowledgement.

I spent Christmas with Lord and Lady Gowrie at Canberra, endured an unpleasant bout of colitis, and then spent a week by myself in a lovely little house on an estuary belonging to an old gentleman called Mr Allen. This kind man, having heard that I needed a few days' rest, put his house and housekeeper at my disposal. We had never met until he drove me out to instal me in it. I shall always be grateful to him because, although I spent only a few days there, the peace of it ironed me out and gave me a little time to review the last few weeks and conserve energy with which to face the next few weeks.

On December the 31st there was no sun until the evening at about five-thirty, when it suddenly emerged and seemed to set the estuary on fire. I went down and swam in the pool which was netted to keep out the sharks, and then settled myself with my back to a rock, with a packet of cigarettes by me, and looked out across the silver-grey water and yellow sandbanks to the farther shore. There was a fishing-boat a little way off and the chugging of its Diesel engine and the squalling of seagulls were the only sounds in the stillness. I looked back over the year that was just ending; at its ups and downs, its hopes, disappointments, excitements and despairs, and wondered rather bleakly if 1941 was going to be so supercharged with emotions and frustrations and so overcrowded with events and people.

1940, in immediate retrospect, seemed to me to be the most difficult, complicated year I had ever lived, so many adjustments and re-adjustments and changing circumstances. The first months of the year in Paris; the office routine, the propaganda conferences, the agitations over Radio Fécamp, the flights back and forth between Paris and London in snow and sleet, the inter-office policy discussions and arguments; then the six weeks' visit to America and the Clipper flight home. The return to America to still more irritations and frustrations. The emigration of the Orphanage; the endless train and plane journeys across the States. The voyage across the Pacific; Honolulu, Japan, China; the arrival in Australia. The handshakes, Press interviews, rehearsals, performances, bazaars, Rotary lunches, troop concerts, broadcasts, civic receptions and speeches of thanks. Above all, the people, the innumerable thousands of people. Individual faces flickered across my memory like a montage sequence in a movie: Blanche Prenez, my French teacher, convulsed with laughter at my misuse of the subjunctive; the nun crossing herself as the plane took off from Bordeaux; the sneering little Japanese officials refusing to let me land in Yokohama; Madame Birt weeping for lost years in Shanghai; Dick Casey describing Australia to me, his eyes alight with enthusiasm; ex-President Hoover abusing England to me, his eyes beady with anger; Marlene seeing me off at Pasadena; Robert Menzies welcoming me in Canberra. Kind faces, suspicious faces, famous faces, unknown faces; rows and rows of quite expressionless faces staring at me like plates; my own face leering at me from Press photographs, grinning, smirking, performing – the routine smile, so simple, so human, 'so unspoiled by his great success'; the camera angles so unpredictable, the results so often nauseating. How invaluable it would be, I reflected, if just once, just for a brief spell, I could see myself clearly from the outside, as others saw me. How helpful it would be, moving so continually across the public vision, to know what that vision really observed, to note objectively what it was in my personality that moved some people to like and applaud me and aroused in others such irritation and resentment. How salutary it would be to watch the whole performance through from the front of the house, to see to what extent the mannerisms were effective and note when and where they should be cut down. I know, as all public performers know, that it is impossible to please everyone, but it would be a comfort to know for certain, just once, that I was at least pleasing myself. I tried, lying there in the fading light, to put myself in the place of an ordinary Australian Digger, a true product of the wide open spaces, suddenly asked to sit on a hard bench in a stuffy Nissen hut and enjoy the restrained antics of a forty-year-old Englishman with no voice and a red carnation in his buttonhole. What, in the songs I sang, in the allusions I made, could possibly be entertaining to him? He obviously would have preferred a really fine singer or a saucy blonde in a décolletée evening gown, or an experienced low comedian who could convulse him with slapstick and funny stories. I was always aware of this every time I stepped on to the stage, always conscious of my inability to give my audience what it really wanted. The public performances in theatres and cinemas and Town Halls were, of course, quite different. On these occasions the audiences were urban and mixed and my stardom was an asset rather than a defect, but those poor Diggers were the ones who really commanded my sympathy and my gratitude. That I was able to keep them quiet for an hour was certainly a great tribute to my personality, but a still greater tribute to their natural courtesy and good-humour. Had I known at that moment how much those anxious misgivings were destined to torment me during the next four years I think I should have plunged into the water outside the shark net and prayed for the worst. As it was, the interminable troop concerts of the future were mercifully veiled from me. I knew I had a certain amount of them to get through in New Zealand, but that would only be for a month, after which I could relax for a bit and go home.

The last light went from the sky, the stars came out and, girding my towel round me, I walked up to the quiet house. That night, after dinner, I wrote out

the final draft of my farewell broadcast, which was scheduled for the evening
before I sailed, and went to bed. When the year 1940 actually came to end with
its toast-drinkings and handshakings and bell ringings I was fast asleep in blissful,
peaceful solitude.

5

My ship, the *Mariposa*, arrived at Auckland on Monday, January 13th, at seven-
thirty in the morning. The anchor was dropped about a mile from the dock and
so I had a leisurely breakfast and proceeded to bath and shave in good order.
While I was shaving there was a knock on the door and thinking it was the
steward I called 'Come in'. After a moment I emerged from the bathroom stark
naked and came face to face with a completely strange man clutching a Homburg
hat and looking, naturally enough, rather startled. I apologised lightly for my
casual appearance, put on my dressing-gown and offered him a cigarette. He
then told me that his name was Stevens and that he had been accredited to me as
a sort of A.D.C. by Mr Fraser, the Prime Minister, from whom he brought
cordial greetings. He had also brought the Mayor of Auckland (Sir Ernest Davis)
and three Press gentlemen, who were waiting on deck. I hurried into my clothes
as quickly as I could while Stevens gave me a rough outline of my itinerary for
the next few days. He was an affable young man and inclined to be perky.

The itinerary sounded reasonable enough, a good deal less strenuous than my
Australian programme, and my spirits lightened considerably. By the time I had
met the Mayor and been photographed on gangways waving archly to imaginary
crowds the ship had drawn alongside the harbour. We drove sedately to the hotel
and I was both relieved and a little dunched to observe that my arrival in New
Zealand had apparently caused little stir among the population. Sefton Daly had
arrived before me, delighted to be visiting his homeland under my glittering
auspices, and was waiting for me in my suite with a young man called Jack
Maclean who was to be my secretary. We ordered coffee immediately and settled
down to study the order of the day. Lunch with Lord Galway, the Governor-
General, a civic reception in the Town Hall, then my first broadcast at seven
o'clock, and that was all. I could hardly believe my eyes. Sefton giggled
sympathetically at my astonishment and reminded me that New Zealand was less
dashing and go-ahead than Australia and that I must be prepared for a slower
tempo.

I questioned Stevens about the civic reception, whereupon he looked rather
glum and said he hoped it would be all right. I gathered from his manner, that
however much he hoped, he was fairly certain that it would be far from all right. I
then asked how the tickets were selling for my first public concert in two days'
time, and he said 'So-so'. This was altogether too much for Sefton, who retired
hurriedly to the bathroom. Later, when Stevens and Jack Maclean had gone, we

had some coffee and looked the situation squarely in the eye. Evidently someone had blundered. Either there hadn't been enough advance publicity or the people of Auckland just weren't interested. In any case it seemed probable that we were in for a flop. God knows I wasn't exactly yearning for a repetition of the non-stop run-around I had been given in Australia, but a happy mean would have been acceptable. This felt like the doldrums. Envisaging a quarterful Town Hall and an almost empty theatre I started to laugh, and by the time the waiter came to fetch the tray we were both scarlet in the face.

My lunch with the Governor-General was pleasant enough. He was agreeable but seemed a little vague when I questioned him about New Zealand. Perhaps he was sick of it.

The civic reception, contrary to expectations, was a triumph. The Town Hall was packed to the ceiling and I was given an enthusiastic welcome. Not only this, but the streets were lined with people to see me drive away, which astounded Stevens almost as much as it astounded me. It also cheered me a great deal. There is nothing so damping to a publicised visitor, keyed up to expect a hullabaloo, as to be faced with no hullabaloo at all. I drove smugly back to the hotel to run through my broadcast.

From that first bleak morning onwards everything was fine. My first two troop concerts the next day were highly successful, and my public concert on the Wednesday evening was a riot. The first part of the programme consisted of Heddle Nash, a tenor, and Mary Pratt, a fine contralto. Both of them were great favourites and sang beautifully. The last half as usual I had to myself and sang for an hour. There were three thousand people in the house, and Sefton and I debated whether or not we should have to give Stevens first aid.

The Prime Minister and the Government had really taken trouble to make my visit as pleasant as possible. Sight-seeing trips had been arranged and sometimes two or three days had been left free of engagements, for which I was grateful. The whole New Zealand trip, as Sefton had predicted, was taken at a much slower tempo. In the principal towns there was, of course, a great deal to be got through – the usual public lunches and dinners and speechmaking, but in between times I was allowed to rest and enjoy the glorious scenery of both islands. In Rotorua I was given a Maori welcome. This was very special and took place in a church hall. I was met at the door by a painted warrior who capered round me for some minutes and finally made me pick up two sticks from the floor. After I had achieved this not impossible feat a great uproar broke out and I was presented to the chiefs and the local belles, with whom I rubbed noses; this was damp but convivial. Then came the entertainment, which consisted of native songs and dances, slightly spoilt for me by the fact that the male dancers wore ordinary grey flannel trousers under their straw skirts, which, I thought, vitiated the primitive barbarity of the occasion. The younger Maori maidens obliged with some modern Tin-Pan alley tunes which they sang with more enthusiasm than accuracy. The old guard, however, when the party got really going, sang some of the vintage Maori songs, which were entrancing. At the end of all this I sang a few numbers myself, which were listened to with polite bewilderment, and was presented with a carved wooden box and an ink-stand.

Rotorua is famous for its geysers, hot springs and thermal baths. I was taken through a Maori village where they cook, work and bathe in pools of different temperatures provided considerately by the Great Redeemer. Ocassionally the Great Redeemer goes too far and a bit of ground caves in and someone gets scalded to death. Personally I felt that to be able to boil an egg in a puddle outside your front door, although undoubtedly labour-saving, was not really enough compensation for having to live immediately on top of the earth's hidden fires.

Stevens accompanied us everywhere. He was really a nice young man, but desperately jocular. He invariably greeted me every morning with 'Good morrow, kind sir. How are we this merry morn?' He alluded to any hotel proprietor as Mine Host and referred to any female, regardless of age or size, as Girlie.

We were driven through rich green country; we visited the Waitomo caves and saw millions of glow-worms glittering on the rocks overhead like stars; we picnicked, on our journeys between airfields and training camps, among vast ferns. 'Down with the jolly old rug,' Stevens would say with a merry laugh, and down went the jolly old rug.

The South Island is more spectacularly beautiful than the North Island because of its vivid snow capped mountains. Christchurch is a lovely town, gently reminiscent of an English cathedral city. This is Sefton's birthplace and he played two of his own compositions at my concert, which were, rightly, received enthusiastically. The high spot of the whole tour for me was a troop concert in the Town Hall at Dunedin. The audience of several thousand men had marched from surrounding camps, some of which were as far as fifty miles away. They marched through the town with bands playing about an hour before the concert was due to begin. This, although a thrilling spectacle, filled me with dread, for I had no symphony orchestra and no other artists to help me through the evening. All those gallent men were going to get was just me and Sefton's two compositions. They were quick-witted and wonderful; one of the most receptive all-male audiences I have ever performed to. I sang for an hour and forty minutes and then, as they still seemed eager for me, went on for a further quarter of an hour. At the end I felt so exhilarated that I could cheerfully have given another performance then and there.

Wellington was hectic and crowded and there was a fuss about my public concert being broadcast because it had been hinted that some of my lyrics might not be quite proper enough to be blown out over the ether. As I detest aggressive puritanism, or indeed any kind of puritanism, this flung me into a rage and I said firmly that either the concert must be broadcast in its entirety as arranged or not broadcast at all. The battle raged for several hours and I was ultimately victorious. The concert was a success and there was a reception afterwards in the Mayor's parlour, during which I had a slight set-to with the Mayoress. She was, I am sure, an excellent Mayoress, but seemed to me to suffer from delusions of grandeur, or perhaps she was a prey to agonising shyness and, like many such unfortunate people, sought to conceal it beneath an over-forthright manner. At all events, whatever subconscious motives prompted her behaviour, the result was gratuitously rude. She said to me in ringing tones that I was never to dare to sing 'The Stately Homes of England' again as it was an insult to the homeland and that neither she nor anybody else liked it. I replied coldly that for many years it had been one of my greatest successes, whereupon she announced triumphantly to everyone within earshot: 'You see – he can't take criticism!' Irritated beyond endurance I replied that I was perfectly prepared to take intelligent criticism at any time, but I was not prepared to tolerate bad manners. With this I bowed austerely and left the party.

Afterwards when my rage evaporated, I regretted having been so quick to take offence. It is the duty of a visitor to remain unmoved in such situations and, on the whole, I think I have succeeded pretty well in restraining my feelings in public. Every now and then, however, some little incident happens, some particular inanity flicks my nerves, snaps my control and, to my dismay, sends me stamping down into the arena. A sudden, unprovoked attack is always startling, especially when one is on show and 'observing the niceties'. Apparently for certain individuals men and women in the public eye are regarded as fair game. There they stand, the admired and the envied, smirking and bowing, surrounded with gushing sycophants: why shouldn't they be knocked off their balance occasionally, taken down a peg or two, made to look foolish? It does not occur to such mutinous observers that the poor beasts may be a great deal more vulnerable than they appear to be. A central figure at a social function isn't always as happy as he looks: he is seldom permitted to talk for more than a few minutes with anyone he wants to talk to, and very often is bogged down, for what seems like hours, with someone whom he doesn't. Then there is his own degree of natural poise to be considered. Is he really as much at ease as appears on the surface? Is that attentive smile, that charming assurance, really genuine? Or is it perhaps masking an inward shyness, a desolate boredom, a frustrated longing to spit in the face of cackling pleasantries and rush screaming from the room? In Hollywood and other parts of the United States husbands and wives obtain divorces every day of the week on the grounds of mental cruelty. I have often thought of founding a society for the 'Prevention of Mental Cruelty to Celebrities'. To me the worst offenders are those women whose self-righteous egocentricity makes them wish to impress the celebrity rather than be impressed by him. These crusaders cherish the belief that forthright criticism, preferably in public, is more admirable than conventional politeness. They feel, I am sure, by saying what they think, straight-from-the-shoulder-and-no-nonsense, that their devastating honesty provides a refreshing breeze in a stuffy atmosphere, and that they will be gratefully remembered for it. 'Who was that attractive little woman in the mauve hat? She actually told me that she loathed my plays and that I over-acted! I should like to see *her* again.' In this belief they are, alas, misguided. They will be remembered certainly, but not quite in the way they would have wished. They will be remembered for having made the task of the guest of honour just a little harder than it need have been. They will be remembered for having placed him in a position of acute embarrassment. They will also be remembered, not for their moral courage, but for their lack of social grace.

Happily my progress through the years has been fairly untroubled by such idiots, but they crop up every now and then. Usually a sort of conditioned reflex, a personal radar, warns me of their approach and I am able to mow them down before they can get far. Occasionally, however, they take me completely by surprise and there I am with a brawl on my hands.

The official part of my New Zealand tour finished in Wellington, and I flew back to Auckland to wait for a day or two for the Clipper to take me to Canton Island, where I had arranged to stop off for a week to catch my breath and get some sun. I occupied the few days by writing some long-delayed letters home; luxuriating in the knowledge that I had no more speeches to make and no more songs to sing, and that I could stay in bed late in the morning and return to it early at night with enough vitality left over to enjoy reading a book. Stevens and Sefton were still with me and we went to a jolly old movie or two. At one of these the manager, in a fit of misguided enthusiasm, flashed on the screen an announcement that I was present in the cinema. This produced gratifying applause and finally resulted in a free-for-all in the lobby at the end of the performance. It was a Saturday night and the theatre was full, and it took us about twenty minutes to get out on to the pavement and into the car. Once in it there was near tragedy. A mother, obviously in the grip of mass hysteria, handed me her baby through the window, screaming: 'Kiss my little girlie, go on, kiss her!' At this moment the car started to move and I was caught with the little girlie's head while the mother hung on to its legs. With commendable presence of mind I struck the mother sharply on the head with my left hand and yanked the child into the car with me before its back was broken. There was a great deal of shrieking, the car stopped, and I handed back girlie unhurt and unkissed. She had, however, utilised her brief moment of perilous reflected glory by wetting me to the skin.

6

My Clipper left Auckland at 7.30 a.m. on February 3rd and arrived at New Caledonia in the afternoon, where the passengers were allowed to go ashore, drive about, bathe, and dine aboard the Pan-American yacht *Southern Seas*. There was no point in going to bed because we had to leave again at three-thirty in the morning, so I spent the hours enjoying a light drinking bout with the

Captain, a homesick North Countryman called Beardsall, Crowther, a pilot who had flown me from Batavia to Singapore in 1936, and a couple of others. It was a pleasant interlude, romantic too in its own way because it had a quality familiar to all travellers – an evanescence, a 'here today and gone tomorrow' friendliness enhanced by tropical stars, lights glimmering in the distant town and the small waves of the lagoon slapping gently against the side of the ship.

The plane was due to arrive at Canton Island at 7 p.m. the following evening, but owing to head-winds there was a delay of three hours; there was also a feeling of tension because there were no other islands within hundreds of miles and the passengers (perhaps the crew as well) were beginning to wonder how much longer the fuel would hold out. At last, however, there was a gleeful shout from the forward end of the plane and we all pressed our foreheads against the tiny circular windows and stared down into the blackness where, thousands of feet below us, was a small cluster of winking lights looking like a Cartier bracelet flung on to black velvet. Canton Island is a coral reef, one degree south of the equator, twenty-nine miles round and no wider than a few hundred yards at any point. It enclosed a lagoon into which there is only one narrow entrance from the open sea, not wide enough to give passage to anything larger than a launch. The Clipper made a perfect landing, the doors were opened and the warm tropical night air came swirling in. The passengers walked along a little wooden jetty and straight into the lounge of a typical American luxury hotel. The effect was startling. I had settled in my mind for a ramshackle bamboo guest-house with wide tumble-down verandas and inadequate plumbing, and was prepared to endure all manner of creature discomforts for the sake of rest and sun. I had certainly not bargained for private showers, luxurious beds, shining Fifth Avenue chintzes and a chromium cocktail bar. The Clipper took off again at noon the following day, leaving me behind in the empty hotel with seven clear days in which to swim and read and enjoy myself.

The island, although scenically disappointing, for there was no scenery beyond a few palms was exactly what I wanted. A glorious lagoon a few feet away full of vivid tropical fish, pounding surf a few yards away to supply a permanent lullaby, a tennis court, a small sailing-boat belonging to Dick Danner, the island entomologist, and, above all, time and to spare.

The hotel was run by a young American couple called Jack and Lordee Bramham. In addition to them there was a sprinkling of men concerned with the running of the airport, and the ground staff for servicing the planes. A hundred yards or so away from the hotel was the British Residency and a radio station. The official British residents were a Mr and Mrs Fleming. Frank Fleming had built the house, aided by some Chamarro boys, virtually with his own hands. He ran the radio office, raised the Union Jack solemnly every morning and lowered it every night. They were two very nice people. My note about them in my diary reads as follows: 'Called on Flemings after dinner and had a drink with them. Typically English in the best possible sense, simple, unpretentious and getting on with the job. They came here alone, before Pan American, from Fiji, or rather he did. He built the house they live in and she joined him later. They have relatives in London and Sussex and suffer occasionally from bad bouts of homesickness coupled with a certain irritation at the Americans, who have so much luxury such a little way away. They have no official photograph of the King and Queen, only a framed reproduction from the *Illustrated London News* which has buckled because the rain-water got into the frame during the last cyclone. Promised to report this when I get home. Feel there is a story in them.'

A few months after my return to London I had the opportunity of telling the Queen about the buckled reproduction, and a few days later received a letter from her lady-in-waiting informing me that a photograph of Their Majesties had been sent to Mr and Mrs Fleming. Later still, in 1949, I made an approximation of their characters and situation the basis of a story called 'Mr and Mrs Edgehill' (*Star Quality*: Heinemann). I sent it to them the moment it was published, but I don't know if they ever received it.

There were other story possibilities on Canton Island – there always are in small isolated communities. Local conflicts and dramas and comedies swell to terrific proportions when there is nothing but surf and sky, the elements surrounding you and no escape, not even for a week-end. Even during the short time I spent on Canton Island there were several excitements. One was the arrival, three weeks late, of the supply ship. This was a great moment; we had lived on fish for days and were right out of cigarettes. The ship was sighted in the early afternoon. Everyone cheered. There was, as usual, a heavy sea running. The launch put out through the narrow channel and managed to reach the ship safely, but on the way back, loaded to the gunwales with much-needed stores, it capsized in the surf and sank like a stone. Fortunately no one was drowned, although some of the crew were badly battered by the reefs. The cigarettes, thank God, floated ashore in their tin containers.

There was also the episode of the cyclone. The New Zealand-bound Clipper was due one evening at 8 p.m., but owing to a cyclone blowing up between it and Canton Island, it was delayed for several hours, too far from Honolulu to be able to turn back and too far from any other possible landing place. The evident drama of the situation was made even more poignant on the island because the wife of Hal Graves, the airport manager, was on board the plane with their newly-born child. From eight until one in the morning we all sat about, either in the hotel or the airport office, waiting for news. Radio messages occasionally got through, but the weather was so appalling that they were mostly unintelligible. Then came the news which we both hoped for and dreaded – the Clipper was coming in to land. Hal Graves, white and shaking but in perfect control, rushed out to the launch followed by me and Jack Bramham. I was wearing bathing trunks and a mackintosh because the rain was torrential and there was no sense in wearing anything else. The launch, with its revolving circular light, chugged up and down the lagoon in the blackness. We on the deck were straining our eyes to try and spot the plane through the mist and the rain. Suddenly there it was immediately above our heads; it zoomed low over the hotel, missing the roof by inches, disappeared completely and then, a few seconds later, reappeared and dropped gently down on to the water. I remember yelling violently with relief. Mrs Graves and the baby emerged unscathed and so did the rest of the passengers. They looked shaken I thought, but cheered up after some whisky and hot soup.

The same prowling cyclone that had provided us with this drama kept everyone weatherbound in the hotel for four days. The America-bound Clipper which was to take me away managed to land two days later, but was unable to take off again, and so there we were, two full passenger loads and two crews all milling about, and all, in varying degrees, frustrated, uncomfortable and cross. Lordee and Jack kept their heads; extra beds were made up in odd places, the meals were staggered and general chaos reigned until the morning of the fifth day, when the weather lifted enough for the New Zealand-bound Clipper to take off. With relief we waved it up into the clouds. The relief, however, was short-lived, for the plane was back again in two hours with engine trouble. Early the next morning, after several hours of conflicting rumours, my Clipper finally took off. As it taxied along the lagoon I looked out through the spray at the dawn coming up. The plane circled round once and headed back to the world. The week's holiday I had planned had lasted sixteen days, but seemed somehow much longer than that. I felt that I had been living on that coral strip for months. Australia and New Zealand had dropped into the far past. I craned my head to look back just before we flew into a cloudbank. There it lay, that tiny coral circlet in the blue water; the jetty, the lagoon, the coloured fish, the little white terns so tame that they perched on your hand, Lordee and Jack, Hal Graves's baby screaming its lungs out and Frank Fleming, wearing an old pair of khaki shorts, hauling up the flag.

6a

The cyclone which had been causing everyone such inconvenience had either gone off in another direction or blown itself out of existence, for after only an hour or so in cloud the plane was droning along through clear sky with the sea far below glittering in the sunlight. I read and dozed fitfully, reflecting how agreeable air travel can be when the weather is good and how excessively disagreeable when it isn't. We were due to arrive in Honolulu in the late afternoon, where I hoped to spend a few hours with the Dillinghams before taking off again at midnight for Los Angeles. This hope was more than gratified, for I was forced, owing to weather conditions, to spend four days with them. However, on that bright morning, poised between infinity and the sea, there seemed to be no cloud in the universe, until a distinguished-looking gentleman with a beard came over and sat next to me. He introduced himself as Professor

Fischel and explained that he was the nephew of King Feisal. We had, he said, a great mutual friend in the late Lord Lloyd. I stared at him in astonishment and said: 'Why late?' He then went on to tell me that George Lloyd had died a few days previously in London. The bitter surprise of this made me speechless for a moment, and seeing from my expression how upset I was, he apologised for giving me bad news so abruptly and left me to myself. I was grateful to him for this consideration and lay back with my eyes closed trying to adjust my mind to the shock. I have been told that when the body suffered a sharp blow the entire organism reacts immediately; all gland secretions are affected, first-aid units are automatically sent scurrying through ducts and channels to the scene of the trouble and the bloodstream itself changes its consistency. In fact a 'Calling all cars' state of emergency is declared and a combined therapeutic operation is set in motion in a split second. When the mind suffers a sharp blow I presume that something of the same kind occurs; a general rally is sounded, an immediate anaesthesia administered, either in the form of a fainting fit or temporary incredulity, or just merciful numbness. Very few civilised people give way to transports of noisy grief on the receipt of bad news. It is later that the heart aches and the eyes fill with tears.

Up until 1941 Fate had been considerate to me. I had suffered no sudden bereavements, lost no really close friends since the death of John Ekins in 1916. People I had known and liked had died from time to time, causing me momentary regrets but touching me with only the shadow of real sadness. The death of George Lloyd was a horrible shock to me. He was a great man in many ways. He had dynamic vitality, humour, tremendous executive ability and, to me, always a kind and generous heart. He was an Imperialist, in the best sense because his passionate love of England and his unshakable belief in the British Empire were based on common sense. He taught me much in the fortunate years that I knew him, and I was aware then, in the trans-Pacific Clipper, faced with the fact of his sudden death, that if ever I did anything in my life to change his good opinion of me I should be very ashamed.

7

Three weeks later I was in another Clipper heading across the Atlantic to England via Bermuda, the Azores and Lisbon. The ceiling was low but my spirits were high. I was bearing a pouch with some letters for the Foreign Office and a courier's passport, which gave me a sense of mysterious importance. Little Bill had offered me a job which, in his opinion and in mine, would be of real value to the war effort, and would utilise not only my celebrity value by my intelligence as well. I had had some intensive briefing in New York and Washington and was now in a state of, alas, premature exaltation. It is not my intention in this book to give an account of the work for which I was being groomed, because the whole enterprise was nipped in the bud by High Authority in London before my plane had reached Bermuda. There the crushing news was broken to me in a cable from Little Bill. He gave no explanations, merely a brief message announcing that the whole thing was off, but I gathered from the very terseness of the message that 'A greater power than we could contradict had thwarted our intents'. It was a horrid disappointment and cost me some black hours, but there was obviously nothing to do but rise above it, figuratively and literally, and fly on home as soon as possible. On looking back over those difficult, enraging moments in 1940 and 1941 it is curious to reflect that, in the long run, fate always proved to be on my side. If the Duff Cooper American scheme had come off I should never have had the rewarding experience of Australia and New Zealand. If Little Bill's job had materialised I should never have written *Blithe Spirit*, *In Which We Serve* or *London Pride*. When I received that devastating message in Bermuda, however, all these were in the future and I returned to England with my spirits lower than they had been when I started.

On arrival at Bristol I was met by Gladys, looking very smart in her M.T.C. uniform, and when the Immigration and Customs officials had finished with me we drove up to London. During that two hours' drive all inner anxieties and disappointments were elbowed out of my mind by the sheer pleasure of being home again. My studio in Gerald Road was still occupied by Dallas Brooks, who had been living in it while I was away, so we drove to Claridge's, where Lorn was waiting for me in an elaborate suite. So vast and imposing was it that I decided there and then to give it up the following morning and return to my own spare room at the studio. On that first night home, however, after a gay reunion party at Clemence Dane's, I retired to bed slightly fried blissfully happy and in excessive luxury.

The next day the Press had been invited to meet me at Gerald Road. All the little men who had been busy vilifying me when I was at the other side of the world – I had been looking forward to meeting them face to face and telling them exactly what I thought of them for months, but, of course, when they actually arrived nothing happened at all. I found, when confronted with them on my own ground, that the whole occasion was utterly without importance. Instead of the white-heat of self-righteous indignation with which I had intended to sear them there was nothing in my heart but boredom. They were all polite and most of them seemed to be quite amiably disposed. When they had all been given drinks they sat about expectantly, and so I told them, rather dully I fear, the accurate story of my activities since September 1939. I explained, mildly, that I had *not* run away from the perils of war; that I had *not* worn a uniform to which I was not entitled; that I *had* been officially appointed as Sir Campbell's representative in Paris; that I *had* been sent to America by the Minister of Information and that my visit to Australia and New Zealand had been at the express invitation of the Governments of those Dominions. I then went on to remind them, without heat, that whereas it was perfectly within their rights as newspaper men to comment as unfavourably as they wished on my talents, either creative or interpretative, they had no right whatsoever, without incontrovertible proof, to impugn my private character or my personal integrity. They listened attentively to all this, and when I had finished one or two of them asked some uninspired questions, which I managed to answer without any undue strain on my temper, after which they each had another drink and went away.

The reports in the newspapers the next day were quite civil, although only one of them was an accurate statement of what I had said. This account was written by the only woman reporter present. I suspected when I read it that she would either go far in her profession or get the sack immediately. I have never discovered if either of these surmises were correct.

In due course I moved back into the studio. Dallas was no trouble as a tenant-guest, and as he was out most of the time that I was in, and vice versa, we got along very happily for a few days until the Luftwaffe intervened and blew our agreeable little ménage to pieces. This occurred on the evening of April the 16th. When the raid started I was dining at the Hungaria. The restaurant was underground and all we could hear at first was a series of distant thumps. Presently the manager came to our table and said that the raid was becoming serious and that we had better stay where we were. This advice was immediately disregarded, our party dispersed and I walked down towards the Admiralty with Robert Neville, who at that time was Deputy Director of Naval Intelligence. There had been a few minor raids since my return six days before, but this one was obviously on a much bigger scale. Having left Robert Neville at the Admiralty I hailed a taxi in Trafalgar Square and drove off along the Mall. The sky above Carlton House Terrace was red with the reflected glow of fires, presumably in the Piccadilly district, and the rooftops and chimney-pots were etched black against it. There was a lot of noise and gunfire and, every so often, a shattering explosion. My taxi-driver drove hell for leather, keeping up a breathless running commentary as he did so. I was interested to note, this being my first experience of a blitz, that I was not frightened at all. This surprised me, because physical courage has never been one of my strong points. I can only suppose that I was so inured to the terrors of air raids by listening to the over-dramatic accounts of them on the American radio, that the actual experience was an anti-climax. This curious detachment under bombardment remained with me throughout the war, and I have never been able to understand it. I do hope that, to the reader, this does not appear to be retrospective smugness, because it is actually true. I have been far more frightened flying in the ordinary aeroplane between London and Paris than I ever was in an air raid. To me the feeling of inevitability, the knowledge that there was nothing I could possibly do about it, numbed any fears I might have had and induced a form of objective fatalism. I wish I could achieve this same immunity from sickening fright when I am in a car with a dangerous driver. I was badly frightened on several occasions during the war, but those occasions had nothing to do with anything so impersonally lethal as bombs and landmines and doodle-bugs.

As my taxi rattled along Ebury Street I saw ahead of me the four corners by South Eaton Place blazing to the skies. This I realised was too near the studio for comfort. The taxi deposited me at my door in Gerald Road. I invited the driver in for a drink, but he refused and drove away, leaving me to scramble over rubble and broken glass in the alleyway to get to my front door. Fortunately my electric torch was new and bright and its beam saved me the trouble of fumbling for my latchkey by disclosing that only a little of the front door was there. The stairs inside were a shambles because the skylight had fallen in. I crackled up them and into the studio, where I found Dallas Brooks, also with a torch, wearing a grey dressing-gown and rubbing a slight bump on his forehead where the bedroom chandelier had struck him. Before he had had time to register my arrival a bomb fell near-by and the whole house shook. 'The buggers,' he said laconically and went to the whisky decanter. After we had each had a quick drink I told him I had some morphine capsules in my pocket, that I was going out to see if I could help the wounded, and that he'd better dress and come too. He replied with some grandeur that he would with pleasure, but that he had lost his glasses. While we were both groping about looking for them there was another louder explosion which brought down the main skylight, shattered the high windows and sent two oak doors skittering past us like ballet dancers. This was followed by a slower, more ominous noise from the direction of the Mews. 'That,' I said, 'sounds like the office.' I stumbled down the three steps leading to the Mews side of the house, where there is a sliding door. This stuck fast, but I managed to move it enough to peer with my torch into the darkness and verify my suspicions. It was indeed the office. The whole ceiling had fallen in and was lying on the floor. I went back through the studio and out of the house, calling to Dallas to follow me as soon as he could. I raced round the corner into South Eaton Place gripping my box of morphine capsules in the pocket of my coat. The spectacle at the corner of Elbury Street was horrifying. Houses were blazing, the road was a mass of rubble: some fire-fighters were standing quite silently with a hose directing streams of water on to the flames. There was a momentary lull in the raid and the sudden cessation of noise was eerie. I asked an A.R.P. warden if I could be of any help with the injured and he said all who could be got out had been taken away an hour ago. At this moment I noticed, coming towards me rather mincingly across the rubble, two smartly-dressed young girls in high-heeled shoes. As they passed close by me I heard one say to the other: 'You know, dear, the trouble with all this is you could rick your ankle.' This example of British understatement so enchanted me that I laughed out loud. The warden looked sharply at me, obviously suspecting hysteria, and said hadn't I better get indoors. I explained gently that at the moment there was very little indoors to get into, then we exchanged cigarettes and a little light conversation until Dallas joined us wearing full Marine regalia and a tin hat.

Later on, after we had got a couple of gallant old girls out of a tobacconist's and led them into the house next door to my studio, where they were wrapped in blankets and given some whisky, we made our way to Gladys Calthrop's house in Spenser Street, I on a bicycle and Dallas on foot. She received us with relief and we sat drinking hot tea while the raid started up again. Presently I dropped off to sleep on the sofa and was awakened by the All Clear.

The next morning Gladys and I went round to Gerald Road to see by daylight the real extent of the damage. Lorn, to whom I had telephoned, met us there with Ann, my housekeeper, who made us some coffee. We sat gingerly in the studio itself, on the edge of a soot-covered sofa, and shook our heads like mandarins. The skylights were all down; the main windows, which were enormous, had shattered inside their heavy curtains, so that the curtains were bulging out over the two grand pianos. In my bedroom, where Dallas had been sleeping, the chandelier was down, also a lot of plaster. Lorn's office was in the worst mess. The ceiling was on the floor and up out of it was rearing a tall filing cabinet on which stood an uncracked photograph of Jack and Natasha, smiling. The spare room, which I was occupying until Dallas moved out, was undamaged. The bed was neatly turned down with my pyjamas laid out on it, but everything, bed and furniture and pyjamas, were so thick with soot that they looked like black velvet. On the whole the damage was much less than I feared, but the place obviously couldn't be lived in even if we could get the windows boarded up, so I telephoned to the Savoy and reserved a room for that night, and we all trooped out to look at the wreck of the streets. The houses on the corner were still smouldering and groups of people were standing about staring aimlessly, their faces looking wan and papery in the cold morning light. There was a hopeless, beastly smell in the air. I suddenly felt miserable and most profoundly angry.

8

The day-to-day account in my diary of those weeks immediately following my homecoming is inadequate to say the least of it – nothing but a telegraphic jumble of people's names, half-formed impressions, visits to the movies with Joyce, discussions with Lorn, lunches, teas and dinners with so-and-so and such-and-such, and hardly any indication whatsoever of what was really going on in my mind. A stranger reading it in the hope of finding some clue to my character would, after the first few pages, dismiss me for ever as illiterate, incoherent and trivial to the point of idiocy. Even my own efforts to recapture from it, for the purposes of this book, a gleam of genuine significance, a hint of what I really felt, have resulted in bewildered exasperation. 'Discussion with Lorn' – what about? 'Long talk with Duff, very satisfactory' – why? 'Lunched with Joyce and Arthur, laughed hilariously' – what at? 'Bought bicycle at Fortnum's and ordered tin hat at shop in Victoria Street.' 'Tea with the Cranbornes; what a dear she is!' – what did she murmur to me over tea that so endeared her? 'Drinks at the Berkeley with Eric and Bob' — Eric and Bob who? 'Fell off bicycle' — where? After grim concentration and a great deal of brain-racking I have managed to fish out of this irrelevant welter an occasional clue, a slight spur to memory, but the overall picture is blurred and confused and gives me very little to go on. I can remember clearly two genuine emotions that illuminated that particular period. One was my relief at being home again and among my friends, and the other was a completely new appreciation of the charm and quality of London. London as a city had in the past never attracted me much. It was my home, of course, and I knew it intimately, perhaps too intimately. In my early days I had known its seamy side and later on more of its graces, but it had always seemed to me a little dull and smug compared with the romantic gaiety of Paris and the sharp vitality of New York. Now suddenly, in my early forties, I saw it for the first time as somewhere where I belonged. This sentimental revelation was made clearer to me by the fact that I was staying in a London hotel for the first time in my life. It was a strange sensation to step out of the comfortable impersonality of the Savoy into the personal, familiar streets of my childhood. I felt a sudden urge to visit the Tower and the Abbey and Madame Tussaud's and go to the Zoo. The move from Gerald Road to the Strand had transformed me overnight into a tourist in my own home, and as such it seemed more attractive to me and more genuinely gay than it had ever been before. I am not sure that that particular quality of gaiety survived the war. The rigours of peace and post-war party politics have done much to dim its glow, but in 1941, the real lights of London shone through the blackout with a steady brilliance that I shall never forget.

Three days after I had moved into the Savoy, Gladys and Bill Taylor and I were dining in the Grill, which was crowded. The usual Alert had sounded and we were half-way through dinner when two bombs dropped near-by, the second of which blew in one of the doors of the restaurant. There was dead silence for a split second after the crash and then everyone started talking again. With gallantry, tinged, I suspect, with a strong urge to show off, I sprang on to the orchestra platform where Carroll Gibbons was playing the piano, and sang several songs before anyone could stop me. The startled diners had little chance, anyhow, because Carroll was on my side and I had the microphone. Faced with the limited choice of staying where they were or rushing out into the blitz, the majority resigned themselves to the inevitable and we had quite a little party. Judy Campbell joined me on the platform and sang 'A Nightingale in Berkeley Square', and a group of slightly drunk but charmingly vocal Scotch-Canadians in kilts obliged with 'Shenandoah' and 'Billy Boy' in loose harmony. The whole occasion was a great success and there was a lot of cheering.

A day or two later the management of the Savoy courteously offered me a 'River Suite' at the same rate that I was paying for my single room. I suspected Carroll's wily hand in this, but I accepted gratefully without quibbling. It was a nice suite and I lived in it happily for several months.

During the next two weeks I see in my diary (one of its rare moments of coherence) that I spent a week-end with Gladys at her Mill near Ashford. The weather was nippy and the house, as usual, freezing, for Gladys is famous for her imperviousness to temperature. However, I grabbed two hot-water bottles and slept blissfully, sniffing up the fresh Kentish air. We drove over to Goldenhurst, a melancholy experience. All my furniture was in store at Whitstable and the house looked pathetic and derelict with only trestle tables and camp beds. On the whole it had been well cared for and the Commanding Officer, with whom we had tea, couldn't have been nicer, but I left with a feeling of nostalgia. My diary reports as follows: 'Visited G. Garden in fine condition but house oppressed by ghosts. Captain M. nice. Tea in what used to be Mother's sitting-room. Poor old Goldenhurst, I wonder if I shall ever see it again – have a strong feeling that I shall not. It seems that that is all over.'

On Friday, May the 2nd, Joyce Carey and I caught a morning train from Paddington, bound for Port Meirion in North Wales. For some time past an idea for a light comedy had been rattling at the door of my mind and I thought the time had come to let it in and show it a little courtesy. Joyce was engaged in writing a play about Keats, so here we were, 'Hurrah for the Holidays', without buckets and spades but with typewriters, paper, carbons, bathing-suits, sun-tan oil and bezique cards. We arrived on a golden evening, sighed with pleasure at the mountains and the sea in the late sunlight, and settled ourselves into a pink guest-house. The next morning we sat on the beach with our backs against the sea wall and discussed my idea exclusively for several hours. Keats, I regret to say, was not referred to. By lunch-time the title had emerged together with the names of the characters, and a rough, very rough, outline of the plot. At seven-thirty the next morning I sat, with the usual nervous palpitations, at my typewriter. Joyce was upstairs in her room wrestling with Fanny Brawne. There was a pile of virgin paper on my left and a box of carbons on my right. The table wobbled and I had to put a wedge under one of its legs. I smoked several cigarettes in rapid succession, staring gloomily out of the window at the tide running out. I fixed the paper into the machine and started: *Blithe Spirit*. A Light Comedy in Three Acts.

For six days I worked from eight to one each morning and from two to seven each afternoon. On Friday evening, May the 9th, the play was finished and, disdaining archness and false modesty, I will admit that I knew it was witty, I knew it was well constructed and I also knew that it would be a success. My gift for comedy dialogue, which I feared might have atrophied from disuse, had obviously profited from its period of inactivity. Beyond a few typographical errors I made no corrections, and only two lines of the original script were ultimately cut. I take pride in these assertions, but it is a detached pride, natural enough in the circumstances and not to be confused with boastfulness. I was not attempting to break any records, to prove how quickly I could write and how clever I was. I was fully prepared to revise and re-write the whole play had I thought it necessary, but I did not think it necessary. I knew from the first morning's work that I was on the right track and that it would be difficult, with that situation and those characters, to go far wrong. I can see no particular virtue in writing quickly; on the contrary, I am well aware that too great a facility is often dangerous, and should be curbed where it shows signs of getting the bit too firmly between its teeth. No reputable writer should permit his talent to bolt with him. I am also aware though, from past experience, that when the right note is struck and the structure of a play is carefully built in advance, it is both wise and profitable to start at the beginning and write through to the end in as short a time as possible. On the occasions when I have followed this procedure with other plays, notably *Private Lives* (four days) and *Present Laughter* (six days), the results have, I believe, justified the method. *Blithe Spirit* was exceptional from these two that I have mentioned only because its conception was followed immediately by the actual writing of it. *Private Lives* lived in my mind several months before it emerged. *Present Laughter* had waited about, half formulated, for nearly three years before I finally wrote it. Somerset Maugham has laid down that a good short story should have a beginning, a middle and an end. To me this is unassailable common sense and applies even more sternly to playwriting. Before the first word of the first act is written, the last act should be clearly in the author's mind, if not actually written out in the form of a synopsis. Dialogue, for those who have a talent for it, is easy; but construction, with or without talent, is difficult and is of paramount importance. I know this sounds like heresy in this era of highly-praised, half-formulated moods, but no mood, however exquisite, is likely to hold the attention of an audience for two hours and a half unless it is based on a solid structure.

Between May the 9th, when *Blithe Spirit* was finished at Port Meirion, and June the 16th, when it opened its preliminary tour in Manchester, several things happened. Rudolf Hess arrived in Scotland, which affected me very little, although it flung the Press boys at the Savoy into a frenzy of excitement and wild surmise. The Metro-Goldwyn-Mayer epic film of *Bitter Sweet* in violent Technicolor arrived at the Empire, which affected me even less, for I had already seen it in a projection room in Hollywood and had decided, sensibly, to wipe it from my mind. It was directed with gusto by Mr Victor Saville and sung with even more gusto by Miss Jeanette Macdonald and Mr Nelson Eddy. It was vulgar, lacking in taste and bore little relation to my original story. What did affect me, however, was the news on May the 27th of the sinking of H.M.S. *Kelly*, although naturally I had no idea at the time how much more this was destined to affect me in the future. Immediately the news broke I telephoned to Robert Neville at the Admiralty, and he told me that Mountbatten had survived and was coming home. This was a great relief, but knowing how much his ship meant to him, and remembering with what pride he had taken me over her only a short while ago, I felt miserable.

Blithe Spirit, after the usual casting troubles and complications, duly opened in Manchester and was an enormous success. The London opening night was on July the 2nd at the Piccadilly Theatre, and a very curious opening night it was.

The audience, socially impeccable from the journalistic point of view and mostly in uniform, had to walk across planks laid over the rubble caused by a recent air raid to see a light comedy about death. They enjoyed it, I am glad to say, and it ran from that sunny summer evening through the remainder of the war and out the other side. A year later it transferred to the St James's Theatre for a while, and then finally went to the Duchess, where at last it closed on March the 9th, 1946.

Later on, the play was produced in New York by Jack Wilson, where it ran for eighteen months, and I am prepared to say, here and now, with the maximum of self-satisfaction that those six days in Port Meirion in May 1941 were not wasted.

A few days after the *Blithe Spirit* opening, a deputation of three gentlemen, Filippo del Giudice, Anthony Havelock-Allan and Charles Thorpe, called on me at the Savoy Hotel. I received them warily because I knew that the object of their visit was to persuade me to make a film, and I had no intention of making a film then or at any other time. I had generated in my mind a strong prejudice against the moving-picture business, a prejudice compounded of small personal experience and considerable intellectual snobbery. I had convinced myself, with easy sophistry, that it was a soul-destroying industry in which actors of mediocre talent were publicised and idolised beyond their deserts, and authors, talented or otherwise, were automatically massacred. Of all my plays only one, *Cavalcade*, had been filmed with taste and integrity. The rest, with the possible exception of *Private Lives*, which was passable, had been re-written by incompetent hacks, vulgarised by incompetent directors and reduced to common fatuity. My only experience as a film actor had been *The Scoundrel*, which was made in New York, or rather at the Astoria Studios, Brooklyn, in 1935. It was written and directed by Ben Hecht and Charles MacArthur and I agreed to do it because I thought the idea was good and, most particularly, because I was promised that Helen Hayes, whom I love and admire, would play the young poetess. However, at the last minute she was unable to get out of some contract and the part had to be re-cast. Finally, after much trial and error, Julie Haydon walked into the office, read the part sensitively and was engaged. The picture was made quickly and fairly efficiently; most of its speed and efficiency being due to Lee Garmes, the cameraman. The direction of Charlie MacArthur and Ben Hecht was erratic, and I, who had never made a picture before, was confused and irritated from the beginning to the end. *The Scoundrel* was hailed with critical acclaim. I made a success in it and so did everyone concerned, but I still wish that it and they and I had been better.

It can be seen therefore, with this annoying episode strong in my memory, why I received del Giudice and his confrères with a certain lack of enthusiasm. The interview passed off pleasantly enough. Del Giudice was flattering and persuasive, Tony Havelock-Allan equally persuasive and rather more articulate, while Thorpe, who represented Columbia Pictures – why I shall never know – remained watchful and uncommunicative. This non-committal attitude was explained later on when he and Columbia Pictures withdrew their support from the enterprise because they did not consider that my name had sufficient drawing power. When the three of them had filed out I had agreed to think the proposition over carefully and give them my answer in a week's time. The actual proposition they had put to me was that if I agreed to write and appear in a picture for them I should have complete control of cast, director, subject, cameraman, etc., and that all financial aspects would be, they assured me, settled to my satisfaction once I had consented. It would have been churlish not to appreciate that this was a very flattering offer indeed, and although all my instincts were against it, I was forced to admit to myself that, provided I could think of a suitable idea, there was a good deal to be said for it. The very next evening Fate obligingly intervened and rang a bell so loudly in my brain that I was unable to ignore it. I happened to dine in Chester Street with Dickie and Edwina Mountbatten. Dickie had only been home in England for a little over a week, and although I had seen him briefly at the first night of *Blithe Spirit* I had not had an opportunity to talk to him. After dinner, he told me the whole story of the sinking of the *Kelly* off the island of Crete. He told it without apparent emotion, but the emotion was there, poignantly behind every word he uttered. I was profoundly moved and impressed. The Royal Navy, as I have explained elsewhere in this book, means a great deal to me, and here, in this Odyssey of one destroyer, was the very essence of it. All the true sentiment, the comedy, the tragedy, the casual valiance, the unvaunted heroism, the sadness without tears and the pride without end. Later on that night, in my bed at the Savoy, I knew that this was a story to tell if only I could tell it without sentimentality but with simplicity and truth.

Within the next few weeks *In Which We Serve* was conceived, although it was not until much later, after passing through various metamorphoses, that it achieved its final script form. The first stumbling-block was that although Dickie was all for a film which would be good propaganda for the Navy, he was not unnaturally afraid of my basing my story too exactly on the *Kelly* lest the film should in any sense become a boost for himself. After I had reassured him on this point, and in particular had made it clear that I had no intention of copying his own particular character, he undertook that he and some of the survivors of the *Kelly* would give me that help without which it would have been very difficult to have produced a convincing film. First of all, the Royal Navy's permission was asked for and willingly given. Dickie's personal enthusiasm cut through many strings of red tape and set many wheels turning on my behalf. From the beginning he saw the idea as a tribute to the Service he loved, and he supported me through every difficulty and crisis until the picture was completed. But that happy moment was over a year away and, in the meantime, there were many tiresome obstacles to be surmounted. I could never have surmounted them without his constructive criticism, his gift for concentration, his confidence in the film and in me. This might so easily have been strained beyond bearing within the ensuing few months, for neither of us dreamed in those first days of enthusiasm what a variety of dim-witted ogres we should have to vanquish. To begin with, the Press, led exultantly by the section which had proved hostile to me before, proceeded to sabotage the project from the moment the news broke that I was going to do it. There were sneering articles, contemptuous little innuendoes in the gossip columns, letters of protest written, I suspect, editorially, and the suggestion that I was going to portray Lord Louis Mountbatten on the screen, a suggestion for which no possible evidence had been furnished, was reiterated *ad nauseam* until even the Admiralty became restive and, I believe although I am not certain, protested strongly to the Ministry of Information. I only know that after a few weeks the clamour died down. The fact that there had never been any question of my portraying Lord Louis Mountbatten on the screen was, of course, ignored. 'Captain (D)' in *In Which We Serve* was conceived, written and acted to the best of my ability as an average naval officer, whereas Mountbatten was then, and is now, very far from being an average naval officer. He is definitely one of the most outstanding men of our times and showed every sign of becoming so when I first knew him in the early 'twenties. My 'Captain (D)' was a simpler character altogether, far less gifted than he, far less complicated, but in no way, I hope, less gallant. The story of the film was certainly based on H.M.S. *Kelly*, for the simple reason that through Mountbatten himself, and his shipmates who survived, I was able to get first-hand information and accurate details, both technical and psychological. The story, however, could have applied to any other destroyer sunk in action during the war. In all of them were the same potentialities, the same bravery, the same humour and the same spirit.

It would be wearisome to recapitulate all the irritations, frustrations and tiresomeness which had to be coped with during those difficult weeks. It would also involve undignified recrimination and possibly several libel suits. One thing I cannot forbear to mention was a letter to the Lords of the Admiralty from the head of the film department in the Ministry of Information. This letter, written on receipt of the final script, stated unequivocally that in the Ministry's opinion the story was exceedingly bad propaganda for the Navy, as it showed one of H.M.'s ships being sunk by enemy action, and that permission would never be granted for it to be shown outside this country. The contents of this letter were communicated to me over the telephone by the head of the Ministry of Information's film department himself and, I need hardly say, left me speechless with rage. It was also made known by some means or other to the Two Cities Film Company, which had already invested a great deal of money in the production. The information, naturally enough, terrified them, and if I had not acted quickly the whole project would probably have been abandoned, at considerable financial loss, a few weeks before the actual shooting was due to begin. Fortunately for me this serious setback occurred later on in the production of the picture, when Mountbatten was back in England again, having been recalled from his command of the *Illustrious* to take over Combined Operations. I telephoned him immediately and he asked me to have a script delivered to him right away, and that he would show it to the Member of the Board of Admiralty who would be most likely to be called upon to make a decision in this matter. This gallant Admiral, who was afterwards lost in action, took the view that the story was very good propaganda indeed, and that the fact that the film portrayed a destroyer being sunk in war-time was certainly not necessarily a reflection on the Navy, where so many gallant ships were fighting to the end in the defence of the country's vital sea-lines of communication.

So, upheld by this moral support, Dickie and I went to the Ministry of Information, where we were received by Brendan Bracken, who kindly sent for the writer of the letter. Dickie went off like a time bomb and it was one of the most startling and satisfactory scenes I have ever witnessed. I actually felt a pang of compassion for the wretched official, who wilted under the tirade like a tallow candle before a strong fire. The upshot of it all was that from that moment onwards I had to endure no more nonsense from the Ministry of Information. In the following September, when *In Which We Serve* opened at the Gaumont, I received a congratulatory letter from this very official saying that the film was as moving and impressive as he had always known it would be. A curious missive.

In the meantime the Two Cities Film Company's fluttering hearts were stilled and on we went with the production.

At the very beginning of the whole enterprise I had been warned that the British Film Industry was a jungle of intrigue, politics and treachery, and a breeding ground of desperate chicaneries. Actually I found it none of these things. What I did find was that it was extravagant to the point of lunacy and, on the whole, fairly inefficient. The people who worked with me on the picture, however, were hand-picked and, with one or two exceptions, one hundred per cent efficient. It would have been difficult to go far astray with David Lean as my co-director, Tony Havelock-Allan in charge of production and Ronald Neame as director of photography. From these three I had whole-hearted, intelligent, and affectionate co-operation from the beginning to the end, and we have been close friends ever since. I was sorry, later on, when the three of them split up to go their different ways. They were a formidable trio together, and I owe to them much of the success of *In Which We Serve*, *This Happy Breed*, and above all, *Brief Encounter*. I will draw a light, spangled veil over *Blithe Spirit*, which they made while I was away in South Africa. It wasn't entirely bad, but it was a great deal less good than it should have been.

Apart from these three, there was the over-exuberant and most lovable Filippo del Giudice. His English was appalling and his enthusiasm boundless. He was another who, in spite of all storms and stresses and difficulties, never allowed his faith in me and the picture to be shaken for a moment. I find, on looking back, that I entered the jungle of the movie business with exceedingly staunch native bearers. They knew every inch of the perilous terrain and, I am convinced, saved my life repeatedly.

There is a French word that has been appropriated to describe a necessary technical expedient in the making of a moving picture: the word is 'montage'. Montage is usually employed to convey a lapse of days, weeks or years by telescoping events into the shortest possible screen time. For instance, if the heroine has abandoned the static domesticity of her home life in Omaha, Nebraska, and decided to go to Europe and become an opera singer, and it is essential for a few months to elapse before we see her making her début at La Scala, montage is used to cover those pregnant months. There will be a series of quick shots dissolving into one another – the wheels of the train bearing her to New York; an Atlantic liner steaming past the Statue of Liberty; a lightning glimpse of her practising in a Montmartre attic; a panoramic flash of the city of Milan dissolving into an empty theatre where she is seen struggling to master a difficult aria; a few fleeting visions of her trudging wearily through empty, alien streets with her music case; being fitted for her dresses; staring with tear-filled eyes at a photograph of her mother; a shot of the orchestra tuning up; another of the Opera House itself, crammed to the roof with Hollywood extras in deep evening dress applauding wildly; then finally a long shot of her bowing to her ovation and preparing to get on with the story at a more leisurely pace. From this brief description it will be readily understood that montage is a most convenient trick and can be used as effectively in writing as on the screen.

On looking back on the seven months between the original conception of *In Which We Serve* and the day on which we actually began shooting, I find I can see them only in terms of montage – endless conferences; hours in Wardour Street projection-rooms looking at British films; casting discussions, technical discussions; days at sea in destroyers; drives to and from Denham Studios in winter weather; arguments about the budget of the picture; moving into a dank cottage so as to be near the studios; crises, triumphs, despairs, exultations; tests in the Gaumont British studios at Shepherds Bush; hours of staring at myself on the screen – heavy jowls, no eyes at all; lighting wrong, lighting better; visits to shipyards in Newcastle; to dockyards at Plymouth and Portsmouth; endless discussions with experts – naval experts, film experts, shipbuilding experts, gunnery experts; and last, but by no means least, the nerve-racking business of my court proceedings at Bow Street and the Mansion House, which I will deal with more fully later.

On February 5th, 1942, we had our first shooting day of *In Which We Serve*. David and Ronnie and I were quivering with nerves, but, as the day went on, they evaporated as they usually do under stress of intensive work, and in the evening we had a drink in my dressing-room to celebrate the fact that at last, at long last, our preliminary troubles were over and we were under way.

From then on for five months the world outside Denham Studios virtually ceased to exist for me. Gladys Calthrop, who was my personal art director for the picture, had rented a cottage next door to mine. The two crouched together in a grove of morose trees which dripped in the rain, moaned in the wind and, in the spring, robbed us of the daylight. In the winter this didn't matter so much, for except on Sundays we never saw the daylight; we left for the studios in the black-out at about 7.30 a.m. and usually got home in the evening in time to hear the nine o'clock news, have dinner and go to bed.

I made occasional trips to London on days when for some reason or other I was not wanted at the studios. It felt strange and almost alien and it was often a relief to get into the Tube at Piccadilly Circus, get out at Uxbridge, pick up my car from the hotel garage and drive back to the familiarity of that beastly little cottage. Later on I moved into a much nicer one near Fulmer, but in the dark days 'Pine Cottage' was my hearth and home and I couldn't have disliked it more.

Work on the picture proceeded slowly but steadily. There were good days and bad days, cheerful days and bad-tempered days. There were nine very uncomfortable days when John Mills, Bernard Miles and I, and twenty others, spent from 8.30 a.m. to 6.30 p.m, clinging to a Carley float in a tank of warm but increasingly filthy water; also we were smeared from head to foot with synthetic fuel oil, only a little of which we were able to scrape off for the lunch break.

At certain times we had two hundred and fifty cheerful British sailors, kindly supplied by the Royal Naval Barracks, Portsmouth. At others, serried ranks of Coldstream Guardsmen greeted us briskly when we arrived on the floor. Those 'Big Scene' days were enjoyable, and David and Ronnie, with their various assistants, handled them with calmness and efficiency. Other days were devoted to small dialogue scenes in cramped circumstances (in moving-pictures dialogue scenes are almost invariably played in cramped circumstances). These days were sometimes less happy. I was, and still am, prone to become irritable when forced to say the same few sentences over and over again in long shots, medium shots and finally close-ups, with the camera a couple of inches from my nose and the microphone dangling one inch above my forehead. I got more and more used to it after a while, but for the first few weeks I was fairly fractious. I still think that *In Which We Serve* was one of the best acted pictures I ever saw. The leading actors, Celia Johnson, Kay Walsh, Joyce Carey, Johnnie Mills, Bernard Miles and Kathleen Harrison were impeccable (modesty compels me to dissociate myself from this assessment), but all the, at that time, smaller-part actors, including Richard Attenborough, Michael Wilding, Philip Friend, James Donald, Hubert Gregg, Derek Elphinstone, Dora Barton, Walter Fitzgerald, Gerald Case and a number of others, played with the utmost integrity.

There were many heated discussions concerning naval procedure. My 'Ward-room and Bridge' adviser was an ex-Destroyer Commander, 'Bushy' Clarke. My 'Lower Deck' adviser, a diminutive young man called Terry Lawlor, had served with Mountbatten as his cabin hand and had been burnt practically to death when the *Kelly* was sunk. Later, he was returning home in a hospital ship when it was torpedoed and he was burnt all over again. The plastic surgeons had done a miraculous job for him, and unless you looked closely you would never have realised that the skin of his face was almost entirely grafted. He was altogether a remarkable character and invaluable to us. I realised from the outset that it was essential to the accuracy of the picture that the lower deck and fo'c'sle should be represented as accurately as the quarterdeck, the bridge and the ward-room. The arguments between Bushy Clarke and Lawlor were frequent and sometimes very funny. They each held on to their ends of the controversial point like bull-terriers with a bone. Occasionally I was even forced to telephone to Dickie Mountbatten for impartial arbitration. Half-way through the picture, to our dismay Bushy was called back to do a course. His successor was Charles Compton, an amiable young lieutenant who obliged with advice when wanted, but by that time most of the important advice-giving had been done by Bushy, so there was not really much for him to do. However, I think on the whole he enjoyed himself.

In the middle of August, before embarking on the actual writing of the script, I decided to assist inspiration by absorbing some authentic naval atmosphere. Captain Brojah Brooking, my staunchest supporter at the Admiralty, arranged for me to visit the Home Fleet at Scapa Flow for a week or two. At the same time I was invited by another of my old friends, Admiral Philip Vian, to go for a short cruise with him in his flagship H.M.S. *Nigeria*. As the *Nigeria* happened to be at Scapa this fitted in conveniently, so I travelled to Edinburgh by night, arriving at 4 a.m., caught the five o'clock train for Inverkeithing, where I was met by a car in the pouring rain and driven to the naval air-base at Donnibristle. Here I shaved and washed and was given breakfast by a pretty W.R.E.N. In due course Vian arrived and we discovered to our irritation that the plane which was to fly us to Thurso could not take off owing to the weather. There was nothing for it but to scramble into a crowded train on which we had no reservations. Appointing myself as the Admiral's unofficial flag-lieutenant, I forced the guard to accommodate us in his van, where the Admiral sat in a baby's perambulator all the way to Inverness. In pre-war years I had often been to sea with Vian when he was Captain of H.M.S. *Arethusa*. Since then he had distinguished himself in many ways, notably in the episode of the *Altmark*. He is a man of charm, sardonic humour, occasional irascibility and immense kindness. He also, like so many of his colleagues, is a stranger to fear. This was exemplified only too clearly to me during our nightmare drive from Inverness to Thurso. The roads were like glass, the visibility almost nil owing to the deluge, and the driver obviously a homicidal maniac. Being temperamentally unable to share Vian's immunity from stark terror, I arrived shaking like a leaf and moaning for gin. Happily in H.M.'s ships this is usually procurable, and after an hour or so in the ward-room of H.M.S. *Lively*, which was at Thurso to meet us, my nerves were soothed. The *Lively* deposited me on board the *King George V*, where I was to be the guest of the C.-in-C., Admiral Tovey, and took Vian on to his own ship, in which I was to join him two days later. From then on the atmosphere which I had come to absorb proceeded as usual to absorb me, to the exclusion of all other considerations. Even the primary object of my being there, which was to gather as much technical information as possible for the film, was forgotten in the pleasure of being with the Navy again. I was entertained in various ships; I opened a new cinema for the troops in Thurso; I watched, through the scuttle of the Admiral's cabin, H.M.S. *Prince of Wales* come to anchor, bearing Winston Churchill home after the signing of the Atlantic Charter. In fact it wasn't until a week later, when I arrived in Iceland on board the *Nigeria*, that it occurred to me to ask Vian where we were going and how long we should be away. He replied cheerfully that our immediate destination was Murmansk and that we might be away anything from two weeks to two months. This startled me into a sudden realisation of my own self-indulgence and my own responsibilities. I had promised the film unit before leaving London that I would not be away for longer than three weeks at the outside, and here I was, heading for Russia, with no way of communicating with them, for it was obviously impossible, for security reasons, to send home reassuring radiograms from a cruiser at sea in war-time. Vian, I regret to say, showed little concern with my problem and said gaily that the film could wait and that the sea air would do me good. Fortunately at this moment we were sharing an Icelandic fjord with H.M.S. *Shropshire*, which was on her way home from South Africa. I managed, with some difficulty, to persuade Vian that it really was essential for me to get back, and so signals were exchanged and I was transferred to the charge of Captain Borrett. I hated leaving *Nigeria* just as I was beginning to know the ship and become part of the ward-room family, but it had to be done and I spent a dismal hour going round and saying good-bye to everyone. Later that evening after dinner with 'Jacko' Borrett, who had received me with the usual naval hospitality, we watched the *Nigeria* sail out of the fjord and into the dark night. It subsequently turned out that had I only been able to sail in her I should have been in an exciting action during which half her bows were shot away. I should also have been out of contact with the film boys for more than seven weeks.

The trip home in the *Shropshire* was uneventful except that we sailed blithely through a minefield regardless of the fact that our Asdic apparatus had packed up. Back in Scapa, I stayed on in the ship for a few days, laughed a lot, drank a lot, engaged in further naval junketings, and was finally flown in a seaplane to Inverness, where, after badgering the R.T.O. at the station, I managed to get into the train for London.

9

On Thursday, October 16th, when I was hard at work in my studio in Gerald Road on the second draft of *In Which We Serve*, I was interrupted by the arrival of two police inspectors with two summonses from the Finance Defence Department. They told me, politely enough, that I was to appear, on Friday the 24th, before a court and that I was liable to a fine of £22,000 for having broken certain rules, the very existence of which I knew nothing about. They also informed me that another summons was on the way. This, naturally, was a shattering blow and I was horrified and extremely angry. I realised that unless I could get the case postponed, pending further investigations, I should be landed with a Press scandal which not only would smear my personal reputation, but might quite conceivably damage my relations with the Admiralty, Mountbatten and the Navy, and place the whole film in serious jeopardy. As it subsequently transpired, I needn't have worried about the Admiralty, Mountbatten or the Navy because, I am proud to say, they held me in too much honour to pay any attention to such palpable celebrity-baiting. Nevertheless it was a black moment and had to be dealt with firmly and swiftly. I immediately telephoned Nicholas Lawford, Anthony Eden's secretary at the Foreign Office, and asked him for the name of a good lawyer. The one he suggested, although sympathetic, was unable to represent me, for he was representing the other side, i.e., the Bank of England and the Treasury, but he was kind enough to ring up another lawyer, Dingwall Bateson, who agreed to deal with my case. A few days later I was served with three further summonses. These dealt with currency. I was told for the first time – my accountants having maintained a stately silence on the point – that on August 26th, 1939, a law was passed decreeing that all English people with money in America must declare it and not spend it in any circumstances whatever. This was entirely news to me, and exceedingly unpleasant news, for it meant that by spending the money I had spent from my personal account in New York, principally on work for my Government, I had been committing a criminal offence.

Bateson, who was understanding and shrewd, took a gloomy view. I gathered from his manner that he suspected somebody high up was specifically gunning for me. He said, at all events, that the Treasury was out for well-known blood, but that he hoped at least to be able to get a temporary adjournment. This he succeeded in doing, and my case was ultimately tried at Bow Street Police Court on October 30th. In the meantime Geoffrey Roberts ('Khaki' Roberts) had been engaged to defend me. Four days before the case I was surprised and most touched to receive out of the blue the following letter from George Bernard Shaw:

4, Whitehall Court,
London, S.W.I.
26/10/1941

DEAR NOËL COWARD,

The other day George Arliss, being in trouble about his American securities, pleaded Guilty under the impression that he was only admitting the facts and saving the Lord Mayor useless trouble. There was nothing for it then but to fine him £3,000.

He should have admitted the facts and pleaded Not Guilty, being as innocent as an unborn lamb. Of course the facts have to be established before that question arises; but when they are admitted or proved they leave the question of innocence or guilt unsettled. There can be no guilt without intention. Arliss knew nothing about the Finance Clauses, and did not even know that he owned American securities. He was Not Guilty, and should have said so and thereby put his defence in order.

Therefore let nothing induce you to plead Guilty. If your lawyers advise you to do so, tell them that *I* advise you not to. You may know all this as well as I do; but after the Arliss case I think it safer to warn you.

G.B.S.

Armed with this I went straight to Roberts and declared my intention of pleading Not Guilty. He explained to me patiently and at length that legally, not morally, I was guilty and that, as the maximum fine on all the charges might conceivably be £61,000 and the minimum £5,000, it would be much wiser to plead Guilty and hope for the latter. With the phrase from Shaw's letter, 'There can be no guilt without intention', stuck firmly in my mind, I held to my decision. He warned me that I should have to endure cross-examination, to which I replied that if all the most brilliant K.C.s in England cross-examined me until they dropped in their tracks they would be unable to prove me guilty when I bloody well knew I was innocent. I added defiantly that I would rather go to prison than pay the smallest fine for an offence about which I knew nothing. He thought poorly of this idea and the argument went on for a long time until finally I won my point.

On the morning of that unpleasant day I arrived with Lorn and Bateson at Bow Street at ten o'clock. Gladys and Joyce were in the body of the court to give me moral support. The counsel for the prosecution led off with the statement that I was liable to a £61,000 fine. The Magistrate looked, I thought, both disgruntled and unyielding, and I was in no way comforted when someone hissed in my ear that he was one of the most dreaded magistrates on the bench. Actually, as far as I was concerned he proved to be neither disgruntled nor unyielding; on the contrary he was, after the first few minutes of my evidence, both courteous and considerate. Under cross-examination I kept my head and answered briefly and to the point. It was apparent to me early on that the prosecution was anxious to prove that I had not been sent to America by the Ministry of Information, but had wangled my way out of the country by some means or other, presumably to live in sophisticated luxury on my illicit American earnings, and as far away from the discomforts of war-time England as possible. The letter, or what purported to be the letter, I had taken to Lord Lothian was suddenly produced and I was asked if I recognised it. I replied that it was a private communication between the Minister of Information and the British Ambassador, that naturally I hadn't read it and so, obviously, couldn't recognise it. The production of this letter in Court puzzled me at the time and has puzzled me ever since. It was not offered to me to look at closely, but, as far as I can recall, it was on one sheet of thin paper, whereas the letter I actually delivered to Lord Lothian was quite bulky. A reference to my courier's passport agitated me rather. I was determined not to mention Little Bill's name whatever happened to me, but I reasoned that, the passport having been officially issued by the British Embassy in Washington at his request, it was fairly certain that nothing would be said likely to compromise him in any way.

The hearing of the case was a dreary business and seemed to drag on interminably. Roberts made an excellent, if somewhat embarrassing, speech about my honour and integrity, and I felt myself assuming the kind of expression I wear when I am obliged to listen to a eulogistic mayoral address at a civic function. The upshot of the whole business was that the Magistrate, after some scathing but, I fear justified, comments on my financial vagueness, fined me £200 with £20 costs. Considering that the minimum fine was assessed at £5,000, this was more in the nature of an accolade than a penalty, and I left the court relieved beyond words and went back to my script.

A week later I was summoned at the Mansion House on the charges relating to my American securities. The difference between the conduct of the court at the Mansion House and the court at Bow Street was as marked as the difference between the production of a play by a first-rate West End management and a production of the same play by a suburban Amateur Dramatic Society. The same questions which had been put to me at Bow Street were reiterated *ad nauseam*, and the Bench, struggling in a welter of dates and figures, interjected comments from time to time of quite startling irrelevance. The one fact that struck like a burr in their minds was that I had failed, while in America, to discuss finance, lease-lend and international economics with the British Purchasing Commission which had happened to be there at the time. In spite of my repeated assurances that I had not the faintest knowledge of such matters, and that had I attempted to discuss them with anybody at all I should merely have made a cracking ass of myself, they returned valiantly to the charge until I gave up all attempts to convince them and confined my answers to weary 'Yes's' and 'Noes'.

Having adjourned my case once for an hour while they tried a minor one, adjourned it again for lunch, and still a third time whilst they retired to consider their verdict, they finally imposed on me a fine of £1,600, graciously adding that they would allow me a month in which to pay it.

It seemed to me then, and it seems to me now, a curious reflection on British justice that whereas a trained lawyer had fined me £200 when the country had lost, through my ignorance, £11,000, an unprofessional Bench fined me £1,600 when the country had lost absolutely nothing.

At all events, the whole nasty business was mercifully over; the Press had treated me with unexpected kindness throughout both cases, and I was now free to wipe the whole thing from my mind and get on with my work. I still wonder if the Lord Mayor ever received the £2,000 sent to his Relief Fund by the Mayor of Sydney after my farewell concert.

10

The miserable winter of 1941–2 dragged on with the war news getting worse and worse. Gladys and I, crouching over the radio in the smoky discomfort of Pine Cottage, listened every morning to the clipped, impartial voices of the B.B.C. announcers telling us of further defeats and further disasters. The *Prince of Wales* and the *Repulse* were lost, Singapore fell, the Japanese began their invasion of Sumatra and Burma and the Germans advanced again in Libya. Two other warships that I knew well were lost, the *Cornwall* and the *Dorsetshire*. I remembered a gay dance on *Cornwall's* quarterdeck with coloured lights, a marine band and a full moon shining over Hong Kong harbour. I remembered the warm friendliness of *Dorsetshire's* ward-room. Most of those cheerful, kindly young men who had entertained me so hospitably were now drowned or burnt and lying at the bottom of the sea.

One day Gladys, who had been in London, arrived at the studio having heard the night before that her only son Hugo had been killed in Burma. Hugo, was young, good-looking and finely intelligent, and on the day in July 1940 when I had sailed for America he was in one of the other ships in the convoy, bound for Egypt. That was the last Gladys had seen of him. She demanded no pity and got on with the job as usual, and I knew that there was nothing to be done but to play up to her own integrity; it was not until several weeks had passed that we talked of him.

The picture progressed. There were, inevitably, troubles and crises and arguments, and on one occasion, when the entire electrical staff had descended from their perches at ten-thirty in the morning to have tea, leaving me with two hundred sailors waiting for the lights, I lost my temper and let fly. The result of this fracas was greatly increased efficiency for the remainder of the picture.

On April the 8th, I note in my diary, we had a proud and pleasant day. The King and Queen arrived in the afternoon with Princess Elizabeth, Princess Margaret and Dickie and Edwina Mountbatten. I met them with Arthur Rank and the Directors. We took them first to Stage Five, the big set, to see H.M.S. *Torrin*, our magnificent life-sized replica of a destroyer. Bushy Clarke called the sailors to attention and His Majesty, in his uniform of Admiral of the Fleet, took the salute. The Royal party were then installed on a rostrum to watch me do the 'Dunkirk' speech. The ship rolled, the wind machine roared and everything went beautifully. After three short 'takes' I took them all over the ship, presenting various people to them on the way. Then they inspected the Pattern shop and Stage One and spent half an hour in the projection-room looking at some rough-cut sections of the picture. Throughout their whole visit they were charming and easy and interested in everything, and I was amused to observe the impact of their perfect manners on some of the 'pinker' members of the staff. Altogether their visit was an unqualified success, from every point of view, and I hoped that it impressed the studio as much as it should have. Not because of Royal grandeur, but because the King and Queen and the Princesses of England had put themselves out to make everyone they met happy and at ease.

To quote Mr Bernard Shaw, the most ardent Socialist of his day: 'The constitutional King of England stands for: "the future and the past, the posterity that has no vote, and the tradition that never had any ... for the great abstractions, for conscience and virtue, for the eternal against the expedient, for the evolutionary appetite against the day's gluttony, for intellectual integrity, for humanity. ..."'

The truth of these words seemed to me to be very apparent on that 'proud and pleasant' day.

Spring gave way, rather grudgingly, I thought, to summer and in late June we were about to complete the last shot of the film. It was an uncomfortable shot that was almost lethal for me. A replica of the bridge of the destroyer had been made of light wood and real glass and placed on the edge of the large outside tank at Denham Studios. Above it, a few hundred yards away on a scaffolding, were perched two enormous tanks filled with thousands of gallons of water. On a given signal a lever would be pulled, whereupon the tanks would disgorge their load down a chute, and overturn and capsize the bridge with me on it. Shivering in the bitter summer weather, I looked at the flimsy structure on which I was to stand and then up at the vast tanks and said 'No'. David and Ronnie, whose nonchalant attitude to human endurance had been engendered by years of film-making, looked at me with rather contemptuous disappointment. If I was frightened, David said, a stand-in would do it first, although this would entail a three hours' wait while the tanks were filled up again. These words, obviously intended as a spur to my failing courage, fell on stony ground for the simple reason that I knew a great deal more about the weight of water than they did. I replied that in no circumstances would I either do it myself or allow any living creature to stand on the bridge until I saw what the impact of water would do to it. Finally, after some grumbling at the time waste, they gave in to my insistence and ordered the signal to be given. The whistle blew and we all stood back and watched. There was a loud roar as the released water came hurtling down the chute and, in a split second, there was nothing left of the bridge at all. It was immediately obvious to all concerned that anyone standing on it would have been killed instantly. David and Ronnie, pale and trembling, returned silently with me to my dressing-room, where we each of us downed a strong tot of brandy.

A few days later the bridge was rebuilt, breakwaters were installed and tested, and on June the 27th the shot was at last taken. I cannot say that I enjoyed it and the moment before the whistle blew I was terrified. From that moment on, all was chaos. I flattened myself against the Pelorus; the water struck me in the small of the back, knocking all the breath out of me; the structure slowly capsized as planned and after a few desperate moments I fought my way to the surface. Happily the cameras had been efficient, so the shot did not have to be repeated. On the screen the episode is over in a flash, but I have never looked at it without a retrospective shudder.

II

Earlier in the year, when the routine of the film studio was beginning to get me down, I had decided, after a conversation with Hugh Beaumont, the managing director of H.M. Tennent, to return to the stage. Hugh (Binkie) Beaumont, one of my closest friends and my business associate for many years, was delighted with the idea and it was arranged that I should do a twenty-eight weeks' provincial tour with a repertoire of three plays, *Present Laughter, This Happy Breed* and *Blithe Spirit*, opening in September. From July onwards therefore, I bade a relieved and respectful good-bye to Denham Studios, and, with the exception of a few days here and there of dubbing and post-synching, plunged back into the familiar, comforting business of planning, auditioning and casting.

On August 20th, having agreed to replace Cecil Parker in the London production of *Blithe Spirit* for two weeks, I appeared on the stage for the first time since 1937, when I had concluded the run of *Tonight at Eight-Thirty* in New York. I arrived at the St James's Theatre in the evening after a reasonably slick midday rehearsal feeling apprehensive and troubled with the thought that I might have lost the knack of being a light comedian. After I had been on the stage for a few minutes, however, the old-well-remembered magic began to happen and I felt myself beginning to time my lines and movements. After the initial strain had worn off, it was wonderful to be able once more to play consecutive scenes of more than a few sentences, and to get laughter and applause from actual audiences, after months of acting my heart out before a preoccupied production unit and the silent regard of disinterested property-men and electricians.

I was delighted to be back in the theatre and undaunted by the prospect of a long tour through the provincial cities in war-time, when the hotel amenities were likely to be austere and travelling accommodations erratic.

My life seemed to have fallen into place again in spite of the fact that all the fine schemes I had had at the beginning of the war for doing important work for the country had been temporarily frustrated. It had certainly not been my fault. I had done my best, or what I thought was my best. Perhaps that was where the trouble lay. My best might more certainly be achieved in my own job after all. Possibly I had been over-sanguine and even a trifle conceited to imagine that my abilities could be transferred immediately and successfully to such very different milieux. At least, on my own ground, I would not have to endure bureaucratic pomposity and attacks on my personal character. I think I realised, even in that mood of rosy introspect, that the time would come when I would be restless again, yearning to be up and away, to be doing a little more for the war effort than merely earning my living in slightly more uncomfortable circumstances than usual. But such rebellious urges were far in the future and I knew I should be much too occupied during the next eight months to allow them to disturb me.

During the two weeks that I was playing at the St James's, the Duke of Kent was killed in an air crash in Scotland. I had first met him during the run of *London Calling* in 1923, and we had been friends ever since. My cottage near Fulmer was only a couple of miles away from Coppins, the house of the Duke and Duchess of Kent, and I had dined with them there on an average of once a fortnight since the beginning of the film. I had actually talked to him on the telephone two days before he was killed, and made a date for him to come on the following Friday to see me in the play and have supper afterwards. The news was announced over the air on the evening of August 25th, but I was supping out and knew nothing of it until the following morning when I read the newspaper headlines. It was an appalling shock and, as often happens at such moments, my mind at first refused to believe it, which of course was foolish, because in those dark years we were all of us learning by bitter experience that it was only too easy to believe someone young and gay and kind was dead. They were dying all the time. My heart ached for the poor Duchess and I could think of no articulate words to write to her. I did my best, but on such occasions there is little to be said or written. Memories of her unfailing sweetness to me ever since I had first met her in London, just after her engagement was announced, flooded into my mind; memories of all the happy times the three of us had had together in the following years; the twinkle in the eye suddenly caught and registered on grand occasions; the absurd word games played on quiet evenings in the country; the irrelevant jokes, all the fun, now suddenly tragically over. It was a black and miserable day, and when I arrived at the theatre for the evening performance I was grateful to Fay Compton for warning me, just before I went on, to be on my guard against certain lines in the play which might surprise me, by their dreadful appositeness, into a betrayal of my feelings. She was right to warn me. *Blithe Spirit* certainly treats the subject of death lightly, and although I still maintain that Death in the abstract is not nearly so solemn and lachrymose as many people would have us believe, it is not always possible to treat it with the proper disdain when the personal heart is quivering with a sense of loss.

A few days later I drove down to Windsor for the funeral service in St George's Chapel. The service was impressive and supremely dignified. I tried hard not to cry, but it was useless. When the Duchess came in with the Queen and Queen Mary, and when the coffin passed with a simple bunch of flowers from the garden at Coppins and Prince George's R.A.F. cap on it, I was finished. At the end, when the King had sprinkled the earth and the Royalties had gone away, we all went up, one by one, to the vault and bowed and secretly said our good-byes to him. Then we filed out into the strong sunshine and, for me, a nineteen-year-old friendship was over for ever except in my memory.

12

On September the 20th my tour opened at Blackpool with *Present Laughter*. On the two subsequent evenings we opened *This Happy Breed* and *Blithe Spirit*. My cast was excellent: Joyce Carey, Judy Campbell, Beryl Measor, Jennifer Gray, Molly Johnson, Meg Titheradge, Gwendolyn Floyd, Dennis Price, Billy Thatcher, Gerald Case and James Donald. All three plays were successful, and my satisfaction was only slightly offset by a violent cold which I had started at the Monday morning word-rehearsal. The theatre was packed at every performance and the Blackpool audiences, although a trifle confused by the 'brittle sophistication' of *Present Laughter*, were, on the whole, receptive.

From then on our Odyssey continued until the following April. The routine was broken from time to time by week-end visits to London. The first of these came at the end of the first week because I had promised, and was indeed eager, to be in London for the first showing of *In Which We Serve*, which took place on Sunday evening, September the 17th. The Press showing, a few days previously, had resulted in ecstatic reviews in all the papers. The première was given in aid of Naval Charities and the preponderance of naval uniforms and gold lace gave a considerable *cachet* to the occasion, and I was moved and proud to see the impact of the picture on that distinguished audience. Towards the end there was a great deal of gratifying nose-blowing and one stern-faced Admiral in the row behind me was unashamedly in tears. For me it was a wonderful experience. I had, of course, seen the film in all its phases, but I had never seen it entirely completed nor heard an audience react to it. I felt that it was a fine piece of work which more than justified all the troubles, heartburnings, disappointments and frustrations we had endured in the making of it. There it was, once and for all, well directed, well photographed and well played and, above all, as far as I was concerned, an accurate and sincere tribute to the Royal Navy.

When it was over there was a party at the Savoy, and David and Ronnie and I received happily most of the superlatives in the English language, several in French, Norwegian, Danish and American, and none in Russian or German.

The following morning, blown up with triumph, Joyce and I travelled to Bristol to carry on with the tour. I would not have missed those months of flogging through the provinces for anything in the world, for although there were many moments of bitter cold, discomforts, exhaustion and near-starvation, there were also many compensations and we were an exceedingly happy company. There were no scenes or squabbles or unpleasantnesses from the beginning of the tour to the end. My stage staff, Peggy Dear, Charles Russell and Lance Hamilton, achieved miracles by successfully getting the plays lit and set in time for each

Monday evening performance on stages that varied in size and shape from the vastness of the Bristol Hippodrome to the tiny intimacy of the Theatre Royal, Exeter. In Inverness we opened *Blithe Spirit* in a small converted cinema which had been closed for two months and was like a frigidaire, which was not surprising as it was January and there was a blizzard raging. After the first act I complained to Joyce and Judy that I had been unable to hear myself speaking owing to the chattering of their teeth. In the second act, to our immense relief, the theatre caught on fire; clouds of acrid black smoke rose from the orchestra pit and we chokingly carried on with the play, longing for the flames. It turned out to be merely a stoppage in the wardrobe chimney and we were obliged to press on, to an audience coughing its lungs out.

I had agreed, at the request of the Director of Naval Intelligence, to give a five-minutes security speech at the end of each performance. This was a good idea in theory, but it is not actually easy, when you have been striving all the evening to make people laugh and enjoy themselves, suddenly to turn on them at the end and admonish them sternly with grim little anecdotes of death and betrayal resulting from their not keeping their traps shut. In addition to this, one speech was not enough, for I was playing three plays consecutively which were attended, as a general rule, by the same audiences. I had to invent three entirely different security speeches to save myself the embarrassment of seeing my public gathering up their hats and coats and programmes and walking out on me as I began to speak. The Admiralty promised to supply me with a series of true incidents concerning the losing of lives by careless talk. The incidents they produced were meagre from the dramatic point of view, so I was forced to invent myself a few hair-raising stories about ships being sunk, spies being landed from submarines and munition factories being sabotaged because some garrulous citizen in a pub or a shop had said something indiscreet. Fortunately the audiences took these little tirades in good part and, of course, the company adored them. Whether or not they did the slightest good I shall never know.

There was still in my mind a core of discontent because I was engaged on a pleasant and profitable acting job which contributed nothing actually to the war effort. This perhaps was silly, because at least I was amusing people who were having a dreary time and making them laugh and forget their problems for a few hours. But there it was, this nebulous dissatisfaction, and in order to quell it I rashly agreed to give an average of four to six concerts a week in munition factories and hospitals in each town we visited. Judy agreed to appear with me and I engaged an accompanist in London, Robb Stewart, to tour with us and be available when required. He was an excellent musician and played beautifully for me when he was in the mood, but owing to a certain inherent vagueness in his temperament he was not always in the mood. Those concerts, all in all, were shattering experiences. Usually we appeared in factories during the lunch hour and had to bellow desperately to make ourselves heard above the din of crockery and the clangour of metal plates. Our audiences were apathetic as a rule and were flung into a state of leaden bewilderment when Judy sang to them that Arthur Murray had taught her dancing in a hurry and that there was a nightingale singing incessantly in Berkeley Square. I confused them still further with 'Don't Put Your Daughter on the Stage, Mrs Worthington' and 'Mad Dogs and Englishmen'. We fully realised that our songs were not entirely appropriate and tried to vary them with more popular favourites. These were received with much the same apathy, excepting 'If You were the Only Girl in the World' and 'There'll Always be an England', which they generally knew and were able to sing themselves. After a few weeks of these uninspired entertainments I was forced to the conclusion that I would rather sing to an audience of hostile aborigines than to a group of over-tired, and obviously ravenous, factory girls. The hospitals were a bit better, but somehow or other there was always something wrong with the organisation. Either the car didn't arrive to fetch us in time, or there was no microphone, or the microphone there was shrieked like a banshee and broke down. At all events my conscience, which, although perhaps over-sensitive, is not entirely an ass, finally persuaded me that if I continued to beat my brains out giving concerts four or five times a week as well as playing eight performances of three plays, I should probably crack up and have to cancel the tour, thereby throwing my company out of work and disappointing a large number of people. The common sense of this was obvious, and so bit by bit we cut out the dreadful concerts and by Christmas time we had dropped them entirely, although we later gave a few troop shows in Scotland.

We spent a happy Christmas in Aberdeen. On Christmas morning I gave a party for the company in my hotel sitting-room, and for days before it we were continually meeting each other in Union Street, furtively darting in and out of shops and buying each other identical presents. *George Bernard Shaw*, by Hesketh Pearson, and drinking-flasks were the most popular purchases. We all gave and received several of them. Mary Garden, as dynamic as ever, came to the plays and I saw to it that she was treated as Royalty. There were flowers in her box, and Hugh Kingston-Hardy, our business manager, received her with his usual charm. In my opinion she was one of the greatest operatic actresses in the world. The years had left no apparent mark on her and when I asked after her voice she said gaily she had given up singing for ever and preferred smoking and bridge.

The tour pursued its course through the dark winter months into the spring. Each town we visited had its surprises for us, some of which were agreeable and some very much the reverse. In Hull there was no heating in the hotel; although there were fires temptingly laid in our rooms we were not permitted to light them without a doctor's certificate to prove we were ill. The promptitude with which Joyce, Judy and I arrived at Death's Door between Sunday evening and Monday morning was remarkable. We all three arrived at the nearest doctor's consulting-room palpably on the verge of pneumonia and returned triumphantly to the hotel clutching our certificates.

In most towns our evening performance coincided with the hotel dinner hour and we seldom got a hot meal after the show, in fact in certain places it needed all our persuasions to get some cold spam and damp salad left out for us. Those of the company who were in digs were, on the whole, better off, although even they frequently suffered from conscientiously austere landladies who seized gleefully on war-time conditions to starve them to death. In Scotland the situation was happier and we were given sausages, bacon, kippers, eggs and even occasional steaks. Our luck still held in Carlisle owing to the kindness of our hotel proprietor, but as we progressed further down into the depressing English Midlands our treats became fewer and much further between. Our Sundays, of course, we spent in unheated trains, except on one occasion, when, bundled up like Eskimos in woollies and coats and fleece-lined boots, we found ourselves in a train so over-heated that we could scarcely breathe. There were seldom restaurant cars and, when there were, the food served in them was inedible. In many towns the transport problem was a serious trial. The few trams there were had usually stopped by the time we emerged from the stage-door, and as taxis were frequently unobtainable we had to foot it through pitch-black, unfamiliar streets, and stumble along with our electric torches, the bulbs of which had to be painted blue and therefore gave hardly any light at all. We generally managed to rise above these inconveniences with fortitude, but occasionally, when we had colds or headaches or were over-tired, they got us down. We played through a certain number of air raids, but neither the audiences nor ourselves were unduly agitated by them.

For me the tour fizzled out ignominiously. I had managed to keep reasonably well ever since my original cold in Blackpool. Some of the company fell by the wayside at different times and missed a performance or two, but most of us continued to keep on our feet until our opening performance in Exeter, when, to my dismay, I knew beyond a doubt that I was running a temperature. I got through to the end of the play, *This Happy Breed*, though my head was spinning and my voice sounded as though it belonged to somebody else. When I took my temperature it was 102, and had risen the next morning to 104. A doctor arrived at the hotel and told me there was no question of my playing. Dennis Price, who was my understudy, played *Blithe Spirit* that evening, after which, when it was realised that I was really ill with a bad attack of jaundice the rest of the tour was cancelled with the exception of a week in Bournemouth, where Dennis played for me very well. Jaundice is a depressing disease and I do not wish to dwell on it. I was wretched with it for several weeks and lay yellow and desolate in the Imperial Hotel, Torquay. Bert Lister, my dresser, nursed me with a fervour that Florence Nightingale would have envied. Lorn, Gladys, Binkie and others came down from London to visit me and did their best to cheer me, but it was not until I had spent a month convalescing at Tintagel on a rigid diet that I felt well enough to contemplate without dismay my forthcoming season at the Haymarket.

My room in the King Arthur's Castle Hotel at Tintagel looked out over stormy seas, cliffs, gorse and seagulls. Bert came with me for the first few days, then I sent him to London and gave myself up gratefully to solitude. I went for a brief walk every day, read numberless books and, for the only time in my life, listened consistently to the radio. It was a good radio and it tuned in easily to foreign stations. I listened to Spanish politicians, German sopranos and French collaborators. Occasionally I even listened to the B.B.C. entertainment programme. The war news was brighter but not bright enough to give any illusions of swift victory. The world was still suffering and fighting and dying, and the ordinary years that we had lived and enjoyed and taken for granted receded further and further into the limbo, until I began to feel they were figments of imagination that had never existed at all. It was difficult to realise that only three years ago the Germans had overrun Europe, that our Army had been driven back to the beaches of Dunkirk, and that France had fallen. I had the feeling that my life had retreated into a vacuum, comfortable enough, but without significance. I also realised, for not even jaundice had entirely submerged my common sense, that these bouts of melancholy introspection were the inevitable results of months of hard work followed by a depressing illness; nevertheless something at the back of my mind was nagging at me and after a little while, when the process of recuperation was almost completed, I was able to identify it. It was my old familiar urge to change my course and do something different and to go somewhere different. I had agreed with Binkie to play an eight-week season at the Haymarket with *This Happy Breed* and *Present Laughter*. I had also agreed to tack on an extra week in Plymouth to compensate for the one cancelled on account of my illness. After this, however, I was without commitments and free to go where I wanted, provided I was adroit enough to steer clear of officialdom and wriggle through a few bureaucratic fences. I am certain, on looking back over the war years, that much of the irritation and obstructiveness I aroused in official breasts was due to my determination to play a lone hand; to do what I considered the best thing to do in my own way and on my own responsibility. This resolute individualism is seldom a popular quality, but it happens to be an essential part of my character. I had no intention of offering my services to E.N.S.A., for I was suspicious of its efficiency and my instincts rebelled, as usual, against the idea of being subject to the whims of any Government department. I decided therefore to get myself to the Middle East by some means or other, entertain troops in places where I considered I would be most needed, and visit hospitals whenever and wherever I found them. I knew that, once out of England, I could rely on the Fighting Services for transport. I also knew that on my own I could get to certain obscure places where officially organised entertainments had not penetrated. The moment I had arrived at this decision my spirits lightened and I strode out on to the edge of the cliffs and recited Clemence Dane's 'Trafalgar Day' defiantly to the seagulls.

13

On April the 20th my mother celebrated with suitable rejoicing her eightieth birthday. Aunt Vida, with whom she shared a flat in Eaton Mansions, was a trifle supercilious over such a fuss being made, as she herself was several years older and spry as a grasshopper. I gave Mother a silver fox cape, in which she swaggered up and down the room like a mannequin.

On Thursday, April the 29th, *Present Laughter* opened at the Haymarket Theatre, and on the following evening *This Happy Breed*. Both plays were successes and we played happily to capacity for the entire season. To me the Theatre Royal, Haymarket, is not only the nicest theatre in London but probably the nicest in the world. It is neither too large nor too small, its acoustics are perfect and it is rich in tradition.

During those weeks my days, excepting Wednesdays and Saturdays when we played matinées, were largely occupied by discussing with David, Ronnie and Tony at Denham the film script of *Blithe Spirit* and looking at the rushes and rough-cuts of *This Happy Breed*, which was in course of production.

I usually went down to my cottage near Fulmer after the evening performance, travelling by Tube to Uxbridge and by car from then onwards. It was pleasant to be concerned with the picture but not trapped by it. I could never quite prevent a sinking of the heart every time I drove through the gates of Denham Studios – they recalled so many leaden and difficult days; but at least in these circumstances, with David and Ronnie doing all the actual work, I could say what I had to say and get out again before the atmosphere really defeated me. The picture of *This Happy Breed* was on the whole very well done. Celia Johnson, Kay Walsh, Johnnie Mills and Stanley Holloway were first rate, and the technicolour, after much discussion, was reduced to its minimum, delicately balanced and for once did not sear the eyeballs with oleographic oranges and reds and yellows.

The war, meanwhile, was becoming increasingly dramatic and increasingly hopeful. We were achieving staggering victories in the Desert. The Russians were holding their own, Italy was disintegrating. The papers were full of premature clamour for a Second Front and it looked, at long last, as though the tide really was turning in the Allies' favour.

Our Haymarket season closed on July the 3rd and we played our final week of all at Plymouth as promised. The audiences were wonderful and, casting aside my security speeches, I recited at the end of the play a poem by Clemence Dane called 'Plymouth Hoe'. She had been most impressed the year before when I had described to her the people of Plymouth dancing on the Hoe every evening at a time when the town was enduring intensive air raids every night. The poem she wrote was simple, touching and to the point, and needless to say it was a triumphant success. The idea of the people dancing had been conceived by Lady

Astor, the Mayoress, in the summer of 1942. It was a fine idea and she fought with all her extraordinary vitality and determination to get it carried out. Much has been written and said about Lady Astor as a politician, she is renowned for throwing monkey wrenches into debates, attacking Winston Churchill and inveighing, occasionally tiresomely, about the evils of intemperance, but nobody who saw her, as I did, when Plymouth was being bombed almost out of existence could feel for her anything but profound and affectionate admiration. I remember in 1942 walking with her through the devastated streets of the town one morning after a bad blitz, and her effect on the weary people was electrifying. She indulged in no facile sentimentality; she was cheerful, friendly, aggressive, and at moments even a little governessy. She dashed here and there and everywhere, encouraging, scolding, making little jokes. In the sitting-room of one pathetic house, the roof and kitchen of which had been demolished, she ordered a pale young man to take the cigarette out of his mouth. With remarkable presence of mind he held out his hand in the Nazi salute and said with a giggle: 'Heil Hitler, my Lady!' My Lady, not in the least nonplussed, laughed, told him he would ruin his morals and his lungs with nicotine, slapped him on the back and on we went. Occasionally we encountered hopelessness and tears and desolation. At these moments Lady Astor discarded her morale-lifting cheerfulness and, from the depths of her genuine kindliness, found the right words to say. I have little reverence for the teachings of Christian Science; as a religion it has always seemed to me to induce a certain arid superiority in its devotees, as well as encouraging them to swish their skirts aside from many of life's unspiritual, but quite unquestionable, realities. But, like many other sects which are offshoots of Christianity, some of its tenets are based on solid ground. Lady Astor is, I know, an ardent Christian Scientist, but I feel that she would be equally kind, dynamic, gallant, intolerant and warm hearted had she been a Bhuddist, a Seventh Day Adventist or a Holy Roller.

During our week in Plymouth Judy and I did various concerts for the Navy, all of which were enjoyable. On the last night of our final performance of *Present Laughter*, in spite of a very dressy audience, the company was high and, I fear, rather badly behaved, but we were all feeling sad inside and so perhaps a little carrying on was permissible. At the end the company assembled on the stage for me to say 'Good-bye', and to present me with two very fine eighteenth-century cannon heads and a ship's lantern. Meg Titheradge, being the smallest member of the cast, had been chosen to make the presentation, which she did with tears running down her cheeks. The emotion of the moment was catching, and I found that I could only stammer out a strangulated 'Thank you', say how much I loved them all, and retire hurriedly to my dressing-room.

They were a dear company, we had worked happily together for many months and it was a suitably sentimental finale.

It had been arranged, through the kindness of Brendan Bracken, that I should fly to Gibraltar the following week under the aegis of the Ministry of Information.

From then onwards, I was told, to my relief, that I could fend for myself. It was also arranged that I should carry traveller's cheques, duly approved by the Treasury, so that there could be no further questions asked about my betraying my country by the wild expenditure of my own hard-earned money in the middle of the Sahara desert.

A few days before I was due to leave, a message arrived from the Ministry of Information informing me that I was to submit for censorship the words of all the songs I intended to sing. Realising this meant that the songs would probably not be returned to me in time to take with me I telephoned the Ministry of Information censorship department and protested. The gentleman at the other end of the telephone, who I suspected was wearing bottle-green corduroy trousers and an oatmeal tie, assured me in thin, Bloomsbury tones that in the event of delay the songs would be sent on to me in Gibraltar. Aware that the mills of bureaucracy grind even more slowly than the mills of God, I thanked him graciously, selected at random from my files at least a hundred lyrics that I had not the slightest intention of singing and despatched them to the Ministry of Information by special messenger. I then telephoned the Commander-in-Chief at Plymouth, Admiral Forbes, told him that I was flying to Gibraltar at the end of the week, but would much prefer to go by sea. He replied that nothing could be easier and that if I could get myself to Plymouth on the night train I could leave the following evening.

The rest of that day was devoted to saying good-byes and packing a great deal more than I should have been allowed to take in a plane. My farewell scene with Mother passed off smoothly; she behaved beautifully and didn't shed a tear. My Aunt Vida enquired if I had to wear a special boating costume when travelling with the Navy, to which I replied that the usual formalities were relaxed in time of war, so I would be required to wear only a sword and a cocked hat in harbour, and only the hat at sea.

Gladys, Lorn, Joyce and Bert saw me off at Paddington after a gay dinner at The Ivy, and with a light heart I set off on my travels once more.

The next morning I breakfasted with the C.-in-C. and Lady Forbes. Several Admirals came to lunch, also Captain Voelcker, who had agreed to give me a passage in his ship, H.M.S. *Charybdis*. I warmed to him immediately and felt fairly certain, judging by his personality and the way he talked, that the ship would be a happy one. In the late afternoon he called for me in his boat, my bags were put inboard by two grinning ratings, I said good-bye to the C.-in-C. and Lady Forbes and we chugged across the Sound to where the *Charybdis* was lying, grey and purposeful, with steam up.

About an hour later, when I had been comfortably installed in the Captain's day cabin, introduced to the Commander, John Whitfeld, and the ward-room officers and, at my own firm request, been made an honorary member of the bar, we upped anchor and sailed. From the bridge I watched Plymouth fade into the distance and the cliffs of Cornwall pass by. It was the first time I had been on the bridge of a warship since H.M.S. *Torrin* in Denham Studios. I fell automatically into my 'Captain (D)' postures and it was only with a great effort that I restrained myself from pushing Captain Voelcker out of the way and shouting orders down the voice pipes.

14

The next three months of my life I have already dealt with in a small book called *Middle East Diary*, published in 1944. It achieved only a moderate success and I find on re-reading it that it is only moderately interesting. My original intention in writing it was to describe what, to me, was a memorable experience, and at the same time to pay a tribute to the fighting men I met in ships, camps, air-bases, and hospitals. Unfortunately it was done too hurriedly, with neither sufficient selectiveness nor sufficient perspective, and it relies too much on actual quotations from my day-to-day diary, many of which, though valid enough for a private record, emerge on the printed page as trite, sentimental and, at moments, trivial. Also it suffers from a rash of pompous footnotes which helped to damn the book in the eyes of the American critics. At all events, the book was never intended for American consumption and it was foolish of me to allow it to be published there. I have regretted this ever since because, apart from the damning notices it received, it involved me in an unpleasant and entirely unexpected fracas. On page 106 of this ill-starred little volume I made a careless mistake. In describing a visit to a large hospital in Tripoli, soon after the landings at Salerno, I explained at some length how impressed I was with the superb spirit and courage of the United States soldiers I talked to, most of whom had been grievously wounded and were in great pain. Gallantry in the face of suffering always moves me and it was only with difficulty that I prevented my feelings from showing on my face. On my way out of that crowded and agonised ward I stopped beside two beds near the door in which two young men were weeping bitterly. When I had talked to them for a few moments and done my best to cheer them up, I asked them where they came from and they replied, Brooklyn. I then discovered that one of them had had a bullet through his toe and the other a fractured arm. Both these wounds, although perhaps painful, seemed hardly to justify such abandonment of grief. My mind, although well conditioned by this time to tragedy, was still quivering from the gruesome horrors I had seen at the other end of the ward and, I must honestly admit, the commotion these two were making irritated me. I controlled my irritation, wished them well and left them, but the incident remained in my memory and was duly recorded in my diary. The offensive paragraph which ultimately caused such a storm read as follows: 'There was a mixed lot in this particular hospital, among them about a hundred Americans in from Salerno. I talked to some tough men from Texas and Arizona, they were magnificent specimens and in great heart, but I was less impressed by some of the mournful little Brooklyn boys lying there in tears amidst the alien corn with nothing less than a bullet wound in the leg or a fractured arm.' That the people of Brooklyn should have been bitterly offended by this was more than understandable, for it is careless and inaccurate: the word 'some' implies that all Brooklyn boys are craven, whereas in this case there were only two and although, unfortunately, they both happened to come from Brooklyn they might just as easily have come from anywhere else. Neither courage nor cowardice belong exclusively to the people of any city, state or country, and loose generalisation is a trap into which we all fall far too frequently. It still astonishes me, however, that this admittedly unwarranted phrase should have caused so violent a storm. It was of course exacerbated by newspaper columnists and also by the late Mayor la Guardia, who delivered a vituperative broadcast about me with, I suspect, the object of increasing his Brooklyn vote. The general hysteria finally reached such a pitch that a club was formed, I think by the Mayor of Brooklyn, for the 'Prevention of Noël Coward re-entering America'. I still have in my possession a card of membership kindly procured for me by Beatrice Lillie. It is not surprising that by this time my friends in America were seriously perturbed, although not any more than I was myself. I apologised publicly to Brooklyn with complete sincerity, which I am happy to say damped down the flames until at last they fizzled out. It was not until a long while later that Leonard Lyons and Edna Ferber both told me in London that the term 'Brooklyn Boys' had been generally understood to be a snarling reference on my part to the Jewish Race. This, although palpably idiotic, shocked me more than anything else, for I have always detested any form of racial discrimination and consider anti-Semitism to be silly, inconsistent, cruel and entirely beneath contempt. At all events, I have been to America many times since and passed through Brooklyn unmolested, which proves, I sincerely hope, that I have genuinely been forgiven.

Middle East Diary, in spite of its apparent triviality and occasional triteness, is not entirely without merit. There are certain descriptive passages and recorded observations that convey at least a little of what I was feeling and thinking at the time. Some of these I intend to incorporate into this book, for it would be waste of time to attempt to paraphrase them. I will, however, refrain from placing any of these extracts in inverted commas, and if any of my readers should detect here and there a few paragraphs that they have already read, I must ask them to forgive me and press on.

15

I enjoyed every moment of my voyage to Gibraltar in H.M.S. *Charybdis*. I roamed the ship from stem to stern, talked to ordinary seamen, able seamen, leading seamen, stokers, torpedo-men, signal-men, gun ratings, engine-room artificers, petty officers and ward-room officers. I had cocoa and rum with them, shared jokes with them, sang songs to them and on the last day, when we had abandoned the convoy we were escorting and were only a few hours from land, I was asked formally if I would consent to be godfather to the ship. I accepted with pride and we sailed through the sunset into Gibraltar harbour with the Marine Band playing the *Bitter Sweet* waltz.

Gibraltar is an extraordinary place and I have always been fond of it, not only because of the happy times I have had there with the Navy in the past, but because of its own very definite personality. There is charm in its narrow streets and some of the old houses are lovely. It was enjoyable to climb again up to the Rock at sunset and look across the bay to Algeciras and the purple mountains behind, or across the narrows to the coast of Africa; to watch little ships, minute as toys from that height, making pencil marks across the darkening sea and to hear the distant bugles blowing and see the lights come up in the town.

Two days after I arrived the Governor received a signal from Lord Gort saying that he was expecting me in Malta as soon as possible, and so on August the 2nd I took off with H.E. in his private Hudson for Oran, where we touched down at about three o'clcok. We drove through the town and out to a Battle School by the sea which H.E. was going to inspect. Here at last the real heat for which I had been pining for so long began to seep into my bones. Freezing memories of Hull in November, Inverness in January, and even London in June, melted away under the burning sun as we drove through the hot streets. The familiar French North African atmosphere was unchanged. Arabs were scurrying about in tarbooshes; camels wandered along the side of the road in the sparse shade of the dusty trees; faded, striped sunblinds shaded the windows of ornate French villas; and I noticed a waiter doing his accounts under the awning of a deserted café that might have been transplanted, lock, stock and barrel, from the Boulevard Raspail; there were French names over all the shops, and in the centre of the town, of course, stood that inevitable, imperishable monument to French provincialism, the Municipal Opera House. This one looked a bit decayed: its façade was battered, either by bombardment or climate, and a lot of its plaster work was cracking, but there was still a weary old playbill of *La Bohème* pasted on to one of its columns. There was a new note, however, in this dusty French Colonial symphony, and a pretty sharp note at that. This was struck by the American occupation. There were evidences of it on all sides. Over a 'Café-Tabac' was a sign with 'Doughnuts' printed on it; there were khaki-clad figures everywhere; and outside a canteen was a billboard announcing 'To-Nite Bing Crosby and Dorothy Lamour'. I really felt quite sorry for the poor old Municipal Opera House.

The next day we flew to Algiers, where I said good-bye to Mason-Mac, who was going off for a series of conferences. It had been arranged for me to stay at A.F.H.Q., which, translated, means Allied Forces Headquarters.

I lunched in the mess, which had an air of cheerful informality about it. There were five resident American officers and five English, and if only the larger issues of Anglo-American relationships could be run as smoothly the future would offer few problems.

My three days in Algiers were fully occupied. I gave three troop concerts, comparatively small ones, to only five or six hundred men, at which I played for myself, there being no accompanist available, and got away with it reasonably well. I was taken to a couple of French cocktail-parties, one Giraudist and one de Gaullist, both chirrupy and rather tiresome.

I visited one of the larger military hospitals. This was not an unqualified success. The matron was nice, but the commanding officer received me with bored casualness, as though I had just come in to get out of the rain. After I had been through two wards he said, stifling a yawn, that we had better go and have tea. I explained, perhaps rather tartly, that I had not come to tea but to see the patients, and so we went on and I am delighted to say I ran him off his feet.

The day before I left I went to call on General Eisenhower, armed with a letter of introduction from Dickie Mountbatten. I waited a bit in a light, sunny ante-room, signed several autographs for members of the Staff, and was eventually shown in to the inner room where General Eisenhower was seated at his desk. I delivered my letter of introduction and he read it through quickly and offered me a cigarette. He had a tough manner and a warm, Middle Western voice, and after I had told him where I was going and what I proposed to do and asked him for a few facilities here and there, I got up to go, but he made me sit down again, offered me another cigarette, and proceeded to talk more horse-sense about Anglo-American relationships than I had heard for a long time. He seemed to me to have most of the points of this vexed, and at moments very vexing, question at his fingertips.

I sailed for Malta in H.M.S. *Haydon* a small 'Hunt' class destroyer, which, together with the *Kelpi* and another destroyer whose name I forget, was escorting a large convoy of twenty-seven ships. They were of all shapes and sizes varying from liners and big freighters to small tankers and coaling vessels. Standing on the bridge that first evening I watched them streaming along under a cloudless sky, on a calm sea that only one short year ago had been the most dangerous route of all. They looked complacent and unflurried, as though submarines and torpedoes had never been invented and the Mediterranean had always been at peace.

At about four o'clock on the afternoon of our second day out, while I was having a cup of tea with the Captain, and he was apologising for the uneventfulness and dullness of the trip, the buzzer rang. I said gaily 'Enemy Submarines!' He lifted up the receiver and said 'Christ! Torpedo!' and rushed up on to the bridge. I went out on to the fo'c'sle and saw, only a little way off, one large old ship sinking. It was all over in three minutes. She seemed to kneel apologetically in the calm sea, linger for a few moments, and then, with desolate resignation, she disappeared utterly. The whole thing was unspectacular, and oddly silent, like a film without the sound track. There were a few bits of wreckage and a few heads bobbing about in the water, but that was all. The convoy streamed on as though nothing had happened; a couple of escort vessels stood off to pick up the survivors; the rest began dropping depth charges and we did too. The dazzling white columns of spray looked beautiful. I returned to the cabin, put on my Gieves waistcoat and most meticulously filled my cigarette-case, reflecting that a cigarette is at least an aid to outward nonchalance. There was tension on the bridge and a great deal of staccato conversation; signals flashed back and forth between the escort vessels; more depth charges were dropped, and presently our sister ship signalled that she had firm contact, which meant that there was a fifty-fifty chance that the depth charges had disabled the submarine. A couple of hours later we saw an immense column of smoke on the horizon.

On the third morning I looked out of the scuttle and saw Malta, like a child's complicated sand-castle, glowing in the sunshine. An Army captain, Jim Holland, came on board to fetch me off. The ship's motor had broken down and so we went ashore in a Dhaiser, got into a car and drove to Government House, a fifteenth-century castle perched on the top of a hill. Lord Gort received me and we had breakfast, after which we listened to the morning news and then marched, quite fast, up and down a cement tennis court for about twenty minutes. I had a suspicion that the object of this was to keep fit, so I tactfully evaded it for the rest of my stay.

A gentle austerity was the keynote of breakfast at Government House. There was a copy of the *Malta Times* for everyone present, but Lord Gort, rightly, was the only one who had a sort of lectern on which to prop it. Conversation was sporadic and consisted mostly of a brisk interchange of questions and answers. On the dot of eight-fifteen we adjourned to the large salon to listen to the news, which came to us very faintly by courtesy of the B.B.C. Regularly as clockwork at eight twenty-five Lord Gort said: 'Padding – turn it off' and marched out for his morning drill on the tennis court.

My activities usually began fairly early with a rehearsal and a visit to a hospital. I gave an average of three shows a day. The hospitals in Malta were well run and, for me, walking through those endless wards was a salutary experience. Right up until the end of the war, by which time I had visited hundreds of hospitals and become accustomed to the sight of sickness and suffering, I never ceased to be impressed by the endurance of those soldiers, sailors and airmen; and by their capacity for overcoming, or at least appearing to overcome, desolation, boredom, homesickness, pain and discomfort. They lay, day after day, week after week and sometimes month after month, with nothing to do but swat flies if they happened to have an uninjured hand to do it with, and I seldom heard them complain. Many of them had snapshots of their wives or mothers or girl friends or children always close at hand so that they could look at them whenever they could bear to. Many of them hadn't been home for two or three years; some of them would never go home again. It was only after I had left them that any sadness came into my mind. In their presence their own good manners made any display of sympathy impossible. I could only hope that by just chatting to them for a few minutes I had at least temporarily mitigated their boredom and given them something to talk about in their letters home.

My flight from Malta to Cairo was uneventful and at about seven in the evening we sighted the Nile Delta in the distance, a spread of dark, rich green lying like a carpet across the desert. The Pyramids showed up clearly in the setting sun, but they looked minute, like models in some Luna Park panorama; behind them, in the further distance, were palm trees and the tiny, clustered doll's-houses of Cairo. We circled round the desert aerodrome and slowly came down; the air became hotter and hotter; we landed smoothly, and by the time we had taxied along to the reception hut the sun had gone and it was dark. I was met by a gentleman from E.N.S.A. and a Major Pennington, who was a Welfare Officer.

It felt strange to be driving along that familiar straight road from the Pyramids to Cairo again. It seemed to be comparatively unchanged except for the addition of a glittering new open-air night-club, called the Auberge des Pyramides, which was conforming very little to the black-out regulations. The air was soft and hot, expensive cars whizzed by and as we crossed the bridge over the Nile I could see the feluccas with their curved white sails gleaming in the moonlight. The crowded pavements of the city were ablaze with light and there was the usual cacophony of street noises: shouts and yells, motor horns, klaxons and a thudding in the background as though a lot of people were banging invisible trays.

Sitting on the terrace at Shepheard's, the next morning before lunch, I observed that restrictions of war-time were unknown; people sat there sipping gin slings and cocktails, and chatting and gossiping, while waiters glided about wearing fezzes and inscrutable Egyptian expressions. Almost everyone was wearing uniform of some sort or other, including Constance Carpenter, who was in a natty sharkskin two-piece with E.N.S.A. on her epaulettes. These uniforms indicated that perhaps somewhere in the vague outside world there might be a war going on. But here, obviously one of the last refuges of the *soi-disant* 'International Set', all the fripperies of pre-war luxury living were still in existence. Rich people, idle people, cocktail parties, dinner-parties, jewels and evening dress; Rolls Royces came purring up to the terrace steps; the same age-old Arabs sold the same age-old carpets and junk; scruffy little boys darted in between the tables shouting *'Bourse! Bourse!'*, which when translated means the Egyptian *Times*. There was the usual undercurrent of social and political feuds and, excepting for a brief period when the 'flap' was on and the Germans were expected to march in at any moment, here these people had stayed, floating about lazily in their humid backwater, for four long years. It was odd to see it all going on again; enjoyable for a brief, a very brief, visit, but it seemed old-fashioned and rather lacking in taste. I spent the rest of the day interviewing various military welfare High-ups. They were all called by complicated initials and I became very confused. H.Q., an over-crowded hive of questionable efficiency, was heavily fortified. Myriads of people were working away in their offices secure in the knowledge that they were surrounded by barbed wire, guns, pill-boxes, and sentries and were still further protected by a bureaucratic system of regulations and passes, which had to be signed and counter-signed. I had a feeling that had I arrived with a smoking bomb in my hands I should have been immediately allowed in with it provided I had filled in the correct forms. There is no doubt that, as a nation, we have a passion for needless formalities. As far as I was concerned everything was comparatively easy, for I was led up and down stairs, along passages and in and out of rooms by Major Pennington. The officers I talked to were pleasant to me, and General Lindsell asked me to go to Iraq and visit 'Paiforce'. He warned me that it was the worst possible time of the year, that the climate was hell, that there was a lot of sand-fly and malaria, and that the whole trip would be the acme of arid discomfort – but, he added, the troops there had had practically nothing in the way of entertainment and needed it desperately. I said I'd go, of course, and that was settled.

I idled about for a few days while H.Q. was working on itineraries, transport forms, signals and other paraphernalia to facilitate my journeys to Syria, Iraq and Iran. Cairo was stuffy, so I went briefly to Alexandria, where I gave several improvised concerts in hospitals and convalescent camps. These were mostly short and only of routine interest, but they were good practice for poor George Worthington, an accompanist procured for me by Major Pennington; he, being unable to play by ear, had to read everything at sight and at the same time become acquainted with some of my vagaries as a performer. I know that I am not easy to play for and it was much to his credit that he did as well as he did. The open-air shows were, of course, an added nightmare for him, because malignant little gusts of wind were liable to blow the music away in the middle of a number. On these occasions I carried on, disregarding the sudden silences and scufflings behind me, and hoping that in God's own time he would catch up with me, which, in fairness to him, he usually did.

On August the 23rd I flew from Cairo to Beirut, where my hosts were General and Lady Spears (Mary Borden). In the summer their 'Spears Mission' house in Beirut was too hot, so they lived at Aley in the mountains. It was only half an hour's drive, but the change of climate was violent. There were strange rock formations surrounding the terrace where we dined which gave it a Wagnerian air. Louis Spears said it always gave him the feeling that he was sitting inside a hollow tooth.

I stayed with them for three days, during which I gave two concerts and made a broadcast. Also I was taken by Mary to a leave camp, which was on the edge of the sea, which had a perfect bathing beach. Here the troops came from all over the country to have a week's rest and do exactly what they liked. There were no restrictions or discipline of any kind and, if they wanted to, they could even go into the town and get happily sozzled, for which the only penalty was imposed by nature in the form of a hangover, and even this could be swiftly mitigated by a plunge into the sea. They were looked after and waited on and allowed to have morning tea brought to them in bed. The atmosphere of genuine cheerfulness and relaxation about the place was impressive; I talked to several of the men. They were homesick, of course, and plied me with questions, many of which I should have been unable to answer if I had not done that twenty-eight-weeks tour. As it was, I could talk to men from Hull, Nottingham, Inverness, Glasgow, Cardiff, etc., with the added authority of having recently been to these towns. Some of their questions were quite routine: 'How's Sauchiehall Street?', 'Is it still raining in the Oxford Road?' or 'Is the Tower still open in Blackpool?', but some were more personal and touching and betrayed a certain unexpressed worry in their minds. I often came across the same uneasiness among the men I talked to in the Middle East. Most of them treated it gaily, of course, and made a joke of it, but I could see it was there, gnawing at them behind their gaiety and light words. This half-formulated unhappiness was concerned with the presence in England of American and Dominion troops. I imagined that a good deal of it had been deliberately fostered by enemy propaganda and also by careless and irresponsible letters from home. The Press too had contributed to it by headlining localised scandals, thereby implying that these incidents were the rule rather than the exception of it. Men in desert camps with nothing much to contend with in the way of enemy action, but a good deal to contend with in the way of loneliness and boredom, had a lot of time in which to think and jump to conclusions. The conclusions they jumped to were fairly obvious and generally wrong, but it was not their fault. They read in the papers that England was overrun by Canadians and Americans, who were flinging money about and striking up friendships with their sisters and sweethearts and wives, and, perfectly naturally, jealousy and doubt began to torment them. I explained to a number of them that they were building up delusions in their minds. During the last nine months I had had many opportunities of seeing, at first hand, conditions in London and in all the principal provincial towns, and I could honestly say that at least ninety per cent of the American and Dominion troops I encountered in pubs, trains, Tubes and so on were behaving with perfect courtesy.

Mary, doubtless feeling that sharp contrast gives a spur to the imagination, also took me to a Lebanese dinner party. This was given on a roof hung with coloured lights and overlooking a ravine. The Arab food was highly spiced, delicious and very rich. The host and hostess and their other guests were even richer. The Lebanese ladies were *mondaine*, ornately dressed, and they wore a great deal of baroque jewellery which I am afraid was real. I enjoyed the evening on the whole, but it had a quality of fantasy about it. I felt as though I were appearing in a novel by Pierre Loti.

From Beirut I flew to Bagdad, which looked fascinating from the air: minarets, mosques, date palms, camels and the Tigris winding through the town, its banks lined with opulent oriental palaces. But the short drive to General Pownall's house was long enough to convince me that, however fascinating and fraught with Eastern glamour it might look from above, close to, Bagdad was stifling, dirty and without charm. General Pownall, however, was friendly, clean and had great charm. We dined on a terrace looking across at the winking lights on the other side of the river; the air, although not cool, was at least cooler and the wail of Arab music came to us intermittently from the town. For a little while, aided by the tactful darkness, the city looked almost as romantic as I had expected it to be.

I gave two concerts on the following evening, the first one at seven-thirty and the second at ten, in a pleasant garden overlooking the river.

The next day we flew to Shaibah. The flight took three hours and was immeasurably boring; just sand, interminable, ever-lasting and stretching to the farthest horizon. However, at last it was over, and the heat rose up from the ground and enveloped us and pressed down from the airless sky on to our heads, and shimmered visibly all around us like fumes from a burning brazier. Shaibah consisted of Nissen huts, hangars and sand. There was nothing else except, of course, aeroplanes to go in the hangars and several thousand men to gasp the hours away both inside and outside the Nissen huts. Upon arrival I gave a concert to several thousand men in a large hangar, after which I was shepherded into a car and driven over a bumpy desert road to Basra. Here, more dead than alive, I gave, almost immediately, my second concert in a garden next to a railway siding. I cannot say that this performance was one of my best. I am capable, if necessary, of handling difficult audiences, of rising above minor production difficulties such as bad acoustics, insecure stages and eccentric lighting, but I had never before had to compete with engine whistles and goods trucks being shunted back and forth only a few yards away from me. I bawled through the microphone and tried frantically to get my points over in the pauses between puffings and whistlings and clankings. I gave such an abandoned display of facial expressions that the audience must have thought me either dotty or blind drunk. I looked occasionally at poor George pounding away on an execrable piano and was rewarded by a pitying smile.

The next morning we flew back to Habbaniya and on to Beirut for three days, because I had promised Mary Spears to give a concert at the Kit Kat Club for about two thousand men, and also to give a show in the hospital at Sidon. The first of these concerts was distinguished by the presence of Alice Delysia and her fiancé, a Commandant in the French Navy. For two years she had been back and forth across the desert, tirelessly entertaining the troops, frequently under conditions that would have driven artistes of less stamina into nervous breakdowns. She had bounced about in lorries and trucks, been under fire and lost in sandstorms, and here she was, chic and cool in a pink linen *tailleur*, looking younger and more vital than I had ever seen her. It gave an added impetus to my performance to know she was there.

The evening before I left Beirut, Gyles Isham, who had been all through the desert war and was now doing an Intelligence job, drove me up to Sofar in the mountains to dine in cooler air.

While we were at dinner in the somewhat baroque hotel dining-room at Sofar, an impressive figure appeared, accompanied by a gravely subservient retinue. Gyles rose to his feet, bowed politely and sat down again. The man, who was in the late thirties, handsome and with the ivory skin of the Bedouin, acknowledged the bow with a slight smile, and I asked who he was. Gyles told me that his name was Fawwaz Ibn Shaalan, and that he was the grandson of Nuri Shaalan, who had been a great friend of Lawrence of Arabia. Fawwaz Ibn Shaalan, the head of the Runwalla tribe, was exceedingly pro-British, and after dinner he invited us to have coffee with him. He spoke French well, but no English. I said that I had known Lawrence during the last few years of his life, whereupon his aloof, almost expressionless face lit up, his eyes ceased to be sleepy and veiled and became alive. It was touching to see how deeply Lawrence was loved in this part of the world, and to know that his name was still so potent a talisman.

Aircraftsman T. E. Shaw 338171. I remembered writing to him early on in our acquaintance and beginning the letter 'Dear 338171, may I call you 338?' He had been delighted with this little gibe at his passion for anonymity, and had sent me by return the typescript of his Air Force Diary, a most curious, self-revelatory, and beautifully written document. He was, to my mind, a great writer of English and in that alone his death was a bitter loss to our world. As a man I found him strange and elusive. He neither drank nor smoked and, as far as I could see, very seldom ate. He was painfully shy at moments, so much so that he seemed to withdraw himself completely from his surroundings and almost achieve invisibility. At other moments, when he was in a good mood, he was gay and loquacious and often didactic. There was, I think, twisted up in his character a certain inverted exhibitionism. I remember one occasion when he arrived at my house in Kent on his motor-cycle, wearing his aircraftsman's uniform. He was on his way to spend the week-end at Lympne with Phillip Sassoon, who at that time was Minister for Air, and visit 601 Squadron at Lympne aerodrome. When the news got around that Lawrence was coming to visit them, there was considerable excitement and preparations were made for a carefully chosen lunch-party in the officers' mess. It was therefore disconcerting for them when he appeared resolutely wearing his aircraftsman's uniform, because it created a ticklish ethical situation. Had he worn an ordinary lounge suit he could be received by the officers as an honoured civilian, whereas 338171 Aircraftsman T. E. Shaw should by rights be entertained in the airmen's mess, which was totally unprepared for the privilege. None of this really was of the least importance and, apart from some whispered consultations and a certain preliminary strain, everything went smoothly, but knowing how he shrank from any form of limelight and how he loathed any attention being called to himself, it was surprising that he should choose the one sure way of getting them. I asked him later about this and he laughed, rather self-consciously, I thought, and changed the subject. What I am trying to analyse in my memory of him is the genuineness of his desire for self-effacement, and whether, by so rigidly disciplining his own definite ego, he was not really gratifying some deep-rooted, subconscious masochism. In most of his writing, particularly *The Seven Pillars of Wisdom*, and the Air Force diary, one can discern a certain bitterness directed against himself, a contempt for his smallness of stature. There was in him, I am sure, a terrible area of discontent. Others who knew him far better than I have ascribed it all to his heartbreak and disillusionment over the Damascus problem, but I am not so sure. I believe that there must always have been, deep down in that strange, mystic, dynamic mind, the seeds of despair and an impulse towards self-martyrdom. To me it is infinitely tragic that all he might have given us in the forthcoming dangerous years, his genius, courage, strength of purpose and vision, should have been snuffed out in one blinding, noisy moment on that idiotic motor-cycle.

Back in Cairo I did a week's tour of the canal zone, the usual routine of hospitals and concerts.

The desert hospitals were remarkable, all things considered. Most of the wards were merely tents and the ingenuity of the staffs was extraordinary; they had thought of so many little ways of making the men as comfortable as possible. The nursing sisters all contrived to look as though they had spent at least two hours on their toilettes; their uniforms were always spotless and looked cool and pleasant. They achieved this in circumstances that would drive ordinary women dotty: the sanitation was usually primitive, the heat terrific and the glare and sand and flies appalling. If I had seen nothing else on that trip, those desert hospitals would have made it worth while.

After this dusty excursion I had a day off, most of which I passed reading in the Caseys' garden at Mena. That evening at dinner a South African General, Frank Theron, appeared. He was tall, distinguished and persuasive. The persuasiveness particularly struck me, for he spent an hour on the terrace when we were having coffee coaxing me to do a tour of South Africa. Dick Casey backed him up, and finally I agreed, with the proviso that I could do it early in the New Year and have two or three months in England first.

The effects of that quiet evening in the suburbs of Cairo were, for me, far-reaching and sent me a good deal further on my travels than I intended to go. At the time, of course, the momentousness of the occasion was not apparent, and I let Theron and Dick Casey draft out cables to Field-Marshal Smuts and Lord Harlech without further protest. I was tired and the thought of an organised tour of the camps and hospitals of South Africa was alarming, but I knew that after a couple of months at home I should probably be straining at the leash again.

During the next week I gave an average of three concerts a day in and around Cairo and Alexandria and flew on to Tripoli, where the hospitals were crammed because the Salerno casualties had been heavy. Only one incident haunts my memory and, I suspect, will always do so. In one of the wards was a young man who had, that morning, had a serious operation. He was still unconscious and was having a blood transfusion. His eyes were closed and he was the colour of wax, so I didn't disturb him and passed on. About an hour later, when I was at the other end of the hospital, a sister came with a message that he was asking to see me. I hurried back at once. He was hardly able to speak, but I held his hand and told him that he would soon be better. He smiled at this and said he was feeling better already, and then he died.

There was a certain air of pathos about the town of Tripoli, the foolish pathos of an expensive tart who has allowed herself to go to seed and forgotten to do her nails. The city had been well laid out; there were gardens and terraces and grandiose buildings, but it all had the impermanence of some over-modern World's Fair exhibit. The coloured plaster was already peeling from the angular, self-conscious architecture and the streets were dusty and woebegone. The whole place was obviously never intended to withstand bombardment and conquest. There could never have been either in its conception or its achievement any real spirit. What pride it ever had, had wilted immediately in adversity; like the Italian Army, it could only have been impressive in peace and fair weather. Now, with truckloads of bronzed, tough British and American soldiers whooping up and down its once immaculate boulevards, it seemed cringing and submissive and utterly lacking in even the dignity of decay.

On September the 27th I landed at Algiers. It was bitterly cold and pouring with rain and I felt shaken and bad-tempered. My tour, so far as work was concerned, was over. I had bidden goodbye to George at Tripoli and presented him with a wrist-watch as a token of my very sincere gratitude for all he had done. Never in all the weeks he had played for me, in all the differences of climate and all the difficult circumstances, had he once complained or even looked disconcerted. He had always been there when I wanted him and faded away with the most unobtrusive tact when I didn't. Now I was alone again, on my way home, and the adventure was nearly over.

The next day I took off in a battered D.C.3 which had just been through a storm and smelt of sick.

The flight was beautiful, for the weather had cleared. I sat in the cockpit with the pilot, a most engaging young tough from Indiana; he switched on the radio and we listened to Judy Garland far away in California crooning faintly through waves of crackling 'static'. The Mediterranean was calm and highly coloured and we flew up the middle of it with Europe on our right and Africa on our left; it was so clear that Gibraltar became visible a hundred and forty miles away.

John Perry, who was A.D.C. to the Governor, met me and told me that Mason-Mac was away and so, with the exception of a few transients, we should have Government House to ourselves. I was actually rather relieved to hear this, for I was dead tired and starting a cold, the inevitable effect of the sudden change of climate between Tripoli and Algiers, and felt more than ready for a few days of relaxation.

One evening John and I went to have a drink in a house halfway up the rock and overlooking the harbour. We sat on a terrace listening to the noises of the town drifting up from below and watching the sunset. H.M.S. *Charybdis*, my 'godship', which I had hoped was going to take me home to England, had received a change of orders at the last minute and was sailing off on another assignment. From that terrace on that lovely gentle evening I watched her putting out to sea, I thought gratefully and affectionately of all my friends on board as she moved smoothly and with dignity out over the darkening water. That was the last time I saw her, or ever shall see her, for she was sunk in action off the coast of France in the early hours of the morning of October the 23rd. There were very few survivors.

A few nights later I got into a plane for England.

The shades were taken off the windows at about six o'clock a.m. and I woke up and looked out. We flew low over the Bristol Channel and the green hills of Somerset; the sun began to dispel the morning mist and mark the long shadows of trees across the fields. I looked back in my mind over the last crowded three months: the seas and mountains and deserts I had crossed; the moving sights I had seen; the different faces, voices and handshakes. I thought of all the thousand men who had talked to me in camps, ships, canteens, airfields and hospitals, and realised how much it would mean to any one of them to be looking at what I was looking at now, the familiar, gentle English countryside, still, after four years of war, waking peacefully to an autumn day.

PART FIVE

I

The weeks I spent in England between October the 10th, when I returned with a cold from the Middle East, and December the 2nd, when, with the same cold, I set off on my travels again, are recorded in my day-to-day diary with even more niggardliness than usual. It gives reluctantly a few staccato reminders of whom I saw, where I went, and what I did, but withholds both comment and explanation and is frequently illegible. I gather from it, however, after much memory-straining and concentration, that my days were fully and variously occupied. There were film conferences with David and Ronnie regarding present activities (*Blithe Spirit*) and future possibilities (undecided); interviews with Brendan Bracken at the Ministry of Information and with officials at South Africa House concerning my forthcoming tour; an interview with Field Marshal Smuts himself at the Hyde Park Hotel, where he made me welcome in advance to South Africa and assured me that my visit was being eagerly looked forward to; and a week-end at Chequers, when the Prime Minister told me, in strictest secrecy, of the loss of the *Charybdis*. This last was a painful shock and robbed the day of all pleasure. The bar of secrecy lay heavily on me until the following Tuesday, when I received a considerate message from 10 Downing Street saying that I was now free to make any enquiries I wished. I telephoned immediately to Commander Whitfield, who fortunately had left the ship a week before the action. He told me that only fifteen ratings and four officers had survived. This saddened me for a long time; even now, after ten years have passed, my heart is heavy when I think of it.

I managed, during those few weeks, to do a few troop concerts here and there, just to keep my hand in. Two were in London, at the Wings Club and the Nuffield Centre, and the rest at airfields in the country. On December the 1st I said all my good-byes again and got into the night train for Glasgow. I had arranged, with Brendan Bracken's consent, to go to New York by sea, do a couple of broadcasts there for Henry Morgenthau, who had specially asked me to, and fly to South Africa on the first of January. I had also arranged for Bert Lister to come with me on the South African tour as a personal representative-cum-secretary. Cole was unavailable, having been in the R.A.F. since 1940, and I felt unequal to facing the stresses of another Dominion tour without someone I knew and who knew me. Bert was to travel by sea to Suez and meet me in Khartoum on January the 5th. Norman Hackforth, who had agreed in Cairo to come with me as my accompanist, was to meet me in Pretoria. So with these essential comforts taken care of, I set off, snuffling but with an easy mind. The name of the ship in which I was sailing had been withheld for security reasons, but I knew, I suspect in common with any enemy agents still at large, that it would be either the *Queen Elizabeth* or the *Queen Mary*, for one or other of these ships sailed regularly once a week from Greenock. It turned out to be the former. I was fetched from the Central Hotel, Glasgow, in the early morning by an M.O.I. representative and we drove out of the city and along by the Clyde. The *Queen Elizabeth* was unmistakable from miles away, towering grey and impressive over the surrounding countryside. I mentioned to my escort that I was glad it was the *Q.E.* because I knew her well. He placed his finger to his lips, said 'Hush' and nodded warningly towards the driver. I looked suitably apologetic and, reflecting that security-mindedness could at no time be carried too far, said loudly: 'Look at that pretty little private yacht with steam up, I expect she is in for repairs.' I do not think that my friend was amused.

The *Queen Elizabeth* was crammed with American troops and was consequently 'dry'. Having been warned of this beforehand I had packed a few bottles of whisky and gin in one of my suitcases. Anthony Biddle, who was also travelling, had done the same, only with more lavishness, and so between us we had enough liquor to keep several people in a drunken coma for five days had we wished to. In our anxiety to forestall the possibility of enforced sobriety we had left out of consideration the ships' officers, who, from the Captain downwards, gave a series of high-powered cocktail parties, sherry parties, egg-nog parties and beer parties in the seclusion of their cabins to the transient V.I.P.s. I seldom remember a more cheerful voyage and we finally landed in New York with our personal 'caches' untouched. Cabins were allotted according to rank, and as Biddle and I were the only civilians on board I asked the purser how it was that we had been given such comfortable accommodation, whereupon he showed me his private passenger list in which both our names appeared with the honorary rank of Admiral tacked on to them. From then on we saluted each other elaborately several times a day. The ship sailed on a zig-zag course, unescorted, and it was hoped that her speed and agility would frustrate any attempt by enemy submarines to torpedo her. Inevitably I was pressed into service to entertain the troops, and I performed in the main lounge, the smoking-room, the cabin class and in the tourist class, in which a section had been transformed into a sort of mental hospital for men suffering from war neuroses. Incidentally they turned out to be the brightest audience of the lot.

Thanks to Anthony Biddle's ex-ambassadorial status he was given the courtesy of the port on arrival, and swept me off the ship and through the Customs with him, in an aura of polite officialdom, in less time than it usually takes to get one's baggage on to the dock, after which we saluted one another breathlessly and drove off to our separate destinations. Mine was in Jack's flat in East 55th Street, where he and Natasha were just on the point of leaving to come and meet me.

I had not been in New York since March 1941, nine months before the tragedy of Pearl Harbour blasted America's neutrality to smithereens. The United States had now been in the war for two years, but New York betrayed no outward signs of conflict. Theatres, restaurants and night-clubs were flourishing; the lights of Broadway were as bright as, if not brighter than, they had ever been. All the comforts and amenities of urban life were easily procurable and it was, of course, a relief to be able to stroll home from a theatre through light streets after the fumbling gloom of the London black-out; to be able to eat steaks, drink orange juice and order omelettes; to be able to hail a taxi when you wanted one, and to sleep at night without an air-raid siren dragging you awake; but my relief, I fear, was tinged with irritation, an unmannerly, irrational resentment. I wished New York no ill fortune, I had no desire to see its hard beauty chipped by bombs and made shabby by paneless windows and dust and rubble. It was only that it seemed almost intolerably shiny, secure and well dressed, as though it was continually going to gay parties while London had to stay at home and do the housework.

My own friends were as dear as ever, but some of the conversations at dinner and lunches seemed unreal. There seemed already to be an assumption in the champagne American air that Britain had muddled through for the last time, that her former greatness together with her die-hard Imperialistic pretensions were flaking off her as dried old paint flakes off a decrepit building. Economically we were done for, and in the general, and particularly the American, view to be economically done for was the end, or at least the beginning of the end. I do not subscribe to this view now any more than I did then in 1943. If, in the next fifty years of wars and revolutions, Great Britain should sink wearily into being economically a third-rate power, so much the worse, but I cannot believe that the quality of its people nor the curious tenacity of its traditions will change.

The fourth day after my arrival in America I was struck down with 'flu and retired to bed with aching limbs and a temperature. This only lasted a day or two, but it left me weak and listless.

I did two broadcasts, and an extra one on Christmas Day to Paris, organised by the Free French.

On Christmas night I dined with Bill Stephenson (Little Bill) and Mary his wife. It was a small party and Bill asked me to stay behind when the other guests left as he had something of importance to say to me. What he had to say turned out to be a firm and uncompromising lecture on my health. He said that I looked awful, that I had obviously been doing far too much far too quickly, and that to contemplate a strenuous tour of South Africa in my present exhausted and almost voiceless condition was fool-hardy to the point of imbecility, and could only end in disaster. He then said, more gently, that he had arranged for me to go to a house in Jamaica for two weeks, where I should see nobody and give myself a thorough rest. I protested that Bert and Norman were waiting for me, that my South African itinerary was probably already set and that to cancel it would cause many troublesome complications, to which he replied, with truth, that the complications would be far more troublesome for everyone concerned if I had a breakdown when I got there and was unable to continue. At all events, he said, two weeks couldn't make all that difference one way or another, that the arrangements for my journey to Jamaica were already made and that he would send the necessary explanatory cables to South Africa; he added that all I had to do was to shut up and obey orders.

On Sunday, January 2nd, Neysa gave a farewell cocktail-party, after which I was escorted to La Guardia Airport and placed on the night plane for Miami. In due course the plane thundered along the runway and zoomed up through the clouds of 1944; the vivid lights of New York flickered out in the mist and rain below and I was once again, in every sense of the word, up and away.

2

My first view of Jamaica was from an altitude of about eight thousand feet. The morning was cloudless and the island was discernible from many miles away. Now, remembering that moment nine years ago, my mind becomes choked with clichés. 'Had I but known then . . .' 'Little did I dream,' 'If only I could have foreseen,' but of course I didn't know or dream or foresee how familiar that particular sight would become, how many times in the future I was destined to see these green hills and blue mountains rising out of the sea. Today, sitting on my Jamaican veranda and looking out across the bay at Port Maria, it is difficult to imagine that I ever saw the island for the first time, for it has become so much a part of my life, and given me such pleasure and peace of mind, that I feel that I have known it always. Leaving aside the lush beauty of its scenery, its lovely climate and the pleasantness of its people, it has given me the most valuable benison of all: Time to read and write and think and get my mind in order; time to be utilised and, above all, time to be wasted without regret. I have always been a staunch upholder of 'early to bed, early to rise', as a theory, although in practice I have only rarely been able to carry it out. In Jamaica it is not only possible but automatic; there is nothing to do in the evenings and the morning hours are the loveliest of the day. To have eight or nine hours of sleep and still to be able to see the sun come up is, to me, a happily recurring miracle, and for at least three months of every year I intend to enjoy it to the end of my days.

My first arrival in 1944 was accomplished, thanks to the efficiency of Little Bill's organisation, with impeccable secrecy. I was met at the plane by a naval officer, who whisked me out of a side entrance at the airport and deposited me in a waiting car. Within a few moments my baggage appeared and we drove through the outer fringes of Kingston and up into the mountains. The N.O., acting on orders from above, suspected, I am sure, that I was engaged on nefarious work of the direst significance, and I forbore from disappointing him by explaining that the whole operation had been set in motion merely to give me a nice lie-down.

'Bellevue' is about thirteen hundred feet above sea-level and looks over the whole valley and town of Kingston to the peninsula of Port Royal in the distance, crawling out like a green snake into the sea. In the old days the house had been the property of the resident Admiral, and at one time Nelson, shivering and racked with fever, was conveyed to it on a litter to regain his health in the cooler air and fresher breezes. Although I was not, like Nelson, shivering and racked with fever, I was certainly over-tired and stuffed with catarrh and I hoped that the cooler air and fresher breezes would do as good a job on me as they had on him. I was received by a smiling, dusky major-domo called Montgomery, and several other equally smiling and equally dusky characters, and when I had explored the house and garden, I settled myself in a hammock slung between an orange tree and a coco-palm and felt peace already beginning.

Later in the day a brisk young woman called Florence Reed appeared with a piano. She was private secretary to Robert Kirkwood, to whom I had a letter of introduction, and it was she who had corralled the staff and put the house in order to receive me. She also had been sworn to secrecy and assured me that although it was already known by the grapevine intelligence that a mysterious gentleman had arrived at Bellevue, no one had the slightest idea who it was. From then on, apart from Florence, two American soldier friends of hers and Sybil and Bobby Kirkwood, I met no one in Jamaica until a day or two before I left. It was a perfect holiday. The house was comfortable, the garden lovely and there were masses of books to read. I sat each evening on the terrace watching the sun set and the lights come up in the town. On the third night the moon was full and fireflies flickered among the silvered trees, in fact no magic was omitted. The spell was cast and held, and I knew I should come back.

By the end of the first week my catarrh had gone, my voice had come back and I was satisfactorily sun-tanned and feeling better than I had felt for ages. The creative urge, seldom long in abeyance, reared its sprightly head again and I wrote a song called 'Uncle Harry'. It was a gay song and I hammered it out interminably on Florence's piano until it was so firmly stamped on my memory that I knew I couldn't forget it. I don't suppose that Montgomery and the staff have forgotten it either.

A few days before I was due to leave, Florence procured some petrol coupons and I went for a tour of the island. The chauffeur was a mine of information, but at that time I had not become used to Jamaican inflections and only understood about a quarter of what he told me. We drove through Kingston and on through Port Antonio by the coast road. From there we followed the North Shore road, through Robin's Bay, Anotto Bay and Port Maria, past the strip of coast which one day was to belong to me – no bell rang, no angel voices warned me, no prescient instinct took the trouble to point it out – and on to Oracabessa, Ocho Rios, St Ann's and the long stretch of Falmouth and Montego Bay. The sun shone, the sea sparkled, the coco trees swayed gently in the light trade-wind and it was altogether enchanting. At the Casablanca Hotel in Montego I met, for the first time, my old friend Carmen Pringle. We sat under the stars and listened to native singers and the noise of the surf on the reef. The next morning I drove back via the south coast to Bellevue, and girded myself for my last day in Jamaica, which included a Press reception in Kingston and lunch at King's House.

The following day I was called at four a.m. and drove through the still darkness to the airport. The plane took off just as dawn was breaking and, pressing my forehead against the glass of the window, I murmured a silent *au revoir* to the island that had done much for me even in two short weeks.

At Barranquilla another of Bill's representatives met me and took me to the Hotel del Prado, where a reception and dinner-party had been arranged in my honour. I had to make a speech at the reception, half in English and half in Spanish. I cannot for the life of me remember what I spoke about, but it seemed to go down all right. The dinner-party was large, impressive and bilingual and it went on for a long time.

In Trinidad I was weatherbound for three days and stayed with Sir Bede Clifford at Government House. I utilised one of those days by making a tour of the Naval Base and giving two concerts in the evening.

On January the 21st I drove out to the airport at midnight in a tropical deluge, climbed into a Liberator which was occupied only by four other bodies, and flew off into the storm. The other bodies were cheerful American Air Force technicians and, after a fairly bumpy night, we made ourselves hot egg sandwiches and coffee. We came down briefly at Belem in Brazil, where we had a larger breakfast and drove for half an hour through the haunted tumbledown streets that once, when the town was originally reclaimed from the jungle, had been prosperous and well cared for. Now wealth had wandered away from Belem and the jungle was most decidedly getting its own back.

We got to Natal at six-thirty in the evening. Here I was met by still another of Bill's men, Lieutenant Dick, who took me to an officers' mess. By this time I had become devoted to the Liberator; it was friendly although it certainly couldn't be described as the last word in smooth luxury. It was carrying, in addition to the Americans and me, a heavy load of technical equipment, and although we had managed to make ourselves comfortable enough by twining ourselves round pieces of machinery and sleeping on mailbags, when we emerged from the plane we were all fairly grubby. The 'wash and brush up' I had in that officers' mess was bliss; after dinner in the mess there was a soldiers' dance, at which the commanding officer asked me to make a brief appearance. There was only time for one number, so I obliged breathlessly with 'I'll See You Again', accompanied by the dance band in the wrong key, and got back into the plane. At seven-thirty next morning we came down for an hour on Ascension Island, where we were given breakfast in a large mess-room while the refuelling was going on. Ascension Island seemed strange and desolate, with two sharply pointed hills, one deep red and the other purple. The sea looked wonderful, curling in over orange sands, and, excepting for a clump of trees on top of a low hill where I was told the

Resident lived, the whole landscape might have been painted by Vlaminck or Matisse at the peak of their 'Fauve' period.

In Accra I had a twenty-four-hours breather. Lord Swinton's A.D.C. met me and I stayed in the mess. The next morning the A.D.C. drove me to a dusty beach where we bathed in coffee-coloured surf. The coast was flat and sinister and a shrill, warm wind blew the sand into our eyes. After a lunch-party at Government House with several pukka sahibs, a few drained-looking ladies in flowered chiffon and, surprisingly enough, Walter Elliot, who was passing through on some unspecified mission, I flew off in a D.C.3 to Lagos. Here the lush, tropical, 'white man's grave' atmosphere was very strong. I stayed the night in the house of the Acting Secretary, a dim cool house with punkahs creaking over the dining-table and black lizards coughing on the veranda like old bishops in the Athenaeum Club.

Having dragged myself awake at six a.m. and driven out to the airport, I was told that my plane would not take off until midday, if then, for the weather was very bad. Although well accustomed to the capriciousness of air travel, this depressed me. I was already late on my schedule and South Africa was still a long way away. I sat in the B.O.A.C. Club for an hour, drinking coffee and gloomily visualising several days of maddening inactivity, when a message came to say that a large Ensign was about to take off and that they were holding it for me. Within five minutes I was back at the airport and in the plane. I fastened my seat belt tightly and looked out at the appalling weather: thick rain drove horizontally across the airfield, the visibility was practically nil and although my relief at leaving was considerable it was offset by several minutes of stark terror. The Ensign was enormous and carrying a heavy load, and as it lumbered along the sodden runway preparatory to taking off into the full force of the storm my heart sank and, like the wife of a famous statesman on her wedding night, I closed my eyes and thought of England.

That evening we came down at Maiduguri, a town of mud huts in the north-west corner of Nigeria. The day's flight had been uneventful except for a hair-raising landing and take-off at Kano. The weather was clear at Maiduguri, and the Resident, an agreeable man called Thompstone, came to meet me and drive me back to his house. On the way we stopped off for a drink at the club, which as an example of the 'Outpost of Empire' tradition was accurate to the last detail. There were bead curtains, faded chintz covers and a rack full of months-old English newspapers and magazines. There was a mixed tennis foursome going on which might have been lifted bodily, court and players, from Cheltenham and set down in one piece in this savage, alien land. 'Well played,' 'Yours, partner,' 'Love-fifteen'. Clear English voices echoed across the dusty grass separating the veranda from the edge of the court, while from the village near-by came the thud of native drums and the thin wail of reed instruments. The natives of Maiduguri move beautifully and wear robes of the most lovely shades of blue which they dye themselves. The resident British moved perhaps less beautifully and their apparel was nondescript, but their quality was unmistakable. That small club, so very far away from home, was touching and curiously impressive.

At four a.m. I flew off again and, as the long hours of the day passed, the land beneath us changed shape and colour until there was nothing but desert sand. In the early evening we had arrived in Khartoum.

Bert Lister, after various vicissitudes, had got himself and my heavier baggage to Khartoum two weeks before. When I arrived I found him thrashing about in the hotel bedroom with tonsilitis and a high temperature. He was in a suicidal rage, having been perfectly well until the preceding morning. This of course was a maddening setback. I couldn't very well go on and leave him alone and ill, so I was forced to postpone our flight to Pretoria for three days. By this time I was getting panic-stricken. In addition to my pre-arranged two weeks' holiday in Jamaica, I had been delayed three days in Trinidad, another night and day in Accra and here was a still further hold up. I sent an explanatory cable to Norman Hackforth, who had already arrived in South Africa, and fortunately received a reassuring one back. Happily the three days were enough to bring Bert's temperature down and get him up and about, and on January the 30th I set off on the last lap of my journey. Our plane was crowded with gay homeward-bound South Africans and our first night stop was at a strange place called Mallakel, where we were put up at a rest-house. Before dinner we went for a stroll along a river bank, hoping to encounter some of the Dinkas whose terrain it was. The Dinkas' claim to fame is that they are very tall, have the longest penises in the world and dye their hair with urine; doubtless cause and effect. We only saw two standing listlessly on the opposite side of the river and, as far as we could judge from that distance, they were right up to standard.

Part of the next day we flew low over animal country: the wings of our plane made swift shadows on the land, which startled herds of static elephants into sudden activity and sent hippos and crocodiles slithering hurriedly from sandbanks into the gleaming rivers. We dropped down at Juba in the Congo for refuelling, and in the evening got to Totara, Tanganyika. Here a young Station-Commander took Bert and me for a drive and to dinner in the mess, thereby annoying the local Resident, who had apparently come down to the rest-house to look me over but had neither met me nor invited me to anything. I was told later that there had been a fine shindy over this and that our friend had got into trouble. I certainly hope that it wasn't true, because we were much in his debt for welcoming us so enthusiastically and giving us such a good time.

Finally, on Feburary the 1st, after a long day of very rough flying, we arrived at Bulawayo. The hotel was modern and comfortable and I was able to telephone to Myles Bourke, who was to be my host in Pretoria and was also in charge of my itinerary. He sounded charming on the telephone, and assured me that I needn't worry about being late, and that everything was under control. This was comforting and I was able, with a light heart, to put myself down and relax. Unhappily the light-heartedness and relaxation didn't last, for we spent the next three days driving to the airport, getting into planes, getting out again and driving back to the hotel. The weather reports from Pretoria were bad on the first day and so we didn't take off; on the second and third days the weather had cleared in Pretoria, but was vile in Bulawayo and so we didn't take off. At last, when I was practically a nervous wreck with frustration, a Captain von Roon arrived in a Lodestar and told us that he had two vacant seats and would take us on the following day. This was too good to believe, but sure enough on that next afternoon off we went at three-forty-five and at long last arrived in Pretoria at seven o'clock in the evening. Myles Bourke was at the airport to greet us, with Norman and several others, including the Quartermaster-General with a welcoming message from Field-Marshal Smuts. A horde of Pressmen rushed at me, flash-bulbs seared my eyeballs, I mumbled a few words into a microphone and drove off with Myles and Norman, leaving Bert to follow in another car with the luggage.

3

A chronological, day-by-day, account of my three months in South Africa, although fraught with personal interest to me who lived through them, would, I fear, be fraught with impersonal tedium for any reader who had not. I will try therefore to be as concise as possible and fish out of the welter of routine, troop concerts, Rotarian lunches, rehearsals, public performances, bazaar openings, arrivals, departures and civic receptions a few outstanding incidents, agreeable or otherwise, a few hurried but very definite impressions of that remarkable country and the people who live in it. It was inevitable, I suppose, that at first I should compare it in my mind with Australia, but after a while I realised that such a facile comparison was neither valid nor intelligent. The Union of South Africa is comparable to other Dominions of the British Commonwealth only in its most superficial aspects; beneath these seethes a ferment of racial problems and political unrest. Between the Afrikaans and the British there is distrust, and between the blacks and the whites a deadly fear. This underlying, perilous discontent soon becomes apparent even to the most casual visitor. The air is deceptively clear and the country beautiful, but even in its beauty there is a quality of potential danger as though the land itself was beginning to lose patience with its fractious tenants and might at any moment heave itself up and send the whole lot tumbling into the sea. As soon as my instincts recognised this fundamental disharmony I resolved to guard my tongue, watch my step and strain every nerve to be as tactful as possible. I was the guest of Smuts and the Government, and therefore an obvious target for the Opposition Press, so it would be wise to steel myself against some inevitable slings and arrows; aware also that my strong contempt for any sort of racial discrimination might if expressed, however casually, imperil the success of my tour, I decided to sidetrack the subject whenever possible and, when not possible, to keep my mouth firmly shut. In this I succeeded on the whole, although there was a bad moment when I unthinkingly suggested in my farewell broadcast that the 'Cape Coloureds' should be encouraged to start a repertory company of their own. Fortunately an official of the South African Consolidated Theatres spotted this heresy in the nick of time and it was hurriedly deleted from the script. Heavens knows I would be the last to upset dear African Consolidated Theatres, for without their co-operation and efficiency my tour might have been a dire flop. On my first morning in Pretoria, when, with Norman and Bert and Myles Bourke, I went through my proposed itinerary, I saw clearly that it would have to be entirely reorganised. Myles, who was officially in control of entertainments for the Forces, had either not understood or been misinformed about my requirements. He had arranged for me to open in Durban at a time when the Government and everyone of importance was in Cape Town. He had also engaged an Air Force dance band to accompany me wherever I went. This band, complete with a crooner, was to precede my own appearance at every concert. Even for troop shows this would have been unsatisfactory, because much of my performance depended on a microphone, and to have someone else moaning into it, possibly more effectively, immediately before I came on, would be redundant to say the least, but for my big public concerts which I was to give in every big city in aid of Mrs Smuts' Comforts Fund, an Air Force band of twelve pieces would be ineffective from the point of view of balance and inadequate for the size of the theatres. My own intention, needless to say, was to make my first public appearance in Cape Town at the height of the season with a symphony orchestra or nothing. Poor Myles, who took my fairly acrid criticisms of his itinerary charmingly, was shocked at such an exhibition of brash showmanship, and when I added that Field-Marshal Smuts, Mrs Smuts and the entire Cabinet should attend my opening performance his eyes glazed, he muttered: 'True, O King,' in a strangulated voice and retired from the arena.

Marguerite Bourke, Myles's wife, received the news of this preliminary skirmish with a twinkle in her eyes. She was a small, grey-haired woman, humorous, intelligent, always impeccably dressed and, to me, a unique and enchanting character. She also ran her house so well, and provided us with such perfectly cooked food, that wherever we stayed afterwards seemed an anti-climax. I expect she will laugh when she reads this glowing description of herself, but it will, I know, be a laugh of deep affection. At all events, I had pangs of conscience about the itinerary. Myles had taken so much trouble, and, with my usual ruthlessness where my own professional interests are concerned, I had virtually torn it up and flung it in his teeth. Marguerite, understanding swiftly that right or wrong I intended to get my own way, proceeded with exquisite tact to dispel all traces of friction and, unlike the Union of South Africa as a whole, the atmosphere of that house vibrated with dulcet harmony until the day we regretfully said good-bye to it.

Realising that if everything had to be reorganised from scratch there was no time to be wasted, I set out with Bert immediately to beard the South African Consolidated Theatres in their den in Johannesburg. Dick Harmel, a shrewd and kindly man, received us, and when I had explained my dilemma, agreed to take control of all my public appearances, rearrange my whole tour so that I could make the maximum amount of money for the Fund, provide through his organisation the requisite publicity and draft and have printed an expensive and attractive souvenir programme.

The next ten days hurried by, panting and breathless, as though they were running to catch a train, which in a sense they were, the train to be caught being February the 21st, the date set for my opening in Cape Town. Fortunately we were staying in the Bourkes' peaceful house and we were able to get to bed early, for there was no time during the day to relax for a moment. There was a great deal of driving back and forth between Pretoria and Johannesburg, an endless series of conferences – planning conferences, Press conferences, souvenir programme conferences – and Norman and I spent several hours in a dilapidated film studio being photographed, informally rehearsing, for the newsreels. Our actual rehearsals also took up a lot of time. It was many years since Norman had played for me and although, to me, he is the best and most sensitive accompanist in the world, he has to know each number thoroughly before either he or I can feel really secure. The Cape Town Symphony Orchestra had agreed by telegram to take over the first part of each of my three public concerts at the Alhambra. The arrangement was that the orchestra should play a forty-five-minutes programme of discreetly classical music, there would then be a ten minute *entr'acte*, and then Norman and me for an hour and a half. That ominous hour and a half haunted our waking hours and troubled our dreams. We knew, having seen the seating plan, that the theatre was enormous, and to hope to keep a vast, and presumably fashionable, audience happy and amused for such a long time seemed rashly optimistic. However, Dick Harmel had assured me that all would be well, though why he was so certain I shall never know, as he had never heard me in his life, and so we overrode our quaking fears and rehearsed feverishly. I decided to break the monotony of my adroit but thin singing by reciting these verses in the middle of my programme: 'Trafalgar Day' and 'Plymouth Hoe' by Clemence Dane and a short piece of my own called 'Lie in the Dark and Listen'. During this brief patriotic interlude Norman was to leave the stage for a breather and return refreshed to play a five-minute medley of my tunes. This medley, known affectionately as 'Scrambled Father', would allow me to retire to my dressing-room and decide whether or not to shoot myself. Then, provided the audience was still present, I would come back and round off the evening with the strongest comedy numbers in my repertoire. Bert, throughout all these anguished plannings, struck and maintained a note of breezy confidence. He pooh-poohed the least suggestion that I could be anything but a triumphant success and swirled away our misgivings in a spate of Cockney invective. Bert's phraseology was rich and varied, and although in public an acquired sense of propriety stemmed its flow, in private his command of the more idiomatic ebulliences of the English language was truly remarkable. Abetted by a slight stammer and deep-rooted indestructible Cockney humour he could charm a bird off a tree, provided the bird was familiar with race-track jargon, rhyming slang and the more trenchant four-letter words of our native tongue. Besides this enviable talent he had other gifts, among them tact and understanding. He was also entirely undisciplined, an inveterate gambler, and, in spite of his determined efforts to appear tough, an incurable sentimentalist. Throughout the whole arduous South African tour he was invaluable to me. He upbraided me when I was over-nervous, laughed me out of tantrums, upheld me staunchly when there was a battle to be fought and very seldom irritated me at all. An extraordinary achievement.

As the time drew near for our departure for the Cape I thought it wise, both for Norman's sake and my own, to try out our programme in military camps in and around Pretoria. We did five shows in three days, all of which were hearteningly successful except the first one. This went down all right on the whole, but I was nervous and put off by a glum-faced Padre in the front row who so obviously disapproved of my performances that I became fascinated by him like a rabbit with a python. I heard afterwards that he complained that my songs were suggestive and lowering to the morale of the troops. Bert's summing up of this gentleman was hilarious and would have sent the morale of those troops soaring.

At last, on the evening of February the 17th, we drove over to Johannesburg and got into the evening train for Cape Town. The Government had provided me with a private coach, which was just as well, for my entourage had swollen. In addition to Norman and Bert and myself there were Frank Rogali, my troops entertainment organiser appointed by Myles Bourke, his assistant and a Press representative. Through the whole of the next day we traversed the flat plains known as the Karoo. Small humpy hills, kopjes, broke the monotony, and the light was extraordinary. At eight-thirty a.m. on the morning of the second day we arrived at Paarl, a town apparently a hundred per cent Afrikaans and notorious for its anti-British feeling. However, for some reason or other, possibly the efficient advance publicity of African Consolidated Theatres, it decided to rise above all nationalistic prejudice and come and meet me. As the train drew in to the station I looked out of the window and saw a small boy scout holding a banner twice as big as himself with on it a Victory V and 'Welcome to Noël Coward' in scarlet letters. I stepped out of the train, was presented with a bouquet by a little girl in a pink dress and received by the Mayor in full regalia. The Mayor read me a letter of welcome in halting English, to which I replied with a few even more halting phrases of Afrikaans which I had been practising with Frank Rogali during the journey. After this polite exchange we stood, rather uneasily, and stared at one another. A small but interested crowd watched the proceedings from a roped off section of the platform, and out of the corner of my eye I caught a glimpse of Bert's face, convulsed with laughter, at a lavatory window. Having exhausted my meagre stock of Afrikaans and realising that the Mayor couldn't understand English, I became slightly panic-stricken and fought down an impulse to laugh madly in his face. Fortunately at this moment I noticed some large crates being loaded into my coach. I pointed to them and enquired in exaggerated sign language what they were. He responded gravely by pouring imaginary wine from a bottle and drinking it, with every sign of enjoyment, from an imaginary glass. This endeared him to me and, remembering suddenly that Frank had told me that Paarl was celebrated for its wine, I clapped my hands with pleasure, capered about and gave an overdone display of simulated drunkenness, which went with such a swing that the Mayor's gravity melted, the crowd applauded and cheered and I climbed back into the train flushed with triumph.

My reception at Cape Town lacked the cosy intimacy of my welcome in Paarl. The train arrived at eleven-thirty instead of nine-thirty and consequently the crowds had been waiting in the streets for over two hours. I was received at the station by the Mayor and a group of local dignitaries, including a representative of Field-Marshal Smuts, several officers, a lot of Press and, curiously enough, Marie Ney, who had greeted me on my arrival in Melbourne. She looked charming in a shantung suit and a large white hat, and I had the feeling that whatever Dominions I was destined to visit in future, however far away and inaccessible, there would be Marie Ney, smiling and friendly, ready to help and advise and warn me against local pitfalls.

When we had all shaken hands and the cameras had clicked, we walked sedately through lines of onlookers to the exit. The station yard was packed with people who cheered and waved flags and handkerchiefs. The Mayor ushered me into an open car, and at this moment unfortunately a hitch occurred. Norman, who should have been with me, had completely disappeared. I didn't want to leave without him, and Bert, frantic with irritation and hissing obscenities out of the corner of his mouth, flew off to look for him. Meanwhile the Mayor and I sat in the car conversing nervously. The plaudits of the crowd, naturally enough, dwindled into silence and I have seldom felt so acutely uncomfortable. After a few minutes Norman appeared, looking sheepish, having been snatched from the embraces of an ex-Principal Boy who had waylaid him by the bookstall. The outriders revved up their motor-cycles, the crowd kindly lashed itself to a final outburst of enthusiasm, and the procession moved off. We drove at a snail's pace through the town until we arrived at Adderley Street, which was so densely packed that I could only assume African Consolidated Theatres had threatened any Cape Town citizens who showed unwillingness to greet me with mass execution.

The Mayor asked me to stand up in the car as we drove along and so I complied, steadying myself with my left hand on the windscreen, waving graciously with my right hand and feeling fairly silly. The houses and shops were hung with welcoming flags and banners and the crowd cheered like mad. I was told afterwards that it numbered thirty thousand people, but at the time these appeared, to my startled eyes, to be at least thirty million. At a given moment the procession halted and I was led through a shop, up some stairs and out on to a flower- and flag-bedecked balcony; the Mayor made a speech of welcome, handed the microphone to me, and I embarked, with outward urbanity but inward panic, on a short string of clichés, dragging in my Afrikaans phrases whenever I could. After this the crowds melted away with almost disconcerting swiftness and I was driven to the Mount Nelson Hotel.

When the dignitaries had departed the last Pressman gone and Norman, Bert and I were left alone in my suite, we had a large horse's neck each and laughed. This was not, I hasten to say, lack of appreciation of the warmth of my welcome. I hope and believe that amid all that organised hullabaloo there was a lot of genuine interest and kindliness, but I could not help feeling that the scale of the demonstration had been slightly out of proportion. But having asked African Consolidated Theatres to see to it that my tour was efficiently publicised, it would have been ungrateful to complain, so I resigned myself then and there to accept my place on the band-wagon with as good grace as possible. In this I was wise, because a similar ballyhoo took place, in varying degrees, in every town I visited, though never quite to the same extent as in Cape Town. Perhaps by the time I reached the other cities the word had gone round that although my performances were pleasant and entertaining they hardly merited a public holiday.

The following day I lunched with Field-Marshal Smuts in the House of Assembly and enjoyed it enormously. Only having met him, briefly, once before in London, I had no idea of the true quality of that extraordinary man. His memory was fantastic and the range of his general knowledge remarkable. We discussed books, painting, politics and even the Boer War. His mind was as swift and agile as that of a dynamic young man of thirty. He exuded physical health, and apparently walked up to the top of Table Mountain and down again several times a week for the sheer pleasure of it. I was told afterwards that his house-guests were warned, on arrival, never to accept an invitation from him to go for a little stroll before lunch. Fortunately he was too busy to suggest going for a walk with me.

My opening performance at the Alhambra was nerve-racking but, I am more than thankful to say, a triumphant success. To have failed after that majestic parade through the streets would have been too humiliating. The theatre was packed to the doors, which, considering that over half of the tickets were five guineas each, was gratifying, not only to me, but to Mrs Smuts' Comfort Fund. Both Field-Marshal and Mrs Smuts were present, together with the entire Cabinet, the Crown Princess of Greece and all the bigwigs of Cape Town. Such an array of social *crème de la crème* usually makes for a bad audience, but this occasion was certainly an exception. They were a very good audience indeed and saved me, in the first ten minutes, from ruining my performance by my own nervousness. I have never been so miserably nervous in my life and I hope and pray I will never be so again. The hour I spent with Norman and Bert sitting in my dressing-room while the Symphony Orchestra was on is branded for ever on my memory. Then came the *entr'acte*, which seemed an eternity, then the lights went down, Norman banged out the opening chords of 'I'll See You Again', the curtain rose and on I went. They gave me a wonderful reception and I finally started to sing, shakily and with neither precision nor taste. I got through my opening waltz medley somehow, with the sweat running off the back of my head and down my back, and my hands trembled so much when I held them out that I had to keep them to my sides. I knew I was doing badly and seriously contemplated pretending to be ill and having the curtain rung down. Happily, 'Don't Put Your Daughter on the Stage, Mrs Worthington' was my second number, a fairly solid standby. Before I was half through it the audience's obvious enjoyment began to relax me and from then on all was well. I sang ten songs in the first half, did my three recitations reasonably well, Norman played 'Scrambled Father' better than he had ever played it before, and then I came on again, sang eight more songs, finishing with Cole Porter's 'Let's Do It', which brought the house down. The applause was terrific, I made a brief 'Thank you' speech and went to my dressing-room, where Bert was waiting for me with a large whisky and soda and hopping up and down with excitement, but he wasn't so carried away that he didn't say what he had steeled himself to say. When the crowd of visitors had left and I was taking off my make up he told me, stammering a bit but with great firmness, that I had buggered up my first number completely, only just managed to put 'Worthington' over, and that if I ever allowed nerves to take such a hold on me again he would look on me not as a professional but as a—— amateur. Curiously enough the virulence of this attack, which had a great deal more to it than I have quoted, had a lasting effect on me. I have never been so nervous again. I have suffered, as we all do, on opening nights, but never since that agonising experience in Cape Town have I permitted my nerves to jeopardise my performance.

After the concert there was a supper-party given in the theatre restaurant upstairs. This was my first meeting with Mrs Smuts ('Ouma') and I loved her at once. She had curly grey hair, twinkling eyes, a dress that conceded little to any specified mode, and a downright, entirely beguiling manner. During supper the crowd was still yelling outside and the Field-Marshal and 'Ouma' tried to push me out on to the balcony by myself, but I wasn't having any of that nonsense and dragged them with me. It was a happy moment, and if blood and sweat and tears are any guarantee of an accolade I had certainly earned it.

I spent nineteen days in Cape Town, during which I gave three consecutive public performances at the Alhambra, and about thirty-five camp and hospital shows within a radius of fifty miles or so. This was hard going for Norman and I changed the programme constantly to avoid getting stale, but the results were rewarding. At several of the earlier troop shows I was surprised to see the same civilian sitting in the audience, a nice-looking man in a navy-blue suit. Puzzled by his recurrent presence I sent Bert to find out who he was and ask him round for a drink at the hotel. In due course he arrived and we talked pleasantly of this and that. I found the conversation a bit of an effort because there seemed to be something withdrawn, almost taciturn, in his manner. Presently when the whisky had mellowed him and he had begun to suspect that I was not quite the clipped, ultra-sophisticated, affected type that he had expected me to be, he broke down and confessed that he was the local representative of a prominent London newspaper and had been ordered to attend all my troop concerts until he was lucky enough to see me booed off the stage. I received this fascinating information with the correct smile and warned him that judging by results hitherto his assignment looked like being a long and tough one. I then chided him gently for being so conscientious. 'Why not,' I said, 'use a little imagination and invent a nice degrading incident in which I am howled down by enraged Service men and pelted with ripe tomatoes?' His paper would be quite satisfied, never having been exactly renowned for its veracity, and he himself would be saved a great deal of boredom and frustration. He laughed, a trifle shamefacedly, at this and we had another drink. He was really quite an agreeable character. A day or two later he was rewarded for his conscientiousness, though perhaps not quite in the way he had hoped, for a member of the Government Opposition rose up in the House and asked why a 'Music Hall crooner' (me) should be accorded a private car on the train. The gentleman's name was Sauer and his question was headlined immediately in the Press. It was also answered immediately, by Smuts himself, who explained that I was a distinguished guest of the Government, that I had, on his request, agreed to entertain troops all over the Union in addition to giving my services in aid of the Comforts Fund, and that in the circumstances it was the Government's duty to facilitate my efforts with every possible courtesy. This, I need hardly say, was never reported in the London Press, although Mr Sauer's unmannerly question was given considerable space. As a matter of fact I believe it was the only time that my South African tour was ever referred to in the English newspapers.

Before I arrived in the Union someone concerned with my proposed itinerary – I never discovered who – suggested to several prominent hostesses that they invite me to stay in their houses during my visits to the different cities. With typical South African hospitality they agreed, and at once proceeded to make plans for my social entertainment. This was one of the earlier dilemmas with which I had to grapple. I was touched by the kindness, but appalled at the idea of staying in a series of strange houses with people, who, however friendly and charming they might be, could not be expected to understand that any free time I had would have to be devoted to resting and conserving my energies. I am naturally gregarious and would have enjoyed being their guest and meeting their friends had I been on a casual holiday, but this was far from being a casual holiday. I had come to South Africa to do a job and, with memories of Australia and New Zealand fresh in my mind, I knew in advance that it would be strenuous. It is always difficult to convince people outside the world of the theatre that performing in public is a dedicated and arduous business. To act a long part in a relaxed manner, to sing a few songs, bow to applause, make gracious little speeches of thanks, all this looks, or should look, so effortless, so easy, but actually it isn't. The conscience of a true artist always stands like an implacable barrier between him and peace of mind. The process is very, very rarely as gay and enjoyable as it appears to be. Out of all the hundreds of troop concerts I gave during the war I can only remember a half a dozen that were, to me, entirely satisfactory. There was always a strain, always a lurking fear, not of failure exactly, but of inadequacy, of not being absolutely at my best. The amount of vitality expended in playing even to a quick and receptive audience is considerable, but when, as is the case nine times out of ten, you are faced with a dull audience, an audience that has to be coaxed, cajoled and won over, it is not to be wondered at that all sensible performers dread and evade any wastage of their nervous energy.

It was for this reason that I was forced to forgo the pleasure of staying with those kindly hostesses, and I am afraid that some of them were rather put out, but it couldn't be helped and I hope that by now they have forgiven me. One of them, a vivacious and attractive social leader in Cape Town, evinced such bitter disappointment that I should prefer the Mount Nelson hotel to her very lovely house that she finally prevailed on me to spend a restful week-end in it. 'Restful' was the operative word as far as I was concerned, and like an ass I fell for it and accepted her invitation. I arrived, fairly worn out, on Saturday, in time for lunch, which was an intimate affair for twenty people. This was followed by a bathing-party at somebody's pool, a tea-party, a cocktail-party and a large dinner-party. The house was delightful, but it contained, apart from the family and the other guests, four cats, three large dogs, a six-months-old baby and apparently no servants. I spent a troubled night in a glorious early Dutch four-poster on what I can only conclude was an early Dutch mattress. At ten-thirty the next morning there was a tea-party in the garden for about twenty ladies, which went on until some anxious-looking Kaffir servants miraculously appeared and served a buffet lunch at one-thirty. In the afternoon we piled into cars and went visiting returning at six o'clock for a cocktail-party for thirty souls. Dinner was the *bonne bouche* of the whole gay adventure. My hostess had corralled six socially prominent young women of various degrees of attractiveness and placed them at six small tables. It was my privilege and pleasure to eat one course of the meal *tête-à-tête* with each of them. My convulsive progress from table to table occasioned considerable merriment, and the whole thing was regarded by everyone but me as a delightful social innovation. Very shortly after this I managed to slip away and telephone Bert at the hotel. Fortunately he was in and a half-hour later he arrived in a car with some garbled tale about an important telephone call from London. Evincing the most poignant regret at having to leave so suddenly, I bade my hostess and the assembled company a fond adieu and was out of the house like a flash.

This, over and above a few pleasant semi-official lunch-parties and a quiet week-end with Lord Harlech, the High Commissioner, was the peak of my social activities in Cape Town. Norman, Bert and I did contrive, however, to spend some gentle evenings with the Cameron McClures, Kiki and Mac, whose house was always open to us and with whom we could put ourselves down after a hard day's work. Gwen ffrangcon-Davies and Marda Vanne had introduced us into this less demanding milieu, and the hours I passed in that pleasant unpretentious little house are among my happiest memories of South Africa.

Our next date after Cape Town was Durban, and Field-Marshal Smuts urged me, as there were a few days to spare, to go by train along the coast route and enjoy some spectacular scenery. This sounded restful and would give me time to prepare myself for any further excesses the A.C.T. publicity department might have in store for me, and so in due course Bert and I left, waved away by a group of new and old friends including the McClures, Gwen, Marda and Norman, who was going to Durban via Johannesburg. This time, possibly out of deference to Mr Sauer, the private car was not quite so spacious, but it was comfortable and the journey was fascinating. The Field-Marshal had been right about the scenery. The train crept along for the whole of the first day between the bright sea on one side and sinister Wagnerian mountains on the other. It rained for a great part of the time, but this gave an added quality of mystery to that fantastic landscape. Bert and I slept, read and played rummy, occasionally getting out at isolated stations to stretch our legs. At one of these a woman appeared with her ten-year-old son. They had driven eighteen miles in a farm cart so that the little boy could get my autograph. Bert rooted about among the suitcases and produced the largest photograph he could find; happily the train stopped at that particular station for nearly half an hour and so we had time to talk to them. The boy's father was a farmer and they lived in a lonely valley in the interior. There were no neighbours nearer than eleven miles, where there was a small Kaffir village with a general store. The mother asked a number of questions about England, and once or twice I thought I detected a tear of homesickness glistening in her eye. The little boy, with his brown face and sun-bleached hair, was startlingly English. I asked him if he could speak Afrikaans, whereupon his mother said 'No' almost sharply and changed the subject. When the train bore us away I leant out of the window and waved. They waved back violently until they looked like two little fair dolls in the distance. Bert, whose emotions were never far below the surface, was moved to tears. 'Christ!' he said, sitting down at the table and shuffling the cards with unnecessary vigour, 'the poor sods, the poor lonely sods. Living in this —— place, —— year in and —— year out.'

The journey took four days and five nights. We had a few hours in Port Elizabeth, where we visited a snake farm, in a deluge of rain, and watched the attendant twining deadly cobras and mambas round his neck as though they were knitted scarves; an evening in Bloemfontein, very European in atmosphere, where we sat and had a drink in a tree-fringed public square with an illuminated fountain in the middle; and three hours in Ladysmith, where we drove out and bathed in a very cold river. We arrived at Durban at seven-fifteen on a Sunday morning and as my official entry was planned for the next day our car was shunted on to a siding. This depressed us, but presently a Major Leon arrived and banished melancholy by driving us to Umdoni Park, fifty miles away. Here we stayed in a rest house for officers on the edge of the sea. There was an enormous bathing pool blasted out of the rock which was refilled daily by the tide, and there was no one in the house except two pleasant naval officers and Mr and Mrs Reynolds who ran the place. It was lovely to be in the tropics again. Monkeys chattered in the trees; a large iguana, looking like a toy dragon, ambled across the drive as we arrived; and after the bracing but sharp air of Cape Town the heat was wonderfully soothing.

The next morning we rose at dawn and drove back to Durban, where we slipped unobtrusively into the King Edward Hotel by the back way.

In due course the inevitable open car arrived, accompanied by outriders, and off we went. The streets were fairly crowded, but not as densely as they had been in Cape Town. The Mayor was away in Johannesburg and so I was received on the red-carpeted steps of the Town Hall by the Deputy Mayor, who was trembling. A Ladies' Orchestra was sawing away at *Bitter Sweet* under a striped awning and the square facing the Town Hall was crammed. The whole thing passed off without a hitch. The Deputy Mayor delivered his welcoming address, I thanked him and everyone within sight, the Ladies' Orchestra attacked 'Someday I'll Find You' with unparalleled fervour, and we all retired into the Mayor's parlour for iced coffee. My public concerts in Durban took place at Ye Playhouse, a large cinema, the interior of which had been got up, surprisingly, to represent a medieval castle. It was full of battlements and turrets and false stone work, and the ceiling was a deep blue sky studded with stars, some of which fused from time to time, but the acoustics were good and the concerts successful. From then on, our tour proceeded at an increasing tempo. My diary records a jumble of Rotarian luncheons, civic receptions, rehearsals, journeys in trains, journeys in planes, journeys in cars, performances in camps, hospitals, cinemas, Town Halls, Institutes and hangars. I also opened bazarrs, flower shows, photographic exhibitions, art exhibitions, boys' clubs and girls' clubs. I inspected sea cadets, air cadets, land cadets, nurses and voluntary workers, and on one occasion, owing to my royal determination not to miss anything, I inspected a ladies' lavatory in a Victoria League hostel before anyone could stop me.

We appeared in Pietermaritzburg, Bloemfontein, Kimberley, Pretoria and, finally, Johannesburg. From all these places we drove out daily to outlying camps and air-bases.

On the night journey from Bloemfontein to Pretoria I was suddenly aware of a rather tiresome South American rhythm thumping in my head. This went on intermittently all night and emerged next morning as 'Nina'. Both Norman and I were delighted with it and, gaily ignoring the fact that both the lyric and the accompaniment were complicated, we decided to put it into the second half of our programme the following evening. Unfortunately during the day I had to make a long speech at a public luncheon, open something or other in the afternoon and attend a reception in my honour at the Country Club, and so, apart from an hour or two in the morning, I had had no time to rehearse it. Experience should have warned me that to attempt to sing a new song when it was still hot from the oven was dangerous, but the voice of experience was silenced by over-confidence and it was only when I heard myself announcing to a packed audience that black fear descended on me. I shot Norman a hunted look while he was bashing out the introductory chords, started on the first verse and dried up dead. Norman, with misguided presence of mind, prompted me loudly with what I knew to be a phrase from the second verse. There was a dreadful moment of silence during which my heart pounded and my brain searched vainly for the right words, then, realising that the game was up, I laughed with agonised nonchalance, asked the audience to forgive me, and started again from the beginning, praying that when I came to the forgotten phrase it would drop automatically into my mind. This was a desperate risk, but it worked; I scampered through the whole number without a further hitch and the audience were delighted with it. I, on the other hand, was furious with myself and ashamed at my casual non-professionalism, and before I attempted 'Nina' again it had been rehearsed two hours a day for a week.

Johannesburg was our last date. We made our usual official entrance with open cars, outriders, crowds and speeches. By this time it was generally known that the whole tour had been a success, and our reception was tremendous. The two weeks we spent there were more crowded and hectic than anything we had experienced hitherto. We had one Sunday off, which we spent in Mrs Baillie-Southwell's house. Erica Baillie-Southwell was one of the hostesses who had originally been asked to entertain me. She was elegant and charming and understood completely my reasons for preferring to stay in the Carlton Hotel rather than with her. We had a quiet, restful day with her and her family, picnicked in the garden and returned to our tasks and occupations greatly refreshed. Apart from this oasis the going was heavy; heavy from the point of view of actual work, but highly satisfactory on all other counts. Barragwanath Hospital alone took the best part of three days. It was a fine hospital but enormous, and we did four shows in different sections of it, besides visiting all the wards. We flew to Kimberley for a day and a night; reception and speech outside City Hall – visit to diamond mines – early morning tea-party in somebody's garden – civic lunch with speech – concert at aerodrome – cocktail-party – public concert in local cinema – further speeches – after-concert reception – five hours' sleep in the local club – up at dawn and back to Johannesburg.

Our two farewell public concerts took place in the Empire Theatre, which was vast and packed to the roof. These two performances netted six thousand pounds for the Fund. Combined symphony orchestras played for an hour, after which Norman and I took over. They were, I think, the best performances we gave; the piano was good and the lighting excellent. I was not nervous and consequently sang with authority and enjoyed myself. The audience apparently enjoyed themselves too and it was with very real regret that I bade them good-bye.

On my last day of all in South Africa I went over to Pretoria in the morning to say good bye to the Field-Marshal and Mrs Smuts, and returned to Johannesburg to make my farewell broadcast in the evening. That interlude with the Smuts stays pleasantly in my memory. They lived in complete simplicity in a ramshackle old house which had been, ironically enough, a British barracks during the Boer War. The Field-Marshal was wearing faded shorts and an open-necked shirt; 'Ouma' was shuffling about happily in carpet slippers and a sort of overall. The inside of the house was cosily untidy; books were piled up indiscriminately all over the furniture and I observed, sticking out from under the sofa, a heavily embossed but dusty piece of paper which stated that General Smuts had been given the freedom of somewhere or other. I refrained from asking which city because it might have been London, which would have been faintly embarrassing: only faintly however, because no embarrassment could exist for long in the presence of Ouma Smuts, her kindness and humour would whisk it away and up the chimney before you had time to think. We sat round a wooden table on an enclosed 'stoep' and had coffee and biscuits. They questioned me about my tour and laughed appropriately at some of the funnier episodes, the conversation was gay, irrelevant and, I fear, without significance. They made me feel as though I were one of the family and that anything of importance could be said later. When I rose to go 'Ouma' kissed me lightly and thanked me for helping her Fund; the Field-Marshal rummaged in a desk stacked with papers and produced a photograph of himself which he signed and gave me. As the car bore me away those two most remarkable characters came on to the front steps and waved. That was the last I saw of them.

4

After a two-days holiday with Bert at Victoria Falls, which, as a wonder of nature, resolutely defy description, we returned to Bulawayo, where Norman was waiting for us, and started off on our tour of Rhodesia. This, after the strenuousness of South Africa, was a rest cure. We only gave nine shows in the whole eleven days we were there, and these included our two public performances in Bulawayo and Salisbury. There were, of course, the usual civic receptions and lunches and a few social functions, but the sense of urgency had gone; the power of the African Consolidated Theatres publicity department did not extend to the uplands of Rhodesia, the air was gentle, the streets clear of crowds and outriders, the whole atmosphere so English and parochial that I felt no one would have been surprised had I arrived at my first civic reception on a bicycle. There was no uneasy awareness at the back of my mind that sinister forces were at work below the surface. There was certainly no lurking fear of an anti-British demonstration, for all the people we met were British from the tops of their heads to the soles of their boots and, as audiences, cheerful and appreciative.

It had been arranged for us to fly to Bulawayo to Nairobi, give a few shows there and in Mombasa, then to fly on to Cairo and straight home to England. The last part of this plan was drastically changed by the arrival of a cable from Dickie Mountbatten in Ceylon, asking us to come out and entertain the Fourteenth Army in Assam and Burma. This cable was a bombshell. I had been out of England for five months and was longing to get home. Also I was very tired and felt that I needed at least a month's rest. On the other hand Mountbatten's cable stressed very strongly the need of entertainment in the Burma area, and I knew he would not have asked me to go unless he considered it really important. Norman, Bert and I sat up in the hotel in Bulawayo until three in the morning discussing the pros and cons, but I knew, and I think they did too, that there was no question of refusing. Admittedly we had done a good job in South Africa. The Comforts Fund had made twenty-two thousand pounds from our twelve public performances; the Flag had been shown with reasonable dignity all over the Union, and the Fighting Services and hospitals had, I hoped, benefited by my visit. But the fact remained that the troops we had entertained and the hospitals we had visited were in South Africa, many miles away from the war, and surrounded by far more creature comforts than England had enjoyed since 1939, whereas the troops and hospitals Mountbatten had invited us to visit were virtually in the front line. We drafted a cable to be sent first thing in the morning saying that we would come immediately we had finished with Nairobi and Mombasa, and would let him know as soon as possible how we proposed to accomplish the journey. I remember, before I went to sleep that night, envisaging Mother's and Lorn's disappointment when they heard I was not coming home after all, wondering which was the swiftest and least complicated way I could get Norman, Bert and myself across the Indian Ocean to Ceylon, and hoping against hope that by agreeing to Dickie's request I was not, in my present state of tiredness, taking on an assignment that I was not physically capable of carrying through.

5

Ten days later, on the evening of May the 16th, I sailed from Mombasa in one of H.M.'s destroyers, the *Rapid*, for Ceylon. Norman and Bert were flying direct to Cairo, where they were to wait until I sent for them. After three performances in Nairobi we had flown to Mombasa, where a kindly man called Granville Roberts lent us his beach house for four days. It was a small wooden bungalow looking out over a coral reef, and although far from luxurious it had, for me, the greatest luxury of all, absolute quiet except for the sound of the surf on the reef. The sea was almost too warm in the heat of the day, but in the early morning and in the evening before sundown it was delicious. I re-read Lytton Strachey's *Queen Victoria* and *Bleak House*, and slept twelve hours a night.

On the evening I sailed we gave a performance in Mombasa. The theatre was stuffy, the microphone bad and the piano vile, but realising that it was the last time we should have to rise above such horrors for at least three weeks, we pressed on cheerfully, and the audience, although a bit sticky at first, cheered at the end, stamped its feet and gave every indication of being a great deal more satisfied than we were.

The voyage in the *Rapid* took twelve days. The ship was not belying her name and could easily have done it in five, but we had to escort a convoy for part of the way. For me, at any rate, the time was all too short; after the first three days, when the sea was so rough that I had to lash myself into my bunk at night, we slid out on to the bosom of the Indian Ocean into halcyon weather. I lunched *tête-à-tête* every day with the Captain, and spent the rest of the time lying on the fo'c'sle in the sun, or wandering about the ship and talking to whoever was interested. As is usually the case in small ships the atmosphere was friendly and informal. There were terrific arguments in the ward-room after dinner on various subjects; the problems of the tortured world, the colour question, the Indian question, Communism, Toryism, Socialism, sex, music, literature and, when I was allowed my head, the Theatre were all analysed and discussed with passionate zeal. Sometimes, after one of these intellectual free-for-alls, I felt disinclined for sleep and went up to the bridge to chat with the Officer of the Watch and have some ship's cocoa under the vivid stars.

I also managed during these twelve days to write a short story called 'Mr and Mrs Edgehill'. To have time, even so little time, after the overcrowded, hectic scramble of the last few months, was a great pleasure to me. I had begun to think that I should never be able to write again, and that, even were I to try, the gift would have atrophied and no words come. However, the words did come and I scribbled and typed for hours daily in the Captain's cabin until, two days before we were due to arrive at Colombo, the story was finished. It was an imaginary tale based loosely on Mr and Mrs Fleming at Canton Island. The story was ultimately published with five others in my book *Star Quality*, which can be bought for the modest price of five shillings, by anyone who has been careless enough to overlook it.

At last the voyage was over and the island of Ceylon appeared on the horizon, its mountains blue and purple in the morning light. The day before, I had given two improvised shows for the ship's company and been given a farewell party in the ward-room, and now the moment had come for another regretful good-bye. Mike Umfreville, one of Mountbatten's A.D.C.s, came on board to fetch me; we had a cup of coffee with the Captain and went ashore. Umfreville told me, in the course of our drive up to Kandy, that he had been accredited to me for the whole tour of Assam, India and Burma, and as he was friendly and appeared to be pleased at the prospect, I was pleased too and we had a nip out of his flask to cement the deal.

On my first evening in the King's Pavilion in Kandy, which Dickie Mountbatten had made his G.H.Q., he and I dined quietly. He outlined to me all the arrangements he had made for my tour and briefed me about the different units I was to visit, warning me at the same time that in certain sections I should find conditions fairly tough, for I should be in Assam and Burma at the peak of the monsoon period, and must be prepared to be wet and muddy and uncomfortable for days on end. The valley of Imphal, for instance, had been under siege for three months, and he had arranged for us to be flown in over the Japanese lines in one of the transport planes that delivered supplies to the beleaguered troops. This sounded dashing enough to erase from my conscience all memories of private cars and social junketings in South Africa. He talked as usual with utter concentration and high-powered enthusiasm, but although he looked sunburnt and outwardly fit I detected a strain in his eyes. He was on a difficult wicket in his position as Supreme Commander. Portions of the American Press were gunning for him, his administrative problems were considerable, and a large percentage of the war equipment he had been promised had failed to materialise owing to the preparations in England for the launching of the Second Front. In addition to this, as is now well known, the American General Stilwell (Vinegar Joe), who was in command of the United States and Chinese troops in North-Eastern Burma, must have been an added problem for Mountbatten – although Mountbatten was far too tactful even to hint that there was any sort of trouble. I myself experienced one of the reasons why Stilwell was called Vinegar Joe, because although Mountbatten had persuaded him to allow me to visit his troops on the Ledo Road, he personally refused to allow me to go on up to the front line. I lay awake for a long time that night under my mosquito-net looking back over the years I had known Dickie Mountbatten, and reflecting on our enduring and curiously unlikely friendship. Temperamentally we were diametrically opposed; practically all our interests and pleasures and ambitions were so divergent that it was difficult to imagine how, over such a long period of time, we could have found one another such good company. We had, I knew, a mutual respect for one another, admiration too for our respective achievements, but although respect and admiration may form a basis for affection they do not explain it. I respect and admire many people with whom I have no personal contact whatever. Dickie is exactly six months younger than I. I met him and Edwina in the early 'twenties, when he had just returned from a world tour with the Prince of Wales. For several years our acquaintanceship was only casual; he was fully occupied in being an up-and-coming sailor, and I was equally concentrated on being an up-and-coming playwright. How and when we really began to know one another I cannot remember, perhaps suddenly at some forgotten dinner-party a conversation started up that rang a bell; there was certainly no mutually endured crisis to strike the spark, so it must have been something light, a song or a well-timed witticism, possibly a betrayal of my hero-worship for the Royal Navy, but most certainly not a betrayal of Dickie's hidden passion for the theatre, for he has little more than a cursory interest in it. However, in due course and much to my surprise I found myself in the summer of 1932 traipsing across Greece during a series of earthquakes to join him in the *Queen Elizabeth* at Mudros. From then on, our relationship stabilised itself, and whenever I wanted a holiday I went to wherever his ship happened to be. I spent one of the gayest months I have ever spent with him and Edwina in Malta. It was the first time he had ever had command of a ship and *Daring*, one of the new 'D' class destroyers, was the first nautical apple of his eye. There have been many progressively larger, apples since. In the late 'thirties he asked me to work with him in forming the Royal Naval Film Corporation, which was to equip all the ships of the Navy, excepting sloops and submarines, with film-projectors and films. This, owing to Mountbatten's drive and determination, was a *fait accompli* by the end of 1938. My own contributions to the carrying out of the whole scheme were, I am afraid, fairly negligible, and consisted mainly in visiting all the ships of the Mediterranean and Home Fleets and questioning the sailors about what sort of films they preferred. This assignment although it took quite a time, came under the heading of enjoyment rather than hard work. In after years, when the showing of movies on board H.M. ships had become an accepted routine, I have felt proud, I must admit, to have been even lightly associated with such a wise and important innovation.

Now, after all the storms and stresses of *In Which We Serve* in 1941, here I was in Ceylon, of all places, in the fourth year of the war, swirling once more in the orbit of Mountbatten's unpredictable star, and viewing the immediate future with excitement tinged with dismay. More troop concerts, more rows and rows of amiable but sometimes bewildered faces, more hospitals, more bad pianos and defective microphones, more commanding officers making speeches of thanks, more jolly parties in messes when we were worn out and longing for sleep. Only this time, of course, there would be the added fillip of monsoons, mosquitoes and mud.

On the fifth day after my arrival in Ceylon I took to the air again. Mike Umfreville was with me, looking angular and distinguished in a khaki bush jacket. Dickie Mountbatten waved us away into the morning sky and returned to more austere responsibilities, and thus began my most arduous and certainly most interesting adventure of the war.

For anyone who wishes to experience an authentic foretaste of hell and damnation, I heartily recommend the city of Calcutta in the weeks immediately preceding the breaking of the monsoons. The heat was more appalling, more inescapable, more utterly disintegrating than any I had known in my life. It burned all oxygen from the air and left us limp, drained of vitality and gasping for breath. The nights were as hot as, if not hotter than, the days. The large old fashioned punkah in my hotel room revolved very slowly like an aged ballerina and, far from cooling the room, seemed to make it even more stifling.

Norman arrived from Cairo having left poor Bert behind in a hospital in Alexandria with a bad attack of malaria. This, we agreed sadly, was not to be surprised at, because in spite of our remonstrances he had contemptuously refused to take any of the necessary precautions. The little bungalow we had been lent outside Mombasa was near a mangrove swamp and every evening at sundown, while Norman and I sensibly sweltered in mosquito boots, long-sleeved shirts and scarves, Bert had laughed at us for being fussy. Sundown was the time for his evening swim, after which he liked to sit naked on the veranda rail and enjoy a cigarette. We warned him repeatedly that by so doing he was presenting a fascinating area for the Anopholes to explore, but with his inherent gambler's belief that everything would be all right he had persisted. Now, to his own and our bitter disappointment, he was separated from us and would have to return sadly to England when he was strong enough. In the meantime we had much to do and only three days in which to do it. To begin with, we had to find a portable piano, no easy task in Calcutta. Norman was gloomily prepared to make do with a miniature piano if there was nothing else procurable, but fortunately a kind lady agreed to lend us her small upright which was not too ungainly and in excellent condition. I fear, however, that by the time she got it back its condition was fairly critical. It went with us everywhere, in aeroplanes, trains and trucks, and once it made an eighty-mile journey in a jeep. It was known as the Little Treasure and Norman tuned it lovingly every day. We also managed to find a travelling microphone that in no circumstances ever merited the name of Little Treasure. It was from first to last a malign, temperamental little monster.

Our tour began at Chittagong with two highly successful shows, one at five and the second at eight, and from then on, life was real, life was earnest, and although the grave was not actually the goal it seemed at moments as though it quite possibly might be. The monsoons broke and we drove, usually in a jeep, through sheets of heavy warm rain, along the jungle roads of the Arakan. We slept at nights in 'Bashas', which are bamboo huts, generally open at one side. Our camp beds and mosquito-nets travelled in a lorry with the Little Treasure. As a rule they left before us, but occasionally we would get to some isolated camp and discover that they hadn't arrived, which, of course, meant hours of feverish agitation as the time for the show drew nearer and nearer. Only once did we have to do a performance without a piano at all. This fortunately was at a small gun emplacement on a rain-sodden hilltop. There were only about sixty men, so I rendered a few comedy numbers unaccompanied, talked, told archaic funny stories and finally started them off on community singing. Throughout this curious entertainment Norman sat on an ammunition box and applauded politely.

The Arakan place names fascinated us: Dozahri, Deuchapalong, Tambru Gat and, most surprisingly, Cox's Bazaar. The latter was by the sea, a turgid dun-coloured sea, and was one of the most squalid places I have ever been to. In Tambru Gat I was having half an hour's rest in my 'Basha' before the evening show when I heard a sinister rustling sound and watched, without enthusiasm, a long green snake, wriggle from under my bed and disappear outside. After a moment or two, when I was about to go out and see where it had gone, I heard some shots, and by the time I had emerged on to the little bamboo veranda I had the pleasure of seeing it borne away draped over a pole like a bright ribbon.

After about ten days in the Arakan we returned to Chittagong and thence to Comilla, where we were to wait until circumstances were favourable enough for us to be flown over the mountains into the valley of Imphal. Comilla, after the jungle and the 'Bashas', was luxurious. There was an actual theatre to play in; the microphone (not ours) was perfect and the audiences at the two shows we gave them really wonderful. It was suffocatingly hot, of course, and I sweated through three shirts, but it was well worth it. By this time Mike Umfreville had gathered two batmen for us. They were B.O.R.s – British Other Ranks; one was tall, the other short, and both were lugubrious. Neither of them betrayed the faintest sign of emotion in any of the adventures they shared with us; we might be bogged down in mud, cowering in trenches during a Jap air raid, or strapped to our seats in a bucketing plane during an electric storm, but they remained silent and solid as the cliffs of their native Yorkshire. They looked after us with routine efficiency but little initiative; they listened to our, at times unconventional, dialogue with never the slightest twitch of the ear or gleam in the eye. I think they liked us all right, because when we finally parted from them they presented each of us solemnly with a photograph of themselves in lurid colour. They were known privately by Norman and me as The Ball of Fire and The Spirit of Jazz. I don't think they ever knew this, but even if they did they would undoubtedly have ignored the irony as stolidly as they ignored the wayward circumstances in which they found themselves.

In Comilla I lunched with General Slim and he talked, unsentimentally but with moving sincerity, of the Fourteenth Army. He referred with sudden bitterness to the phrase 'Forgotten Army' which had been coined by some zealous newspaper man who was evidently more interested in *mots justes* than *noblesse oblige*. The General explained that, although the morale of the troops had remained astonishingly high throughout all the vicissitudes of their repeated advances and retreats, this label 'Forgotten Army' had really stuck in their minds like a prickly burr and hurt them out of all proportion to its actual significance. The trouble was that there was a germ of truth in it. They realised, when papers were sent them from home, that, as far as news value was concerned, the war they were grimly fighting year in year out was apparently not important. Columns were devoted to raids on European strongholds, to air battles and sea battles, but their exploits, if mentioned at all, were usually relegated to the back page.

General Slim asked me if I could do anything to remedy this situation when I got back to England and I promised to do a broadcast at the earliest opportunity.

A day or two later, after several false starts entailing early morning drives to the airstrip, hours of waiting about and ignominious retreats back to the officers' club, we finally took off for Imphal in very bad weather indeed. Our plane was a D.C.3 transport and carried, in addition to ourselves and the Little Treasure, a large consignment of food supplies and, I believe, ammunition. We bumped through a bad electric storm, cleared an eleven-thousand-foot mountain range, flew over the Japanese lines and bounced down on the flooded Imphal airstrip with an impressive splash. General Scoones's headquarters, where we were billeted, consisted of a series of wooden huts and 'Bashas' scrambling down a steep hillside. The actual mess-room was on the top and was reached by a stairway of wooden slats embedded in the mud. It was impossible to negotiate these without a stick because the mud was not only thick but very slippery. General Scoones, a gentle and intelligent man, was just saying how do you do to us when a Jap air raid started and he ushered us firmly into a deep trench, where we continued our mutual politenesses until a bugle played a very flat D Flat to announce that the skies were clear again.

I think I am right in saying that the valley of Imphal is an area of approximately fifty square miles. Mountains rise all round it, and on and behind those mountains were the Japs. The siege had lasted for three months, but there were signs that the enemy was retreating and everyone seemed fairly certain that it would not last much longer. During those three months our troops, vulnerable to air attack and continually repelling enemy sorties, had lived on supplies dropped by the R.A.F. air-lift from Comilla. These planes were sometimes shot down, indeed the one immediately preceding ours had been, and I must admit that when they told me this my heart missed a couple of beats.

Our daily routine varied very little. At 6.30 a.m. we were called; we shaved and washed in a tin basin on a tripod and then clambered up to the mess-room for breakfast, after which we slithered down again, and Norman went off in a lorry with the Little Treasure to wherever we were to give our first show of the day. I meanwhile was driven, either in a car or in a jeep to different hospitals. Some of them were comparatively large, consisting of a group of 'Bashas' or wooden huts connected by covered ways; others were small advance clearing stations. There were no matrons or nurses; the men were cared for by surgeons, doctors and orderlies. In many of them there was no flooring and one had to squelch from bed to bed through the pervasive mud. The men lay under mosquito-nets reading magazines if they were well enough, and, if not, just staring up at the roof and listening to the drumming of the rain. There was a preponderance of malaria and other jungle fevers, and the nursing, as far as I could see, was as expert as conditions permitted. Most of the badly wounded were flown to Comilla and thence to better equipped hospitals in India, but the chest cases could not be flown out because it was necessary for the planes to fly at an altitude of fourteen thousand feet to clear the mountain range. These men, left behind in the steamy, oppressive, perpetually moist heat of the valley, were the most pathetic. They were resigned to their fate, few of them complained and all of them made a valiant effort to be cheerful when I talked to them. Even the worst cases, who were too weak and grievously injured to speak above a whisper, managed to smile or wink or give some sign that they were still undefeated.

The advance clearing stations were inevitably gruesome, but the gentleness and efficiency of the Field Surgeons impressed me deeply. Under appallingly difficult conditions I watched emergency operations performed with the same unflurried skill and precision that I have seen in the most lavishly equipped modern operating theatres. It is not my intention to harrow my readers with descriptions of physical horrors – I saw enough of these during the war to last me for a lifetime – but I cannot withhold comment on the routine heroism of those whose interminable job it was to mitigate the horrors and alleviate the suffering. It might be a small comfort to the mothers and wives and friends of those wounded men to know that everything that could be done for them in the circumstances was done and done well.

I usually managed to get through a couple of hospitals each morning, after which I was driven to wherever our first afternoon concert was to take place. The organisation of all this was well handled and there were only a few hitches. We appeared on shaky wooden platforms, tank transports and sometimes on the bare ground. If we were lucky we had a tarpaulin rigged over us, if not we shared the rain with our audience. We gave one show a thousand yards from the Jap lines. This was an uneven performance because the intermittent gunfire made timing very complicated. The men, having been withdrawn from the line for two hours, an hour and a quarter for the entertainment and the remaining forty-five minutes for tea, sat cross-legged in the mud at our feet with their rifles across their knees. At one alfresco show we gave, the sun made a brief and disconcerting appearance, which brought forth dense clouds of Burmese midges which rushed up my nose and into my mouth and settled on the microphone like caraway seeds on a bun. With the capricious sun came a sharp change of wind, and with the change of wind a most horrible, nauseating stink, which emanated from several hundred rotting Japanese bodies stacked in a clearing a quarter of a mile distant. After the concert I was discreetly sick in a bucket before going on to the next show some miles away. Norman remained unmoved and captain of his soul.

Only one unhappy incident occurred during our ten days in Imphal, and as this redounds little to my credit I will recount it with the utmost brevity. On a certain evening, when I had done two hospitals in the morning, two shows in the afternoon and a small extra one on a gun emplacement, Norman and I were invited to drink and dine in a mess hut with about a dozen officers. The C.O. was florrid and affable and we accepted two large drinks gratefully, our day's work being done. At the end of dinner, which was convivial, the C.O. told us that our piano had been placed in the ante-room (an adjoining hut) and that he and his officers would be bitterly disappointed if we did not give them a show. Although we had had a heavy day we knew we couldn't refuse, and so, with a sinking heart, I agreed, signalled to Norman, who stared at me in horror from the other end of the table, and together with our, by this time, vociferous audience we adjourned to the ante-room. The officers, amid much badinage and merriment, settled themselves to their satisfaction and I began to sing. They remained fairly quiet, but their attention was, I felt, divided. There was a good deal of whispering and scuffling and one officer, to everyone's amusement, made a stately but insecure exit through the door at the other end of the hut. Realising that sentimental songs would be out of place in such a cheerful atmosphere I hissed 'Stately Homes' to Norman and we began it. Before I had completed the first refrain I noticed an officer immediately in front of me hand the C.O. a packet of snapshots. The C.O. scrutinised the first one, gave a guffaw, and passed it to his righthand neighbour, who also greeted it with the amusement I have no doubt it merited. From then on no one present paid the faintest attention to me. Faced with this curious display of bad manners I made the mistake of losing my temper. It is one of my ingrained professional principles never to allow myself to betray irritation with an audience however badly behaved it may be. But on this occasion my control snapped, I stopped singing, signalled to Norman to follow me and walked out of the hut. The C.O. after a minute or two came after us and, still convulsed with uninhibited laughter, tried to show me one of the snapshots. I slapped it out of his hand, told him that I considered his manners intolerable, climbed into the waiting jeep with Norman and away we went. I fumed with rage all the way back to our headquarters and went to bed exhausted, depressed and ashamed. In the clearer light of the next morning I told General Scoones the whole episode and endeavoured to remedy my own lack of manners by sending the C.O. a letter of apology. In due course he replied correctly but without warmth, and afterwards, when my acids had simmered down, I realised that my apology had not been to him but to myself. I also realised that such an outburst was a bad sign, a warning indication that my nerves were becoming over-strained and that I had better watch my step. There is no place for artistic temperament in battle areas.

We left Imphal on the day the long siege was raised. The Japs had been finally beaten back and there was great jubilation. From then on, our tour was devoted to the Americans along and about the Ledo Road. We reverted to our Arakan travelling routine: jeeps, trucks and planes. I changed my programme drastically, inserting numbers which were not aggressively British and were likely to be recognised and appreciated by the G.I.s, who were as a general rule excellent audiences. There was one disastrous occasion when I bounced on unannounced to sing to about two thousand coloured troops who had never heard of me in their lives and couldn't have cared less. As a matter of fact they couldn't even hear me then, for the show took place on a small, dimly lit, wooden stage only twenty-five yards from the main Ledo Road along which lorries and tanks rumbled continually. I tried grimly to keep them quiet, but when they began to shout and give catcalls I realised, all too clearly, that I was getting the bird, and so Norman and I beat a dignified retreat. To offset this there was an exhilarating performance in the compound of a convalescent hospital. The stage was under cover, but the men and nurses sat on wooden benches in the mud. About half-way through my performance the skies opened and down came a deluge of rain, which made such a deafening noise on the tin roof of the stage that it was impossible to go on. I stopped and asked them all to get under cover, promising them to finish the show another day, but they roared and shouted, covered their heads with mackintosh capes and refused to budge. For the next hour we all sang songs together, soaked to the skin and happy as mudlarks.

During this phase of our travels I developed a mild fever of some sort. No one ever discovered what it was; I had a check-up in one of the hospitals, but no sinister germs were found, my stool was as fresh as a daisy and my urine cloudless as a summer day This unspecified malaise lasted for about five days and broke the smooth-flowing rhythm of our performances somewhat, for I was unable to get through more than four or five numbers without rushing off the stage and being sick. Fortunately the act of being sick does not prostrate me as it does some people, and I was able to pop back and get on with the programmeee until the next bout. Norman's presence of mind rose to the occasion and he dreamed up some charming little musical interludes to cover up my spasmodic disappearances. At a place called Digboi we stayed in the house of a Scottish planter and his wife, Bill and Jean Fleming, who accepted the invasion of Norman, Mike, me and the two batmen without even wincing. Their house was cool, comfortable, and stood on a hill overlooking a lush valley. To sleep in a proper bed again with a bathroom adjoining and a lulu that worked; to be brought ambrosial breakfasts of crisp bacon, fruit, Cooper's marmalade and china tea; to be valeted and looked after by well trained servants was so unexpected and so deeply enjoyable that with ruthless determination I persuaded the dear Flemings to let us stay a week instead of two nights. The shows we had to give in that sector were all within an area of about eighty miles and, however hard the roads and however turbulent the weather, the thought of bumping home every night to that lovely haven on the hill shone like a star in our minds. At last we had to bid those kind, hospitable people good-bye and press on for our last lap of jungle before flying back to India. Nothing spectacular happened except one nightmare moment when we were sitting at midnight in a Liberator on an airstrip waiting to take off, and the plane in front of ours crashed in flames. It was an ammunition transport carrying twelve men, all of whom were killed. Our take-off was delayed for a couple of hours and we sat wretchedly in a canteen, drinking Coca-Cola and waiting for the wreckage to be cleared away.

The last few days we spent with the American Army in that beautiful but oppressive jungle country were no more strenuous than the others had been, but they seemed so. The fever had left me a bit drained and it was an effort to pump enough vitality to get through the shows. Norman, as usual, was unflagging. He tuned the piano whenever it needed it, which was practically every day; he kept his temper, his sense of humour and his health, which was the most surprising of all, for his looks as resolutely belied his constitution then as they do today. His face is always wan and set in deceptively morose lines, and no burning sun, no stinging wind has ever succeeded in tinting lightly its waxen pallor. Sometimes in these later years, when I am singing in the luxurious intimacy of the Café de Paris, I glance at him sitting impeccably at the grand piano, and my mind flashes back to those rickety wooden stages, to the steaming heat, the wind, the rain, and the insects, and I see him with sudden vivid clarity divested of dinner-jacket, red carnation and brilliantine, and wearing instead an open-neck, sweat-stained khaki shirt, with a lock of damp hair hanging over one eye, and hammering away at the Little Treasure as though he was at his last gasp and this was the last conscious action of his life.

When we had waded through the dozen or so rain-sodden, mud-caked villages with unpronounceable names that remained on our itinerary, we got wearily into a Dakota at a place called Panitola and flew back to Calcutta. It was an uncomfortable and terrifying journey; the plane was crammed with G.I.s going on leave and the electric storms were so violent that we had to be strapped together like trussed fowls throughout the entire flight. At last, only about ten minutes before we were due to land, the weather cleared and we were able to unstrap ourselves, stamp our feet, stretch our legs and ease our aching buttocks from the dreadful grip of the bucket seats. The plane touched down on the wide runway of the Calcutta airfield in a blaze of late afternoon sunlight and, after baking for an interminable quarter of an hour while a bright green official sprayed us with insecticide, we were allowed to clamber out on to the sizzling tarmac

6

A great deal has been written about the vast sub-continent of India and it is not my intention to add more than a few words to it. I was only there for a month all told and I have no particular desire to go there again. I was too tired to be interested in its problems and had no time to appreciate or even take in the beauty of its scenery or the quality of its people. All my energies were concentrated on the performances I had undertaken to give and the camps and hospitals I had promised to visit. My itinerary was fairly formidable but not alarmingly so. My public performances in each city were to be in aid of war charities and, as in South Africa, troop shows were to be given whenever and wherever possible. I knew that both Norman and I needed a rest, and I also knew that there was little likelihood of our getting one beyond a day or two here and there. On the morning of our arrival at Government House, where we were staying with

Richard and Maie Casey, we started rehearsing and reorganising our programme for the first two public performances we were to give a few evenings later in the New Empire Theatre. After the rugged discomforts of the Arakan, Burma and Assam the luxury of Government House was soothing, but I was aware, naturally enough, of a sensation of anti-climax. During those weeks with the advanced Forces we had been upheld by the very fact of having to overcome stresses and strains and difficulties, and also by the knowledge that, however untidy and haphazard our performances might be, we were at least giving them to men who had had no sort of entertainment at all for months and possibly years. There was a deep satisfaction in this, and the enforced 'roughing it', which as a rule I detest, added to rather than detracted from it. India would inevitably be a reversion to more familiar and less stimulating routines. Microphones breaking down, lights fusing and such-like hazards could be laughed away in the presence of entertainment-starved men who were just out of the front line and grateful even for the hour's rest, but we couldn't expect dressy pukka sahibs and memsahibs who had paid heavily for their seats to tolerate such nonchalant improvisation. We should have to be slick and professional once more, reorganise our values as well as our programmes, and see to it that the 'mike' was faultless, the lighting perfect and the veneer smeared on again and polished until it shone. The prospect of this necessary transition dismayed us, because without Bert to handle the technical problems for us we knew that we should have to deal with them ourselves, thus becoming embroiled in arguments with inefficient stage staffs, further arguments with well-meaning but inexperienced charity organisers, and probable hand-to-hand fights with ubiquitous Welfare Officers. These, we had learnt to our cost, had, as a rule, little knowledge of the professional theatre and were more prone to hurt feelings, umbrage-taking and hot flushes than the most temperamental opera singers. Our forebodings were fairly well justified; the irritations occurred, the arguments and frustrations also. The Welfare Officers appeared as predicted, faffed about, used either too much initiative or too little, and retired in due course licking their wounds. Their chief was apparently an old General who sat majestically in Simla, from which cool eminence he controlled a vast network of inefficiency. It is a matter of lasting regret to me that I never met him, for by the end of our Indian tour I could have supplied him with some fascinating information. We appeared in and around Calcutta, Delhi, Bombay, Bangalore and Madras. In Delhi we stayed in the Viceroy's house with Lord and Lady Wavell, who attended our public performance and several of our troop concerts. I had heard that Lord Wavell was taciturn and difficult to talk to and that Lady Wavell was inclined to be remote and unapproachable. Personally I found them both exactly the contrary. Lord Wavell's passion for poetry alone would have been enough to endear him to me; his memory was remarkable and his own anthology, *Other Men's Flowers*, was selected with taste and imagination except, in my opinion, for a preponderance of Macaulay. I remonstrated with him about this, and, far from being taciturn, he merely laughed and said that he found

Macaulay the most satisfactory of all for reciting out loud in a noisy aeroplane. I shall always cherish a mental picture of him flying back and forth across the Sahara during the Egyptian Campaign shouting, 'Oh Tiber! Father Tiber! to whom the Romans pray' at the top of his lungs. Lady Wavell was a dear and allowed me to inaugurate High Tea at five o'clock every day, so that we could get away to do our shows. Not only did she allow it but took to the idea herself with enthusiasm, which, I was told later by an irate A.D.C., disrupted the smooth running of the house and caused a considerable lash-up in the kitchen.

From Delhi we flew to Bombay, where I stayed for three days with an old friend, Eric Dunstan, in a small villa by the sea. We gave our public performance on a Sunday evening, and the next morning I escaped a violent death by a few inches. We were bowling along at about forty-five miles an hour in a sleek limousine belonging to Aly Khan when a naval lorry in front of us turned, without warning, off the parkway. I knew in that split second that we were bound to hit it and shut my eyes. There was a shattering crash, our car ricochetted off the lorry, skidded for ninety yards, crashed into a palm tree, the impact of which wrenched off the back wheels, careered across a patch of grass and crashed finally against the sea wall. If the palm tree had not broken our impetus we should undoubtedly have jumped the sea wall, which was only a few feet high, and hurtled into the sea.

I was knocked out for a few seconds and was brought to by Eric, miraculously unhurt, shaking my shoulder and saying in an anxious voice: 'Are you all right? For Christ's sake say you are all right!' I answered obligingly that I was quite all right, which was not quite true, for I was badly bruised and felt shattered. A crowd collected and we were helped out of the overturned car. The Indian driver, although not seriously hurt, was bleeding profusely. I sat on the ground with my back against a tree and tried to light a cigarette, but my hands were shaking so that somebody had to light it for me. I must still have been concussed, because I don't remember anything more until a half-hour later when we got back to the villa in another car and I had a stiff brandy. I had a shock when I looked at myself in the glass, for Fate, emphasising the comic rather than the tragic aspects of the situation, had arranged for a two-pound packet of freshly-ground coffee to burst on my head during the crash. My hair was full of it and it had streaked down my face in brown stripes, giving me a family resemblance to Pocahontas. I laughed, perhaps too hysterically, at this and was led away to lie down. Later a doctor appeared, examined me and told me it would be wiser to cancel my flight to Bangalore for a few days. I discussed this with Eric and Norman and finally decided against it. I was not injured in any way apart from a few bruises, we only had two more weeks to do and cancellations and postponements would cause a lot of complications, besides putting us behind on our schedule. This decision I afterwards regretted, for the shock to my whole system had been more serious than I realised. However, I forced myself up at six o'clock the next morning and off we went. On arrival at Bangalore I was in considerable pain and so I went to a hospital to be X-rayed, but no bones were broken and the pain would obviously have to be borne until the bruises went down and the stiffness wore off. We gave a concert to fifteen hundred men that evening which must have looked rather stilted, for I was unable to move my right arm at all.

Our last town in India was Madras, where we stayed in Government House with Lady Hope and went through our usual routines: rehearsals, mike tests, two public performances, several troop shows and finally, after an affectionate farewell to Bill Erskine, who had been with us since Calcutta in the capacity of assistant bottle-washer to Mike Umfreville, we flew back to Ceylon.

We gave a show in Kandy to Dickie Mountbatten's personnel, three or four more in various camps which entailed some long drives, and then what I had been dreading for a long time happened. I collapsed finally and knew that I had come to the end of my rope. The collapse was unspectacular and devoid of drama. It began during a long drive home after a show at a newly built R.A.F. base. I had got through the performance drearily, but without mishap, and been mildly sick afterwards. The C.O. gave me a stomach powder, but the effect of it wore off after a little while and I was seized with agonising indigestion, and felt myself inflating as though I were being blown up by a bicycle pump. The drive took two hours and a half and when I got out of the car I could hardly stand. Norman helped me to bed, which was a slow process because I could neither sit nor lie down without excruciating pain. I remained in this state all through the night and the following day, when a doctor was summoned and administered several remedies, none of which had any effect. On that evening Nature intervened with prodigal generosity, and at last the 'great winds shoreward blew', leaving me weak, uninterested and in deep melancholy. I lay on the edge of sleep, for I dared not take even a Secconal for fear of bringing on another bout of indigestion, and whenever I did manage to drop off for a little I was torn awake by nightmares, most of which were reversions to the car smash in Bombay. I realised in my wakeful moments that I was obviously suffering from delayed reaction, but I also knew that delayed reaction, however unpleasant, could not have brought me so low if I hadn't already been nervously exhausted. I am physically pretty strong; my height is six foot and my average weight eleven stone. At the time of that breakdown I had been working at high pressure for eight months in addition to travelling, not always in the most comfortable circumstances, half round the world, and I weighed exactly nine stone one. This left very little margin for resistance to unexpected shocks, my vitality had been expended to the last drop and I knew beyond any question that the moment had come to pack up. This meant cancelling about a dozen shows I had promised to give for Dickie in Ceylon; I hated doing this and compromised by giving three, a week later, in the Naval Base in Trincomalee, but they were forced and not very good.

I stayed for a few days in the Galle Face Hotel in Colombo, waiting for a plane to take me home. Norman had got off, through the kindness of Air Marshal Garrod, the morning after our return from Trincomalee. I hated to see him go, but comforted myself with the thought that without him I had an excellent excuse for refusing to do any more concerts. The few days at the Galle Face were peaceful and without incident. I spent most of the time lying by the swimming pool and reading. Eventually I took off at dawn, a very overdone tropical dawn with scarlet clouds piled against a lemon and blue sky, and flew home to England in a succession of different planes via Karachi, Shasah, Bahrein, Cairo, Tripoli, Rabat and Casablanca.

7

The remainder of 1944, although eventful for the world, was not particular eventful for me beyond the fact that I adapted *Still Life*, one of my *Tonight at Eight-Thirty* plays, into a film script, rechristened it *Brief Encounter* and persuaded David Lean and Ronnie Neame to put it into production. This, after some argument, they agreed to do, which was lucky from all points of view, for it turned out to be a very good picture.

After the strenuousness of South Africa and the rigours of the Far East it was pleasant to have nothing to do but read the increasingly heartening war news, make plans for the future, and dodge doodlebugs. My plans for the future were vague and fluid and only one or two of them materialised. I recovered my health and put on weight. I attended Peter Glenville's production of *Point Valaine*, played by the Liverpool Old Vic Company. Mary Ellis and Frederick Valk played very well the parts created in America by Lynn Fontanne and Alfred Lunt, and the production was good; in spite of which I saw more clearly than ever the fundamental weakness of the play was its basic theme. It was neither big enough for tragedy nor light enough for comedy; the characters were well drawn, but not one of them was either interesting or kind. The young man, the only one with any claims to sympathy from the audience, although played well in both productions, struck me on closer analysis as silly, over-idealistic and a prig. The play had opened originally in Boston on Christmas night, 1934, with an excellent cast: Osgood Perkins, a subtle and fine actor, and Louis Hayward, whom I had imported from England to play the young man, in addition to Lynn and Alfred. Somehow everything seemed to go wrong from the beginning. Alfred and Lynn and I were irritable with each other, which we had never been before and seldom have since; Gladys Calthrop's sets were too heavy for the quick changes and had to be cut down at the last minute. There was a disastrous rain machine which flooded the whole stage at the dress-rehearsal and had to be scrapped. We all pressed on with 'Old Trouper' determination, but none of us was happy, and none of us quite knew why until sometime afterwards, and the revelation burst on us that what was really wrong was the play. The New York critics gleefully encouraged us in this belief after one of those doomed opening nights that occur, I think, more in New York than anywhere else. The first-nighters were soggy and comatose if not actually hostile. Lynn and Alfred received only a spatter of applause when they came on, and Gladys, Jack Wilson and I sat at the back of the theatre and watched the play march with unfaltering tread down the drain. It was not surprising that seeing it again, however well done, should give me a few pangs of rather embittered nostalgia.

On November the 1st another, less poignant, revival of my work opened at the Apollo Theatre. This was John Clements' and Kay Hammond's production of *Private Lives*, and it was, as it usually is, a great success. They both played it wittily and well for a very long time. I am deeply attached to *Private Lives*, for although it has always been patronised by the American and English critics, it has also been enthusiastically and profitably patronised by the public wherever and in whatever language it has been played.

In addition to enjoying these reminders of the past, I fulfilled my promise to General Slim, by writing and delivering a broadcast on the subject of the Fourteenth Army. The response to this was varied. I was congratulated by the King and Queen, received over two thousand letters of thanks in one week from relatives of the men in the Forgotten Army, and a full page of unqualified abuse from Mr John Gordon in the *Sunday Express*.

In November I dismounted graciously from my high horse and agreed to appear in Paris and Brussels for E.N.S.A. It was, on the whole, a tiresome experience and almost entirely uninteresting. The company included, as well as myself, Geraldo and his band, Bobby Howes, Nervo and Knox (for one performance only), Frances Day and, later, Josephine Baker. We played at the Marigny Theatre in Paris, in a rococo eighteenth-century frigidaire in Versailles and an Olympian Music Hall in Brussels. The organisation was slap-dash and the audiences, as a rule, slow but appreciative. Field-Marshal Montgomery came to our last performance in Brussels, and there was a moving incident when Frances Day sang 'Thanks for All You've Done' at him and roguishly presented him with a pair of her drawers. He received both the sentiment and the drawers with dignified restraint.

To return to Paris after its four years' humiliation was a curious and sad experience. Not entirely sad, of course, because the city itself was unharmed and as beautiful as ever, but there was, to me at any rate, a feeling of malaise in the atmosphere, a malaise compounded of recrimination, shame and bitterness. Outwardly all was bright, perhaps a trifle over-bright, but I couldn't help being aware of much cynicism and distrust below the surface. I soon gave up enquiring from my French friends as to who had been collaborators and who had not, for, with a few notable exceptions, they all seemed to be accusing each other. In any event it was none of my business, although it confirmed my belief that worse things than bombardment can happen to civilians in war-time.

Back in England, on Christmas Day I drove up from the country, where I was staying with Larry and Vivien Olivier, and appeared at the Stage Door Canteen. Although it was annoying, having to leave my friends and crawl into London through a yellow fog, virtue for once was rewarded because the Canteen was packed with troops who had nowhere else to go and greeted all of us who appeared with boisterous enthusiasm. There was a lightness in the air, a tacit awareness that this might conceivably be the last Christmas of the war. The show started at eight and continued until one-thirty, by which time a great deal of beer had been drunk and so many cigarettes smoked that the atmosphere inside was almost as thick as the pea-soup fog outside. The combination of fog and the black-out in London was awe-inspiring. I don't know how the audience or my fellow artists managed to get home that night, but it took me an hour and a half to grope my way from Piccadilly to Gerald Road through familiar streets that had been entirely obliterated. Occasionally the concrete blackness was broken by the gleam of somebody's electric torch, or the dim blue light of a car, but only very occasionally, for there was very little traffic about. The rest was silence; silence and darkness so profound that I felt that the world had come to an end, quietly and without fuss, while we were singing our songs in the stuffy, brightly-lit Canteen, and that I was now stumbling away into eternity.

The first few weeks of the New Year, 1945, Victory Year, were punctuated by rocket bombs as well as doodlebugs. Of the two I favoured the latter because at least you could hear them coming and lie down briskly in the gutter when they cut out immediately over your head, whereas the V.2s dropped without warning and seemed to shake the universe.

In February I went to Tintagel for a week by myself, remembering gratefully how it had comforted me and restored me to health in 1943 when I was convalescing after jaundice. This time I required no comforting and my health was perfect, but it was good nevertheless to be completely idle for a few days, to read books, to go for walks along the cliffs and look at the sea and the sky and the gulls wheeling in the winter sunshine. It also gave me time to assemble some ideas for a revue I was planning for the summer. The planning was then only tentative, because although it was generally presumed that the war would end within a few months, this was by no means certain, and if it didn't end I knew that I should have to be up and away again. At all events I had thought of a good title, *Sigh No More*, which later, I regret to say, turned out to be the best part of the revue. However, that was all in the indefinite future and in the meantime there were other chores to do. One of them was the opening of a Stage Door Canteen in Paris in March. Marlene Dietrich, Maurice Chevalier and I inaugurated the three opening performances, and it was a tough assignment for me particularly, because a cold I had been warding off for several days finally caught up with me and crouched, with gleeful malignity, on my vocal chords three hours before I was to appear. Fortunately, with the aid of Dr Leme, a famous throat specialist, I managed to get through all three shows without utterly disgracing myself, but I loathed every minute of them.

On April the 14th came the tragic news of Roosevelt's death, which was a personal sadness to me, because although I did not know him really well he had been friendly, kind and unpompous and had treated me with respect at a moment when I most needed it. On April the 29th came the less tragic but macabre news that Mussolini had been tried, shot and hung upside down in the streets to be spat at.

On May the 3rd, when the complete surrender of Germany was imminent, I dined quietly with Juliet Duff in her flat in Belgrave Place. There were only the four of us: Juliet, Venetia Montagu, Winston Churchill and myself. The Prime Minister was at his most benign, and suddenly, towards the end of dinner, looking across the table at the man who had carried England through her dark years, I felt an upsurge of gratitude that melted into hero worship. This was a profoundly significant moment in the history of our country; the long, long hoped-for victory was so very near, and the fact that we were in the presence of the man who had contributed so much foresight, courage and genius to winning it struck Juliet and Venetia at the same instant that it struck me. Emotion submerged us and without exchanging a word, as simultaneously as though we had carefully rehearsed it, the three of us rose to our feet and drank Mr Churchill's health.

8

On the morning of Victory Day I visited my mother and then wandered about the London streets in the hot sunshine. The crowds were gay and good-humoured, the bells clanged and the flags fluttered. In the evening I went along to have a drink with the *Blithe Spirit* company and then to Clemence Dane's flat, where we had cold food and drinks and listened to the King's broadcast, followed by speeches by Eisenhower, Tovey, Montgomery and Alexander. Various people came and went: Joyce, Lilian Braithwaite, Lynn and Alfred, Dick Addinsell, Lorn, Gladys, etc. The room looked as comforting and relaxed in victory as it had in disaster. Winnie and Olwen bustled about, looking after everybody as they had always done. In the later evening some of us went out into the streets again and wandered down the Mall through the orderly London crowds to Buckingham Palace, the whole façade of which was illuminated. The people sang and cheered, and presently the King and Queen came out on to the balcony and we cheered still more. There was, as in all celebrations of victory, an inevitable undertow of sadness. Parades generate only a superficial gaiety because we all know that they cannot last, and although this was the end of the war it was far from being the end of the world's troubles. Japan was still unconquered and even when she was vanquished there was still the future to be fought.

Chronology

1899   Born on 16 December in Teddington, Middlesex.

1911   Made first stage appearance in *The Goldfish*, London.

1914   Began writing songs, sketches and short stories (with Esmé Wynne).

1917   His play *Ida Collaborates* (written with Esmé Wynne) produced on a British tour.

1918   Wrote first play as sole author, *The Rat Trap*, produced in Britain in 1926.

1919   Wrote *I'll Leave It To You*, produced in Britain in 1920 and in USA in 1923.

1920   Appeared in London in *I'll Leave It To You*.

1921   Wrote *The Young Idea*, produced in Britain in 1922 and in USA in 1932, and *Sirocco*, produced in Britain in 1927.

1922   Appeared in *The Young Idea*. Wrote songs and sketches for the revue *London Calling!*, produced in 1923, and *The Queen Was in the Parlour*, produced in Britain in 1926 and in USA in 1929. *A Withered Nosegay* published in Britain and (in an expanded version as *Terribly Intimate Portraits*) in USA.

1923   Appeared in London in *London Calling!* Wrote *The Vortex*, produced in Britain in 1924 and in USA in 1925, and *Fallen Angels*, produced in Britain in 1925 and in USA in 1927.

1924   Directed and appeared in *The Vortex* in London. Wrote *Hay Fever*, produced in Britain and USA in 1925, and *Easy Virtue*, produced in USA in 1925 and in Britain in 1926.

1925   Continued appearing in *The Vortex* in London and also in USA. Wrote book, music and lyrics for *On With the Dance*, produced that year in Britain. *Chelsea Buns* published in Britain.

1926   Wrote *This Was A Man*, produced that year in USA, *The Marquise*, produced in Britain and USA in 1927, and *Semi-Monde*, produced in Britain in 1977.

1927   *Easy Virtue*, *The Vortex* and *The Queen Was in the Parlour* filmed. Wrote *Home Chat*, produced in Britain that year and in USA in 1932.

1928   Wrote book, music and lyrics for *This Year of Grace!*, produced in Britain and USA that year – also appeared in American production.

1929   Completed operetta *Bitter Sweet*, produced in Britain and USA that year. Wrote *Private Lives*, produced in Britain in 1930 and USA in 1931.

1930   Appeared in *Private Lives* in Britain. Wrote *Post-Mortem*, first professional production on British television in 1968, and started *Cavalcade*.

1931   Appeared in *Private Lives* in USA. *Cavalcade* produced in Britain. *Private Lives* filmed. *Collected Sketches and Lyrics* published in Britain (USA 1932).

1932   Wrote book, music and lyrics for *Words and Music*, produced in Britain that year. Also wrote *Design for Living*, produced in USA in 1933 and in Britain in 1939. *The Queen Was in the Parlour* filmed again under the title *Tonight is Ours*. *Cavalcade* filmed. *Spangled Unicorn* published in Britain.

1933   Appeared in USA in *Design for Living*. Wrote *Conversation Piece*, produced in Britain and USA in 1934. *Design for Living* and *Bitter Sweet* both filmed.

1934   Appeared in *Conversation Piece* in Britain. Wrote *Point Valaine*, produced in USA that year and in Britain in 1944.

1935   Wrote *Tonight at 8.30*, produced in Britain that year and in USA in 1936. He appeared in both productions.

1937   Wrote *Operette*, produced in Britain in 1938. First volume of autobiography, *Present Indicative*, published in Britain and USA.

1938   Adapted *Words and Music* for its American production, entitled *Set to Music*.

1939   Wrote *Present Laughter* and *This Happy Breed*. Rehearsals for both interrupted by the war and not produced in Britain until 1942. *Present Laughter* produced in USA in 1946 and *This Happy Breed* in 1949. *To Step Aside* (short stories) published in Britain and USA.

1940   Toured Australia and also wrote *Time Remembered (Salute to the Brave)*, unproduced to date.

1941   Wrote and directed *Blithe Spirit*, produced in Britain and USA that year. Wrote screenplay for *In Which We Serve*.

1942   Appeared in and co-directed (with David Lean) *In Which We Serve*. Toured Britain in *Blithe Spirit*, *Present Laughter* and *This Happy Breed*. *We Were Dancing* (from *Tonight at 8.30*) filmed.

1943   Appeared in London in *Present Laughter* and *This Happy Breed* and co-produced film version of the latter.

1944   Toured extensively in South Africa, Far East and Europe. Co-produced film of *Blithe Spirit*. Wrote screenplay for *Brief Encounter* (based on *Still Life* from *Tonight at 8.30*). *Middle East Diary* published in Britain and USA.

1945   Wrote *Sigh No More*, produced in Britain that year, and started writing *Pacific 1860*, produced in Britain in 1946.

1946   Started writing *Peace in Our Time*, produced in Britain in 1947

1947   Appeared in *Present Laughter* in Britain. Wrote *Long Island Sound*, unproduced to date.

1948   Appeared in French production of *Present Laughter* (*Joyeux Chagrins*). Wrote screenplay for *The Astonished Heart* (from *Tonight at 8.30*).

1949   Appeared in *The Astonished Heart*. Wrote *Ace of Clubs*, produced in Britain in 1950, and *Home and Colonial*: as *Island Fling* it was produced in USA in 1951 and revised as *South Sea Bubble* in Britain in 1956.

1951   Wrote *Relative Values*, produced in Britain that year, and *Quadrille*, produced in Britain in 1952 and in USA in 1954. Made first cabaret appearance at Café de Paris, London. *Star Quality* (short stories) published in Britain and USA.

1952   Three plays from *Tonight at 8.30* filmed as *Meet Me Tonight*.

1953   Wrote *After the Ball*, produced in Britain in 1954 and in USA in 1955.

1954   Wrote *Nude with Violin* produced in Britain in 1956 and in USA in 1957. *Future Indefinite* published in Britain and USA.

1955   Cabaret season in Las Vegas, USA. Wrote and appeared in *Together with Music* for US television.

1956   Appeared in *Blithe Spirit* and *This Happy Breed* on US television. Wrote *Volcano*, unproduced to date.

1957   Appeared in USA in *Nude with Violin*.

1958   Appeared in USA in *Present Laughter* and *Nude with Violin*. Adapted Feydeau's *Occupe-toi d'Amélie* as *Look After Lulu*, produced in USA and Britain in 1959. Composed score for the ballet *London Morning*, produced in Britain in 1959.

1959   Wrote *Waiting in the Wings*, produced in Britain in 1960.

1960   His novel *Pomp and Circumstance* published in Britain and USA.

1961   Completed *Sail Away*, produced in USA that year and in Britain in 1962.

1962   Wrote music and lyrics for *The Girl Who Came to Supper*, produced in USA in 1963. *The Collected Short Stories* published in Britain.

1964   Directed *High Spirits* (musical of *Blithe Spirit*) in USA and *Hay Fever* in Britain. *Pretty Polly Barlow* (short stories) published in Britain.

1965   Wrote *Suite in Three Keys*, produced in Britain in 1966 and (as *Noël Coward in Two Keys*) in USA in 1974. *The Lyrics of Noël Coward* published in Britain (USA 1967).

1966   Appeared in Britain in *Suite in Three Keys*. Started writing stage version of *Star Quality*, produced in Britain in 1982.

1967   *Bon Voyage* (short stories) and *Not Yet The Dodo* (verses) published in Britain (USA 1968).

1970   Received knighthood in the British New Year Honours List.

1972   *Cowardy Custard* produced in Britain and *Oh! Coward* in USA.

1973   Died on 26 March in Jamaica.

Index

* indicates that Coward also appeared as an actor

* indicates that Coward also appeared as an actor

Biography and Memoirs
also available in Methuen Paperbacks
are listed on the following pages

Maeve Gilmore
A WORLD AWAY

Christopher Isherwood
CHRISTOPHER AND HIS KIND
MY GURU AND HIS DISCIPLE

Philippe Jullian and John Phillips
VIOLET TREFUSIS

John Lahr
NOTES ON A COWARDLY LION

Virginia Leng
GINNY

Arthur Miller
SALESMAN IN BEIJING

Christopher Milne
THE ENCHANTED PLACES
THE HOLLOW ON THE HILL
THE PATH THROUGH THE TREES

H. Montgomery Hyde
OSCAR WILDE

Olga Pyne Clarke
SHE CAME OF DECENT PEOPLE

Shelley Rohde
A PRIVATE VIEW OF L. S. LOWRY

A. L. Rowse
MEMORIES AND GLIMPSES

Keith Sagar
THE LIFE OF D. H. LAWRENCE

Captain Robert Falcon Scott
SCOTT'S LAST EXPEDITION

Ernest Shepard
DRAWN FROM MEMORY / DRAWN FROM
LIFE

Edith Templeton
THE SURPRISE OF CREMONA

Norman Thelwell
A MILLSTONE ROUND MY NECK
A PLANK BRIDGE BY A POOL

Tomi Ungerer
FAR OUT ISN'T FAR ENOUGH

Marie 'Missie' Vassiltchikov
THE BERLIN DIARIES 1940 – 1945

Vivienne de Watteville
SPEAK TO THE EARTH